Introduction to the Law of Corporations

ISBN-13: 9781075963391

Introduction to the Law of Corporations:
Cases and Materials

Brian JM Quinn

Boston College Law School
Fall 2019

Table of Contents

Introduction

This open-source casebook is the sixth edition of a casebook using the H2O/ OpenCasebook platform of Harvard's Berkman Center. This casebook is intended to be used as the main casebook for an introductory course on the law of corporations. Because is subject to a Creative Commons license and can be printed via Amazon, it is available to students at a very modest cost. Alternatively, students can read and access the cases and materials online via the H2O platform at opencasebook.org at no cost. This casebook and the H2O/ OpenCasebook platform are part of an effort by educators to make high quality course materials and casebooks available to students at reasonable prices.

Although this course is called an *Introduction to the Law of Corporations*, it is better understood as a more general business organizations course. The materials in this casebook cover Delaware corporate code exclusively. However, your learning during this semester long course will not be limited to the corporate law. We will start the class with an online course covering the basic concepts of Agency. Agency is the single most important building block required to understand the corporate law. Agency is also an essential building block to understand the laws governing other forms of business organization.

During the course of this semester, you will be introduced to other forms of business organization, including Partnership, Limited Liability Companies, Nonprofit Corporations, and Public Benefit Corporations. Most of your introduction to these other forms will come through a series of online courses covering the basic concepts and rules for each of the forms. You should plan to complete all of these courses, including the accompanying quizzes in Canvas, by the dates set forth in the syllabus. As you are working on the online courses, in class we will focus on the corporate form, the Delaware corporate code, and the Delaware common law of corporations.

Because the corporate law is so much more extensive than the laws of other business forms, like for example the law governing LLCs, courts often lean heavily on the corporate law and apply it by analogy to other forms when they are in search of persuasive authority. By becoming expert in the corporate law, you will find it easy to translate that knowledge and apply it other business organizations.

Much of the work of the corporate lawyer starts with the code. As such, we will start with an in depth examination of the corporate code. Although we could study the Model Code or the Massachusetts code, for most corporate lawyers, the Delaware corporate law will be central to their practice. Sixty percent of all publicly traded corporations are Delaware corporations. With respect to private corporations, they are typically incorporated in the state in which they are physically located, or they are incorporated in Delaware.

Beyond the code, Delaware has a very deep corporate common law. It is in the corporate common law that the courts have developed the law of corporate fiduciary duties. It is through fiduciary duties that the corporate law attempts to regulate the relationship between stockholders and the corporation, between managers and the corporation, as well as the relationships of controlling stockholders and minority stockholders. Delaware's treatment of the corporate common law is so extensive that it is not at all uncommon at all for the courts of other states to refer to, or cite Delaware corporate law cases, when deciding questions involving their own corporate law. The Delaware corporate law is the closest we have to a lingua franca in the US for corporate law.

The fiduciary duties of corporate directors are tested most often in the context of corporate takeovers. The corporate takeover materials in this casebook attempt to highlight the most important issues in takeover situations as well as the court's doctrinal efforts to mitigate the transaction costs that arise in these situations.

1. Building Your Business Vocabulary

Before we dive into the corporate law, a quick word about what corporate law is and, perhaps more importantly, what it isn't. Many law students take corporate law thinking that it will equip them with enough business background, including finance and accounting, so that they can be successful in a corporate/transactional law practice. Unfortunately, if you're hoping that a course in the corporate law will substitute for an MBA, then you're mistaken. This course will focus on certain legal relationships that are central to the corporate form.

That said, a good corporate/transactional lawyer will be very conversant with the language of business and will understand what it is his or her clients are doing. If you wish to be an effective business lawyer, it is extremely important, therefore, to develop the vocabulary of business and some basic business skills while in law school or soon there after. Don't worry. Building this vocabulary can be easier than you might expect. First things first, you should begin to read the things that your clients will read. I recommend subscribing to the New York Times Dealbook newsletter delivered by email everyday. If you begin to read it regularly, the business and legal issues that are central to your business clients will become apparent to you over time.

In addition to this informal education, you should take advantage of your time in law school to take at least one accounting/finance class at the business school. If you cannot enroll in courses at the business school, I recommend adding the Wharton Foundation Series (http://blog.coursera.org/post/60889088289/the-wharton-foundation-series) to your list of things to do before graduating or maybe in lieu of a bar trip after gradutation. The foundation series is a series of four online courses available through Coursera and conducted by the faculty of the Wharton School at UPenn. The courses are as follows:

> 1. Introduction to Financial Accounting;
> 2. Introduction to Corporate Finance;
> 3. Introduction to Marketing; and
> 4. Introduction to Operations Management

Start with Financial Accounting and then Corporate Finance. Good luck!

2. The Delaware General Corporation Law
2.1 Introduction to the Delaware Corporations Law

Although every state has its own corporate law, we will focus on the Delaware General Corporation Law. We do this for one very important reason: two-thirds of all publicly-traded U.S. companies, including more than 60% of the Fortune 500, and a significant number of private corporations are incorporated in Delaware. A study by Robert Daines found that when private companies are incorporated that there are only two incorporation choices. First, they tend to incorporate in the state in which they are headquartered and in which they do their business. Second, they incorporate in Delaware.

You might well ask how is it possible that a corporation that is headquartered in Massachusetts and does business in Massachusetts should be governed by Delaware law? This seemingly odd result is a function of a variety of factors, including historical developments as well as our federal system.

In the earliest days of our Republic, the power to incorporate corporations was reserved to the states. Prior to the adoption of general incorporation statutes, the incorporation of a corporation required state legislatures to adopt a law incorporating the entity. These incorporation statutes laid out the powers and responsibilities of the corporation, including the rights of corporate stockholders with respect to the entity formed by the state legislature. It was not uncommon at the time for the state grants of corporate charters to reserve some monopoly power within the state to the corporation - typically to facilitate the development of some critical infrastructure like a canal, roadway, or railroad. Over time, the process of incorporation was simplified as states adopted general incorporation statutes, which took legislatures out of the business of incorporating individual businesses. General incorporation statutes laid out default powers and responsibilities of the corporation as well as describing the default powers and rights of the corporation's stockholders vis a vis the corporation.

When one combines the power of states to incorporate businesses with constitutional prohibitions against states impeding interstate commerce and Article IV's full faith and credit clause (requiring each state to provide full faith and credit to public acts of every other state) with a state's power to incorporate, then one makes it possible for a corporation to be incorporated in one state and then do business in another.

Of course, a corporation's outward acts - acts other than those related to their relationships with their stockholders, for example with respect to employment law or the environment - are subject to the jurisdiction of the law in which the acts occur. However, the internal affairs of the corporation (relations among the stockholders, and managers with the corporation itself) are the stuff of the law of the state of incorporation. In a 1982 case, *Edgar v Mite Corp.* (457 US 624 (1982)) the US Supreme Court recognized the "internal affairs doctrine" as well settled law in the US:

> The internal affairs doctrine is a conflict of laws principle which recognizes that only one State should have the authority to regulate a corporation's internal affairs — matters peculiar to the relationships among or between the corporation and its current officers, directors, and shareholders — because otherwise a corporation could be faced with conflicting demands. See Restatement (Second) of Conflict of Laws § 302, Comment *b*, pp. 307-308 (1971).

But *Edgar* is not a unique application of the internal affairs doctrine by the US Supreme Court. In an earlier case, *Cort v. Ash* (422 US 66, 1975), the court described the doctrine and the primacy of state law in the following way:

> Corporations are creatures of state law, and investors commit their funds to corporate directors on the understanding that, except where federal law expressly requires certain responsibilities of directors with respect to stockholders, state law will govern the internal affairs of the corporation. If, for example, state law permits corporations to use corporate funds as contributions in state elections, see *Miller, supra,* at 763 n. 4, shareholders are on notice that their funds may be so used and have no recourse under any federal statute.

The ability of entrepreneurs to elect to incorporate their businesses in one of any number of states gave way to something of a competition among states in the early 20th century for the revenue associated with incorporation of businesses. In corporate governance circles, this competitive environment was criticized as a "race to the bottom" with states competing with each other to reduce management accountability to its lowest possible level in order to attract incorporations. While this race to the bottom logic is by now slightly overblown, at one point in the past states aggressively competed for incorporations. Although some states occasionally attempt to revive their incorporation business, the age of active competition for incorporations is long since over with Delaware decisively winning. As Daines noted, the incorporation decision these days is more likely to be binary - incorporate where you do business or in Delaware.

Rather than see itself in competition against other state jurisdictions, Delaware sees itself in tension with the SEC and federal regulators for dominance in corporate governance. Delaware is protective of its position as a leader in the law of corporations. To the extent the SEC and federal regulators adopt, or threaten to adopt, rules that affect corporate governance, Delaware reacts. Over the course of this semester we will see various examples of federal movement in the corporate governance area along with reactions by the state of Delaware as it reacts to protect its position.

For now, though, we will focus on the basics of the Delaware corporate law, starting with formation.

2.2 Formation
2.2.1 The beginnings of incorporation

Prior to the late 19th century, few states had general enabling laws with respect incorporations. Incorporation was not a right, but rather a privilege granted by state governments on individual groups of promoters. At that time, the incorporation of a business required a legislative act by the state in which the corporation was to do its business. As a consequence, there were few corporations in the US. When legislatures granted incorporations, the majority of incorporations were limited to enterprises intended to engage in infrastructure development. The earliest corporations in the US were corporations formed to develop canals, turnpikes and bridges. It was not uncommon for state legislatures to grant monopoly rights to develop certain critical infrastructure. It was also not uncommon for states to invest in these enterprises by way of a contribution of land for the use of the infrastructure corporation.

By the early 20th century, general enabling laws, which granted everyone the right to incorporate, began to take hold in states across the country. One of the motivations for the switch to general enabling laws was a backlash to the high degree of corruption in state legislatures. Promoters seeking support for acts of incorporation often found that support the old-fashioned way - by means of a bribe. By turning the power dynamic on its head and making the act of incorporation ministerial rather than discretionary, state legislatures were robbed of an important motivation for corruption.

In his dissent in a 1933 case, *Ligget v Lee* (288, US 517), Justice Brandeis discussed the development of general enabling laws and the related concepts of "charter mongering" (or, competition amongst the states for incorporations in the period following adoption of the general enabling laws):

> The prevalence of the corporation in America has led men of this generation to act, at times, as if the privilege of doing business in corporate form were inherent in the citizen; and has led them to accept the evils attendant upon the free and unrestricted use of the corporate mechanism as if these evils were the inescapable price of civilized life and, hence, to be borne with resignation. Throughout the greater part of our history a different view prevailed. Although the value of this instrumentality in commerce and industry was fully recognized, incorporation for business was commonly denied long after it had been freely granted for religious, educational and charitable purposes. It was denied because of fear. Fear of encroachment upon the liberties and opportunities of the individual. Fear of the subjection of labor to capital. Fear of monopoly. Fear that the absorption of capital by corporations, and their perpetual life, might bring evils similar to those which attended mortmain. There was a sense of some insidious menace inherent in large aggregations of capital, particularly when held by corporations. So, at first, the corporate privilege was granted sparingly; and only when the grant seemed necessary in order to procure for the community some specific benefit otherwise unattainable. The later enactment of general incorporation laws does not signify that the apprehension of corporate domination had been overcome. The desire for business expansion created an irresistible demand for more charters; and it

was believed that under general laws embodying safeguards of universal application the scandals and favoritism incident to special incorporation could be avoided. The general laws, which long embodied severe restrictions upon size and upon the scope of corporate activity, were, in part, an expression of the desire for equality of opportunity.

(a) Limitation upon the amount of the authorized capital of business corporations was long universal. The maximum limit frequently varied with the kinds of business to be carried on, being dependent apparently upon the supposed requirements of the efficient unit. Although the statutory limits were changed from time to time this principle of limitation was long retained. Thus in New York the limit was at first $100,000 for some businesses and as little as $50,000 for others. Until 1881 the maximum for business corporations in New York was $2,000,000; and until 1890, $5,000,000. In Massachusetts the limit was at first $200,000 for some businesses and as little as $5,000 for others. Until 1871 the maximum for mechanical and manufacturing corporations was $500,000; and until 1899, $1,000,000. The limit of $100,000 was retained for some businesses until 1903. In many other states, including the leading ones in some industries, the removal of the limitations upon size was more recent. Pennsylvania did not remove the limits until 1905. Its first general act not having contained a maximum limit that of $500,000 was soon imposed. Later, it was raised to $1,000,000; and, for iron and steel companies, to $5,000,000. Vermont limited the maximum to $1,000,000 until 1911 when no amount over $10,000,000 was authorized if, in the opinion of a judge of the supreme court, such a capitalization would tend "to create a monopoly or result in restraining competition in trade." Maryland limited until 1918 the capital of mining companies to $3,000,000; and prohibited them from holding more than 500 acres of land (except in Allegany County, where 1,000 acres was

16

allowed). New Hampshire did not remove the maximum limit until 1919. It had been $1,000,000 until 1907, when it was increased to $5,000,000. Michigan did not remove the maximum limit until 1921. The maximum, at first $100,000, had been gradually increased until in 1903 it became $10,000,000 for some corporations and $25,000,000 for others; and in 1917 became $50,000,000. Indiana did not remove until 1921 the maximum limit of $2,000,000 for petroleum and natural gas corporations. Missouri did not remove its maximum limit until 1927. Texas still has such a limit for certain corporations.

(b) Limitations upon the scope of a business corporation's powers and activity were also long universal. At first, corporations could be formed under the general laws only for a limited number of purposes — usually those which required a relatively large fixed capital, like transportation, banking, and insurance, and mechanical, mining, and manufacturing enterprises. Permission to incorporate for "any lawful purpose" was not common until 1875; and until that time the duration of corporate franchises was generally limited to a period of 20, 30, or 50 years. All, or a majority, of the incorporators or directors, or both, were required to be residents of the incorporating state. The powers which the corporation might exercise in carrying out its purposes were sparingly conferred and strictly construed. Severe limitations were imposed on the amount of indebtedness, bonded or otherwise. The power to hold stock in other corporations was not conferred or implied. The holding company was impossible.

(c) The removal by the leading industrial States of the limitations upon the size and powers of business corporations appears to have been due, not to their conviction that maintenance of the restrictions was undesirable in itself, but to the conviction that it was futile to insist upon them; because local restriction would be circumvented by foreign incorporation. Indeed, local restriction

17

seemed worse than futile. Lesser States, eager for the revenue derived from the traffic in charters, had removed safeguards from their own incorporation laws. Companies were early formed to provide charters for corporations in states where the cost was lowest and the laws least restrictive. The states joined in advertising their wares. The race was one not of diligence but of laxity. Incorporation under such laws was possible; and the great industrial States yielded in order not to lose wholly the prospect of the revenue and the control incident to domestic incorporation. The history of the changes made by New York is illustrative. The New York revision of 1890, which eliminated the maximum limitation on authorized capital, and permitted intercorporate stockholding in a limited class of cases, was passed after a migration of incorporation from New York, attracted by the more liberal incorporation laws of New Jersey. But the changes made by New York in 1890 were not sufficient to stem the tide. In 1892, the Governor of New York approved a special charter for the General Electric Company, modelled upon the New Jersey Act, on the ground that otherwise the enterprise would secure a New Jersey charter. Later in the same year the New York corporation law was again revised, allowing the holding of stock in other corporations. But the New Jersey law still continued to be more attractive to incorporators. By specifically providing that corporations might be formed in New Jersey to do all their business elsewhere, the state made its policy unmistakably clear. Of the seven largest trusts existing in 1904, with an aggregate capitalization of over two and a half billion dollars, all were organized under New Jersey law; and three of these were formed in 1899. During the first seven months of that year, 1336 corporations were organized under the laws of New Jersey, with an aggregate authorized capital of over two billion dollars. The Comptroller of New York, in his annual report for 1899, complained that "our tax list reflects little of the great wave of organization that has swept over the country during the past year and to which this state contributed more capital than any other state in the Union." "It is time," he declared, "that great corporations having their actual headquarters in this State and a nominal office elsewhere, doing nearly all of their business within our borders, should be brought within the jurisdiction of this State not only as to matters of taxation but in respect to other and equally important affairs." In 1901 the New York corporation law was again revised. The history in other states was similar. Thus, the Massachusetts revision of 1903 was precipitated by the fact that "the possibilities of incorporation in other states have become well known, and have been availed of to the detriment of this Commonwealth."... Able, discerning scholars have pictured for us the economic and social results of thus removing all limitations upon the size and activities of business corporations and of vesting in their managers vast powers once exercised by stockholders — results not designed by the States and long unsuspected. They show that size alone gives to giant corporations a social significance not attached ordinarily to smaller units of private enterprise. Through size, corporations, once merely an efficient tool employed by individuals in the conduct of private business, have become an institution — an institution which has brought such concentration of economic power that so-called private corporations are sometimes able to dominate the State. The typical business corporation of the last century, owned by a small group of individuals, managed by their owners, and limited in size by their personal wealth, is being supplanted by huge concerns in which the lives of tens or hundreds of thousands of employees and the property of tens or hundreds of thousands of investors are subjected, through the corporate mechanism, to the control of a few men. Ownership has been separated from control; and this separation has removed many of the checks which formerly operated to curb the misuse of wealth and power. And as ownership of the shares is becoming continually more dispersed, the power which formerly accompanied ownership is becoming increasingly

19

concentrated in the hands of a few. The changes thereby wrought in
the lives of the workers, of the owners and of the general public, are
so fundamental and far-reaching as to lead these scholars to
compare the evolving "corporate system" with the feudal system;
and to lead other men of insight and experience to assert that this
"master institution of civilised life" is committing it to the rule of a
plutocracy.

Questions for discussion

1. Justice Brandeis observed that recently some had come to believe that the "privilege
of doing business in the corporate form were inherent in the citizen." Should the people
have the "right to incorporate" or should incorporation remain a "privilege?"

2. Why might a state engage in "charter mongering", otherwise known as the "race to
the bottom?"

2.2.2 DGCL Sec. 101 - Formation

A certificate of incorporation is the functional equivalent of a corporation's constitution.
The certificate goes by different names in different states. In other states it is known as
the articles of incorporation or the corporate charter, or the articles of organization. All
of these refer to the same document. As the corporation's constitution, the certificate
may limit or define the power of the corporation and the corporation's board of
directors. Drafter's of certificates have a great deal of flexibility when drafting these
documents. Although most certificates are "plain vanilla" certificates that rely almost
entirely on the state corporate law default rules to define the power of the corporation
and its directors as well as delineate the rights of stockholders. Of course, such a
minimal approach to drafting corporate documents is not required. The corporate law is
"enabling" in nature. Incorporators are free to tailor the internal governance of
the corporation in any way they might like, provided it does not conflict with other
provisions of the statute.

For example, some corporations, like the Green Bay Packers professional football team, have highly tailored certificates of incorporation. The Green Bay Packers' certificate is available on the course website. Promoters of the Green Bay Packers corporation tailored the rights of shareholders so that no shareholder can expect to receive any portion of the profits of the Packers - those have to be donated to a charity - and that no shareholder can expect their shares of the Packers to have any resale value on a stock exchange - any attempt to transfer shares to someone other than a family member will result in the corporation redeeming the shares for pennies.

In addition to permitting the corporation's promoters a high degree of freedom in the design of their internal governance mechanisms, enabling statutes upend the 19th Century view that a corporation is a special act of the state that requires legislative action. Rather, section 101 that follows below makes it clear that the filing of a certificate of incorporation is sufficient to form a corporation. This is the essence of an enabling statute.

This subtle, but important, change is more important than you might imagine at first glance. To the extent government control over decisions about who can form a corporation and under what circumstances gives rise to incentives for corruption and generally mucks up the business environment, the switch to a bottom-up incorporation regime can be seen as a valuable contribution of the Progressive Era.

§ 101. Incorporators; how corporation formed; purposes.

(a) Any person, partnership, association or corporation, singly or jointly with others, and without regard to such person's or entity's residence, domicile or state of incorporation, may incorporate or organize a corporation under this chapter by filing with the Division of Corporations in the Department of State a certificate of incorporation which shall be executed, acknowledged and filed in accordance with § 103 of this title.

(b) A corporation may be incorporated or organized under this chapter to conduct or promote any lawful business or purposes, except as may otherwise be provided by the Constitution or other law of this State.

[…]

2.2.3 DGCL Sec. 102 - Contents of Certificate of Incorporation

The certificate of incorporation is the corporation's basic governing document. It lays out the basic understanding about governance of the corporation and the corporation's powers. It also limits the power and discretion of the corporation's board of directors in the management of the corporation. To the extent they comply with the requirements of the corporation law, the promoters of a corporation have the flexibility to tailor the internal governance of the corporation as well as to limit the powers of the board of directors. The certificate of incorporation is contractual in nature. Initial stockholders have the ability, at least in theory, to negotiate the terms of their relationship with the corporation. Later stockholders take their stock pursuant to the terms of the certificate of incorporation already in place.

DGCL §102 describes the contents of every corporation's certificate of incorporation. Section 102 has two basic components. First, §102(a) lays out the required elements of every certificate of incorporation. Many of the required elements relate to notice (e.g. how can the state contact responsible parties in the corporation). To the extent some of the required elements of §102 seem out of place (e.g. par value), remember they were first included in the code following the transition from discretionary charters to general enabling laws. Consequently, they may reflect a number of vestigal elements of the corporate law.

Second, §102(b) lays out the optional elements of every certificate of incorporation. Many of the optional elements in a certificate relate to corporate governance rights of stockholders and/or the board of directors. Section 102(b) does not generally limit promoters' ability to tailor governance structures, but it does often provide promoters with menus of options that they can choose from as they draft certificates.

§ 102. Contents of certificate of incorporation.

(a) The certificate of incorporation shall set forth:

(1) The name of the corporation, which (i) shall contain 1 of the words "association," "company," "corporation," "club," "foundation," "fund," "incorporated," "institute," "society," "union," "syndicate," or "limited," (or abbreviations thereof, with or without punctuation), or words (or abbreviations thereof, with or without punctuation) of like

import of foreign countries or jurisdictions (provided they are written in roman characters or letters); […];

(2) The address (which shall be stated in accordance with § 131(c) of this title) of the corporation's registered office in this State, and the name of its registered agent at such address;

(3) The nature of the business or purposes to be conducted or promoted. It shall be sufficient to state, either alone or with other businesses or purposes, that the purpose of the corporation is to engage in any lawful act or activity for which corporations may be organized under the General Corporation Law of Delaware, and by such statement all lawful acts and activities shall be within the purposes of the corporation, except for express limitations, if any;

(4) If the corporation is to be authorized to issue only 1 class of stock, the total number of shares of stock which the corporation shall have authority to issue and the par value of each of such shares, or a statement that all such shares are to be without par value. If the corporation is to be authorized to issue more than 1 class of stock, the certificate of incorporation shall set forth the total number of shares of all classes of stock which the corporation shall have authority to issue and the number of shares of each class and shall specify each class the shares of which are to be without par value and each class the shares of which are to have par value and the par value of the shares of each such class. The certificate of incorporation shall also set forth a statement of the designations and the powers, preferences and rights, and the qualifications, limitations or restrictions thereof, which are permitted by § 151 of this title in respect of any class or classes of stock or any series of any class of stock of the corporation and the fixing of which by the certificate of incorporation is desired, and an express grant of such authority as it may then be desired to grant to the board of directors to fix by resolution or resolutions any thereof that may be desired but which shall not be fixed by the certificate of incorporation. […];

(5) The name and mailing address of the incorporator or incorporators;

(6) If the powers of the incorporator or incorporators are to terminate upon the filing of the certificate of incorporation, the names and mailing addresses of the persons who are

to serve as directors until the first annual meeting of stockholders or until their successors are elected and qualify.

(b) In addition to the matters required to be set forth in the certificate of incorporation by subsection (a) of this section, the certificate of incorporation may also contain any or all of the following matters:

(1) Any provision for the management of the business and for the conduct of the affairs of the corporation, and any provision creating, defining, limiting and regulating the powers of the corporation, the directors, and the stockholders, or any class of the stockholders, or the governing body, members, or any class or group of members of a nonstock corporation; if such provisions are not contrary to the laws of this State. Any provision which is required or permitted by any section of this chapter to be stated in the bylaws may instead be stated in the certificate of incorporation; […]

(3) Such provisions as may be desired granting to the holders of the stock of the corporation, or the holders of any class or series of a class thereof, the preemptive right to subscribe to any or all additional issues of stock of the corporation of any or all classes or series thereof, or to any securities of the corporation convertible into such stock. No stockholder shall have any preemptive right to subscribe to an additional issue of stock or to any security convertible into such stock unless, and except to the extent that, such right is expressly granted to such stockholder in the certificate of incorporation. […];

(4) Provisions requiring for any corporate action, the vote of a larger portion of the stock or of any class or series thereof, or of any other securities having voting power, or a larger number of the directors, than is required by this chapter;

(5) A provision limiting the duration of the corporation's existence to a specified date; otherwise, the corporation shall have perpetual existence;

(6) A provision imposing personal liability for the debts of the corporation on its stockholders to a specified extent and upon specified conditions; otherwise, the stockholders of a corporation shall not be personally liable for the payment of the corporation's debts except as they may be liable by reason of their own conduct or acts;

(7) A provision eliminating or limiting the personal liability of a director to the corporation or its stockholders for monetary damages for breach of fiduciary duty as a

director, provided that such provision shall not eliminate or limit the liability of a director: (i) For any breach of the director's duty of loyalty to the corporation or its stockholders; (ii) for acts or omissions not in good faith or which involve intentional misconduct or a knowing violation of law; (iii) under § 174 of this title; or (iv) for any transaction from which the director derived an improper personal benefit. […]

(c) It shall not be necessary to set forth in the certificate of incorporation any of the powers conferred on corporations by this chapter.

2.2.4 Exculpation Provision

Section 102(b)(7) was added to the statute in 1985 following *Smith v Van Gorkom* where directors were found liable for monetary damages for violating their fiduciary duty of care to the corporation. Although §102(b)(7) provides a blank exculpation from monetary liability for any violation of fiduciary duties, it carves out various flavors of loyalty violations. In effect, §102(b)(7) provides that where such a provision is present in a certificate of incorporation, directors will face no monetary liability to stockholders for any violations of their duty of care.

Although a §102(b)(7) exculpation provision is an optional provision, the protection granted to directors of §102(b)(7) is so powerful that this provision is ubiquitous in corporate charters.

2.2.5 DGCL Sec. 103 - Filing requirements

Section 103 describes the requirements for filing corporate documents, where to file, what to file, and who has to sign which documents. Although this section may seem boring, it is actually an important one for practicing attorneys. As we work our way through the code, you will notice that some provisions will require documents be filed with the state in order for them to take effect. All such documents, including the certificate of incorporation, must be filed in compliance with §103. You should familiarize yourself with §103's requirements.

§103. Execution, acknowledgment, filing, recording and effective date of original certificate of incorporation and other instruments; exceptions.

(a) Whenever any instrument is to be filed with the Secretary of State or in accordance with this section or chapter, such instrument shall be executed as follows:

(1) The certificate of incorporation, and any other instrument to be filed before the election of the initial board of directors if the initial directors were not named in the certificate of incorporation, shall be signed by the incorporator or incorporators[…]

(2) All other instruments shall be signed:

a. By any authorized officer of the corporation; or

b. If it shall appear from the instrument that there are no such officers, then by a majority of the directors or by such directors as may be designated by the board; or

c. If it shall appear from the instrument that there are no such officers or directors, then by the holders of record, or such of them as may be designated by the holders of record, of a majority of all outstanding shares of stock; or

d. By the holders of record of all outstanding shares of stock.

(b) Whenever this chapter requires any instrument to be acknowledged, such requirement is satisfied by either:

(1) The formal acknowledgment by the person or 1 of the persons signing the instrument that it is such person's act and deed or the act and deed of the corporation, and that the facts stated therein are true. […]

(2) The signature, without more, of the person or persons signing the instrument, in which case such signature or signatures shall constitute the affirmation or acknowledgment of the signatory, under penalties of perjury, that the instrument is such person's act and deed or the act and deed of the corporation, and that the facts stated therein are true.

(c) Whenever any instrument is to be filed with the Secretary of State or in accordance with this section or chapter, such requirement means that:

(1) The signed instrument shall be delivered to the office of the Secretary of State;

(2) All taxes and fees authorized by law to be collected by the Secretary of State in connection with the filing of the instrument shall be tendered to the Secretary of State; and

(3) Upon delivery of the instrument, the Secretary of State shall record the date and time of its delivery. Upon such delivery and tender of the required taxes and fees, the Secretary of State shall certify that the instrument has been filed in the Secretary of State's office by endorsing upon the signed instrument the word "Filed", and the date and time of its filing. This endorsement is the "filing date" of the instrument, and is conclusive of the date and time of its filing in the absence of actual fraud. [...]

(4) Upon request made upon or prior to delivery, the Secretary of State may, to the extent deemed practicable, establish as the filing date of an instrument a date and time after its delivery. If the Secretary of State refuses to file any instrument due to an error, omission or other imperfection, the Secretary of State may hold such instrument in suspension, and in such event, upon delivery of a replacement instrument in proper form for filing and tender of the required taxes and fees within 5 business days after notice of such suspension is given to the filer, the Secretary of State shall establish as the filing date of such instrument the date and time that would have been the filing date of the rejected instrument had it been accepted for filing. [...]

(h) Any signature on any instrument authorized to be filed with the Secretary of State under this title may be a facsimile, a conformed signature or an electronically transmitted signature. [...]

2.2.6 Amendment of Certificate of Incorporation

2.2.6.1 DGCL Sec. 242 - Amendments to Certificate

Like a constitution, a corporation's certificate of incorporation may be amended at any point in the future. It is not a "forever" contract. A board of directors together with the corporation's stockholders can amend a certificate of incorporation. Section 242 outlines the procedures for amending a certificate.

There are two features of the amendment process that are worth pointing out. First, any amendment to a corporation's certificate of incorporation must be initiated by the corporation's board of directors and requires the board's assent. A certificate

27

amendment may not be initiated by stockholders. A certificate may not be amended against the will of the board of directors. Second, any amendments recommended by the board of directors must be approved by a vote of a majority of the outstanding shares of the corporation. A certificate may not be amended against the will of the majority of the stockholders. These dual requirements can make the process of amending a certificate of incorporation difficult. Thus, the limitations placed on a board or a corporation's stockholders by the certificate of incorporation are effective constraints.

Although any portion of the certificate may be amended, the most common amendment to certificates of incorporation involves increases to the number of authorized shares. Such amendments are usually, but not always, noncontroversial.

§ 242. Amendment of certificate of incorporation after receipt of payment for stock; nonstock corporations

(a) After a corporation has received payment for any of its capital stock, or after a nonstock corporation has members, it may amend its certificate of incorporation, from time to time, in any and as many respects as may be desired, so long as its certificate of incorporation as amended would contain only such provisions as it would be lawful and proper to insert in an original certificate of incorporation filed at the time of the filing of the amendment; and, if a change in stock or the rights of stockholders, or an exchange, reclassification, subdivision, combination or cancellation of stock or rights of stockholders is to be made, such provisions as may be necessary to effect such change, exchange, reclassification, subdivision, combination or cancellation. In particular, and without limitation upon such general power of amendment, a corporation may amend its certificate of incorporation, from time to time, so as:

(1) To change its corporate name; or

(2) To change, substitute, enlarge or diminish the nature of its business or its corporate powers and purposes; or

(3) To increase or decrease its authorized capital stock or to reclassify the same, by changing the number, par value, designations, preferences, or relative, participating, optional, or other special rights of the shares, or the qualifications, limitations or restrictions of such rights, or by changing shares with par value into shares without par value, or shares without par value into shares with par value either with or without

increasing or decreasing the number of shares, or by subdividing or combining the outstanding shares of any class or series of a class of shares into a greater or lesser number of outstanding shares; or

(4) To cancel or otherwise affect the right of the holders of the shares of any class to receive dividends which have accrued but have not been declared; or

(5) To create new classes of stock having rights and preferences either prior and superior or subordinate and inferior to the stock of any class then authorized, whether issued or unissued; or

(6) To change the period of its duration; or

(7) To delete:

a. Such provisions of the original certificate of incorporation which named the incorporator or incorporators, the initial board of directors and the original subscribers for shares; and

b. Such provisions contained in any amendment to the certificate of incorporation as were necessary to effect a change, exchange, reclassification, subdivision, combination or cancellation of stock, if such change, exchange, reclassification, subdivision, combination or cancellation has become effective.

Any or all such changes or alterations may be effected by 1 certificate of amendment.

(b) Every amendment authorized by subsection (a) of this section shall be made and effected in the following manner:

(1) If the corporation has capital stock, its board of directors shall adopt a resolution setting forth the amendment proposed, declaring its advisability, and either calling a special meeting of the stockholders entitled to vote in respect thereof for the consideration of such amendment or directing that the amendment proposed be considered at the next annual meeting of the stockholders; provided, however, that unless otherwise expressly required by the certificate of incorporation, no meeting or vote of stockholders shall be required to adopt an amendment that effects only changes described in paragraph (a)(1) or (7) of this section. […]If no vote of stockholders is required to effect such amendment, or if a majority of the outstanding stock entitled to vote thereon, and a majority of the outstanding stock of each class entitled to vote

thereon as a class has been voted in favor of the amendment, a certificate setting forth the amendment and certifying that such amendment has been duly adopted in accordance with this section shall be executed, acknowledged and filed and shall become effective in accordance with § 103 of this title.

(2) The holders of the outstanding shares of a class shall be entitled to vote as a class upon a proposed amendment, whether or not entitled to vote thereon by the certificate of incorporation, if the amendment would increase or decrease the aggregate number of authorized shares of such class, increase or decrease the par value of the shares of such class, or alter or change the powers, preferences, or special rights of the shares of such class so as to affect them adversely. If any proposed amendment would alter or change the powers, preferences, or special rights of 1 or more series of any class so as to affect them adversely, but shall not so affect the entire class, then only the shares of the series so affected by the amendment shall be considered a separate class for the purposes of this paragraph. The number of authorized shares of any such class or classes of stock may be increased or decreased (but not below the number of shares thereof then outstanding) by the affirmative vote of the holders of a majority of the stock of the corporation entitled to vote irrespective of this subsection, if so provided in the original certificate of incorporation, in any amendment thereto which created such class or classes of stock or which was adopted prior to the issuance of any shares of such class or classes of stock, or in any amendment thereto which was authorized by a resolution or resolutions adopted by the affirmative vote of the holders of a majority of such class or classes of stock. […]

(c) The resolution authorizing a proposed amendment to the certificate of incorporation may provide that at any time prior to the effectiveness of the filing of the amendment with the Secretary of State, notwithstanding authorization of the proposed amendment by the stockholders of the corporation or by the members of a nonstock corporation, the board of directors or governing body may abandon such proposed amendment without further action by the stockholders or members.

2.2.6.2 DGCL Sec. 245 - Restating the Certificate

When certificates are amended, the amendments are simply "stapled" to the back of the original certificate. The result is often a document that is cumbersome to read. Rather than rely on a potentially confusing set of documents, a certificate may be "restated" in its entirety reading all the amendments into the certificate so that the document is easier to read and more understandable. Section 245 lays out the process by which a certificate may be restated.

§ 245. Restated certificate of incorporation.

(a) A corporation may, whenever desired, integrate into a single instrument all of the provisions of its certificate of incorporation which are then in effect and operative as a result of there having theretofore been filed with the Secretary of State 1 or more certificates or other instruments pursuant to any of the sections referred to in § 104 of this title, and it may at the same time also further amend its certificate of incorporation by adopting a restated certificate of incorporation.

(b) If the restated certificate of incorporation merely restates and integrates but does not further amend the certificate of incorporation, as theretofore amended or supplemented by any instrument that was filed pursuant to any of the sections mentioned in § 104 of this title, it may be adopted by the board of directors without a vote of the stockholders[…]. If the restated certificate of incorporation restates and integrates and also further amends in any respect the certificate of incorporation, as theretofore amended or supplemented, it shall be proposed by the directors and adopted by the stockholders in the manner and by the vote prescribed by § 242 of this title or, if the corporation has not received any payment for any of its stock, in the manner and by the vote prescribed by § 241 of this title.

(c) A restated certificate of incorporation shall be specifically designated as such in its heading. It shall state, either in its heading or in an introductory paragraph, the corporation's present name, and, if it has been changed, the name under which it was originally incorporated, and the date of filing of its original certificate of incorporation with the Secretary of State. A restated certificate shall also state that it was duly adopted in accordance with this section. If it was adopted by the board of directors without a vote of the stockholders (unless it was adopted pursuant to § 241 of this title or without a vote of members pursuant to § 242(b)(3) of this title), it shall state that it only restates and integrates and does not further amend the provisions of the corporation's certificate of incorporation as theretofore amended or supplemented, and that there is no discrepancy between those provisions and the provisions of the restated certificate. A restated certificate of incorporation may omit (a) such provisions of the original certificate of incorporation which named the incorporator or incorporators, the initial board of directors and the original subscribers for shares, and (b) such provisions contained in any amendment to the certificate of incorporation as were necessary to effect a change, exchange, reclassification, subdivision, combination or cancellation of stock, if such change, exchange, reclassification, subdivision, combination or cancellation has become effective. Any such omissions shall not be deemed a further amendment.

(d) A restated certificate of incorporation shall be executed, acknowledged and filed in accordance with § 103 of this title. […]

2.2.7 DGCL Sec. 107 - Powers of Incorporators

Corporations cannot incorporate themselves. The parties who incorporate a business are known as "incorporators" or "promoters". An incorporator need not be a person. An incorporator may also be another corporation.

Typically, the incorporator names the initial board of directors of the corporation immediately as part of the incorporation process, but if not, the incorporator has plenary power to manage the corporation until such time as the incorporator appoints the initial board of directors.

§ 107. Powers of incorporators.

If the persons who are to serve as directors until the first annual meeting of stockholders have not been named in the certificate of incorporation, the incorporator or incorporators, until the directors are elected, shall manage the affairs of the corporation and may do whatever is necessary and proper to perfect the organization of the corporation, including the adoption of the original bylaws of the corporation and the election of directors.

2.2.8 DGCL Sec. 108 - Organization Meeting

Once a corporation is incorporated, a formal organization meeting of the initial board of directors is required to adopt corporate bylaws, and ratify any actions taken by the incorporator. This organizational meeting may be in person, or as is often the case, undertaken by relying on written consent of the directors.

§ 108. Organization meeting of incorporators or directors named in certificate of incorporation.

(a) After the filing of the certificate of incorporation an organization meeting of the incorporator or incorporators, or of the board of directors if the initial directors were named in the certificate of incorporation, shall be held, either within or without this State, at the call of a majority of the incorporators or directors, as the case may be, for the purposes of adopting bylaws, electing directors (if the meeting is of the incorporators) to serve or hold office until the first annual meeting of stockholders or until their successors are elected and qualify, electing officers if the meeting is of the directors, doing any other or further acts to perfect the organization of the corporation, and transacting such other business as may come before the meeting. [...]

(c) Any action permitted to be taken at the organization meeting of the incorporators or directors, as the case may be, may be taken without a meeting if each incorporator or director, where there is more than 1, or the sole incorporator or director where there is only 1, signs an instrument which states the action so taken.

2.2.9 Doctrine of Preincorporation Adoption

Lots of things go into the formation of a business. In addition, to the incorporation one can reasonably expect that a not-yet-formed business might enter into contracts incident to incorporation. For example, the not-yet-formed business might contract with lawyers to undertake the incorporation itself. In addition, there may be a sales contract that could be the impetus for the formation of the corporation that is signed or entered into prior to incorporation. The fact that a contract was entered into prior to incorporation does not mean that the contract fails.

Courts have developed the "doctrine of preincorporation adoption" is applied. The doctrine of preincorporation adoption as it is applied to preincorporation agreements is relatively straightforward. According to a leading treatise:

> American courts generally hold that promoters' contracts made on the corporation's behalf may be adopted, accepted or ratified by the corporation when organized, and that the corporation is then liable, both at law and in equity, on the contract itself, and not merely for the benefits which it has received. *Accordingly, if the corporation accepts the contract's benefits, the corporation will be required to perform its obligations.*

Under Delaware law, if the subsequently-formed corporation expressly adopts the preincorporation agreement or implicitly adopts it by accepting its benefits with knowledge of its terms, the corporation is bound by it.

See: Alf v Lorillard Tobacco Co., 831 A.2d 335, 350 (Del. Ch. Ct, 2003).

2.2.10 Piercing the Corporate Veil

Legal personality and limited liability are two critical features of the modern corporate structure. Although these two features are often described as different, they are in fact two sides of the same coin. The "coin" in this case is the principal of separateness. Legal personality means that the corporate entity stands on its own, independent of its stockholders, such that the debts and other liabilities of the stockholders of the corporation are not the debts or liabilities of the corporation.

Equally important, limited liability (the default rule, provided under 102(b)(6)) means that the debts and other liabilities of the corporation are the debts and liabilities of the corporation and not the stockholders. The separate life of the corporation and the power of limited liability are extremely powerful policy choices that have implications for third parties as well as for corporate decision-makers.

Businesses can and do fail. When they do, limited liability means that the costs of that failure will mostly be borne by third party creditors of the firm and not by the directors or the stockholders of the firm. This may create incentives for third parties to careful when dealing with corporations. Before agreeing to a contract with a corporation, it is not uncommon for counterparties to engage in some "due diligence" to investigate the capabilities of the corporation. But, limited liability also creates incentives that improve the liquidity of capital markets and encourage corporate risk-taking - a stockholder can feel free to invest in a risky business, like a start-up, safe in the knowledge that should it fail, the stockholder will not be risking all of her assets, including the college fund she has saved for her kids.

"Piercing the corporate veil" is an equitable doctrine that is the exception to the limited liability rule. In extreme cases, courts may look through the protective barrier of limited liability and assign the corporation's liabilities to the stockholders. The following cases raise of the issues common in veil piercing cases.

Although the concept of corporate separateness is well understood at the state level, in recent years a series of First Amendment cases have provided the US Supreme Court the opportunity to give its own view on the traditional state law question of corporate separateness. Unlike state level courts, the US Supreme Court has taken a much more malleable view towards the doctrine of corporate separateness as that concept relates to the First Amendment.

2.2.10.1 Walkovszky v. Carlton

The default rule for the corporation is that stockholders face limited liability for the debts of the corporation. The liability of stockholders is limited to the capital they contributed to the corporation. For instance, if a stockholder contributes $100 in equity capital to the corporation by buying stock from the corporation for $100 (assume this represents all the equity capital available to the corporation), and if the corporation has $150 in debts, the corporation may be required to pay all of its equity capital (i.e. $100) to settle the corporation's debts. In most circumstances, stockholders will not be liable for the balance of the corporation's debt of $50. The liability of stockholders is thus limited to only their capital contributions.

Although limited liability as described above is the default rule, in extreme cases courts may look through the corporate form, or "pierce the corporate veil", and assign liability for corporate debts to stockholders.

The following case is paradigmatic. The owner of the corporation has obviously established the corporations in question specifically to limit his exposure to debts of each of the corporations he controls. In deciding whether the stockholder should receive the benefit of corporate limited liability, the court lays out an equitable test to determine whether it should look through the veil of limited liability protection and find the shareholders liable for the debts of the corporation.

If the corporation is a mere "alter ego" of the stockholders (e.g. if the corporation is operated without formality and for mere convenience of its stockholders) and the stockholder used the corporate form to engage in some injustice, it is more likely, though not certain, that a court will look through the corporate form and assign corporate liabilities to stockholders in order to prevent a fraud or inequitable result.

18 N.Y.2d 414 (1966)
WALKOVSKY v. CARLTON

Fuld, J

This case involves what appears to be a rather common practice in the taxicab industry of vesting the ownership of a taxi fleet in many corporations, each owning only one or two cabs.

The complaint alleges that the plaintiff was severely injured four years ago in New York City when he was run down by a taxicab owned by the defendant Seon Cab Corporation and negligently operated at the time by the defendant Marchese. The individual defendant, Carlton, is claimed to be a stockholder of 10 corporations, including Seon, each of which has but two cabs registered in its name, and it is implied that only the minimum automobile liability insurance required by law (in the amount of $10,000) is carried on any one cab. Although seemingly independent of one another, these corporations are alleged to be "operated * * * as a single entity, unit and enterprise" with regard to financing, supplies, repairs, employees and garaging, and all are named as defendants.[1] The plaintiff asserts that he is also entitled to hold their stockholders personally liable for the damages sought because the multiple corporate structure constitutes an unlawful attempt "to defraud members of the general public" who might be injured by the cabs. […]

The law permits the incorporation of a business for the very purpose of enabling its proprietors to escape personal liability […] but, manifestly, the privilege is not without its limits. Broadly speaking, the courts will disregard the corporate form, or, to use accepted terminology, "pierce the corporate veil", whenever necessary "to prevent fraud or to achieve equity". […] In determining whether liability should be extended to reach assets beyond those belonging to the corporation, we are guided, as Judge CARDOZO noted, by "general rules of agency". […]In other words, whenever anyone uses control of the corporation to further his own rather than the corporation's business, he will be liable for the corporation's acts "upon the principle of *respondeat superior* applicable even where the agent is a natural person". […]

In the case before us, the plaintiff has explicitly alleged that none of the corporations "had a separate existence of their own" and, as indicated above, all are named as defendants. However, it is one thing to assert that a corporation is a fragment of a larger corporate combine which actually conducts the business. […] It is quite another to claim that the corporation is a "dummy" for its individual stockholders who are in reality carrying on the business in their personal capacities for purely personal rather than corporate ends. […] Either circumstance would justify treating the corporation as an agent and piercing the corporate veil to reach the principal but a different result would follow in each case. In the first, only a larger *corporate* entity would be held financially responsible […] while, in the other, the stockholder would be personally liable. […] Either the stockholder is conducting the business in his individual capacity or he is not. If he is, he will be liable; if he is not, then, it does not matter — insofar as his personal liability is concerned — that the enterprise is actually being carried on by a larger "enterprise entity". […]

 Reading the complaint in this case most favorably and liberally, we do not believe that there can be gathered from its averments the allegations required to spell out a valid cause of action against the defendant Carlton.

The individual defendant is charged with having "organized, managed, dominated and controlled" a fragmented corporate entity but there are no allegations that he was conducting business in his individual capacity. Had the taxicab fleet been owned by a single corporation, it would be readily apparent that the plaintiff would face formidable barriers in attempting to establish personal liability on the part of the corporation's stockholders. The fact that the fleet ownership has been deliberately split up among many corporations does not ease the plaintiff's burden in that respect. The corporate form may not be disregarded merely because the assets of the corporation, together with the mandatory insurance coverage of the vehicle which struck the plaintiff, are insufficient to assure him the recovery sought. If Carlton were to be held individually liable on those facts alone, the decision would apply equally to the thousands of cabs which are owned by their individual drivers who conduct their businesses through corporations organized pursuant to section 401 of the Business Corporation Law and carry the minimum insurance required by subdivision 1 (par. [a]) of section 370 of the Vehicle and Traffic Law. These [420] taxi owner-operators are entitled to form such corporations […], and we agree with the court at Special Term that, if the insurance coverage required by statute "is inadequate for the protection of the public, the remedy lies not with the courts but with the Legislature." It may very well be sound policy to require that certain corporations must take out liability insurance which will afford adequate compensation to their potential tort victims. However, the responsibility for imposing conditions on the privilege of incorporation has been committed by the Constitution to the Legislature (N. Y. Const., art. X, § 1) and it may not be fairly implied, from any statute, that the Legislature intended, without the slightest discussion or debate, to require of taxi corporations that they carry automobile liability insurance over and above that mandated by the Vehicle and Traffic Law.[2]

This is not to say that it is impossible for the plaintiff to state a valid cause of action against the defendant Carlton. However, the simple fact is that the plaintiff has just not done so here. While the complaint alleges that the separate corporations were undercapitalized and that their assets have been intermingled, it is barren of any "sufficiently particular[ized] statements" […] that the defendant Carlton and his associates are actually doing business in their individual capacities, shuttling their personal funds in and out of the corporations "without regard to formality and to suit their immediate convenience." […] Such a "perversion of the privilege to do business in a corporate form" […] would justify imposing personal liability on the individual stockholders. […] Nothing of the sort has in fact been charged, and it cannot reasonably or logically be inferred from the happenstance that the business of Seon […] Cab Corporation may actually be carried on by a larger corporate entity composed of many corporations which, under general principles of agency, would be liable to each other's creditors in contract and in tort.[3]

In point of fact, the principle relied upon in the complaint to sustain the imposition of personal liability is not agency but fraud. Such a cause of action cannot withstand analysis. If it is not fraudulent for the owner-operator of a single cab corporation to take out only the minimum required liability insurance, the enterprise does not become either illicit or fraudulent merely because it consists of many such corporations. The plaintiff's injuries are the same regardless of whether the cab which strikes him is owned by a single corporation or part of a fleet with ownership fragmented among many corporations. Whatever rights he may be able to assert against parties other than the registered owner of the vehicle come into being not because he has been defrauded but because, under the principle of *respondeat superior*, he is entitled to hold the whole enterprise responsible for the acts of its agents.

In sum, then, the complaint falls short of adequately stating a cause of action against the defendant Carlton in his individual capacity.

The order of the Appellate Division should be reversed, with costs in this court and in the Appellate Division, the certified question answered in the negative and the order of the Supreme Court, Richmond County, reinstated, with leave to serve an amended complaint.

KEATING, J. (dissenting).

The defendant Carlton, the shareholder here sought to be held for the negligence of the driver of a taxicab, was a principal shareholder and organizer of the defendant corporation which owned the taxicab. The corporation was one of 10 organized by the defendant, each containing [422] two cabs and each cab having the "minimum liability" insurance coverage mandated by section 370 of the Vehicle and Traffic Law. The sole assets of these operating corporations are the vehicles themselves and they are apparently subject to mortgages.[*]

From their inception these corporations were intentionally undercapitalized for the purpose of avoiding responsibility for acts which were bound to arise as a result of the operation of a large taxi fleet having cars out on the street 24 hours a day and engaged in public transportation. And during the course of the corporations' existence all income was continually drained out of the corporations for the same purpose.

The issue presented by this action is whether the policy of this State, which affords those desiring to engage in a business enterprise the privilege of limited liability through the use of the corporate device, is so strong that it will permit that privilege to continue no matter how much it is abused, no matter how irresponsibly the corporation is operated, no matter what the cost to the public. I do not believe that it is.

Under the circumstances of this case the shareholders should all be held individually liable to this plaintiff for the injuries he suffered. (See *Mull v. Colt Co.*, 31 F. R. D. 154, 156; *Teller v. Clear Serv. Co.*, 9 Misc 2d 495.) At least, the matter should not be disposed of on the pleadings by a dismissal of the complaint. "If a corporation is organized and carries on business without substantial capital in such a way that the corporation is likely to have no sufficient assets available to meet its debts, it is inequitable that shareholders should set up such a flimsy organization to escape personal liability. The attempt to do corporate business without providing any sufficient basis of financial responsibility to creditors is an abuse of the separate entity and will be ineffectual to exempt the shareholders from corporate debts. It is coming to be recognized as the policy of law that shareholders should in good faith put at the risk of the business unincumbered capital reasonably adequate for its prospective liabilities. If capital is illusory or trifling compared with the business to be done and the risks [423] of loss, this is a ground for denying the separate entity privilege." (Ballantine, Corporations [rev. ed., 1946], § 129, pp. 302-303.)

In *Minton v. Cavaney* (56 Cal. 2d 576) the Supreme Court of California had occasion to discuss this problem in a negligence case. The corporation of which the defendant was an organizer, director and officer operated a public swimming pool. One afternoon the plaintiffs' daughter drowned in the pool as a result of the alleged negligence of the corporation.

Justice ROGER TRAYNOR, speaking for the court, outlined the applicable law in this area. "The figurative terminology `alter ego' and `disregard of the corporate entity'", he wrote, "is generally used to refer to the various situations that are an abuse of the corporate privilege * * * The equitable owners of a corporation, for example, are personally liable when they treat the assets of the corporation as their own and add or withdraw capital from the corporation at will * * *; when they hold themselves out as being personally liable for the debts of the corporation * * *; *or when they provide inadequate capitalization and actively participate in the conduct of corporate affairs*". (56 Cal. 2d, p. 579; italics supplied.)

Examining the facts of the case in light of the legal principles just enumerated, he found that "[it was] undisputed that there was no attempt to provide adequate capitalization. [The corporation] never had any substantial assets. It leased the pool that it operated, and the lease was forfeited for failure to pay the rent. Its capital was `trifling compared with the business to be done and the risks of loss'". (56 Cal. 2d, p. 580.)

It seems obvious that one of "the risks of loss" referred to was the possibility of drownings due to the negligence of the corporation. And the defendant's failure to provide such assets or any fund for recovery resulted in his being held personally liable.

In *Anderson v. Abbott* (321 U. S. 349) the defendant shareholders had organized a holding company and transferred to that company shares which they held in various national banks in return for shares in the holding company. The holding company did not have sufficient assets to meet the double liability requirements of the governing Federal statutes which provided that the owners of shares in national [424] banks were personally liable for corporate obligations "to the extent of the amount of their stock therein, at the par value thereof, in addition to the amount invested in such shares" (U. S. Code, tit. 12, former § 63).

The court had found that these transfers were made in good faith, that other defendant shareholders who had purchased shares in the holding company had done so in good faith and that the organization of such a holding company was entirely legal. Despite this finding, the Supreme Court, speaking through Mr. Justice DOUGLAS, pierced the corporate veil of the holding company and held all the shareholders, even those who had no part in the organization of the corporation, individually responsible for the corporate obligations as mandated by the statute.

"Limited liability", he wrote, "is the rule, not the exception; and on that assumption large undertakings are rested, vast enterprises are launched, and huge sums of capital attracted. But there are occasions when the limited liability sought to be obtained through the corporation will be qualified or denied. Mr. Justice CARDOZO stated that

41

a surrender of that principle of limited liability would be made 'when the sacrifice is essential to the end that some accepted public policy may be defended or upheld.' * * * The cases of fraud make up part of that exception * * * But they do not exhaust it. *An obvious inadequacy of capital, measured by the nature and magnitude of the corporate undertaking, has frequently been an important factor in cases denying stockholders their defense of limited liability * * * That rule has been invoked even in absence of a legislative policy which undercapitalization would defeat.* It becomes more important in a case such as the present one where the statutory policy of double liability will be defeated if impecunious bank-stock holding companies are allowed to be interposed as non-conductors of liability. *It has often been held that the interposition of a corporation will not be allowed to defeat a legislative policy, whether that was the aim or only the result of the arrangement* * * * 'the courts will not permit themselves to be blinded or deceived by mere forms of law' but will deal 'with the substance of the transaction involved as if the corporate agency did not exist and as the justice of the case may require.'" (321 U. S., pp. 362-363; emphasis added.)

The policy of this State has always been to provide and facilitate recovery for those injured through the negligence of others. The automobile, by its very nature, is capable of causing severe and costly injuries when not operated in a proper manner. The great increase in the number of automobile accidents combined with the frequent financial irresponsibility of the individual driving the car led to the adoption of section 388 of the Vehicle and Traffic Law which had the effect of imposing upon the owner of the vehicle the responsibility for its negligent operation. It is upon this very statute that the cause of action against both the corporation and the individual defendant is predicated.

In addition the Legislature, still concerned with the financial irresponsibility of those who owned and operated motor vehicles, enacted a statute requiring minimum liability coverage for all owners of automobiles. The important public policy represented by both these statutes is outlined in section 310 of the Vehicle and Traffic Law. That section provides that: "The legislature is concerned over the rising toll of motor vehicle accidents and the suffering and loss thereby inflicted. The legislature determines that it is a matter of grave concern that motorists shall be financially able to respond in damages for their negligent acts, so that innocent victims of motor vehicle accidents may be recompensed for the injury and financial loss inflicted upon them."

The defendant Carlton claims that, because the minimum amount of insurance required by the statute was obtained, the corporate veil cannot and should not be pierced despite the fact that the assets of the corporation which owned the cab were "trifling compared with the business to be done and the risks of loss" which were certain to be encountered. I do not agree.

The Legislature in requiring minimum liability insurance of $10,000, no doubt, intended to provide at least some small fund for recovery against those individuals and corporations who just did not have and were not able to raise or accumulate assets sufficient to satisfy the claims of those who were injured as a result of their negligence. It certainly could not have intended to shield those individuals who organized corporations, with the specific intent of avoiding responsibility to the public, where the operation of the corporate enterprise yielded profits sufficient to purchase additional insurance. Moreover, it is reasonable [426] to assume that the Legislature believed that those individuals and corporations having substantial assets would take out insurance far in excess of the minimum in order to protect those assets from depletion. Given the costs of hospital care and treatment and the nature of injuries sustained in auto collisions, it would be unreasonable to assume that the Legislature believed that the minimum provided in the statute would in and of itself be sufficient to recompense "innocent victims of motor vehicle accidents * * * for the injury and financial loss inflicted upon them".

The defendant, however, argues that the failure of the Legislature to increase the minimum insurance requirements indicates legislative acquiescence in this scheme to avoid liability and responsibility to the public. In the absence of a clear legislative statement, approval of a scheme having such serious consequences is not to be so lightly inferred.

The defendant contends that the court will be encroaching upon the legislative domain by ignoring the corporate veil and holding the individual shareholder. This argument was answered by Mr. Justice DOUGLAS in *Anderson v. Abbot* (*supra*, pp. 366-367) where he wrote that: "In the field in which we are presently concerned, judicial power hardly oversteps the bounds when it refuses to lend its aid to a promotional project which would circumvent or undermine a legislative policy. To deny it that function would be to make it impotent in situations where historically it has made some of its most notable

43

contributions. If the judicial power is helpless to protect a legislative program from schemes for easy avoidance, then indeed it has become a handy implement of high finance. *Judicial interference to cripple or defeat a legislative policy is one thing; judicial interference with the plans of those whose corporate or other devices would circumvent that policy is quite another.* Once the purpose or effect of the scheme is clear, once the legislative policy is plain, we would indeed forsake a great tradition to say we were helpless to fashion the instruments for appropriate relief." (Emphasis added.)

The defendant contends that a decision holding him personally liable would discourage people from engaging in corporate enterprise.

What I would merely hold is that a participating shareholder of a corporation vested with a public interest, organized with capital insufficient to meet liabilities which are certain to arise in the ordinary course of the corporation's business, may be held personally responsible for such liabilities. Where corporate income is not sufficient to cover the cost of insurance premiums above the statutory minimum or where initially adequate finances dwindle under the pressure of competition, bad times or extraordinary and unexpected liability, obviously the shareholder will not be held liable (Henn, Corporations, p. 208, n. 7).

The only types of corporate enterprises that will be discouraged as a result of a decision allowing the individual shareholder to be sued will be those such as the one in question, designed solely to abuse the corporate privilege at the expense of the public interest.

For these reasons I would vote to affirm the order of the Appellate Division.

Order reversed, etc.

2.2.10.2
KINNEY SHOE CORP. v. POLAN

Courts have long recognized that a corporation is an entity, separate and distinct from its officers and stockholders, and the individual stockholders are not responsible for the debts of the corporation.

In the following case, a Federal court lays out its approach to the question of whether a court should depart from the limited liability norm and "pierce the corporate veil" thus making stockholders liable for the debts of the corporation. The approach taken by the Federal court here differs only slightly from the approach to piercing taken by various state courts, including *Walkovszky*.

Central to a court's inquiry will be whether the stockholders treated the corporation as a separate entity with respect for the formalities due to a separate entity such that a court should also respect the corporation's limited liability.

Although the court in this case provides us with a convenient "test" it is worth remembering that piercing the corporate veil is an equitable remedy, therefore courts can – at times – appear to be inconsistent in their application of these tests. Success will usually require highly idiosyncratic facts and very sympathetic plaintiffs. In the most general terms, piercing the corporate veil is never going to be a court's first instinct.

939 F.2d 209 (1991)
KINNEY SHOE CORPORATION v. POLAN

CHAPMAN, Senior Circuit Judge:

Plaintiff-appellant Kinney Shoe Corporation ("Kinney") brought this action in the United States District Court for the Southern District of West Virginia against Lincoln M. Polan ("Polan") seeking to recover money owed on a sublease between Kinney and Industrial Realty Company ("Industrial"). Polan is the sole shareholder of Industrial. The district court found that Polan was not personally liable on the lease between Kinney and Industrial. Kinney appeals asserting that the corporate veil should be pierced, and we agree. […]

In 1984 Polan formed two corporations, Industrial and Polan Industries, Inc., for the purpose of re-establishing an industrial manufacturing business. […] Polan was the owner of both corporations. Although certificates of incorporation were issued, no organizational meetings were held, and no officers were elected.

In November 1984 Polan and Kinney began negotiating the sublease of a building in which Kinney held a leasehold interest. […]

The term of the sublease from Kinney to Industrial commenced in December 1984, even though the written lease was not signed by the parties until April 5, 1985. On April 15, 1985, Industrial subleased part of the building to Polan Industries for fifty percent of the rental amount due Kinney. Polan signed both subleases on behalf of the respective companies.

Other than the sublease with Kinney, Industrial had no assets, no income and no bank account. Industrial issued no stock certificates because nothing was ever paid in to this corporation. Industrial's only income was from its sublease to Polan Industries, Inc. The first rental payment to Kinney was made out of Polan's personal funds, and no further payments were made by Polan or by Polan Industries, Inc. to either Industrial or to Kinney.

Kinney filed suit against Industrial for unpaid rent and obtained a judgment in the amount of $166,400.00 on June 19, 1987. […]. Kinney then filed this action against Polan individually to collect the amount owed by Industrial to Kinney. Since the amount to which Kinney is entitled is undisputed, the only issue is whether Kinney can pierce the [211] corporate veil and hold Polan personally liable. […]

We have long recognized that a corporation is an entity, separate and distinct from its officers and stockholders, and the individual stockholders are not responsible for the debts of the corporation. […] This concept, however, is a fiction of the law "`and it is now well settled, as a general principle, that the fiction should be disregarded when it is urged with an intent not within its reason and purpose, and in such a way that its retention would produce injustices or inequitable consequences.'" *Laya v. Erin Homes, Inc.,* 352 S.E.2d 93, 97-98 (W.Va.1986) […].

Piercing the corporate veil is an equitable remedy, and the burden rests with the party asserting such claim. *DeWitt Truck Brokers,* 540 F.2d at 683. A totality of the circumstances test is used in determining whether to pierce the corporate veil, and each case must be decided on its own facts. The district court's findings of facts may be overturned only if clearly erroneous. *Id.*

Kinney seeks to pierce the corporate veil of Industrial so as to hold Polan personally liable on the sublease debt. The Supreme Court of Appeals of West Virginia has set forth a two prong test to be used in determining whether to pierce a corporate veil in a breach of contract case. This test raises two issues: first, is the unity of interest and ownership such that the separate personalities of the corporation and the individual shareholder no longer exist; and second, would an equitable result occur if the acts are treated as those of the corporation alone. […] Numerous factors have been identified as relevant in making this determination.[1] […]

It is undisputed that Industrial was not adequately capitalized. Actually, it had no paid in capital. Polan had put nothing into this corporation, and it did not observe any corporate formalities. As the West Virginia court stated in *Laya*, "`[i]ndividuals who wish to enjoy limited personal liability for business activities under a corporate umbrella should be expected to adhere to the relatively simple formalities of creating and maintaining a corporate entity.'" [ … ] This, the court stated, is "`a relatively small price to pay for limited liability.'" *Id.* Another important factor is adequate capitalization. "[G]rossly inadequate capitalization combined with disregard of corporate formalities, causing basic unfairness, are sufficient to pierce the corporate veil in order to hold the shareholder(s) actively participating in the operation of the business personally liable for a breach of contract to the party who entered into the contract with the corporation.[…].

In this case, Polan bought no stock, made no capital contribution, kept no minutes, and elected no officers for Industrial. In addition, Polan attempted to protect his assets by placing them in Polan Industries, Inc. and interposing Industrial between Polan Industries, Inc. and Kinney so as to prevent Kinney from going against the corporation with assets. Polan gave no explanation or justification for the existence of Industrial as the intermediary between Polan Industries, Inc. and Kinney. Polan was obviously trying to limit his liability and the liability of Polan Industries, Inc. by setting up a paper curtain constructed of nothing more than Industrial's certificate of incorporation. These facts present the classic scenario for an action to pierce the corporate veil so as to reach the responsible party and produce an equitable result. Accordingly, we hold that the district court correctly found that the two prong test in *Laya* had been satisfied. […]

For the foregoing reasons, we hold that Polan is personally liable for the debt of Industrial. […]

FOOTNOTE [1] The following factors were identified in *Laya:*

(1) commingling of funds and other assets of the corporation with those of the individual shareholders;(2) diversion of the corporation's funds or assets to noncorporate uses (to the personal uses of the corporation's shareholders);(3) failure to maintain the corporate formalities necessary for the issuance of or subscription to the corporation's stock, such as formal approval of the stock issue by the board of directors;(4) an individual shareholder representing to persons outside the corporation that he or she is personally liable for the debts or other obligations of the corporation;(5) failure to maintain corporate minutes or adequate corporate records;(6) identical equitable ownership in two entities;(7) identity of the directors and officers of two entities who are responsible for supervision and management (a partnership or sole proprietorship and a corporation owned and managed by the same parties);(8) failure to adequately capitalize a corporation for the reasonable risks of the corporate undertaking;(9) absence of separately held corporate assets;(10) use of a corporation as a mere shell or conduit to operate a single venture or some particular aspect of the business of an individual or another corporation;(11) sole ownership of all the stock by one individual or members of a single family;(12) use of the same office or business location by the corporation and its individual shareholder(s);(13) employment of the same employees or attorney by the corporation and its shareholder(s);(14) concealment or misrepresentation of the identity of the ownership, management or financial interests in the corporation, and concealment of personal business activities of the shareholders (sole shareholders do not reveal the association with a corporation, which makes loans to them without adequate security);(15) disregard of legal formalities and failure to maintain proper arm's length relationships among related entities;(16) use of a corporate entity as a conduit to procure labor, services or

48

merchandise for another person or entity;(17) diversion of corporate assets from the corporation by or to a stockholder or other person or entity to the detriment of creditors, or the manipulation of assets and liabilities between entities to concentrate the assets in one and the liabilities in another;(18) contracting by the corporation with another person with the intent to avoid risk of nonperformance by use of the corporate entity; or the use of a corporation as a subterfuge for illegal transactions;(19) the formation and use of the corporation to assume the existing liabilities of another person or entity.

Laya, 352 S.E.2d at 98-99 […]

2.2.10.3
FLETCHER v. ATEX, INC.

A subsidiary corporation is a corporation whose shares are owned entirely (or mostly) by another corporation. As between parent corporations and their subsidiaries, the default rule of limited liability still applies. A parent corporation will not normally be held liable for the debts of its subsidiary corporations.

In *Fletcher*, tort victims are asking the court to pierce the corporate veil of one of its defunct subsidiaries in order to make Kodak liable for the subsidiaries debts that resulted from an alleged product defect that caused repetitive stress disorders in customers.

The *Fletcher* court uses two different theories to test whether it should pierce the corporate veil and make Kodak, the sole stockholder of Atex, liable for the damages caused by Atex. The first theory is the same two prong test applied in other piercing the corporate veil cases. The second theory relies on more straightforward concepts of agency law. These theories are not necessarily mutually exclusive.

68 F.3d 1451 (1995)
FLETCHER v. ATEX, INC.

JOSÉ A. CABRANES, Circuit Judge:

The plaintiffs-appellants filed suit against Atex, Inc. ("Atex") and its parent, Eastman Kodak Company ("Kodak"), to recover for repetitive stress injuries that they claim were caused by their use of computer keyboards manufactured by Atex. […]

The *Fletcher* and *Hermanson* plaintiffs filed their respective complaints on December 4, 1992, and February 25, 1994, seeking recovery from Atex and Kodak, among others, for repetitive stress injuries that they claim were caused by their use of Atex computer keyboards. From 1981 until December 1992, Atex was a wholly-owned subsidiary of Kodak. In 1987, Atex's name was changed to Electronic Pre-Press Systems, Inc., ("EPPS"), but its name was changed back to Atex in 1990. In December 1992, Atex sold substantially all of its assets to an independent third party and again changed its name to 805 Middlesex Corp., which holds the proceeds from the sale. Kodak continues to be the sole shareholder of 805 Middlesex Corp.

After extensive discovery, Kodak moved for summary judgment in *Fletcher* on April 21, 1994, and in *Hermanson* on April 28, 1994. The plaintiffs opposed Kodak's motion, arguing that genuine issues of material fact existed as to Kodak's liability under any number of theories, including (1) that Atex was merely Kodak's alter ego or instrumentality; (2) that Atex was Kodak's agent in the manufacture and marketing of the keyboards; (3) that Kodak was the "apparent manufacturer" of the Atex keyboards [...]

B. Theories of Liability

1. Alter Ego Liability

The plaintiffs claim that the district court erred in granting Kodak's motion for summary judgment on their alter ego theory of liability. […]

The district court correctly noted that "[u]nder New York choice of law principles, `[t]he law of the state of incorporation determines when the corporate form will be disregarded and liability will be imposed on shareholders.'" […] Because Atex was a

Delaware corporation, Delaware law determines whether the corporate veil can be pierced in this instance.

Delaware law permits a court to pierce the corporate veil of a company "where there is fraud or where [it] is in fact a mere instrumentality or alter ego of its owner." [...]. Although the Delaware Supreme Court has never explicitly adopted an alter ego theory of parent liability for its subsidiaries, lower Delaware courts have applied the doctrine on several occasions, as has the United States District Court for the District of Delaware. [...]Thus, under an alter ego theory, there is no requirement of a showing of fraud. *Id.* at 1085. To prevail on an alter ego claim under Delaware law, a plaintiff must show (1) that the parent and the subsidiary "operated as a single economic entity" and (2) that an "overall element of injustice or unfairness ... [is] present." [...]

In the New York state action of *King v. Eastman,* the court granted Kodak's motion for summary judgment, relying on an erroneous interpretation of Delaware's alter ego doctrine. The court noted that although the plaintiffs had raised "ample questions of fact regarding the first element of the piercing theory — domination," they made "no showing that Kodak used whatever dominance it had over Atex to perpetrate a fraud or other wrong that proximately cause[d] injury to them." This was an error; under Delaware law, the alter ego theory of liability does not require any showing of fraud. [...]

To prevail on an alter ego theory of liability, a plaintiff must show that the two corporations "`operated as a single economic entity such that it would be inequitable ... to uphold a legal distinction between them.'" [...]. Among the factors to be considered in determining whether a subsidiary and parent operate as a "single economic entity" are:

> "[W]hether the corporation was adequately capitalized for the corporate undertaking; whether the corporation was solvent; whether dividends were paid, corporate records kept, officers and directors functioned properly, and other corporate formalities were observed; whether the dominant shareholder siphoned corporate funds; and whether, in general, the corporation simply functioned as a facade for the dominant shareholder."

As noted above, a showing of fraud or wrongdoing is not necessary under an alter ego theory, but the plaintiff must demonstrate an overall element of injustice or unfairness. […]

A plaintiff seeking to persuade a Delaware court to disregard the corporate structure faces "a difficult task." […] Courts have made it clear that "[t]he legal entity of a corporation will not be disturbed until sufficient reason appears."[…] Although the question of domination is generally one of fact, courts have granted motions to dismiss as well as motions for summary judgment in favor of defendant parent companies where there has been a lack of sufficient evidence to place the alter ego issue in dispute. […]

Kodak has shown that Atex followed corporate formalities, and the plaintiffs have offered no evidence to the contrary. Significantly, the plaintiffs have not challenged Kodak's assertions that Atex's board of directors held regular meetings, that minutes from those meetings were routinely prepared and maintained in corporate minute books, that appropriate financial records and other files were maintained by Atex, that Atex filed its own tax returns and paid its own taxes, and that Atex had its own employees and management executives who were responsible for the corporation's day-to-day business. The plaintiffs' primary arguments regarding domination concern (1) the defendant's use of a cash management system; (2) Kodak's exertion of control over Atex's major expenditures, stock sales, and the sale of Atex's assets to a third party; (3) Kodak's "dominating presence" on Atex's board of directors; (4) descriptions of the relationship between Atex and Kodak in the corporations' advertising, promotional literature, and annual reports; and (5) Atex's assignment of one of its former officer's mortgage to Kodak in order to close Atex's asset-purchase agreement with a third party. The plaintiffs argue that each of these raises a genuine issue of material fact about Kodak's domination of Atex, and that the district court therefore erred in granting summary judgment to Kodak on the plaintiffs' alter ego theory. We find that the district court correctly held that, in light of the undisputed factors of independence cited by Kodak, "the elements identified by the plaintiffs ... [were] insufficient as a matter of law to establish the degree of domination necessary to disregard Atex's corporate identity." […]

First, the district court correctly held that "Atex's participation in Kodak's cash management system is consistent with sound business practice and does not show undue domination or control." […]The parties do not dispute the mechanics of Kodak's cash management system. Essentially, all of Kodak's domestic subsidiaries participate in the system and maintain zero-balance bank accounts. All funds transferred from the subsidiary accounts are recorded as credits to the subsidiary, and when a subsidiary is in need of funds, a transfer is made. At all times, a strict accounting is kept of each subsidiary's funds.

Courts have generally declined to find alter ego liability based on a parent corporation's use of a cash management system. *See, e.g., In re Acushnet River & New Bedford Harbor Proceedings,* 675 F.Supp. 22, 34 (D.Mass.1987) (Without "considerably more," "a centralized cash management system ... where the accounting records always reflect the indebtedness of one entity to another, is not the equivalent of intermingling funds" and is insufficient to justify disregarding the corporate form.); […]The plaintiffs offer no facts to support their speculation that Kodak's centralized cash management system was actually a "complete commingling" of funds or a means by which Kodak sought to "siphon[] all of Atex's revenues into its own account."

Second, the district court correctly concluded that it could find no domination based on the plaintiffs' evidence that Kodak's approval was required for Atex's real estate leases, major capital expenditures, negotiations for a sale of minority stock ownership to IBM, or the fact that Kodak played a significant role in the ultimate sale of Atex's assets to a third party. Again, the parties do not dispute that Kodak required Atex to seek its approval and/or participation for the above transactions. However, this evidence, viewed in the light most favorable to the plaintiffs, does not raise an issue of material fact about whether the two corporations constituted "a single economic entity." […] In *Akzona,* the Delaware district court noted that a parent's "general executive responsibilities" for its subsidiary's operations included approval over major policy decisions and guaranteeing bank loans, and that that type of oversight was insufficient to demonstrate domination and control. […]

The plaintiffs' third argument, that Kodak dominated the Atex board of directors, also fails. Although a number of Kodak employees have sat on the Atex board, it is undisputed that between 1981 and 1988, only one director of Atex was also a director of Kodak. Between 1989 and 1992, Atex and Kodak had no directors in common. Parents and subsidiaries frequently have overlapping boards of directors while maintaining separate business operations. In *Japan Petroleum,* the Delaware district court held that the fact that a parent and a subsidiary have common officers and directors does not necessarily demonstrate that the parent corporation dominates the activities of the subsidiary. […] Since the overlap is negligible here, we find this evidence to be entirely insufficient to raise a question of fact on the issue of domination. […]

Finally, even if the plaintiffs did raise a factual question about Kodak's domination of Atex, summary judgment would still be appropriate because the plaintiffs offer no evidence on the second prong of the alter ego analysis. The plaintiffs have failed to present evidence of an "overall element of injustice or unfairness" that would result from respecting the two companies' corporate separateness. *See Harper,* 743 F.Supp. at 1085 (holding that plaintiff cannot prevail on alter ego theory "because he has failed to allege any unfairness or injustice which would justify the court in disregarding the [companies'] separate legal existences"). In the instant case, the plaintiffs offer nothing more than the bare assertion that Kodak "exploited" Atex "to generate profits but not to safeguard safety." There is no indication that Kodak sought to defraud creditors and consumers or to siphon funds from its subsidiary. The plaintiffs' conclusory assertions, without more, are not evidence […] and are completely inadequate to support a finding that it would be unjust to respect Atex's corporate form. […]

2. Agency Liability

The plaintiffs next contend that a genuine issue of fact was raised as to whether Kodak could be held liable on an agency theory — that is, whether Kodak, as principal, could be liable for the tortious acts of Atex, its agent. The plaintiffs rely on statements in Atex/ EPPS literature to support their theory: (1) the statement in the Atex document "Setting Up TPE 6000 on the Sun 3 Workstation" that "Atex is an unincorporated division of Electronic Pre-Press Systems, Inc., a Kodak company"; and (2) the statements in the EPPS promotional pamphlet that "EPPS serves as Kodak's primary agent to supply electronic pre-press products" and that "Atex is the largest of the EPPS business units." In granting Kodak's motion for summary judgment, the district court rejected the plaintiffs' agency theory of liability, finding that there was no evidence that Kodak authorized the statements. […]

The plaintiffs contend that the fact that Kodak permitted the use of its logo on these documents raises a question of fact as to whether Kodak authorized or appeared to authorize the references to Atex/EPPS as its agent. First, the plaintiffs' argument fails under a theory of actual authority. The Restatement (Second) of Agency states: "Authority is the power of the agent to affect the legal relations of the principal by acts done in accordance with the principal's manifestations of consent to him." RESTATEMENT (SECOND) OF AGENCY § 7 (1958). "Manifestation of consent" is "the expression of the will to another as distinguished from the undisclosed purpose or intention." […]. A close reading of the record reveals no evidence that Kodak conferred actual authority upon Atex to act on its behalf. The plaintiffs have offered no evidence that either document was produced by Kodak; in fact, it appears that Atex and EPPS published and disseminated the documents at issue. The presence of a parent's logo on documents created and distributed by a subsidiary, standing alone, does not confer authority upon the subsidiary to act as an agent.

For similar reasons, plaintiffs' arguments fail under a theory of apparent authority. New York's Court of Appeals has made it clear that "apparent authority is dependent upon verbal or other acts *by a principal* which reasonably give an appearance of authority to conduct the transaction." […] "Key to the creation of apparent authority," the court continued, "is that the third person, accepting the appearance of authority as true, has relied upon it." *Id.* The plaintiffs offer no evidence that Kodak authorized or gave the appearance of having authorized the statements in the Atex/EPPS documents. Atex's/EPPS's use of the Kodak logo is not a "verbal or other act[] by a *principal,*" but rather, an act by the purported agent. Furthermore, the record contains no evidence that the plaintiffs relied on the documents at issue. If there were evidence that the plaintiffs relied on these documents and if there were evidence that Kodak uttered or authorized them, then there would be an issue of material fact as to the existence of apparent authority. However, there is neither. We affirm the district court's order granting summary judgment to the defendant on the plaintiffs' agency theory of liability.

III. CONCLUSION

To summarize:

We affirm the district court's order granting summary judgment for the defendant on each of the plaintiffs' four theories of liability.

1. We agree with the district court's conclusion that the defendant was entitled to summary judgment on the plaintiffs' alter ego theory of liability. The collateral estoppel doctrine does not preclude relitigation of the question of Kodak's domination over Atex because the state court's finding of material facts in dispute was not essential to its judgment and because the defendant did not have a full and fair opportunity to litigate the issue. The elements identified by the plaintiffs were insufficient to raise a material issue of fact regarding domination, and further, the plaintiffs failed to offer evidence of injustice that would justify disregarding Atex's corporate form.

2. We affirm the district court's conclusion that the defendant was entitled to summary judgment on the plaintiffs' agency theory of liability because the plaintiffs offered no evidence that Kodak authorized or appeared to authorize Atex to act on its behalf in the manufacturing and marketing of keyboards or that the plaintiffs relied on the documents in question. […]

2.2.10.4 First Amendment, the Corporation, and "Reverse Veil Piercing"

In recent years, the US Supreme Court has pursued an aggressive expansion of First Amendment rights for corporations. Underlying all of the court's opinions in this area is the proposition that a corporation's rights under the First Amendment are derived from the rights of the corporation's stockholders and that there is no separation between stockholders and the corporation for purposes of the First Amendment and regulation of corporate speech. It is important to recognize that this view of the corporation - as one and the same with its stockholders - is at odds with state corporate law where the default is legal separation between the existence of the corporation and its stockholders. This default rule is also known as the "doctrine of corporate separateness."

In arriving at its present view of the First Amendment rights for corporations, the Roberts Court has had to basically ignore this doctrine. If one were to arrive at where the Roberts Court presently is, and still comport with basic conceptions of the corporate law and the doctrine of corporate separateness, one would first have to develop a theory of "reverse veil piercing". In neither of the two landmark First Amendment cases in recent years in which the court has imputed the First Amendment rights of stockholders, managers and employees to the corporation has the court done so through a reverse veil piercing theory.

First Amendment and Corporation

In *Citizens United*, the court protected speech rights of corporations by analogizing that corporations are nothing more than "associations of citizens." Let us leave to the side the court's assumption that corporations are associations of "citizens", which clearly they are not. It is well established that corporations can hold stock in other corporations. There is also no statutory requirement that limits stock ownership to citizens versus say, non-resident aliens. Nevertheless, in *Citizens United* the court would not sanction government restrictions on corporate speech because "citizens" had decided associate themselves together in the corporate form. The court reasoned in the same way the government could not restrict speech of persons under the constitution that corporations had rights derivative of the citizen stockholders associated with the corporation.

In *Hobby Lobby*, the Roberts Court imputes the religious views of stockholders to the corporation. Much like in *Citizens United*, Justice Alito rationalizes extending constitutional rights to corporations because of the people associated with the corporation. Justice Alito is, however, more expansive in his derivation of corporate rights:

> A corporation is simply a form of organization used by human
> beings to achieve desired ends. An established body of law specifies
> the rights and obligations of the *people* (including shareholders,
> officers, and employees) who are associated with a corporation in
> one way or another. When rights, whether constitutional or
> statutory, are extended to corporations, the purpose is to protect the
> rights of these people.

In the view of Justice Alito in *Hobby Lobby*, the motivation for extension of the First Amendment to the corporation is to protect the right of a various constituents of the incorporation, specifically including shareholders, officers, and employees of the corporation. Although the court in *Hobby Lobby* uses this rationale to impute the religious views of the shareholders of Hobby Lobby to the corporation itself, nowhere in the court's opinion does the court describe how it weighs the diverse religious views of the thousands of Hobby Lobby's employees.

In another recent high-profile case involving the First Amendment and the corporate form, *Masterpiece Cakeshop Ltd v. Colorado Civil Rights Commission* (2018), the Roberts Court ignored the doctrine of corporate separateness entirely. Throughout the opinion, which was decided on other grounds, the majority equated the controlling shareholder of Masterpiece Cakeshop Ltd with the corporation. Whether this was by accident or design is unclear. One thing that is clear is that were this case about assigning the financial liabilities of the corporation to the shareholder, the court would have been much less cavalier.

Citizens United, Hobby Lobby, and *Masterpiece Cakeshop* represent a distinct departure from earlier cases where the Supreme Court expressed a high degree of deference for the corporate form and the doctrine of corporate separateness. Take, for example *Domino's Pizza v. McDonald* (546 US 470, 2006). In *Domino's,* John W. McDonald, the sole shareholder and employee of JWM, Inc., brought a civil rights claim against Domino's arguing that Domino's discriminated against JWM, Inc. (a Domino's vendor) because McDonald himself was African-American. In that case, the Supreme Court had no problem in seeing a clear difference between the sole shareholder and the corporation and dismissed McDonald's claim for lack of standing because McDonald had signed the contracts in question in his capacity as an officer of JWM, Inc. and *not* in his personal capacity.

> McDonald's complaint does identify a contractual relationship, the one between Domino's and JWM. But it is fundamental corporation and agency law—indeed, it can be said to be the whole purpose of corporation and agency law—that the shareholder and contracting officer of a corporation has no rights and is exposed to no liability under the corporation's contracts. McDonald now makes light of the law of corporations and of agency—arguing, for instance, that because he "negotiated, signed, performed, and sought to enforce the contract," Domino's was wrong to "insist that [the contract] somehow was not his `own.'" Brief for Respondent 4. This novel approach to the law contradicts McDonald's own experience. Domino's filed a proof of claim against JWM during its corporate bankruptcy; it did *not* proceed against McDonald personally. The

corporate form and the rules of agency protected his personal assets, even though he "negotiated, signed, performed, and sought to enforce" contracts for JWM. The corporate form and the rules of agency similarly deny him rights under those contracts.

On the one hand, the court is happy to look through the corporate form in order to impute shareholders' religious views to the legal fiction we call the corporation. On the other hand, when stockholders seek to asserts civil rights claims on behalf of the corporation, the court refuses to impute the rights of the stockholders to corporation. If it seems hard to make sense of the Robert Court's approach to the corporate form that is because, frankly, it does not make much sense.

Reverse Veil Piercing Theory

If one were to create a doctrinally sound path for a court to impute the constitutional rights of stockholders to the corporation, one would have to do much more work than the Roberts Court has done in preparing the way. One would have to "pierce the corporate veil" but in reverse.

Remember, in the context of traditional veil piercing, courts will rely on a two prong test to overcome the partition between stockholders and the corporation. First, stockholders must have operated the corporation as an "alter ego." In practice, that means stockholders must have disregarded the simple corporate formalities required by the statute that give a separate life to the corporation: articles of incorporation, bylaws, meetings of a board of directors, etc. Second, the court must determine that not piercing the corporate veil of limited liability would result in some inequity or injustice.

Any theory of looking through the corporate form and pierce the corporate veil in reverse, as the Supreme Court would have us do, must require a test that is an analogue of the traditional veil piercing test: a unity of interest between the corporation and the corporation and whether not permitting a reverse veil piercing would result in some injustice to the stockholders.

Where stockholders treat the corporation as no more than their alter ego (due to lack of formality, etc.) and where the failure of the court to impute the constitutional rights of the stockholders to the corporation would result in some inequity or injustice, then a court would be right to impute the constitutional rights of the shareholder to the corporation. Of course, application of this reverse veil piercing standard to corporations would be a two-edge sword for the corporations that avail themselves of this. Corporations seeking to disregard the doctrine of corporate separateness for the purposes of imputing the constitutional rights of stockholders to the corporation would also give up, in effect, the benefits of limited liability.

***

If the Supreme Court were to apply state-level veil piercing doctrines to the question of imputing a group of stockholders' religious views to the corporation, what might that "reverse veil piercing" doctrine look like? In that case, what would have to be true before the court might impute the religious views of stockholders to the corporation?

2.3 Corporate Powers

Prior to the passage of general enabling laws, the explication of corporate power through the corporate charter was extremely important. State legislatures could tailor corporate charters to provide corporations significant powers, including monopoly rights over markets or territories. Although states no longer grant corporations such unique powers, explication of corporate powers (e.g. right to own property, right sue and be sued, etc.) nevertheless remains important in establishing a corporation's legal personality.

Sections 121 and 122 are authorizing provisions that grant corporate entities both explicit and implicit authority to act and conduct business. While §122 provides explicit authority for certain activities of the corporation, §121 is a catch-all provision that provides implied authority to the corporation to undertake all other actions required to conduct business. Taken together, the corporation has a great deal of flexibility to act.

2.3.1 DGCL Sec. 121 - General Powers

Section 121 provides for the general powers of a corporation. The corporation has implied authority to undertake all actions required in order to conduct its business as determined by the board of directors and as limited by the corporation's certificate of incorporation and the statute.

§ 121. General powers.

(a) In addition to the powers enumerated in § 122 of this title, every corporation, its officers, directors and stockholders shall possess and may exercise all the powers and privileges granted by this chapter or by any other law or by its certificate of incorporation, together with any powers incidental thereto, so far as such powers and privileges are necessary or convenient to the conduct, promotion or attainment of the business or purposes set forth in its certificate of incorporation.

(b) Every corporation shall be governed by the provisions and be subject to the restrictions and liabilities contained in this chapter.

2.3.2 DGCL Sec. 122 - Specific Powers

In addition to a corporation's general powers, the statute lays out a series of specific powers available to every corporation. Many of these specific powers are critical to the life of a corporation. These specific powers under §122 were once controversial, but by now are almost taken for granted.

For example, the corporate power to make charitable donations is one such specific corporate power that was once controversial. In the early years of the corporate form, donations to charitable causes were deemed to be *ultra vires* – or beyond the power of boards of directors. Through a series of changes – in the code and the common law – charitable contributions are now permissible.

Section 122 grants the corporation other specific powers, all of which are calculated to facilitating the ability of the corporation to act in its own behalf as a corporate person separate from its stockholders.

§ 122. Specific powers.

Every corporation created under this chapter shall have power to:

(1) Have perpetual succession by its corporate name, unless a limited period of duration is stated in its certificate of incorporation;

(2) Sue and be sued in all courts and participate, as a party or otherwise, in any judicial, administrative, arbitrative or other proceeding, in its corporate name;

(3) Have a corporate seal, which may be altered at pleasure, and use the same by causing it or a facsimile thereof, to be impressed or affixed or in any other manner reproduced;

(4) Purchase, receive, take by grant, gift, devise, bequest or otherwise, lease, or otherwise acquire, own, hold, improve, employ, use and otherwise deal in and with real or personal property, or any interest therein, wherever situated, and to sell, convey, lease, exchange, transfer or otherwise dispose of, or mortgage or pledge, all or any of its property and assets, or any interest therein, wherever situated;

(5) Appoint such officers and agents as the business of the corporation requires and to pay or otherwise provide for them suitable compensation;

(6) Adopt, amend and repeal bylaws;

(7) Wind up and dissolve itself in the manner provided in this chapter;

(8) Conduct its business, carry on its operations and have offices and exercise its powers within or without this State;

(9) Make donations for the public welfare or for charitable, scientific or educational purposes, and in time of war or other national emergency in aid thereof;

(10) Be an incorporator, promoter or manager of other corporations of any type or kind;

(11) Participate with others in any corporation, partnership, limited partnership, joint venture or other association of any kind, or in any transaction, undertaking or arrangement which the participating corporation would have power to conduct by itself, whether or not such participation involves sharing or delegation of control with or to others;

(12) Transact any lawful business which the corporation's board of directors shall find to be in aid of governmental authority;

(13) Make contracts, including contracts of guaranty and suretyship, incur liabilities, borrow money at such rates of interest as the corporation may determine, issue its notes, bonds and other obligations, and secure any of its obligations by mortgage, pledge or other encumbrance of all or any of its property, franchises and income, and make

contracts of guaranty and suretyship which are necessary or convenient to the conduct, promotion or attainment of the business of (a) a corporation all of the outstanding stock of which is owned, directly or indirectly, by the contracting corporation, or (b) a corporation which owns, directly or indirectly, all of the outstanding stock of the contracting corporation, or (c) a corporation all of the outstanding stock of which is owned, directly or indirectly, by a corporation which owns, directly or indirectly, all of the outstanding stock of the contracting corporation, which contracts of guaranty and suretyship shall be deemed to be necessary or convenient to the conduct, promotion or attainment of the business of the contracting corporation, and make other contracts of guaranty and suretyship which are necessary or convenient to the conduct, promotion or attainment of the business of the contracting corporation;

(14) Lend money for its corporate purposes, invest and reinvest its funds, and take, hold and deal with real and personal property as security for the payment of funds so loaned or invested;

(15) Pay pensions and establish and carry out pension, profit sharing, stock option, stock purchase, stock bonus, retirement, benefit, incentive and compensation plans, trusts and provisions for any or all of its directors, officers and employees, and for any or all of the directors, officers and employees of its subsidiaries;

(16) Provide insurance for its benefit on the life of any of its directors, officers or employees, or on the life of any stockholder for the purpose of acquiring at such stockholder's death shares of its stock owned by such stockholder.

(17) Renounce, in its certificate of incorporation or by action of its board of directors, any interest or expectancy of the corporation in, or in being offered an opportunity to participate in, specified business opportunities or specified classes or categories of business opportunities that are presented to the corporation or 1 or more of its officers, directors or stockholders. […]

2.3.3 THEODORA HOLDING CORP. v. HENDERSON

Theodora deals with the issue of corporate charity. Until the post-World War II period, there was some question whether a corporation had the power to make donations to charity. On the one hand, there were those who felt that a board's sole duty was to maximize profits for stockholders and that absent express authority to make corporate charitable contributions in the corporation's certificate of incorporation, that a board does not have the authority to make such contributions. On the other hand, there were those who recognized corporations had – even back to the pre-enabling laws period – a broader social role beyond maximizing profit for stockholders in the short run.

Eventually, states legislatures put this question to rest by amending their corporate statutes to recognize the power of boards to make charitable corporate gifts. A series of court cases, including *Theodora*, reinforced the importance of corporate charitable contributions and the role of corporate charitable contributions in the corporate social compact.

The power of a corporation to make charitable contributions is not unlimited, however. *Theodora* and *AP Smith*, cited in *Theodora*, hint at the limits to corporate largesse.

The debate about the extent of corporate power to make charitable donations runs parallel to a modern debate about corporate purpose. On the one side, there are those who argue that boards should be focused exclusively on maximizing stockholder value. On the other are those who argue that corporations have responsibilities to a broader group of stakeholders. Managing the tension that is reflected in this ongoing debate is central to understanding the corporate law and how modern boards make decisions.

257 A.2d 398 (1969)
THEODORA HOLDING
CORPORATION v. HENDERSON

Plaintiff, which was formed in May of 1967 by the defendant Girard B. Henderson's former wife, Theodora G. Henderson, is the holder of record of 11,000 of the 40,500 issued and outstanding shares of common stock of the defendant Alexander Dawson, Inc. It sues derivatively as well as on its own behalf for an accounting by the individual defendants for the losses allegedly sustained by the corporate defendant and the concomitant improper gains allegedly received by the individual defendants as a result of certain transactions of which plaintiff complains.[…]

As of September 30, 1968, Theodora G. Henderson, in addition to her interest in [400] the plaintiff corporation, was the holder of the following shares of preferred stock of the corporate defendant, namely, 3,000 of first preferred, 12,000 of second preferred, and 22,000 of third preferred. She continues to receive dividends on such shares. Prior to plaintiff's formation in 1967 Mrs. Henderson had received dividends on both common and preferred shares of the corporate defendant until she transferred her 11,000 shares of the common stock of said company to plaintiff during the year 1967. Corporate dividends paid to Mrs. Henderson in recent years and now to plaintiff and Mrs. Henderson have increased substantially in recent years. As of December 3, 1968, dividends paid to plaintiff and Mrs. Henderson in that year totalled $385,240. In 1966, Mrs. Henderson had received dividends in the amount of $292,840, and in 1967, a year in which Alexander Dawson, Inc., made a controversial charitable contribution having a value of $528,000, the combined dividends of plaintiff and Mrs. Henderson totalled $286,240.

In January of 1955, the defendant Girard B. Henderson and his then wife, Theodora G. Henderson, had entered into a separation agreement looking towards a divorce, at which time Mrs. Henderson's dividends from the corporate defendant totalled approximately $50,000 per annum. Under the terms of such agreement Mrs. Henderson acknowledged that she had received from her then husband the shares of common stock of Alexander Dawson, Inc., here in issue as well as a number of shares of preferred stock of such corporation. Upon plaintiff's organization, it became the owner of Mrs. Henderson's 11,000 shares of common stock[1] on May 3, 1967. As of April 30, 1967, the shares of Alexander Dawson, Inc., to be turned over to the plaintiff corporation had a fair market value of $15,675,000 and an underlying net asset value of $28,996,000. […]

The individual defendant Henderson by reason of the extent of his combined majority holdings of common and preferred stock of Alexander Dawson, Inc., each class of which has voting rights, exercises effective control over the affairs of such corporation, the net worth of the assets of which, at the time of the filing of this suit, was approximately $150,000,000.

It is claimed and the evidence supports such contention that on December 8, 1967, the defendant Girard B. Henderson, by virtue of his voting control over the affairs of Alexander Dawson, Inc., caused the board of directors of such corporation to be reduced in number from eight to three persons, namely himself, the defendant Bengt Ljunggren,[2] an employee of the corporate defendant, and Mr. Henderson's daughter,

Theodora H. Ives. It is alleged that thereafter the defendant Girard B. Henderson (over the objection of the director, Mrs. Ives) caused the board and the majority of the voting stock of Alexander [401] Dawson, Inc., improperly to contribute stock held by it in the approximate value of $550,000 to the Alexander Dawson Foundation, a charitable trust, the affairs of which were then controlled and continue to be controlled by Mr. Henderson. […]

Alexander Dawson, Inc. has functioned as a personal holding company since 1935 when Mr. Henderson's mother exchanged a substantial number of shares held by her in a company which later became Avon Products, Inc., for all of the shares of her own company known as Alexander Dawson, Inc. Mr. Henderson and a brother later succeeded to their mother's interest in Alexander Dawson, Inc., the brother thereafter permitting his shares to be redeemed by the corporation. As noted earlier, Mr. Henderson, by reason of his combined holdings of common and preferred stock of the corporate defendant, is in clear control of the affairs of such corporation, which, for the most part, has been operated informally by Mr. Henderson with scant regard for the views of other board members. Some seventy-five percent of its assets consist of shares of Avon Products, Inc. stock, there having been some diversification, particularly in 1967, largely through the urging of officers of the United States Trust Company of New York who have served as advisors. Through exercise of such control, Mr. Henderson has, since 1957, [402] caused the corporate defendant to donate varying amounts to a charitable trust organized in that year by Mr. Henderson, namely the Alexander Dawson Foundation. In 1957, $10,610 was donated to such trust. From 1960 to 1966 (except for the year 1965) gifts were in the range of approximately $63,000 to $70,000 or higher in each year other than 1963 when $27,923 was donated. In 1966, however, a gift in the form of a large tract of land in Colorado, having a value of some $467,750, was made.[3] All of these gifts through 1966 were unanimously approved by all of the stockholders of Alexander Dawson, Inc., including Mrs. Theodora G. Henderson. The gift now under attack, namely one of the shares of stock of the corporate defendant having a value of some $528,000, was made to the Alexander Dawson Foundation in December of 1967. Such gift was first proposed by Mr. Henderson in April, 1967 before the board of the corporate defendant was reduced in number from eight to three. However, director reaction was thereafter confused, one of the directors, Mrs. Henderson's daughter,

Theodora H. Ives, having expressed a desire that a corporate gift also be made to her own charitable corporation and that of her mother, Theodora G. Henderson. Accordingly, the matter was not pressed by Mr. Henderson until late December when the reduced board had taken over management of the corporate defendant. It is claimed and admitted that such gift had an effect on the equity and dividends of shareholders of the corporate defendant although the tax consequences of such gift clearly soften the apparent impact of such transaction. It is significant, however, as noted above, that the 1966 corporate gift, consisting of a ranch located in Colorado, had been approved by all of the directors and stockholders of the corporate defendant, and that the gift here under attack was apparently intended to be a step towards consummation of the purpose behind such grant of land, namely to provide a fund for the financing of a western camp for under privileged boys, particularly members of the George Junior Republic, a self-governing institution which has served the public interest for some seventy-five years at a school near Freeville, New York. Thus, in the summer of 1967, a small group of under privileged children had enjoyed the advantages of such camp in a test of the feasibility of such an institution. However, it is apparently Mr. Henderson's intention to continue and expand his interest in such camp where he maintains an underground home which he occupies at a $6,000 rental per annum, such house being occupied by him during some three months of the year. Plaintiff initially attacked such use. However[…] plaintiff seeks no accounting from the individual defendants[…] plaintiff asks that all actions undertaken by Mr. Henderson which demonstrate a course of irresponsible corporate conduct as well as misuse of corporate power and assets should be considered by the Court in reaching an ultimate decision on the question of whether or not a liquidating receiver for Alexander Dawson, Inc., should be appointed. […]

The next matter to be considered is the propriety of the December 1967 gift made by Alexander Dawson, Inc. to the Alexander Dawson Foundation of shares of stock of the corporate defendant having a value in excess of $525,000, an amount within the limits of the provisions of the federal tax law having to do with deductible corporate gifts, Internal Revenue Code of 1954 §§ 170(b) (2), 545(b) (2).

Title 8 Del.C. § 122 provides as follows:

"Every corporation created under this chapter shall have power to
—

* * * * * *

(9) Make donations for the public welfare or for charitable, scientific or educational purposes, and in time of war or other national emergency in aid thereof."

There is no doubt but that the Alexander Dawson Foundation is recognized as a legitimate charitable trust by the Department of Internal Revenue. It is also clear that it is authorized to operate exclusively in the fields of "* * * religious, charitable, scientific, literary, or educational purposes, or for the prevention of cruelty to children or animals * * *". Furthermore, contemporary courts recognize that unless corporations carry an increasing share of the burden of supporting charitable and educational causes that the business advantages now reposed in corporations by law may well prove to be unacceptable to the representatives of an aroused public. The recognized obligation of corporations towards philanthropic, educational and artistic causes is reflected in the statutory law of all of the states, other than the states of Arizona and Idaho.

In A. P. Smith Mfg. Co. v. Barlow, 13 N.J. 145, 98 A.2d 681, 39 A.L.R.2d 1179, appeal dismissed, 346 U.S. 861, 74 S.Ct. 107, 98 L.Ed. 373, a case in which the corporate donor had been organized long before the adoption of a statute authorizing corporate gifts to charitable or educational institutions, the Supreme Court of New Jersey upheld a gift of $1500 by the plaintiff corporation to Princeton University, being of the opinion that the trend towards the transfer of wealth from private industrial entrepreneurs to corporate institutions, the increase of taxes on individual income, coupled with steadily increasing philanthropic needs, necessitate corporate giving for educational needs even were there no statute permitting such gifts, and this was held to be the case apart from the question of the reserved power of the state to amend corporate charters. The court also noted that the gift tended to bolster the free enterprise system and the general social climate in which plaintiff was nurtured. And while the court pointed out that there was no showing that the gift in question was made indiscriminately or to a pet charity in furtherance of personal rather than corporate ends, the actual holding of the opinion appears to be that a corporate charitable or educational gift to be valid must merely be within reasonable limits both as to amount and purpose. Compare Union Pacific R. R. v. Trustees, Inc., 8 Utah 2d 101, 329 P.2d 398.

The New Jersey statute in force and effect at the time of the Smith case gift provided that directors might cause their corporation to contribute for charitable and educational purposes and the like "* * such reasonable sum or sums as they may determine * * *" provided, however, that such contributions might not be made in situations where the proposed donee owned more than 10% of the voting stock of the donor and provided further that such gifts be limited to 5% of capital and surplus unless "* * * authorized by the stockholders."

[405] Whether or not these statutory limitations on corporate giving were the source of the limiting language of the New Jersey Supreme Court is not clear, the point being that the Delaware statute contains no such limiting language and therefor must, in my opinion, be construed to authorize any reasonable corporate gift of a charitable or educational nature. Significantly, Alexander Dawson, Inc. was incorporated in Delaware in 1958 after 8 Del.C. § 122(9) was cast in its present form, therefor no constitutional problem arising out of the effect on a stockholder's property rights of the State's reserved power to amend corporate charters is presented.

I conclude that the test to be applied in passing on the validity of a gift such as the one here in issue is that of reasonableness, a test in which the provisions of the Internal Revenue Code pertaining to charitable gifts by corporations furnish a helpful guide. The gift here under attack was made from gross income and had a value as of the time of giving of $528,000 in a year in which Alexander Dawson, Inc.'s total income was $19,144,229.06, or well within the federal tax deduction limitation of 5% of such income. The contribution under attack can be said to have "cost" all of the stockholders of Alexander Dawson, Inc. including plaintiff, less than $80,000, or some fifteen cents per dollar of contribution, taking into consideration the federal tax provisions applicable to holding companies as well as the provisions for compulsory distribution of dividends received by such a corporation. In addition, the gift, by reducing Alexander Dawson, Inc.'s reserve for unrealized capital gains taxes by some $130,000, increased the balance sheet net worth of stockholders of the corporate defendant by such amount. It is accordingly obvious, in my opinion, that the relatively small loss of immediate income otherwise payable to plaintiff and the corporate defendant's other stockholders, had it not been for the gift in question, is far out-weighed by the overall benefits flowing from the placing of such gift in channels where it serves to benefit those in need of philanthropic or educational support, thus providing justification for large private holdings, thereby benefiting plaintiff in the long run. Finally, the fact that the interests of the Alexander Dawson Foundation appear to be increasingly directed towards the rehabilitation and education of deprived but deserving young people is peculiarly appropriate in an age when a large segment of youth is alienated even from parents who are not entirely satisfied with our present social and economic system.

[…]

2.3.4 DGCL Sec. 123 - Ownership of securities

Prior to the adoption of general incorporation statutes, corporations were regularly prohibited from owning stock or securities of other corporations. By specifically permitting a corporation to own and vote the stock of another corporation, §123 makes possible the "holding company" structure.

A holding company is a corporation that has no operations but holds assets in the form of stock of subsidiary operating corporations. This hierarchical business structure is now quite common in the US and has a number of obvious benefits. First and foremost, the holding company structure permits the parent corporation to hold risky assets at arm's length, utilizing the subsidiary's limited liability shield to prevent an adverse risk in one business unit from affecting the entire business operation. The holding company structure also makes it easier to buy and sell corporate assets. Rather than engage in an corporate level merger or sale, the board of directors of a holding company can buy or sell divisions by simply transferring the shares of the division to or from a buyer. For these reasons, and others, the holding company structure has become ubiquitous.

§ 123. Powers respecting securities of other corporations or entities.

Any corporation organized under the laws of this State may guarantee, purchase, take, receive, subscribe for or otherwise acquire; own, hold, use or otherwise employ; sell, lease, exchange, transfer or otherwise dispose of; mortgage, lend, pledge or otherwise deal in and with, bonds and other obligations of, or shares or other securities or interests in, or issued by, any other domestic or foreign corporation, partnership, association or individual, or by any government or agency or instrumentality thereof. A corporation while owner of any such securities may exercise all the rights, powers and privileges of ownership, including the right to vote.

2.3.5 Public Benefit Corporations

The development of corporate social responsibility and social entrepreneurship has given rise to demand for a different kind of corporate form, the "public benefit corporation". The public benefit corporation is a for-profit corporation established with a specific public purpose. The certificate of incorporation of a public benefit corporation requires that incorporators specify some public benefit against which the pecuniary interests of the corporation's business must be balanced. Public benefit corporations as a specific form are a relatively new addition to corporate laws of states in response to a growing desire by promoters to have a corporate form that outwardly signals a credible commitment by managers to a more publicly-minded business.

Although the form is relatively new, there is very little in the public benefit form that could not also be accomplished using a regular corporation. For many years, non-profit corporations were nothing more than corporations in which the certificate of incorporation prohibited the board from making a profit for stockholders. In fact, the Green Bay Packers' certificate of incorporation prohibits stockholders from ever receiving a dividend and requires the board of the Packers to donate any profits the team might have to a community foundation.

In recent years, there has been a proliferation of public benefit corporations. For example, Ello, a Delaware public benefit corporation (social networking site), specifies as its public benefit that it will not share the private information of its customers with third parties. Plum Organics, another Delaware public benefit corporation (a baby food manufacturer), specifies that its public benefit includes "the delivery of nourishing, organic food to the nation's little ones." Finally, Kickstarter, PBC, a New York public benefit corporation, specifies a number of public benefits that it will be guided by. The certificates of incorporation for Kickstarter is available in the Appendix.

2.3.5.1 Public Benefit Corporations

The following amendments to the Delaware corporation code became effective on August 1, 2013 and provide for the establishment of public benefit corporations under the Delaware General Corporation Law. Section 362 requires public benefit corporations to identify a public benefit in its certificate of incorporation. Section 365 requires boards of directors to manage the business in a manner that balances profit with the best interests of those affected by the corporation's conduct as well as the specific public benefit identified in the certificate of incorporation.

BE IT ENACTED BY THE GENERAL ASSEMBLY OF THE STATE OF DELAWARE:

SUBCHAPTER XV, PUBLIC BENEFIT CORPORATIONS

§ 362. Public benefit corporation defined; contents of certificate of incorporation.

(a)   A public benefit corporation is a for-profit corporation organized under and subject to the requirements of this chapter that is intended to produce a public benefit or public benefits and to operate in a responsible and sustainable manner. To that end, a public benefit corporation shall be managed in a manner that balances the stockholders' pecuniary interests, the best interests of those materially affected by the corporation's conduct, and the public benefit or public benefits identified in its certificate of incorporation. In the certificate of incorporation, a public benefit corporation shall (i) identify within its statement of business or purpose pursuant to§ 102(a)(3) of this title one or more specific public benefits to be promoted by the corporation, and (ii) state within its heading that it is a public benefit corporation.

(b)   "Public benefit" means a positive effect (or reduction of negative effects) on one or more categories of persons, entities, communities or interests (other than stockholders in their capacities as stockholders) including, but not limited to, effects of an artistic, charitable, cultural, economic, educational, environmental, literary, medical, religious, scientific or technological nature. "Public benefit provisions" means the provisions of a certificate of incorporation contemplated by this subchapter.

(c)   The name of the public benefit corporation shall, without exception, contain the words "public benefit corporation", or the abbreviation "P.B.C.", or the designation "PBC", which shall be deemed to satisfy the requirements of § 102(a)(l)(i) of this title.

§ 363. Certain amendments and mergers; votes required; appraisal rights.

(a)   Notwithstanding any other provisions of this chapter, a corporation that is not a public benefit corporation, may not, without the approval of ninety percent of the outstanding shares of each class of the stock of the corporation of which there are outstanding shares, whether voting or non-voting, (i) amend its certificate of incorporation to include a provision authorized by § 362(a)(i) of this title or (ii) merge or consolidate with or into another entity if, as a result of such merger or consolidation, the shares in such corporation would become, or be converted into or exchanged for the right to receive, shares or other equity interests in a domestic or foreign public benefit corporation or similar entity. The restrictions of this § 363 shall not apply prior to the time that the corporation has received payment for any of its capital stock, or in the case of a nonstock corporation, prior to the time that it has members.

(b)   Any stockholder of a corporation that is not a public benefit corporation that holds shares of stock of such corporation immediately prior to the effective time of (1) an amendment to the corporation's certificate of incorporation to include a provision authorized by § 362(a)(i) of this title, or (2) a merger or consolidation that would result in the conversion of the corporation's stock into or exchange of the corporation's stock for the right to receive shares or other equity interests in a domestic or foreign public benefit corporation or similar entity, and has neither voted in favor of such amendment or such merger or consolidation nor consented thereto in writing pursuant to § 228 of this title, shall be entitled to an appraisal by the Court of Chancery of the fair value of the stockholder's shares of stock.

(c)   Notwithstanding any other provisions of this chapter, a corporation that is a public benefit corporation may not, without the approval of two-thirds of the outstanding shares of each class of the stock of the corporation of which there are outstanding shares, whether voting or non-voting, (i) amend its certificate of incorporation to delete or amend a provision authorized by § 362(a)(i) or § 366(c) of this title or (ii) merge or consolidate with or into another entity if, as a result of such merger or consolidation, the shares in such corporation would become, or be converted into or exchanged for the right to receive, shares or other equity interests in a domestic or foreign corporation that is not a public benefit corporation or similar entity and the certificate of incorporation (or similar governing instrument) of which does not contain the identical provisions identifying the public benefit or public benefits pursuant to § 362(a) or imposing requirements pursuant to § 366(c) of this title.

§ 365. Duties of directors.

(a)   The board of directors shall manage or direct the business and affairs of the public benefit corporation in a manner that balances the pecuniary interests of the stockholders, the best interests of those materially affected by the corporation's conduct, and the specific public benefit or public benefits identified in its certificate of incorporation.

(b)   A director of a public benefit corporation shall not, by virtue of the public benefit provisions or § 362(a) of this title, have any duty to any person on account of any interest of such person in the public benefit or public benefits identified in the certificate of incorporation or on account of any interest materially affected by the corporation's conduct and, with respect to a decision implicating the balance requirement in subsection (a) of this section, will be deemed to satisfy such director's fiduciary duties to stockholders and the corporation if such director's decision is both informed and disinterested and not such that no person of ordinary, sound judgment would approve.

(c)   The certificate of incorporation of a public benefit corporation may include a provision that any disinterested failure to satisfy this section shall not, for the purposes of § 102(b)(7) or § 145 of this title, constitute an act or omission not in good faith, or a breach of the duty of loyalty.

§ 366. Periodic statements and third party certification.

[…]

(b)   A public benefit corporation shall no less than biennially provide its stockholders with a statement as to the corporation's promotion of the public benefit or public benefits identified in the certificate of incorporation and of the best interests of those materially affected by the corporation's conduct. The statement shall include: (i) the objectives the board of directors has established to promote such public benefit or public benefits and interests; (ii) the standards the board of directors has adopted to measure the corporation's progress in promoting such public benefit or public benefits and interests; (iii) objective factual information based on those standards regarding the corporation's success in meeting the objectives for promoting such public benefit or public benefits and interests; and (iv) an assessment of the corporation's success in meeting the objectives and promoting such public benefit or public benefits and interests.

§ 367. Derivative suits.

Stockholders of a public benefit corporation owning individually or collectively, as of the date of instituting such derivative suit, at least two percent of the corporation's outstanding shares or, in the case of a corporation with shares listed on a national securities exchange, the lesser of such percentage or shares of at least two million dollars in market value, may maintain a derivative lawsuit to enforce the requirements set forth in § 365(a) of this title.

2.4 Corporate Bylaws

The corporate bylaws, in addition to the certificate of incorporation, make up the core of any corporation's governance documents. Whereas the subject matter of the certificate of incorporation deals with the basic relationships between stockholders and the corporation, the substance of corporate bylaws is typically limited to issue of governance process within the corporation. Bylaws typically do not contain substantive mandates, but direct how the corporation, the board, and its stockholders may take certain actions.

The corporate bylaws are subordinate to the certificate of incorporation. To the extent bylaws and the certificate or the DGCL are in conflict, the certificate and/or the DGCL will take precedence over the bylaws. Because they are subordinate, corporate bylaws are also easier to amend. Typically, corporate bylaws may be amended by a corporation's board of directors or its stockholders. When stockholders amend the bylaws, they need only achieve a majority of a quorum rather than the more exacting majority of the outstanding shares as is the case in an amendment to the corporation's certificate of incorporation.

Whereas the certificate of incorporation must be filed with the state, a corporation is not required to file its bylaws with any state authority.

2.4.1 DGCL Sec. 109

This provision authorizes the corporation to adopt bylaws governing the conduct of the affairs of the corporation. The provision provides that the power to adopt and amend bylaws lies with the stockholders. However, if a corporation provides for such in its certificate of incorporation - as most corporate certificates do - then the board of directors may also amend the bylaws. As you might guess, issues may arise when stockholders and directors adopt conflicting bylaws.

§ 109. Bylaws.

(a) The original or other bylaws of a corporation may be adopted, amended or repealed by the incorporators, by the initial directors of a corporation […] if they were named in the certificate of incorporation, or, before a corporation […] has received any payment for any of its stock, by its board of directors. After a corporation […]has received any payment for any of its stock, the power to adopt, amend or repeal bylaws shall be in the stockholders entitled to vote. […] Notwithstanding the foregoing, any corporation may, in its certificate of incorporation, confer the power to adopt, amend or repeal bylaws upon the directors[…]. The fact that such power has been so conferred upon the directors or governing body, as the case may be, shall not divest the stockholders or members of the power, nor limit their power to adopt, amend or repeal bylaws.

(b) The bylaws may contain any provision, not inconsistent with law or with the certificate of incorporation, relating to the business of the corporation, the conduct of its affairs, and its rights or powers or the rights or powers of its stockholders, directors, officers or employees.

2.4.2 Boilermakers Local 154 v. Chevron Corp.

In *Boilermakers*, the court answers the question whether directors can unilaterally adopt bylaws to restrict the rights of stockholders. The bylaw in question is an 'exclusive forum provision' bylaw that purports to limit the rights of stockholders to bring certain kinds of litigation against the corporation and its board to courts in Delaware. Forum selection provisions are common in commercial contracts.

In this case, the board – and not the stockholders – adopted an exclusive forum bylaw. This case raises important questions about the ability of directors to act unilaterally in the context of corporate bylaws as well as the nature of the "corporate contract" that stockholders enter into when they purchase shares of any corporation.

This case also reviews the standards of review a court will apply to judicial challenges to bylaws as well as the typical subject matter appropriate for bylaws.

BOILERMAKERS LOCAL 154 RETIREMENT FUND v. CHEVRON CORPORATION

Civil Action Nos. 7220-CS, 7238-CS
Court of Chancery of Delaware.

STRINE, Chancellor.

I. Introduction

The board of Chevron, the oil and gas major, has adopted a bylaw providing that litigation relating to Chevron's internal affairs should be conducted in Delaware, the state where Chevron is incorporated and whose substantive law Chevron's stockholders know governs the corporation's internal affairs. The board of the logistics company FedEx, which is also incorporated in Delaware and whose internal affairs are also therefore governed by Delaware law, has adopted a similar bylaw providing that the forum for litigation related to FedEx's internal affairs should be the Delaware Court of Chancery. The boards of both companies have been empowered in their certificates of incorporation to adopt bylaws under 8 *Del. C.* § 109(a).[1]

The plaintiffs, stockholders in Chevron and FedEx, have sued the boards for adopting these "forum selection bylaws." The plaintiffs' complaints are nearly identical and were filed only a few days apart by clients of the same law firm. In Count I, the plaintiffs claim that the bylaws are statutorily invalid because they are beyond the board's authority under the Delaware General Corporation Law ("DGCL"). In Count IV, the plaintiffs allege that the bylaws are contractually invalid, and therefore cannot be enforced like other contractual forum selection clauses under the test adopted by the Supreme Court of the United States in *The Bremen v. Zapata Offshore Co.*,[2] because they were unilaterally adopted by the Chevron and FedEx boards using their power to make bylaws. […]

In this opinion, the court resolves the defendants' motion for judgment on the pleadings on the counts relating to the statutory and contractual validity of the bylaws. Because the two bylaws are similar, present common legal issues, and are the target of near-identical complaints, the court decided to address them together. This is efficient, and is also in the interests of the parties, because a decision on the legal validity of the bylaws under the DGCL will moot the plaintiffs' other challenges if the bylaws are found to be invalid. And, it also aids the administration of justice, because a foreign court that respects the internal affairs doctrine, as it must,[3] when faced with a motion to enforce the bylaws will consider, as a first order issue, whether the bylaws are valid under the "chartering jurisdiction's domestic law."[4] Furthermore, the plaintiffs' facial statutory invalidity claim and their related contention that, as a matter of law, the bylaws are not contractually enforceable, have cast a cloud over the defendants' bylaws and those of other corporations. A decision as to the basic legal questions presented by the plaintiffs' complaints will provide efficiency benefits to not only the defendants and their stockholders, but to other corporations and their investors. […]

II. Background and Procedural Posture

A. The Chevron and FedEx Forum Selection Bylaws

Critical to the resolution of this motion is an understanding of who has the power to adopt, amend, and repeal the bylaws, and what subjects the bylaws may address under the DGCL. 8 *Del. C.* § 109(a) identifies who has the power to adopt, amend, and repeal the bylaws:

> [T]he power to adopt, amend or repeal bylaws shall be in the
> stockholders entitled to vote . . . . Notwithstanding the foregoing,

> any corporation may, in its certificate of incorporation, confer the
> power to adopt, amend or repeal bylaws upon the directors . . . .
> The fact that such power has been so conferred upon the directors .
> . . shall not divest the stockholders . . . of the power, nor limit their
> power to adopt, amend or repeal bylaws.

8 *Del. C.* § 109(b) states the subject matter the bylaws may address:

> The bylaws may contain any provision, not inconsistent with law or
> with the certificate of incorporation, relating to the business of the
> corporation, the conduct of its affairs, and its rights or powers or
> the rights or powers of its stockholders, directors, officers or
> employees.

Both Chevron's and FedEx's certificates of incorporation conferred on the boards the power to adopt bylaws under 8 *Del. C.* § 109(a). Thus, all investors who bought stock in the corporations whose forum selection bylaws are at stake knew that (i) the DGCL allows for bylaws to address the subjects identified in 8 *Del. C.* § 109(b), (ii) the DGCL permits the certificate of incorporation to contain a provision allowing directors to adopt bylaws unilaterally, and (iii) the certificates of incorporation of Chevron and FedEx contained a provision conferring this power on the boards.

Acting consistent with the power conferred to the board in Chevron's certificate of incorporation, the board amended the bylaws and adopted a forum selection bylaw. Generally speaking, a forum selection bylaw is a provision in a corporation's bylaws that designates a forum as the exclusive venue for certain stockholder suits against the corporation, either as an actual or nominal defendant, and its directors and employees. On September 29, 2010, the board of Chevron, a Delaware corporation headquartered in California, adopted a forum selection bylaw that provided:

> Unless the Corporation consents in writing to the selection of an
> alternative forum, the Court of Chancery of the State of Delaware
> shall be the sole and exclusive forum for (i) any derivative action or
> proceeding brought on behalf of the Corporation, (ii) any action
> asserting a claim of breach of a fiduciary duty owed by any director,

officer or other employee of the Corporation to the Corporation or the Corporation's stockholders, (iii) any action asserting a claim arising pursuant to any provision of the Delaware General Corporation Law, or (iv) any action asserting a claim governed by the internal affairs doctrine. Any person or entity purchasing or otherwise acquiring any interest in shares of capital stock of the Corporation shall be deemed to have notice of and consented to the provisions of this [bylaw].[19]

Several months later, on March 14, 2011, the board of FedEx, a Delaware corporation headquartered in Tennessee, adopted a forum selection bylaw identical to Chevron's.[...]

In their briefing, the boards of Chevron and FedEx state that the forum selection bylaws are intended to cover four types of suit, all relating to internal corporate governance:

- *Derivative suits.* The issue of whether a derivative plaintiff is qualified to sue on behalf of the corporation and whether that derivative plaintiff has or is excused from making demand on the board is a matter of corporate governance, because it goes to the very nature of who may speak for the corporation.

- *Fiduciary duty suits.* The law of fiduciary duties regulates the relationships between directors, officers, the corporation, and its stockholders.

- *D.G.C.L. suits.* The Delaware General Corporation Law provides the underpinning framework for all Delaware corporations. That statute goes to the core of how such corporations are governed.

- *Internal affairs suits.* As the U.S. Supreme Court has explained, "internal affairs," in the context of corporate law, are those "matters peculiar to the relationships among or between the corporation and its current officers, directors, and shareholders."[23]

That is, the description of the forum selection bylaws by the Chevron and FedEx boards is consistent with what the plain language of the bylaws suggests: that these bylaws are not intended to regulate *what* suits may be brought against the corporations, only *where* internal governance suits may be brought.[…]

B. The Defendant Boards Have Identified Multiforum Litigation Over Single Corporate Transactions Or Decisions As The Reason Why They Adopted The Bylaws

The Chevron and FedEx boards say that they have adopted forum selection bylaws in response to corporations being subject to litigation over a single transaction or a board decision in more than one forum simultaneously, so-called "multiforum litigation."[25] The defendants' opening brief argues that the boards adopted the forum selection bylaws to address what they perceive to be the inefficient costs of defending against the same claim in multiple courts at one time.[26] The brief describes how, for jurisdictional purposes, a corporation is a citizen both of the state where it is incorporated and of the state where it has its principal place of business.[27] Because a corporation need not be, and frequently is not, headquartered in the state where it is incorporated, a corporation may be subject to personal jurisdiction as a defendant in a suit involving corporate governance matters in two states.[28] Therefore, any act that the corporation or its directors undertake is potentially subject to litigation in at least two states.[29] Furthermore, both state and federal courts may have jurisdiction over the claims against the corporation. The result is that any act that the corporation or its directors undertake may be challenged in various forums within those states simultaneously.[30] The boards of Chevron and FedEx argue that multiforum litigation, when it is brought by dispersed stockholders in different forums, directly or derivatively, to challenge a single corporate action, imposes high costs on the corporations and hurts investors by causing needless costs that are ultimately born by stockholders, and that these costs are not justified by rational benefits for stockholders from multiforum filings.[31] […]

III. The Standard of Review

As our Supreme Court held in the *Frantz Manufacturing* case, "[t]he bylaws of a corporation are presumed to be valid, and the courts will construe the bylaws in a manner consistent with the law rather than strike down the bylaws."[54] Thus, the plaintiffs' burden on this motion challenging the facial statutory and contractual validity of the bylaws is a difficult one: they must show that the bylaws cannot operate lawfully or equitably *under any circumstances*.[55] So, the plaintiffs must show that the bylaws do not address proper subject matters of bylaws as defined by the DGCL in 8 *Del. C.* § 109(b), and can never operate consistently with law.[56] The plaintiffs voluntarily assumed this burden by making a facial validity challenge,[57] and cannot satisfy it by pointing to some future hypothetical application of the bylaws that might be impermissible.[58] […]

IV. Legal Analysis

A. The Board-Adopted Forum Selection Bylaws Are Statutorily Valid

Given this procedural context, the court structures its analysis to mirror the two facial claims of invalidity as they have been presented in the complaints. First, the court looks at Count I's challenge that the "bylaw[s are] invalid because [they are] beyond the authority granted in 8 *Del. C.* § 109(b)."[63] As to that claim, the court must determine whether the adoption of the forum selection bylaws was beyond the board's authority in the sense that they do not address a proper subject matter under 8 *Del. C.* § 109(b), which provides that:

> The bylaws may contain any provision, not inconsistent with law or
> with the certificate of incorporation, relating to the business of the
> corporation, the conduct of its affairs, and its rights or powers or
> the rights or powers of its stockholders, directors, officers or
> employees.

Thus, the court must decide if the bylaws are facially invalid under the DGCL because they do not relate to the business of the corporations, the conduct of their affairs, or the rights of the stockholders.

After first making that determination, the court then addresses Count IV's challenge that "the bylaw[s are] not a valid and enforceable forum selection provision."[64] That is, even if forum selection bylaws regulate proper subject matter under 8 *Del. C.* § 109(b), the plaintiffs allege that forum selection bylaws are contractually invalid because they have been unilaterally adopted by the board.[…]

1. The Forum Selection Bylaws Regulate A Proper Subject Matter Under 8 *Del. C.* § 109(b)

[…]As a matter of easy linguistics, the forum selection bylaws address the "rights" of the stockholders, because they regulate where stockholders can exercise their right to bring certain internal affairs claims against the corporation and its directors and officers.[68] They also plainly relate to the conduct of the corporation by channeling internal affairs cases into the courts of the state of incorporation, providing for the opportunity to have internal affairs cases resolved authoritatively by our Supreme Court if any party wishes to take an appeal.[69] That is, because the forum selection bylaws address internal affairs claims, the subject matter of the actions the bylaws govern relates quintessentially to "the corporation's business, the conduct of its affairs, and the rights of its stockholders [*qua* stockholders]."

The bylaws of Delaware corporations have a "procedural, process-oriented nature."[74] It is doubtless true that our courts have said that bylaws typically do not contain substantive mandates, but direct how the corporation, the board, and its stockholders may take certain actions.[75] 8 *Del. C.* § 109(b) has long been understood to allow the corporation to set "self-imposed rules and regulations [that are] deemed expedient for its convenient functioning.[…] The forum selection bylaws here fit this description. They are process-oriented, because they regulate *where* stockholders may file suit, not *whether* the stockholder may file suit or the kind of remedy that the stockholder may obtain on behalf of herself or the corporation. The bylaws also clearly address cases of the kind that address "the business of the corporation, the conduct of its affairs, and . . . the rights or powers of its stockholders, directors, officers or employees," because they govern where internal affairs cases governed by state corporate law may be heard.[77] These are the kind of claims most central to the relationship between those who manage the corporation and the corporation's stockholders. […]

Nor is it novel for bylaws to regulate how stockholders may exercise their rights as stockholders. For example, an advance notice bylaw "requires stockholders wishing to make nominations or proposals at a corporation's annual meeting to give notice of their intention in advance of so doing."[79] Like such bylaws, which help organize what could otherwise be a chaotic stockholder meeting, the forum selection bylaws are designed to bring order to what the boards of Chevron and FedEx say they perceive to be a chaotic filing of duplicative and inefficient derivative and corporate suits against the directors and the corporations. The similar purpose of the advance notice bylaws and the forum selection bylaws reinforce that forum selection bylaws have a proper relationship to the business of the corporation and the conduct of its affairs under 8 *Del. C.* § 109(b).[…]

The plaintiffs' argument, then, reduces to the claim that the bylaws do not speak to a "traditional" subject matter, and should be ruled invalid for that reason alone. For starters, the factual premise of this argument is not convincing. The bylaws cannot fairly be argued to regulate a novel subject matter: the plaintiffs ignore that, in the analogous contexts of LLC agreements and stockholder agreements, the Supreme Court and this court have held that forum selection clauses are valid.[…] But in any case, the Supreme Court long ago rejected the position that board action should be invalidated or enjoined simply because it involves a novel use of statutory authority. […] Merely because the General Corporation Law is silent as to a specific matter does not mean that it is prohibited."[84] […]

Therefore, the court concludes that forum selection bylaws are statutorily valid under Delaware law, and Count I of the plaintiffs' complaints is dismissed. The court now considers whether a forum selection bylaw is contractually invalid when adopted by the board unilaterally.

2. The Board-Adopted Bylaws Are Not Contractually Invalid As Forum Selection Clauses Because They Were Adopted Unilaterally By the Board

Despite the contractual nature of the stockholders' relationship with the corporation under our law, the plaintiffs argue, in Count IV of their complaints, that the forum selection bylaws by their nature are different and cannot be adopted by the board unilaterally. The plaintiffs' argument is grounded in the contention that a board-adopted forum selection bylaw cannot be a *contractual* forum selection clause because the stockholders do not vote in advance of its adoption to approve it.[…] The plaintiffs acknowledge that contractual forum selection clauses are "prima facie valid" under *The Bremen v. Zapata Off-Shore Co.* and *Ingres Corp. v. CA, Inc.,* and that they are presumptively enforceable.[92] But, the plaintiffs say, the forum selection bylaws are contractually invalid in this case, because they were adopted by a board, rather than by Chevron's and FedEx's dispersed stockholders. The plaintiffs argue that this method of adopting a forum selection clause is invalid as a matter of contract law, because it does not require the assent of the stockholders who will be affected by it. Thus, in the plaintiffs' view, there are two types of bylaws: (i) contractually binding bylaws that are adopted by stockholders; (ii) non-contractually binding bylaws that are adopted by boards using their statutory authority conferred by the certificate of incorporation.[...]

By this artificial bifurcation, the plaintiffs misapprehend fundamental principles of Delaware corporate law. Our corporate law has long rejected the so-called "vested rights" doctrine.[94] That vested rights view, which the plaintiffs have adopted as their own, "asserts that boards cannot modify bylaws in a manner that arguably diminishes or divests pre-existing shareholder rights absent stockholder consent."[95] As then-Vice Chancellor, now Justice, Jacobs explained in the *Kidsco* case, under Delaware law, where a corporation's articles or bylaws "put all on notice that the by-laws may be amended at any time, *no vested rights can arise that would contractually prohibit an amendment.*"[...]

In an unbroken line of decisions dating back several generations, our Supreme Court has made clear that the bylaws constitute a binding part of the contract between a Delaware corporation and its stockholders.[97] Stockholders are on notice that, as to those subjects that are subject of regulation by bylaw under 8 *Del. C.* § 109(b), the board itself may act unilaterally to adopt bylaws addressing those subjects.[...] Such a change by the board is not extra-contractual simply because the board acts unilaterally; rather it is the kind of change that the overarching statutory and contractual regime the stockholders buy into explicitly allows the board to make on its own.[...] Therefore, when stockholders have authorized a board to unilaterally adopt bylaws, it follows that the bylaws are not contractually invalid simply because the board-adopted bylaw lacks the contemporaneous assent of the stockholders.[...]

Even so, the statutory regime provides protections for the stockholders, through the indefeasible right of the stockholders to adopt and amend bylaws themselves. "[B]y its terms Section 109(a) vests in the shareholders a power to adopt, amend or repeal bylaws that is legally sacrosanct, *i.e.,* the power cannot be non-consensually eliminated or limited by anyone other than the legislature itself."[104] Thus, even though a board may, as is the case here, be granted authority to adopt bylaws, stockholders can check that authority by repealing board-adopted bylaws. And, of course, because the DGCL gives stockholders an annual opportunity to elect directors,[105] stockholders have a potent tool to discipline boards who refuse to accede to a stockholder vote repealing a forum selection clause.[106]

Thus, a corporation's bylaws are part of an inherently flexible contract between the stockholders and the corporation under which the stockholders have powerful rights they can use to protect themselves if they do not want board-adopted forum selection bylaws to be part of the contract between themselves and the corporation. […]

In sum, stockholders contractually assent to be bound by bylaws that are valid under the DGCL—that is an essential part of the contract agreed to when an investor buys stock in a Delaware corporation. Where, as here, the certificate of incorporation has conferred on the board the power to adopt bylaws, and the board has adopted a bylaw consistent with 8 *Del. C.* § 109(b), the stockholders have assented to that new bylaw being contractually binding. Thus, Count IV of the complaints cannot survive and the bylaws are contractually valid as a facial matter.

2.4.3 Proxy Access and Expense Bylaws

Although corporate bylaws are typically limited to process, they can still be extremely powerful in determining the balance of internal corporate governance. For example, although stockholders are required to vote for the board of directors, unless stockholders have the ability to nominate candidates the director positions, the power to vote might appear somewhat meaningless. Consequently, the ability to nominate directors to the corporate ballot is an extremely important power. Without access to the corporate-sponsored ballot, stockholders are often left only rubberstamping board decisions about who is able to run for a seat on the board of directors.

Of course stockholders are always free to run a "proxy contest" by sponsoring their own proxy ballot, however the mechanics of such a contest are prohibitively expensive for all but the largest stockholders.

In response to efforts by the SEC to enforce a blanket rule opening up access to the corporate-sponsored proxy to all stockholders, Delaware adopted permissive rules that on the one hand make it possible for corporations to opt to adopt bylaws making access to the corporate proxy available to stockholders under certain conditions.

Delaware also adopted rules that allow corporations to adopt bylaws to permit the reimbursement of election expenses for successful candidates. Reimbursement bylaws are intended to reduce the financial hurdles for independent board candidates to run against incumbent directors.

Both of these changes – proxy access and reimbursement bylaws - are intended to reduce the incentives against stockholders nominating and running their own candidates for seats on boards and thereby make boards more responsive to stockholder interests.

2.4.3.1 DGCL Sec. 112 - Proxy Access Bylaw

Section 112 permits boards to adopt bylaws that give stockholders the right, under certain conditions, to nominate their own directors who will appear on the corporate sponsored proxy.

§ 112. Access to proxy solicitation materials.

The bylaws may provide that if the corporation solicits proxies with respect to an election of directors, it may be required, to the extent and subject to such procedures or conditions as may be provided in the bylaws, to include in its proxy solicitation materials (including any form of proxy it distributes), in addition to individuals nominated by the board of directors, 1 or more individuals nominated by a stockholder. Such procedures or conditions may include any of the following:

(1) A provision requiring a minimum record or beneficial ownership, or duration of ownership, of shares of the corporation's capital stock, by the nominating stockholder, and defining beneficial ownership to take into account options or other rights in respect of or related to such stock;

(2) A provision requiring the nominating stockholder to submit specified information concerning the stockholder and the stockholder's nominees, including information concerning ownership by such persons of shares of the corporation's capital stock, or options or other rights in respect of or related to such stock;

(3) A provision conditioning eligibility to require inclusion in the corporation's proxy solicitation materials upon the number or proportion of directors nominated by stockholders or whether the stockholder previously sought to require such inclusion;

(4) A provision precluding nominations by any person if such person, any nominee of such person, or any affiliate or associate of such person or nominee, has acquired or

publicly proposed to acquire shares constituting a specified percentage of the voting power of the corporation's outstanding voting stock within a specified period before the election of directors;

(5) A provision requiring that the nominating stockholder undertake to indemnify the corporation in respect of any loss arising as a result of any false or misleading information or statement submitted by the nominating stockholder in connection with a nomination; and

(6) Any other lawful condition.

2.4.3.2 DGCL Sec. 113 - Proxy Expense Bylaw

Section 113 reduces the economic incentives against stockholders engaging in proxy contests by permitting expense reimbursement following proxy contest for successful candidates.

§ 113. Proxy expense reimbursement.

(a) The bylaws may provide for the reimbursement by the corporation of expenses incurred by a stockholder in soliciting proxies in connection with an election of directors, subject to such procedures or conditions as the bylaws may prescribe, including:

(1) Conditioning eligibility for reimbursement upon the number or proportion of persons nominated by the stockholder seeking reimbursement or whether such stockholder previously sought reimbursement for similar expenses;

(2) Limitations on the amount of reimbursement based upon the proportion of votes cast in favor of 1 or more of the persons nominated by the stockholder seeking reimbursement, or upon the amount spent by the corporation in soliciting proxies in connection with the election;

(3) Limitations concerning elections of directors by cumulative voting pursuant to § 214 of this title; or

(4) Any other lawful condition.

2.5 Board of Directors

Stockholders – as we will see later – have a number of rights with respect to the corporation. However, one right that stockholders do not have is the right to directly manage the day-to-day operations of the business. The general corporation law, as well as the common law, vests exclusive responsibility for corporate management and decisionmaking not with the stockholders, but rather with the corporation's board of directors.

We might like to think that shareholders own and run the business, but they do not. The authority to manage and oversee the operation of the business on a day to day basis is vested exclusively with the board. To the extent stockholders have rights to oversee the operations of the business, those rights are attenuated. Perhaps the most important provision of the Delaware corporate law is §141. Delaware is by no means unique; *every state* has its equivalent to §141. Section 141 centralizes decisionmaking authority to the board.

The statutory authority granted to the board by §141 lies at the heart of the business judgment presumption, or the "business judgment rule." The business judgment presumption is judicial presumption that exists as an acknowledgment of the statutory authority vested in boards, and not shareholders, to run the corporation. The effect of this judicial presumption is to cause courts to defer to decisions of the board in most matters when those decisions are challenged by stockholders.

This presumption is quite powerful and have effects beyond the courtroom. Because courts will generally abstain from intervening in disputes between stockholders and boards about most business decisions, boards will feel a great deal of latitude and independence in their decision making process. The insulation from stockholders afforded by this judicial presumption encourages boards to take business risk.

2.5.1 DGCL Sec. 141 - Board of directors

Section 141 deals with the power and the structure of the board of directors. Of all the provisions in the corporate law, §141(a) is perhaps the single most important. Section 141(a) grants plenary power over the management of the corporation – not the stockholders – but to the board of directors. Among other things, §141(a) provides the statutory basis for the business judgment presumption.

Sections 141(b) & (f) describe the requirements for the conduct of regular business at board meetings or actions by the board without a meeting. Under §141(c), a board is authorized to delegate almost all of its authority to committees of directors. Section 141(d) permits the creation of staggered, or classified, board structures.

Section 141(e) creates a safe harbor from liability for boards that reasonably rely on experts when making decisions. Section 141(h) provides boards the statutory authority to set their own compensation, while §141(k) describes the circumstances under which stockholders may dismiss a director.

§ 141. Board of directors; powers; number, qualifications, terms and quorum; committees; classes of directors; nonstock corporations; reliance upon books; action without meeting; removal.

(a) The business and affairs of every corporation organized under this chapter shall be managed by or under the direction of a board of directors, except as may be otherwise provided in this chapter or in its certificate of incorporation. If any such provision is made in the certificate of incorporation, the powers and duties conferred or imposed upon the board of directors by this chapter shall be exercised or performed to such extent and by such person or persons as shall be provided in the certificate of incorporation.

(b) The board of directors of a corporation shall consist of 1 or more members, each of whom shall be a natural person. The number of directors shall be fixed by, or in the manner provided in, the bylaws, unless the certificate of incorporation fixes the number of directors, in which case a change in the number of directors shall be made only by amendment of the certificate. Directors need not be stockholders unless so required by the certificate of incorporation or the bylaws. The certificate of incorporation or bylaws may prescribe other qualifications for directors. Each director shall hold office until such director's successor is elected and qualified or until such director's earlier resignation or removal. Any director may resign at any time upon notice given in writing or by electronic transmission to the corporation. A resignation is effective when the resignation is delivered unless the resignation specifies a later effective date or an effective date determined upon the happening of an event or events. A resignation which is conditioned upon the director failing to receive a specified vote for reelection as a director may provide that it is irrevocable. A majority of the total number of directors shall constitute a quorum for the transaction of business unless the certificate of incorporation or the bylaws require a greater number. Unless the certificate of incorporation provides otherwise, the bylaws may provide that a number less than a majority shall constitute a quorum which in no case shall be less than 1/3 of the total number of directors except that when a board of 1 director is authorized under this section, then 1 director shall constitute a quorum. The vote of the majority of the directors present at a meeting at which a quorum is present shall be the act of the board of directors unless the certificate of incorporation or the bylaws shall require a vote of a greater number.

(c)(2) The board of directors may designate 1 or more committees, each committee to consist of 1 or more of the directors of the corporation. The board may designate 1 or more directors as alternate members of any committee, who may replace any absent or disqualified member at any meeting of the committee. […] Any such committee, to the extent provided in the resolution of the board of directors, or in the bylaws of the corporation, shall have and may exercise all the powers and authority of the board of directors in the management of the business and affairs of the corporation, and may authorize the seal of the corporation to be affixed to all papers which may require it; but no such committee shall have the power or authority in reference to the following matter: (i) approving or adopting, or recommending to the stockholders, any action or matter (other than the election or removal of directors) expressly required by this chapter to be submitted to stockholders for approval or (ii) adopting, amending or repealing any bylaw of the corporation.

(3) Unless otherwise provided in the certificate of incorporation, the bylaws or the resolution of the board of directors designating the committee, a committee may create 1 or more subcommittees, each subcommittee to consist of 1 or more members of the committee, and delegate to a subcommittee any or all of the powers and authority of the committee.

(d) The directors of any corporation organized under this chapter may, by the certificate of incorporation or by an initial bylaw, or by a bylaw adopted by a vote of the stockholders, be divided into 1, 2 or 3 classes; the term of office of those of the first class to expire at the first annual meeting held after such classification becomes effective; of the second class 1 year thereafter; of the third class 2 years thereafter; and at each annual election held after such classification becomes effective, directors shall be chosen for a full term, as the case may be, to succeed those whose terms expire. The certificate of incorporation or bylaw provision dividing the directors into classes may authorize the board of directors to assign members of the board already in office to such classes at the time such classification becomes effective. The certificate of incorporation may confer upon holders of any class or series of stock the right to elect 1 or more directors who shall serve for such term, and have such voting powers as shall be stated in the certificate of incorporation. The terms of office and voting powers of the directors elected separately by the holders of any class or series of stock may be greater than or less than those of any other director or class of directors. In addition, the certificate of incorporation may confer upon 1 or more directors, whether or not elected separately by the holders of any class or series of stock, voting powers greater than or less than those of other directors. Any such provision conferring greater or lesser voting power shall apply to voting in any committee or subcommittee, unless otherwise provided in the certificate of incorporation or bylaws. If the certificate of incorporation provides that 1 or more directors shall have more or less than 1 vote per director on any matter, every reference in this chapter to a majority or other proportion of the directors shall refer to a majority or other proportion of the votes of the directors.

(e) A member of the board of directors, or a member of any committee designated by the board of directors, shall, in the performance of such member's duties, be fully protected in relying in good faith upon the records of the corporation and upon such information, opinions, reports or statements presented to the corporation by any of the corporation's officers or employees, or committees of the board of directors, or by any other person as to matters the member reasonably believes are within such other person's professional or expert competence and who has been selected with reasonable care by or on behalf of the corporation.

(f) Unless otherwise restricted by the certificate of incorporation or bylaws, any action required or permitted to be taken at any meeting of the board of directors or of any committee thereof may be taken without a meeting if all members of the board or committee, as the case may be, consent thereto in writing, or by electronic transmission and the writing or writings or electronic transmission or transmissions are filed with the minutes of proceedings of the board, or committee. Such filing shall be in paper form if the minutes are maintained in paper form and shall be in electronic form if the minutes are maintained in electronic form.

(g) Unless otherwise restricted by the certificate of incorporation or bylaws, the board of directors of any corporation organized under this chapter may hold its meetings, and have an office or offices, outside of this State.

(h) Unless otherwise restricted by the certificate of incorporation or bylaws, the board of directors shall have the authority to fix the compensation of directors.

(i) Unless otherwise restricted by the certificate of incorporation or bylaws, members of the board of directors of any corporation, or any committee designated by the board, may participate in a meeting of such board, or committee by means of conference telephone or other communications equipment by means of which all persons participating in the meeting can hear each other, and participation in a meeting pursuant to this subsection shall constitute presence in person at the meeting.

[...]

(k) Any director or the entire board of directors may be removed, with or without cause, by the holders of a majority of the shares then entitled to vote at an election of directors, except as follows:

(1) Unless the certificate of incorporation otherwise provides, in the case of a corporation whose board is classified as provided in subsection (d) of this section, stockholders may effect such removal only for cause; or

(2) In the case of a corporation having cumulative voting, if less than the entire board is to be removed, no director may be removed without cause if the votes cast against such director's removal would be sufficient to elect such director if then cumulatively voted at an election of the entire board of directors, or, if there be classes of directors, at an election of the class of directors of which such director is a part.

Whenever the holders of any class or series are entitled to elect 1 or more directors by the certificate of incorporation, this subsection shall apply, in respect to the removal without cause of a director or directors so elected, to the vote of the holders of the outstanding shares of that class or series and not to the vote of the outstanding shares as a whole.

2.5.2 DGCL Sec. 223 - Director Vacancies

When a director resigns from the board of directors, such resignations may not be contemporaneous with a stockholder meeting. Unless otherwise specified in the certificate of incorporation or bylaw, during the interim period before the stockholder meeting, boards have the power to appoint replacement directors.

§ 223. Vacancies and newly created directorships.

(a) Unless otherwise provided in the certificate of incorporation or bylaws:

(1) Vacancies and newly created directorships resulting from any increase in the authorized number of directors elected by all of the stockholders having the right to vote as a single class may be filled by a majority of the directors then in office, although less than a quorum, or by a sole remaining director;

(2) Whenever the holders of any class or classes of stock or series thereof are entitled to elect 1 or more directors by the certificate of incorporation, vacancies and newly created directorships of such class or classes or series may be filled by a majority of the directors elected by such class or classes or series thereof then in office, or by a sole remaining director so elected. [...]

(b) In the case of a corporation the directors of which are divided into classes, any directors chosen under subsection (a) of this section shall hold office until the next election of the class for which such directors shall have been chosen, and until their successors shall be elected and qualified. [...]

2.5.3 The Nature of the Board of Directors

Corporations are managed by boards of directors. It's important to note that no director, acting individually, is empowered to speak or act on behalf of the corporation. Individual directors, in that sense, are not agents of the corporation, nor are they principals. The board of directors - as group - is the only party statutorily authorized to manage the corporation.

Individual directors have no authority to speak on behalf of the corporation unless they have been specifically delegated such authority by the board. Along the same lines, unless otherwise outlined in the certificate of incorporation, no director is superior or has more rights than any other director. Each member of a corporate board has the right to consultation with the others and has the right to be heard upon all questions considered by the board. Absent a governance agreement to the contrary, each director is entitled to receive the same information furnished to his or her fellow board members.

While stockholders are permitted to act at a stockholders meeting by "proxy" - that is they need not be present, but may authorize someone else to act on their behalf pursuant to instructions - directors are not permitted to delegate their proxy to another at a board meeting. If a director is not present at a meeting, that director's vote may not be counted. There is important reasons for not permitting directors to act by proxy. A director cannot authorize anyone to act for her, because her associates are entitled to their own judgment, experience and business ability, just as her associates cannot deprive her of her rights and powers as director.

Delaware corporate law embraces a "board-centric" model of governance. This model expects that all directors - and not their proxies - will participate in a collective and deliberative decision-making process.

Given that the DGCL allocates fundamental decision-making power to the board as a whole, and not to any individual director *qua* director, all directors must have an equal opportunity to participate meaningfully in any matter brought before the board and to discharge their oversight responsibilities. In more granular terms, directors must be afforded, at a minimum, (i) proper notice of all board meetings, (ii) the opportunity to attend and to express their views at board meetings, and (iii) access to all information that is necessary or appropriate to discharge their fiduciary duties, including the opportunity to consult with officers, employees, and other agents of the corporation. *OptimisCorp v Waite* (Del. Sup. Ct., April 20, 2016) at Footnote 9.

The Delaware corporate law does not generally follow a rule that permits "super directors": the size of a director's stock ownership does not convey additional powers. However, consistent with the enabling nature of the statute and pursuant to Section 141(d), the certificate of incorporation may confer upon 1 or more directors, voting powers greater than or less than those of other directors. Any such provision conferring greater or lesser voting power shall apply to voting in any committee, unless otherwise provided in the certificate of incorporation or bylaws.

2.5.4 Shlensky v. Wrigley

In this iconic case, a stockholder challenges a decision of the board of directors of the Chicago Cubs not to install lights at the field and to only play games during daylight hours.

For many years, the Chicago Cubs, a Delaware corporation, were controlled by Philip K. Wrigley – also known for his success as a chewing gum manufacturer. In many respects, Wrigley was an innovative businessman. During World War II he founded the All American Girls Baseball League to fill the void created when many professional baseball players went to war. The film, A League of Their Own, was a fictionalized account of the experiences of the AAGBL. In addition, Wrigley made a decision to increase the value of the Cubs brand by effectively giving away the rights to radio broadcasts of Cubs games.

In *Shlensky v Wrigley*, a stockholder sued the board of the Cubs, including Philip Wrigley, for the board's decision not to install lights and refusal to play night games at Wrigley Field.The stockholder alleged that the board's decision to only play day games at Wrigley caused the corporation to make less money than had the board installed lights and permitted the team to play night games.

This case highlights a very typical board decision and a common tension between the managers of the corporation and its stockholders. In this case we also see the degree of deference that courts will pay to a board's business judgment when that decision is made in an informed manner at arm's length.

95 Ill. App.2d 173 (1968)
Shlensky v. Philip K. Wrigley, et al., and Chicago National League Ball Club (Inc.)

[handwritten: Mangers v. Stoke holders] *[handwritten: Del & Chic, IL]*

This is an appeal from a dismissal of plaintiff's amended complaint on motion of the defendants. […]

Plaintiff is a minority stockholder of defendant corporation, Chicago National League Ball Club (Inc.), a Delaware corporation with its principal place of business in Chicago, Illinois. […] The individual defendants are directors of the Cubs and have served for varying periods of years. Defendant Philip K. Wrigley is also president of the corporation and owner of approximately 80% of the stock therein.

Plaintiff alleges that since night baseball was first played in 1935 nineteen of the twenty major league teams have scheduled night games. In 1966, out of a total of 1,620 games in the major leagues, 932 were played at night. Plaintiff alleges that every member of the major leagues, other than the Cubs, scheduled substantially all of its home games in 1966 at night, exclusive of opening days, Saturdays, Sundays, holidays and days prohibited by league rules. Allegedly this has been done for the specific purpose of maximizing attendance and thereby maximizing revenue and income.

The Cubs, in the years 1961-65, sustained operating losses from its direct baseball operations. Plaintiff attributes those losses to inadequate attendance at Cubs' home games. He concludes that if the directors continue to refuse to install lights at Wrigley Field and schedule [176] night baseball games, the Cubs will continue to sustain comparable losses and its financial condition will continue to deteriorate.

Plaintiff alleges that, except for the year 1963, attendance at Cubs' home games has been substantially below that at their road games, many of which were played at night.

Plaintiff compares attendance at Clubs' games with that of the Chicago White Sox, an American League club, whose weekday games were generally played at night. The weekend attendance figures for the two teams were similar; however, the White Sox week-night games drew many more patrons than did the Cubs' weekday games.

Plaintiff alleges that the funds for the installation of lights can be readily obtained through financing and the cost of installation would be far more than offset and recaptured by increased revenues and incomes resulting from the increased attendance.

Plaintiff further alleges that defendant Wrigley has refused to install lights, not because of interest in the welfare of the corporation but because of his personal opinions "that baseball is a `daytime sport' and that the installation of lights and night baseball games will have a deteriorating effect upon the surrounding neighborhood." It is alleged that he has admitted that he is not interested in whether the Cubs would benefit financially from such action because of his concern for the neighborhood, and that he would be willing for the team to play night games if a new stadium were built in Chicago. [...]

The question on appeal is whether plaintiff's amended complaint states a cause of action. It is plaintiff's position that fraud, illegality and conflict of interest are not the only bases for a stockholder's derivative action against the directors. Contrariwise, defendants argue that the courts will not step in and interfere with honest business judgment of the directors unless there is a showing of fraud, illegality or conflict of interest. [...]

The standards set in Delaware are clearly stated in the cases. [...]

> "We have then a conflict in view between the responsible managers
> of a corporation and an overwhelming majority of its stockholders
> on the one hand and a dissenting minority on the other — a conflict
> touching matters of business policy, such as has occasioned
> innumerable applications to courts to intervene and determine
> which of the two conflicting views should prevail. The response
> which courts make to such applications is that it is not their
> function to resolve for corporations questions of policy and
> business management. The directors are chosen to pass upon such
> questions and their judgment *unless shown to be tainted with fraud* is
> accepted as final. The judgment of the directors of corporations
> enjoys the benefit of a presumption that it was formed in good faith

and was designed to promote the best interests of the corporation they serve." (Emphasis supplied.)

Similarly, the court in Toebelman v. Missouri-Kansas Pipe Line Co., 41 F Supp 334, said at page 339:

> "The general legal principle involved is familiar.[...] Reference may be made to the statement of the rule in Helfman v. American Light & Traction Company, 121 NJ Eq 1, 187 A 540, 550, in which the Court stated the law as follows: `In a purely business corporation ... the authority of the directors in the conduct of the business of the corporation must be regarded as absolute when they act within the law, and the court is without authority to substitute its judgment for that of the directors.'"

[...]

Plaintiff in the instant case argues that the directors are acting for reasons unrelated to the financial interest and welfare of the Cubs. However, we are not satisfied that the motives assigned to Philip K. Wrigley, and through him to the other directors, are contrary to the best interests of the corporation and the stockholders. For example, it appears to us that the effect on the surrounding neighborhood might well be considered by a director who was considering the patrons who would or would not attend the games if the park were in a poor neighborhood. Furthermore, the long run interest of the corporation in its property value at Wrigley Field might demand all efforts to keep the neighborhood from deteriorating. By these thoughts we do not mean to say that we have decided that the decision of the directors was a correct one. That is beyond our jurisdiction and ability. We are merely saying that the decision is one properly before directors and the motives alleged in the amended complaint showed no fraud, illegality or conflict of interest in their making of that decision. [...]

There is no allegation that the night games played by the other nineteen teams enhanced their financial position or that the profits, if any, of those teams were directly related to the number of night games scheduled. There is an allegation that the installation of lights and scheduling of night games in Wrigley Field would have resulted in large amounts of additional revenues and incomes from increased attendance and related sources of income. Further, the cost of installation of lights, funds for which are allegedly readily available by financing, would be more than offset and recaptured by increased revenues. However, no allegation is made that there will be a net benefit to the corporation from such action, considering all increased costs.

Plaintiff claims that the losses of defendant corporation are due to poor attendance at home games. However, it appears from the amended complaint, taken as a whole, that factors other than attendance affect the net earnings or losses. For example, in 1962, attendance at home and road games decreased appreciably as compared with 1961, and yet the loss from direct baseball operation and of the whole corporation was considerably less.

The record shows that plaintiff did not feel he could allege that the increased revenues would be sufficient to cure the corporate deficit. The only cost plaintiff was at all concerned with was that of installation of lights. No mention was made of operation and maintenance of the lights or other possible increases in operating costs of night games and we cannot speculate as to what other factors might influence the increase or decrease of profits if the Cubs were to play night home games. […]

Finally, we do not agree with plaintiff's contention that failure to follow the example of the other major league clubs in scheduling night games constituted negligence. Plaintiff made no allegation that these teams' night schedules were profitable or that the purpose for which night baseball had been undertaken was fulfilled. Furthermore, it cannot be said that directors, even those of corporations that are losing money, must follow the lead of the other corporations in the field. Directors are elected for their business capabilities and judgment and the courts cannot require them to forego their judgment because of the decisions of directors of other companies. Courts may not decide these questions in the absence of a clear showing of dereliction of duty on the part of the specific directors and mere failure to "follow the crowd" is not such a dereliction.

For the foregoing reasons the order of dismissal entered by the trial court is affirmed.

2.5.5 Aronson v. Lewis

In *Shlensky*, the court described its policy of deferring to the decisions of the board of directors absent some evidence of fraud or wrongdoing. Aronson is the leading case for the restatement of the principle highlighted in *Shlensky*: the business judgment presumption, or the business judgment rule.

This presumption, which is rooted in §141(a)'s allocation of exclusive management authority to the board of directors, requires that court leave board decisions undisturbed unless complaining stockholders present some evidence that the board made the challenged decisions in an <u>uninformed manner</u>, or in a manner <u>not in good faith</u>, or for reasons otherwise <u>not in the best interests of the corporation</u> (e.g. board self-dealing).

Note that the pleading burden is on the complaining stockholders. In the absence of facts to undermine the business judgment presumption, courts will leave board decisions, even bad ones, in place.

473 A.2d 805 (1984)
ARONSON v. LEWIS

[…] A cardinal precept of the General Corporation Law of the State of Delaware is that directors, rather than shareholders, manage the business and affairs of the corporation. 8 *Del.C.* § 141(a). Section 141(a) states in pertinent part:

> "The *business and affairs* of a corporation organized under this
> chapter *shall be managed by or under the direction* of a board of directors
> except as may be otherwise provided in this chapter or in its
> certificate of incorporation."

8 *Del.C.* § 141(a) (Emphasis added). The existence and exercise of this power carries with it certain fundamental fiduciary obligations to the corporation and its shareholders. […]

The business judgment rule is an acknowledgment of the managerial prerogatives of Delaware directors under Section 141(a). S[…]. It is a presumption that in making a business decision the directors of a corporation acted on an informed basis, in good faith and in the honest belief that the action taken was in the best interests of the company.[…] The burden is on the party challenging the decision to establish facts rebutting the presumption.

First, its protections can only be claimed by disinterested directors whose conduct otherwise meets the tests of business judgment. From the standpoint of interest, this means that directors can neither appear on both sides of a transaction nor expect to derive any personal financial benefit from it in the sense of self-dealing, as opposed to a benefit which devolves upon the corporation or all stockholders generally.[…]

Second, to invoke the rule's protection directors have a duty to inform themselves, prior to making a business decision, of all material information reasonably available to them. Having become so informed, they must then act with requisite care in the discharge of their duties. While the Delaware cases use a variety of terms to describe the applicable standard of care, our analysis satisfies us that under the business judgment rule director liability is predicated upon concepts of gross negligence.[…]

However, it should be noted that the business judgment rule operates only in the context of director action. Technically speaking, it has no role where directors have either abdicated their functions, or absent a conscious decision, failed to act.[7] But it also follows that under applicable principles, a conscious decision to refrain from acting may nonetheless be a valid exercise of business judgment and enjoy the protections of the rule. […]

2.5.6 Gagliardi, v. Trifoods International, Inc.

In this case, a stockholder brings suit to challenge a series of what turned out ultimately to be ill-advised board decisions. As in *Shlensky*, we see the degree of deference that courts will pay to a board's business judgment. The court in *Gagliardi* also offers up a rationale for why a high degree of deference for disinterested board decisions might generally be good policy.

683 A.2d 1049 (1996)
GAGLIARDI v. TRIFOODS INTERNATIONAL, INC.

ALLEN, Chancellor.

Plaintiff, Eugene Gagliardi, is the founder of the TriFoods, Inc. and in 1990 he induced certain persons to invest in the company by buying its stock. In 1993 he was removed as

Chairman of the board and his employment with the company terminated. He continues to own approximately 13% of the company's common stock. The business of the company has, according to the allegations of the complaint, deteriorated very badly since Mr. Gagliardi's ouster.

The suit asserts that defendants are liable to the corporation and to plaintiff individually on a host of theories, most importantly for mismanagement. […]

Count IV: Negligent Mismanagement:

This count, which is asserted against all defendants, alleges that "implementation of their grandiose scheme for TriFoods' future growth ... in only eighteen months destroyed TriFoods." Plaintiff asserts that the facts alleged, which sketch that "scheme" and those results, constitute mismanagement and waste.

The allegations of Count IV are detailed.

They assert most centrally that prior to his dismissal Gagliardi disagreed with Hart concerning the wisdom of TriFoods manufacturing its products itself and disagreed strongly that the company should buy a plant in Pomfret, Connecticut and move its operations to that state. Plaintiff thought it foolish (and he alleges that it was negligent judgment) to borrow funds from CDA for that purpose. ¶¶ 71-74; 77-81.

Plaintiff also alleges that Hart caused the company to acquire and fit-out a research or new product facility in Chadds Ford Pennsylvania, which "duplicated one already available and under lease to Designer Foods [the predecessor name of TriFoods], and which was therefore, a further waste of corporate assets." ¶ 76.

Next, it is alleged that "defendants either acquiesced in or approved a reckless or grossly negligent sales commission to build volume." ¶ 82.

Next, it is alleged that "Hart and the other defendants caused TriFoods to purchase [the exclusive rights to produce and sell a food product known as] Steak-umms from Heinz in April 1994." ¶ 85. The price paid compared unfavorably with a transaction in 1980 in which this product had been sold and which earlier terms are detailed. ¶ 86. "Defendants recklessly caused TriFoods to pay $15 million for Steak-umms alone (no plant, no equipment, etc) which was then doing annual sales of only $28 million." *Id.*

Next, it is alleged that "Hart caused TriFoods... to pay $125,000 to a consultant for its new name, logo and packaging." ¶ 87.

Next, it is alleged that Hart destroyed customer relationships by supplying inferior products. [...]

Next, it is alleged that "Hart refused to pay key manufacturers and suppliers ... thus injuring TriFoods' trade relations." ¶ 92.

Next, it is alleged that "defendants entered into a transaction whereby TriFoods was to acquire "Lloyd's Ribs" at a grossly excessive price, knowing (or recklessly not knowing) that the Company could not afford the transaction." [...]

Do these allegations of Count IV state a claim upon which relief may be granted? In addressing that question, I start with what I take to be an elementary precept of corporation law: in the absence of facts showing self-dealing or improper motive, a corporate officer or director is not legally responsible to the corporation for losses that may be suffered as a result of a decision that an officer made or that directors authorized in good faith.[2][...] Thus, to allege that a corporation has suffered a loss as a result of a lawful transaction, within the corporation's powers, authorized by a corporate fiduciary *acting in a good faith pursuit of corporate purposes,* does not state a claim for relief against that fiduciary no matter how foolish the investment may appear in retrospect.

The rule could rationally be no different. Shareholders can diversify the risks of their corporate investments. Thus, it is in their economic interest for the corporation to accept in rank order all positive net present value investment projects available to the corporation, starting with the *highest risk adjusted rate of return first*. Shareholders don't want (or shouldn't rationally want) directors to be risk averse. Shareholders' investment interests, across the full range of their diversifiable equity investments, will be maximized if corporate directors and managers honestly assess risk and reward and accept for the corporation the highest risk adjusted returns available that are above the firm's cost of capital.

But directors will tend to deviate from this rational acceptance of corporate risk *if* in authorizing the corporation to undertake a risky investment, the directors must assume some degree of personal risk relating to *ex post facto* claims of derivative liability for any resulting corporate loss.

Corporate directors of public companies typically have a very small proportionate ownership interest in their corporations and little or no incentive compensation. Thus, they enjoy (as residual owners) only a very small proportion of any "upside" gains earned by the corporation on risky investment projects. If, however, corporate directors were to be found liable for a corporate loss from a risky project on the ground that the investment was too risky (foolishly risky! stupidly risky! egregiously risky! — you supply the adverb), their liability would be joint and several for the whole loss (with I suppose a right of contribution). Given the scale of operation of modern public corporations, this stupefying disjunction between risk and reward for corporate directors threatens undesirable effects. Given this disjunction, only a very small probability of director liability based on "negligence", "inattention", "waste", etc., could induce a board to avoid authorizing risky investment projects to any extent! Obviously, it is in the shareholders' economic interest to offer sufficient protection to directors from liability for negligence, etc., to allow directors to conclude that, as a practical matter, there is no risk that, if they act in good faith and meet minimal proceduralist standards of attention, they can face _Good faith_ liability as a result of a business loss.

The law *protects shareholder investment interests* against the uneconomic consequences that the presence of such second-guessing risk would have on director action and shareholder wealth in a number of ways. It authorizes corporations to pay for director and officer liability insurance and authorizes corporate indemnification in a broad range of cases, for example. But the first protection against a threat of sub-optimal risk acceptance is the so-called business judgment rule. That "rule" in effect provides that where a director is independent and disinterested, there can be no liability for corporate loss, unless the facts are such that no person could possibly authorize such a transaction if he or she were attempting in good faith to meet their duty. [...]

Thus, for example it does not state a claim to allege that: (1) Hart caused the corporation to pay $125,000 to a consultant for the design of a new logo and packaging. On what possible basis might a corporate officer or director be put to the expense of defending such a claim? Nothing is alleged except that an expenditure of corporate funds for a corporate purpose was made. Whether that expenditure was wise or foolish, low risk or high risk is of no concern to this Court. [...] Nor does an allegation that defendants acquiesced in a reckless commission structure "in order to build volume" state a claim; it alleges no conflicting interest or improper motivation[. .]. It alleges only an ordinary business decision with a pejorative characterization added. (3) The allegation of "duplication" of existing product research facilities similarly simply states a matter that falls within ordinary business judgment; that plaintiff regards the decision as unwise, foolish, or even stupid in the circumstances is not legally significant; indeed that others may look back on it and agree that it was stupid is legally unimportant, in my opinion. (4) That the terms of the purchase of "Steak-umms" seem to plaintiff unwise (especially when compared to the terms of a 1980 transaction involving that product) again fail utterly to state any legal claim. No self-interest, nor facts possibly disclosing improper motive or judgment satisfying the waste standard are alleged. Similarly, (5) the allegations of corporate loss resulting from harm to customer relations by delivery of poor product and (6) harm to supplier relations by poor payment practices, again state nothing that constitutes a legal claim. Certainly these allegations state facts that, if true, constitute either mistakes, poor judgment, or reflect hard choices facing a cash-pressed company, but where is the allegation of conflicting interest or suspect motivation? […] There are none. Nothing is alleged other than poor business practices. To permit the possibility of director liability on that basis would be very destructive of shareholder welfare in the long-term.

A similar analysis holds for the allegations concerning a contract to acquire the product "Lloyd's Ribs" (7); nothing is alleged other than that the price was excessive and the directors knew (or recklessly didn't know) that "the company could not afford such a transaction." More importantly, the complaint does not allege that the contract was ever closed! Indeed in Count V it is alleged that certain defendants diverted the opportunity to acquire Lloyd's Ribs from TriFoods! Thus, with respect to this possible transaction, not only does the amended complaint contain no allegation of conflict of interest or improper motivation in TriFoods' acquiring "Lloyd's Ribs," but it contains no allegation that a transaction involving the company ever occurred.

Finally, (8) there is the allegation that despite warnings from plaintiff and despite the alleged fact that the Pomfret facility "was not reasonably fit" for the purpose, the directors authorized the purchase of the facility at a "grossly excessive" price in order to implement a business plan that would have the company manufacture some or all of its food products and that defendants caused the company to borrow substantial funds to accomplish that task. Once more there is no allegation of conflict of interest with respect to this transaction[4], nor is there any allegation [1054] of improper motivation in authorizing the transactions. There is, in effect, only an allegation that plaintiff believes the transaction represents poor business judgment and the conclusion that "no reasonable business person would have engaged in it." […]

For the foregoing reason Count IV of the amended complaint will be dismissed.

2.5.7 Kamin v. American Express Co.

The business judgment presumption creates a great deal of space for boards to make decisions related to the operation and strategic direction of the business. Provided boards are disinterested and act in good faith in an informed manner, courts will give those board decisions great latitude when they are challenged by stockholders. The following case is an example of a stockholder challenge to a board decision and the court's implementation of the business judgment presumption.

86 Misc.2d 809 (1976)
Kamin v. American Express Company

EDWARD J. GREENFIELD, J.

The complaint alleges that in 1972 American Express acquired for investment 1,954,418 shares of common stock of Donaldson, Lufken and Jenrette, Inc. (hereafter DLJ), a publicly traded corporation, at a cost of $29,900,000. It is further alleged that the current market value of those shares is approximately $4,000,000. On July 28, 1975, it is alleged, the board of directors of American Express declared a special dividend to all stockholders of record pursuant to which the shares of DLJ would be distributed in kind. Plaintiffs contend further that if American Express were to sell the DLJ shares on the market, it would sustain a capital loss of $25,000,000 which could be offset against taxable capital gains on other investments. Such a sale, they allege, would result in tax savings to the company of approximately $8,000,000, which would not be available in the case of the distribution of DLJ shares to stockholders. […]

It is apparent that all the previously-mentioned allegations of the complaint go to the question of the exercise by the board of directors of business judgment in deciding how to deal with the DLJ shares. [...]

Examination of the complaint reveals that there is no claim of fraud or self-dealing, and no contention that there was any bad faith or oppressive conduct. The law is quite clear as to what is necessary to ground a claim for actionable wrongdoing. "In actions by stockholders, which assail the acts of their directors or trustees, courts will not interfere unless the powers have been illegally or unconscientiously executed, or unless it be made to appear that the acts were fraudulent or collusive and destructive of the rights of the stockholders. Mere errors of judgment are not sufficient as grounds for equity interference; for the powers of those entrusted with corporate management are largely discretionary." [...]

More specifically, the question of whether or not a dividend is to be declared or a distribution of some kind should be made is exclusively a matter of business judgment for the board of directors. "Courts will not interfere with such discretion unless it be first made to appear that the directors have acted or are about to act in bad faith and for a dishonest purpose. It is for the directors to say, acting in good faith of course, when and to what extent dividends shall be declared * * * The statute confers upon the directors this power, and the minority stockholders are not in a position to question this right, so long as the directors are acting in good faith" [...]

Thus, a complaint must be dismissed if all that is presented is a decision to pay dividends rather than pursuing some other course of conduct. [...]A complaint which alleges merely that some course of action other than that pursued by the board of directors would have been more advantageous gives rise to no cognizable cause of action. Courts have more than enough to do in adjudicating legal rights and devising remedies for wrongs. The directors' room rather than the courtroom is the appropriate forum for thrashing out purely business questions [813] which will have an impact on profits, market prices, competitive situations, or tax advantages. [...]

It is not enough to allege, as plaintiffs do here, that the directors made an imprudent decision, which did not capitalize on the possibility of using a potential capital loss to offset capital gains. More than imprudence or mistaken judgment must be shown. "Questions of policy of management, expediency of contracts or action, adequacy of consideration, lawful appropriation of corporate funds to advance corporate interests, are left solely to their honest and unselfish decision, for their powers therein are without limitation and free from restraint, and the exercise of them for the common and general interests of the corporation may not be questioned, although the results show that what they did was unwise or inexpedient." […]

Nor does this appear to be a case in which a potentially valid cause of action is inartfully stated. The defendants have moved alternatively for summary judgment and have submitted affidavits under CPLR 3211 (subd [c]), and plaintiffs likewise have submitted papers enlarging upon the allegations of the complaint. The affidavits of the defendants and the exhibits annexed thereto demonstrate that the objections raised by the plaintiffs to the proposed dividend action were carefully considered and unanimously rejected by the board at a special meeting called precisely for that purpose at the plaintiffs' request. The minutes of the special meeting indicate that the [814] defendants were fully aware that a sale rather than a distribution of the DLJ shares might result in the realization of a substantial income tax saving. Nevertheless, they concluded that there were countervailing considerations primarily with respect to the adverse effect such a sale, realizing a loss of $25,000,000, would have on the net income figures in the American Express financial statement. Such a reduction of net income would have a serious effect on the market value of the publicly traded American Express stock. This was not a situation in which the defendant directors totally overlooked facts called to their attention. They gave them consideration, and attempted to view the total picture in arriving at their decision. While plaintiffs contend that according to their accounting consultants the loss on the DLJ stock would still have to be charged against current earnings even if the stock were distributed, the defendants' accounting experts assert that the loss would be a charge against earnings only in the event of a sale, whereas in the event of distribution of the stock as a dividend, the proper accounting treatment would be to charge the loss only against surplus. While the chief accountant for the SEC raised some question as to the appropriate accounting treatment of this transaction, there was no basis for any action to be taken by the SEC with respect to the American Express financial statement.

2.5.8 DGCL Sec. 145 - Indemnification of Officers and Directors

As we learned in the Agency Course, agents acting within the scope of their agency have a common law right of indemnification. Section 145 authorizes the corporation to indemnify agents of the corporation (including directors, officers, and other agents) under certain conditions.

Section 145(a) gives the corporation the power to indemnify agents of the corporation in suits by third parties. In such suits, the corporation may pay any judgments, fines or settlements that result from the agents actions with respect to third parties. Section 145(b) empowers the corporation to indemnify agents of the corporation in derivative suits. In the context of derivative suits, a corporation does not have the power to indemnify agents for any judgments, fines or settlements except upon application to the Chancery Court where there has not been an adjudication of liability. Under Section 145(c), where the corporate agent has successfully defended an action, the corporation is required to indemnify the agent.

The statute envisions that directors seeking indemnification under (a) or (b) may well create conflicts as directors seek the approval of their fellow directors for indemnification. Consequently, the statute requires specific procedures prior to board approval of any such payments. These procedures attempt to mimic an arm's length approval of such payments by enlisting independent directors and/or unaffiliated stockholders. Note the analogue between an approval for purposes of §145 and agency law's approach to approving conflicted agent transactions.

§ 145. Indemnification of officers, directors, employees and agents; insurance.

(a) A corporation shall have power to indemnify any person who was or is a party or is threatened to be made a party to any threatened, pending or completed action, suit or proceeding, whether civil, criminal, administrative or investigative (other than an action by or in the right of the corporation) by reason of the fact that the person is or was a director, officer, employee or agent of the corporation, or is or was serving at the request of the corporation as a director, officer, employee or agent of another corporation, partnership, joint venture, trust or other enterprise, against expenses (including attorneys' fees), judgments, fines and amounts paid in settlement actually and reasonably incurred by the person in connection with such action, suit or proceeding if the person acted in good faith and in a manner the person reasonably believed to be in or not opposed to the best interests of the corporation, and, with respect to any criminal action or proceeding, had no reasonable cause to believe the person's conduct was unlawful. The termination of any action, suit or proceeding by judgment, order, settlement, conviction, or upon a plea of nolo contendere or its equivalent, shall not, of itself, create a presumption that the person did not act in good faith and in a manner which the person reasonably believed to be in or not opposed to the best interests of the corporation, and, with respect to any criminal action or proceeding, had reasonable cause to believe that the person's conduct was unlawful.

(b) A corporation shall have power to indemnify any person who was or is a party or is threatened to be made a party to any threatened, pending or completed action or suit by or in the right of the corporation to procure a judgment in its favor by reason of the fact that the person is or was a director, officer, employee or agent of the corporation, or is or was serving at the request of the corporation as a director, officer, employee or agent of another corporation, partnership, joint venture, trust or other enterprise against expenses (including attorneys' fees) actually and reasonably incurred by the person in connection with the defense or settlement of such action or suit if the person acted in good faith and in a manner the person reasonably believed to be in or not opposed to the best interests of the corporation and except that no indemnification shall be made in respect of any claim, issue or matter as to which such person shall have been adjudged to be liable to the corporation unless and only to the extent that the Court of Chancery or the court in which such action or suit was brought shall determine upon application that, despite the adjudication of liability but in view of all the circumstances of the case, such person is fairly and reasonably entitled to indemnity for such expenses which the Court of Chancery or such other court shall deem proper.

(c) To the extent that a present or former director or officer of a corporation has been successful on the merits or otherwise in defense of any action, suit or proceeding referred to in subsections (a) and (b) of this section, or in defense of any claim, issue or matter therein, such person shall be indemnified against expenses (including attorneys' fees) actually and reasonably incurred by such person in connection therewith.

(d) Any indemnification under subsections (a) and (b) of this section (unless ordered by a court) shall be made by the corporation only as authorized in the specific case upon a determination that indemnification of the present or former director, officer, employee or agent is proper in the circumstances because the person has met the applicable standard of conduct set forth in subsections (a) and (b) of this section. Such determination shall be made, with respect to a person who is a director or officer of the corporation at the time of such determination:

(1) By a majority vote of the directors who are not parties to such action, suit or proceeding, even though less than a quorum; or

(2) By a committee of such directors designated by majority vote of such directors, even though less than a quorum; or

(3) If there are no such directors, or if such directors so direct, by independent legal counsel in a written opinion; or

(4) By the stockholders.

(e) Expenses (including attorneys' fees) incurred by an officer or director of the corporation in defending any civil, criminal, administrative or investigative action, suit or proceeding may be paid by the corporation in advance of the final disposition of such action, suit or proceeding upon receipt of an undertaking by or on behalf of such director or officer to repay such amount if it shall ultimately be determined that such person is not entitled to be indemnified by the corporation as authorized in this section. Such expenses (including attorneys' fees) incurred by former directors and officers or other employees and agents of the corporation or by persons serving at the request of the corporation as directors, officers, employees or agents of another corporation, partnership, joint venture, trust or other enterprise may be so paid upon such terms and conditions, if any, as the corporation deems appropriate.

(f) The indemnification and advancement of expenses provided by, or granted pursuant to, the other subsections of this section shall not be deemed exclusive of any other rights to which those seeking indemnification or advancement of expenses may be entitled under any bylaw, agreement, vote of stockholders or disinterested directors or otherwise, both as to action in such person's official capacity and as to action in another capacity while holding such office. A right to indemnification or to advancement of expenses arising under a provision of the certificate of incorporation or a bylaw shall not be eliminated or impaired by an amendment to the certificate of incorporation or the bylaws after the occurrence of the act or omission that is the subject of the civil, criminal, administrative or investigative action, suit or proceeding for which indemnification or advancement of expenses is sought, unless the provision in effect at the time of such act or omission explicitly authorizes such elimination or impairment after such action or omission has occurred.

(g) A corporation shall have power to purchase and maintain insurance on behalf of any person who is or was a director, officer, employee or agent of the corporation, or is or was serving at the request of the corporation as a director, officer, employee or agent of another corporation, partnership, joint venture, trust or other enterprise against any liability asserted against such person and incurred by such person in any such capacity, or arising out of such person's status as such, whether or not the corporation would have the power to indemnify such person against such liability under this section.

(h) For purposes of this section, references to "the corporation" shall include, in addition to the resulting corporation, any constituent corporation (including any constituent of a constituent) absorbed in a consolidation or merger which, if its separate existence had continued, would have had power and authority to indemnify its directors, officers, and employees or agents, so that any person who is or was a director, officer, employee or agent of such constituent corporation, or is or was serving at the request of such constituent corporation as a director, officer, employee or agent of another corporation, partnership, joint venture, trust or other enterprise, shall stand in the same position under this section with respect to the resulting or surviving corporation as such person would have with respect to such constituent corporation if its separate existence had continued. [...]

(k) The Court of Chancery is hereby vested with exclusive jurisdiction to hear and determine all actions for advancement of expenses or indemnification brought under this section or under any bylaw, agreement, vote of stockholders or disinterested directors, or otherwise. The Court of Chancery may summarily determine a corporation's obligation to advance expenses (including attorneys' fees).

2.6 Stock and Dividends

The following provisions of the corporate law are enabling provisions related the corporation's stock. In general terms, a corporation may issue shares with a variety of rights and powers. Unless the certificate reserves to the board of directors the right designate stock rights, such rights must be stipulated in the corporation's certificate of incorporation.

Where the certificate has reserved to the board the power to designate rights, when a board issues shares it may designate special rights, including voting power and dividend rights, for the stock it issues. Boards have used this power to create high vote shares and other types of stock with preferences and rights. This power to tailor the rights of stock is central to the board's ability to adopt "poison pills", also known as shareholder rights plans.

A common right built in a share of stock is the "liquidation preference". In firms funded by venture capital, venture capitalists will often demand that the shares they are issued come with liquidation preferences. A liquidation preference is a right that grants certain preferential payments to stockholder in the event the corporation undertakes any one of a series of different liquidation events (e.g. a merger, sale of the corporation, or a dissolution). Below is an example of a liquidation preference that might appear in a certificate of incorporation of venture backed start up firm:

> Upon the occurrence of a Liquidation, the holders of the Preferred Stock shall be entitled to receive, prior and in preference to any distribution of any of the assets or surplus funds of the Corporation to the holders of the Common Stock by reason of their ownership thereof, the amount of $5 per share (as adjusted for any stock dividends, combinations or splits with respect to such shares) plus all declared or accumulated but unpaid dividends on such share for each share of Preferred Stock then held by them.

This preference ensures that in the event of a liquidation event like a sale of the corporation, the venture investor receives $5 per share of the transaction consideration before any other stockholder is paid. Once the preference is paid, then stockholders share the balance of the transaction proceeds ratably.

When a board issues shares, this chapter of the code also permits boards to restrict the ability of stockholders to buy and sell shares of the corporation – making such shares subject to redemption rights, rights of first offer, and also prohibiting in some circumstances interested stockholder transactions.

With respect to dividends, the provisions in this chapter makes it clear that decisions with respect to the declaration of dividends are ones that lie wholly within the discretion of the board of directors and are not the realm of stockholder action.

2.6.1 DGCL Sec. 151 - Classes and series of stock

A corporation may issue shares in more than one class, with each class having separate rights and powers. In addition to the liquidation preference, discussed previously, a board can use §151 to issue shares with variable voting rights. For example, Facebook, Google, Twitter and other tech firms have used §151 to issue shares classes of stock to founders with 10 votes per share. Stock issued to the public have 1 vote per share, or in some cases, no votes at all.

Shares issued by the corporation, may also be subject to redemption should that right be stipulated in the certificate of incorporation or the certificate of designation. In a redemption, the board may at any time make a "call" on the stock and can redeem the stock for a price determined in the certificate. A redemption differs from a stock repurchase in the a number of ways. First, a stock repurchase involves a decision by the stockholder to sell their stock. Absent consent of the stockholder, no one can force a stockholder to sell into a stock repurchase. A redemption can lack a certain degree of voluntariness. Stockholders take the stock knowing that the board has the power to redeem stock against the will of stockholders. Second, the stock repurchase can be done at any price. Presumably, the board will want a sufficient number of stockholders to voluntarily tender their shares, consequently the repurchase is typically done a premium to the market price. In a redemption, the redemption price, or at least a formula to calculate the price is set in the certificate of incorporation.

§ 151. Classes and series of stock; redemption; rights.

(a) Every corporation may issue 1 or more classes of stock or 1 or more series of stock within any class thereof, any or all of which classes may be of stock with par value or stock without par value and which classes or series may have such voting powers, full or limited, or no voting powers, and such designations, preferences and relative, participating, optional or other special rights, and qualifications, limitations or restrictions thereof, as shall be stated and expressed in the certificate of incorporation or of any amendment thereto, or in the resolution or resolutions providing for the issue of such stock adopted by the board of directors pursuant to authority expressly vested in it by the provisions of its certificate of incorporation. Any of the voting powers, designations, preferences, rights and qualifications, limitations or restrictions of any such class or series of stock may be made dependent upon facts ascertainable outside the certificate of incorporation or of any amendment thereto, or outside the resolution or resolutions providing for the issue of such stock adopted by the board of directors pursuant to authority expressly vested in it by its certificate of incorporation, provided that the manner in which such facts shall operate upon the voting powers, designations, preferences, rights and qualifications, limitations or restrictions of such class or series of stock is clearly and expressly set forth in the certificate of incorporation or in the resolution or resolutions providing for the issue of such stock adopted by the board of directors. The term "facts," as used in this subsection, includes, but is not limited to, the occurrence of any event, including a determination or action by any person or body, including the corporation. The power to increase or decrease or otherwise adjust the capital stock as provided in this chapter shall apply to all or any such classes of stock.

(b) Any stock of any class or series may be made subject to redemption by the corporation at its option or at the option of the holders of such stock or upon the happening of a specified event; provided however, that immediately following any such redemption the corporation shall have outstanding 1 or more shares of 1 or more classes or series of stock, which share, or shares together, shall have full voting powers. [...]

Any stock which may be made redeemable under this section may be redeemed for cash, property or rights, including securities of the same or another corporation, at such time or times, price or prices, or rate or rates, and with such adjustments, as shall be stated in the certificate of incorporation or in the resolution or resolutions providing for the issue of such stock adopted by the board of directors pursuant to subsection (a) of this section.

(c) The holders of preferred or special stock of any class or of any series thereof shall be entitled to receive dividends at such rates, on such conditions and at such times as shall be stated in the certificate of incorporation or in the resolution or resolutions providing for the issue of such stock adopted by the board of directors as hereinabove provided, payable in preference to, or in such relation to, the dividends payable on any other class or classes or of any other series of stock, and cumulative or noncumulative as shall be so stated and expressed. […]

(d) The holders of the preferred or special stock of any class or of any series thereof shall be entitled to such rights upon the dissolution of, or upon any distribution of the assets of, the corporation as shall be stated in the certificate of incorporation or in the resolution or resolutions providing for the issue of such stock adopted by the board of directors as hereinabove provided.

(e) Any stock of any class or of any series thereof may be made convertible into, or exchangeable for, at the option of either the holder or the corporation or upon the happening of a specified event, shares of any other class or classes or any other series of the same or any other class or classes of stock of the corporation, at such price or prices or at such rate or rates of exchange and with such adjustments as shall be stated in the certificate of incorporation or in the resolution or resolutions providing for the issue of such stock adopted by the board of directors as hereinabove provided.

2.6.2 DGCL Sec. 157 - Rights and options

By now, stock options have become well known as a device for employee compensation in corporations. A stock option provides the holder with the right to purchase a share of the corporation at a stated price. When this "strike price" is below the price of the shares trading in the stock market, the options are considered "in the money" and the optionholder has an economic incentive to exercise the stock option. When the strike price is above the market price for the stock, the optionholder does not have an incentive to exercise the options.

Because stock options increase in value with an increase in the stock price, options are thought to be reasonably efficient incentive mechanisms, delivering value to employees when the firm succeeds. Because stock options issued to employees also vest over time, the existence of unvested options as part of an employee's compensation package creates a bonding mechanism between the corporation and the employee.

§ 157. Rights and options respecting stock.

(a) Subject to any provisions in the certificate of incorporation, every corporation may create and issue, whether or not in connection with the issue and sale of any shares of stock or other securities of the corporation, rights or options entitling the holders thereof to acquire from the corporation any shares of its capital stock of any class or classes, such rights or options to be evidenced by or in such instrument or instruments as shall be approved by the board of directors.

(b) The terms upon which, including the time or times which may be limited or unlimited in duration, at or within which, and the consideration (including a formula by which such consideration may be determined) for which any such shares may be acquired from the corporation upon the exercise of any such right or option, shall be such as shall be stated in the certificate of incorporation, or in a resolution adopted by the board of directors providing for the creation and issue of such rights or options, and, in every case, shall be set forth or incorporated by reference in the instrument or instruments evidencing such rights or options.[...]

2.6.3 DGCL Sec. 160 - Corporate ownership of its own stock

Corporations, as entities separate from their stockholders, are empowered by the statute to hold and maintain all sorts of assets, including holding stock of other corporations (making the holding company possible). But can a corporation own its own stock? And, if it does, what are the implications?

The short answer is that a corporation can indeed buy and own its own stock. However, the implications of the corporation buying its own stock are significant. When a corporation buys or redeems its own stock that stock is deemed to be "treasury stock" and is no longer outstanding stock. Treasury stock may not be voted and does not count towards determining a quorum at stockholder meetings.

Any corporation stock held by wholly-owned subsidiary of the corporation is also deemed treasury stock. However, corporation stock held by the corporation in a fiduciary capacity (corporation stock held as part of an employee retirement plan managed by the corporation, for example), is not deemed to be treasury stock.

§ 160. Corporation's powers respecting ownership, voting, etc., of its own stock; rights of stock called for redemption.

(a) Every corporation may purchase, redeem, receive, take or otherwise acquire, own and hold, sell, lend, exchange, transfer or otherwise dispose of, pledge, use and otherwise deal in and with its own shares; provided, however, that no corporation shall: [...]

(2) Purchase, for more than the price at which they may then be redeemed, any of its shares which are redeemable at the option of the corporation; [...]

(c) Shares of its own capital stock belonging to the corporation or to another corporation, if a majority of the shares entitled to vote in the election of directors of such other corporation is held, directly or indirectly, by the corporation, shall neither be entitled to vote nor be counted for quorum purposes. Nothing in this section shall be construed as limiting the right of any corporation to vote stock, including but not limited to its own stock, held by it in a fiduciary capacity.

(d) Shares which have been called for redemption shall not be deemed to be outstanding shares for the purpose of voting or determining the total number of shares entitled to vote on any matter on and after the date on which written notice of redemption has been sent to holders thereof and a sum sufficient to redeem such shares has been irrevocably deposited or set aside to pay the redemption price to the holders of the shares upon surrender of certificates therefor. [...]

2.6.4 DGCL Sec. 161 - Issuance of stock

The board of directors has the authority to issuance of new shares of the corporation. Provided the shares have been authorized in the certificate of incorporation, the board need not seek stockholder approval prior to issuing such shares.

§ 161. Issuance of additional stock; when and by whom.

The directors may, at any time and from time to time, if all of the shares of capital stock which the corporation is authorized by its certificate of incorporation to issue have not been issued, subscribed for, or otherwise committed to be issued, issue or take subscriptions for additional shares of its capital stock up to the amount authorized in its certificate of incorporation. […]

2.6.5 DGCL Sec. 170 - Dividends

When a corporation has profits, it may distribute those profits back to stockholders. These profit distributions back to stockholders are known as "dividends".

The decision whether or not to issue dividends to stockholders lies wholly within the discretion of the board of directors. Unless the certificate of incorporation states otherwise, stockholders have no right to corporate dividends.

Some old-line corporations, like G.E. are well-known for a long-standing board policy of making dividend payments to their stockholders. Other corporations, like start-up corporations or corporations in high-growth stages of development, have the exact opposite policy. Companies like Alphabet or Facebook have board policies against making dividend payments to stockholders, opting to reinvest all their profits into the company.

§ 170. Dividends; payment; wasting asset corporations.

(a) The directors of every corporation, subject to any restrictions contained in its certificate of incorporation, may declare and pay dividends upon the shares of its capital stock either:

(1) Out of its surplus, as defined in and computed in accordance with §§ 154 and 244 of this title; or

(2) In case there shall be no such surplus, out of its net profits for the fiscal year in which the dividend is declared and/or the preceding fiscal year.

If the capital of the corporation, computed in accordance with §§ 154 and 244 of this title, shall have been diminished by depreciation in the value of its property, or by losses, or otherwise, to an amount less than the aggregate amount of the capital represented by the issued and outstanding stock of all classes having a preference upon the distribution of assets, the directors of such corporation shall not declare and pay out of such net profits any dividends upon any shares of any classes of its capital stock until the deficiency in the amount of capital represented by the issued and outstanding stock of all classes having a preference upon the distribution of assets shall have been repaired. [...]

2.6.6 DGCL Sec. 202 - Restrictions on transfer of stock

When a board issues new shares, in addition assigning voting rights to the shares, the board may also, pursuant to §202, place reasonable restrictions on the ability of stockholders to transfer or sell such shares. There are a variety of common restrictions placed on shares, particularly shares of private corporations. For example, a board might include a right of first refusal restriction on shares it issues to ensure that existing stockholders the opportunity to purchase any shares that a stockholder would like to sell. Another common restriction prevents accumulation of shares by any one stockholder. For example, the Green Bay Packers restrict any one shareholder from owning more than 5% of the outstanding shares of the corporation. The ability of boards to design restrictions on the transfer of stock is fairly broad. Of course, this power is not without limits. For example, restrictions against selling stock to based on racial or gender categories would run afoul of Federal law and thus not be enforceable.

§ 202. Restrictions on transfer and ownership of securities.

(a) A written restriction or restrictions on the transfer or registration of transfer of a security of a corporation, or on the amount of the corporation's securities that may be owned by any person or group of persons[...] may be enforced against the holder of the restricted security or securities or any successor or transferee of the holder including an executor, administrator, trustee, guardian or other fiduciary entrusted with like responsibility for the person or estate of the holder.[...]

(b) A restriction on the transfer or registration of transfer of securities of a corporation, or on the amount of a corporation's securities that may be owned by any person or group of persons, may be imposed by the certificate of incorporation or by the bylaws or by an agreement among any number of security holders or among such holders and the corporation. [...]

(c) A restriction on the transfer or registration of transfer of securities of a corporation or on the amount of such securities that may be owned by any person or group of persons is permitted by this section if it:

(1) Obligates the holder of the restricted securities to offer to the corporation or to any other holders of securities of the corporation or to any other person or to any combination of the foregoing, a prior opportunity, to be exercised within a reasonable time, to acquire the restricted securities; or

(2) Obligates the corporation or any holder of securities of the corporation or any other person or any combination of the foregoing, to purchase the securities which are the subject of an agreement respecting the purchase and sale of the restricted securities; or

(3) Requires the corporation or the holders of any class or series of securities of the corporation to consent to any proposed transfer of the restricted securities or to approve the proposed transferee of the restricted securities, or to approve the amount of securities of the corporation that may be owned by any person or group of persons; or

(4) Obligates the holder of the restricted securities to sell or transfer an amount of restricted securities to the corporation or to any other holders of securities of the corporation or to any other person or to any combination of the foregoing, or causes or results in the automatic sale or transfer of an amount of restricted securities to the corporation or to any other holders of securities of the corporation or to any other person or to any combination of the foregoing; or

(5) Prohibits or restricts the transfer of the restricted securities to, or the ownership of restricted securities by, designated persons or classes of persons or groups of persons, and such designation is not manifestly unreasonable. [...]

2.6.7 DGCL Sec. 203 - State anti-takeover legislation

Section 203 is an example of state anti-takeover legislation. Section 203 is a flavor of the kinds of restrictions on stock transfer as we saw in §202. In §203 restrictions a board may prohibit a stockholder from purchasing additional shares in the corporation for a period of time once they have completed a transaction that gives them control of the corporation. These restrictions are intended to delay the ability of a hostile acquirer to quickly complete a hostile acquisition of the corporation unless the corporation's board consents.

§ 203. Business combinations with interested stockholders.

(a) Notwithstanding any other provisions of this chapter, a corporation shall not engage in any business combination with any interested stockholder for a period of 3 years following the time that such stockholder became an interested stockholder, unless:

(1) Prior to such time the board of directors of the corporation approved either the business combination or the transaction, which resulted in the stockholder becoming an interested stockholder;

(2) Upon consummation of the transaction which resulted in the stockholder becoming an interested stockholder, the interested stockholder owned at least 85% of the voting stock of the corporation outstanding at the time the transaction commenced, excluding for purposes of determining the voting stock outstanding (but not the outstanding voting stock owned by the interested stockholder) those shares owned (i) by persons who are directors and also officers and (ii) employee stock plans in which employee participants do not have the right to determine confidentially whether shares held subject to the plan will be tendered in a tender or exchange offer; or

(3) At or subsequent to such time the business combination is approved by the board of directors and authorized at an annual or special meeting of stockholders, and not by written consent, by the affirmative vote of at least 66 2/3% of the outstanding voting stock which is not owned by the interested stockholder.

(b) The restrictions contained in this section shall not apply if:

(1) The corporation's original certificate of incorporation contains a provision expressly electing not to be governed by this section; [...]

 (c) As used in this section only, the term: [...]

(3) "Business combination," when used in reference to any corporation and any interested stockholder of such corporation, means:

(i) Any merger or consolidation of the corporation or any direct or indirect majority-owned subsidiary of the corporation with (A) the interested stockholder, or (B) with any other corporation, partnership, unincorporated association or other entity if the merger or consolidation is caused by the interested stockholder and as a result of such merger or consolidation subsection (a) of this section is not applicable to the surviving entity;

(ii) Any sale, lease, exchange, mortgage, pledge, transfer or other disposition (in 1 transaction or a series of transactions), except proportionately as a stockholder of such corporation, to or with the interested stockholder, whether as part of a dissolution or otherwise, of assets of the corporation or of any direct or indirect majority-owned subsidiary of the corporation which assets have an aggregate market value equal to 10% or more of either the aggregate market value of all the assets of the corporation determined on a consolidated basis or the aggregate market value of all the outstanding stock of the corporation; [...]

2.7 Stockholder Meetings and Voting for Directors

Stockholders do not have a general right to manage the business and affairs of the corporation. Nor do they have a general right to vote on matters related to the operation of the corporation's business. The principle power of stockholders is the power to vote for directors and certain corporate transactions which for which there is a statutory stockholder vote required. Stockholders who disagree with the strategy or direction of the corporation have generally have two choices: vote in favor of a different board and thus change the composition of the board of directors; or sell their shares. In many cases, institutional stockholders or indexed stockholders will not be in a position to sell their shares. Thus, the corporate ballot box becomes a fulcrum to affect a change in corporate strategy.

Nominations for membership on the board of directors are typically made by the board itself through a nominations and governance committee of the board created for that purpose. Stockholder activists will often use the threat of a contested election in which they nominate their own directors to sway incumbent directors with respect to corporate strategy. In that sense, stockholder control over corporations can be better described as a "bank shot" (to use a basketball description). While stockholders cannot dictate business decisions to boards of directors, when a board feels sufficiently vulnerable to expulsion at the ballot box, boards will become more amenable to activists' suggestions about the strategic direction of the business.

The importance of the stockholder franchise and votes for control over the board of directors are the central tension in modern corporate governance. Boards are free to manage corporations in any manner they see fit, subject to regular votes of confidence by stockholders. To the extent boards stray far from the interests of stockholders, boards are vulnerable to replacement through regular stockholder votes.

The following provisions lay out the requirements for stockholder meetings as well as stockholder voting at these meetings.

2.7.1 DGCL Sec. 211 - Stockholder meetings

The following provision lays out the requirements for a corporation to hold an annual meeting of the stockholders. The principle business of any corporation's annual meeting is the election of the directors. It is through the annual election of directors that stockholders have their biggest voice and influence in the running of the corporation's business and affairs.

§ 211. Meetings of stockholders.

(a)(1) Meetings of stockholders may be held at such place, either within or without this State as may be designated by or in the manner provided in the certificate of incorporation or bylaws, or if not so designated, as determined by the board of directors.[...]

(b) Unless directors are elected by written consent in lieu of an annual meeting as permitted by this subsection, an annual meeting of stockholders shall be held for the election of directors on a date and at a time designated by or in the manner provided in the bylaws. […]

(c) A failure to hold the annual meeting at the designated time or to elect a sufficient number of directors to conduct the business of the corporation shall not affect otherwise valid corporate acts or work a forfeiture or dissolution of the corporation except as may be otherwise specifically provided in this chapter. If the annual meeting for election of directors is not held on the date designated therefor or action by written consent to elect directors in lieu of an annual meeting has not been taken, the directors shall cause the meeting to be held as soon as is convenient. If there be a failure to hold the annual meeting or to take action by written consent to elect directors in lieu of an annual meeting for a period of 30 days after the date designated for the annual meeting, or if no date has been designated, for a period of 13 months after the latest to occur of the organization of the corporation, its last annual meeting or the last action by written consent to elect directors in lieu of an annual meeting, the Court of Chancery may summarily order a meeting to be held upon the application of any stockholder or director. The shares of stock represented at such meeting, either in person or by proxy, and entitled to vote thereat, shall constitute a quorum for the purpose of such meeting, notwithstanding any provision of the certificate of incorporation or bylaws to the contrary. The Court of Chancery may issue such orders as may be appropriate, including, without limitation, orders designating the time and place of such meeting, the record date or dates for determination of stockholders entitled to notice of the meeting and to vote thereat, and the form of notice of such meeting.

(d) Special meetings of the stockholders may be called by the board of directors or by such person or persons as may be authorized by the certificate of incorporation or by the bylaws.

(e) All elections of directors shall be by written ballot unless otherwise provided in the certificate of incorporation; […]

2.7.2 DGCL. Sec. 228 - Action by written consent

Stockholders may act by providing their written consent rather than at a meeting. Taking action by written consent rather than at a formal meeting may be preferable in corporations, like start-up companies, where the number of stockholders is relatively small and easily identifiable. Any action that can be taken at a meeting of the stockholders can also be accomplished by written consent of the majority of the outstanding shares.

This default right to act by written consent can be stripped from stockholders. It is not uncommon for larger, publicly-traded corporations to include a prohibition against acting by written consent in the corporation's certificate of incorporation. By requiring stockholders to act only at a meeting - the time and place of which is controlled by the board of directors - managers of the corporation make it difficult for stockholder activists or for potential hostile acquirers of the corporation to organize stockholders against the incumbent board of directors and managers.

§ 228. Consent of stockholders or members in lieu of meeting.

(a) Unless otherwise provided in the certificate of incorporation, any action required by this chapter to be taken at any annual or special meeting of stockholders of a corporation, or any action which may be taken at any annual or special meeting of such stockholders, may be taken without a meeting, without prior notice and without a vote, if a consent or consents in writing, setting forth the action so taken, shall be signed by the holders of outstanding stock having not less than the minimum number of votes that would be necessary to authorize or take such action at a meeting at which all shares entitled to vote thereon were present and voted and shall be delivered to the corporation by delivery to its registered office in this State, its principal place of business or an officer or agent of the corporation having custody of the book in which proceedings of meetings of stockholders are recorded. [...]

(c) Every written consent shall bear the date of signature of each stockholder or member who signs the consent, and no written consent shall be effective to take the corporate action referred to therein unless, within 60 days of the earliest dated consent delivered in the manner required by this section to the corporation[...]

(e) Prompt notice of the taking of the corporate action without a meeting by less than unanimous written consent shall be given to those stockholders or members who have not consented in writing and who, if the action had been taken at a meeting, would have been entitled to notice of the meeting if the record date for notice of such meeting had been the date that written consents signed by a sufficient number of holders or members to take the action were delivered to the corporation as provided in subsection (c) of this section. [...]

2.7.3 DGCL Sec. 212 - Stockholder voting rights

The default rule is that each share of stock gets one vote unless the certificate of incorporation provides otherwise. A stockholder may vote in person or may delegate authority to another person to vote as their proxy.

§ 212. Voting rights of stockholders; proxies; limitations.

(a) Unless otherwise provided in the certificate of incorporation and subject to § 213 of this title, each stockholder shall be entitled to 1 vote for each share of capital stock held by such stockholder. If the certificate of incorporation provides for more or less than 1 vote for any share, on any matter, every reference in this chapter to a majority or other proportion of stock, voting stock or shares shall refer to such majority or other proportion of the votes of such stock, voting stock or shares.

(b) Each stockholder entitled to vote at a meeting of stockholders or to express consent or dissent to corporate action in writing without a meeting may authorize another person or persons to act for such stockholder by proxy. [...]

2.7.4 Stock with Multiple Voting Classes

According to §212, the default is that every share of stock has one vote. However, because the corporate code provides for parties to tailor their arrangements, it is possible for boards to issue different classes or series of stock with different rights. The most common, though certainly not the only, customization of stock in recent years is the creation of multiple classes of stock with different voting power. In recent years, multiple class voting structures have become popular with founder-led tech companies when they go public. For example, corporations like Alphabet (Google), Facebook, Snap, and Uber, among others, all have multiple classes of stock, each with different voting rights. High vote stock, held by the controlling stockholders in these corporations, typically have ten votes per share, while stock held by the public has stock with a lower number of votes per share.

Alphabet (Google) has a relative complex share structure. Alphabet's Class A shares are the shares commonly held by the public. These shares have one vote each. Alphabet's Class B shares are high vote shares held by the founders. These shares have 10 votes each. The final Class of shares in Alphabet at no-vote Class C shares. Class C shares do not have the right to vote. Alphabet uses these shares as acquisition currency. Class C shares permit the founders to purchase other companies for using Alphabet stock as the currency without risking reduction in the voting power of the founders. By holding high vote Class B shares, Google's founders can control the outcome of stockholder votes without holding an equivalent economic interest in the corporation.

Snap went public in 2017 with its own version of multiple classes of shares. In Snap's case, the company has three classes of common stock: Class A, Class B, and Class C. Holders of Snap's Class A common stock are not entitled to vote on matters submitted to the stockholders. Holders of Snap's Class B common stock (mostly made up of employees and venture investors) are entitled to one vote per share. And holders of Snap's Class C common stock (held by Snap's founders: Evan Spiegal and Robert Murphy) and are entitled to ten votes per share. Holders of shares of Class B common stock and Class C common stock will vote together as a single class on all matters (including the election of directors) submitted to a vote of stockholders. As a result of this voting structure founders Evan Spiegel and Robert Murphy are able to exercise voting rights with respect to approximately 88.5% of the voting power of Snap's outstanding capital stock.

How to read votes and shares: Pursuant to Section 212(a), where a corporation has multiple classes of stock with different voting power, then the entire code should be re-read and where the code calls for *"share"* (with respect to required votes or quorum, etc) that must be read to read *"votes"*.

2.7.5 DGCL Sec. 213 - Record dates

Prior to any stockholder meeting, the board must set a "record date" for determining who are the stockholders of the corporation who have the right to vote at the meeting.

Determining who is a stockholder for the purposes of notice and the right to vote at a meeting can be more complex than you might initially think. in a private corporation, like a start-up, determining who are the record stockholders entitled to notice and to vote at a meeting is, typically, a simple matter. Shares of a private corporation are not transferrable and are held by a relatively small number of easily identifiable persons. One need only refer to the corporation's stock ledger (usually an Excel spreadsheet) to determine who are the stockholders.

On the other hand, determining who is a stockholder in a modern publicly-traded corporation is an altogether different matter. In publicly-traded corporations, there are potentially millions of stockholders and the demographic of the stockholding base turns over regularly as traders in the market buy and sell shares of the corporation. Determining who is a stockholder for purposes of receiving notice of a meeting and then being entitled to vote at that meeting is difficult. For one thing, a stockholder who is given notice today may very well not be a stockholder of the corporation in 45 when the meeting is actually held.

Later, when we discuss stockholder lists and §219, you will be introduced to the complexities of the system that has been gerry-rigged to try to deal with the question of record ownership in a fast paced trading environment. For now, though, note that §213 tries to deal with some obvious issues.

By permitting a board to separate a stockholder's right to receive notice of a meeting and the identification of stockholders entitled to vote at a meeting. by delaying the identification of those stockholders entitled to vote, the statute acknowledges the reality that in many corporations there will be significant turnover in the stockholding demographic between notice and the meeting. By identifying stockholders entitled to vote at a later point closer in time to the meeting, drafters of the statute hope the actual stockholding demographic more closely resembles those who have been identified as having the right to vote at a meeting.

§ 213. Fixing date for determination of stockholders of record.

(a) In order that the corporation may determine the stockholders entitled to notice of any meeting of stockholders or any adjournment thereof, the board of directors may fix a record date, which record date shall not precede the date upon which the resolution fixing the record date is adopted by the board of directors, and which record date shall not be more than 60 nor less than 10 days before the date of such meeting. If the board of directors so fixes a date, such date shall also be the record date for determining the stockholders entitled to vote at such meeting unless the board of directors determines, at the time it fixes such record date, that a later date on or before the date of the meeting shall be the date for making such determination. If no record date is fixed by the board of directors, the record date for determining stockholders entitled to notice of and to vote at a meeting of stockholders shall be at the close of business on the day next preceding the day on which notice is given, or, if notice is waived, at the close of business on the day next preceding the day on which the meeting is held. A determination of stockholders of record entitled to notice of or to vote at a meeting of stockholders shall apply to any adjournment of the meeting; provided, however, that the board of directors may fix a new record date for determination of stockholders entitled to vote at the adjourned meeting, and in such case shall also fix as the record date for stockholders entitled to notice of such adjourned meeting the same or an earlier date as that fixed for determination of stockholders entitled to vote in accordance with the foregoing provisions of this subsection (a) at the adjourned meeting.

[…] If no record date has been fixed by the board of directors, the record date for determining stockholders entitled to consent to corporate action in writing without a meeting, when no prior action by the board of directors is required by this chapter, shall be the first date on which a signed written consent setting forth the action taken or proposed to be taken is delivered to the corporation by delivery to its registered office in this State, its principal place of business or an officer or agent of the corporation having custody of the book in which proceedings of meetings of stockholders are recorded. […] If no record date has been fixed by the board of directors and prior action by the board of directors is required by this chapter, the record date for determining stockholders entitled to consent to corporate action in writing without a meeting shall be at the close of business on the day on which the board of directors adopts the resolution taking such prior action. […]

2.7.6 DGCL Sec. 222 - Notice of meetings

A meeting may not be called unless all stockholders of record have received adequate notice under the provisions of the statute. Section 222 below outlines the notice requirements for stockholder meetings.

§ 222. Notice of meetings and adjourned meetings.

(a) Whenever stockholders are required or permitted to take any action at a meeting, a written notice of the meeting shall be given which shall state the place, if any, date and hour of the meeting, the means of remote communications, if any, by which stockholders and proxy holders may be deemed to be present in person and vote at such meeting, the record date for determining the stockholders entitled to vote at the meeting, if such date is different from the record date for determining stockholders entitled to notice of the meeting, and, in the case of a special meeting, the purpose or purposes for which the meeting is called.

(b) Unless otherwise provided in this chapter, the written notice of any meeting shall be given not less than 10 nor more than 60 days before the date of the meeting to each stockholder entitled to vote at such meeting as of the record date for determining the stockholders entitled to notice of the meeting. […]

(c) When a meeting is adjourned to another time or place, unless the bylaws otherwise require, notice need not be given of the adjourned meeting if the time, place, if any, thereof, and the means of remote communications, if any, by which stockholders and proxy holders may be deemed to be present in person and vote at such adjourned meeting are announced at the meeting at which the adjournment is taken. […] If the adjournment is for more than 30 days, a notice of the adjourned meeting shall be given to each stockholder of record entitled to vote at the meeting. If after the adjournment a new record date for stockholders entitled to vote is fixed for the adjourned meeting, the board of directors shall fix a new record date for notice of such adjourned meeting in accordance with § 213(a) of this title, and shall give notice of the adjourned meeting to each stockholder of record entitled to vote at such adjourned meeting as of the record date fixed for notice of such adjourned meeting.

2.7.7 Who Gets to Vote - 219 and Lists of Record Stockholders

In advance of a meeting, stockholders have the right to seek a list of fellow stockholders of record for the purpose of communicating with them about the upcoming meeting. In the typical private corporation, identifying the stockholders of record is a relatively simple matter: every time the corporation issues a share, the corporate secretary records the name of the stockholder into the corporation's stock ledger. In order to determine the stockholders of record, one need only refer to the stock ledger.

This exercise is more complex when one wishes to determine the stockholders of record of a corporation which has its stock trading on the public markets, like the NASDAQ or the NYSE. In the *Dell* case that follows, Vice Chancellor Laster provides an overview of the US system of recording beneficial and record stockholders for public corporations.

2.7.7.1 DGCL Sec. 219 - Stockholder lists

Stockholders of a corporation have a right to access the list of stockholders in anticipation of a stockholder meeting. A corporation that wishes to prevent a stockholder from inspecting this list bears a burden of proving to the court why it should not be required to permit inspection.

§ 219. List of stockholders entitled to vote; penalty for refusal to produce; stock ledger.

(a) The officer who has charge of the stock ledger of a corporation shall prepare and make, at least 10 days before every meeting of stockholders, a complete list of the stockholders entitled to vote at the meeting; provided, however, if the record date for determining the stockholders entitled to vote is less than 10 days before the meeting date, the list shall reflect the stockholders entitled to vote as of the tenth day before the meeting date, arranged in alphabetical order, and showing the address of each stockholder and the number of shares registered in the name of each stockholder. […]

Such list shall be open to the examination of any stockholder for any purpose germane to the meeting for a period of at least 10 days prior to the meeting: […]

(b) If the corporation, or an officer or agent thereof, refuses to permit examination of the list by a stockholder, such stockholder may apply to the Court of Chancery for an order to compel the corporation to permit such examination. The burden of proof shall be on the corporation to establish that the examination such stockholder seeks is for a purpose not germane to the meeting. The Court may summarily order the corporation to permit examination of the list upon such conditions as the Court may deem appropriate, and may make such additional orders as may be appropriate, including, without limitation, postponing the meeting or voiding the results of the meeting.

(c) The stock ledger shall be the only evidence as to who are the stockholders entitled by this section to examine the list required by this section or to vote in person or by proxy at any meeting of stockholders. […]

2.7.7.2 In re Appraisal of Dell Inc.

In this appraisal opinion, Vice Chancellor Laster provides an overview of stockholder record keeping for public companies.

IN RE APPRAISAL OF DELL INC.
Consol. C.A. No. 9322-VCL.

LASTER, Vice Chancellor.

The petitioners are five institutions[1] who owned common stock of Dell, Inc. They sought appraisal after Dell announced a going-private merger. Dell contends that they did not hold their shares continuously through the effective date of the merger and therefore lost their appraisal rights.

The Funds held their shares through custodial banks. By virtue of this relationship, the Funds did not have legal title to the shares; they were beneficial owners. But the custodial banks did not have legal title either. The shares they held were registered in the name of Cede & Co., which is the nominee of the Depository Trust Company ("DTC").[2]

DTC's place in the ownership structure results from the federal response to a paperwork crisis on Wall Street during the late 1960s and early 1970s. Increased trading volume in the securities markets overwhelmed the back offices of brokerage firms and the capabilities of transfer agents. No one could cope with the burdens of documenting stock trades using paper certificates. The markets were forced to declare trading holidays so administrators could catch up. With trading volumes continuing to climb, it was obvious that reform was needed. Congress directed the SEC to evaluate alternatives that would facilitate trading.

After studying the issue, the SEC adopted a national policy of share immobilization. To carry out its policy, the SEC placed a new entity—the depository institution—at the bottom the ownership chain. DTC emerged as the only domestic depository. Over 800 custodial banks and brokers are participating members of DTC and maintain accounts with that institution. DTC holds shares on their behalf in fungible bulk, meaning that none of the shares are issued in the names of DTC's participants. Instead, all of the shares are issued in the name of Cede. Through a Fast Automated Securities Transfer account (the "FAST Account"), DTC uses an electronic book entry system to track the number of shares of stock that each participant holds.

By adding DTC to the bottom of the ownership chain, the SEC eliminated the need for the overwhelming majority of legal transfers. Before share immobilization, custodial banks and brokers held shares through their own nominees, so new certificates had to be issued frequently when shares traded. With share immobilization, legal title remains with Cede. No new certificates are required. […]

A. The Funds' Ownership Of Dell Shares

On February 5, 2013, Dell agreed to a merger in which each publicly held share of Dell common stock would be converted into the right to receive $13.75 in cash, subject to the right of stockholders to seek appraisal. The Funds held at least 922,975 shares of Dell common stock. Like most investors, the Funds did not hold legal title to their shares. The Funds owned the shares indirectly through accounts at custodial banks. Two of the Funds used J.P. Morgan Chase ("JP Morgan") as their custodian. The others used The Bank of New York Mellon ("BONY").

The custodial banks did not own record title either. JP Morgan and BONY are two of more than 800 custodial banks and brokers who are participating members of DTC.

> The vast majority of publicly traded shares in the United States are registered on the companies' books not in the name of beneficial owners— i.e., those investors who paid for, and have the right to vote and dispose of, the shares—but rather in the name of "Cede & Co.," the name used by The Depository Trust Company ("DTC").Shares registered in this manner are commonly referred to as being held in "street name." . . . DTC holds the shares on behalf of banks and brokers, which in turn hold on behalf of their clients (who are the underlying beneficial owners or other intermediaries).

John C. Wilcox, John J. Purcell III, & Hye-Won Choi, *"Street Name" Registration & The Proxy Solicitation Process, in A Practical Guide to SEC Proxy and Compensation Rules* 10-3, 10-3 (Amy Goodman et al. eds., 4th ed. 2007 & 2008 Supp.) [hereinafter *Street Name*] (footnote omitted).

The history of how we arrived at this ownership structure is important and informative.[4]

> Prior to 1970, negotiation was the most common method used to transfer stock in the United States. The owner would endorse the physical certificate to the name of the assignee on the back of the certificate. This endorsement instruct[ed] the corporation, upon notification, [about] the change in ownership of the shares on its corporate books. If the parties used the services of a broker, the seller would transfer the certificate to his brokerage firm. The brokerage firm representing the customer buying the security would receive the physical certificate and transfer it to the buyer as the new record owner of the security. Occasionally, the new owner might request that the physical certificate remain at the street address of the brokerage firm to facilitate the transfer of the certificate in a subsequent sale.

Wolfe, *supra,* at 180 (footnotes omitted).

Transfer of securities in the traditional certificate-based system was a complicated, labor-intensive process. Each time securities were traded, the physical certificates had to be delivered from the seller to the buyer, and in the case of registered securities the certificates had to be surrendered to the issuer or its transfer agent for registration of transfer.

Prefatory Note at 2.

By the late 1960s, increased trading rendered the certificate system obsolete. The paperwork burden reached "crisis proportions." *Id.*

Stock certificates and related documents were piled "halfway to the ceiling" in some offices; clerical personnel were working overtime, six and seven days a week, with some firms using a second or even a third shift to process each day's transaction. Hours of trading on the exchange and over the counter were curtailed to give back offices additional time after the closing bell. Deliveries to customers and similar activities dropped seriously behind, and the number of errors in brokers' records, as well as the time to trace and correct these errors, exacerbated the crisis.

Wolfe, *supra,* at 181 n.49 (quoting *SEC Study* at 219 n.1). "The difficulty that brokers and dealers experienced in keeping their records due to the volume of transactions and their thin capitalization caused many brokerage firms to declare bankruptcy and many investors to realize losses." *Id.* at 182.

Congress responded by passing the Securities Investor Protection Act of 1970, which directed the SEC to study the practices leading to the growing crisis in securities transfer. 15 U.S.C. § 78kkk(g). The SEC recommended discontinuing the physical movement of certificates and adopting a depository system. Wolfe, *supra,* at 182 n.58 (citing *SEC Study* at 13). Congress then passed the Securities Acts Amendments of 1975, which directed the SEC to "use its authority under this chapter to end the physical movement of securities certificates in connection with the settlement among brokers and dealers of transactions in securities consummated by means of the mails or any means or instrumentalities of interstate commerce." 15 U.S.C. § 78q-1(e). In a resulting report, the SEC found that "registering securities in other than the name of the beneficial owner" was essential to establishing "a national system for the prompt and accurate clearance and settlement of securities transactions." Kahan & Rock, *supra,* at 1237 n.49.

Thus was born the federal policy of immobilizing share certificates through a depository system. "Congress called for a more efficient process for comparison, clearing, and settlement in a national market system, and for the end of the physical movement of securities certificates in connection with the settlement of transactions among brokers and dealers." Egon Guttman, *Transfer of Securities: State and Federal Interaction,* 12 Cardozo L. Rev. 437, 447 (1990); *accord* S. REP. NO. 94-75 at 5 (1975) ("A national clearance and settlement system is clearly needed."). To comply, "[b]rokerages and banks created [depositories] to allow them to deposit certificates centrally (so-called `jumbo certificates,' often representing tens or hundreds of thousands of shares) and leave them at rest." Larry T. Garvin, *The Changed (And Changing?) Uniform Commercial Code,* 26 Fla. St. U. L. Rev. 285, 315 (1999).

In 1973, just after the paperwork crisis and with the federal writing on the wall, the members of the New York Stock Exchange created DTC to serve as a depository and clearing agency. Originally there were three regional depositories in addition to DTC: the Midwest Securities Depository Trust Company, which held through its nominee, Kray & Co.; the Pacific Securities Depository Trust Company, which held through its nominee, Pacific & Co; and the Philadelphia Depository Trust Company, which held through its nominee, Philadep & Co. "[I]n the 1990's DTC . . . assumed the activities of the [other] depositories." Carnell & Hanks, *supra,* at 26. Today DTC is the world's largest securities depository and the only domestic depository. Kahan & Rock, *supra,* at 1238 n.50. "DTC is owned by its `participants,' which are the member organizations of the various national stock exchanges (*e.g.,* State Street Bank, Merrill Lynch, Goldman Sachs & Co.)." *Street Name* at 10-6 to 10-7.

DTC has been estimated to hold "about three-quarters of [the] shares in publicly traded companies." Garvin, *supra,* at 315; *accord* Kahan & Rock, *supra,* at 1236; *Street Name* at 10-4 n.2. "The shares of each company held by DTC are typically represented by only one or more `immobilized' jumbo stock certificates held in DTC's vaults." *Street Name* at 10-7. "The immobilized jumbo certificates are the direct result of Section 17A(e) of the

Exchange Act, in which Congress instructed the SEC to `use its authority . . . to end the physical movement of securities certificates. . . .'" *Id.* at 10-7 n.10.

The depository system is what enables public trading of securities to take place. In 2014, the NYSE reported average *daily* volume of approximately 1 *billion* shares and approximately 4 *million* separate trades. *See* NYSE Factbook, http://www.nysedata.com/factbook (last visited June 19, 2015). The failure of the certificate-based system to keep up with much lower trading volumes in the 1960s demonstrates that it cannot meet current demand. *Prefatory Note* at 2. Without immobilization and DTC, "implementing a system to settle securities within five business days (T+5), much less today's norm of T+3 or the current goals of T+1 or T+0, would simply be impossible." Kahan & Rock, *supra,* at 1238. Trading at current levels is only possible because of share immobilization and DTC. *Street Name* at 10-7; *accord* Garvin, *supra,* at 315-16; *Prefatory Note* at 2-3.

Because of the federal policy of share immobilization, it is now Cede—not the ultimate beneficial owner and not the DTC-participant banks and brokers—that appears on the stock ledger of a Delaware corporation. Cede is typically the largest holder on the stock ledger of most publicly traded Delaware corporations. *Street Name* at 10-6. To preserve the pre-immobilization status quo—at least at the federal level—the SEC provided that for purposes of federal law, the custodial banks and brokers remain the record holders. Depositories are defined as "clearing agencies." 15 U.S.C. § 78c(23)(A). The term "record holder" is defined as "any broker, dealer, voting trustee, bank, association or other entity that exercises fiduciary powers which holds securities of record in nominee name or otherwise or as a participant in a clearing agency registered pursuant to section 17A of the Act." 17 C.F.R. § 240.14c-1(i). The term "entity that exercises fiduciary powers" is similarly defined as "any entity that holds securities in nominee name or otherwise on behalf of a beneficial owner but does not include a clearing agency registered pursuant to section 17A of the Act or a broker or a dealer." *Id.* § 240.14c-1(c). Federal law thus looks through DTC when determining a corporation's record holders. For example, when determining whether an issuer has 500 or more record holders of a class of its equity securities such that it must register under 15 U.S.C. § 78l(g), DTC does not count as a single holder of record. Each DTC participant member counts as a holder of record. Michael K. Molitor, *Will More Sunlight Fade The Pink Sheets?*, 39 Ind. L. Rev. 309, 315-16 (2006) (citing SEC interpretive releases).

The federal regulations also ensure that a corporation can easily find out the identities of the banks and brokers who hold shares through DTC. Federal regulations require that DTC "furnish a securities position listing promptly to each issuer whose securities are held in the name of the clearing agency or its nominee." 17 C.F.R. § 240.17Ad-8(b). The participant listing is known colloquially as the "Cede breakdown," and it identifies for a particular date the custodial banks and brokers that hold shares in fungible bulk as of that date along with the number of shares held. A Delaware corporation can obtain a Cede breakdown with ease. In 1981, this court noted that a Cede breakdown could be obtained in a matter of minutes. *Hatleigh Corp. v. Lane Bryant, Inc.*, 428 A.2d 350, 354 (Del. Ch. 1981). A Cede breakdown can now be obtained through DTC's website or by calling the DTC "Proxy Services Hotline." Issuers use the Cede breakdown to understand their stockholder profile, and proxy solicitors use it when advising clients. Commentary regards the information as reliable. *Handbook for the Conduct of Shareholders' Meetings* 40 (ABA Business Law Section, Corporate Governance Committee ed., 2000) (identifying the "lists of holders obtained from depositories" as one of the documents that can be relied on in "determining the shares entitled to vote and tabulating the vote").

A publicly traded corporation cannot avoid going through DTC. Federal law requires that when submitting a matter for a stockholder vote, an issuer must send a broker search card at least twenty business days prior to the record date to any "broker, dealer, voting trustee, bank, association, or other entity that exercises fiduciary powers in nominee name" that the company "knows" is holding shares for beneficial owners. 17 C.F.R. § 240.14a-13(a). Rule 14a-13 provides that "[i]f the registrant's list of security holders indicates that some of its securities are registered in the name of a clearing agency registered pursuant to Section 17A of the Act (e.g., `Cede & Co.,' nominee for Depository Trust Company), the registrant *shall make* appropriate inquiry of the clearing agency and thereafter of the participants in such clearing agency." *Id.* § 240.14a-13(a) n.1 (emphasis added). An issuer cannot look only at its own records and treat Cede as a single, monolithic owner.

B. The Funds Seek Appraisal, And DTC Certificates The Shares.

140

Dell was a publicly traded company and the merger involved a stockholder vote, so Dell had to go through the federally mandated process to identify the custodial banks and brokers that held its shares through DTC, then send information through them to the beneficial holders. The list of DTC-participants included JP Morgan and BONY. Through JP Morgan and BONY, information reached the Funds.

The Funds exercised appraisal rights for the 922,975 shares that are the subject of this motion. Because they owned their shares in street name through their custodial banks, the Funds caused Cede to demand appraisal on their behalf. On July 12, 2013, before the vote on the merger, Cede made appraisal demands for the Funds.

DTC held all of the Dell shares registered in street name in fungible bulk, which enabled DTC to track their ownership through electronic bookkeeping entries in the FAST Account. When the Funds caused Cede to make appraisal demands for their shares, DTC moved a corresponding number of shares out of the FAST Account by directing Dell's transfer agent to issue uniquely numbered certificates. By issuing paper certificates, DTC sought to avoid inadvertently surrendering the shares for the merger consideration along with other shares in the FAST Account. This procedure protected Dell, which effectively had "the responsibility of overseeing the surrender of shares after a merger." *Ala. By-Prods.,* 857 A.2d at 263.

Dell's transfer agent is the American Stock Transfer & Trust Company, LLC (the "Transfer Agent"). On July 24, 2013, at DTC's request, the Transfer Agent issued paper stock certificates in Cede's name for the shares owned beneficially by the Funds.

2.7.8 DGCL Sec. 216 - Quorum and required votes

For any stockholder meeting to be a valid meeting, there must be sufficient representation of the corporation's underlying stockholder base. Quorum requirements exist to ensure that when a corporation's stockholders meet they are sufficiently representative such that their votes reflect the will of the stockholders as a whole.

This §216 also sets out the default rules for voting for directors.

§ 216. Quorum and required vote for stock corporations.

Subject to this chapter in respect of the vote that shall be required for a specified action, the certificate of incorporation or bylaws of any corporation authorized to issue stock may specify the number of shares and/or the amount of other securities having voting power the holders of which shall be present or represented by proxy at any meeting in order to constitute a quorum for, and the votes that shall be necessary for, the transaction of any business, but in no event shall a quorum consist of less than 1/3 of the shares entitled to vote at the meeting, except that, where a separate vote by a class or series or classes or series is required, a quorum shall consist of no less than 1/3 of the shares of such class or series or classes or series. In the absence of such specification in the certificate of incorporation or bylaws of the corporation:

(1) A majority of the shares entitled to vote, present in person or represented by proxy, shall constitute a quorum at a meeting of stockholders;

(2) In all matters other than the election of directors, the affirmative vote of the majority of shares present in person or represented by proxy at the meeting and entitled to vote on the subject matter shall be the act of the stockholders;

(3) Directors shall be elected by a plurality of the votes of the shares present in person or represented by proxy at the meeting and entitled to vote on the election of directors; and

(4) Where a separate vote by a class or series or classes or series is required, a majority of the outstanding shares of such class or series or classes or series, present in person or represented by proxy, shall constitute a quorum entitled to take action with respect to that vote on that matter and, in all matters other than the election of directors, the affirmative vote of the majority of shares of such class or series or classes or series present in person or represented by proxy at the meeting shall be the act of such class or series or classes or series.

A bylaw amendment adopted by stockholders which specifies the votes that shall be necessary for the election of directors shall not be further amended or repealed by the board of directors. […]

2.7.9 DGCL Sec. 214 - Cumulative voting option for directors

Although plurality voting is the default rule for the election of directors under §216, a corporation may, in its certificate of incorporation, opt into a cumulative voting structure. The cumulative voting structure gives minority blockholders the power to elect representatives to the board in a manner that would be impossible under plurality voting. It does so by permitting stockholders to accumulate all their votes into a single (or multiple) block and then allocate that block of votes to a single candidate.

For example, if the election is for four directors and the stockholder has 500 shares, under the default plurality voting regime, the stockholder can vote a maximum of 500 shares for each one candidate. Under a cumulative voting regime, the stockholder has that number of votes equal to the number of shares owned by the stockholder multiplied by the number of available board seats in the election. In this case: 500 * 4 = 2,000 votes. The stockholder is then free to allocate those votes in any many she pleases, for example all 2,000 votes on candidate A, splitting her votes 1,000 each between candidate A and B while giving no votes to candidates C and D.

Under §141(k), the director removal provision, a director may be removed under cumulative voting, however, remova of a director may be blocked by minority stockholders. Under §141(k), no director in a cumulative voting regime may be removed when the votes cast against removal would be sufficient to elect the director if voted cumulatively at an election where all memberships entitled to vote were voted.

§ 214. Cumulative voting.

The certificate of incorporation of any corporation may provide that at all elections of directors of the corporation, or at elections held under specified circumstances, each holder of stock or of any class or classes or of a series or series thereof shall be entitled to as many votes as shall equal the number of votes which (except for such provision as to cumulative voting) such holder would be entitled to cast for the election of directors with respect to such holder's shares of stock multiplied by the number of directors to be elected by such holder, and that such holder may cast all of such votes for a single director or may distribute them among the number to be voted for, or for any 2 or more of them as such holder may see fit.

2.7.10 Shareholder Proposals

At the annual stockholder meeting, directors ask stockholders to vote on certain matters, including the election of directors and other matters, like the ratification of the board's selection of a corporate auditor. But, directors do not have exclusive control over the agenda at a stockholder meeting. Stockholders also have the right to put proposals and questions before the meeting. Some matters that are proposed by stockholders, including amendments to bylaws are expressly permitted by the state corporate law. Others are governed by bylaws, for example stockholder nomination of candidates for the position of director.

For publicly-traded corporations, the process by which a stockholder can get access to the company's proxy statement to put a question before the shareholders at a meeting is governed by SEC regulation. The SEC's 14a-8 rules have been developed to govern when a board is required to put a shareholder proposal on the corporate proxy statement, or to be more precise rules governing when a board is permitted to exclude a shareholder proposal from the corporation's proxy materials sent to stockholders.

Although many shareholder proposals are focused on traditional corporate governance issues, there is a long history of social activists using the shareholder proposal process to put important social issues on the agendas of corporate America. For example, during the 1970s and 1980s, the anti-Apartheid movement used the shareholder proposal process to raise awareness of the evils of Apartheid in South Africa.

2.7.10.1 14a-8 Shareholder Proposals

A "proxy statement" is a required disclosure document that publicly traded companies must send to all beneficial stockholders prior to any meeting of the stockholders. The proxy statement lays describes for beneficial stockholders the business of the upcoming meeting and include a voting proxy that a beneficial stockholder can return to the record holder. The most common business at a meeting is the annual election of directors. However, a board can bring any business or question to the stockholders for consideration and a vote.

The contents of this document are laid out in a series of rules under the '34 Act. The rules governing how a stockholder can get access to a corporation's proxy statement for the purpose of presenting proposals to fellow shareholders for their consideration at annual shareholder meetings are presented below in a unique FAQ format.

The default rule is that any proposal put forward by an eligible stockholder in a timely manner must be included in the corporate proxy. However, the board is not required to include all proposals in the proxy. There are a number of very important exceptions to the inclusion requirement, and they are laid out in the 14a-8 rules that follow.

§ 240.14a-8 Shareholder proposals.

This section addresses when a company must include a shareholder's proposal in its proxy statement and identify the proposal in its form of proxy when the company holds an annual or special meeting of shareholders. In summary, in order to have your shareholder proposal included on a company's proxy card, and included along with any supporting statement in its proxy statement, you must be eligible and follow certain procedures. Under a few specific circumstances, the company is permitted to exclude your proposal, but only after submitting its reasons to the Commission. We structured this section in a question-and-answer format so that it is easier to understand. The references to "you" are to a shareholder seeking to submit the proposal.

(a) Question 1: What is a proposal? A shareholder proposal is your recommendation or requirement that the company and/or its board of directors take action, which you intend to present at a meeting of the company's shareholders. Your proposal should state as clearly as possible the course of action that you believe the company should follow. If your proposal is placed on the company's proxy card, the company must also provide in the form of proxy means for shareholders to specify by boxes a choice between approval or disapproval, or abstention. Unless otherwise indicated, the word "proposal" as used in this section refers both to your proposal, and to your corresponding statement in support of your proposal (if any).

(b) Question 2: Who is eligible to submit a proposal, and how do I demonstrate to the company that I am eligible? (1) In order to be eligible to submit a proposal, you must have continuously held at least $2,000 in market value, or 1%, of the company's securities entitled to be voted on the proposal at the meeting for at least one year by the date you submit the proposal. You must continue to hold those securities through the date of the meeting.

(2) If you are the registered holder of your securities, which means that your name appears in the company's records as a shareholder, the company can verify your eligibility on its own, although you will still have to provide the company with a written statement that you intend to continue to hold the securities through the date of the meeting of shareholders. However, if like many shareholders you are not a registered holder, the company likely does not know that you are a shareholder, or how many shares you own. In this case, at the time you submit your proposal, you must prove your eligibility to the company in one of two ways:

(i) The first way is to submit to the company a written statement from the "record" holder of your securities (usually a broker or bank) verifying that, at the time you submitted your proposal, you continuously held the securities for at least one year. You must also include your own written statement that you intend to continue to hold the securities through the date of the meeting of shareholders; or

(ii) The second way to prove ownership applies only if you have filed a Schedule 13D (§ 240.13d-101), Schedule 13G (§ 240.13d-102), Form 3 (§ 249.103 of this chapter), Form 4 (§ 249.104 of this chapter) and/or Form 5 (§ 249.105 of this chapter), or amendments to those documents or updated forms, reflecting your ownership of the shares as of or before the date on which the one-year eligibility period begins. If you have filed one of these documents with the SEC, you may demonstrate your eligibility by submitting to the company:

(A) A copy of the schedule and/or form, and any subsequent amendments reporting a change in your ownership level;

(B) Your written statement that you continuously held the required number of shares for the one-year period as of the date of the statement; and

(C) Your written statement that you intend to continue ownership of the shares through the date of the company's annual or special meeting.

(c) Question 3: How many proposals may I submit? Each shareholder may submit no more than one proposal to a company for a particular shareholders' meeting.

(d) Question 4: How long can my proposal be? The proposal, including any accompanying supporting statement, may not exceed 500 words.

(e) Question 5: What is the deadline for submitting a proposal? (1) If you are submitting your proposal for the company's annual meeting, you can in most cases find the deadline in last year's proxy statement. However, if the company did not hold an annual meeting last year, or has changed the date of its meeting for this year more than 30 days from last year's meeting, you can usually find the deadline in one of the company's quarterly reports on Form 10-Q (§ 249.308a of this chapter), or in shareholder reports of investment companies under § 270.30d-1 of this chapter of the Investment Company Act of 1940. In order to avoid controversy, shareholders should submit their proposals by means, including electronic means, that permit them to prove the date of delivery.

(2) The deadline is calculated in the following manner if the proposal is submitted for a regularly scheduled annual meeting. The proposal must be received at the company's principal executive offices not less than 120 calendar days before the date of the company's proxy statement released to shareholders in connection with the previous year's annual meeting. However, if the company did not hold an annual meeting the previous year, or if the date of this year's annual meeting has been changed by more than 30 days from the date of the previous year's meeting, then the deadline is a reasonable time before the company begins to print and send its proxy materials.

(3) If you are submitting your proposal for a meeting of shareholders other than a regularly scheduled annual meeting, the deadline is a reasonable time before the company begins to print and send its proxy materials.

(f) Question 6: What if I fail to follow one of the eligibility or procedural requirements explained in answers to Questions 1 through 4 of this section? (1) The company may exclude your proposal, but only after it has notified you of the problem, and you have failed adequately to correct it. Within 14 calendar days of receiving your proposal, the company must notify you in writing of any procedural or eligibility deficiencies, as well as of the time frame for your response. Your response must be postmarked, or transmitted electronically, no later than 14 days from the date you received the company's notification. A company need not provide you such notice of a deficiency if the deficiency cannot be remedied, such as if you fail to submit a proposal by the company's properly determined deadline. If the company intends to exclude the proposal, it will later have to make a submission under § 240.14a-8 and provide you with a copy under Question 10 below, § 240.14a-8(j).

(2) If you fail in your promise to hold the required number of securities through the date of the meeting of shareholders, then the company will be permitted to exclude all of your proposals from its proxy materials for any meeting held in the following two calendar years.

(g) Question 7: Who has the burden of persuading the Commission or its staff that my proposal can be excluded? Except as otherwise noted, the burden is on the company to demonstrate that it is entitled to exclude a proposal.

(h) Question 8: Must I appear personally at the shareholders' meeting to present the proposal? (1) Either you, or your representative who is qualified under state law to present the proposal on your behalf, must attend the meeting to present the proposal. Whether you attend the meeting yourself or send a qualified representative to the meeting in your place, you should make sure that you, or your representative, follow the proper state law procedures for attending the meeting and/or presenting your proposal.

(2) If the company holds its shareholder meeting in whole or in part via electronic media, and the company permits you or your representative to present your proposal via such media, then you may appear through electronic media rather than traveling to the meeting to appear in person.

(3) If you or your qualified representative fail to appear and present the proposal, without good cause, the company will be permitted to exclude all of your proposals from its proxy materials for any meetings held in the following two calendar years.

(i) Question 9: If I have complied with the procedural requirements, on what other bases may a company rely to exclude my proposal? (1) Improper under state law: If the proposal is not a proper subject for action by shareholders under the laws of the jurisdiction of the company's organization;

Note to paragraph (i)(1): Depending on the subject matter, some proposals are not considered proper under state law if they would be binding on the company if approved by shareholders. In our experience, most proposals that are cast as recommendations or requests that the board of directors take specified action are proper under state law.

Accordingly, we will assume that a proposal drafted as a recommendation or suggestion is proper unless the company demonstrates otherwise.

(2) Violation of law: If the proposal would, if implemented, cause the company to violate any state, federal, or foreign law to which it is subject;

Note to paragraph (i)(2): We will not apply this basis for exclusion to permit exclusion of a proposal on grounds that it would violate foreign law if compliance with the foreign law would result in a violation of any state or federal law.

(3) Violation of proxy rules: If the proposal or supporting statement is contrary to any of the Commission's proxy rules, including § 240.14a-9, which prohibits materially false or misleading statements in proxy soliciting materials;

(4) Personal grievance; special interest: If the proposal relates to the redress of a personal claim or grievance against the company or any other person, or if it is designed to result in a benefit to you, or to further a personal interest, which is not shared by the other shareholders at large;

(5) Relevance: If the proposal relates to operations which account for less than 5 percent of the company's total assets at the end of its most recent fiscal year, and for less than 5 percent of its net earnings and gross sales for its most recent fiscal year, and is not otherwise significantly related to the company's business;

(6) Absence of power/authority: If the company would lack the power or authority to implement the proposal;

(7) Management functions: If the proposal deals with a matter relating to the company's ordinary business operations;

(8) Director elections: If the proposal:

(i) Would disqualify a nominee who is standing for election;

(ii) Would remove a director from office before his or her term expired;

(iii) Questions the competence, business judgment, or character of one or more nominees or directors;

(iv) Seeks to include a specific individual in the company's proxy materials for election to the board of directors; or

(v) Otherwise could affect the outcome of the upcoming election of directors.

(9) Conflicts with company's proposal: If the proposal directly conflicts with one of the company's own proposals to be submitted to shareholders at the same meeting;

Note to paragraph (i)(9): A company's submission to the Commission under this section should specify the points of conflict with the company's proposal.

(10) Substantially implemented: If the company has already substantially implemented the proposal;

Note to paragraph (i)(10): A company may exclude a shareholder proposal that would provide an advisory vote or seek future advisory votes to approve the compensation of executives as disclosed pursuant to Item 402 of Regulation S-K (§ 229.402 of this chapter) or any successor to Item 402 (a "say-on-pay vote") or that relates to the frequency of say-on-pay votes, provided that in the most recent shareholder vote required by § 240.14a-21(b) of this chapter a single year (i.e., one, two, or three years) received approval of a majority of votes cast on the matter and the company has adopted a policy on the frequency of say-on-pay votes that is consistent with the choice of the majority of votes cast in the most recent shareholder vote required by § 240.14a-21(b) of this chapter.

(11) Duplication: If the proposal substantially duplicates another proposal previously submitted to the company by another proponent that will be included in the company's proxy materials for the same meeting;

(12) Resubmissions: If the proposal deals with substantially the same subject matter as another proposal or proposals that has or have been previously included in the company's proxy materials within the preceding 5 calendar years, a company may exclude it from its proxy materials for any meeting held within 3 calendar years of the last time it was included if the proposal received:

(i) Less than 3% of the vote if proposed once within the preceding 5 calendar years;

(ii) Less than 6% of the vote on its last submission to shareholders if proposed twice previously within the preceding 5 calendar years; or

(iii) Less than 10% of the vote on its last submission to shareholders if proposed three times or more previously within the preceding 5 calendar years; and

(13) Specific amount of dividends: If the proposal relates to specific amounts of cash or stock dividends.

(j) Question 10: What procedures must the company follow if it intends to exclude my proposal? (1) If the company intends to exclude a proposal from its proxy materials, it must file its reasons with the Commission no later than 80 calendar days before it files its definitive proxy statement and form of proxy with the Commission. The company must simultaneously provide you with a copy of its submission. The Commission staff may permit the company to make its submission later than 80 days before the company files its definitive proxy statement and form of proxy, if the company demonstrates good cause for missing the deadline.

(2) The company must file six paper copies of the following:

(i) The proposal;

(ii) An explanation of why the company believes that it may exclude the proposal, which should, if possible, refer to the most recent applicable authority, such as prior Division letters issued under the rule; and

(iii) A supporting opinion of counsel when such reasons are based on matters of state or foreign law.

(k) Question 11: May I submit my own statement to the Commission responding to the company's arguments?

Yes, you may submit a response, but it is not required. You should try to submit any response to us, with a copy to the company, as soon as possible after the company makes its submission. This way, the Commission staff will have time to consider fully your submission before it issues its response. You should submit six paper copies of your response.

(l) Question 12: If the company includes my shareholder proposal in its proxy materials, what information about me must it include along with the proposal itself?

(1) The company's proxy statement must include your name and address, as well as the number of the company's voting securities that you hold. However, instead of providing that information, the company may instead include a statement that it will provide the information to shareholders promptly upon receiving an oral or written request.

(2) The company is not responsible for the contents of your proposal or supporting statement.

(m) Question 13: What can I do if the company includes in its proxy statement reasons why it believes shareholders should not vote in favor of my proposal, and I disagree with some of its statements?

(1) The company may elect to include in its proxy statement reasons why it believes shareholders should vote against your proposal. The company is allowed to make arguments reflecting its own point of view, just as you may express your own point of view in your proposal's supporting statement.

(2) However, if you believe that the company's opposition to your proposal contains materially false or misleading statements that may violate our anti-fraud rule, § 240.14a-9, you should promptly send to the Commission staff and the company a letter explaining the reasons for your view, along with a copy of the company's statements opposing your proposal. To the extent possible, your letter should include specific factual information demonstrating the inaccuracy of the company's claims. Time permitting, you may wish to try to work out your differences with the company by yourself before contacting the Commission staff.

(3) We require the company to send you a copy of its statements opposing your proposal before it sends its proxy materials, so that you may bring to our attention any materially false or misleading statements, under the following timeframes:

(i) If our no-action response requires that you make revisions to your proposal or supporting statement as a condition to requiring the company to include it in its proxy materials, then the company must provide you with a copy of its opposition statements no later than 5 calendar days after the company receives a copy of your revised proposal; or

(ii) In all other cases, the company must provide you with a copy of its opposition statements no later than 30 calendar days before its files definitive copies of its proxy statement and form of proxy under § 240.14a-6.

2.7.10.2 Lovenheim v. Iroquois Brands, Ltd.

When a stockholder presents a proposal to a board of directors, the default rule is that such proposals shall be included in the proxy unless the board of the subject company has a legitimate reason to exclude the proposal.

In the case that follows, animal rights activists sought to include a proposal relating to the inhumane treatment of animals in the preparation of food products sold by the subject company. The board of subject company sought to exclude the proposal. In seeking a no-action letter from the SEC, the board Iroquois argued that the stockholder's proposal lacked relevance and thus could properly be excluded.

In this opinion, the court provides guidance on how the SEC will typically treat these kinds of social proposals.

618 F.Supp. 554 (1985)
LOVENHEIM v. IROQUOIS BRANDS, LTD.

GASCH, District Judge.

Plaintiff Peter C. Lovenheim, owner of two hundred shares of common stock in Iroquois Brands, Ltd. (hereinafter "Iroquois/Delaware"),[1] seeks to bar Iroquois/Delaware from excluding from the proxy materials being sent to all shareholders in preparation for an upcoming shareholder meeting information concerning a proposed resolution he intends to offer at the meeting. Mr. Lovenheim's proposed resolution relates to the procedure used to force-feed geese for production of paté de foie gras in France,[2] a type of paté imported by Iroquois/Delaware. Specifically, his resolution calls upon the Directors of Iroquois/Delaware to:

> form a committee to study the methods by which its French
> supplier produces paté de foie gras, and report to the shareholders
> its findings and opinions, based on expert consultation, on whether
> this production method causes undue distress, pain or suffering to
> the animals involved and, if so, whether further distribution of this
> product should be discontinued until a more humane production
> method is developed.

[...]

Mr. Lovenheim's right to compel Iroquois/Delaware to insert information concerning his proposal in the proxy materials turns on the applicability of section 14(a) of the Securities Exchange Act of 1934, 15 U.S.C. § 78n(a) ("the Exchange Act"), and the shareholder proposal rule promulgated by the Securities and Exchange Commission ("SEC"), Rule 14a-8.[3] That rule states in pertinent part:

> If any security holder of an issuer notifies the issuer of his intention to present a proposal for action at a forthcoming [557] meeting of the issuer's security holders, the issuer shall set forth the proposal in its proxy statement and identify it in its form of proxy and provide means by which security holders [presenting a proposal may present in the proxy statement a statement of not more than 200 words in support of the proposal[4]].

Iroquois/Delaware has refused to allow information concerning Mr. Lovenheim's proposal to be included in proxy materials being sent in connection with the next annual shareholders meeting. In doing so, Iroquois/Delaware relies on an exception to the general requirement of Rule 14a-8, Rule 14a-8(c)(5). That exception provides that an issuer of securities "may omit a proposal and any statement in support thereof" from its proxy statement and form of proxy:

> if the proposal relates to operations which account for less than 5 percent of the issuer's total assets at the end of its most recent fiscal year, and for less than 5 percent of its net earnings and gross sales for its most recent fiscal year, and is not otherwise significantly related to the issuer's business.

Applicability of Rule 14a-8(c)(5) Exception

[...] The likelihood of plaintiff's prevailing in this litigation turns primarily on the applicability to plaintiff's proposal of the exception to the shareholder proposal rule contained in Rule 14a-8(c)(5).

Iroquois/Delaware's reliance on the argument that this exception applies is based on the following information contained in the affidavit of its president: Iroquois/Delaware has annual revenues of $141 million with $6 million in annual profits and $78 million in assets. In contrast, its paté de foie gras sales were just $79,000 last year, representing a net loss on paté sales of $3,121. Iroquois/Delaware has only $34,000 [559] in assets related to paté. Thus none of the company's net earnings and less than .05 percent of its assets are implicated by plaintiff's proposal. [...]

Plaintiff does not contest that his proposed resolution relates to a matter of little economic significance to Iroquois/Delaware. Nevertheless he contends that the Rule 14a-8(c)(5) exception is not applicable as it cannot be said that his proposal "is not otherwise significantly related to the issuer's business" as is required by the final portion of that exception. In other words, plaintiff's argument that Rule 14a-8 does not permit omission of his proposal rests on the assertion that the rule and statute on which it is based do not permit omission merely because a proposal is not economically significant where a proposal has "ethical or social significance."[8]

Iroquois/Delaware challenges plaintiff's view that ethical and social proposals cannot be excluded even if they do not meet the economic or five percent test. Instead, Iroquois/Delaware views the exception solely in economic terms as permitting omission of any proposals relating to a de minimis share of assets and profits. Iroquois/Delaware asserts that since corporations are economic entities, only an economic test is appropriate.

The Court would note that the applicability of the Rule 14a-8(c)(5) exception to Mr. Lovenheim's proposal represents a close question given the lack of clarity in the exception itself. In effect, plaintiff relies on the word "otherwise," suggesting that it indicates the drafters of the rule intended that other noneconomic tests of significance be used. Iroquois/Delaware relies on the fact that the rule examines other significance in relation to the issuer's business. Because of the apparent ambiguity of the rule, the Court considers the history of the shareholder proposal rule in determining the proper interpretation of the most recent version of that rule.

Prior to 1983, paragraph 14a-8(c)(5) excluded proposals "not significantly related to the issuer's business" but did not contain an objective economic significance test such as the five percent of sales, assets, and earnings specified in the first part of the current version.[9] Although a series of SEC decisions through 1976 allowing issuers to exclude proposals challenging compliance with the Arab economic boycott of Israel allowed exclusion if the issuer did less than one percent of their business with Arab countries or Israel,[10] the Commission stated later in 1976 that it did "not believe that subparagraph (c)(5) should be hinged solely on the economic relativity of a proposal." […] Thus the Commission required inclusion "in many situations in which the related business comprised less than one percent" of the company's revenues, profits or assets "where the proposal has raised *policy questions* important enough to be [560] considered `significantly related' to the issuer's business.[…]

The 1983 revision adopted the five percent test of economic significance in an effort to create a more objective standard. Nevertheless, in adopting this standard, the Commission stated that proposals will be includable notwithstanding their "failure to reach the specified economic thresholds if a significant relationship to the issuer's business is demonstrated on the face of the resolution or supporting statement." […] Thus it seems clear based on the history of the rule that "the meaning of `significantly related' is not *limited* to economic significance."[…]

2.7.10.3 "Say on Pay" Vote

In the wake of the Financial Crisis of 2008, Congress adopted the Frank-Dodd bill. Section 951 of Frank-Dodd requires regular votes by shareholders to approve executive compensation. Note that the structure and effect of the vote are sensitive to the 14a-8 process and comport with what one might expect of other shareholder proposals. When approving the "say on pay" votes, Congress was sensitive to the traditional preeminence of the state corporate law. Consequently, "say on pay" votes are precatory in nature.

SEC. 951. SHAREHOLDER VOTE ON EXECUTIVE COMPENSATION DISCLOSURES.

 (a)(1) In general.--Not less frequently than once every 3 years, a proxy or consent or authorization for an annual or other meeting of the shareholders for which the proxy solicitation rules of the Commission require compensation disclosure shall include a separate resolution subject to shareholder vote to approve the compensation of executives, as disclosed pursuant to section 229.402 of title 17, Code of Federal Regulations, or any successor thereto.

(2) Frequency of vote.--Not less frequently than once every 6 years, a proxy or consent or authorization for an annual or other meeting of the shareholders for which the proxy solicitation rules of the Commission require compensation disclosure shall include a separate resolution subject to shareholder vote to determine whether votes on the resolutions required under paragraph (1) will occur every 1, 2, or 3 years.

(b) Shareholder Approval of Golden Parachute Compensation.--

(1) Disclosure.-- At a meeting at which shareholders are asked to approve an acquisition, merger, consolidation, or proposed sale or other disposition of all or substantially all the assets of an issuer, the person making such solicitation shall disclose in the proxy or consent solicitation material, in a clear and simple form in accordance with regulations to be promulgated by the Commission, any agreements or understandings that such person has with any named executive officers of such issuer (or of the acquiring issuer, if such issuer is not the acquiring issuer) concerning any type of compensation (whether present, deferred, or contingent) that is based on or otherwise relates to the acquisition, merger, consolidation, sale, or other disposition of all or substantially all of the assets of the issuer and the aggregate total of all such compensation that may (and the conditions upon which it may) be paid or become payable to or on behalf of such executive officer.

(2) Shareholder approval.--Any proxy or consent or authorization relating to the proxy or consent solicitation material containing the disclosure required by paragraph (1) shall include a separate resolution subject to shareholder vote to approve such agreements or understandings and compensation as disclosed, unless such agreements or understandings have been subject to a shareholder vote under subsection (a).

 (c) Rule of Construction.--The shareholder vote referred to in subsections (a) and (b) shall not be binding on the issuer or the board of directors of an issuer, and may not be construed--

   (1) as overruling a decision by such issuer or board of directors;

(2) to create or imply any change to the fiduciary duties of such issuer or board of directors;

(3) to create or imply any additional fiduciary duties for such issuer or board of directors; or

(4) to restrict or limit the ability of shareholders to make proposals for inclusion in proxy materials related to executive compensation.

3 Stockholder Litigation

Before we turn to too much more case law, it is important to understand the particular procedural aspects of the stockholder litigation that we will be reading. Because the litigation involves stockholders, directors, and the corporation, it is procedurally different than litigation you may have seen until now in law school.

The source of these differences is often a question about who gets to speak for and vindicate the rights of the corporation - the board or the stockholder. Resolution of this question is especially important when it is the board itself that is accused of wrong-doing against the corporation.

3.1 Direct and Derivative Suits

Officers and directors of Delaware corporations are subject to the jurisdiction of Delaware courts under Delaware's long-arm statute for lawsuits related to the corporation and their duties as directors and officers of the corporation. By virtue of incorporating in Delaware and maintaining an agent in Delaware for service of process, directors of a Delaware corporation, no matter where they are, can be served by making service on the corporation's agent as listed in the corporation's certificate of incorporation.

Stockholders may bring different kinds of litigation against the corporation. **Direct suits** are brought on behalf of the stockholder in the stockholder's capacity as a stockholder and seek to vindicate the rights of the stockholder. **Derivative suits** are brought by stockholders on behalf of the corporation and seek to vindicate the rights of the corporation. Stockholders seeking to bring a derivative action on behalf of the corporation must comply with the requirements of Chancery Rule 23.1.

Many times the most important question in stockholder litigation turns on the type of litigation that is at issue. Stockholders may attempt to characterize the litigation as direct in order to maintain control, while boards may attempt to characterize the question before the court as derivative in order to assert control over the litigation and end it.

Understanding the distinction between direct and derivative suits can be confusing. However, there is a coherent test *(Tooley v. DLJ)* for determining which is which.

3.1.1 Historical Development of Derivative Litigation

It is black-letter law that the board of directors of a Delaware corporation exercises all corporate powers and manages, or directs others in the management of, the business and affairs of the corporation. One corporate power exercised by the board of directors is the conduct of litigation that seeks to redress harm inflicted upon the corporation, including harm inflicted upon the corporation by its officers or directors from a breach of fiduciary duty owed to the corporation and its shareholders. Recognizing, however, that directors and officers of a corporation may not hold themselves accountable to the corporation for their own wrongdoing, courts of equity have created an ingenious device to police the activities of corporate fiduciaries: the shareholder's derivative suit. Chancellor Wolcott described this device:

> Generally a cause of action belonging to a corporation can be asserted only by the corporation. However, whenever a corporation possesses a cause of action which it either refuses to assert or, by reason of circumstances, is unable to assert, equity will permit a stockholder to sue in his own name for the benefit of the corporation solely for the purpose of preventing injustice when it is apparent that the corporation's rights would not be protected otherwise.

As the above description reveals, a derivative action may not be pursued if the corporation is willing and able to assert the suit on its own behalf, *i.e.,* the complaining shareholder must give the board of directors the opportunity to manage the litigation to its satisfaction or the board of directors must for some reason be incapable of pursuing the litigation.

The requirement that shareholders exhaust their remedies within the corporation before pursuing derivative litigation is found in Court of Chancery Rule 23.1. Rule 23.1 requires that the complaint in a derivative action "allege with particularity the efforts, if any, made by the plaintiff to obtain the action the plaintiff desires from the directors or comparable authority and the reasons for the plaintiff's failure to obtain the action or for not making the effort." Even if attempting to obtain the action that the plaintiff desires from the board of directors would be futile because a majority of the directors suffer some disabling interest, the board may appoint a special litigation committee of disinterested directors that may recommend dismissal of the derivative action after a reasonable investigation. Rule 23.1 also requires, as does Section 327 of the Delaware General Corporation Law, that the complaint allege that "the plaintiff was a stockholder of the corporation at the time of the transaction." Rule 23.1 further provides that a derivative action generally may not be dismissed or settled without approval of this Court and notice to other shareholders. The requirements of Rule 23.1, while burdensome to the equitable device created by the courts to remedy harm inflicted upon a corporation, are necessary to prevent the potentially disruptive effects of derivative litigation on the ability of a board of directors to direct the business and affairs of a corporation. The prerequisites to a derivative action, developed over time, have attempted to balance the Delaware prerogative that directors manage the affairs of a corporation with the realization that shareholder policing, via derivative actions, is a necessary check on the behavior of directors that serve in a fiduciary capacity to shareholders.

The exacting procedural prerequisites to the prosecution of a derivative action create incentives for plaintiffs to characterize their claims as "direct" or "individual" in the sense that they seek recovery not for harm done to the corporation, but for harm done to them. A decision finding that a complaint alleges direct claims allows plaintiffs to bypass the ability of the corporation's board to decide, in the best interests of the corporation, how to proceed with the litigation. In clear-cut cases, where the corporation has not been harmed by the conduct at issue in the litigation but the plaintiff has suffered injury, bypassing the board's involvement in the litigation is of little concern. In fact, it seems wholly inappropriate to allow a board of directors to control litigation where the corporation's concerns are only tangential and the corporation would not share any eventual recovery.

3.1.2 Delaware's long arm statute

You might wonder how it is the case that a corporate director sitting in New York or Massachusetts could be subject to the jurisdiction of the courts of Delaware. The short answer is that all persons who agree to become corporate directors also consent to jurisdiction of the Delaware courts under Delaware's "long arm statute."

§ 3114 Service of process on nonresident directors, trustees, members of the governing body or officers of Delaware corporations.

(b) Every nonresident of this State who after January 1, 2004, accepts election or appointment as an officer of a corporation organized under the laws of this State, or who after such date serves in such capacity, and every resident of this State who so accepts election or appointment or serves in such capacity and thereafter removes residence from this State shall, by such acceptance or by such service, be deemed thereby to have consented to the appointment of the registered agent of such corporation (or, if there is none, the Secretary of State) as an agent upon whom service of process may be made in all civil actions or proceedings brought in this State, by or on behalf of, or against such corporation, in which such officer is a necessary or proper party, or in any action or proceeding against such officer for violation of a duty in such capacity, whether or not the person continues to serve as such officer at the time suit is commenced. Such acceptance or service as such officer shall be a signification of the consent of such officer that any process when so served shall be of the same legal force and validity as if served upon such officer within this State and such appointment of the registered agent (or, if there is none, the Secretary of State) shall be irrevocable.

3.1.3 DGCL § 321 Service of process on corporations

Certificates of incorporation all require the corporation to name a registered agent, along with an address in the state of Delaware where the agent may be contacted. The registered agent plays an important role in ensuring corporate officers and directors (their principles) are subject to the jurisdiction of the Delaware courts for the purpose of stockholder litigation and other litigation related to the corporation.

§ 321 Service of process on corporations.

(a) Service of legal process upon any corporation of this State shall be made by delivering a copy personally to any officer or director of the corporation in this State, or the registered agent of the corporation in this State, or by leaving it at the dwelling house or usual place of abode in this State of any officer, director or registered agent (if the registered agent be an individual), or at the registered office or other place of business of the corporation in this State.[…]

(b) In case the officer whose duty it is to serve legal process cannot by due diligence serve the process in any manner provided for by subsection (a) of this section, it shall be lawful to serve the process against the corporation upon the Secretary of State, and such service shall be as effectual for all intents and purposes as if made in any of the ways provided for in subsection (a) of this section.[…]

3.1.4 DGCL Sec. 327 - Derivative actions

In order to have standing in derivative litigation, a stockholder must have already been a stockholder at the time of the bad act that gave rise to the litigation. This requirement prevents people from observing some bad act and then buying into a lawsuit.

§ 327. Stockholder's derivative action; allegation of stock ownership.

In any derivative suit instituted by a stockholder of a corporation, it shall be averred in the complaint that the plaintiff was a stockholder of the corporation at the time of the transaction of which such stockholder complains or that such stockholder's stock thereafter devolved upon such stockholder by operation of law.

3.1.5 Delaware Rules of Civil Procedure, Rule 23.1

The Delaware Rules of Civil Procedure lay out rules for bringing and maintaining a stockholder derivative action. Compliance with these rules is necessary in order for a claim to stay in court. Often times, defendants will move to dismiss a plaintiff's claim for failure to comply with the requirements of Rule 23.1.

The Rule 23.1 Motion to Dismiss often revolves around the characterization of the claim (direct v. derivative) and the independence of the directors (demand required/demand futility).

Rule 23.1. Derivative actions by shareholders.

(a) In a derivative action brought by one or more shareholders or members to enforce a right of a corporation or of an unincorporated association, the corporation or association having failed to enforce a right which may properly be asserted by it, the complaint shall allege that the plaintiff was a shareholder or member at the time of the transaction of which the plaintiff complains or that the plaintiff's share or membership thereafter devolved on the plaintiff by operation of law. The complaint shall also allege with particularity the efforts, if any, made by the plaintiff to obtain the action the plaintiff desires from the directors or comparable authority and the reasons for the plaintiff's failure to obtain the action or for not making the effort.

(b) Each person seeking to serve as a representative plaintiff on behalf of a corporation or unincorporated association pursuant to this Rule shall file with the Register in Chancery an affidavit stating that the person has not received, been promised or offered and will not accept any form of compensation, directly or indirectly, for prosecuting or serving as a representative party in the derivative action in which the person or entity is a named party except (i) such fees, costs or other payments as the Court expressly approves to be paid to or on behalf of such person, or (ii) reimbursement, paid by such person's attorneys, of actual and reasonable out-of-pocket expenditures incurred directly in connection with the prosecution of the action. The affidavit required by this subpart shall be filed within 10 days after the earliest of the affiant filing the complaint, filing a motion to intervene in the action or filing a motion seeking appointment as a representative party in the action. An affidavit provided pursuant to this subpart shall not be construed to be a waiver of the attorney-client privilege.

(c) The action shall not be dismissed or compromised without the approval of the Court, and notice by mail, publication or otherwise of the proposed dismissal or compromise shall be given to shareholders or members in such manner as the Court directs; except that if the dismissal is to be without prejudice or with prejudice to the plaintiff only, then such dismissal shall be ordered without notice thereof if there is a showing that no compensation in any form has passed directly or indirectly from any of the defendants to the plaintiff or plaintiff's attorney and that no promise to give any such compensation has been made. At the time that any party moves or otherwise applies to the Court for approval of a compromise of all or any part of a derivative action, each representative plaintiff in such action shall file with the Register in Chancery a further affidavit in the form required by subpart (b) of this rule.

3.1.6 Tooley v. Donaldson, Lufkin, & Jenrette, Inc.

In *Tooley*, the court was asked to determine whether shareholder litigation is direct or derivative. Rather than rely on a more traditional, and cumbersome, "special injury" test, the court in *Tooley* announced a new, simpler test for determining whether a stockholder action is direct or derivative. Since *Tooley* other jurisdictions, like New York, have abandoned their own versions of the special injury in favor of specifically adopting Delaware's *Tooley* standard.

845 A.2d 1031 (2004)
TOOLEY v. DONALDSON, LUFKIN, & JENRETTE, INC.

Plaintiff-stockholders brought a purported class action in the Court of Chancery, alleging that the members of the board of directors of their corporation breached their fiduciary duties by agreeing to a 22-day delay in closing a proposed merger. Plaintiffs contend that the delay harmed them due to the lost time-value of the cash paid for their shares. The Court of Chancery granted the defendants' motion to dismiss on the sole ground that the claims were, "at most," claims of the corporation being asserted derivatively. They were, thus, held not to be direct claims of the stockholders, individually. Thereupon, the Court held that the plaintiffs lost their standing to bring this action when they tendered their shares in connection with the merger.

Although the trial court's legal analysis of whether the complaint alleges a direct or derivative claim reflects some concepts in our prior jurisprudence, we believe those concepts are not helpful and should be regarded as erroneous. We set forth in this Opinion the law to be applied henceforth in determining whether a stockholder's claim is derivative or direct. That issue must turn *solely* on the following questions: (1) who suffered the alleged harm (the corporation or the suing stock-holders, individually); and (2) who would receive the benefit of any recovery or other remedy (the corporation or the stock-holders, individually)? [...]

Facts

Patrick Tooley and Kevin Lewis are former minority stockholders of Donaldson, Lufkin & Jenrette, Inc. (DLJ), a Delaware corporation engaged in investment banking. DLJ was acquired by Credit Suisse Group (Credit Suisse) in the Fall of 2000. Before that acquisition, AXA Financial, Inc.(AXA), which owned 71% of DLJ stock, controlled DLJ. Pursuant to a stockholder agreement between AXA and Credit Suisse, AXA agreed to exchange with Credit Suisse its DLJ stockholdings for a mix of stock and cash. The consideration [1034] received by AXA consisted primarily of stock. Cash made up one-third of the purchase price. Credit Suisse intended to acquire the remaining minority interests of publicly-held DLJ stock through a cash tender offer, followed by a merger of DLJ into a Credit Suisse subsidiary.

The tender offer price was set at $90 per share in cash. The tender offer was to expire 20 days after its commencement. The merger agreement, however, authorized two types of extensions. First, Credit Suisse could unilaterally extend the tender offer if certain conditions were not met, such as SEC regulatory approvals or certain payment obligations. Alternatively, DLJ and Credit Suisse could agree to postpone acceptance by Credit Suisse of DLJ stock tendered by the minority stockholders.

Credit Suisse availed itself of both types of extensions to postpone the closing of the tender offer. The tender offer was initially set to expire on October 5, 2000, but Credit Suisse invoked the five-day unilateral extension provided in the agreement. Later, by agreement between DLJ and Credit Suisse, it postponed the merger a second time so that it was then set to close on November 2, 2000.

Plaintiffs challenge the second extension that resulted in a 22-day delay. They contend that this delay was not properly authorized and harmed minority stockholders while improperly benefitting AXA. They claim damages representing the time-value of money lost through the delay.

The ruling before us on appeal is that the plaintiffs' claim is derivative, purportedly brought on behalf of DLJ. The Court of Chancery, relying upon our confusing

166

jurisprudence on the direct/derivative dichotomy, based its dismissal on the following ground: "Because this delay affected all DLJ shareholders equally, plaintiffs' injury was not a special injury, and this action is, thus, a derivative action, at most."[3]

Plaintiffs argue that they have suffered a "special injury" because they had an alleged contractual right to receive the merger consideration of $90 per share without suffering the 22-day delay arising out of the extensions under the merger agreement. But the trial court's opinion convincingly demonstrates that plaintiffs had no such contractual right that had ripened at the time the extensions were entered into:

> *Here, it is clear that plaintiffs have no separate contractual right to bring a direct claim, and they do not assert contractual rights under the merger agreement.* First, the merger agreement specifically disclaims any persons as being third party beneficiaries to the contract. Second, any contractual shareholder right to payment of the merger consideration did not ripen until the conditions of the agreement were met. The agreement stated that Credit Suisse Group was not required to accept any shares for tender, or could extend the offer, under certain conditions — one condition of which included an extension or termination by agreement between [1035] Credit Suisse Group and DLJ. *Because Credit Suisse Group and DLJ did in fact agree to extend the tender offer period, any right to payment plaintiffs could have did not ripen until this newly negotiated period was over. The merger agreement only became binding and mutually enforceable at the time the tendered shares ultimately were accepted for payment by Credit Suisse Group.* It is at that moment in time, November 3, 2000, that the company became bound to purchase the tendered shares, making the contract mutually enforceable. *DLJ stockholders had no individual contractual right to payment until November 3, 2000, when their tendered shares were accepted for payment.* Thus, they have no contractual basis to challenge a delay in the closing of the tender offer up until November 3. *Because this is the date the tendered shares were accepted for payment, the contract was not breached and plaintiffs do not have a contractual basis to bring a direct suit.*[4]

Moreover, no other individual right of these stockholder-plaintiffs was alleged to have been violated by the extensions.

That conclusion could have ended the case because it portended a definitive ruling that plaintiffs have no claim whatsoever on the facts alleged. But the defendants chose to argue, and the trial court chose to decide, the standing issue, which is predicated on an assertion that this claim is a derivative one asserted on behalf of the corporation, DLJ.

The Court of Chancery correctly noted that "[t]he Court will independently examine the nature of the wrong alleged and any potential relief to make its own determination of the suit's classification.... Plaintiffs' classification of the suit is not binding."[5] The trial court's analysis was hindered, however, because it focused on the confusing concept of "special injury" as the test for determining whether a claim is derivative or direct. The trial court's premise was as follows:

> In order to bring a *direct* claim, a plaintiff must have experienced some "special injury." [citing *Lipton v. News Int'l*, 514 A.2d 1075, 1079 (Del.1986)]. A special injury is a wrong that "is separate and distinct from that suffered by other shareholders, ... or a wrong involving a contractual right of a shareholder, such as the right to vote, or to assert majority control, which exists independently of any right of the corporation." [citing *Moran v. Household Int'l. Inc.,* 490 A.2d 1059, 1070 (Del.Ch.1985), *aff'd* 500 A.2d 1346 (Del.1986 [1985])].[6]

In our view, the concept of "special injury" that appears in some Supreme Court and Court of Chancery cases is not helpful to a proper analytical distinction between direct and derivative actions. We now disapprove the use of the concept of "special injury" as a tool in that analysis.

The Proper Analysis to Distinguish Between Direct and Derivative Actions

The analysis must be based solely on the following questions: Who suffered the alleged harm — the corporation or the suing stockholder individually — and who would receive the benefit of the recovery or other remedy? This simple analysis is well imbedded in our jurisprudence,[7] but some cases have complicated it by injection of the amorphous and confusing concept of "special injury."

A Brief History of Our Jurisprudence

The derivative suit has been generally described as "one of the most interesting and ingenious of accountability mechanisms for large formal organizations."[10] It enables a stockholder to bring suit on behalf of the corporation for harm done to the corporation.[11] Because a derivative suit is being brought on behalf of the corporation, the recovery, if any, must go to the corporation. A stockholder who is directly injured, however, does retain the right to bring an individual action for injuries affecting his or her legal rights as a stockholder. Such a claim is distinct from an injury caused to the corporation alone. In such individual suits, the recovery or other relief flows directly to the stockholders, not to the corporation.

Determining whether an action is derivative or direct is sometimes difficult and has many legal consequences, some of which may have an expensive impact on the parties to the action.[12] For example, if an action is derivative, the plaintiffs are then required to comply with the requirements of Court of Chancery Rule 23.1, that the stockholder: (a) retain ownership of the shares throughout the litigation; (b) make presuit demand on the board; and (c) obtain court approval of any settlement. Further, the recovery, if any, flows only to the corporation. The decision whether a suit is direct or derivative may be out-come-determinative. Therefore, it is necessary that a standard to distinguish such actions be clear, simple and consistently articulated and applied by our courts.

Thus, two confusing propositions have encumbered our caselaw governing the direct/derivative distinction. The "special injury" concept, […] can be confusing in identifying the nature of the action. The same is true of the proposition […] that an action cannot be direct if all stockholders are equally affected or unless the [1039] stockholder's injury is separate and distinct from that suffered by other stockholders. The proper analysis has been and should remain that […] a court should look to the nature of the wrong and to whom the relief should go. The stockholder's claimed direct injury must be independent of any alleged injury to the corporation. The stockholder must demonstrate that the duty breached was owed to the stockholder and that he or she can prevail without showing an injury to the corporation.

Standard to be Applied in This Case

In this case it cannot be concluded that the complaint alleges a derivative claim. There is no derivative claim asserting injury to the corporate entity. There is no relief that would go the corporation. Accordingly, there is no basis to hold that the complaint states a derivative claim.

But, it does not necessarily follow that the complaint states a direct, individual claim. While the complaint purports to set forth a direct claim, in reality, it states no claim at all. The trial court analyzed the complaint and correctly concluded that it does not claim that the plaintiffs have any rights that have been injured.[27] Their rights have not yet ripened. The contractual claim is nonexistent until it is ripe, and that claim will not be ripe until the terms of the merger are fulfilled, including the extensions of the closing at issue here. Therefore, there is no direct claim stated in the complaint before us.

Accordingly, the complaint was properly dismissed. But, due to the reliance on the concept of "special injury" by the Court of Chancery, the ground set forth for the dismissal is erroneous, there being no derivative claim. That error is harmless, however, because, in our view, there is no direct claim either.

Conclusion

For purposes of distinguishing between derivative and direct claims, we expressly disapprove both the concept of "special injury" and the concept that a claim is necessarily derivative if it affects all stockholders equally. In our view, the tests going forward should rest on those set forth in this opinion.

3.1.7 Gentile v. Rossette

Because there are important procedural hurdles to bringing a derivative suit, it oftentimes becomes an important point of contention between the parties whether the particular litigation is direct or derivative. This case is an example of that problem in action. Note how the court applies the Tooley test to assist it in answering the question whether the claims are direct (and thus properly brought by the stockholder) or are derivative in nature (requiring the stockholder to make a demand on the board and thus lose control over the litigation).

This opinion is a decision on a Rule 23.1 Motion to Dismiss ("MTD"). Much shareholder litigation lives or dies at this stage. The 23.1 MTD battle is typically fought on two grounds: 1) character of the litigation; and 2) demand futility.

With respect to the character of the litigation, the defendant board will typically attempt characterize the litigation as derivative and then will argue since the plaintiff failed to make a demand on the board as required under Rule 23.1 for derivative litigation, and for that reason the court should dismiss the litigation in favor of the defendant board. For its part, plaintiff will attempt to characterize the litigation as direct, thus ensuring that the case cannot be dismissed on procedural grounds.

We will take up demand futility later in this chapter.

906 A.2d 91 (2006)
GENTILE v. ROSSETTE

JACOBS, Justice.

The plaintiffs, who are former minority shareholders of SinglePoint Financial, Inc. ("SinglePoint" or "the company"), appeal from a grant of summary judgment by the Court of Chancery dismissing their claim for breach of fiduciary duty against SinglePoint's former directors and its CEO/controlling stockholder. The claim arises from a self-dealing transaction in which the CEO/controlling stockholder forgave the corporation's debt to him, in exchange for being issued stock whose value allegedly exceeded the value of the forgiven debt. The transaction, it is claimed, wrongfully reduced the cash-value and the voting power of the public stockholders' minority interest, and increased correspondingly the value and voting power of the controller's majority interest. After the debt conversion, SinglePoint was later acquired by another company ("Cofiniti") in a merger. Shortly thereafter, the acquirer, Cofiniti, filed for bankruptcy and was liquidated. The plaintiffs then brought this action in the Court of Chancery, seeking to recover the value of which they claimed to have been wrongfully deprived in the debt conversion. The Court of Chancery dismissed the action on the ground that the claim was exclusively derivative, and that as a result of the Cofiniti merger the plaintiffs had lost standing to assert the claim on behalf of SinglePoint.

171

The issue presented on this appeal is one purely of law: can SinglePoint's former minority stockholders bring a direct claim against the fiduciaries responsible for the debt conversion transaction complained of, or is such a claim exclusively derivative? We hold, for the reasons discussed herein, that the claim is not exclusively derivative and can be brought by the (former) minority shareholders directly. We must, therefore, reverse the contrary ruling of the Court of Chancery.

III. THE PARTIES' CONTENTIONS

This appeal concerns only the grant of summary judgment dismissing the claim for breach of fiduciary duty arising out of the debt conversion.[12] The issue that we must decide is whether that claim was *exclusively* derivative in character. If it was, then the summary judgment grant must be affirmed; if not, then the summary judgment must be reversed.

The defendant-appellees argue that the plaintiffs' debt conversion fiduciary duty claim is exclusively derivative, and that the Vice Chancellor correctly so held. Under *Tooley*,[13] whether a claim is derivative or direct depends solely upon two questions: "(1) who suffered the alleged harm (the corporation or the suing stockholders individually); and (2) who would receive the benefit of the recovery or other remedy (the corporation or the stockholders, individually)?"[14]

Here, the defendants maintain, the only harm arguably resulting from the debt conversion was to the corporation, because in essence, the debt conversion claim is that SinglePoint was caused to overpay for the debt forgiveness. More specifically, the claim is that the debt conversion rate [98] ($.05 per share) was unfair and resulted in SinglePoint issuing "vastly more stock [to Rossette] than it should have."[15] No harm from that overpayment resulted to any stockholder individually (defendants argue), because to the extent the overpayment invalidly increased the number of outstanding shares, the resulting dilution affected each and all of the pre-debt conversion shares identically—including the shares owned by Rossette. Moreover, defendants assert, whatever form any damages recovery or other remedy might take—whether it be to cancel the "excess" shares or to require the acquirer to pay their fair value—the only beneficiary of that remedy would be the company. Lastly, defendants contend that to the extent the plaintiffs' claim is for wrongful dilution of their voting power, restoration of that voting power is no longer possible because, as a result of the Cofiniti merger and the Cofiniti bankruptcy, for all practical purposes SinglePoint and Cofiniti no longer exist.

The defendants concede that a "stock dilution" claim may be brought as a direct claim if voting rights are harmed. They insist, however, that that can only occur where the loss of voting power is "material." The defendants conclude that the Court of Chancery correctly found that the plaintiffs never had any material voting power to lose, because both before and after the debt conversion, the public shareholders of SinglePoint held only a minority interest.

The plaintiffs vigorously contest these arguments. They claim that under *Tooley* their claim is direct, for two alternative reasons. First, their debt conversion claim cannot be derivative because only the shareholder minority—but not the corporation—was injured. The reason (plaintiffs say) is that the company was insolvent, and therefore suffered no harm by issuing its valueless stock to expunge a sizeable portion of its debt to Rossette.[16] But, even if economically worthless, the SinglePoint stock did have voting power, and the debt conversion reduced the minority shareholders' ownership percentage, and voting power, from about 39% to 7%. Moreover, because of the significant (over 80%) reduction in their share ownership percentage, the minority stockholders also suffered a corresponding reduction of the proceeds they would have otherwise received in the Cofiniti merger. The plaintiffs contend that because SinglePoint no longer exists, only the former minority stockholders can benefit from a judicial remedy. The only remedy now available would be a recovery of the fair value of the Cofiniti merger proceeds the plaintiffs would have received but for the extraction of value resulting from the debt conversion. Any such recovery would benefit only the (former) SinglePoint minority.

[99] Second, and alternatively, the plaintiffs contend that their claim is direct under *In re Tri-Star Pictures, Inc. Litigation*.[17] Their argument runs as follows: even if the SinglePoint shares had value, the debt conversion was a self-dealing corporate transaction with a significant stockholder, that increased the voting power and economic value of that significant stockholder's interest in SinglePoint, at the expense and to the corresponding detriment of the minority shareholders. The plaintiffs claim that the Court of Chancery erred by reading into *Tri-Star* a requirement that for such a transaction to give rise to a direct claim, the loss of voting power must be "material," *i.e.,* that it must reduce the

public stockholders' voting power from majority to minority status. We conclude that the plaintiffs are correct and that *Tooley* and *Tri-Star,* properly applied, compel the conclusion that the debt conversion claim was both derivative and direct.[…]

The defendants respond (and the Court of Chancery agreed) that […]for a loss of voting power to give rise to a direct claim, the loss must be "material," meaning that the challenged transaction must reduce the holdings of the plaintiff class from majority to minority stockholder status[24]—a reduction that did not occur here.

Because the defendants do not claim that this case is distinguishable from *Tri-Star* in any other respect, the issue is a narrow one that may be stated thusly: where a *Tri-Star* type transaction reduces the voting power of the corporation's public shareholders, must the reduction be from majority to minority stockholder status, for the public shareholders to have standing to assert a direct claim against the fiduciaries responsible? We hold that the answer is no. We so conclude for three separate reasons.

First, a requirement of a reduction from majority to minority status finds no support in our case law. The Court of Chancery cited no authority supporting that conclusion,[25] and nothing in *Tri-Star,* which created the analytical framework for this issue, compels it.[…]

Second, the requirement of a "material" reduction in voting power should play no part in any analysis of whether a claim is direct, derivative, or both. Such a requirement distracts from—and obscures— the nature of the harm inflicted upon the minority in a *Tri-Star* transaction, and denigrates the seriousness of the breach of fiduciary duty causing that harm. The *Tri-Star* type of transaction was found to be wrongful because it resulted in an improper extraction or expropriation, by the controlling shareholder, of economic value and voting power that belonged to the minority stockholders. The specific manner in which this was accomplished was causing the corporation to issue, to the controlling stockholder, shares having more value than the value of what the corporation received in exchange. The consequence was to increase the controlling stockholder's percentage of stock ownership at the expense of the minority.[26] The resulting reduction in economic value and voting power affected the minority stockholders uniquely, and the corresponding benefit to the controlling stockholder was the product of a breach of the duty of loyalty well recognized in other forms of self-dealing transactions.[27] A rule that focuses on the degree or extent of the expropriation, and requires that the expropriation attain a certain level before the minority stockholders may seek a judicial remedy directly, denigrates the gravity of the fiduciary breach and condones overreaching by fiduciaries—at least in cases where the resulting harm to the minority falls below the prescribed threshold for "materiality." No principle of fiduciary law or policy justifies any condonation of fiduciary misconduct, even where the resulting harm is not "material" in the sense used by the trial court.

Third, the result reached here fits comfortably within the analytical framework mandated by *Tooley*.[...]

V. CONCLUSION

The judgment of the Court of Chancery granting summary judgment dismissing Count I of the Complaint (the debt conversion claim) is reversed, and the case is remanded for proceedings consistent with this Opinion.

3.2 Demand and Demand Futility

As we know, the corporate law places the board of directors in a central place with respect to the management of the corporation. Section 141(a) and its mandate that the board manage the business and affairs of the corporation extends naturally to control over any legal claims that the corporation may have. Claims of the corporation against third parties are relatively simple to deal with. Stockholders have little reason to worry that a board might not pursue claims against third parties. Legal claims against the corporation's own board of directors or the corporation's own agents, on the other hand, are more troublesome.

It may not be realistic to expect the board to pursue potential legal claims owned by the corporation against themselves. The derivative action permits stockholders in certain circumstances to stand in the shoes of the corporation to vindicate rights of the corporation that its own directors will not pursue.

The ability of stockholders to take up litigation on behalf of the corporation is not unlimited.

In order to preserve the central importance of the board in the management of the corporation, courts will require shareholders who wish to sue on behalf the corporation to jump through certain procedural hoops.

Consequently, procedure plays an extremely important role in derivative litigation. This section provides an overview to procedural requirements in derivative cases. In particular, Rule 23.1 requires that in any complaint, a statement that the stockholder made a "demand" to the corporation or if they did not why such a demand would have been "futile". Many cases will be resolved on a Rule 23.1 Motion to Dismiss for failure of the stockholder to make a demand when a demand was required.

3.2.1 Aronson v. Lewis

Because derivative litigation is properly litigation that "belongs" to the corporation, stockholders bringing derivative litigation should be the exception rather than the rule. The requirement that a stockholder make a demand on the board prior to bringing derivative litigation is a recognition of this fact.

The court in Aronson lays out one test for determining whether a plaintiff in a derivative suit will be relieved of the "demand" requirement. If making a demand on the board would be "futile", a stockholder plaintiff will be free to bring a derivative claim on behalf of the corporation without first asking the board to take action. In order to establish that demand is futile under Rule 23.1 and the Aronson test, plaintiffs must allege sufficient facts in the complaint as to call into question the business judgment presumption.

473 A.2d 805 (1984)
ARONSON v. LEWIS

MOORE, Justice:

When is a stockholder's demand upon a board of directors, to redress an alleged wrong to the corporation, excused as futile prior to the filing of a derivative suit? We granted this interlocutory appeal to the defendants, Meyers Parking System, Inc. (Meyers), a Delaware corporation, and its directors, to review the Court of Chancery's denial of their motion to dismiss this action, pursuant to Chancery Rule 23.1, for the [808] plaintiff's failure to make such a demand or otherwise demonstrate its futility.[1] The Vice Chancellor ruled that plaintiff's allegations raised a "reasonable inference" that the directors' action was unprotected by the business judgment rule. Thus, the board could not have impartially considered and acted upon the demand. See *Lewis v. Aronson*, Del.Ch., 466 A.2d 375, 381 (1983).

We cannot agree with this formulation of the concept of demand futility. In our view demand can only be excused where facts are alleged with particularity which create a reasonable doubt that the directors' action was entitled to the protections of the business judgment rule. Because the plaintiff failed to make a demand, and to allege facts with particularity indicating that such demand would be futile, we reverse the Court of Chancery and remand with instructions that plaintiff be granted leave to amend the complaint. […]

The plaintiff, Harry Lewis, is a stockholder of Meyers. The defendants are Meyers and its ten directors, some of whom are also company officers.

In 1979, Prudential Building Maintenance Corp. (Prudential) spun off its shares of Meyers to Prudential's stockholders. Prior thereto Meyers was a wholly owned subsidiary of Prudential. Meyers provides parking lot facilities and related services throughout the country. Its stock is actively traded over-the-counter.

This suit challenges certain transactions between Meyers and one of its directors, Leo Fink, who owns 47% of its outstanding stock. Plaintiff claims that these transactions were approved only because Fink personally selected each director and officer of Meyers.[2]

Prior to January 1, 1981, Fink had an employment agreement with Prudential which provided that upon retirement he was to become a consultant to that company for ten years. This provision became operable when Fink retired in April 1980.[3] Thereafter, Meyers agreed with Prudential to share Fink's consulting services and reimburse Prudential for 25% of the fees paid Fink. Under this arrangement Meyers paid Prudential $48,332 in 1980 and $45,832 in 1981.

On January 1, 1981, the defendants approved an employment agreement between Meyers and Fink for a five year term with provision for automatic renewal each year thereafter, indefinitely. Meyers agreed to pay Fink $150,000 per year, plus a bonus of 5%

of its pre-tax profits over $2,400,000. Fink could terminate the contract at any time, but Meyers could do so only upon six months' notice. At termination, Fink was to become a consultant to Meyers and be paid $150,000 per year for the first three years, $125,000 for the next three years, and $100,000 thereafter for life. Death benefits were also included. Fink agreed to devote his best efforts and substantially his entire business time to advancing Meyers' interests. The agreement also provided [809] that Fink's compensation was not to be affected by any inability to perform services on Meyers' behalf. Fink was 75 years old when his employment agreement with Meyers was approved by the directors. There is no claim that he was, or is, in poor health. […]

The complaint charges that these transactions had "no valid business purpose", and were a "waste of corporate assets" because the amounts to be paid are "grossly excessive", that Fink performs "no or little services", and because of his "advanced age" cannot be "expected to perform any such services". The plaintiff also charges that the existence of the Prudential consulting agreement with Fink prevents him from providing his "best efforts" on Meyers' behalf. Finally, it is alleged that the loans to Fink were in reality "additional compensation" without any "consideration" or "benefit" to Meyers.

The complaint alleged that no demand had been made on the Meyers board because:

> 13. … such attempt would be futile for the following reasons:
>
> (a) All of the directors in office are named as defendants herein and they have participated in, expressly approved and/or acquiesced in, and are personally liable for, the wrongs complained of herein.
>
> (b) Defendant Fink, having selected each director, controls and dominates every member of the Board and every officer of Meyers.
>
> (c) Institution of this action by present directors would require the defendant-directors to sue themselves, thereby placing the conduct of this action in hostile hands and preventing its effective prosecution.

[…]

The relief sought included the cancellation of the Meyers-Fink employment contract and an accounting by the directors, including Fink, for all damage sustained by Meyers and for all profits derived by the directors and Fink. […]

Defendants moved to dismiss for plaintiff's failure to make demand on the Meyers board prior to suit, or to allege with factual particularity why demand is excused.[…]

After recounting the allegations, the trial judge noted that the demand requirement of Rule 23.1 is a rule of substantive right designed to give a corporation the opportunity to rectify an alleged wrong without litigation, and to control any litigation which does arise. *Lewis,* 466 A.2d at 380. According to the Vice Chancellor, the test of futility is "whether the Board, at the time of the filing of the suit, could have impartially considered and acted upon the demand". […]

As part of this formulation, the trial judge stated that interestedness is one factor affecting impartiality, and indicated that the business judgment rule is a potential defense to allegations of director interest, and hence, demand futility. *Id.* However, the court observed that to establish demand futility, a plaintiff need not allege that the challenged transaction could never be deemed a product of business judgment. *Id.* Rather, the Vice Chancellor maintained that a plaintiff "must only allege facts which, if true, show that there is a reasonable inference that the business judgment rule is not applicable for purposes of considering a pre-suit demand pursuant to Rule 23.1".[…]

The trial judge correctly noted that futility is gauged by the circumstances existing at the commencement of a derivative suit. […]

The defendants make two arguments, one policy-oriented and the other, factual. First, they assert that the demand requirement embraces the policy that directors, rather than stockholders, manage the affairs of the corporation. They contend that this fundamental principle requires the strict construction and enforcement of Chancery Rule 23.1. Second, the defendants point to four of plaintiff's basic allegations and argue that they lack the factual particularity necessary to excuse demand. Concerning the allegation that Fink dominated and controlled the Meyers board, the defendants point to the absence of any facts explaining how he "selected each director". With respect to Fink's 47% stock interest, the defendants say that absent other facts this is insufficient to indicate domination and control. Regarding the claim of hostility to the plaintiff's suit, because defendants would have to sue themselves, the latter assert that this bootstrap argument ignores the possibility that the directors have other [811] alternatives, such as cancelling the challenged agreement. As for the allegation that directorial approval of the agreement excused demand, the defendants reply that such a claim is insufficient, because it would obviate the demand requirement in almost every case. The effect would be to subvert the managerial power of a board of directors. Finally, as to the provision guaranteeing Fink's compensation, even if he is unable to perform any services, the defendants contend that the trial court read this out of context. Based upon the foregoing, the defendants conclude that the plaintiff's allegations fall far short of the factual particularity required by Rule 23.1.

A cardinal precept of the General Corporation Law of the State of Delaware is that directors, rather than shareholders, manage the business and affairs of the corporation. 8 *Del.C.* § 141(a). Section 141(a) states in pertinent part:

> "The *business and affairs* of a corporation organized under this
> chapter *shall be managed by or under the direction* of a board of directors
> except as may be otherwise provided in this chapter or in its
> certificate of incorporation."

8 *Del.C.* § 141(a) (Emphasis added). The existence and exercise of this power carries with it certain fundamental fiduciary obligations to the corporation and its shareholders.[…]Moreover, a stockholder is not powerless to challenge director action which results in harm to the corporation. The machinery of corporate democracy and the derivative suit are potent tools to redress the conduct of a torpid or unfaithful management. The derivative action developed in equity to enable shareholders to sue in the corporation's name where those in control of the company refused to assert a claim belonging to it. The nature of the action is two-fold. First, it is the equivalent of a suit by the shareholders to compel the corporation to sue. Second, it is a suit by the corporation, asserted by the shareholders on its behalf, against those liable to it.

By its very nature the derivative action impinges on the managerial freedom of directors.[5] Hence, the demand requirement of Chancery Rule 23.1 exists at the threshold, first to insure that a stockholder exhausts his intracorporate remedies, and [812] then to provide a safeguard against strike suits. Thus, by promoting this form of alternate dispute resolution, rather than immediate recourse to litigation, the demand requirement is a recognition of the fundamental precept that directors manage the business and affairs of corporations.

In our view the entire question of demand futility is inextricably bound to issues of business judgment and the standards of that doctrine's applicability. The business judgment rule is an acknowledgment of the managerial prerogatives of Delaware directors under Section 141(a). See *Zapata Corp. v. Maldonado,* 430 A.2d at 782. It is a presumption that in making a business decision the directors of a corporation acted on an informed basis, in good faith and in the honest belief that the action taken was in the best interests of the company. *Kaplan v. Centex Corp.,* Del.Ch., 284 A.2d 119, 124 (1971); *Robinson v. Pittsburgh Oil Refinery Corp.,* Del.Ch., 126 A. 46 (1924). Absent an abuse of discretion, that judgment will be respected by the courts. The burden is on the party challenging the decision to establish facts rebutting the presumption. See *Puma v. Marriott,* Del.Ch., 283 A.2d 693, 695 (1971).

Delaware courts have addressed the issue of demand futility on several earlier occasions. […]

Our view is that in determining demand futility the Court of Chancery in the proper exercise of its discretion must decide whether, under the particularized facts alleged, a reasonable doubt is created that: (1) the directors are disinterested and independent and (2) the challenged transaction was otherwise the product of a valid exercise of business judgment. Hence, the Court of Chancery must make two inquiries, one into the independence and disinterestedness of the directors and the other into the substantive nature of the challenged transaction and the board's approval thereof. As to the latter inquiry the court does not assume that the transaction is a wrong to the corporation requiring corrective steps by the board. Rather, the alleged wrong is substantively reviewed against the factual background alleged in the complaint. As to the former inquiry, directorial independence and disinterestedness, the court reviews the factual allegations to decide whether they raise a reasonable doubt, as a threshold matter, that the protections of the business judgment rule are available to the board. [815] Certainly, if this is an "interested" director transaction, such that the business judgment rule is inapplicable to the board majority approving the transaction, then the inquiry ceases. In that event futility of demand has been established by any objective or subjective standard.[8][...]

However, the mere threat of personal liability for approving a questioned transaction, standing alone, is insufficient to challenge either the independence or disinterestedness of directors, although in rare cases a transaction may be so egregious on its face that board approval cannot meet the test of business judgment, and a substantial likelihood of director liability therefore exists.[...] In sum the entire review is factual in nature. The Court of Chancery in the exercise of its sound discretion must be satisfied that a plaintiff has alleged facts with particularity which, taken as true, support a reasonable doubt that the challenged transaction was the product of a valid exercise of business judgment. Only in that context is demand excused. [...]

Having outlined the legal framework within which these issues are to be determined, we consider plaintiff's claims of futility here: Fink's domination and control of the directors, board approval of the Fink-Meyers employment agreement, and board hostility to the plaintiff's derivative action due to the directors' status as defendants.

Plaintiff's claim that Fink dominates and controls the Meyers' board is based on: (1) Fink's 47% ownership of Meyers' outstanding stock, and (2) that he "personally selected" each Meyers director. Plaintiff also alleges that mere approval of the employment agreement illustrates Fink's domination and control of the board. [...]

Such contentions do not support any claim under Delaware law that these directors lack independence. In *Kaplan v. Centex Corp.,*[...] the Court of Chancery stated that "[s]tock ownership alone, at least when it amounts to less than a majority, is not sufficient proof of domination or control".[...]Moreover, in the demand context even proof of majority ownership of a company does not strip the directors of the presumptions of independence, and that their acts have been taken in good faith and in the best interests of the corporation. There must be coupled with the allegation of control such facts as would demonstrate that through personal or other relationships the directors are beholden to the controlling person.[...]

The requirement of director independence interest in the conception and rationale of the business judgment rule. The presumption of propriety that flows from an exercise of business judgment is based in part on this unyielding precept. Independence means that a director's decision is based on the corporate merits of the subject before the board rather than extraneous considerations or influences. While directors may confer, debate, and resolve their differences through compromise, or by reasonable reliance upon the expertise of their colleagues and other qualified persons, the end result, nonetheless, must be that each director has brought his or her own informed business judgment to bear with specificity upon the corporate merits of the issues without regard for or succumbing to influences which convert an otherwise valid business decision into a faithless act.

Thus, it is not enough to charge that a director was nominated by or elected at the behest of those controlling the outcome of a corporate election. That is the usual way a person becomes a corporate director. It is the care, attention and sense of individual responsibility to the performance of one's duties, not the method of election, that generally touches on independence.

We conclude that in the demand-futile context a plaintiff charging domination and control of one or more directors must allege particularized facts manifesting "a direction of corporate conduct in such a way as to comport with the wishes or interests of the corporation (or persons) doing the controlling". [...]

Here, plaintiff has not alleged any facts sufficient to support a claim of control. The personal-selection-of-directors allegation stands alone, unsupported. At best it is a conclusion devoid of factual support. The causal link between Fink's control and approval of the employment agreement is alluded to, but nowhere specified. The director's approval, alone, does not establish control, even in the face of Fink's 47% stock ownership. [...] Therefore, we cannot conclude that the [817] complaint factually particularizes any circumstances of control and domination to overcome the presumption of board independence, and thus render the demand futile. [...]

Turning to the board's approval of the Meyers-Fink employment agreement, plaintiff's argument is simple: all of the Meyers directors are named defendants, because they approved the wasteful agreement; if plaintiff prevails on the merits all the directors will be jointly and severally liable; therefore, the directors' interest in avoiding personal liability automatically and absolutely disqualifies them from passing on a shareholder's demand.

Such allegations are conclusory at best. In Delaware mere directorial approval of a transaction, absent particularized facts supporting a breach of fiduciary duty claim, or otherwise establishing the lack of independence or disinterestedness of a majority of the directors, is insufficient to excuse demand.[11][…]

Plaintiff's final argument is the incantation that demand is excused because the directors otherwise would have to sue themselves, thereby placing the conduct of the litigation in hostile hands and preventing its effective prosecution. This bootstrap argument has been made to and dismissed by other courts. […] Unless facts are alleged with particularity to overcome the presumptions of independence and a proper exercise of business judgment, in which case the directors could not be expected to sue themselves, a bare claim of this sort raises no legally cognizable issue under Delaware corporate law. […]

In sum, we conclude that the plaintiff has failed to allege facts with particularity indicating that the Meyers directors were tainted by interest, lacked independence, or took action contrary to Meyers' best interests in order to create a reasonable doubt as to the applicability of the business judgment rule. Only in the presence of such a reasonable doubt may a demand be deemed futile. […]

3.2.2 Rales v. Blasband

In *Rales*, the court announces a second, alternative, test for demand futility. The focus on the inquiry under the *Aronson* test is the challenged transaction and questions the interestedness and independence of directors with respect to the challenged transaction. In *Rales* the court's focus of analysis is different because *Rales* is applied in circumstances where there is no particular transaction to challenge. Rather, the focus of the analysis is on whether board would be able to fairly consider the stockholder's demand had it been made.

The claim here involves a "double derivative suit." In a double derivative suit, stockholders of a parent corporation bring suit against the parent of a wholly-owned subsidiary on behalf of the subsidiary corporation.

Notice that this case is presented as a certified question. The Delaware Supreme Court is one of the very few state supreme courts in the country that accepts certified questions.

It often does so to resolve novel questions of the Delaware corporate law that arise before other courts. In *Rales*, the question presented to the Delaware Supreme Court was raised by a US federal district court.

634 A.2d 927 (1993)
Steven M. RALES v. Alfred BLASBAND

VEASEY, Chief Justice:

This certified question of law comes before the Court pursuant to Article IV, Section 11(9) of the Delaware Constitution and Supreme Court Rule 41. The question of law was certified by the United States District Court for the District of Delaware (the "District Court"), and was accepted by this Court on June 16, 1993. See Rales v. Blasband, Del.Supr., 626 A.2d 1364 (1993). Briefing and oral argument in this Court followed. This is the decision of the Court on the certified question.

The underlying action pending in the District Court is a stockholder derivative action [930] filed on March 25, 1991, by Alfred Blasband ("Blasband") on behalf of Danaher Corporation, a Delaware corporation ("Danaher"). Blasband's original complaint was dismissed by the District Court on August 15, 1992, based on Blasband's lack of standing, but the United States Court of Appeals for the Third Circuit (the "Third Circuit") vacated the District Court's order and permitted Blasband to amend his complaint. Blasband v. Rales, 971 F.2d 1034 (3d Cir.1992) ("Blasband I"). Following Blasband's filing of an amended complaint (the "amended complaint"), the defendants filed a motion to dismiss and moved to certify the following question of law to this Court:

> In the context of this novel action, which is neither a simple derivative suit nor a double derivative suit, but which the United States Court of Appeals for the Third Circuit describes as a "first cousin to a double derivative suit," has plaintiff Alfred Blasband, in accordance with the substantive law of the State of Delaware, alleged facts to show that demand is excused on the board of directors of Danaher Corporation, a Delaware corporation?

After consideration of the allegations of the amended complaint, the briefs, and the oral argument of the parties in this Court, it is our conclusion that the certified question must be answered in the affirmative. Because the amended complaint does not challenge a decision of the board of directors of Danaher (the "Board"), the test enunciated in Aronson v. Lewis, Del.Supr., 473 A.2d 805 (1984) is not implicated. In the unusual context of this case, demand on the Board is excused because the amended complaint alleges particularized facts creating a reasonable doubt that a majority of the Board would be disinterested or independent in making a decision on a demand. [...]

II. SCOPE AND STANDARD OF REVIEW

The parties have raised a threshold issue regarding this Court's ability to consider the legal standards which are applicable to the certified question. Blasband contends that the role of this Court in responding to the certified question is limited to a mechanical application of the two-part test[6] set forth in Aronson v. Lewis, Del.Supr., 473 A.2d 805, 814 (1984). The defendants disagree, and argue that the Court should apply a test more stringent than the Aronson test to protect corporations against strike suits.

Consideration of this issue must begin with the language of the certified question itself:

> In the context of this novel action, which is neither a simple
> derivative suit nor a double derivative suit, but which the United
> States Court of Appeals for the Third Circuit describes as a "first
> cousin to a double derivative suit," has plaintiff Alfred Blasband, in
> accordance with the substantive law of the State of Delaware,
> alleged facts to show that demand is excused on the board of
> directors of Danaher Corporation, a Delaware corporation?

(Emphasis added). The certified question does not limit the issue presented to the mere application of the Aronson test, but instead calls upon this Court to decide whether Blasband's amended complaint establishes that demand is excused under the "substantive law of the State of Delaware." It is therefore necessary for this Court to determine what the applicable "substantive law" is before we can decide whether demand on the Board should be excused. Accordingly, the language of the question certified to this Court requires a consideration of the appropriate legal principles, including the applicability of the Aronson test in this unusual context, so that we may properly decide the issue presented to us.

III. THE STANDARDS FOR DETERMINING WHETHER DEMAND IS EXCUSED IN THIS DERIVATIVE SUIT

The stockholder derivative suit is an important and unique feature of corporate governance. In such a suit, a stockholder asserts a cause of action belonging to the corporation. […] In a double derivative suit, such as the present case, a stockholder of a parent corporation seeks recovery for a cause of action belonging to a subsidiary corporation. […] Because directors are empowered to manage, or direct the management of, the business and affairs of the corporation, 8 Del.C. § 141(a), the right of a stockholder to prosecute a derivative suit is limited to situations where the stockholder has demanded that the directors pursue the corporate claim and they have wrongfully refused to do so or where demand is excused because the directors are incapable of making an impartial decision regarding such litigation. […]Chancery Court Rule 23.1, constitutes the procedural embodiment of this substantive principle of corporation law.[7]

[933] Derivative suits have been used most frequently as a means of redressing harm to a corporation allegedly resulting from misconduct by its directors. As we observed in Aronson:

> [A] stockholder is not powerless to challenge director action which results in harm to the corporation. The machinery of corporate democracy and the derivative suit are potent tools to redress the conduct of a torpid and unfaithful management.

473 A.2d at 811. In such instances, stockholders often do not make a demand on the board of directors, and instead file suit claiming that demand is excused.

Because such derivative suits challenge the propriety of decisions made by directors pursuant to their managerial authority, we have repeatedly held that the stockholder plaintiffs must overcome the powerful presumptions of the business judgment rule before they will be permitted to pursue the derivative claim. […]Our decision in Aronson enunciated the test for determining a derivative plaintiff's compliance with this fundamental threshold obligation: "whether, under the particularized facts alleged, a reasonable doubt is created that: (1) the directors are disinterested and independent [or] (2) the challenged transaction was otherwise the product of a valid exercise of business judgment."*[...]

Although these standards are well-established, they cannot be applied in a vacuum. Not all derivative suits fall into the paradigm addressed by Aronson and its progeny. The essential predicate for the Aronson test is the fact that a decision of the board of directors is being challenged in the derivative suit.**[...]

> Directorial interest exists whenever divided loyalties are present, or a director has received, or is entitled to receive, a personal financial benefit from the challenged transaction which is not equally shared by the stockholders. The question of independence flows from an analysis of the factual allegations pertaining to the influences upon the directors' performance of their duties generally, and more specifically in respect to the challenged transaction.
>
> The second, or business judgment inquiry of Aronson, focuses on the substantive nature of the challenged transaction and the board's approval thereof.

Under the unique circumstances of this case, an analysis of the Board's ability to consider a demand requires a departure here from the standards set forth in Aronson. The Board did not approve the transaction which is being challenged by Blasband in this action. In fact, the Danaher directors have made no decision relating to the subject of this derivative suit. Where there is no conscious decision by directors to act or refrain from acting, the business judgment rule has no application.***[...]The absence of board action, therefore, makes it impossible to perform the essential inquiry contemplated by Aronson — whether the directors have acted in conformity with the business judgment rule in approving the challenged transaction. [...]

Consistent with the context and rationale of the Aronson decision, a court should not apply the Aronson test for demand futility where the board that would be considering the demand did not make a business decision which is being challenged in the [934] derivative suit. This situation would arise in three principal scenarios: (1) where a business decision was made by the board of a company, but a majority of the directors making the decision have been replaced;[8] (2) where the subject of the derivative suit is not a business decision of the board;[9] and (3) where, as here, the decision being challenged was made by the board of a different corporation.

Instead, it is appropriate in these situations to examine whether the board that would be addressing the demand can impartially consider its merits without being influenced by improper considerations. Thus, a court must determine whether or not the particularized factual allegations of a derivative stockholder complaint create a reasonable doubt that, as of the time the complaint is filed, the board of directors could have properly exercised its independent and disinterested business judgment in responding to a demand. If the derivative plaintiff satisfies this burden, then demand will be excused as futile.

IV. WHETHER THE BOARD IS INTERESTED OR LACKS INDEPENDENCE

In order to determine whether the Board could have impartially considered a demand at the time Blasband's original complaint was filed, it is appropriate to examine the nature of the decision confronting it. A stockholder demand letter would, at a minimum, notify the directors of the nature of the alleged wrongdoing and the identities of the alleged wrongdoers. The subject of the demand in this case would be the alleged breaches of fiduciary duty by the Easco board of directors in connection with Easco's investment in Drexel "junk bonds." The allegations of the amended complaint, which must be accepted as true in this procedural context, claim that the investment was made solely for the benefit of the Rales brothers, who were acting in furtherance of their business relationship with Drexel and not with regard to Easco's best interests. Such conduct, if proven, would constitute a breach of the Easco directors' duty of loyalty. [...]

The task of a board of directors in responding to a stockholder demand letter is a two-step process. First, the directors must determine the best method to inform themselves of the facts relating to the alleged wrongdoing and the considerations, both legal and financial, bearing on a response to the demand. If a factual investigation is required,[11] it must be conducted reasonably and in good faith.[...] Second, the board must weigh the alternatives available to it, including the advisability of implementing internal corrective action and commencing legal proceedings. [...]In carrying out these tasks, the board must be able to act free of personal financial interest and improper extraneous influences.[12] We [936] now consider whether the members of the Board could have met these standards.

189

A. Interest

The members of the Board at the time Blasband filed his original complaint were Steven Rales, Mitchell Rales, Sherman, Ehrlich, Caplin, Kellner, Stephenson, and Lohr. The Rales brothers and Caplin were also members of the Easco board of directors at the time of the alleged wrongdoing. Blasband's amended complaint specifically accuses the Rales brothers of being the motivating force behind the investment in Drexel "junk bonds." The Board would be obligated to determine whether these charges of wrongdoing should be investigated and, if substantiated, become the subject of legal action.

A director is considered interested where he or she will receive a personal financial benefit from a transaction that is not equally shared by the stockholders. […]Directorial interest also exists where a corporate decision will have a materially detrimental impact on a director, but not on the corporation and the stockholders. In such circumstances, a director cannot be expected to exercise his or her independent business judgment without being influenced by the adverse personal consequences resulting from the decision.

We conclude that the Rales brothers and Caplin must be considered interested in a decision of the Board in response to a demand addressing the alleged wrongdoing described in Blasband's amended complaint. Normally, "the mere threat of personal liability for approving a questioned transaction, standing alone, is insufficient to challenge either the independence or disinterestedness of directors...." […]Nevertheless, the Third Circuit has already concluded that "Blasband has pleaded facts raising at least a reasonable doubt that the [Easco board's] use of proceeds from the Note Offering was a valid exercise of business judgment." […]This determination is part of the law of the case, […] and is therefore binding on this Court. Such determination indicates that the potential for liability is not "a mere threat" but instead may rise to "a substantial likelihood."****[13][…]

Therefore, a decision by the Board to bring suit against the Easco directors, including the Rales brothers and Caplin, could have potentially significant financial consequences for those directors. Common sense dictates that, in light of these consequences, the Rales brothers and Caplin have a disqualifying financial interest that disables them from impartially considering a response to a demand by Blasband.

B. Independence

Having determined that the Rales brothers and Caplin would be interested in a decision on Blasband's demand, we must now examine whether the remaining Danaher directors are sufficiently independent to make an impartial decision despite the fact that they are presumptively disinterested. As explained in Aronson, "[i]ndependence means that a director's decision is based on the corporate merits of the subject before the board rather than extraneous considerations or influences." […]To establish lack of independence, Blasband must show that the directors are "beholden" to the Rales brothers or so under their influence that their discretion would be sterilized.[…]stockholder). We conclude that the amended complaint alleges particularized facts sufficient to create a reasonable doubt that Sherman and Ehrlich, as members of the Board, are capable of acting independently of the Rales brothers.

Sherman is the President and Chief Executive Officer of Danaher. His salary is approximately $1 million per year. Although Sherman's continued employment and substantial remuneration may not hinge solely on his relationship with the Rales brothers, there is little doubt that Steven Rales' position as Chairman of the Board of Danaher and Mitchell Rales' position as Chairman of its Executive Committee place them in a position to exert considerable influence over Sherman. In light of these circumstances, there is a reasonable doubt that Sherman can be expected to act independently considering his substantial financial stake in maintaining his current offices.

Ehrlich is the President of Wabash National Corp. ("Wabash"). His annual compensation is approximately $300,000 per year. Ehrlich also has two brothers who are vice presidents of Wabash. The Rales brothers are directors of Wabash and own a majority of its stock through an investment partnership they control. As a result, there is a reasonable doubt regarding Ehrlich's ability to act independently since it can be inferred that he is beholden to the Rales brothers in light of his employment.

Therefore, the amended complaint pleads particularized facts raising a reasonable doubt as to the independence of Sherman and Ehrlich. Because of their alleged substantial financial interest in maintaining their employment positions, there is a reasonable doubt that these two directors are able to consider impartially an action that is contrary to the interests of the Rales brothers.

V. CONCLUSION

We conclude that, under the "substantive law" of the State of Delaware, the Aronson test does not apply in the context of this double derivative suit because the Board was not involved in the challenged transaction. […] Instead, the appropriate inquiry is whether Blasband's amended complaint raises a reasonable doubt regarding the ability of a majority of the Board to exercise properly its business judgment in a decision on a demand had one been made at the time this action was filed. Based on the existence of a reasonable doubt that the Rales brothers and Caplin would be free of a financial interest in such a decision, and that Sherman and Ehrlich could act independently in light of their employment with entities affiliated with the Rales brothers, we conclude that the allegations of Blasband's amended complaint establish that DEMAND IS EXCUSED on the Board.

Rales Notes

**The key for the application of *Aronson* is that there is a specific decision or transaction undertaken by the board that is the subject of the derivative suit.
***The difficulty of the facts in this case is that there is no specific board decision or transaction that is in question. *Aronson* as understood by the court is an ill fit.
****Potential liability has to be more than a "mere threat" and had to rise to the level of a "substantial likelihood" of liability before a director can be considered interested for demand purposes.

3.2.3 Guttman v. Huang

In *Guttman*, the court applies the *Rales* standard in the context of a Rule 23.1 Motion to Dismiss. One question the court deals with here is whether it is sufficient under *Rales* to merely name a director as a defendant in a complaint in order to establish that the director is interested to the extent that the director cannot fairly decide on a demand.

823 A.2d 492 (2003)
GUTTMAN v. HUANG

STRINE, Vice Chancellor.

In this case, the plaintiffs bring a derivative action on behalf of NVIDIA Corporation, a technology firm. They allege that the defendants — all NVIDIA directors and/or officers — either sold stock at a time when they knew material, non-public information about the company and/or are culpable for failing to prevent accounting irregularities that caused the company to restate its financial statements for the period during which the stock sales took place. The plaintiffs seek relief for NVIDIA for harm relating to this supposed malfeasance and nonfeasance.

The defendants have moved for dismissal for failure to make a demand under Court of Chancery Rule 23.1. In support of that contention, they point to the conclusory allegations of the amended complaint[1] as being insufficient to cast a doubt on the impartiality of NVIDIA's majority independent board.[...]

B. The Essence of the Plaintiffs' Claims

The plaintiffs allege that the defendants engaged in a variety of misconduct related to NVIDIA's failure to accurately account for and disclose its financial results for the period from February 15, 2000 to July 30, 2002 — what I shall call the "Contested Period." During the Contested Period, NVIDIA allegedly released bullish disclosures regarding its results and future prospects.

These optimistic statements were, the plaintiffs contend, materially misleading because they were premised on improper accounting. According to them, NVIDIA "used `cookie jar' reserves (bad debt, sales returns, and account[s] payable) to even out earnings in bad times, used `back-in' accounting to ensure that forecasted margins were achieved and managed profit margins by manipulating shipments at the end of quarters."[2] The plaintiffs contend that this conduct was intended to inflate NVIDIA's stock price.

Also during the Contested Period, the defendants as a class sold $194.6 million in company stock at diverse times. Four of the defendants were responsible for over $157 million of this sum:

> • Defendant Jen-Hsun Huang sold almost 1.2 million shares,
> reaping proceeds of over $50 million. Huang is a co-founder of
> NVIDIA, and has been the company's President, Chief Executive
> Officer and a director at all relevant times.

• Defendant Christine B. Hoberg was NVIDIA's Chief Financial Officer from December 1998 until April 29, 2002. She sold $22.3 million worth of stock during the Contested Period.

• Defendant Jeffrey Fisher has been, at all relevant times, NVIDIA's Vice President of Worldwide Sales. During the Contested Period, Fisher sold $36.3 million worth of NVIDIA stock.

• Defendant Chris A. Malachowsky, at all relevant times, has been NVIDIA's Vice President of Hardware Engineering. Malachowsky co-founded the company with Huang. During the Contested Period, he sold $48.6 million in company shares.

[...]

C. The Allegations of Wrongdoing in the Complaint

The complaint makes two alternative arguments about the various defendants. The first — and more aggressive — is that each of the defendants who sold during the Contested Period was in possession of material, non-public information and traded to his personal advantage using that information. Specifically, the defendants allegedly knew that NVIDIA's improper accounting practices were propping up its stock price artificially and they thus reaped unfair profits by selling to buyers who were in the dark about the reality of NVIDIA's (impliedly more troubled) financial status.

The plaintiffs buttress this argument by contending that:

• Each of the defendants was in a position to know of the improper accounting practices engaged in by NVIDIA [497] during the Contested Period. This allegation is made cursorily.

• Each of the defendants engaged in trades shortly after NVIDIA released a financial statement that was later restated.

• Aside from the sale by defendant Gaither, all of the defendants' sales resulted in proceeds of millions of dollars.

• The sales did not result from a regular, preplanned trading
  program and were not consistent with the defendants' trading
  patterns for the year immediately before the sales. This allegation is
  made cursorily.

The plaintiffs' alternative argument is that the defendants — primarily those who were non-management directors of NVIDIA — breached their fiduciary duty to NVIDIA by failing to ensure that there was an adequate system of financial controls in place at the company. Because the outside directors were allegedly indolent in the fulfillment of their duty to make sure that the company had in place a functioning system to guarantee compliance with legally mandated accounting standards, certain managers at NVIDIA caused the company to issue materially misleading financial statements. Advertently or not, the outside director-defendants benefited because of the failure of oversight, by being able to sell large amounts of stock into a market artificially inflated by the company's false financials.

D. The Harm Suffered by NVIDIA and the Relief Sought by the Plaintiffs

The complaint alleges that the defendants' breaches of fiduciary duty caused NVIDIA injury in several related ways. First, their conduct has exposed NVIDIA itself to federal securities liability for misleading investors about its financial health, and has caused NVIDIA to incur substantial costs in responding to the suits and to the SEC's investigation. Second, NVIDIA's credibility as an entity has allegedly been damaged, leading investors to be skeptical of its statements about its performance.

To remedy this injury, the plaintiffs seek a judgment holding the defendants responsible to, among other things: (1) repay or otherwise indemnify NVIDIA for any damages it must pay or costs it must incur as a result of the federal securities suits and the SEC investigation; (2) repay all salaries and other remuneration they received from NVIDIA during the time they were committing breaches of fiduciary duty; and (3) disgorge all profits they made from trades in NVIDIA stock during the Contested Period. […]

II. Legal Analysis

This matter comes before me now on the defendants' motion to dismiss, which is primarily predicated on Court of Chancery Rule 23.1, because the claims asserted by the plaintiffs are derivative in nature and belong to NVIDIA itself.[…]

I will consider their motion against a record confined to the well-pled allegations of the complaint. Likewise, I will draw all reasonable inferences from the non-conclusory factual allegations of the complaint in the plaintiffs' favor.[7] But I cannot accept cursory contentions of wrongdoing as a substitute for the pleading of particularized facts.[8] Mere notice pleading is insufficient to meet the plaintiffs' burden to show demand excusal in a derivative case.[9]

Here, both the plaintiffs and the defendants agree that the standard set forth in *Rales v. Blasband*[10] applies to the determination of whether demand on the NVIDIA board is excused and this action can proceed. The reason that they agree that *Rales* applies is that the plaintiffs do not challenge any particular business decision made by the NVIDIA board as a whole.

Instead, the plaintiffs allege that the defendant-directors individually breached their fiduciary duties by either purposely trading in their individual capacities while possessing material, non-public information about NVIDIA's improper accounting practices and financial results and/or by failing to ensure that NVIDIA had in place the financial control systems necessary to ensure compliance with applicable accounting standards. As this court held in *In re Baxter Internatational, Inc. Shareholders Litigation* — and both parties concur — these kinds of allegations do not attack a [500] specific business judgment of the board,[11] and, therefore, the *Rales* test, and not the two-pronged demand excusal test of *Aronson v. Lewis*,[12] is applied determine whether demand is excused.

As I will soon describe, the differences between the *Rales* and the *Aronson* tests in the circumstances of this case are only subtly different, because the policy justification for each test points the court toward a similar analysis. To show why, it is useful to remember that the second prong of *Aronson* permits a plaintiff suing a board that is structurally independent and presumptively capable of acting impartially on a demand to proceed with its lawsuit — *i.e.,* a board that passes muster under *Aronson*'s first prong, which focuses on board disinterest and independence — if it pleads a claim for breach of fiduciary duty with particularity.[13]

In simple terms, the second prong of *Aronson* can be said to fulfill two important integrity-assuring functions in our law. First, but somewhat less relevant to this case, the second *Aronson* prong addresses concerns regarding the inherent "structural bias" of corporate boards, by allowing suits to go forward even over a putatively independent board's objection if the plaintiff can meet a heightened pleading standard that provides confidence that there is a substantial basis for the suit.[14]

Second, and particularly pertinent here, the second *Aronson* prong responds to the related concern that a derivative suit demand asks directors to authorize a suit against themselves — *i.e.,* asks them to take an act against their personal interests. The conundrum for the law in this area is well understood. If the legal rule was that demand was excused whenever, by mere notice pleading, the plaintiffs could state a breach of fiduciary duty claim against a majority of the board, the demand requirement of the law would be weakened and the settlement value of so-called "strike suits" would greatly increase, to the perceived detriment of the best interests of stockholders as investors. But, if the demand excusal test is too stringent, then stockholders may suffer as a class because the deterrence effects of meritorious derivative suits on faithless conduct may be too weak. The second prong of *Aronson* therefore balances the conflicting policy interests at stake by articulating a safety valve that releases a suit for prosecution when the complaint meets a heightened pleading standard of particularity, because in these circumstances the threat of liability to the directors required to act on the demand is sufficiently substantial to cast a reasonable doubt over their impartiality.[15]

[501] At first blush, the *Rales* test looks somewhat different from *Aronson,* in that involves a singular inquiry into:

> [W]hether the board that would be addressing the demand can impartially consider its merits without being influenced by improper considerations. Thus, a court must determine whether or not the particularized factual allegations of a derivative stockholder complaint create a reasonable doubt that, as of the time the complaint is filed, the board of directors could have properly exercised its independent and disinterested business judgment in responding to a demand. If the derivative plaintiff satisfies this burden, then demand will be excused as futile.[16]

Upon closer examination, however, that singular inquiry makes germane all of the concerns relevant to both the first and second prongs of *Aronson.* For example, in a situation when a breach of fiduciary duty suit targets acts of self-dealing committed, for example, by the two key managers of a company who are also on a nine-member board, and the other seven board members are not alleged to have directly participated or even approved the wrongdoing (*i.e.,* it was not a board decision), the *Rales* inquiry will concentrate on whether five of the remaining board members can act independently of the two interested manager-directors. This looks like a first prong *Aronson* inquiry.

When, however, there are allegations that a majority of the board that must consider a demand acted wrongfully, the *Rales* test sensibly addresses concerns similar to the second prong of *Aronson.* To wit, if the directors face a "substantial likelihood" of personal liability, their ability to consider a demand impartially is compromised under *Rales,* excusing demand.[17]

In the *Baxter* case, this court recognized that the threat of liability that directors face can be influenced in a substantial way if the corporate charter contains an exculpatory charter provision authorized by 8 *Del. C.* § 102(b)(7). *Baxter* held that in the event that the charter insulates the directors from liability for breaches of the duty of care, then a serious threat of liability may only be found to exist if the plaintiff pleads a *non-exculpated* claim against the directors based on particularized facts.[18]*Baxter* has relevance here because the NVIDIA charter indisputably contains an exculpatory charter provision that immunizes the NVIDIA directors from liability for duty of care violations.

Taken together, the principles I have just discussed provide the framework for the proper disposition of this motion. In order to analyze the motion, I must consider whether the NVIDIA board in place at the time of this suit could impartially consider a demand. This requires me to analyze whether the underlying conduct complained of in the complaint […] renders any of the board members "interested," and, if so, whether any of the [502] other members of the board are compromised in their ability to act independently of the directors found to be interested. If a majority of the board is impartial under this initial analysis, I must next consider whether the complaint sets forth particularized facts that plead a non-exculpated claim of breach of fiduciary duty against a majority of the board, thereby stripping away their first-blush veneer of impartiality.

I turn to that analysis now.

A. Are Any of the Directors Interested?

The NVIDIA board is comprised of seven members. The plaintiffs allege that each of the seven is "interested" for purposes of considering a demand because each traded stock during the Contested Period. As such, each supposedly had a personal "interest" in a challenged transaction that is separate from NVIDIA's and therefore cannot be impartial.

I reject this attempt to extend concepts designed to fit classic self-dealing transactions into another context that is quite different. In a typical derivative suit involving a transaction between a director and her corporation, that director is interested because she is on the other side of the transaction from the corporation and faces liability if the entire fairness standard applies, regardless of her subjective good faith, so long as she cannot prove that the transaction was fair to the corporation. In those circumstances, the director has always been considered "interested"[19] and it displays common sense for the law to consider that director unable to consider a demand to set aside the transaction between the corporation and herself.

In this case, the plaintiffs attack a myriad of stock sales, not between the defendant-directors and NVIDIA, but between the defendant-directors and market-place buyers. As a matter of course, corporate insiders sell company stock and such sales, in themselves, are not quite as suspect as a self-dealing transaction in which the buyer and seller can be viewed as sitting at both sides of the negotiating table. Although insider sales are (rightly) policed by powerful forces — including the criminal laws — to prevent insiders from unfairly defrauding outsiders by trading on non-public information, it is unwise to formulate a common law rule that makes a director "interested" whenever a derivative plaintiff cursorily alleges that he made sales of company stock in the market at a time when he possessed material, non-public information.

This would create the same hair-trigger demand excusal that *Aronson* and *Rales* eschewed. The balanced approach that is more in keeping with the spirit of those important cases is to focus the impartiality analysis on whether the plaintiffs have pled particularized facts regarding the directors that create a sufficient likelihood of personal liability because they have engaged in material trading activity at a time when (one can infer from particularized pled facts that) they knew material, non-public information about the company's financial condition.

With this concept in mind, a quick review of the composition of the NVIDIA board is in order. Of the seven members, only defendant Huang is a member of company management.[20] Only one other board member is alleged to have any relationship [503] with the company other than as a director — *i.e.*, director Gaither, a former partner and current senior counsel to Cooley Godward, a law firm that allegedly has represented the company for years and represented the company's audit committee in responding to the SEC investigation. The complaint fails to allege the amount of the fees that Cooley Godward received for that work, or that Gaither's compensation as senior counsel depends on the work he helps bring in. That is, the complaint fails to allege the materiality of these factors to Gaither.

In any event, even if one assumes that these allegations compromised Huang and Gaither,[21] the plaintiffs have failed to mount any challenge to the other five directors' independence, other than that those directors traded in NVIDIA stock during the Contested Period. From the complaint, it appears that these five directors — defendants Coxe, Jones, Miller, Seawell, and Stevens — are not materially dependent on Huang's good graces to make a living or beholden to him for any other personal reason.

As a result, the key inquiry in the *Rales* analysis is whether the plaintiffs have pled facts that show that these five directors face a sufficiently substantial threat of personal liability to compromise their ability to act impartially on a demand. I turn to that question now.

B. Is the Board's Impartiality Compromised by the Threat of Personal Liability?

In order for the five directors — *i.e.*, those other than Huang and Gaither[22] — to have their impartiality compromised, they must face a substantial likelihood of liability for breach of fiduciary duty for one of two alternative reasons: (1) that they personally profited from stock sales while in knowing possession of material, non-public information or (2) that they committed a non-exculpated breach of fiduciary duty by failing to oversee the company's compliance with legally mandated accounting and disclosure standards.

1. The Plaintiffs' Insider Trading Claims

Although the plaintiffs allege that Coxe, Jones, Miller, Seawell and Stevens had reason to know that the company's financial statements were misstated, this allegation is wholly conclusory. Entirely absent from the complaint are well-pled, particularized allegations of fact detailing the precise roles that these directors played at the company,[23] the information that would have come to their attention in those roles, and any indication as to why they would have perceived the accounting irregularities.

Likewise, while it is true that the dollar proceeds reaped by these directors from their sales was substantial, the complaint cannot be fairly said to contain particularized facts providing an inference of insider trading. For example, the timing of the defendants' trades is quite disparate, having only the common pattern of coming after the filing of a certified financial statement. No inference can be drawn from [504] that simple fact because it is more obviously consistent with the idea that NVIDIA permitted stock sales in such periods because it diminished the possibility that insiders could exploit outside market buyers. Similarly, the complaint alleges that the defendants' trades were inconsistent with their trading practices for the prior year. The prior year measure in itself is a weak one, covering as it does a temporally brief period. But, in any event, the complaint fails to specify what trades, if any, these directors made in that prior year. Not only that, the complaint fails to address whether the directors traded because options were expiring or because IPO-related restrictions on liquidity had recently ended.

It is no doubt true that some of the sales by certain of these five directors comprised a substantial portion of their NVIDIA holdings. For example, director Sea-well sold his entire position in NVIDIA and director Miller sold half of his holdings. But the others — directors Stevens (32%), Coxe (20%), and Jones (10%) — sold much smaller stakes. In the absence of any fact pleading that supports a rational inference that any of these directors had some basis to believe that NVIDIA's financial statements were materially misleading in a manner that inflated the company's stock price, the mere fact that two of the directors sold large portions of their stock does not, in my view, support the conclusion that those two directors face a real threat of liability.[24]

In this respect, it is important to note that none of these five defendants is even named as a defendant in the pending federal securities suits. The complaints in those suits — which were recently dismissed without prejudice for failing to state a claim — were the primary source of information used by the plaintiffs in this action. The plaintiffs admitted as much at oral argument.

At oral argument, the plaintiffs also conceded that they had failed to seek NVIDIA's books and records under 8 *Del. C.* § 220. These books and records could have provided the basis for the pleading of particularized facts — *i.e.,* for the filing of a complaint that meets the legally required standard. Rather than pursue that option, the plaintiffs, after confronting a motion to dismiss their original complaint, were content to simply amend their complaint in reliance upon the (now dismissed) federal complaints, which did not even name the NVIDIA outside directors as defendants. They have thus ignored the repeated admonitions of the Delaware Supreme Court and this court for derivative plaintiffs to proceed deliberately and to use the books and records device to gather the materials necessary to prepare a solid complaint.[25]

The cursory allegations of the complaint in this action do not come close to meeting the plaintiffs' burden to show that these five defendants face a substantial threat of liability for insider trading-based fiduciary duty violations. Nothing in the complaint provides any particularized basis to infer that these outside directors had any idea about the questionable accounting practices. This is fatal to the plaintiffs' effort to show demand excusal. […]

III. Conclusion and Final Order

The defendants' motion to dismiss under Rule 23.1 is hereby GRANTED.
IT IS SO ORDERED.

Footnotes

[15] *Aronson,* 473 A.2d at 815 ("[T]he mere threat of personal liability for approving a questioned transaction, standing alone, is insufficient to challenge either the independence or disinterestedness of directors, although in rare cases a transaction may be so egregious on its face that board approval cannot meet the test of business judgment, and a substantial likelihood of director liability therefore exists."); *Ash v. McCall,* 2000 WL 1370341, at *10 (Del.Ch. Sept. 15, 2000) ("Directors who are sued for failure to oversee subordinates have a disabling interest for presuit demand purposes when the potential for liability is not a mere threat but instead may rise to a substantial

likelihood." (internal quotation marks and footnote omitted)); *Kohls v. Duthie,* 791 A.2d 772, 782 (Del.Ch.2000) (suggesting that a "`substantial threat' of personal liability" can make a director interested with respect to whether litigation should be brought); *see also* 1 Donald J. Wolfe, Jr. & Michael A. Pittenger, *Corporate and Commercial Practice in the Delaware Court of Chancery* § 9-2(b)(3)(iii) (2003) (stating that directors will be deemed interested for demand purposes when the complaint alleges specific facts that makes directorial liability "a substantial likelihood" and not just "a mere threat"); Leo E. Strine, Jr., *The Inescapably Empirical Foundation of the Common Law of Corporations,* 27 Del. J. Corp. L. 499, 508 (2002) (describing *Aronson*'s second prong as "a safety valve permitting a derivative plaintiff to not make a demand if he can show with particularity that the board decision under attack ... is not entitled to business judgment rule protection").

3.2.4 Beam v. Stewart

Beam is a ruling on a defendant's 23.1 motion to dismiss. In the 23.1 motion, the defendants are arguing that demand was not futile under the relevant test (*Rales* in this case), and plaintiffs should have properly made demand. Plaintiffs argue that they didn't make demand because doing so would have been futile because of the board's lack of independence from Martha Stewart and the fact that Stewart was interested in the transaction.

The Chancery Court articulated the standard at issue here in the following way:

"Because this claim does not challenge an action of the board of directors of MSO, the appropriate test for demand futility is that articulated in *Rales v. Blasband.* Particularly, the Court's task is to evaluate whether the particularized allegations "create a reasonable doubt that, as of the time the complaint [was] filed, the board of directors could have properly exercised its independent and disinterested business judgment in responding to a demand." *Rales* requires that a majority of the board be able to consider and appropriately to respond to a demand "free of personal financial interest and improper extraneous influences." Demand is excused as futile if the Court finds there is "a reasonable doubt that a majority of the Board would be disinterested or independent in making a decision on demand.""

It is important to your understanding of *Beam* to remember that when the court approaches the question of interestedness and independence of the board in a 23.1 motion to dismiss, the board enjoys the benefit of the business judgment presumption. That means the plaintiff in its pleadings must allege facts to overcome that presumption. Mere statements that board members are either interested or not independent will not be sufficient to establish demand futility.

845 A.2d 1040 (2004)
BEAM v. Martha STEWART, Sharon L. Patrick, Arthur C. Martinez, Naomi O. Seligman, Darla D. Moore; Jeffrey W. Ubben, L. John Doerr, and Martha Stewart Living Omnimedia, Inc.

In this appeal we review and affirm the judgment of the Court of Chancery in dismissing under Rule 23.1 a claim in a derivative suit because the plaintiff failed to make presuit demand on the corporation's board of directors and failed to demonstrate demand futility.[…]. The single issue before us is that of demand futility, no appeal having been taken on the other issues.

Facts

The plaintiff, Monica A. Beam, owns shares of Martha Stewart Living Omnimedia, Inc. (MSO). Beam filed a derivative action in the Court of Chancery against Martha Stewart, the five other members of MSO's board of directors, and former board member L. John Doerr. […]

In the single claim at issue on appeal (Count 1), Beam alleged that Stewart breached her fiduciary duties of loyalty and care by illegally selling ImClone stock in December of 2001 and by mishandling the media attention that followed, thereby jeopardizing the financial future of MSO. The Court of Chancery dismissed Count 1 under Court of Chancery Rule 23.1 because Beam failed to plead particularized facts demonstrating presuit demand futility.

When Beam filed the complaint in the Court of Chancery, the MSO board of directors consisted of six members: Stewart, Sharon L. Patrick, Arthur C. Martinez, Darla D. Moore, Naomi O. Seligman, and Jeffrey W. Ubben. The Chancellor concluded that the complaint alleged sufficient facts to support the conclusion that two of the directors, Stewart and Patrick, were not disinterested or independent for purposes of considering a presuit demand.

The Court of Chancery found that Stewart's potential civil and criminal liability for the acts underlying Beam's claim rendered Stewart an interested party and therefore unable to consider demand.[3] The Court also found that Patrick's position [1045] as an officer and inside director,[4] together with the substantial compensation she receives from the company, raised a reasonable doubt as to her ability objectively to consider demand.[5] The defendants do not challenge the Court's conclusions with respect to Patrick and Stewart.

We now address the plaintiff's allegations concerning the independence of the other board members. We must determine if the following allegations of the complaint, and the reasonable inferences that may flow from them, create a reasonable doubt of the independence of either Martinez, Moore or Seligman:[6]

> 4. Defendant Arthur C. Martinez ("Martinez") is a director of the Company, a position that he has held since January 2001. Until December 2000, Martinez served as Chairman of the board of directors of Sears Roebuck and Co., and was its Chief Executive Officer from August 1995 until October 2000. Martinez joined Sears, Roebuck and Co. in September 1992 as the Chairman and Chief Executive Officer of Sears Merchandise Group, Sears's former retail arm. From 1990 to 1992, he was Vice Chairman of Saks Fifth Avenue and was a member of Saks Fifth Avenue's board of directors. Martinez is currently a member of the board of directors of PepsiCo, Inc., Liz Claiborne, Inc. and International Flavors & Fragrances, Inc., and is the Chairman of the Federal Reserve Bank of Chicago. *Martinez is a longstanding personal friend of defendants Stewart and Patrick. While at Sears, Martinez established a relationship with the Company, which marketed a substantial volume of products through Sears. Martinez was recruited for the board by Stewart's longtime personal friend, Charlotte Beers. Defendant Patrick was quoted in an*

article dated March 22, 2001 appearing in Directors & Board as follows: *"Arthur is an old friend to both me and Martha."*

5. Defendant Darla D. Moore ("Moore") is a director of the Company, a position she has held since September 2001. Moore has been a partner of Rainwater, Inc., a private investment firm, since 1994. Before that, Moore was a Managing Director of Chase Bank. Moore is also a trustee of Magellan Health Services, Inc. *Moore is a longstanding friend of defendant Stewart. In November 1995, she attended a wedding reception hosted by Stewart's personal lawyer, Allen Grubman, for his daughter. Also in attendance were Stewart and Stewart's friend, Samuel Waksal. In August 1996, Fortune carried an article highlighting Moore's close personal relationship with Charlotte Beers and defendant Stewart. When Beers, a longtime friend and confidante to Stewart, resigned from the Company's board in September 2001, Moore was nominated to replace her.*

6. Defendant Naomi O. Seligman ("Seligman") is a director of the Company, a position that she has held since [1046] September 1999. Seligman was a co-founder of Cassius Advisers, an e-commerce consultancy, where she has served as a senior partner since 1999, and is a co-founder of the Research Board, Inc., an information technology research group, where she served as a senior partner from 1975 until 1999. Seligman currently serves as a director of Akamai Technologies, Inc., The Dun & Bradstreet Corporation, John Wiley & Sons and Sun Microsystems, Inc. *According to a story appearing on July 2, 2002 in The Wall Street Journal, Seligman contacted the Chief Executive Officer of John Wiley & Sons (a publishing house) at defendant Stewart's behest last year to express concern over its planned publication of a biography that was critical of Stewart.*

* * *

8. Martinez, Moore, Seligson [sic], and Ubben are hereinafter referred to collectively as the Director Defendants. By reason of Stewart's overwhelming voting control over the Company, each of

the Director Defendants serves at her sufferance. Each of the Director Defendants receive [sic] valuable perquisites and benefits by reason of their service on the Company's Board....

* * *

DEMAND ALLEGATIONS

73..... No demand on the Board of Directors was made prior to institution of this action, as a majority of the Board of Directors is not independent or disinterested with respect to the claims asserted herein.

* * *

77. *Defendant Martinez is not disinterested in view of his longstanding personal friendship with both Patrick and Stewart.*

78. *Defendant Moore is not disinterested in view of her longstanding personal relationship with defendant Stewart.*

79. *Defendant Seligman is not disinterested; she has already shown that she will use her position as a director at another corporation to act at the behest of defendant Stewart when she contacted the Chief Executive Officer of John Wiley & Sons in an effort to dissuade the publishing house from publishing a biography that was critical of Stewart.*

80. The Director Defendants are not disinterested as they are jointly and severally liable with Stewart in view of their failure to monitor Stewart's actions. Moreover, pursuit of these claims would imperil the substantial benefits that accrue to them by reason of their service on the Board, given Stewart's voting control.[7]

Decision of the Court of Chancery

The Chancellor found that Beam had not alleged sufficient facts to support the conclusion that demand was futile because he determined that the complaint failed to raise a reasonable doubt that these outside directors are independent of Stewart. Because

207

Patrick and Stewart herself are not independent for demand purposes, all the plaintiff need show is that one of the remaining directors is not independent, there being only six board members.[8] The allegations relating to Moore, Seligman and Martinez are set forth above.

It is appropriate here to quote the Chancellor's analysis of the allegations regarding these three directors:

> The factual allegations regarding Stewart's friendship with Martinez are inadequate to raise a reasonable doubt of his independence. While employed by Sears, Martinez developed business ties to MSO due to Sears' marketing of a substantial quantity of MSO products. Martinez was recruited to serve on MSO's board of directors by Beers, who is described as Stewart's longtime personal friend and confidante and who was at that time an MSO director. Shortly after Martinez joined MSO's board, Patrick was quoted in a magazine article saying, "Arthur [Martinez] is an old friend to both me and Martha [Stewart]." Weighing against these factors, the amended complaint discloses that Martinez has been an executive and director for major corporations since at least 1990. At present he serves as a director for four prominent corporations, including MSO, and is the chairman of the Federal Reserve Bank of Chicago. One might say that Martinez's reputation for acting as a careful fiduciary is essential to his career — a matter in which he would surely have a material interest. *Furthermore, the amended complaint does not give a single example of any action by Martinez that might be construed as evidence of even a slight inclination to disregard his duties as a fiduciary for any reason. In this context, I cannot reasonably infer, on the basis of several years of business interactions and a single affirmation of friendship by a third party, that the friendship between Stewart and Martinez raises a reasonable doubt of Martinez's ability to evaluate demand independently of Stewart's personal interests.*

The allegations regarding the friendship between Moore and Stewart are somewhat more detailed, yet still fall short of raising a reasonable doubt about Moore's ability properly to consider demand on Count I. In 1995, Stewart's lawyer, Allen Grubman, hosted a wedding reception for his daughter. Among those in attendance at the reception were Moore, Stewart, and Waksal. In addition, *Fortune* magazine published an article in 1996 that focused on the close personal friendships among Moore, Stewart, and Beers. In September 2001, when Beers resigned from MSO's board of directors, Moore was selected to replace her. *Although the amended complaint lists fewer positions of fiduciary responsibility for Moore than were listed for Martinez, it is clear that Moore's professional reputation similarly would be harmed if she failed to fulfill her fiduciary obligations. To my mind, this is quite a close call. Perhaps the balance could have been tipped by additional, more detailed allegations about the closeness or nature of the friendship, details of the business and social interactions between the two, or allegations raising additional considerations that might inappropriately affect Moore's ability to impartially consider pursuit of a lawsuit against Stewart. On the facts pled, however, I cannot say that I have a reasonable doubt of Moore's ability to properly consider demand.*

No particular felicity is alleged to exist between Stewart and Seligman. The amended complaint reports in ominous tones, however, that Seligman, who is a director both for MSO and for JWS, contacted JWS' chief executive officer about an unflattering biography of Stewart slated for publication. From this, the Court is asked to infer that Seligman acted in a way that preferred the protection of Stewart over her fiduciary duties to one or both of these [1048] *companies. Without details about the nature of the contact, other than Seligman's wish to "express concern," it is impossible reasonably to make this inference. Stewart's public image, as plaintiff persistently asserts, is critical to the fortunes of MSO and its shareholders. As a fiduciary of MSO, Seligman may have felt obligated to express concern and seek additional information about the publication before its release. As a fiduciary of JWS, she could well have anticipated* some risk of liability if any of the unflattering characterizations of Stewart proved to be insufficiently researched or made carelessly. *There is no allegation that Seligman made any inappropriate attempt to prevent the publication of the biography.* Nor does the amended complaint indicate whether the biography was ultimately published and, if so, whether Seligman's inquiry is believed to have resulted in any changes to the content of the book. *As alleged, this matter does not serve to raise a reasonable doubt of Seligman's independence or ability to consider demand on Count I.*

In sum, plaintiff offers various theories to suggest reasons that the outside directors might be inappropriately swayed by Stewart's wishes or interests, but fails to plead sufficient facts that could permit the Court reasonably to infer that one or more of the theories could be accurate.[9]

Demand Futility and Director Independence

Under the first prong of *Aronson*,[14] a stockholder may not pursue a derivative suit to assert a claim of the corporation unless: (a) she has first demanded that the directors pursue the corporate claim and they have wrongfully refused to do so; or (b) such demand is excused because the directors are deemed incapable of making an impartial decision regarding the pursuit of the litigation.[15] The issue in this case is the quantum of doubt about a director's independence that is "reasonable" in order to excuse a presuit demand.[...]

The key principle upon which this area of our jurisprudence is based is that the directors are entitled to a *presumption* that they were faithful to their fiduciary duties.[16] In the context of presuit demand, the burden is upon the plaintiff in a derivative action to overcome that presumption.[17] The Court must determine whether a plaintiff has alleged particularized facts creating a reasonable doubt of a director's independence to rebut the presumption at the pleading stage.[18] If the Court determines that the pleaded facts create a reasonable doubt that a majority of the board could have acted independently in responding to the demand, the presumption is rebutted for pleading purposes and demand will be excused as futile.[19]

A director will be considered unable to act objectively with respect to a presuit demand if he or she is interested in the outcome of the litigation or is otherwise not independent.[20] A director's interest may be shown by demonstrating a potential personal benefit or detriment to the director as a result of the decision.[21] "In such circumstances, a director cannot be expected to exercise his or her independent business judgment without being influenced by the ... personal consequences resulting from the decision."[22] The primary basis upon which a director's independence must be measured is whether the director's decision is based on the corporate merits of the subject before the board, rather than extraneous considerations or influences.[23] This broad statement of the law requires an analysis of whether the director is disinterested in the underlying transaction and, even if disinterested, whether the director is otherwise independent. More precisely in the context of the present case, the independence inquiry requires us to determine whether there is a reasonable doubt that any one of these three directors is capable of objectively making a business decision to assert or not assert a corporate claim against Stewart.

Independence Is a Contextual Inquiry

In order to show lack of independence, the complaint of a stockholder-plaintiff must create a reasonable doubt that a director is not so "beholden" to an interested director (in this case Stewart) that his or her "discretion would be sterilized. [...]

The "reasonable doubt" standard "is sufficiently flexible and workable to provide the stockholder with `the keys to the courthouse' in an appropriate case where the claim is not based on mere suspicions or stated solely in conclusory terms."[26]

Personal Friendship

A variety of motivations, including friendship, may influence the demand futility inquiry. But, to render a director unable to consider demand, a relationship must be of a bias-producing nature. Allegations of mere personal friendship or a mere outside business relationship, standing alone, are insufficient to raise a reasonable doubt about a director's independence.[27] In this connection, we adopt as our own the Chancellor's analysis in this case:

> [S]ome professional or personal friendships, which may border on
> or even exceed familial loyalty and closeness, may raise a reasonable

211

doubt whether a director can appropriately consider demand. This is particularly true when the allegations raise serious questions of either civil or criminal liability of such a close friend. Not all friendships, or even most of them, rise to this level and the Court cannot make a *reasonable* inference that a particular friendship does so without specific factual allegations to support such a conclusion.

The facts alleged by Beam regarding the relationships between Stewart and these other members of MSO's board of directors largely boil down to a "structural bias" argument, which presupposes that [1051] the professional and social relationships that naturally develop among members of a board impede independent decisionmaking.[29] This Court addressed the structural bias argument in *Aronson v. Lewis:*

> Critics will charge that [by requiring the independence of only a majority of the board] we are ignoring the structural bias common to corporate boards throughout America, as well as the other unseen socialization processes cutting against independent discussion and decisionmaking in the boardroom. The difficulty with structural bias in a demand futile case is simply one of establishing it in the complaint for purposes of Rule 23.1. We are satisfied that discretionary review by the Court of Chancery of complaints alleging specific facts pointing to bias on a particular board will be sufficient for determining demand futility.[30]

In the present case, the plaintiff attempted to plead affinity beyond mere friendship between Stewart and the other directors, but her attempt is not sufficient to demonstrate demand futility. Even if the alleged friendships may have preceded the directors' membership on MSO's board and did not necessarily arise out of that membership, these relationships are of the same nature as those giving rise to the structural bias argument.

Allegations that Stewart and the other directors moved in the same social circles, attended the same weddings, developed business relationships before joining the board, and described each other as "friends," even when coupled with Stewart's 94% voting power, are insufficient, without more, to rebut the presumption of independence. They

212

do not provide a sufficient basis from which reasonably to infer that Martinez, Moore and Seligman may have been beholden to Stewart. Whether they arise before board membership or later as a result of collegial relationships among the board of directors, such affinities — standing alone — will not render presuit demand futile.

[The trial court] must review the complaint on a case-by-case basis to determine whether it states with particularity facts indicating that a relationship — whether it preceded or followed board membership — is so close that the director's independence may *reasonably* be doubted. This doubt might arise either because of financial ties, familial affinity, a particularly close or intimate personal or business affinity or because of evidence that in the past the relationship caused the director to act non-independently vis à vis an interested director. No such allegations are made here. Mere allegations that they move in the same business and social circles, or a characterization that they are close friends, is not [1052] enough to negate independence for demand excusal purposes.

That is not to say that personal friendship is always irrelevant to the independence calculus. But, for presuit demand purposes, friendship must be accompanied by substantially more in the nature of serious allegations that would lead to a reasonable doubt as to a director's independence. That a much stronger relationship is necessary to overcome the presumption of independence at the demand futility stage becomes especially compelling when one considers the risks that directors would take by protecting their social acquaintances in the face of allegations that those friends engaged in misconduct.[31] To create a reasonable doubt about an outside director's independence, a plaintiff must plead facts that would support the inference that because of the nature of a relationship or additional circumstances other than the interested director's stock ownership or voting power, the non-interested director would be more willing to risk his or her reputation than risk the relationship with the interested director.[32]

Specific Allegations Concerning Seligman and Moore

1. Seligman

Beam's allegations concerning Seligman's lack of independence raise an additional [1053] issue not present in the Moore and Martinez relationships. Those allegations are not

213

necessarily based on a purported friendship between Seligman and Stewart. Rather, they are based on a specific past act by Seligman that, Beam claims, indicates Seligman's lack of independence from Stewart. Beam alleges that Seligman called John Wiley & Sons (Wiley) at Stewart's request in order to prevent an unfavorable publication reference to Stewart. The Chancellor concluded, properly in our view, that this allegation does not provide particularized facts from which one may reasonably infer improper influence.

The bare fact that Seligman contacted Wiley, on whose board Seligman also served, to dissuade Wiley from publishing unfavorable references to Stewart, even if done at Stewart's request, is insufficient to create a reasonable doubt that Seligman is capable of considering presuit demand free of Stewart's influence. Although the court should draw all *reasonable* inferences in Beam's favor, neither improper influence by Stewart over Seligman nor that Seligman was beholden to Stewart is a reasonable inference from these allegations.

Indeed, the reasonable inference is that Seligman's purported intervention on Stewart's behalf was of benefit to MSO and *its* reputation, which is allegedly tied to *Stewart's* reputation, as the Chancellor noted.[34] A motivation by Seligman to benefit the company every bit as much as Stewart herself is the only reasonable inference supported by the complaint, when all of its allegations are read in context.[35]

2. Moore

The Court of Chancery concluded that the plaintiff's allegations with respect to Moore's social relationship with Stewart [1054] presented "quite a close call" and suggested ways that the "balance could have been tipped."[36] Although we agree that there are ways that the balance could be tipped so that mere allegations of social relationships would become allegations casting reasonable doubt on independence, we do not agree that the facts as alleged present a "close call" with respect to Moore's independence. These allegations center on: (a) Moore's attendance at a wedding reception for the daughter of Stewart's lawyer where Stewart and Waksal were also present; (b) a *Fortune* magazine article focusing on the close personal relationships among Moore, Stewart and Beers; and (c) the fact that Moore replaced Beers on the MSO board. In our view, these bare social relationships clearly do not create a reasonable doubt of independence.

3. Stewart's 94% Stock Ownership

Beam attempts to bolster her allegations regarding the relationships between Stewart and Seligman and Moore by emphasizing Stewart's overwhelming voting control of MSO. That attempt also fails to create a reasonable doubt of independence. A stockholder's control of a corporation does not excuse presuit demand on the board without particularized allegations of relationships between the directors and the controlling stockholder demonstrating that the directors are beholden to the stockholder.[37] As noted earlier, the relationships alleged by Beam do not lead to the inference that the directors were beholden to Stewart and, thus, unable independently to consider demand. Coupling those relationships with Stewart's overwhelming voting control of MSO does not close that gap.[38] […]

Conclusion

Because Beam did not plead facts sufficient to support a reasonable inference that at least one MSO director in addition to Stewart and Patrick was incapable of considering demand, Beam was required to make demand on the board before pursuing a derivative suit. Hence, presuit demand was not excused. The Court of Chancery did not err by dismissing Count 1 under Rule 23.1. The judgment of the Court of Chancery is AFFIRMED.

3.2.5 Spiegel v. Buntrock

If a board receives and then refuses demand, the stockholder may not bring a derivative claim on behalf of the corporation. Of course, if a board could just refuse demand without regard to the merits of the demand, the demand requirement would devolve into a toothless exercise. Consequently, when a board refuses demand, the good faith and reasonableness of the board's refusal may still be examined by the courts.

However, a board's decision to refuse demand is a business decision, like any other. As a result, such decisions receive the protection of the business judgment presumption. In challenging a demand refusal, a stockholder will have to plead particularized facts with respect to the board's decision to refuse demand as to overcome the business judgment presumption.

571 A.2d 767 (1990)
Ted SPIEGEL v. Dean L. BUNTROCK

HOLLAND, Justice:

This is an appeal from an order of the Court of Chancery dismissing a derivative action filed by the plaintiff-appellant, Ted Spiegel ("Spiegel"), a shareholder of Waste Management, Inc. ("Waste Management"). In his complaint, Spiegel alleged that Dean L. Buntrock ("Buntrock"), Chairman of the Board of Directors and Chief Executive Officer of Waste Management; Jerry E. Dempsey ("Dempsey"), Vice Chairman; Peter H. Huizenga ("Huizenga"), Vice President and Secretary; and James E. Koenig ("Koenig"), Staff Vice President[1] (collectively "management defendants"), improperly acquired stock in ChemLawn Corporation ("ChemLawn"), based upon inside information, during the two years immediately preceding Waste Management's tender offer for ChemLawn. […]

The underlying issue in this controversy is the often debated subject of when the requirement that a stockholder make demand on a board of directors, prior to filing a derivative lawsuit for the benefit of a corporation, is excused and when a demand, which has been made, is properly refused. Superimposed upon the "demand excused/demand refused" debate[2] are additional issues relating to the use of a special litigation committee by the Board of Waste Management, and the propriety of continuing to argue that demand was excused, after a demand has been made. All of the issues raised implicate the proper standard of judicial review.

[…]Spiegel contended that demand was excused. However, when his failure to make a pre-suit demand was raised by the Board of Waste Management ("Board") as a defense, Spiegel responded by filing a demand. The Board contended that demand was required, because it was disinterested and capable of responding to Spiegel's request for legal action. However, when a demand for such action was made by Spiegel, the Board responded by appointing a special litigation committee with complete authority to review and act upon Spiegel's request. Ultimately, each party used their opponent's legal sword as their own legal shield. Spiegel argued that by appointing a special litigation committee, the Board conceded that demand was excused and the Board argued that by filing a demand Spiegel had admitted that one was required.

The Court of Chancery carefully reviewed the allegations in Spiegel's complaint and found that demand was not excused. Thereafter, the Court of Chancery proceeded to examine the post-suit demand for legal action, which was sent to the Board by Spiegel, and the decision to refuse that demand. The Court of Chancery held that the decision to refuse Spiegel's demand was subject to review according to the traditional business judgment rule, notwithstanding the fact that the Board had delegated its authority to act on Spiegel's demand to a special litigation committee. Applying the traditional business judgment rule, the Court of Chancery held that Spiegel's demand, for the Board to take legal action on behalf of Waste Management, was properly refused.

On appeal, Spiegel contends that, even though he made a demand, given the facts of this case, demand was excused nevertheless. […]

Waste Management is a Delaware corporation headquartered in Oak Brook, Illinois. It provides domestic and international waste removal and disposal services. In the spring of 1984, Waste Management decided to diversify its operations by expanding into new service areas. […]

Waste Management's interest in Chem-Lawn gradually intensified until on February 26, 1987, it launched a cash tender offer for ChemLawn at $27.00 per share.[…]The tender offer included a disclosure that the management defendants owned shares of ChemLawn stock, which they had acquired during the prior two years.[5] Waste Management's tender offer proved to be unsuccessful.

ChemLawn was purchased by EcoLab, Inc. for $36.50 per share. On March 30, 1987, the *Wall Street Journal* carried an article entitled "ChemLawn's Sale Could Yield $1 Million In Profit for Officials of Thwarted Suitor."[6] That same day, Spiegel filed the action against Waste Management, and its directors, that is the subject of this appeal.

On April 30, 1987, the Board filed a motion to dismiss Spiegel's complaint pursuant to Court of Chancery Rule 23.1. The basis for that motion was that Spiegel had failed to make a demand upon the Board prior to instituting his derivative suit and had failed to allege with particularity facts demonstrating that such a demand would have been futile. […]

Spiegel did not immediately contest the Board's motion to dismiss in the Court of Chancery.[8] Instead, Spiegel responded by making a demand to the Board in a letter which stated:

> On behalf of Ted Spiegel, a shareholder of Waste Management, Inc., we hereby formally demand that the Board of Directors take all appropriate action to redress the wrongs as alleged in the enclosed complaint.

In response to Spiegel's demand letter, the Board established a special litigation committee of outside directors (the "Committee") "for the purpose of conducting an independent review of the transactions in the common stock of ChemLawn Corporation by officers of the Company.[...]"

The Committee conducted an investigation into Spiegel's allegations that spanned over five months. The Committee was represented by its own independent counsel, a Washington, D.C., [...] The Committee interviewed a great many people, both within and without Waste Management.[10] It also reviewed volumes of documents.

On the basis of its investigation, and its analysis of the applicable law, the Committee concluded that it would not be in the best interests of Waste Management and its stockholders to pursue Spiegel's derivative action.[...]

Consequently, the Committee, acting for the Board, filed a motion on behalf of Waste Management, in the Court of Chancery to dismiss or, alternatively, for summary judgment, along with the affidavits of the Committee members and the entire report which summarized its findings and analysis.

Derivative Action/Demand Requirement

A basic principle of the General Corporation Law of the State of Delaware is that directors, rather than shareholders, manage the business and affairs of the corporation. [...] The decision to bring a law suit or to refrain from litigating a claim on behalf of a corporation is a decision concerning the management of the corporation. [...] Consequently, such decisions are part of the responsibility of the board of directors. 8 *Del.C.* § 141(a).[11]

Nevertheless, a shareholder may file a derivative action to redress an alleged harm to the corporation. The nature of the derivative action is two-fold.

> First, it is the equivalent of a suit by the shareholders to compel the corporation to sue. Second, it is a suit by the corporation, asserted by the shareholders on its behalf, against those liable to it.

"Because the shareholders' ability to institute an action on behalf of the corporation inherently impinges upon the directors' power to manage the affairs of the corporation the law imposes certain prerequisites on a stockholder's right to sue derivatively." [...] Chancery Court Rule 23.1 requires that shareholders seeking to assert a claim on behalf of the corporation must first exhaust intracorporate remedies by making a demand on the directors to obtain the action desired, or to plead with particularity why demand is excused. Ch. Ct.R. 23.1.

The purpose of pre-suit demand is to assure that the stockholder affords the corporation the opportunity to address an alleged wrong without litigation, to decide whether to invest the resources of the corporation in litigation, and to control any litigation which does occur. [...] "[B]y promoting this form of alternate dispute resolution, rather than immediate recourse to litigation, the demand requirement is a recognition of the fundamental precept that directors manage the business and affairs of corporations." [...]

Standard of Review Demand Excused/Demand Refused

Since a conscious decision by a board of directors to refrain from acting [774] may be a valid exercise of business judgment, "where demand on a board has been made and refused, [courts] apply the business judgment rule in reviewing the board's refusal to act pursuant to a stockholder's demand" to file a lawsuit. [...]The business judgment rule is a presumption that in making a business decision, not involving self-interest, the directors of a corporation acted on an informed basis, in good faith and in the honest belief that the action taken was in the best interests of the company. [...]"The burden is on the party challenging the decision to establish facts rebutting th[is] presumption." [...] Thus, the business judgment rule operates as a judicial acknowledgement of a board of directors' managerial prerogatives. [...]

Demand Made/Futility Waived

Spiegel filed a derivative action on behalf of Waste Management, alleging that a presuit demand on the Board was excused, i.e., would have been a futile gesture. However, Spiegel then filed a demand with the Board to take legal action and "redress the wrongs" set forth in his complaint. Spiegel alleges that he was entitled to simultaneously argue these inconsistent arguments. The Board argues that when Spiegel filed his demand, he waived his right to continue asserting that demand was excused. The Court of Chancery gave implicit recognition to the validity of Spiegel's position by examining the merits of both of his arguments.[...]

"When deciding a motion to dismiss for failure to make a demand under Chancery Rule 23.1 the record before the court must be restricted to the allegations of the complaint." [...]. In determining demand futility, the Court of Chancery must decide whether, under the particularized facts alleged in the complaint:

> [A] reasonable doubt is created that: (1) the directors are
> disinterested and independent and (2) the challenged transaction
> was otherwise the product of a valid exercise of business judgment.

Aronson v. Lewis, 473 A.2d at 814. In this case, the Court of Chancery concluded that the facts alleged in Spiegel's complaint did not raise a reasonable doubt that the Board was disabled from responding to Spiegel's demand and passing upon whether it was in Waste Management's interest to pursue Spiegel's claims.

Spiegel argues that, even though he made a demand, the Court of Chancery properly reviewed the merits of his complaint, which alleged that demand was excused. Spiegel submits that demand [775] should be encouraged by permitting a demand to be made, while at the same time permitting the argument, that demand was excused, to be preserved. Spiegel finds some support for his position in other jurisdictions. [...]However, this Court has held that by making a demand, a shareholder thereby makes his original contention, that demand was excused, moot. [...]

This Court has recently held that when a board of directors is confronted with a derivative action asserted on its behalf, it cannot stand neutral. [...]The Board "must affirmatively object to or support the continuation of the [derivative] litigation."[...] Similarly, a stockholder who asserts a derivative claim cannot stand neutral, in effect, with respect to the board of directors' ability to respond to a request to take legal action, by simultaneously making a demand for such action *and* continuing to argue that demand is excused.

By making a demand, a stockholder tacitly acknowledges the absence of facts to support a finding of futility. […] Thus, when a demand is made, the question of whether demand was excused is moot. […] Therefore, we hold once Spiegel made a demand, it was unnecessary for the Court of Chancery to consider the merits of Spiegel's argument that demand was excused.[…]

A shareholder who makes a demand can no longer argue that demand is excused. […]The effect of a demand is to place control of the derivative litigation in the hands of the board of directors.[…]Consequently, stockholders who, [776] like Spiegel, make a demand which is refused, subject the board's decision to judicial review according to the traditional business judgment rule.

Standard of Review Demand Refused/Motion to Dismiss

Whenever any action or inaction by a board of directors is subject to review according to the traditional business judgment rule, the issues before the Court are independence, the reasonableness of its investigation and good faith. By electing to make a demand, a shareholder plaintiff tacitly concedes the independence of a majority of the board to respond. Therefore, when a board refuses a demand, the only issues to be examined are the good faith and reasonableness of its investigation.

Absent an abuse of discretion, if the requirements of the traditional business judgment rule are met, the board of directors' decision not to pursue the derivative claim will be respected by the courts. […] In such cases, a board of directors' motion to dismiss an action filed by a shareholder, whose demand has been rejected, must be granted.[20] "If Courts would not respect the directors' decision not to file suit, then demand would be an empty formality."

Conclusion

For the reasons stated in this opinion, the ultimate decision of the Court of Chancery, dismissing Spiegel's complaint is AFFIRMED.

3.2.6 Brehm v. Eisner

Aronson test include two prongs. The first prong deals with the interestedness and lack of independence of directors who approve a challenged transaction. The second prong deals with transactions that are not the product of a valid business judgment. In the following case, the interestedness of the board of Disney is not seriously at issue. Consequently, plaintiffs are left to argue that the board's approval of the challenged employment agreement was not the product of a valid business judgment so therefore demand upon the board would be futile.

746 A.2d 244 (2000)
William BREHM v. Michael D. EISNER

VEASEY, Chief Justice:

In this appeal from the Court of Chancery, we agree with the holding of the Court of Chancery that the stockholder derivative Complaint[1] was subject to dismissal for failure to set forth particularized facts creating a reasonable doubt that the director defendants were disinterested and independent or that their conduct was protected by the business judgment rule.[…]

The claims before us are that: (a) the board of directors of The Walt Disney Company ("Disney") as it was constituted in 1995 (the "Old Board") breached its fiduciary duty in approving an extravagant and wasteful Employment Agreement of Michael S. Ovitz as president of Disney; (b) the Disney board of directors as it was constituted in 1996 (the "New Board") breached its fiduciary duty in agreeing to a "non-fault" termination of the Ovitz Employment Agreement, a decision that was [249] extravagant and wasteful; and (c) the directors were not disinterested and independent.[3]

A. The 1995 Ovitz Employment Agreement

By an agreement dated October 1, 1995, Disney hired Ovitz as its president. He was a long-time friend of Disney Chairman and CEO Michael Eisner. At the time, Ovitz was an important talent broker in Hollywood. Although he lacked experience managing a diversified public company, other companies with entertainment operations had been interested in hiring him for high-level executive positions. [250] The Employment

Agreement was unilaterally negotiated by Eisner and approved by the Old Board. Their judgment was that Ovitz was a valuable person to hire as president of Disney, and they agreed ultimately with Eisner's recommendation in awarding him an extraordinarily lucrative contract.

Ovitz' Employment Agreement had an initial term of five years and required that Ovitz "devote his full time and best efforts exclusively to the Company," with exceptions for volunteer work, service on the board of another company, and managing his passive investments.[5] In return, Disney agreed to give Ovitz a base salary of $1 million per year, a discretionary bonus, and two sets of stock options (the "A" options and the "B" options) that collectively would enable Ovitz to purchase 5 million shares of Disney common stock.

The "A" options were scheduled to vest in three annual increments of 1 million shares each, beginning on September 30, 1998 (*i.e.,* at the end of the third full year of employment) and continuing for the following two years (through September 2000). The agreement specifically provided that the "A" options would vest immediately if Disney granted Ovitz a non-fault termination of the Employment Agreement. The "B" options, consisting of 2 million shares, differed in two important respects. Although scheduled to vest annually starting in September 2001 (*i.e.,* the year *after* the last "A" option would vest), the "B" options were conditioned on Ovitz and Disney first having agreed to extend his employment beyond the five-year term of the Employment Agreement. Furthermore, Ovitz would forfeit the right to qualify for the "B" options if his initial employment term of five years ended prematurely for any reason, even if from a non-fault termination.

The Employment Agreement provided for three ways by which Ovitz' employment might end. He might serve his five years and Disney might decide against offering him a new contract. If so, Disney would owe Ovitz a $10 million termination payment.[6] Before the end of the initial term, Disney could terminate Ovitz for "good cause" only if Ovitz committed gross negligence or malfeasance, or if Ovitz resigned voluntarily. Disney would owe Ovitz no additional compensation if it terminated him for "good cause." Termination without cause (non-fault termination) would entitle Ovitz to the present value of his remaining salary payments through September 30, 2000, a $10 million severance payment, an additional $7.5 million for each fiscal year remaining under the agreement, and the immediate vesting of the first 3 million stock options (the "A" Options). […]

The Complaint then alleges that the Old Board failed properly to inform itself about the total costs and incentives of the Ovitz Employment Agreement, especially the severance package. This is the key allegation related to this issue on appeal. Specifically, plaintiffs allege that the Board failed to realize that the contract gave Ovitz an incentive to find a way to exit the Company via a non-fault termination as soon as possible because doing so would permit him to earn more than he could by fulfilling his contract. The Complaint alleges, however, that the Old Board had been advised by a corporate compensation expert, Graef Crystal, in connection with its decision to approve the Ovitz Employment Agreement. Two public statements by Crystal form the basis of the allegation that the Old Board failed to consider the incentives and the total cost of the severance provisions, but these statements by Crystal were not made until after Ovitz left Disney in December 1996, approximately 14½ months after being hired.

The first statement, published in a December 23, 1996 article in the web-based magazine *Slate,* quoted Crystal as saying, in part, "Of course, the overall costs of the package would go up sharply in the event of Ovitz's termination (*and I wish now that I'd made a spreadsheet showing just what the deal would total if Ovitz had been fired at any time*)."[7] The second published statement appeared in an article about three weeks later in the January 13, 1997 edition of *California Law Business.* The article appears first to paraphrase Crystal: "With no one expecting failure, the sleeper clauses in Ovitz's contract seemed innocuous, Crystal says, explaining that no one added up the total cost of the severance package." The article then quotes Crystal as saying that the amount of Ovitz' severance was "shocking" and that *"[n]obody quantified this and I wish we had."*[8] One of the charging paragraphs of the Complaint concludes:

> 57. As has been conceded by Graef Crystal, the executive
> compensation consultant who advised the Old Board with respect
> to the Ovitz Employment Agreement, the Old Board *never*
> considered the costs that would be incurred by Disney in the event
> Ovitz was terminated from the Company for a reason other than
> cause prior to the natural expiration of the Ovtiz Employment
> Agreement.

Although repeated in various forms in the Complaint, these quoted admissions by Crystal constitute the extent of the factual support for the allegation that the Old Board failed properly to consider the severance elements of the agreement. This Court, however, must juxtapose these allegations with the legal presumption that the Old Board's conduct was a proper exercise of business judgment. That presumption includes the statutory protection for a board that relies in good faith on an expert advising the Board.[9] We must decide whether plaintiffs' factual allegations, if proven, would rebut that presumption. […]

Soon after Ovitz began work, problems surfaced and the situation continued to deteriorate during the first year of his employment. To support this allegation, [252] the plaintiffs cite various media reports detailing internal complaints and providing external examples of alleged business mistakes. The Complaint uses these reports to suggest that the New Board had reason to believe that Ovitz' performance and lack of commitment met the gross negligence or malfeasance standards of the termination-for-cause provisions of the contract.

The deteriorating situation, according to the Complaint, led Ovitz to begin seeking alternative employment and to send Eisner a letter in September 1996 that the Complaint paraphrases as stating his dissatisfaction with his role and expressing his desire to leave the Company.[10] The Complaint also admits that Ovitz would not actually resign before negotiating a non-fault severance agreement because he did not want to jeopardize his rights to a lucrative severance in the form of a "nonfault termination" under the terms of the 1995 Employment Agreement.

On December 11, 1996, Eisner and Ovitz agreed to arrange for Ovitz to leave Disney on the non-fault basis provided for in the 1995 Employment Agreement. Eisner then "caused" the New Board[11] "to rubber-stamp his decision (by `mutual consent')."[…]

Although the non-fault termination left Ovitz with what essentially was a very lucrative severance agreement, it is important to note that Ovitz and Disney had negotiated for that severance payment at the time they initially contracted in 1995, and in the end the payout to Ovitz did not exceed the 1995 contractual benefits. Consequently, Ovitz received the $10 million termination payment, $7.5 million for part of the fiscal year remaining under the [253] agreement and the immediate vesting of the 3 million stock options (the "A" options). […]

Pleading Requirements in Derivative Suits

Pleadings in derivative suits are governed by Chancery Rule 23.1,[19] just as pleadings alleging fraud are governed by Chancery Rule 9(b).[20] Those pleadings must comply with stringent requirements of factual particularity that differ substantially from the permissive notice pleadings governed solely by Chancery Rule 8(a).[21] Rule 23.1 is not satisfied by conclusory statements or mere notice pleading. On the other hand, the pleader is not required to plead evidence.[22] What the pleader must set forth are particularized factual statements that are essential to the claim. Such facts are sometimes referred to as "ultimate facts," "principal facts" or "elemental facts."[23] […]

Chancery Rule 23.1 requires, in part, that the plaintiff must allege with particularity facts raising a reasonable doubt that the corporate action being questioned was properly the product of [255] business judgment.[25] The rationale of Rule 23.1 is two-fold. On the one hand, it would allow a plaintiff to proceed with discovery and trial if the plaintiff complies with this rule and can articulate a reasonable basis to be entrusted with a claim that belongs to the corporation. On the other hand, the rule does not permit a stockholder to cause the corporation to expend money and resources in discovery and trial in the stockholder's quixotic pursuit of a purported corporate claim based solely on conclusions, opinions or speculation. As we stated in *Grimes v. Donald*:

> The demand requirement serves a salutary purpose. First, by requiring exhaustion of intracorporate remedies, the demand requirement invokes a species of alternative dispute resolution procedure which might avoid litigation altogether. Second, if litigation is beneficial, the corporation can control the proceedings. Third, if demand is excused or wrongfully refused, the stockholder will normally control the proceedings.
>
> The jurisprudence of *Aronson* and its progeny is designed to create a balanced environment which will: (1) on the one hand, deter costly, baseless suits by creating a screening mechanism to eliminate claims where there is only a suspicion expressed solely in conclusory terms; and (2) on the other hand, permit suit by a stockholder who is able to articulate particularized facts showing that there is a reasonable

226

doubt either that (a) a majority of the board is independent for purposes of responding to the demand, or (b) the underlying transaction is protected by the business judgment rule.[26]

Independence of the Disney Board

The test of demand futility is a two-fold test under *Aronson* and its progeny. The first prong of the futility rubric is "whether, under the particularized facts alleged, a reasonable doubt is created that... the directors are disinterested and independent."[31] The second prong is whether the pleading creates a reasonable doubt that "the challenged transaction was otherwise the product of a valid exercise of business judgment."[32] These prongs are in the disjunctive. Therefore, if either prong is satisfied, demand is excused.[33]

In this case, the issues of disinterestedness and independence involved in the first prong of *Aronson* are whether a majority of the New Board, which presumably was in office when plaintiffs filed this action, was disinterested and independent. That is, were they incapable, due to personal interest or domination and control, of objectively evaluating a demand, if made, that the Board assert the corporation's claims that are raised by plaintiffs or otherwise remedy the alleged injury?[34] This rule is premised on the principle that a claim of the corporation should be evaluated by the board of directors to determine if pursuit of the claim is in the corporation's best interests.[35] That is the analysis the Court of Chancery brought to bear on the matter,[36] and it is that analysis we now examine to the extent necessary for appropriate appellate review.

The facts supporting plaintiffs' claim that the New Board was not disinterested or independent turn on plaintiffs' central allegation that a majority of the Board was beholden to Eisner. It is not alleged that they were beholden to Ovitz. Plaintiffs' theory is that Eisner was advancing Ovitz' interests primarily because a lavish contract for Ovtiz would redound to Eisner's benefit since Eisner would thereby gain in his quest to have his own compensation increased lavishly. This theory appears to be in the nature of the old maxim that a "high tide floats all boats." But, in the end, this theory is not supported by well-pleaded facts, only conclusory allegations. Moreover, the Court of Chancery found that these allegations were illogical and counterintuitive:

Plaintiffs' allegation that Eisner was interested in maximizing his compensation at the expense of Disney and its shareholders cannot reasonably be inferred from the facts alleged in Plaintiffs' amended complaint. At all times material to this litigation, Eisner owned several million options to purchase Disney stock. Therefore, it would not be in Eisner's economic interest to cause the Company to issue millions of additional options unnecessarily and at considerable cost. Such a gesture would not, as Plaintiffs suggest, "maximize" Eisner's own compensation package. Rather, it would dilute the value of Eisner's own very substantial holdings. Even if the impact on Eisner's option value were relatively small, such a large compensation package would, and did, draw largely negative attention to Eisner's own performance and compensation. Accordingly, no reasonable doubt can exist as to Eisner's disinterest in the approval of the Employment Agreement, as a matter of law. Similarly, the Plaintiffs have not demonstrated a reasonable doubt that Eisner was disinterested in granting Ovitz a Non-Fault Termination, thus allowing Ovitz to receive substantial severance benefits under the terms of the Employment Agreement. Nothing alleged by Plaintiffs generates a reasonable inference that Eisner would benefit personally from allowing [258] Ovitz to leave Disney without good cause.[37]

The Court of Chancery held that "no reasonable doubt can exist as to Eisner's disinterest in the approval of the Employment Agreement, as a matter of law," and similarly that plaintiffs "have not demonstrated a reasonable doubt that Eisner was disinterested in granting Ovitz a Non-Fault Termination."[38] Plaintiffs challenge this conclusion, but we agree with the Court of Chancery and we affirm that holding. […]

In this case, therefore, that part of plaintiffs' Complaint raising the first prong of *Aronson,* even though not pressed by plaintiffs in this Court,[41] has been dismissed with prejudice. Our affirmance of that dismissal is final and dispositive of the first prong of *Aronson.*[42] We now turn to the primary issues in this case that implicate the second prong of *Aronson:* whether the Complaint sets forth particularized facts creating a reasonable doubt that the decisions of the Old Board and the New Board were protected by the business judgment rule.

Analytical Framework for the Informational Component of Directorial Decisionmaking

Plaintiffs claim that the Court of Chancery erred when it concluded that a board of directors is "not required to be informed of every fact, but rather is required to be reasonably informed."[43][...] Plaintiffs argue that being "reasonably informed" is too lax a standard to satisfy Delaware's legal test for the informational component of board decisions. They contend that the Disney directors on the Old Board did not avail themselves of all material information reasonably available in approving Ovitz' 1995 contract, and thereby violated their fiduciary duty of care.[45]

The "reasonably informed" language used by the Court of Chancery here may have been a short-hand attempt to paraphrase the Delaware jurisprudence that, in making business decisions, directors must consider all material information reasonably available, and that the directors' process is actionable only if grossly negligent.[46] The question is whether the trial court's formulation is consistent with our objective test of reasonableness, the test of materiality and concepts of gross negligence. We agree with the Court of Chancery that the standard for judging the informational component of the directors' decisionmaking does not mean that the Board must be informed of *every* fact. The Board is responsible for considering only *material* facts that are *reasonably available,* not those that are immaterial or out of the Board's reasonable reach.[47]

Presuit demand will be excused in a derivative suit only if the particularized facts in the complaint create a reasonable doubt that the informational component of the directors' decisionmaking process, *measured by concepts of gross negligence,* included consideration of all material information reasonably available.[48] Thus, we now apply this analytical framework to the particularized facts pleaded, juxtaposed with the presumption of regularity of the Board's process.

Plaintiffs' Contention that the Old Board Violated the Process Duty of Care in Approving the Ovitz Employment Agreement

Certainly in this case the economic exposure of the corporation to the payout scenarios of the Ovitz contract was material, particularly given its large size, for purposes of the directors' decisionmaking process.[49] And those dollar exposure [260] numbers were reasonably available because the logical inference from plaintiffs' allegations is that Crystal or the New Board could have calculated the numbers. Thus, the objective tests of reasonable availability and materiality were satisfied by this Complaint. But that is not the end of the inquiry for liability purposes.

The Court of Chancery interpreted the Complaint to allege that only Crystal (the Board's expert) — and *not the Board itself* — failed to bring to bear all the necessary information because he (Crystal) did not quantify for the Board the maximum payout to Ovitz under the non-fault termination scenario. Alternatively, the Court of Chancery reasoned that even if the Old Board failed to make the calculation, that fact does not raise a reasonable doubt of due care because *Crystal* did not consider it critical to ascertain the potential costs of Ovitz' severance package. The Court's language is as follows:

> With regard to the alleged breach of the duty of care, Plaintiffs claim
> that the directors were not properly informed before they adopted
> the Employment Agreement because they did not know the value of
> the compensation package offered to Ovitz. To that end, Plaintiffs
> offer several statements made by Graef Crystal, the financial expert
> who advised the Board on the Employment Agreement, including
> his admission that "[n]obody quantified the total cost of the
> severance package and I wish we had."

> The fact that *Crystal* did not quantify the potential severance
> benefits to Ovitz for terminating early without cause (under the
> terms of the Employment Agreement) does not create a reasonable
> inference that *the Board* failed to consider the potential cost to
> Disney in the event that they decided to terminate Ovitz without
> cause. But, even if the Board did fail to calculate the potential cost
> to Disney, I nevertheless think that this allegation fails to create a
> reasonable doubt that the former Board exercised due care. Disney's
> expert did not consider an inquiry into the potential cost of Ovitz's
> severance benefits to be critical or relevant to the Board's
> consideration of the Employment Agreement. Merely because

Crystal *now* regrets not having calculated the package is not reason enough to overturn the judgment of the Board *then*. It is the essence of the business judgment rule that a court will not apply 20/20 hindsight to second guess a board's decision, except "in rare cases [where] a transaction may be so egregious on its face that the board approval cannot meet the test of business judgment." Because the Board's reliance on Crystal and his decision not to fully calculate the amount of severance lack "egregiousness," this is not that rare case. I think it a correct statement of law that the duty of care is still fulfilled even if a Board does not know the exact amount of a severance payout but nonetheless is fully informed about the manner in which such a payout would be calculated. A board is not required to be informed of every fact, but rather is required to be reasonably informed. Here the Plaintiffs have failed to plead facts giving rise to a reasonable doubt that the Board, as a matter of law, was reasonably informed on this issue.[50]

We believe, however, that the Complaint, fairly read, charges that Crystal admitted that "nobody" — not Crystal *and* not the directors — made that calculation, although all the necessary information presumably was at hand to do so. Thus the reading given by the Court of Chancery to [261] this aspect of the amended complaint was too restrictive because the Court's reading fails to appreciate the breadth of the allegation — *i.e.,* that neither Crystal nor the Old Board made the calculations that Crystal — the expert — *now* believes he should have made. Moreover, the Court's alternative analysis that "Disney's expert did not consider an inquiry into the potential costs ... to be critical or relevant to the board's consideration" is inappropriately simplistic at the pleading stage to state a comprehensive analysis of the issue.

We regard the Court's language as harmless error, however, for the following reason. The Complaint, fairly construed, admits that the directors were advised by Crystal as an expert and that they relied on his expertise. Accordingly, the question here is whether the directors are to be "fully protected" (*i.e.,* not held liable) on the basis that they relied in good faith on a qualified expert under Section 141(e) of the Delaware General

Corporation Law.[51] The Old Board is entitled to the presumption[52] that it exercised proper business judgment, including proper reliance on the expert. […]

Although the Court of Chancery did not expressly predicate its decision on Section 141(e), Crystal is presumed to be an expert on whom the Board was entitled to rely in good faith under Section 141(e) in order to be "fully protected."[55] Plaintiffs must rebut the presumption that the directors properly exercised their business judgment, including their good faith reliance on Crystal's expertise. What Crystal *now* believes *in hindsight* that he and the Board *should have done* in 1995 does not provide that rebuttal. […]

To survive a Rule 23.1 motion to dismiss in a due care case where an expert has advised the board in its decisionmaking process, the complaint must allege particularized facts (not conclusions) that, if proved, would show, for example, that: (a) the directors did not in fact rely on the expert; (b) their reliance was not in good faith; (c) they did not reasonably believe that the expert's advice was within the expert's professional competence; (d) the expert was not selected with reasonable care by or on behalf of the corporation, and the faulty selection process was attributable to the directors; (e) the subject matter (in this case the cost calculation) that was material and reasonably available was so obvious that the board's failure to consider it was grossly negligent regardless of the expert's advice or lack of advice; or (f) that the decision of the Board was so unconscionable as to constitute waste or fraud.[56] This Complaint includes no particular allegations of this nature, and therefore it was subject to dismissal as drafted.[57]

Conclusion

One can understand why Disney stockholders would be upset with such an extraordinarily lucrative compensation agreement and termination payout awarded a company president who served for only a little over a year and who underperformed to the extent alleged. That said, there is a very large — though not insurmountable — burden on stockholders who believe they should pursue the remedy of a derivative suit instead of selling their stock or seeking to reform or oust these directors from office.

Delaware has pleading rules and an extensive judicial gloss on those rules that must be met in order for a stockholder to pursue the derivative remedy. Sound policy supports these rules, as we have noted. This Complaint, which is a blunderbuss of a mostly conclusory pleading, does not meet that burden, and it was properly dismissed.

3.2.7 In Re The Goldman Sachs Group, Inc. Shareholder Litigation

In the case that follows, the Chancery Court considers the defendant's Rule 23.1 motion to dismiss. In a 23.1 motion, the defendant argues that the complaint should be dismissed for lack of standing. The defendant argues that the plaintiff lacks standing because it did not comply with the requirements of 23.1, typically failure to make demand when demand is not futile.

As is required in such cases, the court reviews the interestedness and independence of each director in order to determine whether demand was futile. Remember, in making a ruling on a 23.1 motion to dismiss, the court must go through the exercise of assessing each director's interestedness and independence pursuant to either *Aronson* or *Rales* and not the underlying merits of the claim. In this particular case, the court applies both *Aronson* and *Rales* to each of the directors on the Goldman Sachs board.

IN RE THE GOLDMAN SACHS GROUP, INC. SHAREHOLDER LITIGATION.
(Del. Ch. 2011)

GLASSCOCK, Vice Chancellor.

The Delaware General Corporation Law is, for the most part, enabling in nature. It provides corporate directors and officers with broad discretion to act as they find appropriate in the conduct of corporate affairs. It is therefore left to Delaware case law to set a boundary on that otherwise unconstrained realm of action. The restrictions imposed by Delaware case law set this boundary by requiring corporate officers and directors to act as faithful fiduciaries to the corporation and its stockholders. Should these corporate actors perform in such a way that they are violating their fiduciary obligations—their core duties of care or loyalty—their faithless acts properly become the subject of judicial action in vindication of the rights of the stockholders. Within the boundary of fiduciary duty, however, these corporate actors are free to pursue corporate opportunities in any way that, in the exercise of their business judgment on behalf of the corporation, they see fit. It is this broad freedom to pursue opportunity on behalf of the corporation, in the myriad ways that may be revealed to creative human minds, that has made the corporate structure a supremely effective engine for the production of wealth. Exercising that freedom is precisely what directors and officers are elected by their shareholders to do. So long as such individuals act within the boundaries of their fiduciary duties, judges are ill-suited by training (and should be disinclined by temperament) to second-guess the business decisions of those chosen by the stockholders to fulfill precisely that function. This case, as in so many corporate matters considered by this Court, involves whether actions taken by certain director defendants fall outside of the fiduciary boundaries existing under Delaware case law—and are therefore subject to judicial oversight—or whether the acts complained of are within those broad boundaries, where a law-trained judge should refrain from acting.

This matter is before me on a motion to dismiss, pursuant to Court of Chancery Rule 23.1, for failure to make a pre-suit demand upon the board, and Court of Chancery Rule 12(b)(6) for failure to state a claim. The Plaintiffs contend that Goldman's compensation structure created a divergence of interest between Goldman's management and its stockholders. The Plaintiffs allege that because Goldman's directors have consistently based compensation for the firm's management on a percentage of net revenue, Goldman's employees had a motivation to grow net revenue at any cost and without regard to risk.

The Plaintiffs allege that under this compensation structure, Goldman's employees would attempt to maximize short-term profits, thus increasing their bonuses at the expense of stockholders' interests. The Plaintiffs contend that Goldman's employees would do this by engaging in highly risky trading practices and by over-leveraging the company's assets. If these practices turned a profit, Goldman's employees would receive a windfall; however, losses would fall on the stockholders.

The Plaintiffs allege that the Director Defendants breached their fiduciary duties by approving the compensation structure discussed above. […]

I. FACTS

Defendant Goldman is a global financial services firm which provides investment banking, securities, and investment management services to consumers, businesses, and governments. Goldman is a Delaware corporation with its principal executive offices in New York, NY.

The complaint also names fourteen individual current and former directors and officers of Goldman as defendants: Lloyd C. Blankfein, Gary D. Cohn, John H. Bryan, Claes Dahlback, Stephen Friedman, William W. George, Rajat K. Gupta, James A. Johnson, Lois D. Juliber, Lakshmi N. Mittal, James J. Schiro, Ruth J. Simmons, David A. Viniar, and J. Michael Evans (together with Goldman, "the Defendants"). […]

B. Background

Goldman engages in three principal business segments: investment banking, asset management and securities services, and trading and principal investments. The majority of Goldman's revenue comes from the trading and principal investment segment.[2] In that segment Goldman engages in market making, structuring and entering into a variety of derivative transactions, and the proprietary trading of financial instruments.[3] […]

As the revenue generated by the trading and principal investment segment grew, so did the trading department's stature within Goldman. The traders "became wealthier and more powerful in the bank."[9] The Plaintiffs allege that the compensation for these traders was not based on performance and was unjustifiable because Goldman was doing "nothing more than compensat[ing] employees for results produced by the vast amounts of shareholder equity that Goldman ha[d] available to be deployed."[10]

C. Compensation

Goldman employed a "pay for performance" philosophy linking the total compensation of its employees to the company's performance.[11] Goldman has used a Compensation Committee since at least 2006 to oversee the development and implementation of its compensation scheme.[12] The Compensation Committee was responsible for reviewing and approving the Goldman executives' annual compensation.[13] To fulfill their charge, the Compensation Committee consulted with senior management about management's projections of net revenues and the proper ratio of compensation and benefits expenses to net revenues (the "compensation ratio").[14] Additionally, the Compensation Committee compared Goldman's compensation ratio to that of Goldman's competitors such as Bear Stearns, Lehman Brothers, Merrill Lynch, and Morgan Stanley. The

Compensation Committee would then approve a ratio and structure that Goldman would use to govern Goldman's compensation to its employees.[15]

The Plaintiffs allege that from 2007 through 2009, the Director Defendants approved a management-proposed compensation structure that caused management's interests to diverge from those of the stockholders.[16] According to the Plaintiffs, in each year since 2006 the Compensation Committee approved the management-determined compensation ratio, which governed "the total amount of funds available to compensate all employees including senior executives," without any analysis.[17] Although the total compensation paid by Goldman varied significantly each year, total compensation as a percentage of net revenue remained relatively constant.[18] Because management was awarded a relatively constant percentage of total revenue, management could maximize their compensation by increasing Goldman's total net revenue and total stockholder equity.[19] The Plaintiffs contend that this compensation structure led management to pursue a highly risky business strategy that emphasized short term profits in order to increase their yearly bonuses.[20]

D. Business Risk

The Plaintiffs allege that management achieved Goldman's growth "through extreme leverage and significant uncontrolled exposure to risky loans and credit risks."[21] The trading and principal investment segment is the largest contributor to Goldman's total revenues; it is also the segment to which Goldman commits the largest amount of capital.[22] The Plaintiffs argue that this was a risky use of Goldman's assets, pointing out that Goldman's Value at Risk (VAR) increased between 2007 and 2009, and that in 2007 Goldman had a leverage ratio of 25 to 1, exceeding that of its peers.[23]

The Plaintiffs charge that this business strategy was not in the best interest of the stockholders, in part, because the stockholders did not benefit to the same degree that management did. Stockholders received roughly 2% of the revenue generated in the form of dividends—but if the investment went south, it was the stockholders' equity at risk, not that of the traders. […]

E. The Plaintiffs' Claims

The Plaintiffs allege that the Director Defendants breached their fiduciary duties by (1) failing to properly analyze and rationally set compensation levels for Goldman's employees and (2) committing waste by "approving a compensation ratio to Goldman employees in an amount so disproportionately large to the contribution of management, as opposed to capital as to be unconscionable."[50]

The Plaintiffs also allege that the Director Defendants violated their fiduciary duties by failing to adequately monitor Goldman's operations and by "allowing the Firm to manage and conduct the Firm's trading in a grossly unethical manner."[51]

II. LEGAL STANDARDS

The Plaintiffs have brought this action derivatively on behalf of Goldman "to redress the breaches of fiduciary duty and other violations of law by [the] Defendants."[52] The Defendants have moved to dismiss, pursuant to Court of Chancery Rule 23.1, for failure to make a pre-suit demand upon the board. […]

B. Rule 23.1

"[T]he pleading burden imposed by Rule 23.1 . . . is more onerous than that demanded by Rule 12(b)(6)."[57] Though a complaint may plead a "conceivable" allegation that would survive a motion to dismiss under Rule 12(b)(6), "vague allegations are . . . insufficient to withstand a motion to dismiss pursuant to Rule 23.1."[58] This difference reflects the divergent reasons for the two rules: Rule 12(b)(6) is designed to ensure a decision on the merits of any potentially valid claim, excluding only clearly meritless claims; Rule 23.1 is designed to vindicate the authority of the corporate board, except in those cases where the board will not or (because of conflicts) cannot exercise its judgment in the interest of the corporation. Rule 23.1 requires that "a plaintiff shareholder . . . make a demand upon the corporation's current board to pursue derivative claims owned by the corporation before a shareholder is permitted to pursue legal action on the corporation's behalf."[59] Demand is required because "[t]he decision whether to initiate or pursue a lawsuit on behalf of the corporation is generally within the power and responsibility of the board of directors."[60] Accordingly, the complaint must allege "with particularity the efforts, if any, made by the plaintiff to obtain the action the plaintiff desires from the directors or comparable authority and the reasons for the plaintiff's failure to obtain the action or for not making the effort."[61]

C. Demand Futility

If, as here, a stockholder does not first demand that the directors pursue the alleged cause of action, he must establish that demand is excused by satisfying "stringent [pleading] requirements of factual particularity" by "set[ting] forth particularized factual statements that are essential to the claim" in order to demonstrate that making demand would be futile.[62] Pre-suit demand is futile if a corporation's board is "deemed incapable of making an impartial decision regarding the pursuit of the litigation."[63]

Under the two-pronged test, first explicated in *Aronson,* when a plaintiff challenges a conscious decision of the board, a plaintiff can show demand futility by alleging particularized facts that create a reasonable doubt that either (1) the directors are disinterested and independent or (2) "the challenged transaction was otherwise the product of a valid exercise of business judgment."[64]

On the other hand, when a plaintiff complains of board *inaction,* "there is no `challenged transaction,' and the ordinary *Aronson* analysis does not apply."[65] Instead, the board's inaction is analyzed under *Rales v. Blasband.*[66] Under the *Rales* test, a plaintiff must plead particularized facts that "create a reasonable doubt that, as of the time the complaint [was] filed, the board of directors could have properly exercised its independent and disinterested business judgment in responding to a demand."[67]

Here, the Plaintiffs concede that they have not made demand upon Goldman's board of directors, but they assert that such demand would be futile for numerous reasons. First, they argue that Goldman's board of directors is interested or lacks independence because of financial ties between the Director Defendants and Goldman.[68] Next, they allege that there is a reasonable doubt as to whether the board's compensation structure was the product of a valid exercise of business judgment.**[69] The Plaintiffs further assert that there is a substantial likelihood that the Director Defendants will face personal liability for the dereliction of their duty to oversee Goldman's operations.*[70]

I evaluate the Plaintiffs' claims involving active decisions by the board under *Aronson*. I evaluate the Plaintiffs' oversight claims against the Director Defendants for the failure to monitor Goldman's operations under *Rales*.

III. ANALYSIS

A. Approval of the Compensation Scheme

The Plaintiffs challenge the Goldman board's approval of the company's compensation scheme on three grounds. They allege (1) that the majority of the board was interested or lacked independence when it approved the compensation scheme, (2) the board did not otherwise validly exercise its business judgment, and (3) the board's approval of the compensation scheme constituted waste. Because the approval of the compensation scheme was a conscious decision by the board, the Plaintiffs must satisfy the *Aronson* test to successfully plead demand futility. I find that under all three of their challenges to the board's approval of the compensation scheme, the Plaintiffs have failed to adequately plead demand futility.

1. Independence and Disinterestedness of the Board

A plaintiff successfully pleads demand futility under the first prong of *Aronson* when he alleges particularized facts that create a reasonable doubt that "a `majority' of the directors could [have] impartially consider[ed] a demand" either because they were interested or lacked independence, as of the time that suit was filed.[71] Generally, "[a] director's interest may be shown by demonstrating a potential personal benefit or detriment to the director as a result of the decision."[72] A director is independent if the "director's decision is based on the corporate merits of the subject before the board rather than extraneous considerations or influences."[73]

When the complaint was originally filed, Goldman's board had 12 directors: Blankfein, Cohn, Bryan, Dahlback, Friedman, George, Gupta, Johnson, Juliber, Mittal, Schiro, and Simmons.[74] The Plaintiffs fail to allege that George and Schiro were interested or lacked independence. It can be assumed that Blankfein and Cohn, as officials of Goldman, would be found to be interested or lack independence. Therefore, the Plaintiffs must satisfy *Aronson* with respect to at least four of the remaining eight directors.[75]

The Plaintiffs argue that demand is excused because a majority of the Director Defendants lacked independence or were interested as a result of significant financial relationships with Goldman. The Plaintiffs contend that directors Bryan, Friedman, Gupta, Johnson, Juliber, and Simmons were interested because the private Goldman Sachs Foundation ("the Goldman Foundation") has made contributions to charitable organizations that the directors were affiliated with.[76] The Plaintiffs assert that directors Dahlback, Friedman, and Mittal were interested because of financial interactions with Goldman.

Below I provide the specific allegations found in the complaint about the Director Defendants. Since the Plaintiffs do not allege that the Director Defendants (aside from Blankfein and Cohn) were interested in the compensation decisions, I analyze whether the director lacks independence.

a. Directors and Charitable Contributions.

i. John H. Bryan

Bryan has served as a Goldman director since 1999.[77] He was also a member of Goldman's Audit Committee and Goldman's Compensation Committee.[78] His charitable works included chairing a successful campaign to raise $100 million for the renovation of the Chicago Lyric Opera House and Orchestra Hall, and acting as a life trustee of the University of Chicago.[79] The Plaintiffs state that part of Bryan's responsibility, as a trustee, was to raise money for the University. The Plaintiffs note that Goldman has made "substantial contributions"[80] to the campaign to renovate the Chicago Lyric Opera House and Orchestra Hall and that the Goldman Foundation donated $200,000 to the University in 2006 and allocated an additional $200,000 in 2007.[81]

The Plaintiffs allege that because Goldman and the Goldman Foundation have assisted Bryan in his fund raising responsibilities, Bryan lacks independence.[82]

This Court has previously addressed directorial independence and charitable contributions. *Hallmark*[83] involved a special committee member who served on a variety of charitable boards where the charity received donations from the defendant corporation. The *Hallmark* Court noted that, even though part of the member's role was to act as a fund raiser, the member did not receive a salary for his work and did not actively solicit donations from the defendant corporation; therefore, the plaintiff failed to sufficiently show that the member was incapable of "exercising independent judgment."[84]

This Court also addressed charitable contributions in *J.P. Morgan*.[85] In that case, the plaintiff challenged the independence of a director who was the President and a trustee of the American Natural History Museum, another director who was a trustee of the American Natural History Museum, and a director who was the President and CEO of the United Negro College Fund.[86] The plaintiff alleged that because the defendant corporation made donations to these organizations and was a significant benefactor, the directors lacked independence.[87] The Court decided that without additional facts showing, for instance, how the donations would affect the decision making of the directors or what percentage of the overall contribution was represented by the corporation's donations, the plaintiff had failed to demonstrate that the directors were not independent.[88]

In the case at bar, nothing more can be inferred from the complaint than the facts that the Goldman Foundation made donations to a charity that Bryan served as trustee, that part of Bryan's role as a trustee was to raise money, and that Goldman made donations to another charity where Bryan chaired a renovation campaign. The Plaintiffs do not allege that Bryan received a salary for either of his philanthropic roles, that the donations made by the Goldman Foundation or Goldman were the result of active solicitation by Bryan, or that Bryan had other substantial dealings with Goldman or the Goldman Foundation. The Plaintiffs do not provide the ratios of the amounts donated by Goldman, or the Goldman Foundation, to overall donations, or any other information demonstrating that the amount would be material to the charity. Crucially, the Plaintiffs fail to provide any information on how the amounts given influenced Bryan's decision-making process.[89] Because the complaint lacks such particularized details, the Plaintiffs have failed to create a reasonable doubt as to Bryan's independence.

ii. Rajat K. Gupta

Gupta has served as a Goldman director since 2006.[90] He was also a member of Goldman's Audit Committee and Goldman's Compensation Committee.[91] Gupta is chairman of the board of the Indian School of Business, to which the Goldman Foundation has donated $1.6 million since 2002.[92] Gupta is also a member of the dean's advisory board of Tsinghua University School of Economics and Management, to which the Foundation has donated at least $3.5 million since 2002.[93] Finally, Gupta is a member of the United Nations Commission on the Private Sector and Development and he is a special advisor to the UN Secretary General on UN Reform.[94] Since 2002, the Foundation has donated around $1.6 million to the Model UN program.[95] The Plaintiffs allege that as "a member of these boards and commission, it is part of Gupta's job to raise money."[96]

The Plaintiffs challenge to Gupta's independence fails for reasons similar to Bryan's. The Plaintiffs allegations only provide information that shows that Gupta was engaged in philanthropic activities and that the Goldman foundation made donations to charities to which Gupta had ties. The Plaintiffs do not mention the materiality of the donations to the charities or any solicitation on the part of Gupta. The Plaintiffs do not state how Gupta's decision-making was altered by the donations. Without such particularized allegations, the Plaintiffs fail to raise a reasonable doubt that Gupta was independent.

iii. James A. Johnson

Again the Plaintiffs fail to provide any information other than that a director was affiliated with a charity and the Goldman Foundation made a donation to that charity. Without more, the Plaintiffs fail to provide particularized factual allegations that create a reasonable doubt in regards to Johnson's independence.

iv. Lois D. Juliber

For the same reasons that the Plaintiffs' allegations fall short for directors Bryan, Gupta, and Johnson, the Plaintiffs' allegations fall short here. The Plaintiffs do not plead facts sufficient to create a reasonable doubt whether Juliber was independent.

v. Ruth J. Simmons

Simmons has served as a Goldman director since 2000.[105] She was also a member of Goldman's Compensation Committee.[106] Simmons is President of Brown University, and the Plaintiffs allege that part of her job is to raise money for the University.[107] The Plaintiffs note that "[t]he [Goldman] Foundation has pledged funding in an undisclosed amount to share in the support of a position of Program Director at The Swearer Center for Public Service at Brown University," and so far $200,000 has been allocated to this project.[108]

Simmons differs from the other directors in that, rather than sitting on a charitable board, as the other defendants do, Simmons livelihood as President of Brown University does directly depend on her fundraising abilities;[109] however, the Plaintiffs fail to allege particularized factual allegations that create a reasonable doubt that Simmons was independent.

The Plaintiffs provide the amount donated to Brown University, but do not give any additional information showing the materiality of the donation to Brown University. The Plaintiffs do not provide the percentage this amount represented of the total amount raised by Brown, or even how this amount was material to the Swearer Center. Additionally, the Plaintiffs' allegations do not provide information that Simmons actively solicited this amount or how this or potential future donations would affect Simmons. The facts pled are insufficient to raise the inference that Simmons feels obligated to the foundation or Goldman management. Consequently, the factual allegations pled by the Plaintiffs fail to raise a reasonable doubt that, despite Simmons's position as President of Brown University, she remained independent.

b. Directors with Other Alleged Interests.

The Plaintiffs allege that three directors have, in addition (in the case of Mr. Friedman) to charitable connections to Goldman or the Goldman Foundation, business dealings with Goldman that render them dependent for purposes of the first prong of the *Aronson* analysis. Having already found that a majority of the Goldman board was independent, I could simply omit analysis of the independence of these directors under *Aronson*. I will briefly address the Plaintiffs contentions with respect to the directors below.

i. Stephen Friedman

The Plaintiffs allege that Friedman lacks independence for two reasons. First, the Plaintiffs allege that Friedman is not independent because of his philanthropic work and Goldman's advancement thereof. Second, the Plaintiffs allege that Friedman is not independent due to his business dealings with Goldman.

Taken by themselves, the facts pled, concerning Friedman's charitable connection to the Goldman Foundation, are insufficient to create a reasonable doubt that Friedman was independent. […]

Besides their allegations concerning Friedman's charitable endeavors, the Plaintiffs also allege that Goldman "*has* invested at least $670 million in funds managed by Friedman."[114] This is the entirety of the pleadings regarding Friedman's business involvement with Goldman. Contrary to the contentions in the Plaintiffs' Answering Brief, the complaint does not allege that Friedman relies on the management of these funds for his livelihood; that contention, if buttressed by factual allegations in the complaint, might reasonably demonstrate lack of independence. The complaint is insufficient, as written, for that purpose.

ii. Claes Dahlback

Besides serving on Goldman's board, Dahlback is a senior advisor to an entity described in the complaint as "Investor AB."[117] The Plaintiffs note that Goldman has invested more than $600 million in funds to which Dahlback is an adviser (presumably, but not explicitly, Investor AB).[118] The Plaintiffs contend that because Dahlback had substantial financial relationships with Goldman, he lacked independence.

The Plaintiffs' allegations regarding Dahlback are sparse and tenuous. "[T]he complaint contains no allegations of fact tending to show that [any] fees paid were material to [Dahlback]."[119] The Plaintiffs only note that Dahlback is an advisor to Investor AB, and that Goldman has invested more than $600 million in funds with an entity to which Dahlback is an advisor. Contrary to the statements by the Plaintiffs in the answering brief, the complaint does not allege that Dahlback's "livelihood depends on his full-time job as an advisor." The Plaintiffs fail to allege that Dahlback derives a substantial benefit from being an advisor to Investor AB, that Dahlback solicited funds from Goldman, that Investor AB received funds because of Dahlback's involvement, or any other fact that would tend to raise a reasonable doubt that Dahlback's future employment with Investor AB is independent of Goldman's investment. As with defendant Friedman, the pleadings are insufficient to raise a reasonable doubt as to Dahlback's independence.

iii. Lakshmi N. Mittal

Mittal is the chairman and CEO of ArcelorMittal.[122] The Plaintiffs allege that "Goldman has arranged or provided billions of euros in financing to his company" and that "[d]uring 2007 and 2008 alone, the Company had made loans to AcelorMittal [sic] in the aggregate amount of 464 million euros."[123]

Goldman is an investment bank. The fact "[t]hat it provided financing to large . . . companies should come as no shock to anyone. Yet this is all that the plaintiffs allege."[124] The Plaintiffs fail to plead facts that show anything other than a series of market transactions occurred between ArcelorMittal and Goldman. For instance, the Plaintiffs have not alleged that ArcelorMittal is receiving a discounted interest rate on the loans from Goldman, that Mittal was unable to receive financing from any other lender, or that loans from Goldman compose a substantial part of ArcelorMittal's funding.[125] The pleadings fail to raise a reasonable doubt as to the independence of Mittal.

B. Otherwise the Product of a Valid Exercise of Business Judgment

Having determined that the Plaintiffs have not pled particularized factual allegations that raise a reasonable doubt as to a majority of the Director Defendants' disinterestedness and independence, I must now apply the second prong of *Aronson* and determine whether the Plaintiffs have pled particularized facts that raise a reasonable doubt that Goldman's compensation scheme was otherwise the product of a valid exercise of business judgment.[126] To successfully plead demand futility under the second prong of *Aronson,* the Plaintiffs must allege "particularized facts sufficient to raise (1) a reason to doubt that the action was taken honestly and in good faith or (2) a reason to doubt that the board was adequately informed in making the decision."[...]

The Plaintiffs' main contention is that Goldman's compensation scheme itself was approved in bad faith. The Plaintiffs allege that "[n]o person acting in good faith on behalf of Goldman consistently could approve the payment of between 44% and 48% of net revenues to Goldman's employees year in and year out"[...]

The decision as to how much compensation is appropriate to retain and incentivize employees, both individually and in the aggregate, is a core function of a board of directors exercising its business judgment. The Plaintiffs' pleadings fall short of creating a reasonable doubt that the Directors Defendants have failed to exercise that judgment here. The Plaintiffs acknowledge that the compensation plan authorized by Goldman's board, which links compensation to revenue produced, was intended to align employee interests with those of the stockholders and incentivize the production of wealth. To an extent, it does so: extra effort by employees to raise corporate revenue, if successful, is rewarded. The Plaintiffs' allegations mainly propose that the compensation scheme implemented by the board does not perfectly align these interests; and that, in fact, it may encourage employee behavior incongruent with the stockholders' interest. This may be correct, but it is irrelevant. The fact that the Plaintiffs may desire a different compensation scheme does not indicate that equitable relief is warranted. Such changes may be accomplished through directorial elections, but not, absent a showing unmet here, through this Court.

The Plaintiffs argue that there was an intentional dereliction of duty or a conscious disregard by the Director Defendants in setting compensation levels; however, the Plaintiffs fail to plead with particularity that any of the Director Defendants had the scienter necessary to give rise to a violation of the duty of loyalty.[140] The Plaintiffs do not allege that the board failed to employ a metric to set compensation levels; rather, they merely argue that a different metric, such as comparing Goldman's compensation to that of hedge fund managers rather than to compensation at other investment banks, would have yielded a better result.[141] But this observance does not make the board's decision self-evidently wrong, and it does not raise a reasonable doubt that the board approved Goldman's compensation structure in good faith.

2. Adequately Informed

The Plaintiffs also contend that the board was uninformed in making its compensation decision. "Pre-suit demand will be excused in a derivative suit only if the . . . particularized facts in the complaint create a reasonable doubt that the informational component of the directors' decisionmaking process, *measured by concepts of gross negligence*, included consideration of all material information reasonably available."[142] Here, Goldman's charter has a 8 *Del. C.* § 102(b)(7) provision, so gross negligence, by itself, is insufficient basis upon which to impose liability. The Plaintiffs must allege particularized facts creating a reasonable doubt that the directors acted in good faith.

Rather than suggesting that the Director Defendants acted on an uninformed basis, the Plaintiffs' pleadings indicate that the board adequately informed itself before making a decision on compensation. The Director Defendants considered other investment bank comparables, varied the total percent and the total dollar amount awarded as compensation, and changed the total amount of compensation in response to changing public opinion.[150] None of the Plaintiffs' allegations suggests gross negligence on the part of the Director Defendants, and the conduct described in the Plaintiffs' allegations certainly does not rise to the level of bad faith such that the Director Defendants would lose the protection of an 8 *Del. C.* § 102(b)(7) exculpatory provision.

At most, the Plaintiffs' allegations suggest that there were other metrics not considered by the board that might have produced better results. The business judgment rule, however, only requires the board to *reasonably* inform itself; it does not require perfection or the consideration of every conceivable alternative.[151] The factual allegations pled by the Plaintiffs, therefore, do not raise a reasonable doubt that the board was informed when it approved Goldman's compensation scheme.

D. The Plaintiffs' Caremark Claim

In addition to the claims addressed above, the Plaintiffs assert that the board breached its duty to monitor the company as required under *Caremark*.[170] Because this claim attacks a failure to act, rather than a specific transaction, the *Rales* standard applies.[171] The *Rales* standard addresses whether the "board that would be addressing the demand can impartially consider its merits without being influenced by improper considerations."[172] To properly plead demand futility under *Rales,* a plaintiff must allege particularized facts which create a reasonable doubt that "the board of directors could have properly exercised its independent and disinterested business judgment in responding to a demand."[173]

"Under *Rales,* defendant directors who face a *substantial* likelihood of personal liability are deemed interested in the transaction and thus cannot make an impartial decision."[174] A simple allegation of potential directorial liability is insufficient to excuse demand, else the demand requirement itself would be rendered toothless, and directorial control over corporate litigation would be lost. The likelihood of directors' liability is significantly lessened where, as here, the corporate charter exculpates the directors from liability to the extent authorized by 8 *Del. C.* § 102(b)(7).[175] Because Goldman's charter contains such a provision, shielding directors from liability for breaches of the duty of care (absent bad faith) "a serious threat of liability may only be found to exist if the plaintiff pleads a *non-exculpated* claim against the directors based on particularized facts."[176] This means that "plaintiffs must plead particularized facts showing bad faith in order to establish a substantial likelihood of personal directorial liability."[177]

The Plaintiffs' contentions that the Director Defendants face a substantial likelihood of personal liability are based on oversight liability, as articulated by then-Chancellor Allen in *Caremark.* In *Caremark,* Chancellor Allen held that a company's board of directors could not "satisfy [its] obligation to be reasonably informed . . . without assuring [itself] that information and reporting systems exist[ed] in the organization."[178] These systems are needed to provide the board with accurate information so that the board may reach "informed judgments concerning both the corporation's compliance with law and its business performance."[179] A breach of oversight responsibilities is a breach of the duty of loyalty, and thus not exculpated under section 102(b)(7).

To face a substantial likelihood of oversight liability for a *Caremark* claim, the Director Defendants must have "(a) . . . utterly failed to implement any reporting or information system or controls" (which the Plaintiffs concede is not the case here); "*or* (b) having implemented such a system or controls, consciously failed to monitor or oversee its operations thus disabling themselves from being informed of risks or problems requiring their attention."[180] Furthermore, "where a claim of directorial liability for corporate loss is predicated upon ignorance of liability creating activities within the corporation . . . only a sustained or systematic failure of the board to exercise oversight—such as an utter failure to attempt to assure a reasonable information and reporting system [exists] —will establish the lack of good faith that is a necessary condition to liability."[181]

The Plaintiffs specifically contend that the Director Defendants created a compensation structure that caused management's interests to diverge from the stockholders' interests. As a result, management took risks which eventually led to unethical behavior and illegal conduct that exposed Goldman to financial liability. According to the Plaintiffs, after the Director Defendants created Goldman's compensation structure, they had a duty to ensure protection from abuses by management, which were allegedly made more likely due to the form of that structure. Instead of overseeing management, however, the Director Defendants abdicated their oversight responsibilities.[182]

Unlike the original and most subsequent *Caremark* claims, where plaintiffs alleged that liability was predicated on a failure to oversee corporate conduct leading to violations of law,[183] the Plaintiffs here argue that the Director Defendants are also liable for oversight failure relating to Goldman's business performance.[184][...]

Part of the Plaintiffs' *Caremark* claim stems from the Director Defendants' oversight of Goldman's business practices. As a preliminary matter, this Court has not definitively stated whether a board's *Caremark* duties include a duty to monitor business risk. In *Citigroup,* then-Chancellor Chandler posited that "it may be possible for a plaintiff to meet the burden under some set of facts."[208] Indeed, the *Caremark* court seemed to suggest the possibility of such a claim:

> [I]t would . . . be a mistake to conclude that . . . corporate boards may satisfy their obligation to be reasonably informed concerning the corporation without assuring themselves that information and reporting systems exist in the organization that are reasonably designed to provide to senior management and to the board itself timely, accurate information sufficient to allow management and the board, each within its scope, to reach informed judgments concerning both the corporation's compliance with law *and its business performance.*[209]

As was the case in *Citigroup,* however, the facts pled here do not give rise to a claim under *Caremark,* and thus I do not need to reach the issue of whether the duty of oversight includes the duty to monitor business risk.

As the Court observed in *Citigroup,* "imposing *Caremark*-type duties on directors to monitor business risk is fundamentally different" from imposing on directors a duty to monitor fraud and illegal activity.[210] Risk is "the chance that a return on an investment will be different than expected."[211] Consistent with this, "a company or investor that is willing to take on more risk can earn a higher return."[212] The manner in which a company "evaluate[s] the trade-off between risk and return" is "[t]he essence of . . . business judgment."[213] The Plaintiffs here allege that Goldman was over-leveraged, engaged in risky business practices, and did not set enough money aside for future losses.[214] As a result, the Plaintiffs assert, Goldman was undercapitalized, forcing it to become a bank holding company and to take on an onerous loan from Warren Buffet.[215]

Although the Plaintiffs have molded their claims with an eye to the language of *Caremark,* the essence of their complaint is that I should hold the Director Defendants "personally liable for making (or allowing to be made) business decisions that, in hindsight, turned out poorly for the Company."[216] If an actionable duty to monitor business risk exists, it cannot encompass any substantive evaluation by a court of a board's determination of the appropriate amount of risk. Such decisions plainly involve business judgment.[217]

The Plaintiffs' remaining allegations in essence seek to hold the Director Defendants "personally liable to the Company because they failed to fully recognize the risk posed by subprime securities."[218] The Plaintiffs charge that the entire board was aware of, or should have been aware of, "the details of the trading business of Goldman and failed to take appropriate action."[219] The Plaintiffs note that "[a]s the housing market began to fracture in early 2007, a committee of senior Goldman executives . . . including Defendants Viniar, Cohn, and Blankfein and those helping to manage Goldman's mortgage, credit and legal operations, took an active role in overseeing the mortgage unit."[220] "[This] committee's job was to vet potential new products and transactions, being wary of deals that exposed Goldman to too much risk."[221] This committee eventually decided that housing prices would decline and decided to take a short position in the mortgage market.[222] The Plaintiffs contend that the Director Defendants were "fully aware of the extent of Goldman's RMBS and CDO securities market activities."[223] The Plaintiffs point out that the Director Defendants were informed about the business decisions Goldman made during the year including an "intensive effort to not only reduce its mortgage risk exposure, but profit from high risk RMBS and CDO Securities incurring losses."[224] The Plaintiffs further allege that because of this the Director Defendants "understood that these efforts involved very large amounts of Goldman's capital that exceeded the Company's Value-at-Risk measures."[225] Finally, the Plaintiffs allege that the practices allowed by the board, including transactions in which Goldman's risk was hedged, imposed reputational risk upon the corporation.[226]

Thus, the Plaintiffs do not plead with particularity anything that suggests that the Director Defendants acted in bad faith or otherwise consciously disregarded their *oversight* responsibilities in regards to Goldman's business risk. Goldman had an Audit Committee in place that was "charged with assisting the Board in its oversight of the Company's management of market, credit liquidity and other financial and operational risks."[227] The Director Defendants exercised their business judgment in choosing and implementing a risk management system that they presumably believed would keep them reasonably informed of the company's business risks. As described in detail above, the Plaintiffs admit that the Director Defendants were "fully aware of the extent of Goldman's RMBS and CDO securities market activities."[228] [...]

Goldman's board and management made decisions to hedge exposure during the deterioration of the housing market, decisions that have been roundly criticized in Congress and elsewhere. Those decisions involved taking objectively large risks, including particularly reputational risks. The outcome of that risk-taking may prove ultimately costly to the corporation. The Plaintiffs, however, have failed to plead with particularity that the Director Defendants consciously and in bad faith disregarded these risks; to the contrary, the facts pled indicate that the board kept itself informed of the risks involved. The Plaintiffs have failed to plead facts showing a substantial likelihood of liability on the part of the Director Defendants.

IV. CONCLUSION

The Delaware General Corporation law affords directors and officers broad discretion to exercise their business judgment in the fulfillment of their obligations to the corporation. Consequently, Delaware's case law imposes fiduciary duties on directors and officers to ensure their loyalty and care toward the corporation. When an individual breaches these duties, it is the proper function of this Court to step in and enforce those fiduciary obligations.

Here, the Plaintiffs [...]have failed to allege facts sufficient to demonstrate that the directors were unable to properly exercise this judgment in deciding whether to bring these claims. Since the Plaintiffs have failed to make a demand upon the Corporation, this matter must be dismissed; therefore, I need not reach the Defendant's motion to dismiss under Rule 12 (b)(6).

For the foregoing reasons, the Defendants' motion to dismiss is granted, and the Plaintiffs' claims are dismissed with prejudice.

3.3 Special Litigation Committees

In situations where demand is futile, stockholders can file derivative litigation without making demand. Does that mean that boards have forever lost control over the derivative litigation? In some circumstances the answer is no.

The following cases lay out the doctrine with respect to how a board can retake control over derivative litigation in later stages of litigation. The board through an independent committee, often known as a special litigation committee, may file a pretrial motion to retake control and then dismiss the derivative litigation. The Special Committee must be prepared to meet the burden under Rule 56 (Summary Judgment) that there is no genuine issue as to any material fact and that the moving party is entitled to dismiss as a matter of law.

Remember, unlike in the case of demand and demand futility, at this stage of the litigation, boards bear the burden of proving that notwithstanding the fact that demand was previously futile, the board is now in a position to fairly consider the facts of the complaint. As you will see, this is a heavy burden for a board to bear.

3.3.1 Zapata v. Maldonado

Zapata is the leading case on the legal standard a court will apply to a special litigation committee's motion to take control over derivative litigation following following the 23.1 motion to dismiss and prior to going to trial. Look at the facts related to the interestedness and independence of directors on the special litigation committee. Consider whether under these same facts demand would have been deemed futile with respect to these directors at the 23.1 motion to dismiss stage.

430 A.2d 779 (1981)
ZAPATA CORPORATION v. William MALDONADO

QUILLEN, Justice:

In June, 1975, William Maldonado, a stockholder of Zapata, instituted a derivative action in the Court of Chancery on behalf of Zapata against ten officers and/or directors of Zapata, alleging, essentially, breaches of fiduciary duty. Maldonado did not first demand that the board bring this action, stating instead such demand's futility because all directors were named as defendants and allegedly participated in the acts specified.[...]

By June, 1979, four of the defendant-directors were no longer on the board, and the remaining directors appointed two new outside directors to the board. The board then created an "Independent Investigation Committee" (Committee), composed solely of the two new directors, to investigate Maldonado's actions, as well as a similar derivative action then pending in Texas, and to determine whether the corporation should continue any or all of the litigation. The Committee's determination was stated to be "final, ... not ... subject to review by the Board of Directors and ... in all respects ... binding upon the Corporation."

Following an investigation, the Committee concluded, in September, 1979, that each action should "be dismissed forthwith as their continued maintenance is inimical to the Company's best interests...." Consequently, Zapata moved for dismissal or summary judgment in the three derivative actions. [...]

On March 18, 1980, the Court of Chancery, in a reported opinion, the basis for the order of April 9, 1980, denied Zapata's motions, holding that Delaware law does not sanction this means of dismissal. More specifically, it held that the "business judgment" rule is not a grant of authority to dismiss derivative actions and that a stockholder has an individual right to maintain derivative actions in certain instances. [...]

We limit our review in this interlocutory appeal to whether the Committee has the power to cause the present action to be dismissed.

We begin with an examination of the carefully considered opinion of the Vice Chancellor which states, in part, that the "business judgment" rule does not confer power "to a corporate board of directors to terminate a derivative suit", 413 A.2d at 1257. His conclusion is particularly pertinent because several federal courts, applying Delaware law, have held that the business judgment rule enables boards (or their committees) to terminate derivative suits, decisions now in conflict with the holding below.[4]

As the term is most commonly used, and given the disposition below, we can understand the Vice Chancellor's comment that "the business judgment rule is irrelevant to the question of whether the Committee has the authority to compel the dismissal of this suit". 413 A.2d at 1257. Corporations, existing because of legislative grace, possess authority as granted by the legislature. Directors of Delaware corporations derive their managerial decision making power, which encompasses decisions whether to initiate, or refrain from entering, litigation,[5] from 8 *Del.C.* § 141 (a).[6] This statute is the fount of directorial powers. The "business judgment" rule is a judicial creation that presumes propriety, under certain circumstances, in a board's decision.[7] Viewed defensively, it does not create authority. In this sense the "business judgment" rule is not relevant in corporate decision making until after a decision is made. It is generally used as a defense to an attack on the decision's soundness. The board's managerial decision making power, however, comes from § 141(a). The judicial creation and legislative grant are related because the "business judgment" rule evolved to give recognition and deference to directors' business expertise when exercising their managerial power under § 141(a).

In the case before us, although the corporation's decision to move to dismiss or for summary judgment was, literally, a decision resulting from an exercise of the directors' (as delegated to the Committee) business judgment, the question of "business judgment", in a defensive sense, would not become relevant until and unless the decision to seek termination of the derivative lawsuit was attacked as improper. […]

Thus, the focus in this case is on the power to speak for the corporation as to whether the lawsuit should be continued or terminated. […]

Accordingly, we turn first to the Court of Chancery's conclusions concerning the right of a plaintiff stockholder in a derivative action. We find that its determination that a stockholder, once demand is made and refused, possesses an independent, individual right to continue a derivative suit for breaches of fiduciary duty over objection by the corporation, […], as an absolute rule, is erroneous.[…]

McKee v. Rogers stated "as a general rule" that "a stockholder cannot be permitted… to invade the discretionary field committed to the judgment of the directors and sue in the corporation's behalf when the managing body refuses. This rule is a well settled one."

The *McKee* rule, of course, should not be read so broadly that the board's refusal will be determinative in every instance. Board members, owing a well-established fiduciary duty to the corporation, will not be allowed to cause a derivative suit to be dismissed when it would be a breach of their fiduciary duty. Generally [784] disputes pertaining to control of the suit arise in two contexts.

Consistent with the purpose of requiring a demand, a board decision to cause a derivative suit to be dismissed as detrimental to the company, after demand has been made and refused, will be respected unless it was wrongful.[...] A claim of a wrongful decision not to sue is thus the first exception and the first context of dispute. Absent a wrongful refusal, the stockholder in such a situation simply lacks legal managerial power. But it cannot be implied that, absent a wrongful board refusal, a stockholder can never have an individual right to initiate an action. [...]

A demand, when required and refused (if not wrongful), terminates a stockholder's legal ability to initiate a derivative action.[12] But where demand is properly excused, the stockholder does possess the ability to initiate the action on his corporation's behalf.

These conclusions, however, do not determine the question before us. Rather, they merely bring us to the question to be decided. It is here that we part company with the Court below. Derivative suits enforce corporate rights and any recovery obtained goes to the corporation. [...] We see no inherent reason why the "two phases" of a derivative suit, the stockholder's suit to compel the corporation to sue and the corporation's suit (see 413 A.2d at 1261-62), should automatically result in the placement in the hands of the litigating stockholder sole control of the corporate right throughout the litigation. To the contrary, it seems to us that such an inflexible rule would recognize the interest of one person or group to the exclusion of all others within the corporate entity. Thus, we reject the view of the Vice Chancellor as to the first aspect of the issue on appeal.

The question to be decided becomes: When, if at all, should an authorized board committee be permitted to cause litigation, properly initiated by a derivative stockholder in his own right, to be dismissed? As noted above, a board has the power to choose not to pursue litigation when demand is made upon it, so long as the decision is not wrongful. If the board determines that a suit would be detrimental to the company, the board's determination prevails. Even when demand is excusable, circumstances may arise when continuation of the litigation would not be in the corporation's best interests. Our inquiry is whether, under such circumstances, there is a permissible procedure under § 141(a) by which a corporation can rid itself of detrimental litigation. If there is

255

not, a single stockholder in an extreme case might control the destiny of the entire corporation. […] "To allow one shareholder to incapacitate an entire board of directors merely by leveling charges against them gives too much leverage to dissident shareholders." But, when examining the means, including the committee mechanism examined in this case, potentials for abuse must be recognized. This takes us to the second and third aspects of the issue on appeal.

Before we pass to equitable considerations as to the mechanism at issue here, it must be clear that an independent committee possesses the corporate power to seek the termination of a derivative suit. Section 141(c) allows a board to delegate all of its authority to a committee.[13] Accordingly, a committee with properly delegated authority would have the power to move for dismissal or summary judgment if the entire board did.

Even though demand was not made in this case and the initial decision of whether to litigate was not placed before the board, Zapata's board, it seems to us, retained all of its corporate power concerning litigation decisions. If Maldonado had made demand on the board in this case, it could have refused to bring suit. Maldonado could then have asserted that the decision not to sue was wrongful and, if correct, would have been allowed to maintain the suit. The board, however, never would have lost its statutory managerial authority. The demand requirement itself evidences that the managerial power is retained [786] by the board. When a derivative plaintiff is allowed to bring suit after a wrongful refusal, the board's authority to choose whether to pursue the litigation is not challenged although its conclusion — reached through the exercise of that authority — is not respected since it is wrongful. Similarly, Rule 23.1, by excusing demand in certain instances, does not strip the board of its corporate power. It merely saves the plaintiff the expense and delay of making a futile demand resulting in a probable tainted exercise of that authority in a refusal by the board or in giving control of litigation to the opposing side. But the board entity remains empowered under § 141(a) to make decisions regarding corporate litigation. The problem is one of member disqualification, not the absence of power in the board.

The corporate power inquiry then focuses on whether the board, tainted by the self-interest of a majority of its members, can legally delegate its authority to a committee of two disinterested directors. We find our statute clearly requires an affirmative answer to this question. [...]

We do not think that the interest taint of the board majority is per se a legal bar to the delegation of the board's power to an independent committee composed of disinterested board members. The committee can properly act for the corporation to move to dismiss derivative litigation that is believed to be detrimental to the corporation's best interest.

Our focus now switches to the Court of Chancery which is faced with a stockholder assertion that a derivative suit, properly instituted, should continue for the benefit of the corporation and a corporate assertion, properly made by a board committee acting with board authority, that the same derivative suit should be dismissed as inimical to the best interests of the corporation.

At the risk of stating the obvious, the problem is relatively simple. If, on the one hand, corporations can consistently wrest bona fide derivative actions away from well-meaning derivative plaintiffs through the use of the committee mechanism, the derivative suit will lose much, if not all, of its generally-recognized effectiveness as an intra-corporate means of policing boards of directors. [...]If, on the other hand, corporations are unable to rid themselves of meritless or harmful litigation [787] and strike suits, the derivative action, created to benefit the corporation, will produce the opposite, unintended result. [...] It thus appears desirable to us to find a balancing point where bona fide stockholder power to bring corporate causes of action cannot be unfairly trampled on by the board of directors, but the corporation can rid itself of detrimental litigation.

As we noted, the question has been treated by other courts as one of the "business judgment" of the board committee. If a "committee, composed of independent and disinterested directors, conducted a proper review of the matters before it, considered a variety of factors and reached, in good faith, a business judgment that [the] action was not in the best interest of [the corporation]", the action must be dismissed. [...]. The issues become solely independence, good faith, and reasonable investigation. The ultimate conclusion of the committee, under that view, is not subject to judicial review.

The context here is a suit against directors where demand on the board is excused. We think some tribute must be paid to the fact that the lawsuit was properly initiated. It is not a board refusal case. Moreover, this complaint was filed in June of 1975 and, while the parties undoubtedly would take differing views on the degree of litigation activity, we have to be concerned about the creation of an "Independent Investigation Committee" four years later, after the election of two new outside directors. Situations could develop where such motions could be filed after years of vigorous litigation for reasons unconnected with the merits of the lawsuit.

Moreover, notwithstanding our conviction that Delaware law entrusts the corporate power to a properly authorized committee, we must be mindful that directors are passing judgment on fellow directors in the same corporation and fellow directors, in this instance, who designated them to serve both as directors and committee members. The question naturally arises whether a "there but for the grace of God go I" empathy might not play a role. And the further question arises whether inquiry as to independence, good faith and reasonable investigation is sufficient safeguard against abuse, perhaps subconscious abuse. […]

Whether the Court of Chancery will be persuaded by the exercise of a committee power resulting in a summary motion for dismissal of a derivative action, where a demand has not been initially made, should rest, in our judgment, in the independent discretion of the Court of Chancery. We thus steer a middle course between those cases which yield to the independent business judgment of a board committee and this case as determined below which would yield to unbridled plaintiff stockholder control. […]

After an objective and thorough investigation of a derivative suit, an independent committee may cause its corporation to file a pretrial motion to dismiss in the Court of Chancery. The basis of the motion is the best interests of the corporation, as determined by the committee. The motion should include a thorough written record of the investigation and its findings and recommendations. Under appropriate Court supervision, akin to proceedings on summary judgment, each side should have an opportunity to make a record on the motion. As to the limited issues presented by the motion noted below, the moving party should be prepared to meet the normal burden under Rule 56 that there is no genuine issue as to any material fact and that the moving party is entitled to dismiss as a matter of law.[15] The Court should apply a two-step test to the motion.

First, the Court should inquire into the independence and good faith of the committee and the bases supporting its conclusions. Limited discovery may be ordered to facilitate such inquiries.[16] The corporation should have the burden of proving independence, good faith and a reasonable investigation, rather than presuming independence, good faith and reasonableness.[17] [789] If the Court determines either that the committee is not independent or has not shown reasonable bases for its conclusions, or, if the Court is not satisfied for other reasons relating to the process, including but not limited to the good faith of the committee, the Court shall deny the corporation's motion. If, however, the Court is satisfied under Rule 56 standards that the committee was independent and showed reasonable bases for good faith findings and recommendations, the Court may proceed, in its discretion, to the next step.

The second step provides, we believe, the essential key in striking the balance between legitimate corporate claims as expressed in a derivative stockholder suit and a corporation's best interests as expressed by an independent investigating committee. The Court should determine, applying its own independent business judgment, whether the motion should be granted.[18] This means, of course, that instances could arise where a committee can establish its independence and sound bases for its good faith decisions and still have the corporation's motion denied. The second step is intended to thwart instances where corporate actions meet the criteria of step one, but the result does not appear to satisfy its spirit, or where corporate actions would simply prematurely terminate a stockholder grievance deserving of further consideration in the corporation's interest. The Court of Chancery of course must carefully consider and weigh how compelling the corporate interest in dismissal is when faced with a non-frivolous lawsuit. The Court of Chancery should, when appropriate, give special consideration to matters of law and public policy in addition to the corporation's best interests.

If the Court's independent business judgment is satisfied, the Court may proceed to grant the motion, subject, of course, to any equitable terms or conditions the Court finds necessary or desirable.

The interlocutory order of the Court of Chancery is reversed and the cause is remanded for further proceedings consistent with this opinion.

3.3.2 In re Oracle Corp. Derivative Litigation

At the later stages of stockholder litigation, a board may use a special litigation committee to attempt to take control of litigation back from stockholders. However, at that time the burden of proof with respect to the independence of the board and its special committee have shifted. The special committee bears the burden of proving its independence. At this stage, facts that might not have been troublesome at the 23.1 stage take on a different light.

Oracle puts a spotlight on the difference the procedural posture makes when assessing social relationships amongst directors.

824 A.2d 917 (2003)
In re ORACLE CORP DERIVATIVE LITIGATION

STRINE, Vice Chancellor.

In this opinion, I address the motion of the special litigation committee ("SLC") of Oracle Corporation to terminate this action, "the Delaware Derivative Action," and other such actions pending in the name of Oracle against certain Oracle directors and officers. These actions allege that these Oracle directors engaged in insider trading while in possession of material, non-public information showing that Oracle would not meet the earnings guidance it gave to the market for the third quarter of Oracle's fiscal year 2001. The SLC bears the burden of persuasion on this motion and must convince me that there is no material issue of fact calling into doubt its independence. This requirement is set forth in *Zapata Corp. v. Maldonado*[1] and its progeny.[2]

The question of independence "turns on whether a director is, *for any substantial reason, incapable of making a decision with only the best interests of the corporation in mind.*"[3] That is, the independence test ultimately "focus[es] on impartiality and objectivity."[4] In this case, the SLC has failed to demonstrate that no material factual question exists regarding its independence.

During discovery, it emerged that the two SLC members — both of whom are professors at Stanford University — are being asked to investigate fellow Oracle directors who have important ties to Stanford, too. Among the directors who are accused by the derivative plaintiffs of insider trading are: (1) another Stanford professor, who taught one of the SLC members when the SLC member was a Ph.D. candidate and who serves as a senior fellow and a steering committee member alongside that SLC member at the Stanford Institute for Economic Policy Research or "SIEPR"; (2) a Stanford alumnus who has directed millions of dollars of contributions to Stanford during recent years, serves as Chair of SIEPR's Advisory Board and has a conference center named for him at SIEPR's facility, and has contributed nearly $600,000 to SIEPR and the Stanford Law School, both parts of Stanford with which one of the SLC members is closely affiliated; and (3) Oracle's CEO, who has made millions of dollars in donations to Stanford through a personal [921] foundation and large donations indirectly through Oracle, and who was considering making donations of his $100 million house and $170 million for a scholarship program as late as August 2001, at around the same time period the SLC members were added to the Oracle board. Taken together, these and other facts cause me to harbor a reasonable doubt about the impartiality of the SLC.

It is no easy task to decide whether to accuse a fellow director of insider trading. For Oracle to compound that difficulty by requiring SLC members to consider accusing a fellow professor and two large benefactors of their university of conduct that is rightly considered a violation of criminal law was unnecessary and inconsistent with the concept of independence recognized by our law. The possibility that these extraneous considerations biased the inquiry of the SLC is too substantial for this court to ignore. I therefore deny the SLC's motion to terminate.

A. Summary of the Plaintiffs' Allegations

The Delaware Derivative Complaint centers on alleged insider trading by four members of Oracle's board of directors — Lawrence Ellison, Jeffrey Henley, Donald Lucas, and Michael Boskin (collectively, the "Trading Defendants"). Each of the Trading Defendants had a very different role at Oracle.

Ellison is Oracle's Chairman, Chief Executive Officer, and its largest stockholder, owning nearly twenty-five percent of Oracle's voting shares. By virtue of his ownership position, Ellison is one of the wealthiest men in America. By virtue of his managerial position, Ellison has regular access to a great deal of information about how Oracle is performing on a week-to-week basis.

Henley is Oracle's Chief Financial Officer, Executive Vice President, and a director of the corporation. Like Ellison, Henley has his finger on the pulse of Oracle's performance constantly.

Lucas is a director who chairs Oracle's Executive Committee and its Finance and Audit Committee. Although the plaintiffs allege that Lucas's positions gave him access to material, non-public information about the company, they do so cursorily. On the present record, it appears that Lucas did not receive copies of week-to-week projections or reports of actual results for the quarter to date. Rather, his committees primarily received historical financial data.

Boskin is a director, Chairman of the Compensation Committee, and a member of the Finance and Audit Committee. As with Lucas, Boskin's access to information was limited mostly to historical financials and did not include the week-to-week internal projections and revenue results that Ellison and Henley received.

According to the plaintiffs, each of these Trading Defendants possessed material, non-public information demonstrating that Oracle would fail to meet the earnings and revenue guidance it had provided to the market in December 2000.[...]

In addition, the plaintiffs contend more generally that the Trading Defendants received material, non-public information that the sales growth for Oracle's other products was slowing in a significant way, which made the attainment of the earnings and revenue guidance extremely difficult. [...]

During the time when these disturbing signals were allegedly being sent, the Trading Defendants engaged in the following trades:

> • On January 3, 2001, Lucas sold 150,000 shares of Oracle common stock at $30 per share, reaping proceeds of over $4.6 million. These sales constituted 17% of Lucas's Oracle holdings.

> • On January 4, 2001, Henley sold one million shares of Oracle stock at approximately $32 per share, yielding over $32.3 million. These sales represented 7% of Henley's Oracle holdings.

• On January 17, 2001, Boskin sold 150,000 shares of Oracle stock at over $33 per share, generating in excess of $5 million. These sales were 16% of Boskin's Oracle holdings.

• From January 22 to January 31, 2001, Ellison sold over 29 million shares at prices above $30 per share, producing over $894 million. Despite the huge proceeds generated by these sales, they constituted the sale of only 2% of Ellison's Oracle holdings.

The plaintiffs allege that the Trading Defendants breached their duty of loyalty by misappropriating inside information and using it as the basis for trading decisions. This claim rests its legal basis on the venerable case of *Brophy v. Cities Service Co.*[5] Its factual foundation is that the Trading Defendants were aware (or at least possessed information that should have made them aware) that the company would miss its December guidance by a wide margin and used that information to their advantage in selling at artificially inflated prices. [...]

D. The Formation of the Special Litigation Committee

On February 1, 2002, Oracle formed the SLC in order to investigate the Delaware Derivative Action and to determine whether Oracle should press the claims raised by the plaintiffs, settle the case, or terminate it. Soon after its formation, the SLC's charge was broadened to give it the same mandate as to all the pending derivative actions, wherever they were filed.

The SLC was granted full authority to decide these matters without the need for approval by the other members of the Oracle board.

E. The Members of the Special Litigation Committee

Two Oracle board members were named to the SLC. Both of them joined the Oracle board on October 15, 2001, more than a half a year after Oracle's 3Q FY 2001 closed. The SLC members also share something else: both are tenured professors at Stanford University.

Professor Hector Garcia-Molina is Chairman of the Computer Science Department at Stanford and holds the Leonard Bosack and Sandra Lerner Professorship in the Computer Science and Electrical Engineering Departments at Stanford. [...]

The other SLC member, Professor Joseph Grundfest, is the W.A. Franke Professor of Law and Business at Stanford University. […]

As will be discussed more specifically later, Grundfest also serves as a steering committee member and a senior fellow of the Stanford Institute for Economic Policy Research, and releases working papers under the "SIEPR" banner.

For their services, the SLC members were paid $250 an hour, a rate below that which they could command for other activities, such as consulting or expert witness testimony. Nonetheless, during the course of their work, the SLC members became concerned that (arguably scandal-driven) developments in the evolving area of corporate governance as well as the decision in *Telxon v. Meyerson*,[9] might render the amount of their compensation so high as to be an argument against their independence. Therefore, Garcia-Molina and Grundfest agreed to give up any SLC-related compensation if their compensation was deemed by this court to impair their impartiality.

The SLC members were recruited to the board primarily by defendant Lucas, with help from defendant Boskin.[10] The wooing of them began in the summer of 2001. Before deciding to join the Oracle board, Grundfest, in particular, did a good deal of due diligence. His review included reading publicly available information, among other things, the then-current complaint in the Federal Class Action.

Grundfest then met with defendants Ellison and Henley, among others, and asked them some questions about the Federal Class Action. The claims in the Federal Class Action are predicated on facts that are substantively identical to those on which the claims in the Delaware Derivative Action are based. Grundfest received answers that were consistent enough with what he called the "exogenous" information about the case to form sufficient confidence to at least join the Oracle board. Grundfest testified that this did not mean that he had concluded that the claims in the Federal Class Action had no merit, only that Ellison's and Henley's explanations of their conduct were plausible. Grundfest did, however, conclude that these were reputable businessmen with whom he felt comfortable serving as a fellow director, and that Henley had given very impressive answers to difficult questions regarding the way Oracle conducted its financial reporting operations.[11]

H. The SLC's Investigation and Report

The SLC's investigation was, by any objective measure, extensive. The SLC reviewed an enormous amount of paper and electronic records. SLC counsel interviewed seventy witnesses, some of them twice. SLC members participated in several key interviews, including the interviews of the Trading Defendants.

Importantly, the interviewees included all the senior members of Oracle's management most involved in its projection and monitoring of the company's financial performance, including its sales and revenue growth. These interviews combined with a special focus on the documents at the company bearing on these subjects, including e-mail communications.

The SLC also asked the plaintiffs in the various actions to identify witnesses the Committee should interview. The Federal Class Action plaintiffs identified ten such persons and the Committee interviewed all but one, who refused to cooperate. The Delaware Derivative Action plaintiffs and the other derivative plaintiffs declined to provide the SLC with any witness list or to meet with the SLC.

During the course of the investigation, the SLC met with its counsel thirty-five times for a total of eighty hours. In addition to that, the SLC members, particularly Professor Grundfest, devoted many more hours to the investigation.

In the end, the SLC produced an extremely lengthy Report totaling 1,110 pages (excluding appendices and exhibits) that concluded that Oracle should not pursue the plaintiffs' claims against the Trading Defendants or any of the other Oracle directors serving during the 3Q FY 2001. […]

II. The SLC Moves to Terminate

Consistent with its Report, the SLC moved to terminate this litigation. The plaintiffs were granted discovery focusing on three primary topics: the independence of the SLC, the good faith of its investigative efforts, and the reasonableness of the bases for its conclusion that the lawsuit should be terminated. Additionally, the plaintiffs received a large volume of documents comprising the materials that the SLC relied upon in preparing its Report.

III. The Applicable Procedural Standard

In order to prevail on its motion to terminate the Delaware Derivative Action, the SLC must persuade me that: (1) its members were independent; (2) that they acted in good faith; and (3) that they had reasonable bases for their recommendations.[17] If the SLC meets that burden, I am free to grant its motion or may, in my discretion, undertake my own examination of whether Oracle should terminate and permit the suit to proceed if I, in my oxymoronic judicial "business judgment," conclude that procession is in the best interests of the company.[18] This two-step analysis comes, of course, from *Zapata*.

IV. Is the SLC Independent?

A. The Facts Disclosed in the Report

In its Report, the SLC took the position that its members were independent. In support of that position, the Report noted several factors including:

> • the fact that neither Grundfest nor Garcia-Molina received compensation from Oracle other than as directors;

> • the fact that neither Grundfest nor Garcia-Molina were on the Oracle board at the time of the alleged wrongdoing;

> • the fact that both Grundfest and Garcia-Molina were willing to return their compensation as SLC members if necessary to preserve their status as independent;

> • the absence of any other material ties between Oracle, the Trading Defendants, and any of the other defendants, on the one hand, and Grundfest and Garcia-Molina, on the other; and

> • the absence of any material ties between Oracle, the Trading Defendants, and any of the other defendants, on the one hand, and the SLC's advisors, on the other.

Noticeably absent from the SLC Report was any disclosure of several significant ties between Oracle or the Trading Defendants and Stanford University, the university that employs both members of the SLC. In the Report, it was only disclosed that:

> • defendant Boskin was a Stanford professor;

• the SLC members were aware that Lucas had made certain donations to Stanford; and

• among the contributions was a donation of $50,000 worth of stock that Lucas donated to Stanford Law School after Grundfest delivered a speech to a venture capital fund meeting in response to Lucas's request. It happens that Lucas's son is a partner in the fund and that approximately half the donation was allocated for use by Grundfest in his personal research.

B. The "Stanford" Facts that Emerged During Discovery

In view of the modesty of these disclosed ties, it was with some shock that a series of other ties among Stanford, Oracle, and the Trading Defendants emerged during discovery. [...]

I begin to discuss the specific ties that allegedly compromise the SLC's independence, beginning with those involving Professor Boskin.

1. Boskin

Defendant Michael J. Boskin is the T.M. Friedman Professor of Economics at Stanford University. [...]

During the 1970s, Boskin taught Grundfest when Grundfest was a Ph.D. candidate. Although Boskin was not Grundfest's advisor and although they do not socialize, the two have remained in contact over the years, speaking occasionally about matters of public policy.

Furthermore, both Boskin and Grundfest are senior fellows and steering committee members at the Stanford Institute for Economic Policy Research, which was previously defined as "SIEPR." [...]

Likewise, the SLC contends that Grundfest went MIA as a steering committee member, having failed to attend a meeting since 1997. The SIEPR web site, however, identifies its steering committee as having the role of "advising the director [of SIEPR] and guiding [SIEPR] on matters pertaining to research and academics."[23] Because Grundfest allegedly did not attend to these duties, his service alongside Boskin in that capacity is, the SLC contends, not relevant to his independence.

Lucas's ties with Stanford are far, far richer than the SLC Report lets on. To begin, Lucas is a Stanford alumnus, having obtained both his undergraduate and graduate degrees there. By any measure, he has been a very loyal alumnus.

The Richard M. Lucas Foundation has given $11.7 million to Stanford since its 1981 founding. Among its notable contributions, the Foundation funded the establishment of the Richard M. Lucas Center [932] for Magnetic Resonance Spectroscopy and Imaging at Stanford's Medical School. Donald Lucas was a founding member and lead director of the Center.

The SLC Report did not mention the Richard M. Lucas Foundation or its grants to Stanford. In its briefs on this motion, the SLC has pointed out that Donald Lucas is one of nine directors at the Foundation and does not serve on its Grant Review Committee. Nonetheless, the SLC does not deny that Lucas is Chairman of the board of the Foundation and that the board approves all grants. […]

From these undisputed facts, it is inarguable that Lucas is a very important alumnus of Stanford and a generous contributor to not one, but two, parts of Stanford important to Grundfest: the Law School and SIEPR.

With these facts in mind, it remains to enrich the factual stew further, by considering defendant Ellison's ties to Stanford.

3. Ellison

There can be little doubt that Ellison is a major figure in the community in which Stanford is located. […] Silicon Valley has generated many success stories, among the greatest of which is that of Oracle and its leader, Ellison. One of the wealthiest men in America, Ellison is a major figure in the nation's increasingly important information technology industry. Given his wealth, Ellison is also in a position to make — and, in fact, he has made — major charitable contributions. […]

Although it is not represented on the Scientific Advisory Board, Stanford has nonetheless been the beneficiary of grants from the Ellison Medical Foundation — to the tune of nearly $10 million in paid or pledged funds. […]

During the time Ellison has been CEO of Oracle, the company itself has also made over $300,000 in donations to Stanford. Not only that, when Oracle established a generously endowed educational foundation — the Oracle Help Us Help Foundation — to help further the deployment of educational technology in schools serving disadvantaged populations, it named Stanford as the "appointing authority," which gave Stanford the right to name four of the Foundation's seven directors.[…]

Beginning in the year 2000 and continuing well into 2001 — the same year that Ellison made the trades the plaintiffs contend were suspicious and the same year the SLC members were asked to join the Oracle board — Ellison and Stanford discussed a much more lucrative donation. The idea Stanford proposed for discussion was the creation of an Ellison Scholars Program modeled on the Rhodes Scholarship at Oxford. The proposed budget for Stanford's answer to Oxford: $170 million. The Ellison Scholars were to be drawn from around the world and were to come to Stanford to take a two-year interdisciplinary graduate program in economics, political science, and computer technology. During the summer between the two academic years, participants would work in internships at, among other companies, Oracle.

As part of his proposal for the Ellison Scholars Program, Shoven suggested that three of the four Trading Defendants — Ellison, Lucas, and Boskin — be on the Program board. In the hypothetical curriculum that Shoven presented to Ellison, he included a course entitled "Legal Institutions and the Modern Economy" to be taught by Grundfest. […]

Given the nature of this case, it is natural that there must be yet another curious [935] fact to add to the mix. This is that Ellison told the *Washington Post* in an October 30, 2000 article that he intended to leave his Woodside, California home — which is worth over $100 million — to Stanford upon his death.[33] In an affidavit, Ellison does not deny making this rather splashy public statement. But, he now (again, rather conveniently) says that he has changed his testamentary intent. Ellison denies having "bequeathed, donated or otherwise conveyed the Woodside property (or any other real property that I own) to Stanford University."[34] And, in the same affidavit, Ellison states unequivocally that he has no intention of ever giving his Woodside compound (or any other real property) to Stanford.[35] Shortly before his deposition in this case, Grundfest asked Ellison about the Woodside property and certain news reports to the effect that he was planning to give it to Stanford. According to Grundfest, Ellison's reaction to his inquiry was one of "surprise."[36] Ellison admitted to Grundfest that he said something of that sort, but contended that whatever he said was merely a "passing" comment.[37] Plus, Ellison said, Stanford would, of course, not want his $100 million home unless it came with a "dowry" — *i.e.,* an endowment to support what is sure to be a costly maintenance budget.[...]

In order to buttress the argument that Stanford did not feel beholden to him, Ellison shared with the court the (otherwise private) fact that one of his children had applied to Stanford in October 2000 and was not admitted.[40] If Stanford felt comfortable rejecting Ellison's child, the SLC contends, why should the SLC members hesitate before recommending that Oracle press insider trading-based fiduciary duty claims against Ellison?

C. The SLC's Argument

The SLC contends that even together, these facts regarding the ties among Oracle, the Trading Defendants, Stanford, and the SLC members do not impair the SLC's independence. In so arguing, the SLC places great weight on the fact that none [936] of the Trading Defendants have the practical ability to deprive either Grundfest or Garcia-Molina of their current positions at Stanford. Nor, given their tenure, does Stanford itself have any practical ability to punish them for taking action adverse to Boskin, Lucas, or Ellison — each of whom, as we have seen, has contributed (in one way or another) great value to Stanford as an institution. As important, neither Garcia-Molina nor Grundfest are part of the official fundraising apparatus at Stanford; thus, it is not their on-the-job duty to be solicitous of contributors, and fundraising success does not factor into their treatment as professors. [...]

More subtly, the SLC argues that university professors simply are not inhibited types, unwilling to make tough decisions even as to fellow professors and large contributors. What is tenure about if not to provide professors with intellectual freedom, even in non-traditional roles such as special litigation committee members? No less ardently — but with no record evidence that reliably supports its ultimate point — the SLC contends that Garcia-Molina and Grundfest are extremely distinguished in their fields and were not, in fact, influenced by the facts identified heretofore. Indeed, the SLC argues, how could they have been influenced by many of these facts when they did not learn them until the post-Report discovery process? If it boils down to the simple fact that both

270

share with Boskin the status of a Stanford professor, how material can this be when there are 1,700 others who also occupy the same position?

E. The Court's Analysis of the SLC's Independence

Having framed the competing views of the parties, it is now time to decide.

I begin with an important reminder: the SLC bears the burden of proving its independence. It must convince me.

But of what? According to the SLC, its members are independent unless they are essentially subservient to the Trading Defendants — *i.e.,* they are under the "domination and control" of the interested parties.[45] If the SLC is correct and this is the central inquiry in the independence determination, they would win. Nothing in the record suggests to me that either Garcia-Molina or Grundfest are dominated and controlled by any of the Trading Defendants, by Oracle, or even by Stanford.[46]

But, in my view, an emphasis on "domination and control" would serve only to fetishize much-parroted language, at the cost of denuding the independence inquiry of its intellectual integrity. Take an easy example. Imagine if two brothers were on a corporate board, each successful in different businesses and not dependent in any way on the other's beneficence in order to be wealthy. The brothers are brothers, they stay in touch and consider each other family, but each is opinionated and strong-willed. A derivative action is filed targeting a transaction involving one of the brothers. The other brother is put [938] on a special litigation committee to investigate the case. If the test is domination and control, then one brother could investigate the other. Does any sensible person think that is our law? I do not think it is.

And it should not be our law. Delaware law should not be based on a reductionist view of human nature that simplifies human motivations on the lines of the least sophisticated notions of the law and economics movement. *Homo sapiens* is not merely *homo economicus*. We may be thankful that an array of other motivations exist that influence human behavior; not all are any better than greed or avarice, think of envy, to name just one. But also think of motives like love, friendship, and collegiality, think of those among us who direct their behavior as best they can on a guiding creed or set of moral values.[47]

Nor should our law ignore the social nature of humans. To be direct, corporate directors are generally the sort of people deeply enmeshed in social institutions. Such institutions have norms, expectations that, explicitly and implicitly, influence and channel the behavior of those who participate in their operation.[48] Some things are "just not done," or only at a cost, which might not be so severe as a loss of position, but may involve a loss of standing in the institution. In being appropriately sensitive to this factor, our law also cannot assume — absent some proof of the point — that corporate directors are, as a general matter, persons of unusual social bravery, who operate heedless to the inhibitions that social norms generate for ordinary folk. [...]

In examining whether the SLC has met its burden to demonstrate that there is no material dispute of fact regarding its independence, the court must bear in mind the function of special litigation committees under our jurisprudence. Under Delaware law, the primary means by which corporate defendants may obtain a dismissal of a derivative suit is by showing that the plaintiffs have not met their pleading burden under the test of *Aronson v. Lewis*,[56] or the related standard set forth in *Rales v. Blasband*.[57] In simple terms, these tests permit a corporation to terminate a derivative suit if its board is comprised of directors who can impartially consider a demand.[58]

Special litigation committees are permitted as a last chance for a corporation to control a derivative claim in circumstances when a majority of its directors cannot [940] impartially consider a demand. By vesting the power of the board to determine what to do with the suit in a committee of independent directors, a corporation may retain control over whether the suit will proceed, so long as the committee meets the standard set forth in *Zapata*. [...]

Thus, in assessing the independence of the Oracle SLC, I necessarily examine the question of whether the SLC can independently make the difficult decision entrusted to it: to determine whether the Trading Defendants should face suit for insider trading-based allegations of breach of fiduciary duty. An affirmative answer by the SLC to that question would have potentially huge negative consequences [941] for the Trading Defendants, not only by exposing them to the possibility of a large damage award but also by subjecting them to great reputational harm. To have Professors Grundfest and Garcia-Molina declare that Oracle should press insider trading claims against the Trading Defendants would have been, to put it mildly, "news." Relatedly, it is reasonable to think that an SLC determination that the Trading Defendants had likely engaged in insider trading would have been accompanied by a recommendation that they step down as fiduciaries until their ultimate culpability was decided. […]

2. The SLC Has Not Met Its Burden to Demonstrate the Absence of a Material Dispute of Fact About Its Independence

Using the contextual approach I have described, I conclude that the SLC has not met its burden to show the absence of a material factual question about its independence. I find this to be the case because the ties among the SLC, the Trading Defendants, and Stanford are so substantial that they cause reasonable doubt about the SLC's ability to impartially consider whether the Trading Defendants should face suit. The concern that arises from these ties can be stated fairly simply, focusing on defendants Boskin, Lucas, and Ellison in that order, and then collectively.

As SLC members, Grundfest and Garcia-Molina were already being asked to consider whether the company should level extremely serious accusations of wrongdoing against fellow board members. As to Boskin, both SLC members faced another layer of complexity: the determination of whether to have Oracle press insider trading claims against a fellow professor at their university. Even though Boskin was in a different academic department from either SLC member, it is reasonable to assume that the fact that Boskin was also on faculty would — to persons possessing typical sensibilities and institutional loyalty — be a matter of more than trivial concern. Universities are obviously places of at-times intense debate, but they also see themselves as communities. In fact, Stanford refers to itself as a "community of scholars."[64] To accuse a fellow professor — whom one might see at the faculty club or at inter-disciplinary presentations of academic papers — of insider trading cannot be a small thing — even for the most callous of academics.

As to Boskin, Grundfest faced an even more complex challenge than Garcia-Molina. Boskin was a professor who had taught him and with whom he had maintained contact over the years. […] Grundfest (I infer) would have more difficulty objectively determining whether Boskin engaged in improper insider trading than would a person who was not a fellow professor, had not been a student of Boskin, had not kept in touch with Boskin over the years, and who was not a senior fellow and steering committee member at SIEPR.

In so concluding, I necessarily draw on a general sense of human nature. It may be that Grundfest is a very special person who is capable of putting these kinds of things totally aside. But the SLC has not provided evidence that that is the case. In this respect, it is critical to note that I do not infer that Grundfest would be less likely to recommend suit against Boskin than someone without these ties. Human nature being what it is, it is entirely possible that Grundfest would in fact be tougher on Boskin than the would on someone with whom he did not have such connections. The inference I draw is subtly, but importantly, different. What I infer is that a person in Grundfest's position would find it difficult to assess Boskin's conduct without pondering his own association with Boskin and their mutual affiliations. Although these connections might produce bias in either a tougher or laxer direction, the key inference is that these connections would be on the mind of a person in Grundfest's position, putting him in the position of either causing serious legal action to be brought against a person with whom he shares several connections (an awkward thing) or not doing so (and risking being seen as having engaged in favoritism toward his old professor and SIEPR colleague).

The same concerns also exist as to Lucas. For Grundfest to vote to accuse Lucas of insider trading would require him to accuse SIEPR's Advisory Board Chair and major benefactor of serious wrongdoing — of conduct that violates federal securities laws. Such action would also require Grundfest to make charges against a man who recently donated $50,000 to Stanford Law School after Grundfest made a speech at his request.[65]

In view of the ties involving Boskin and Lucas alone, I would conclude that the SLC has failed to meet its burden on the independence question. The tantalizing facts about Ellison merely reinforce this conclusion. The SLC, of course, argues that Ellison is not a large benefactor of Stanford personally, that Stanford has demonstrated its independence of him by rejecting his child for admission, and that, in any event, the SLC was ignorant of any negotiations between Ellison and Stanford about a large contribution. For these reasons, the SLC says, its ability to act independently of Ellison is clear.

I find differently. The notion that anyone in Palo Alto can accuse Ellison of insider trading without harboring some fear of social awkwardness seems a stretch. That being said, I do not mean to imply that the mere fact that Ellison is worth tens of billions of dollars and is the key force behind a very important social institution in Silicon Valley disqualifies all persons who live there from being independent of him. Rather, it is merely an acknowledgement of the simple fact that accusing such a significant person in that community of such serious wrongdoing is no small thing.

Given that general context, Ellison's relationship to Stanford itself contributes to my overall doubt, when heaped on top of the ties involving Boskin and Lucas. During the period when Grundfest and Garcia-Molina were being added to the Oracle board, Ellison was publicly considering making extremely large contributions to Stanford. Although the SLC denies [946] knowledge of these public statements, Grundfest claims to have done a fair amount of research before joining the board, giving me doubt that he was not somewhat aware of the possibility that Ellison might bestow large blessings on Stanford. This is especially so when I cannot rule out the possibility that Grundfest had been told by Lucas about, but has now honestly forgotten, the negotiations over the Ellison Scholars Program. [...]

Of course, the SLC says these facts are meaningless because Stanford rejected Ellison's child for admission. I am not sure what to make of this fact, but it surely cannot bear the heavy weight the SLC gives it. The aftermath of denying Ellison's child admission might, after all, as likely manifest itself in a desire on the part of the Stanford community never to offend Ellison again, lest he permanently write off Stanford as a possible object of his charitable aims — as the sort of thing that acts as not one, but two strikes, leading the batter to choke up on the bat so as to be even more careful not to miss the next pitch. Suffice to say that after the rejection took place, it did not keep Ellison from making public statements in *Fortune* magazine on August 13, 2001 about his consideration of making a huge donation to Stanford, at the same time when the two SLC members were being courted to join the Oracle board. [...]

Whether the SLC members had precise knowledge of all the facts that have emerged is not essential, what is important is that by any measure this was a social atmosphere painted in too much vivid Stanford Cardinal red for the SLC members to have reasonably ignored it. Summarized fairly, two Stanford professors were recruited to the Oracle board in summer 2001 and soon asked to investigate a fellow professor and two benefactors of the University. On Grundfest's part, the facts are more substantial, because his connections — through his personal experiences, SIEPR, and the Law School — to Boskin and to Lucas run deeper. […]

Rather than form an SLC whose membership was free from bias-creating relationships, Oracle formed a committee fraught with them. As a result, the SLC has failed to meet its *Zapata* burden, and its motion to terminate must be denied. Because of this reality, I do not burden the reader with an examination of the other *Zapata* factors. In the absence of a finding that the SLC was independent, its subjective good faith and the reasonableness of its conclusions would not be sufficient to justify termination. Without confidence that the SLC was impartial, its findings do not provide the assurance our law requires for the dismissal of a derivative suit without a merits inquiry. […]

3.4 220 Actions and Tools at Hand

Stockholders have a statutory right to access the books and records of the corporation. This power is an extremely important tool for stockholders to monitor the actions the board of directors and to root wrong-doing or malfeasance. However, the right to monitor a corporation's books and records is also subject to limitations. In the following cases we learn about using the "tools at hand" and the limits to their use.

Courts – as in *Beam v. Stewart* – regularly exhort plaintiffs to use § 220 to seek out books and records prior to filing derivative complaints. However, the § 220 process can be lengthy. Consequently, the economics of plaintiff litigation make it difficult for plaintiffs to both pursue § 220 litigation and also maintain control positions in early filed derivative litigation. This challenge makes § 220 actions a less than perfect vehicle for curbing the excesses of the litigation industrial complex.

3.4.1 DGCL Sec. 220 - Inspection of books and records

Stockholders who comply with the requirements of §220 can access the books and records of the corporation.

§ 220. Inspection of books and records.

(a) As used in this section:

(1) "Stockholder" means a holder of record of stock in a stock corporation, or a person who is the beneficial owner of shares of such stock held either in a voting trust or by a nominee on behalf of such person. [...]

(b) Any stockholder, in person or by attorney or other agent, shall, upon written demand under oath stating the purpose thereof, have the right during the usual hours for business to inspect for any proper purpose, and to make copies and extracts from:

(1) The corporation's stock ledger, a list of its stockholders, and its other books and records; and

(2) A subsidiary's books and records, to the extent that:

a. The corporation has actual possession and control of such records of such subsidiary; or

b. The corporation could obtain such records through the exercise of control over such subsidiary, provided that as of the date of the making of the demand:

1. The stockholder inspection of such books and records of the subsidiary would not constitute a breach of an agreement between the corporation or the subsidiary and a person or persons not affiliated with the corporation; and

2. The subsidiary would not have the right under the law applicable to it to deny the corporation access to such books and records upon demand by the corporation.

In every instance where the stockholder is other than a record holder of stock in a stock corporation, or a member of a nonstock corporation, the demand under oath shall state the person's status as a stockholder, be accompanied by documentary evidence of beneficial ownership of the stock, and state that such documentary evidence is a true and correct copy of what it purports to be. A proper purpose shall mean a purpose reasonably related to such person's interest as a stockholder. [...] The demand under oath shall be directed to the corporation at its registered office in this State or at its principal place of business.

(c) If the corporation, or an officer or agent thereof, refuses to permit an inspection sought by a stockholder or attorney or other agent acting for the stockholder pursuant to subsection (b) of this section or does not reply to the demand within 5 business days after the demand has been made, the stockholder may apply to the Court of Chancery for an order to compel such inspection. The Court of Chancery is hereby vested with exclusive jurisdiction to determine whether or not the person seeking inspection is entitled to the inspection sought. The Court may summarily order the corporation to permit the stockholder to inspect the corporation's stock ledger, an existing list of stockholders, and its other books and records, and to make copies or extracts therefrom; or the Court may order the corporation to furnish to the stockholder a list of its stockholders as of a specific date on condition that the stockholder first pay to the corporation the reasonable cost of obtaining and furnishing such list and on such other conditions as the Court deems appropriate. Where the stockholder seeks to inspect the corporation's books and records, other than its stock ledger or list of stockholders, such stockholder shall first establish that:

(1) Such stockholder is a stockholder;

(2) Such stockholder has complied with this section respecting the form and manner of making demand for inspection of such documents; and

(3) The inspection such stockholder seeks is for a proper purpose.

Where the stockholder seeks to inspect the corporation's stock ledger or list of stockholders and establishes that such stockholder is a stockholder and has complied with this section respecting the form and manner of making demand for inspection of such documents, the burden of proof shall be upon the corporation to establish that the inspection such stockholder seeks is for an improper purpose. The Court may, in its discretion, prescribe any limitations or conditions with reference to the inspection, or award such other or further relief as the Court may deem just and proper. The Court may order books, documents and records, pertinent extracts therefrom, or duly authenticated copies thereof, to be brought within this State and kept in this State upon such terms and conditions as the order may prescribe.

(d) Any director shall have the right to examine the corporation's stock ledger, a list of its stockholders and its other books and records for a purpose reasonably related to the director's position as a director. The Court of Chancery is hereby vested with the exclusive jurisdiction to determine whether a director is entitled to the inspection sought. The Court may summarily order the corporation to permit the director to inspect any and all books and records, the stock ledger and the list of stockholders and to make copies or extracts therefrom. The burden of proof shall be upon the corporation to establish that the inspection such director seeks is for an improper purpose. The Court may, in its discretion, prescribe any limitations or conditions with reference to the inspection, or award such other and further relief as the Court may deem just and proper.

4 Fiduciary Duties of Directors

Although the Delaware code - and the corporate codes of all the other states for that matter - do a good job of describing the corporate form and the mechanics of operating this form, with the exception of perhaps §144, the code says precious little about the standards to which boards of directors who are managing the corporation will be held. This is so because corporate fiduciary duties are a product of the common law and not statute. In the following sections we examine the various core duties of corporate directors. Although these duties are fewer in number than the fiduciary obligations of agents, they are entirely consistent.

4.1 Standards of Conduct and Standards of Review

Directors of corporations owe fiduciary duties of care and loyalty to the corporation and its residual claimants (stockholders). The duty of care generally requires a director to use the care that a reasonably prudent person in like position would reasonably believe appropriate under the circumstances. The duty of loyalty generally requires a director to discharge her duties in good faith and with the reasonable belief that her actions are in the best interests of the corporation and the residual claimants.

When a court is asked to judge director actions against the obligations the directors owe, the court deploys one of several standards of review depending on the circumstances and the duty being questioned. The excerpt from *In re Trados S'holder Litigation* provides a broad overview of how courts approach the question of evaluating director conduct against the appropriate standard of review.

In re Trados Inc. Shareholder Litigation
73 A. 3d 17, 35 - Del: Court of Chancery 2013

When determining whether directors have breached their fiduciary duties, Delaware corporate law distinguishes between the standard of conduct and the standard of review. *See* William T. Allen, Jack B. Jacobs, & Leo E. Strine, Jr., *Realigning the Standard of Review of Director Due Care with Delaware Public Policy: A Critique of Van Gorkom and its*

Progeny as a Standard of Review Problem, 96 Nw. U.L.Rev. 449, 451-52 (2002) [hereinafter *Realigning the Standard*]. The standard of conduct describes what directors are expected to do and is defined by the content of the duties of loyalty and care. The standard of review is the test that a court applies when evaluating whether directors have met the standard of conduct. It describes what a plaintiff must first plead and later prove to prevail.

Under Delaware law, the standard of review depends initially on whether the board members (i) were disinterested and independent (the business judgment rule), (ii) faced potential conflicts of interest because of the decisional dynamics present in particular recurring and recognizable situations (enhanced scrutiny), or (iii) confronted actual conflicts of interest such that the directors making the decision did not comprise a disinterested and independent board majority (entire fairness). The standard of review may change further depending on whether the directors took steps to address the potential or actual conflict, such as by creating an independent committee, conditioning the transaction on approval by disinterested stockholders, or both. Regardless, in every situation, the standard of review is more forgiving of directors and more onerous for stockholder plaintiffs than the standard of conduct. This divergence is warranted for diverse policy reasons typically cited as justifications for the business judgment rule. *See, e.g.,* Brehm v. Eisner, 746 A.2d 244, 263 (Del.2000) (explaining justifications for business judgment rule).

The Standard of Conduct

Delaware corporate law starts from the bedrock principle that "[t]he business and affairs of every corporation ... shall be managed by or under the direction of a board of directors." 8 *Del. C.* § 141(a). When exercising their statutory responsibility, the standard of conduct requires that directors seek "to promote the value of the corporation for the benefit of its stockholders."

"It is, of course, accepted that a corporation may take steps, such as giving charitable contributions or paying higher wages, that do not maximize profits currently. They may do so, however, because such activities are rationalized as producing greater profits over the long-term." Leo E. Strine, Jr., *Our Continuing Struggle with the Idea that For-Profit*

Corporations Seek Profit, 47 Wake Forest L.Rev. 135, 147 n. 34 (2012) [hereinafter *For-Profit Corporations*]. Decisions of this nature benefit the corporation as a whole, and by increasing the value of the corporation, the directors increase the share of value available for the residual claimants. Judicial opinions therefore often refer to directors owing fiduciary duties "to the corporation and its shareholders."Gheewalla, 930 A.2d at 99; *accord* Mills Acq. Co. v. Macmillan, Inc., 559 A.2d 1261, 1280 (Del.1989) ("[D]irectors owe fiduciary duties of care and loyalty to the corporation and its shareholders ...."); Polk v. Good, 507 A.2d 531, 536 (Del.1986) ("In performing their duties the directors owe fundamental fiduciary duties of loyalty and care to the corporation and its shareholders."). This formulation captures the foundational relationship in which directors owe duties to the corporation for the ultimate benefit of the entity's residual claimants. Nevertheless, "stockholders' best interest must always, within legal limits, be the end. Other constituencies may be considered only instrumentally to advance that end." *For-Profit Corporations, supra,* at 147 n. 34.

A Delaware corporation, by default, has a perpetual existence. 8 *Del. C.* §§ 102(b)(5), 122(1). Equity capital, by default, is permanent capital. In terms of the standard of conduct, the duty of loyalty therefore mandates that directors maximize the value of the corporation over the long-term for the benefit of the providers of equity capital, as warranted for an entity with perpetual life in which the residual claimants have locked in their investment. When deciding whether to pursue a strategic alternative that would end or fundamentally alter the stockholders' ongoing investment in the corporation, the loyalty-based standard of conduct requires that the alternative yield value exceeding what the corporation otherwise would generate for stockholders over the long-term. Value, of course, does not just mean cash. It could mean an ownership interest in an entity, a package of other securities, or some combination, with or without cash, that will deliver greater value over the anticipated investment horizon. *See* QVC, 637 A.2d at 44 (describing how directors should approach consideration of non-cash or mixed consideration).

The duty to act for the ultimate benefit of stockholders does not require that directors fulfill the wishes of a particular subset of the stockholder base. *See* In re Lear Corp. S'holder Litig., 967 A.2d 640, 655 (Del.Ch.2008) ("Directors are not thermometers, existing to register the ever-changing sentiments of stockholders.... During their term of office, directors may take good faith actions that they believe will benefit stockholders, even if they realize that the stockholders do not agree with them.");Paramount Commc'ns Inc. v. Time Inc., 1989 WL 79880, at *30 (Del.Ch. July 14, 1989)("The corporation law does not operate on the theory that directors, in exercising their powers to manage the firm, are obligated to follow the wishes of a majority of shares. In fact, directors, not shareholders, are charged with the duty to manage the firm."),*aff'd in pertinent part,* Time, 571 A.2d at 1150; TW Servs., 1989 WL 20290, at *8 n. 14("While corporate democracy is a pertinent concept, a corporation is not a New England town meeting; directors, not shareholders, have responsibilities to manage the business and affairs of the corporation, subject however to a fiduciary obligation."). Stockholders may have idiosyncratic reasons for preferring decisions that misallocate capital. Directors must exercise their independent fiduciary judgment; they need not cater to stockholder whim. *See* Time, 571 A.2d at 1154 ("Delaware law confers the management of the corporate enterprise to the stockholders' duly elected board representatives. The fiduciary duty to manage a corporate enterprise includes the selection of a time frame for achievement of corporate goals. That duty may not be delegated to the stockholders." (citations omitted)).

More pertinent to the current case, a particular class or series of stock may hold contractual rights against the corporation and desire outcomes that maximize the value of those rights. *See* MCG Capital Corp. v. Maginn, 2010 WL 1782271, at *6 (Del.Ch. May 5, 2010) (noting that preferential contract rights may appear in "the articles of incorporation, the preferred share designations, or some other appropriate document" such as a registration rights agreement, investor rights agreement, or stockholder agreement). By default, "all stock is created equal." *Id.* Unless a corporation's certificate of incorporation provides otherwise, each share of stock is common stock. If the certificate of incorporation grants a particular class or series of stock special "voting powers, ... designations, preferences and relative, participating, optional or other special rights" superior to the common stock, then the class or series holding the rights is known as preferred stock. 8 *Del. C.* § 151(a); *see* Starring v. Am. Hair & Felt Co.,191 A. 887, 890 (Del.Ch.1937) (Wolcott, C.) ("The term `preferred stock' is of fairly definite import. There is no difficulty in understanding its general concept. [It] is of course a stock which in relation to other classes enjoys certain defined rights and privileges."), *aff'd*, 2 A.2d 249 (Del.1937). If the certificate of incorporation is silent on a particular issue, then as to that issue the preferred stock and the common stock have the same rights. Consequently, as a general matter, "the rights and preferences of preferred stock are contractual in nature." Trados I, 2009 WL 2225958, at *7; *accord* Judah v. Del. Trust Co., 378 A.2d 624, 628 (Del.1977) ("Generally, the provisions of the certificate of incorporation govern the rights of preferred shareholders, the certificate of incorporation being interpreted in accordance with the law of contracts, with only those rights which are embodied in the certificate granted to preferred shareholders.").

A board does not owe fiduciary duties to preferred stockholders when considering whether or not to take corporate action that might trigger or circumvent the preferred stockholders' contractual rights. Preferred stockholders are owed fiduciary duties only when they do not invoke their special contractual rights and rely on a right shared equally with the common stock. Under those circumstances, "the existence of such right and the correlative duty may be measured by equitable as well as legal standards." Thus, for example, just as common stockholders can challenge a disproportionate allocation of merger consideration, so too can preferred stockholders who do not possess and are not limited by a contractual entitlement. Under those circumstances, the decision to allocate different consideration is a discretionary, fiduciary determination that must pass muster under the appropriate standard of review, and the degree to which directors own different classes or series of stock may affect the standard of review.

To reiterate, the standard of conduct for directors requires that they strive in good faith and on an informed basis to maximize the value of the corporation for the benefit of its residual claimants, the ultimate beneficiaries of the firm's value, not for the benefit of its contractual claimants. In light of this obligation, "it is the duty of directors to pursue the best interests of the corporation and its common stockholders, if that can be done faithfully with the contractual promises owed to the preferred." LC Capital, 990 A.2d at 452. Put differently, "generally it will be the duty of the board, where discretionary judgment is to be exercised, to prefer the interests of the common stock — as the good faith judgment of the board sees them to be — to the interests created by the special rights, preferences, *etc* .... of preferred stock." Equity-Linked, 705 A.2d at 1042. This principle is not unique to preferred stock; it applies equally to other holders of contract rights against the corporation. Consequently, as this court observed at the motion to dismiss stage, "in circumstances where the interests of the common stockholders diverge from those of the preferred stockholders, it is *possible* that a director could breach her duty by improperly favoring the interests of the preferred stockholders over those of the common stockholders." Trados I, 2009 WL 2225958, at *7; *accord* LC Capital, 990 A.2d at 447 (quoting *Trados I* and remarking that it "summarized the weight of authority very well"). ...

The Standards of Review

To determine whether directors have met their fiduciary obligations, Delaware courts evaluate the challenged decision through the lens of a standard of review. In this case, the Board lacked a majority of disinterested and independent directors, making entire fairness the applicable standard.

"Delaware has three tiers of review for evaluating director decision-making: the business judgment rule, enhanced scrutiny, and entire fairness." Reis v. Hazelett Strip-Casting Corp., 28 A.3d 442, 457 (Del.Ch.2011). Delaware's default standard of review is the business judgment rule. The rule presumes that "in making a business decision the directors of a corporation acted on an informed basis, in good faith and in the honest belief that the action taken was in the best interests of the company." This standard of review "reflects and promotes the role of the board of directors as the proper body to manage the business and affairs of the corporation." Trados I, 2009 WL 2225958, at *6. Unless one of its elements is rebutted, "the court merely looks to see whether the business decision made was rational in the sense of being one logical approach to advancing the corporation's objectives." In re Dollar Thrifty S'holder Litig.,14 A.3d 573, 598 (Del.Ch. 2010). Only when a decision lacks any rationally conceivable basis will a court infer bad faith and a breach of duty.

Enhanced scrutiny is Delaware's intermediate standard of review. Framed generally, it requires that the defendant fiduciaries "bear the burden of persuasion to show that their motivations were proper and not selfish" and that "their actions were reasonable in relation to their legitimate objective." Mercier v. Inter-Tel (Del.), Inc., 929 A.2d 786, 810 (Del.Ch. 2007). Enhanced scrutiny applies to specific, recurring, and readily identifiable situations involving potential conflicts of interest where the realities of the decisionmaking context can subtly undermine the decisions of even independent and disinterested directors. In *Unocal,* the Delaware Supreme Court created enhanced scrutiny to address the potential conflicts of interest faced by a board of directors when resisting a hostile takeover, namely the "omnipresent specter" that target directors may be influenced by and act to further their own interests or those of incumbent management, "rather than those of the corporation and its shareholders."493 A.2d at 954. Tailored for this context, enhanced scrutiny requires that directors who take defensive action against a hostile takeover show (i) that "they had reasonable grounds for believing that a danger to corporate policy and effectiveness existed," and (ii) that the response selected was "reasonable in relation to the threat posed." *Id.* at 955.

In *Revlon,* the Delaware Supreme Court extended the new intermediate standard to the sale of a corporation. *See* 506 A.2d at 180-82 (expressly applying *Unocal* test). Here too, enhanced scrutiny applies because of the potential conflicts of interest that fiduciaries must confront. "[T]he potential sale of a corporation has enormous implications for corporate managers and advisors, and a range of human motivations, including but by no means limited to greed, can inspire fiduciaries and their advisors to be less than faithful." In re El Paso Corp. S'holders Litig., 41 A.3d 432, 439 (Del.Ch.2012). These potential conflicts warrant a more searching standard of review than the business judgment rule:

> The heightened scrutiny that applies in the *Revlon* (and *Unocal*)
> contexts are, in large measure, rooted in a concern that the board
> might harbor personal motivations in the sale context that differ
> from what is best for the corporation and its stockholders. Most
> traditionally, there is the danger that top corporate managers will
> resist a sale that might cost them their managerial posts, or prefer a
> sale to one industry rival rather than another for reasons having
> more to do with personal ego than with what is best for
> stockholders.

Dollar Thrifty, 14 A.3d at 597 (footnote omitted). Consequently, "the predicate question of what the board's true motivation was comes into play," and "[t]he court must take a nuanced and realistic look at the possibility that personal interests short of pure self-dealing have influenced the board ...." *Id.* at 598. Tailored to the sale context, enhanced scrutiny requires that the defendant fiduciaries show that they acted reasonably to obtain for their beneficiaries the best value reasonably available under the circumstances, which may be no transaction at all. *See* QVC, 637 A.2d at 48-49.

Entire fairness, Delaware's most onerous standard, applies when the board labors under actual conflicts of interest. Once entire fairness applies, the defendants must establish "to the court's satisfaction that the transaction was the product of both fair dealing *and* fair price." Cinerama, Inc. v. Technicolor, Inc. (Technicolor III), 663 A.2d 1156, 1163 (Del. 1995) (internal quotation marks omitted). "Not even an honest belief that the transaction was entirely fair will be sufficient to establish entire fairness. Rather, the transaction itself must be objectively fair, independent of the board's beliefs." Gesoff v. IIC Indus., Inc., 902 A.2d 1130, 1145 (Del.Ch.2006).

To obtain review under the entire fairness test, the stockholder plaintiff must prove that there were not enough independent and disinterested individuals among the directors making the challenged decision to comprise a board majority. *See* Aronson, 473 A.2d at 812 (noting that if "the transaction is not approved by a majority consisting of the disinterested directors, then the business judgment rule has no application"). To determine whether the directors approving the transaction comprised a disinterested and independent board majority, the court conducts a director-by-director analysis.

4.2 Duty of Care

4.2.1 Aronson v. Lewis

In an earlier case (*Shlensky v Wrigley*) you were introduced the business judgment presumption. Remember that in *Shlensky*, the court ruled that absent some act of fraud or gross negligence that it would not second guess business decisions of a board of directors. This general deference to the board's statutory role is known as the business judgment presumption and it plays out most commonly in cases where stockholders bring claims that boards have somehow violated their duty of care to the corporation. The case that follows, *Aronson*, is the leading restatement of the business judgment presumption.

473 A.2d 805 (1984)
ARONSON v. LEWIS

MOORE, Justice:

[...]

A cardinal precept of the General Corporation Law of the State of Delaware is that directors, rather than shareholders, manage the business and affairs of the corporation. 8 *Del.C.* § 141(a). Section 141(a) states in pertinent part:

> "The *business and affairs* of a corporation organized under this chapter *shall be managed by or under the direction* of a board of directors except as may be otherwise provided in this chapter or in its certificate of incorporation."

8 *Del.C.* § 141(a) (Emphasis added). The existence and exercise of this power carries with it certain fundamental fiduciary obligations to the corporation and its shareholders. […]

The business judgment rule is an acknowledgment of the managerial prerogatives of Delaware directors under Section 141(a). […]It is a presumption that in making a business decision the directors of a corporation acted on an informed basis, in good faith and in the honest belief that the action taken was in the best interests of the company.[…] The burden is on the party challenging the decision to establish facts rebutting the presumption. […]

First, its protections can only be claimed by disinterested directors whose conduct otherwise meets the tests of business judgment. From the standpoint of interest, this means that directors can neither appear on both sides of a transaction nor expect to derive any personal financial benefit from it in the sense of self-dealing, as opposed to a benefit which devolves upon the corporation or all stockholders generally. […]

Second, to invoke the rule's protection directors have a duty to inform themselves, prior to making a business decision, of all material information reasonably available to them. Having become so informed, they must then act with requisite care in the discharge of their duties. While the Delaware cases use a variety of terms to describe the applicable standard of care, our analysis satisfies us that under the business judgment rule director liability is predicated upon concepts of gross negligence.[...]

However, it should be noted that the business judgment rule operates only in the context of director action. Technically speaking, it has no role where directors have either abdicated their functions, or absent a conscious decision, failed to act.[7] But it also follows that under applicable principles, a conscious decision to refrain from acting may nonetheless be a valid exercise of business judgment and enjoy the protections of the rule. [...]

4.2.2 Smith v. Van Gorkom

Van Gorkom is a controversial case of the duty of care in the context of a corporate acquisition. In *Van Gorkom*, the court found that the board had violated its duty of care to the corporation and awarded damages to stockholders. *Van Gorkom* was the impetus for the adoption of the § 102(b)(7)'s exculpation provision. Consequently, the result in *Van Gorkom* is unlikely to occur again. However, the *Van Gorkom* case is worth reading because it demonstrates the kinds of director failures that may well rise to the level of a violation of the duty of care.

488 A.2d 858 (1985)
SMITH v. VAN GORKOM

HORSEY, Justice (for the majority):

This appeal from the Court of Chancery involves a class action brought by shareholders of the defendant Trans Union Corporation ("Trans Union" or "the Company"), originally seeking rescission of a cash-out merger of Trans Union into the defendant New T Company ("New T"), a wholly-owned subsidiary of the defendant, Marmon Group, Inc. ("Marmon"). Alternate relief in the form of damages is sought against the defendant members of the Board of Directors of Trans Union, [864] New T, and Jay A. Pritzker and Robert A. Pritzker, owners of Marmon.[1]

Following trial, the former Chancellor granted judgment for the defendant directors by unreported letter opinion dated July 6, 1982.[2] Judgment was based on two findings: (1) that the Board of Directors had acted in an informed manner so as to be entitled to protection of the business judgment rule in approving the cash-out merger; and (2) that the shareholder vote approving the merger should not be set aside because the stockholders had been "fairly informed" by the Board of Directors before voting thereon. The plaintiffs appeal. [...]

We hold: (1) that the Board's decision, reached September 20, 1980, to approve the proposed cash-out merger was not the product of an informed business judgment; (2) that the Board's subsequent efforts to amend the Merger Agreement and take other curative action were ineffectual, both legally and factually; and (3) that the Board did not deal with complete candor with the stockholders by failing to disclose all material facts, which they knew or should have known, before securing the stockholders' approval of the merger. [...]

Trans Union was a publicly-traded, diversified holding company, the principal earnings of which were generated by its railcar leasing business. During the period here involved, the Company had a cash flow of hundreds of millions of dollars annually. However, the Company had difficulty in generating sufficient taxable income to offset increasingly large investment tax credits (ITCs).[...]

Beginning in the late 1960's, and continuing through the 1970's, Trans Union pursued a program of acquiring small companies in order to increase available taxable income. In July 1980, Trans Union Management prepared the annual revision of the Company's Five Year Forecast. This report [...]referred to the ITC situation as a "nagging problem" and, given that problem, the leasing company "would still appear to be constrained to a tax breakeven." The report then listed four alternative uses of the projected 1982-1985 equity surplus: (1) stock repurchase; (2) dividend increases; (3) a major acquisition program; and (4) combinations of the above. The sale of Trans Union was not among the alternatives. The report emphasized that, despite the overall surplus, the operation of the Company would consume all available equity for the next several years, and concluded: "As a result, we have sufficient time to fully develop our course of action."

-B-

On August 27, 1980, Van Gorkom met with Senior Management of Trans Union. Van Gorkom reported on his lobbying efforts in Washington and his desire to find a solution

290

to the tax credit problem more permanent than a continued program of acquisitions. Various alternatives were suggested and discussed preliminarily, including the sale of Trans Union to a company with a large amount of taxable income.

Donald Romans, Chief Financial Officer of Trans Union, stated that his department had done a "very brief bit of work on the possibility of a leveraged buy-out." This work had been prompted by a media article which Romans had seen regarding a leveraged buy-out by management. The work consisted of a "preliminary study" of the cash which could be generated by the Company if it participated in a leveraged buyout. As Romans stated, this analysis "was very first and rough cut at seeing whether a cash flow would support what might be considered a high price for this type of transaction."

On September 5, at another Senior Management meeting which Van Gorkom attended, Romans again brought up the idea of a leveraged buy-out as a "possible strategic alternative" to the Company's acquisition program. [...] According to Romans: They did not "come up" with a price for the Company. They merely "ran the numbers" at $50 a share and at $60 a share with the "rough form" of their cash figures at the time. Their "figures indicated that $50 would be very easy to do but $60 would be very difficult to do under those figures." This work did not purport to establish a fair price for either the Company or 100% of the stock. It was intended to determine the cash flow needed to service the debt that would "probably" be incurred in a leveraged buyout, based on "rough calculations" without "any benefit of experts to identify what the limits were to that, and so forth." [...]

At this meeting, Van Gorkom stated that he would be willing to take $55 per share for his own 75,000 shares. He vetoed the suggestion of a leveraged buy-out by Management, however, as involving a potential conflict of interest for Management. Van Gorkom, a certified public accountant and lawyer, had been an officer of Trans Union [866] for 24 years, its Chief Executive Officer for more than 17 years, and Chairman of its Board for 2 years. It is noteworthy in this connection that he was then approaching 65 years of age and mandatory retirement.

For several days following the September 5 meeting, Van Gorkom pondered the idea of a sale. [...]

Van Gorkom decided to meet with Jay A. Pritzker, a well-known corporate takeover specialist and a social acquaintance. However, rather than approaching Pritzker simply to determine his interest in acquiring Trans Union, Van Gorkom assembled a proposed per share price for sale of the Company and a financing structure by which to accomplish the sale. Van Gorkom did so without consulting either his Board or any members of Senior Management except one: Carl Peterson, Trans Union's Controller. Telling Peterson that he wanted no other person on his staff to know what he was doing, but without telling him why, Van Gorkom directed Peterson to calculate the feasibility of a leveraged buy-out at an assumed price per share of $55. Apart from the Company's historic stock market price,[5] and Van Gorkom's long association with Trans Union, the record is devoid of any competent evidence that $55 represented the per share intrinsic value of the Company.

Having thus chosen the $55 figure, based solely on the availability of a leveraged buy-out, Van Gorkom multiplied the price per share by the number of shares outstanding to reach a total value of the Company of $690 million. Van Gorkom told Peterson to use this $690 million figure and to assume a $200 million equity contribution by the buyer. Based on these assumptions, Van Gorkom directed Peterson to determine whether the debt portion of the purchase price could be paid off in five years or less if financed by Trans Union's cash flow as projected in the Five Year Forecast, and by the sale of certain weaker divisions identified in a study done for Trans Union by the Boston Consulting Group ("BCG study"). Peterson reported that, of the purchase price, approximately $50-80 million would remain outstanding after five years. Van Gorkom was disappointed, but decided to meet with Pritzker nevertheless.

Van Gorkom arranged a meeting with Pritzker at the latter's home on Saturday, September 13, 1980. Van Gorkom prefaced his presentation by stating to Pritzker: "Now as far as you are concerned, I can, I think, show how you can pay a substantial premium over the present stock price and pay off most of the loan in the first five years. * * * If you could pay $55 for this Company, here is a way in which I think it can be financed."

Van Gorkom then reviewed with Pritzker his calculations based upon his proposed price of $55 per share. Although Pritzker mentioned $50 as a more attractive figure, no other price was mentioned. However, Van Gorkom stated that to be sure that $55 was the best price obtainable, Trans Union should be free to accept any better offer. Pritzker demurred, stating that his organization would serve as a "stalking horse" for an "auction contest" only if Trans Union would permit Pritzker to buy 1,750,000 shares of Trans Union stock at market price which Pritzker could then sell to any higher bidder. After further discussion on this point, Pritzker told Van Gorkom that he would give him a more definite reaction soon.

Monday, September 15, Pritzker advised Van Gorkom that he was interested in the $55 cash-out merger proposal and requested more information on Trans Union. Van Gorkom agreed to meet privately with Pritzker, accompanied by Peterson, Chelberg, and Michael Carpenter, Trans Union's consultant from the Boston Consulting Group. The meetings took place on September 16 and 17. Van Gorkom was "astounded that events were moving with such amazing rapidity."

On Thursday, September 18, Van Gorkom met again with Pritzker. At that time, Van Gorkom knew that Pritzker intended to make a cash-out merger offer at Van Gorkom's proposed $55 per share. Pritzker instructed his attorney, a merger and acquisition specialist, to begin drafting merger documents. There was no further discussion of the $55 price. However, the number of shares of Trans Union's treasury stock to be offered to Pritzker was negotiated down to one million shares; the price was set at $38-75 cents above the per share price at the close of the market on September 19. At this point, Pritzker insisted that the Trans Union Board act on his merger proposal within the next three days, stating to Van Gorkom: "We have to have a decision by no later than Sunday [evening, September 21] […]

Van Gorkom retained James Brennan, Esquire, to advise Trans Union on the legal aspects of the merger. Van Gorkom did not consult with William Browder, a Vice-President and director of Trans Union and former head of its legal department, or with William Moore, then the head of Trans Union's legal staff.

On Friday, September 19, Van Gorkom called a special meeting of the Trans Union Board for noon the following day. He also called a meeting of the Company's Senior Management to convene at 11:00 a.m., prior to the meeting of the Board. No one, except Chelberg and Peterson, was told the purpose of the meetings. Van Gorkom did not invite Trans Union's investment banker, Salomon Brothers or its Chicago-based partner, to attend.

Of those present at the Senior Management meeting on September 20, only Chelberg and Peterson had prior knowledge of Pritzker's offer. Van Gorkom disclosed the offer and described its terms, but he furnished no copies of the proposed Merger Agreement. Romans announced that his department had done a second study which showed that, for a leveraged buy-out, the price range for Trans Union stock was between $55 and $65 per share. Van Gorkom neither saw the study nor asked Romans to make it available for the Board meeting.

Senior Management's reaction to the Pritzker proposal was completely negative. […] Romans objected to the price as being too low;[6] he was critical of the timing and suggested that consideration should be given to the adverse tax consequences of an all-cash deal for low-basis shareholders; and he took the position that the agreement to sell Pritzker one million newly-issued shares at market price would inhibit other offers, as would the prohibitions against soliciting bids and furnishing inside information [868] to other bidders. Romans argued that the Pritzker proposal was a "lock up" and amounted to "an agreed merger as opposed to an offer." Nevertheless, Van Gorkom proceeded to the Board meeting as scheduled without further delay.

Chelberg, and Van Gorkom) and five outside (defendants Wallis, Johnson, Lanterman, Morgan and Reneker). All directors were present at the meeting, except O'Boyle who was ill. […]

Van Gorkom began the Special Meeting of the Board with a twenty-minute oral presentation. Copies of the proposed Merger Agreement were delivered too late for study before or during the meeting.[7] He reviewed the Company's ITC and depreciation problems and the efforts theretofore made to solve them. He discussed his initial meeting with Pritzker and his motivation in arranging that meeting. Van Gorkom did not disclose to the Board, however, the methodology by which he alone had arrived at the $55 figure, or the fact that he first proposed the $55 price in his negotiations with Pritzker.

Van Gorkom outlined the terms of the Pritzker offer as follows: Pritzker would pay $55 in cash for all outstanding shares of Trans Union stock upon completion of which Trans Union would be merged into New T Company, a subsidiary wholly-owned by Pritzker and formed to implement the merger; for a period of 90 days, Trans Union could receive, but could not actively solicit, competing offers; the offer had to be acted on by the next evening, Sunday, September 21; [...]

Van Gorkom took the position that putting Trans Union "up for auction" through a 90-day market test would validate a decision by the Board that $55 was a fair price. He told the Board that the "free market will have an opportunity to judge whether $55 is a fair price." Van Gorkom framed the decision before the Board not as whether $55 per share was the highest price that could be obtained, but as whether the $55 price was a fair price that the stockholders should be given the opportunity to accept or reject.[8]

Attorney Brennan advised the members of the Board that they might be sued if they failed to accept the offer and that a fairness opinion was not required as a matter of law.

Romans attended the meeting as chief financial officer of the Company. He told the Board that he had not been involved in the negotiations with Pritzker and knew nothing about the merger proposal until [869] the morning of the meeting; [...] Romans testified:

> I told the Board that the study ran the numbers at 50 and 60, and
> then the subsequent study at 55 and 65, and that was not the same
> thing as saying that I have a valuation of the company at X dollars.
> But it was a way — a first step towards reaching that conclusion.

Romans told the Board that, in his opinion, $55 was "in the range of a fair price," but "at the beginning of the range." [...]

The Board meeting of September 20 lasted about two hours. Based solely upon Van Gorkom's oral presentation, Chelberg's supporting representations, Romans' oral statement, Brennan's legal advice, and their knowledge of the market history of the Company's stock,[9] the directors approved the proposed Merger Agreement. [...]

The Merger Agreement was executed by Van Gorkom during the evening of September 20 at a formal social event that he hosted for the opening of the Chicago Lyric Opera. Neither he nor any other director read the agreement prior to its signing and delivery to Pritzker. [...]

On Monday, September 22, the Company issued a press release announcing that Trans Union had entered into a "definitive" Merger Agreement with an affiliate of the Marmon

Group, Inc., a Pritzker holding company. Within 10 days of the public announcement, dissent among Senior Management over the merger had become widespread. Faced with threatened resignations of key officers, Van Gorkom met with Pritzker who agreed to several modifications of the Agreement. […]

Van Gorkom reconvened the Board on October 8 and secured the directors' approval of the proposed amendments — sight unseen. The Board also authorized the employment of Salomon Brothers, its investment [870] banker, to solicit other offers for Trans Union during the proposed "market test" period.

The next day, October 9, Trans Union issued a press release announcing: (1) that Pritzker had obtained "the financing commitments necessary to consummate" the merger with Trans Union; (2) that Pritzker had acquired one million shares of Trans Union common stock at $38 per share; (3) that Trans Union was now permitted to actively seek other offers and had retained Salomon Brothers for that purpose; and (4) that if a more favorable offer were not received before February 1, 1981, Trans Union's shareholders would thereafter meet to vote on the Pritzker proposal.

It was not until the following day, October 10, that the actual amendments to the Merger Agreement were prepared by Pritzker and delivered to Van Gorkom for execution. As will be seen, the amendments were considerably at variance with Van Gorkom's representations of the amendments to the Board on October 8; and the amendments placed serious constraints on Trans Union's ability to negotiate a better deal and withdraw from the Pritzker agreement. Nevertheless, Van Gorkom proceeded to execute what became the October 10 amendments to the Merger Agreement without conferring further with the Board members and apparently without comprehending the actual implications of the amendments. […]

On February 10, the stockholders of Trans Union approved the Pritzker merger proposal. Of the outstanding shares, 69.9% were voted in favor of the merger; 7.25% were voted against the merger; and 22.85% were not voted.

II.

We turn to the issue of the application of the business judgment rule to the September 20 meeting of the Board. […]

Under Delaware law, the business judgment rule is the offspring of the fundamental principle, codified in 8 *Del.C.* § 141(a), that the business and affairs of a Delaware corporation are managed by or under its board of directors.[…]In carrying out their managerial roles, directors are charged with an unyielding fiduciary duty to the corporation and its shareholders. […]The business judgment rule exists to protect and promote the full and free exercise of the managerial power granted to Delaware directors. […] The rule itself "is a presumption that in making a business decision, the directors of a corporation acted on an informed basis, in good faith and in the honest belief that the action taken was in the best interests of the company." *Aronson, supra* at 812. Thus, the party attacking a board decision as uninformed must rebut the presumption that its business judgment was an informed one. *Id.*

The determination of whether a business judgment is an informed one turns on whether the directors have informed themselves "prior to making a business decision, of all material information reasonably available to them." *Id.*[12]

Under the business judgment rule there is no protection for directors who have made "an unintelligent or unadvised judgment." […] A director's duty to inform himself in preparation for a decision derives from the fiduciary capacity in which he serves the corporation and its stockholders. […] Since a director is vested with the responsibility for the management of the affairs of the corporation, he must execute that duty with the recognition that he acts on behalf of others. Such obligation does not tolerate faithlessness or self-dealing. But fulfillment of the fiduciary function requires more than the mere absence of bad faith or fraud. Representation of the financial interests of others imposes on a director an affirmative duty to protect those interests and to proceed with a critical eye in assessing information of the type and under the circumstances present here. […]

Thus, a director's duty to exercise an informed business judgment is in [873] the nature of a duty of care, as distinguished from a duty of loyalty. Here, there were no allegations of fraud, bad faith, or self-dealing, or proof thereof. Hence, it is presumed that the directors reached their business judgment in good faith, […]

The standard of care applicable to a director's duty of care has also been recently restated by this Court. In *Aronson, supra,* we stated:

> While the Delaware cases use a variety of terms to describe the
> applicable standard of care, our analysis satisfies us that under the
> business judgment rule director liability is predicated upon concepts
> of gross negligence. […]

We again confirm that view. We think the concept of gross negligence is also the proper standard for determining whether a business judgment reached by a board of directors was an informed one.[13]

In the specific context of a proposed merger of domestic corporations, a director has a duty under 8 *Del.C.* 251(b),[14] along with his fellow directors, to act in an informed and deliberate manner in determining whether to approve an agreement of merger before submitting the proposal to the stockholders. Certainly in the merger context, a director may not abdicate that duty by leaving to the shareholders alone the decision to approve or disapprove the agreement. […]

It is against those standards that the conduct of the directors of Trans Union must be tested, as a matter of law and as a matter of fact, regarding their exercise of an informed business judgment in voting to approve the Pritzker merger proposal.

III.

The defendants argue that the determination of whether their decision to accept $55 per share for Trans Union represented an informed business judgment requires consideration, not only of that which they knew and learned on September 20, but also of that which they subsequently learned and did over the following four-month [874] period before the shareholders met to vote on the proposal in February, 1981. The defendants thereby seek to reduce the significance of their action on September 20 and to widen the time frame for determining whether their decision to accept the Pritzker proposal was an informed one. Thus, the defendants contend that what the directors did and learned subsequent to September 20 and through January 26, 1981, was properly taken into account by the Trial Court in determining whether the Board's judgment was an informed one. We disagree with this *post hoc* approach.

The issue of whether the directors reached an informed decision to "sell" the Company on September 20, 1980 must be determined only upon the basis of the information then reasonably available to the directors and relevant to their decision to accept the Pritzker merger proposal. This is not to say that the directors were precluded from altering their original plan of action, had they done so in an informed manner. What we do say is that the question of whether the directors reached an informed business judgment in agreeing to sell the Company, pursuant to the terms of the September 20 Agreement presents, in reality, two questions: (A) whether the directors reached an informed business judgment on September 20, 1980; and (B) if they did not, whether the directors' actions taken subsequent to September 20 were adequate to cure any infirmity in their action taken on September 20. We first consider the directors' September 20 action in terms of their reaching an informed business judgment.

-A-

On the record before us, we must conclude that the Board of Directors did not reach an informed business judgment on September 20, 1980 in voting to "sell" the Company for $55 per share pursuant to the Pritzker cash-out merger proposal. Our reasons, in summary, are as follows:

The directors (1) did not adequately inform themselves as to Van Gorkom's role in forcing the "sale" of the Company and in establishing the per share purchase price; (2) were uninformed as to the intrinsic value of the Company; and (3) given these circumstances, at a minimum, were grossly negligent in approving the "sale" of the Company upon two hours' consideration, without prior notice, and without the exigency of a crisis or emergency.

As has been noted, the Board based its September 20 decision to approve the cash-out merger primarily on Van Gorkom's representations. None of the directors, other than Van Gorkom and Chelberg, had any prior knowledge that the purpose of the meeting was to propose a cash-out merger of Trans Union. No members of Senior Management were present, other than Chelberg, Romans and Peterson; and the latter two had only learned of the proposed sale an hour earlier. Both general counsel Moore and former general counsel Browder attended the meeting, but were equally uninformed as to the purpose of the meeting and the documents to be acted upon.

Without any documents before them concerning the proposed transaction, the members of the Board were required to rely entirely upon Van Gorkom's 20-minute oral presentation of the proposal. No written summary of the terms of the merger was presented; the directors were given no documentation to support the adequacy of $55 price per share for sale of the Company; and the Board had before it nothing more than Van Gorkom's statement of his understanding of the substance of an agreement which he admittedly had never read, nor which any member of the Board had ever seen.

Under 8 *Del.C.* § 141(e),[15] "directors are fully protected in relying in [875] good faith on reports made by officers." […] The term "report" has been liberally construed to include reports of informal personal investigations by corporate officers, […] However, there is no evidence that any "report," as defined under § 141(e), concerning the Pritzker proposal, was presented to the Board on September 20.[16] Van Gorkom's oral presentation of his understanding of the terms of the proposed Merger Agreement, which he had not seen, and Romans' brief oral statement of his preliminary study regarding the feasibility of a leveraged buy-out of Trans Union do not qualify as § 141(e) "reports" for these reasons: The former lacked substance because Van Gorkom was basically uninformed as to the essential provisions of the very document about which he was talking. Romans' statement was irrelevant to the issues before the Board since it did not purport to be a valuation study. At a minimum for a report to enjoy the status conferred by § 141(e), it must be pertinent to the subject matter upon which a board is called to act, and otherwise be entitled to good faith, not blind, reliance. Considering all of the surrounding circumstances — hastily calling the meeting without prior notice of its subject matter, the proposed sale of the Company without any prior consideration of the issue or necessity therefor, the urgent time constraints imposed by Pritzker, and the total absence of any documentation whatsoever — the directors were duty bound to make reasonable inquiry of Van Gorkom and Romans, and if they had done so, the inadequacy of that upon which they now claim to have relied would have been apparent.

The defendants rely on the following factors to sustain the Trial Court's finding that the Board's decision was an informed one: (1) the magnitude of the premium or spread between the $55 Pritzker offering price and Trans Union's current market price of $38 per share; (2) the amendment of the Agreement as submitted on September 20 to permit the Board to accept any better offer during the "market test" period; (3) the collective experience and expertise of the Board's "inside" and "outside" directors;[17] and (4) their reliance on Brennan's legal advice that the directors might be sued if they rejected the Pritzker proposal. […]

(1)

A substantial premium may provide one reason to recommend a merger, but in the absence of other sound valuation information, the fact of a premium alone does not provide an adequate basis upon which to assess the fairness of an offering price. Here, the judgment reached as to the adequacy of the premium was based on a comparison between the historically depressed Trans Union market price and the amount of the Pritzker offer. Using market price as a basis for concluding that the premium adequately reflected the true value of the Company was a clearly faulty, indeed fallacious, premise, as the defendants' own evidence demonstrates.

The record is clear that before September 20, Van Gorkom and other members of Trans Union's Board knew that the market had consistently undervalued the worth of Trans Union's stock, despite steady increases in the Company's operating income in the seven years preceding the merger. […]

In the Proxy Statement, however, the directors reversed their position. There, they stated that, although the earnings prospects for Trans Union were "excellent," they found no basis for believing that this would be reflected in future stock prices. With regard to past trading, the Board stated that the prices at which the Company's common stock had traded in recent years did not reflect the "inherent" value of the Company. But having referred to the "inherent" value of Trans Union, the directors ascribed no number to it. Moreover, nowhere did they disclose that they had no basis on which to fix "inherent" worth beyond an impressionistic reaction to the premium over market and an unsubstantiated belief that the value of the assets was "significantly greater" than book value. By their own admission they could not rely on the stock price as an accurate measure of value. Yet, also by their own admission, the Board members assumed that Trans Union's market price was adequate to serve as a basis upon which to assess the adequacy of the premium for purposes of the September 20 meeting. […]

Indeed, as of September 20, the Board had no other information on which to base a determination of the intrinsic value of Trans Union as a going concern. As of September 20, the Board had made no evaluation of the Company designed to value the entire enterprise, nor had the Board ever previously considered selling the Company or consenting to a buy-out merger. Thus, the adequacy of a premium is indeterminate unless it is assessed in terms of other competent and sound valuation information that reflects the value of the particular business. […]

We do not imply that an outside valuation study is essential to support an informed business judgment; nor do we state that fairness opinions by independent investment bankers are required as a matter of law. Often insiders familiar with the business of a going concern are in a better position than are outsiders to gather relevant information; and under appropriate circumstances, such directors may be fully protected in relying in good faith upon the valuation reports of their management. […]

Here, the record establishes that the Board did not request its Chief Financial Officer, Romans, to make any valuation study or review of the proposal to determine the adequacy of $55 per share for sale of the Company. On the record before us: The Board rested on Romans' elicited response that the $55 figure was within a "fair price range" within the context of a leveraged buy-out. No director sought any further information from Romans. No director asked him why he put $55 at the bottom of his range. No director asked Romans for any details as to his study, the reason why it had been undertaken or its depth. No director asked to see the study; and no director asked Romans whether Trans Union's finance department could do a fairness study within the remaining 36-hour[18] period available under the Pritzker offer. […]

Thus, the record compels the conclusion that on September 20 the Board lacked valuation information adequate to reach an informed business judgment as to the fairness of $55 per share for sale of the Company.[20]

(2)

This brings us to the post-September 20 "market test" upon which the defendants ultimately rely to confirm the reasonableness of their September 20 decision to accept the Pritzker proposal. In this connection, the directors present a two-part argument: (a) that by making a "market test" of Pritzker's $55 per share offer a condition of their September 20 decision to accept his offer, they cannot be found to have acted impulsively or in an uninformed manner on September 20; and (b) that the adequacy of the $17 premium for sale of the Company was conclusively established over the following 90 to 120 days by the most reliable evidence available — the marketplace. Thus, the defendants impliedly contend that the "market test" eliminated the need for the Board to perform any other form of fairness test either on September 20, or thereafter.

Again, the facts of record do not support the defendants' argument. There is no evidence: (a) that the Merger Agreement was effectively amended to give the Board freedom to put Trans Union up for auction sale to the highest bidder; or (b) that a public auction was in fact permitted to occur. […]

The Merger Agreement, specifically identified as that originally presented to the Board on September 20, has never been produced by the defendants, notwithstanding the plaintiffs' several demands for production before as well as during trial. No acceptable explanation of this failure to produce documents has been given to either the Trial Court or this Court. Significantly, neither the defendants nor their counsel have made the affirmative representation that this critical document has been produced. Thus, the Court is deprived of the best evidence on which to judge the merits of the defendants' position as to the care and attention which they gave to the terms of the Agreement on September 20.

Van Gorkom, conceding that he never read the Agreement, stated that he was relying upon his understanding that, under corporate law, directors always have an inherent right, as well as a fiduciary duty, to accept a better offer notwithstanding an existing contractual commitment by the Board.[…]

Several of Trans Union's outside directors resolutely maintained that the Agreement as submitted was approved on the understanding that, "if we got a better deal, we had a right to take it." Director Johnson so testified; but he then added, "And if they didn't put that in the agreement, then the management did not carry out the conclusion of the Board. And I just don't know whether they did or not." The only clause in the Agreement as finally executed to which the defendants can point as "keeping the door open" is the following underlined statement found in subparagraph (a) of section 2.03 of the Merger Agreement as executed:

> The Board of Directors shall recommend to the stockholders of
> Trans Union that they approve and adopt the Merger Agreement
> (`the stockholders' approval') and to use its best efforts to obtain
> the requisite votes therefor. *GL acknowledges that Trans Union directors*

may have a competing fiduciary obligation to the shareholders under certain
circumstances.

Clearly, this language on its face cannot be construed as incorporating either of the two "conditions" described above: either the right to accept a better offer or the right to distribute proprietary information to third parties. The logical witness for the defendants to call to confirm their construction of this clause of the Agreement would have been Trans Union's outside attorney, James Brennan. The defendants' failure, without explanation, to call this witness again permits the logical inference that his testimony would not have been helpful to them. The further fact that the directors adjourned, rather than recessed, the meeting without incorporating in the Agreement these important "conditions" further weakens the defendants' position. As has been noted, nothing in the Board's Minutes supports these claims. No reference to either of the so-called "conditions" or of Trans Union's reserved right to test the market appears in any notes of the Board meeting or in the Board Resolution accepting the Pritzker offer or in the Minutes of the meeting itself. That evening, in the midst of a formal party which he hosted for the opening of the Chicago Lyric Opera, Van Gorkom executed the Merger Agreement without he or any other member of the Board having read the instruments. […]

(3)

The directors' unfounded reliance on both the premium and the market test as the basis for accepting the Pritzker proposal undermines the defendants' remaining contention that the Board's collective experience and sophistication was a sufficient basis for finding that it reached its September 20 decision with informed, reasonable deliberation.[…]

(4)

Part of the defense is based on a claim that the directors relied on legal advice rendered at the September 20 meeting by James Brennan, Esquire, who was present at Van Gorkom's request. Unfortunately, Brennan did not appear and testify at trial even though his firm participated in the defense of this action. […]

-B-

We now examine the Board's post-September 20 conduct for the purpose of determining first, whether it was informed and not grossly negligent; and second, if informed, whether it was sufficient to legally rectify and cure the Board's derelictions of September 20.[23] […]

Defendants made no reference to provisions allegedly reserving to the Board the rights to perform a "market test" and to withdraw from the Pritzker Agreement if Trans Union received a better offer before the shareholder meeting. The defendants also concede that Trans Union never made a subsequent public announcement stating that it had in fact reserved the right to accept alternate offers, the Agreement notwithstanding.

The public announcement of the Pritzker merger resulted in an "en masse" revolt of Trans Union's Senior Management. […]

Van Gorkom then advised Senior Management that the Agreement would be amended to give Trans Union the right to solicit competing offers through January, 1981, if they would agree to remain with Trans Union. Senior Management was temporarily mollified; and Van Gorkom then called a special meeting of Trans Union's Board for October 8.

Thus, the primary purpose of the October 8 Board meeting was to amend the Merger Agreement, in a manner agreeable to Pritzker, to permit Trans Union to conduct a "market test."[…] Van Gorkom presumably so represented the amendments to Trans Union's Board members on October 8. In a brief session, the directors approved Van Gorkom's oral presentation of the substance of the proposed amendments, [883] the terms of which were not reduced to writing until October 10. But rather than waiting to review the amendments, the Board again approved them sight unseen and adjourned, giving Van Gorkom authority to execute the papers when he received them.[…]

The next day, October 9, and before the Agreement was amended, Pritzker moved swiftly to off-set the proposed market test amendment. First, Pritzker informed Trans Union that he had completed arrangements for financing its acquisition and that the parties were thereby mutually bound to a firm purchase and sale arrangement. Second, Pritzker announced the exercise of his option to purchase one million shares of Trans Union's treasury stock at $38 per share — 75 cents above the current market price. […]

The next day, October 10, Pritzker delivered to Trans Union the proposed amendments to the September 20 Merger Agreement. Van Gorkom promptly proceeded to countersign all the instruments on behalf of Trans Union without reviewing the instruments to determine if they were consistent with the authority previously granted him by the Board. The amending documents were apparently not approved by Trans Union's Board until a much later date, December 2. The record does not affirmatively establish that Trans Union's directors ever read the October 10 amendments.[26]

The October 10 amendments to the Merger Agreement did authorize Trans Union to solicit competing offers, but the amendments had more far-reaching effects. […] Under the October 10 amendments, a better *offer* was no longer sufficient to permit Trans Union's withdrawal. Trans Union was now permitted to terminate the Pritzker Agreement and abandon the merger only if, prior to February 10, 1981, Trans Union had either consummated a merger (or sale of assets) with a third party or had entered into a "definitive" merger agreement more favorable than Pritzker's and for a greater consideration — subject only to stockholder approval. Further, the "extension" of the market test period to February 10, 1981 was circumscribed by other amendments which required Trans Union to file its preliminary proxy statement on the Pritzker merger proposal by December 5, 1980 and use its best efforts to mail the statement to its shareholders by January 5, 1981. Thus, the market test period was effectively reduced, not extended. […]

In our view, the record compels the conclusion that the directors' conduct on October 8 exhibited the same deficiencies as did their conduct on September 20. […]

We conclude that the Board acted in a grossly negligent manner on October 8. […]

4.2.3 Section 102(b)(7)

The Delaware Supreme Court's decision in *Van Gorkom* was highly controversial at the time – and even now. The imposition of monetary liability for directors' lack of care, while not unheard of, was not a common occurrence. The court's opinion was a divided 3-2 decision. The Delaware Supreme Court has a norm of unanimity, and it is highly unusual for the court - particularly with respect to the corporate law - to issue divided opinions. This gives you a sense how controversial this opinion was at the time.

The decision has been variously derided by observers as a "comedy of errors", a "serious mistake", "dumbfounding", and "surely one of the worst decisions in the history of corporate law." Nevertheless, *Van Gorkom* has endured over the years. In part, that may be because a combination of statutory responses and subsequent developments in the common law have robbed *Van Gorkom* of much of its bite. In the wake of *Van Gorkom*, there was a public outcry by groups and associations representing the interests of corporate directors. They argued loudly that the real - albeit remote - prospect of directors facing monetary liability for violations of their duty of care would open the floodgates to litigation and cause otherwise qualified directors to retreat from the service on boards of directors. In the alternative, directors who remained on boards would face sky-rocketing insurance premiums for D&O insurance, making American businesses uncompetitive on the global stage.

In response to *Van Gorkom* and the public outcry that followed it, the Delaware legislature (as well soon thereafter the legislatures in all 50 states, DC, and Puerto Rico) adopted exculpation provisions, which exculpate from liability for monetary damages violations by directors of their duty of care, as well as reliance provisions like §141(e).

The text of §102(b)(7), which you've seen earlier in this course, follows below.

One can reasonably disagree with the policy of insulating directors from monetary liability for violations of their duty of care. Indeed, other countries impose liability on corporate directors for care violations.

§ 102. Contents of certificate of incorporation.

(b) In addition to the matters required to be set forth in the certificate of incorporation by subsection (a) of this section, the certificate of incorporation may also contain any or all of the following matters: … **(7)** A provision eliminating or limiting the personal liability of a director to the corporation or its stockholders for monetary damages for breach of fiduciary duty as a director, provided that such provision shall not eliminate or limit the liability of a director: (i) For any breach of the director's duty of loyalty to the corporation or its stockholders; (ii) for acts or omissions not in good faith or which involve intentional misconduct or a knowing violation of law; (iii) under § 174 of this title; or (iv) for any transaction from which the director derived an improper personal benefit. No such provision shall eliminate or limit the liability of a director for any act or omission occurring prior to the date when such provision becomes effective. All references in this paragraph to a director shall also be deemed to refer to such other person or persons, if any, who, pursuant to a provision of the certificate of incorporation in accordance with § 141(a) of this title, exercise or perform any of the powers or duties otherwise conferred or imposed upon the board of directors by this title.

Question: Given the elimination of monetary liability, what incentives are there for directors to do a good job? Is potential monetary liability required in order to assure directors live up to the standard of care?

4.2.4 Malpiede v. Townson

The effect of §102(b)(7) provisions on litigation is significant. Exculpation provisions eliminate of monetary liability directors for violations of their duty of care. Consequently, if a plaintiffs alleges only that directors violated their duty of care and that caused them some damage, there is no remedy available at law for these plaintiffs. Where the court is unable to provide a remedy, judicial economy requires that a case be dismissed. In *Malpiede*, the Delaware courts encounter just such a situation. The result is not surprising: a duty of care claim is dismissed for failure to state a claim for which there is a remedy available.

780 A.2d 1075 (2001)
<u>MALPIEDE v. TOWNSON</u>

VEASEY, Chief Justice.

In this appeal, we affirm […] the granting of a motion to dismiss the plaintiffs' due care claim on the ground that the exculpatory provision in the charter of the target corporation authorized by 8 *Del. C.* § 102(b)(7), bars any claim for money damages against the director defendants based solely on the board's alleged breach of its duty of care. […]

With respect to the dismissal based on the exculpatory effect of the Section 102(b)(7) charter provision, we had an initial concern about the propriety of the trial court's consideration of the exculpatory charter provision on a Rule 12(b)(6) motion to dismiss because it is a matter outside the complaint. […] Because the plaintiffs do not contest the existence, terms, validity or authenticity of the Frederick's exculpatory charter provision, we hold that the charter provision was properly before the Court of Chancery, which correctly held that the plaintiffs' due care claim was barred. Accordingly, we affirm the judgment of the Court of Chancery.

Facts

Frederick's of Hollywood ("Frederick's") is a retailer of women's lingerie and apparel with its headquarters in Los Angeles, California.[1] This case centers on the merger of Frederick's into Knightsbridge Capital Corporation ("Knightsbridge") under circumstances where it became a target in a bidding contest. […]

On June 13, 1997, the Frederick's board approved an offer from Knightsbridge to purchase all of Frederick's outstanding Class A and Class B shares for $6.14 per share in cash in a two-step merger transaction.[5] The terms of the merger agreement signed by the Frederick's board prohibited the board from soliciting additional bids from third parties, but the agreement permitted the board to negotiate with third party bidders when the board's fiduciary duties required it to do so.[6] The Frederick's board then sent to stockholders a Consent Solicitation Statement recommending that they approve the transaction, which was scheduled to close on August 27, 1997.

On August 21, 1997, Frederick's received a fully financed, unsolicited cash offer of $7.00 per share from a third party bidder, Milton Partners ("Milton"). […]

On August 27, 1997, the Frederick's board received a fully financed, unsolicited $7.75 cash offer from Veritas Capital Fund ("Veritas"). In light of these developments, the board postponed the Knightsbridge merger in order to arrange a meeting with the two new bidders. On September 2, 1997, the board sent a memorandum to Milton and Veritas outlining the conditions for participation in the bidding process. […]

On September 6, 1997, Knightsbridge increased its bid to match the $7.75 Veritas offer, but on the condition that the board accept a variety of terms designed to restrict its ability to pursue superior offers.[10] On the same day, the Frederick's board approved this agreement and effectively ended the bidding process. […]

On September 11, 1997, Veritas increased its cash offer to $9.00 per share. Relying on (1) the "no-talk" provision in the merger agreement, (2) Knightsbridge's stated intention to vote its shares against third party bids, and (3) Veritas' request for an option to dilute Knightsbridge's interest, the board rejected the revised Veritas bid. […]

Before the merger closed, the plaintiffs filed in the Court of Chancery the purported class action complaint that is the predecessor [1082] of the amended complaint before us. The plaintiffs also moved for a temporary restraining order enjoining the merger. The Court of Chancery denied the requested injunctive relief.[11]

The plaintiffs then amended their complaint to include a class action claim for damages caused by the termination of the auction in favor of Knightsbridge and the rejection of the higher Veritas offer. […]

The Court of Chancery granted the directors' motion to dismiss the amended complaint under Chancery Rule 12(b)(6), concluding that: (1) the complaint did not support a claim of breach of the board's duty of loyalty, (2) the exculpatory provision in the Frederick's charter precluded money damages against the directors for any breach of the board's duty of care, […]

Standard of Review

We review *de novo* the dismissal by the Court of Chancery of a complaint under Rule 12(b)(6).[14] The complaint ordinarily defines the universe of facts from which the trial court may draw in ruling on a motion to dismiss.[15] Because a motion to dismiss under Chancery Rule 12(b)(6) must be decided without the benefit of a factual record, the Court of Chancery may not resolve material factual disputes; instead, the court is required to assume as true the well-pleaded allegations in the complaint.[16] The trial court may dismiss a complaint under Rule 12(b)(6) only where the court determines with "reasonable certainty" that the plaintiff could prevail on [1083] no set of facts that may be inferred from the well-pleaded allegations in the complaint.[17] This standard is based on the "notice pleading" requirement established in Ct. Ch. R. 8(e) and is "less stringent than the standard applied when evaluating whether a pre-suit demand has been excused in a stockholder derivative suit filed pursuant to Chancery Rule 23.1."[18]

Of course, the trial court is not required to accept every strained interpretation of the allegations proposed by the plaintiff, but the plaintiff is entitled to all reasonable inferences that logically flow from the face of the complaint. Moreover, a claim may be dismissed if allegations in the complaint or in the exhibits incorporated into the complaint effectively negate the claim as a matter of law.[19]

The Duty of Loyalty Claim

The central claim in the amended complaint is that the sale of Frederick's to Knightsbridge "constituted a breach of [the Frederick's board's] fiduciary obligation to maximize shareholder value" because the board did not "conduct an auction with a `level playing field'" as required by *Revlon, Inc. v. MacAndrews & Forbes Holdings*.[20] The plaintiffs contend that this sort of allegation cannot be neatly divided into duty of care claims and duty of loyalty claims.

In our view, *Revlon* neither creates a new type of fiduciary duty in the sale-of-control context nor alters the nature of the fiduciary duties that generally apply. Rather, *Revlon* emphasizes that the board must perform its fiduciary duties in the service of a specific objective: maximizing the sale price of the enterprise.[21] Although [1084] the *Revlon* doctrine imposes enhanced judicial scrutiny of certain transactions involving a sale of control, it does not eliminate the requirement that plaintiffs plead sufficient facts to support the underlying claims for a breach of fiduciary duties in conducting the sale.[...]

The Court of Chancery concluded, and the plaintiffs do not appear to contest on appeal, that the amended complaint adequately alleges a conflict of interest with respect to only one of the directors who approved the Knightsbridge merger.[24] The amended complaint does not allege that the lone conflicted director dominated the three other directors who approved the merger on September 6, 1997.[25] The Court of Chancery therefore correctly held that the Knightsbridge merger was approved [1085] by a majority of disinterested directors. [...]

The Due Care Claim

Having concluded that the complaint was properly dismissed under Chancery Rule 12(b)(6) for failure to state a claim on which relief may be granted on other fiduciary duty claims, we now turn to the due care claim. The primary due care issue is whether the board was grossly negligent, and therefore breached its duty of due care, in failing to implement a routine defensive strategy that could enable the board to negotiate for a higher bid or otherwise create a tactical advantage to enhance stockholder value.

In this case, that routine strategy would have been for the directors to use a poison pill to ward off Knightsbridge's advances and thus to prevent Knightsbridge from stopping the auction process. Had they done so, plaintiffs seem to allege that the directors could have preserved the appropriate options for an auction process designed to achieve the best value for the stockholders.

Construing the amended complaint most favorably to the plaintiffs, it can be read to allege that the board was grossly negligent in immediately accepting the Knightsbridge offer and agreeing to various restrictions on further negotiations without first determining whether Veritas would issue a counteroffer. Although the board had conducted a search for a buyer over one year, plaintiffs seem to contend that the board was imprudently hasty in agreeing to a restrictive merger agreement on the day it was proposed — particularly where other bidders had recently expressed interest.[43] Although the board's haste, in itself, might not constitute a breach of the board's duty of care because the board had already conducted a lengthy sale process, the plaintiffs argue that the board's decision to accept allegedly extreme contractual restrictions impacted its ability to obtain a higher sale price. Recognizing that, at the end of the day, plaintiffs would have an uphill battle in overcoming the presumption of the business judgment rule,[44] we must give plaintiffs the benefit of the doubt at this pleading stage to determine if they have stated a due care claim. Because of our ultimate decision, however, we need not finally decide this question in this case.

We assume, therefore, without deciding, that a claim for relief based on gross negligence during the board's auction process is stated by the inferences most favorable to plaintiffs that flow from these allegations. The issue then becomes whether the amended complaint may be dismissed upon a Rule 12(b)(6) motion by reason of the existence and the legal effect of the exculpatory provision of Article TWELFTH of Frederick's certificate of incorporation, adopted pursuant to 8 *Del. C.* § 102(b)(7). That provision would exempt directors from personal liability in damages with [1090] certain exceptions (*e.g.,* breach of the duty of loyalty) that are not applicable here.[45] […]

312

B. *Application of* Emerald Partners

We now address plaintiffs' argument that the trial court committed error, based on certain language in *Emerald Partners,*[57] by barring their due care claims. Plaintiffs' arguments on this point are based on an erroneous premise, and our decision here is not inconsistent with *Emerald Partners.*

In *Emerald Partners,* we made two important points about the raising of Section 102(b)(7) charter provisions. First we said: "[T]he shield from liability provided by a certificate of incorporation provision adopted pursuant to 8 *Del. C.* § 102(b)(7) is in the nature of an affirmative defense."[58] Second, we said:

> [W]here the factual basis for a claim *solely* implicates a violation of
> the duty of care, this court has indicated that the protections of such
> a charter provision may properly be invoked and applied. *Arnold v.*
> *Society for Savings Bancorp.,* Del.Supr., 650 A.2d 1270, 1288 (1994);
> *Zirn v. VLI Corp.,* Del.Supr., 681 A.2d 1050, 1061 (1996).[59]

Based on this language in *Emerald Partners,* plaintiffs make two arguments. First, they argue that the Court of Chancery in this case should not have dismissed their due care claims because these claims are intertwined with, and thus indistinguishable from, the duty of loyalty and bad faith claims.[60] Second, plaintiffs contend that the Court of Chancery incorrectly assigned to them the burden of going forward with proof.

1. The Court of Chancery Properly Dismissed Claims Based Solely on the Duty of Care

Plaintiffs here, while not conceding that the Section 102(b)(7) charter provision may be considered on this Rule 12(b)(6) motion nevertheless, in effect, conceded in oral argument in the Court of Chancery and similarly in oral argument in this Court that if a complaint unambiguously and solely asserted only a due care claim, the complaint is dismissible once the corporation's Section 102(b)(7) provision is invoked.[61] This concession is in line with our holding in *Emerald Partners* quoted above.

Plaintiffs contended vigorously, however, that the Section 102(b)(7) charter provision does not apply to bar their claims in this case because the amended complaint alleges breaches of the duty of loyalty and other claims that are not barred by the charter provision. As a result, plaintiffs maintain, this case cannot be boiled down solely to a due care case. They argue, in effect, that their complaint is sufficiently well-pleaded that — *as a matter of law* — the due care claims are so inextricably intertwined with loyalty and bad faith claims that Section 102(b)(7) is not a bar to recovery of damages against the directors.[62]

We disagree. It is the plaintiffs who have a burden to set forth "a short and plain statement of the claim showing that the pleader is entitled to relief."[63] The plaintiffs are entitled to all reasonable inferences flowing from their pleadings, but if those inferences do not support a valid legal claim, the complaint should be dismissed without the need for the defendants to file an answer and without proceeding with discovery. Here we have assumed, without deciding, that the amended complaint on its face states a due care claim. Because we have determined that the complaint fails properly to invoke loyalty and bad faith claims, we are left with only a due care claim. Defendants had the obligation to raise the bar of Section 102(b)(7) as a defense, and they did. As plaintiffs conceded in oral argument before this Court, if there is only an unambiguous, residual due care claim and nothing else — *as a matter of law* — then Section 102(b)(7) would bar the claim. Accordingly, the Court of Chancery did not err in dismissing the plaintiffs due care claim in this case.

Conclusion

We have concluded that: (1) the amended complaint does not adequately allege a breach of the Frederick's board's duty of loyalty or its disclosure duty; (2) the exculpatory provision in the Frederick's charter operates to bar claims for money damages against the directors caused by the alleged breach of the board's duty of care; […] Accordingly, we affirm the judgment of the Court of Chancery dismissing the amended complaint against the Frederick's board and Knightsbridge.

4.3.2.3 In re Cornerstone Therapeutics, Inc.
In many cases, the entire board is not guilty of a violation of the duty of loyalty. Rather, only one or two directors may have been alleged to have engaged in bad acts. Nevertheless, plaintiffs will often sue the entire board of directors. The question then

arises whether when a plaintiff challenges an interested transaction that is presumptively subject to entire fairness review, must the plaintiff plead a non-exculpated claim against the disinterested, independent directors to survive a motion to dismiss by those directors? Or must those directors remain in the suit. The Cornerstone opinion provides some guidance on this question.

115 A.3d 1173 (2015)
IN RE CORNERSTONE THERAPEUTICS INC, STOCKHOLDER LITIGATION

STRINE, Chief Justice:

I. INTRODUCTION

These appeals were scheduled for argument on the same day because they turn on a single legal question: in an action for damages against corporate fiduciaries, where the plaintiff challenges an interested transaction that is presumptively subject to entire fairness review, must the plaintiff plead a non-exculpated claim against the disinterested, independent directors to survive a motion to dismiss by those directors?[2] We answer that question in the affirmative. A plaintiff seeking only monetary damages must plead non-exculpated claims against a director who is protected by an exculpatory charter provision to survive a motion to dismiss, regardless of the underlying standard of review for the board's conduct—be it *Revlon, Unocal,* the entire fairness standard, or the business judgment rule. […]

In this decision, we hold that even if a plaintiff has pled facts that, if true, would require the transaction to be subject to the entire fairness standard of review, and the interested parties to face a claim for breach of their duty of loyalty, the independent directors do not automatically have to remain defendants. When the independent directors are protected by an exculpatory charter provision and the plaintiffs are unable to plead a non-exculpated claim against them, those directors are entitled to have the claims against them dismissed, in keeping with this Court's opinion in *Malpiede v. Townson*[5] and cases following that decision.[6][…]

II. BACKGROUND

These appeals both involve damages actions by stockholder plaintiffs arising out of mergers in which the controlling stockholder, who had representatives on the board of directors, acquired the remainder of the shares that it did not own in a Delaware public corporation.[7] Both mergers [1177] were negotiated by special committees of independent directors, were ultimately approved by a majority of the minority stockholders, and were at substantial premiums to the pre-announcement market price.[8] Nonetheless, the plaintiffs filed suit in the Court of Chancery in each case, contending that the directors had breached their fiduciary duty by approving transactions that were unfair to the minority stockholders.

[…] In both cases, the defendant directors were insulated from liability for monetary damages for breaches of the fiduciary duty of care by an exculpatory charter provision adopted in accordance with 8 *Del. C.* § 102(b)(7). Despite that provision, the plaintiffs in each case not only sued the controlling stockholders and their affiliated directors, but also sued the independent directors who had negotiated and approved the mergers.

In the first of these cases to be decided, *In re Cornerstone Therapeutics Inc. Stockholder Litigation,* the independent director defendants moved to dismiss on the grounds that the plaintiffs had failed to plead any non-exculpated claim against them.[11] The independent directors argued that although the entire fairness standard applied to the Court of Chancery's review of the underlying transaction, and thus the controlling stockholder and its affiliated directors were at risk of being found liable for breaches of the duty of loyalty, the plaintiffs still bore the burden to plead non-exculpated claims against the independent directors.[12] The independent directors noted that this Court held in *Malpiede v. Townson* that, in the analogous context of review under the *Revlon* standard, plaintiffs seeking damages must plead non-exculpated claims against each individual director or risk dismissal.[13][…]

In response, the plaintiffs argued that the Court of Chancery could not grant the independent directors' motion to dismiss, regardless of whether they had sufficiently pled non-exculpated claims.[15] Under their reading of language in two of the four decisions issued by this Court in the extensive *Emerald Partners* litigation,[16] the plaintiffs contended that they could defeat the independent directors' motions to dismiss solely by establishing that the underlying transaction was subject to the entire fairness standard.[17][…]

In *In re Zhongpin Stockholders Litigation,* the independent director defendants also argued that the claims against them should be dismissed because the plaintiffs had failed to plead any non-exculpated claims.[23] The Court of Chancery in *Zhongpin* deferred to *Cornerstone*'s interpretation of precedent[24] and held that the claims against the independent directors survived their motion to dismiss "regardless of whether the Complaint state[d] a non-exculpated claim" because the transaction was subject to entire fairness review.[25]

In each case, the Court of Chancery did not analyze the plaintiffs' duty of loyalty claims against the independent directors because it determined that it was required to deny their motions to dismiss regardless of whether such claims had been sufficiently pled.[26] But, recognizing the important and uncertain issue of corporate law at stake, the Court of Chancery in each case recommended certification of an interlocutory appeal to this Court to determine whether its reading of precedent was correct.

III. ANALYSIS

In answering the legal question raised by these appeals, we acknowledge that the body of law relevant to these disputes presents a debate between two competing but colorable views of the law. These cases thus exemplify a benefit of careful employment of the interlocutory appeal process: to enable this Court to clarify precedent that could arguably be read in two different ways before litigants incur avoidable costs.

We now resolve the question presented by these cases by determining that plaintiffs must plead a non-exculpated claim for breach of fiduciary duty against an independent director protected by an exculpatory charter provision, or that director will be entitled to be dismissed from the suit. That rule applies regardless of the underlying standard of review for the transaction. When a director is protected by an exculpatory charter provision, a plaintiff can survive a motion to dismiss by that director defendant by pleading facts supporting a rational inference that the [1180] director harbored self-interest adverse to the stockholders' interests, acted to advance the self-interest of an interested party from whom they could not be presumed to act independently, or acted in bad faith.[27] But the mere fact that a plaintiff is able to plead facts supporting the application of the entire fairness standard to the transaction, and can thus state a duty of loyalty claim against the interested fiduciaries, does not relieve the plaintiff of the responsibility to plead a non-exculpated claim against each director who moves for dismissal.[28]

No doubt, the invocation of the entire fairness standard has a powerful pro-plaintiff effect against interested parties.[29] When that standard is invoked at the pleading stage, the plaintiffs will be able to survive a motion to dismiss by interested parties regardless of the presence of an exculpatory charter provision because their conflicts of interest support a pleading-stage [1181] inference of disloyalty.[30] Indeed, as to the interested party itself, a finding of unfairness after trial will subject it to liability for breach of the duty of loyalty regardless of its subjective bad faith.[31]

The stringency of after-the-fact entire fairness review by the court intentionally puts strong pressure on the interested party and its affiliates to deal fairly before-the-fact when negotiating an interested transaction. To accomplish this, the burden of proving entire fairness in an interested merger falls on the "the controlling or dominating shareholder proponent of the transaction."[32] But applying the entire fairness standard against interested parties does not relieve plaintiffs seeking damages of the obligation to plead non-exculpated claims against each of the defendant directors.[33]

In *Malpiede*, this Court analyzed the effect of a Section 102(b)(7) provision on a due care claim against directors who approved a transaction which the plaintiffs argued should be subject to review under the *Revlon* standard. This Court noted that although "plaintiffs are entitled to all reasonable inferences flowing from their pleadings, ... if those inferences do not support a valid legal claim, the complaint should be dismissed."[34] Because a director will only be liable for monetary damages if she has breached a non-exculpated duty, a plaintiff who pleads only a due care claim against that director has not set forth any grounds for relief. In such a case, "*as a matter of law* [] then Section 102(b)(7) would bar the claim."[35]

[1182] Nevertheless, the plaintiffs in each of these cases contend that their exculpated claims against the independent directors cannot be dismissed solely because the transaction at issue is subject to entire fairness review. The plaintiffs argue that they should be entitled to an automatic inference that a director facilitating an interested transaction is disloyal because the possibility of conflicted loyalties is heightened in controller transactions, and the facts that give rise to a duty of loyalty breach may be unknowable at the pleading stage.[36] But there are several problems with such an inference: to require independent directors to remain defendants solely because the plaintiffs stated a non-exculpated claim against the controller and its affiliates would be inconsistent with Delaware law and would also increase costs for disinterested directors, corporations, and stockholders, without providing a corresponding benefit.

First, this Court and the Court of Chancery have emphasized that each director has a right to be considered individually when the directors face claims for damages in a suit challenging board action.[37] And under Delaware corporate law, that individualized consideration does not start with the assumption that each director was disloyal; rather, "independent [1183] directors are presumed to be motivated to do their duty with fidelity."[38] Thus, in *Aronson v. Lewis,* this Court emphasized that the mere fact that a director serves on the board of a corporation with a controlling stockholder does not automatically make that director not independent.[39] This Court has similarly refused to presume that an independent director is not entitled to the protection of the business judgment rule solely because the controlling stockholder may itself be subject to liability for breach of the duty of loyalty if the transaction was not entirely fair to the minority stockholders.[40]

Adopting the plaintiffs' approach would not only be inconsistent with these basic tenets of Delaware law, it would likely create more harm than benefit for minority stockholders in practice.[41] Our common law of corporations has rightly emphasized [1184] the need for independent directors to be willing to say no to interested transactions proposed by controlling stockholders.[42] For that reason, our law has long inquired into the practical negotiating power given to independent directors in conflicted transactions.[43] Although it is wise for our law to focus on whether the independent directors can say no, it does not follow that it is prudent to create an invariable rule that any independent director who says yes to an interested transaction subject to entire fairness review must remain as a defendant until the end of the litigation, regardless of the absence of any evidence suggesting that the director acted for an improper motive.

For more than a generation, our law has recognized that the negotiating efforts of independent directors can help to secure transactions with controlling stockholders that are favorable to the minority.[44] Indeed, respected scholars have found evidence that interested transactions subject to special committee approval are often priced on terms that are attractive to minority stockholders.[45] We decline to adopt an approach that would create incentives for independent directors to avoid serving as special committee members, or to reject transactions solely because their role in negotiating on behalf of the stockholders would cause them to remain as defendants until the end of any litigation challenging the transaction.[46]

[1185] As is well understood, the fear that directors who faced personal liability for potentially value-maximizing business decisions might be dissuaded from making such decisions is why Section 102(b)(7) was adopted in the first place. As this Court explained in *Malpiede,* "Section 102(b)(7) was adopted by the Delaware General Assembly in 1986 following a directors and officers insurance liability crisis and the 1985 Delaware Supreme Court decision in *Smith v. Van Gorkom.*"[47] Because of that "crisis," the General Assembly feared that directors would not be willing to make decisions that would benefit stockholders if they faced personal liability for making them. The purpose of Section 102(b)(7) was to "free[] up directors to take business risks without worrying about negligence lawsuits."[48] Establishing a rule that all directors must remain as parties in litigation involving a transaction with a controlling stockholder would thus reduce the benefits that the General Assembly anticipated in adopting Section 102(b)(7).

We understand that the plaintiffs, and certain members of the Court of Chancery, have read the decisions this Court issued in the complex circumstances of the *Emerald Partners* litigation to support a different conclusion than we reach here. But the Court in *Emerald Partners* was focused on a separate question; namely, whether courts can consider the effect of a Section 102(b)(7) provision before trial when the plaintiffs have pled facts supporting the inference not only that each director breached not just his duty of care, but also his duty of loyalty, when the applicable standard of review of the underlying transaction is entire fairness.[49] In that circumstance, the Court held that the [1186] determination of whether any failure of the putatively independent directors was the result of disloyalty or a lapse in care was best determined after a trial, because the substantive fairness inquiry would shed light on why the directors acted as they did.[50] The sentence in *Emerald II* that the plaintiffs claim is dispositive here must be understood in that context, as referring to a case where there was a viable, non-exculpated loyalty claim against each putatively independent director. The *Emerald Partners* litigation thus did not answer the specific question at issue in these appeals, whether the application of the entire fairness standard requires the Court of Chancery to deny a motion to dismiss by independent directors even when the plaintiffs may not have sufficiently pled a non-exculpated claim against those directors. Indeed, much of the language in the *Emerald Partners* decisions issued by this Court is consistent with the answer we reach here. For example, this Court observed in *Emerald II* that:

> The rationale of *Malpiede* constitutes judicial cognizance of a practical reality: unless there is a violation of the duty of loyalty or the duty of good faith, a trial on the issue of entire fairness is unnecessary because a Section 102(b)(7) provision will exculpate director defendants from paying monetary damages that are exclusively attributable to a violation of the duty of care. The effect of our holding in *Malpiede* is that, in actions against the directors of Delaware corporations with a Section 102(b)(7) charter provision, a shareholder's complaint must allege well-pled facts that, if true, implicate breaches of loyalty or good faith.[51]

Thus, to the extent that other isolated statements in *Emerald Partners* could be interpreted as inconsistent with the result we reach today, we clarify that the *Emerald Partners* decisions should be read in their case-specific context and not for the broad proposition that the plaintiffs advocate. The reading of the *Emerald Partners* decisions we embrace is also the one adopted by the Court of Chancery itself in *DiRienzo v. Lichtenstein*.[52] In that case, the Court of Chancery recognized that the *Emerald Partners* decisions had to be read in the context of their facts, where there was sufficient record evidence to attribute any lack of effectiveness in the putatively independent directors' handling of the transaction to either a breach of the duty of loyalty (*e.g.,* as the result of bad faith) or a lack of care. The Court of Chancery thus observed that "the directors in *Emerald Partners* were precluded from relying on a 102(b)(7) charter provision by virtue of their conduct, not because the transaction was subject to entire fairness review for other reasons."[53] In other words, *DiRienzo* interpreted the *Emerald Partners* decisions as standing for the mundane proposition that a defendant cannot obtain dismissal on the basis of an exculpatory provision when there is evidence that he committed a non-exculpated breach of fiduciary duty.[54]

Thus, when a complaint pleads facts creating an inference that seemingly [1187] independent directors approved a conflicted transaction for improper reasons, and thus, those directors may have breached their duty of loyalty, the pro-plaintiff inferences that must be drawn on a motion to dismiss counsels for resolution of that question of fact only after discovery.[55] By contrast, when the plaintiffs have pled no facts to support an inference that any of the independent directors breached their duty of loyalty, fidelity to the purpose of Section 102(b)(7) requires dismissal of the complaint against those directors. Accordingly, we reverse the judgments of the Court of Chancery denying the independent directors' motions to dismiss, and remand each case for the Court of Chancery to determine if the plaintiffs have sufficiently pled facts suggesting that the independent directors committed a non-exculpated breach of their fiduciary duty.

Footnotes

[13] 780 A.2d 1075, 1083-84 (Del.2001) ("Although the *Revlon* doctrine imposes enhanced judicial scrutiny of certain transactions involving a sale of control, it does not eliminate the requirement that plaintiffs plead sufficient facts to support the underlying claims for a breach of fiduciary duties in conducting the sale."); *id.* at 1094 ("The plaintiffs are entitled to all reasonable inferences flowing from their pleadings, but if those inferences do not support a valid legal claim, the complaint should be dismissed without the need for the defendants to file an answer and without proceeding with discovery. Here we have assumed, without deciding, that the amended complaint on its face states a due care claim. Because we have determined that the complaint fails properly to invoke loyalty and bad faith claims, we are left with only a due care claim. Defendants had the obligation to raise the bar of Section 102(b)(7) as a defense, and they did. As plaintiffs conceded in oral argument before this Court, if there is only an unambiguous, residual due care claim and nothing else—*as a matter of law*—then Section 102(b)(7) would bar the claim. Accordingly, the Court of Chancery did not err in dismissing the plaintiffs due care claim in this case.").

[28]*See Malpiede,* 780 A.2d at 1094; *see also Emerald II,* 787 A.2d at 92 (citing *Malpiede* with approval for the proposition that "unless there is a violation of the duty of loyalty or the duty of good faith, a trial on the issue of entire fairness is unnecessary because a Section

102(b)(7) provision will exculpate director defendants from paying monetary damages that are exclusively attributable to a violation of the duty of care"); *Emerald I,* 726 A.2d at 1224 ("Nonetheless, where the factual basis for a claim *solely* implicates a violation of the duty of care, this Court has indicated that the protections of such a [Section 102(b)(7)] charter provision may properly be invoked and applied.")[...]

[49] In the *Emerald Partners* litigation, the plaintiffs brought a derivative and class action suit following the corporation's merger with its controlling stockholder, alleging that the merger was not entirely fair and that the defendant directors violated disclosure rules. The defendants did not move to dismiss, but moved for summary judgment after discovery. The Court of Chancery granted that motion, concluding that the plaintiff's allegations supported a duty of care violation at most, and that the company's Section 102(b)(7) charter provision exculpated the defendants from liability. *See Emerald Partners v. Berlin,* 1995 WL 600881, *1 (Del. Ch. Sept. 22, 1995). This Court reversed, holding that several issues remained that implicated the independent directors' duty of loyalty, including the plaintiff's claim that the directors had misrepresented that negotiations were arm's-length in the proxy statement. *See Emerald I,* 726 A.2d at 1223. Because "the entire fairness and disclosure claims under [those] circumstances were intertwined," the defendants could not invoke § 102(b)(7) at that stage of the proceedings. *Id.* In other words, this Court found that the plaintiffs had successfully shown that issues of fact remained that implicated the independent directors' duty of loyalty, and because those issues were not separable from the factual issues about whether the transaction was fair, the independent directors' motion for summary judgment was properly denied.

4.3 Duty of Loyalty

The business judgment presumption presumes, among other things, that directors act "in the best interests of the corporation." When a plaintiff can plead facts to suggest that director does not act in the best interests of the corporation, then the defendant director will lose the deferential business judgment presumption and will be required to prove at trial that notwithstanding the facts pleaded by the plaintiff that the challenged decision was nevertheless entirely fair to the corporation (the entire fairness standard).

Factual situations that commonly call into question whether a director acted in the best interests of the corporation include some of the following factual scenarios:

1. A director engages in a commercial transaction with the corporation (a director is "on both sides" of a transaction with the corporation).
2. A director uses his or her position to obtain a benefit for the director rather that the corporation.
3. A director acts secretly acts as an adverse party or in competition with the corporation.
4. A director gets a material personal benefit from a third party in connection with a transaction between the corporation and third party.

In each of these factual situations, a plaintiff can reasonably plead that a director's decision was not in the best interests of the corporation and the director can lose the presumption of business judgment.

Unlike violations of the duty of care, violations of the duty of loyalty are not exculpable. That is to say, if a director violates her duty of loyalty to the corporation, the director may be personally liable to the corporation and its stockholders for damages. Violations of the duty of care, as you will remember, are exculpable. The availability of a monetary remedy consequently draws the attention of plaintiffs' counsel who can be expected to engage in a high degree of scrutiny of interested director transactions.

4.3.1 Dweck v. Nasser

Consider the facts in the following case. Do the agents of the corporation and the corporate directors appear to comport themselves as loyal agents of the corporation? If not, how do their actions fall short of the standard of conduct expected of corporate fiduciaries?

DWECK v. NASSER and KIDS INTERNATIONAL CORPORATION

Consol. C.A. No. 1353-VCL

LASTER, Vice Chancellor.

In 2005, after thirteen years in business together, Gila Dweck and Albert Nasser parted ways. Their messy split spawned nearly seven years of litigation.

Before the split, Dweck was the CEO, a director, and 30% stockholder in Kids International Corporation ("Kids"). Both before and after the split, Nasser was the Chairman and controlling stockholder of Kids. Dweck and Nasser accused each other of breaching their fiduciary duties, and Nasser asserted third-party claims for breach of fiduciary duty against Dweck's colleagues Kevin Taxin, Kids' President, and Bruce Fine, Kids' CFO and corporate secretary.[…]

In this post-trial decision, I find that Dweck and Taxin breached their fiduciary duties to Kids by establishing competing companies that usurped Kids' corporate opportunities and converted Kids' resources to the point of literally using Kids' own employees, office space, letters of credit, customer relationships, and goodwill to conduct their operations. Dweck further breached her fiduciary duties by causing Kids to reimburse her for hundreds of thousands of dollars of personal expenses. Fine breached his fiduciary duties by abdicating his responsibility to review Dweck's expenses and signing off on them wholesale. In the months leading up to the final split, Dweck, Taxin, and Fine again breached their duties by transferring Kids' customer relationships and business expectancies to their competing companies, packing up Kids' documents and other property and moving them to the competing companies, and organizing a mass employee departure that left Kids crippled. Dweck, Taxin, and Fine are liable to Kids for the damages caused by their breaches of duty. […]

Having weighed the parties' testimony, evaluated their demeanor, and considered the evidence as a whole, I make the following factual findings. […]

Morris Dabah had three sons: Haim, Ezra, and Isaac.[1] Morris and his sons founded the Gitano Group, a large, multi-division apparel wholesaler.

Morris' fourth and youngest child was a daughter: Gila Dweck. While still in college, Dweck began working at Gitano as a receptionist. After graduating, Dweck joined the childrenswear division, known as EJ Gitano, as a salesperson. She rose rapidly through the ranks to become President of EJ Gitano.

In 1993, Haim and Isaac pleaded guilty to criminal violations of United States customs regulations and spent time under house arrest. Wal-Mart, Gitano's largest customer, refused to continue selling Gitano's lines of clothing. Gitano defaulted on its debt and teetered on the verge of bankruptcy.

In the debacle, Dweck saw opportunity. She suggested to Haim that they purchase EJ Gitano. It was profitable, and Dweck thought the existing pipeline of orders made the purchase "essentially risk free." Tr. 448.

But there was a problem. Because of Gitano's default, its lender had the right to veto any sale of assets, and the bank would not approve a sale of EJ Gitano to the Dabah family. Dweck needed a third party.

Enter Albert Nasser, a successful entrepreneur with numerous holdings in the apparel sector. Nasser was a cousin of Dweck's mother, and despite maintaining his primary residence in Switzerland, he moved within the same tightly-knit New York community as the Dabah family. […]

In September 1993, Dweck, Haim, and Nasser purchased the assets of EJ Gitano. The basic deal was straightforward. Nasser agreed to provide 100% of the funding, comprising $8.2 million for acquisition financing plus $1 million in start-up capital. In return, Nasser originally would own 100% of the new company's equity. Once Nasser received payments equal to his original investment plus 10% interest, Nasser would transfer 50% of the equity to Dweck and Haim. Nasser would serve as Chairman of the Board; Dweck and Haim would be in charge of day-to-day management. […]

EJ Gitano's trademarks were acquired separately. For this part of the transaction, Woodsford advanced $4.2 million to Hocalar B.V. ("Hocalar"), a Netherlands corporation. Hocalar then paid the money to Gitano for a perpetual license to the Gitano trademarks. Hocalar immediately sub-licensed the trademarks to Kids in return for a 5% royalty on Kids' sales of Gitano products (the "License Agreement"). […]

Kids was profitable from day one. Although the transaction closed at the end of September 1993, the sale was effective as of June and included EJ Gitano's substantial order base from the pre-closing period. Nasser agreed to indemnify EJ Gitano's lender for its letters of credit, which enabled Kids to take the profits on the existing orders. The new company continued selling Gitano-branded products, primarily jeans. Kids also continued as a major supplier of private label (non-branded) childrenswear for Wal-Mart, which originally comprised approximately 90-95% of Kids' business. In the private label business, a retailer like Wal-Mart outsources to a manufacturer like Kids the work of producing a house brand owned by Wal-Mart and sold only in Wal-Mart's stores. […]

Because of its significant sales, Kids was able to distribute substantial amounts via the License Agreement in addition to the interest-only payments on the Maubi Loan. By 1998, Nasser had received back his original investment plus 10% interest, and it was time for Dweck and Haim to receive equity in Kids. Dweck and Haim were issued 45% of Kids' outstanding equity, paid for out of the corporation's retained earnings. The original deal had been 50%, but it turned out that Nasser had issued a warrant to Shiboleth for 5% of the equity as compensation for his role in setting up Kids. Dweck and Haim acquiesced to the new arrangement, and Nasser left it to Dweck and Haim to divvy up their shares. Dweck received 27.5% of Kids' stock, which she held individually and through trusts for the benefit of her children. Haim received the remaining 17.5%. Around the same time, Taxin was promoted to President of Kids. […]

With Kids enjoying continued success under her management, Dweck began to feel exploited. Despite receiving stock in 1998, Dweck believed she was doing all of the work for less than a third of the profits. To Dweck's further frustration, Nasser decided in 1996 that Kids was a *de facto* partnership, that partners should not receive salaries, and that Dweck's salary as Kids' CEO should be deemed a distribution of profits. […]

Dweck felt she should own a percentage of Kids equity that more fairly represented her responsibility for Kids' success. She complained to Nasser and Haim, but to no avail. Nasser would not give Dweck any more equity, nor would he sell her any of his shares. [...]

Unable to gain a greater share of Kids' profits, Dweck decided to bypass Kids by starting a new company into which she would channel "new opportunities." Tr. 461. As she admitted on cross-examination, she decided to compete "because it was [her] only way to . . . receive more income." Tr. 469.

In October 2001, Dweck formed Success Apparel LLC ("Success"), a New York limited liability company, to operate as a wholesaler of children's clothing. The impetus to form Success came from Taxin, who also had grown dissatisfied with his remuneration. Taxin felt that he was primarily responsible for Kids' success and deserved a share of Kids' profits. He asked Dweck repeatedly for equity, but she consistently turned him down on the grounds that Nasser "only takes in family." Tr. 259. When the President of Bugle Boy, Mary Gleason, offered Taxin the opportunity to purchase the Bugle Boy license in 2001, Taxin decided he was "only interested in doing the opportunity with [Dweck], not

Kids . . . ." Tr. 258. Taxin made the decision despite meeting with Gleason in his capacity as President of Kids, and even though Gleason did not restrict the opportunity or indicate that Kids could not pursue it. Taxin discussed the matter with Dweck, and they decided to take it for themselves. Dweck granted Taxin a 20% membership interest in Success and retained 80% for herself.

From 2001 until 2005, Success operated out of Kids' premises using Kids' employees. Success drew on Kids' letters of credit, sold products under Kids' vendor agreements, used Kids' vendor numbers, and capitalized on Kids' relationships. Ostensibly to compensate Kids, Dweck decided that Success would pay an administrative fee equal to 1% of total sales. Dweck selected the 1% figure unilaterally without disclosure to or consultation with Nasser. The only mention of the fee was an opaque entry on Kids' financial statements entitled "Due from affiliates." *See, e.g.,* JX 783. The identity of the affiliates was not specified, and Fine never discussed it with Nasser. The 1% fee appears to have been grossly inadequate.

Success also reimbursed Kids for the salaries of certain employees (but not for their benefits) and for a portion of Kids' rent. The only employees were those Dweck deemed to be working exclusively for Success. Dweck admitted that most Kids employees performed some work for Success. No effort was made to compensate Kids for their services. Taxin estimated at trial that he spent approximately 20% of his time on Success, which likely was a self-interestedly conservative figure. Numerous other Kids employees performed work for Success without reimbursement, including Pauline Pei, Mark Simonetti, Stanley Bernstein, Joseph Ezraty, Steve Golub, Leah Justice, and Kim Epps. Taxin estimated (doubtless conservatively) that these employees spent approximately 10-20% of their time on Success. Success also used Kids' overseas quality control inspectors and internal quality control employees. The rental reimbursements further illustrate the inadequacy of Success' payments to Kids. In 2004, for example, Dweck's companies reimbursed Kids for rent of $14,594. In 2005, after obtaining space of its own, Dweck's companies paid $437,689 for rent.

In its first three years of operation, Success signed license agreements to manufacture and distribute a number of brands, including Bugle Boy, Everlast, and John Deere. In the pitches to obtain the licenses, Success used marketing materials that listed the logos of Kids and Success side by side, cited industry awards won by Kids, and touted Kids' lengthy record in the apparel business. This resulted in confusion amongst the licensors. John Deere originally drafted their license agreement with Kids as the licensee, and the document was only changed to name Success at Dweck's request. The draft agreement for a license to the Mack brand was also prepared in Kids' name. A press release issued by Everlast described its licensee as "Success Apparel Group LLC, also known as Kids International . . . ." JX 531.

Inside Kids' offices, Success and Kids operated so seamlessly that many of the Kids employees who routinely worked for Success never suspected that Success was a separate company or had different ownership from Kids. Kids and Success used the same showroom and displayed their brands in the same space. There were no references to Success, and nothing suggested that the brands were not all owned by Kids. The only name on the door was Kids. […]

In June 2004, Dweck founded Premium Apparel Brands LLC ("Premium"), a New York limited liability company. Like Success, Premium was a clothing wholesaler, operated out of Kids' premises, and used Kids' employees and resources. Dweck owned 100% of Premium and served as its CEO. Taxin had no equity stake in Premium.

Dweck founded Premium to serve as licensee and manufacturer for the Gloria Vanderbilt brand. When Dweck originally negotiated the Gloria Vanderbilt license, the owner of the brand, Jones Apparel, understood that the license could be with Kids. Dweck switched the agreement to Premium. […]

Not content with her compensation from Kids and the profits from her parasitic companies, Dweck billed Kids for a luxurious lifestyle. Between 2002 and 2005, Dweck charged at least $466,948 in expenses to Kids. At trial, she admitted that at least $171,966 was for personal expenses, including Club Med vacations and assorted luxury goods from Armani, Prada, Gucci, and Bergdorf Goodman. Dweck could not determine whether another $170,400 was for business or personal expenses. She asserted that the remaining $124,582 was for legitimate business expenses. During the same period, Dweck was being paid $850,000 to $1.3 million per year in salary. […]

During 2004, Kids stopped sending Nasser quarterly financial reports. Nasser repeatedly requested the reports, but Dweck and Fine ignored him. In November 2004, Lidia Lozovsky, a secretary at Kids who worked for Nasser, Dweck, and Fine, mentioned to

Nasser that Dweck appeared to be handling a Gloria Vanderbilt line. In December, Lozovsky warned Nasser in stronger terms that there was "something going on" at Kids and that "there were other companies" operating out of Kids' offices. […]

To get a handle on what was going on, Nasser had Shiboleth notice formal meetings of the board and stockholders for January 5, 2005. They were the first formal meetings in Kids' history. In advance of the meetings, Dweck and Fine told Nasser that Kids would book $115 million in sales for 2004. Days later, they lowered the sales figure to $95 million. During the January 5 board meeting, Dweck and Fine revealed that the actual sales figure was $72 million, a decline of roughly $18 million from the previous year. Nasser testified that after hearing the sales figure, "everybody looked at each other. And we knew that something [was] wrong because we were not told the truth at the beginning." […]

Because of his growing suspicions, Nasser came to the January 5 meetings ready to take action. Nasser elected Lozovsky and his nephew, Itzhak Djemal, as directors of Kids. He appointed Djemal to the position of Vice Chairman and gave him authority equal to Dweck's: Djemal would handle production and corporate finances while Dweck would handle sales and design. Nasser privately tasked Djemal with uncovering what was going on at Kids.

Dweck was extremely unhappy with Djemal's appointment. […]

Dweck promptly met with Taxin and discussed the prospect of leaving Kids. With Taxin and Fine's assistance, she located separate office space for Success and Premium. More importantly, Dweck and Taxin organized a campaign to divert Kids' future orders to Success. Over the next three months, Kids employees carried out the campaign by contacting Kids' customers on behalf of Success. […]

In early 2005, Kids was working to fill orders for the Fall 2005 season and had started product development and design work for the Holiday 2005 and Spring 2006 seasons. At the direction of Dweck and Taxin, Kids employees systematically switched the vendor information and customer contacts from Kids to Success, thereby ensuring that when the orders came in, they came to Success. Taxin instructed Paul Cohn, the Kids salesperson for Wal-Mart, to switch the Wal-Mart orders. Taxin instructed Pat Zobel, the Kids salesperson for Target, to switch the Target orders. At the time he gave these instructions, Taxin was President of Kids. Taxin also communicated directly with Wal-Mart and Target about switching purchases from Kids to Success.

H. The March 11, 2005 Meetings

Despite active resistance from Dweck, Djemal soon found evidence that Dweck was operating her own businesses from Kids' premises. When pressed for information, Dweck admitted it but insisted that she had Nasser's permission. Djemal reported his findings to Nasser.

Because Dweck disputed whether the January meetings were properly noticed, Nasser had Shiboleth notice a second round of board and stockholder meetings for March 11, 2005. […]

Shiboleth noticed the meetings to be held at Kids' offices. After arriving at Kids, Nasser and Shiboleth were asked to wait in a conference room. Samples for Gloria Vanderbilt and other brands handled by Success and Premium covered the walls. Meanwhile, Haim, Dweck, and Dweck's counsel, Barry Slotnick, showed up at Shiboleth's office. After learning that Nasser and Shiboleth were at Kids, Dweck told Nasser and Shiboleth that they would be right over. She then instructed one of her employees to remove the samples. As Nasser and Shiboleth waited, an employee entered and removed the samples without explanation. It was a less-than-adroit maneuver, but consistent with Dweck's efforts to conceal her activities.

When the stockholder meeting convened, Shiboleth proposed that Dweck stand for re-election as a director. Dweck's lawyer, Slotnick, then announced that Dweck could not serve as a director because she had a conflict of interest as a result of operating competing businesses. Nasser and Shiboleth were nonplussed. Shiboleth assumed Slotnick made a mistake, so he suggested that he and Dweck consult privately. When they returned after fifteen minutes, Slotnick reiterated that Dweck declined to serve as a director because of a potential claim of a conflict of interest from selling competitive product from Kids' premises. All eyes turned to Dweck, who admitted that she was selling "overlapping product" from Kids' premises. Tr. 567. Nasser and Shiboleth were shocked: it was the first time Dweck had indicated that she was competing with Kids from Kids' premises. During the board meeting convened immediately after the stockholder meeting, Nasser observed that Dweck should not be an officer if she declined to serve as a director. The board formally elected a slate of officers that excluded Dweck, with Djemal as President and CEO.

Dweck, Taxin, And Fine Destroy Kids' Business.

Although no longer employed by Kids after the March 11 meetings, Dweck worked out of Kids' offices until April 11, 2005. Dweck and Taxin continued their campaign to divert Kids' business to Success, and they succeeded in transferring all of the Wal-Mart and Target business from the Holiday 2005 season onward. Kids did not receive any orders after May 2005.

Dweck and Taxin also arranged for Kids' employees to join Success. In early May 2005, Dweck and Taxin met with Kids' managers to inform them that Dweck would be operating her own companies separately from Kids and to offer them positions at her companies. Dweck told the managers to make the same offer to the employees under their supervision. She indicated that if they chose to accept her offer, "they would receive word to pack shortly." JX 636. Taxin later met with Kids' managers, reiterated the plan to leave Kids, and promised them jobs at Success. Fine met with at least one Kids employee and offered him a job at Success.

On May 17, 2005, Taxin informed the employees that May 18 was departure day. In the early morning of May 18, Kids employees began loading a moving truck with roughly 100 boxes of Kids' documents and materials. Fine supervised the process and attempted to conceal the move from Nasser and Djemal. Nasser, however, was tipped by a Kids employee the day before, and he arranged for Djemal and Lozovsky to arrive early at Kids' offices. Lozovsky found the move already underway and Kids' materials loaded in the moving truck. Lozovsky called Nasser, who demanded to speak to the driver. Fine took the phone, claimed that he was a driver named "Gregory," and listened while Nasser threatened to summon the police. Djemal arrived at Kids' offices just in time to stop the truck. He could not stop many of the former employees from taking boxes with them. A computer consultant whom Djemal hired later determined that a number of the hard drives from Kids' computers had been wiped clean.

As part of the May 18 mass departure, Taxin resigned to join Dweck at Success. Fine remained at Kids until May 25, 2005, when he too joined Dweck. […]

On May 20, Dweck and Taxin flew to Wal-Mart's headquarters in Bentonville, Arkansas to meet with more senior Wal-Mart managers. After the meeting, Wal-Mart recognized Success as its existing supplier and no longer recognized Kids. Dweck and Taxin then met with Target managers and achieved the same transition.

To protect their customer relationships, Dweck and Taxin made sure that a handful of employees remained at Kids to fill the Fall 2005 orders. Dweck and Taxin oversaw their efforts, effectively running Kids from afar. […]

J. Nasser And Djemal Fail To Revive Kids.

Having lost nearly all its employees and with its pipeline diverted to Success, Kids had to start over from scratch. Djemal began hiring new employees and attempted to solicit orders from the retail giants that had been Kids' customer base. He immediately encountered difficulties. The Hong Kong factory that Kids relied on for samples was working for Success and would not return his calls. The manufacturing facilities Kids used also would not respond. When Djemal visited Wal-Mart headquarters with a new line of samples, Wal-Mart told him that Success was the recognized supplier and that Djemal would have to reestablish Kids as a new vendor. When he met with Target, the representative told Djemal that she only gave him an appointment because "`I thought you were Success.'" Tr. 1081.

A. Success and Premium

Dweck and Taxin formed Success and Premium, took Kids' business opportunities for their new entities, competed directly with Kids, ran their businesses out of Kids' premises, used Kids' employees, and appropriated Kids' resources. In doing so, Dweck and Taxin breached their duty of loyalty to Kids.

1. The Nature of the Breach

"The essence of a duty of loyalty claim is the assertion that a corporate officer or director has misused power over corporate property or processes in order to benefit himself rather than advance corporate purposes." *Steiner v. Meyerson,* 1995 WL 441999, at *2 (Del. Ch. July 19, 1995) (Allen, C.). "At the core of the fiduciary duty is the notion of loyalty—the equitable requirement that, with respect to the property subject to the duty, a fiduciary always must act in a good faith effort to advance the interests of his beneficiary." *US W., Inc. v. Time Warner Inc.,* 1996 WL 307445, at *21 (Del. Ch. June 6,

1996) (Allen, C.). "Most basically, the duty of loyalty proscribes a fiduciary from any means of misappropriation of assets entrusted to his management and supervision." *Id.* "The doctrine of corporate opportunity represents . . . one species of the broad fiduciary duties assumed by a corporate director or officer." *Broz v. Cellular Info. Sys., Inc.,* 673 A.2d 148, 154 (Del. 1996). The doctrine "holds that a corporate officer or director may not take a business opportunity for his own if: (1) the corporation is financially able to exploit the opportunity; (2) the opportunity is within the corporation's line of business; (3) the corporation has an interest or expectancy in the opportunity; and (4) by taking the opportunity for his own, the corporate fiduciary will thereby be placed in a position inimicable to his duties to the corporation." *Id.* at 154-55.

Dweck was a director and officer of Kids. Taxin was an officer of Kids. In these capacities, they owed a duty of loyalty to Kids. *Gantler v. Stephens,* 965 A.2d 695, 708-09 (Del. 2009). Dweck and Taxin breached their duty of loyalty by diverting what they decided were "new opportunities" to Success and Premium, including license agreements with Bugle Boy, Everlast, John Deere, and Gloria Vanderbilt, Wal-Mart private label business, and Target direct import business. Kids was a profitable enterprise with the financial capability to exploit each of these opportunities. Indeed, Dweck and Taxin used Kids' personnel and resources to pursue each opportunity, demonstrating that Kids just as easily could have pursued the opportunities in its own name. After appropriating the opportunities, Dweck and Taxin operated Success and Premium as if the companies were divisions of Kids, but kept the resulting profits for themselves. By doing so, Dweck and Taxin placed themselves "in a position inimicable to [their] duties to [Kids]." *Broz,* 673 A.2d at 155.

Dweck and Taxin's conduct bears a striking resemblance to the continuing exploitation of corporate resources in *Guth v. Loft, Inc.,* 5 A.2d 503 (Del. 1939), the seminal corporate opportunity case in Delaware jurisprudence. In *Guth,* a director and the President of Loft Incorporated, Charles Guth, appropriated for himself the opportunity to purchase the secret formula and trademark for Pepsi-Cola from then-bankrupt National Pepsi-Cola Company. *Guth,* 5 A.2d at 505-06. Guth then operated Pepsi-Cola as a division of Loft, secretly using its employees and resources but keeping all the profits for himself. *Id.* at 507. The Delaware Supreme Court agreed that Guth breached his duty of loyalty and affirmed that Guth was required to disgorge all profits and equity from the venture to Loft. *Id.* at 515. Like Guth, Dweck and Taxin established a competing company into which they channeled new opportunities, then used Kids' "materials, credit, executives and employees as [they] willed." *Id.* at 506. […]

To defend their actions, Dweck and Taxin tried to distinguish between the private label clothing business and the branded clothing business, then argued that Kids only operated in the private label business. Supposedly this distinction left them free to take the branded business. To the contrary, Kids had an interest in the branded business.

When determining whether a corporation has an interest in a line of business, the nature of the corporation's business should be broadly interpreted. […]

It is abundantly clear that Kids could have capitalized on each of the branded opportunities taken by Success and Premium. At trial, Taxin conceded that Kids could have handled the Bugle Boy and John Deere business. Moreover, Success and Premium did not in fact limit themselves to branded opportunities; they also appropriated private label opportunities. When Wal-Mart approached Kids about manufacturing men's clothing for the Wal-Mart private label called No Boundaries, Dweck and Taxin decided it was a "new opportunity" in which Kids had no expectancy. Manufacturing Wal-Mart private label brands had long been Kids' core business, and Kids had manufactured No Boundaries girls' clothing since 2000. At trial, Taxin admitted that Kids could have taken this opportunity. […] When Target offered Kids the opportunity to engage in "direct importing," a process by which a company would have clothing manufactured overseas and shipped directly to Target, Dweck and Taxin again decided to take the opportunity for Success. Taxin obtained the opportunity while visiting Target's headquarters as Kids' President on a business trip for Kids. At trial, Taxin admitted that Kids could have handled the Target direct business. […]

3. The Consent Defense

As their next defense, Dweck and her colleagues claimed that Nasser gave Dweck permission to compete. According to Dweck, she approached Nasser before forming Success and disclosed that she was planning to start a company that would compete with Kids. In her direct testimony, she claimed to remember "very vividly" a meeting with Nasser in February 2002, at his offices, when she sat with him at "a little round table by the window." […] She recalled telling Nasser that "I'm not motivated to kill myself, continue to work, you know, so many hours a day and weekends, and therefore I would take any new opportunities outside of Kids." Tr. 461. She asserted that Nasser encouraged her to start her own business, declaring "`I'm not standing in your way for improving yourself.'" Tr. 495. According to Dweck, this statement gave her the go-ahead to use Kids' employees and Kids' resources to run a business out of Kids' offices that competed directly with Kids.

On cross-examination, Dweck admitted that [...]Nasser was out of the country, likely in Tel Aviv. She admitted never discussing with Nasser what new opportunities she might pursue. She admitted never suggesting to Nasser that she would take opportunities from Wal-Mart or Target, Kids' largest customers. She admitted never mentioning that her business would operate from Kids' premises, use Kids' resources, or compete with Kids.

Nasser did not recall any meeting or conversation with Dweck. Instead, he remembered a call from Shiboleth, who told him that Dweck wanted to start her own business. After Nasser expressed concern that Dweck's new venture would compete with Kids, Shiboleth assured him that Dweck planned to operate in the upscale department store market. This would have differentiated Dweck's new company from Kids, which sold almost exclusively to discount retailers. Having been assured that Dweck's business would not compete with Kids, Nasser offered to help Dweck and told Shiboleth to advise her on how to set up the business. [...]

Having considered the witnesses' testimony and demeanor, I reject Dweck's version of events. [...]

Nasser never consented to Dweck competing directly with Kids, using Kids' employees and resources, and operating out of Kids' premises. In a real sense, that was not competition at all. It was conversion and theft. Regardless, Dweck and Taxin cannot rely on Nasser's purported consent to justify their conduct. [...]

6. The Remedy

As damages for usurping Kids' corporate opportunities, Dweck, Taxin, Success, and Premium are jointly and severally liable to Kids for the lost profits Kids would have generated from business diverted to Success and Premium. [...]

Dweck, Taxin, Success, and Premium also are jointly and severally liable for profits generated by Success and Premium after May 18, 2005 for the duration of the license agreements then in effect, including any rights of renewal or extension. If Dweck and Taxin had been faithful fiduciaries, those license agreements would have been in Kids' name, and Kids could have continued to perform under the agreements together with any renewals or extensions contemplated by the then-existing contracts. [...]

B. The Mass Departure and the Taking of Kids' Property And Business Expectancies

Dweck, Taxin, and Fine breached their fiduciary duties by directing Kids employees to transfer Kids' expected orders and customer accounts to Success, taking Kids' property and files, and arranging a mass employee departure on May 18, 2005. "A breach of fiduciary duty occurs when a fiduciary commits an unfair, fraudulent, or wrongful act, including . . . misuse of confidential information, solicitation of employer's customers before cessation of employment, conspiracy to bring about mass resignation of an employer's key employees, or usurpation of the employer's business opportunity." [...] Dweck cannot limit her liability by citing the termination of her relationship with Kids on March 11. Before that point, Dweck breached her own duties as a fiduciary. After that point, Dweck actively conspired with Taxin and Fine, thereby aiding and abetting Taxin and Fine's breaches of fiduciary duty. [...]

In my view, Kids' remedy for the departure-related breaches of fiduciary duty should be limited to the damages Kids suffered over and above where Kids would have been had Dweck and Taxin resigned in an appropriate manner. To approximate this loss, I award Kids the profits generated by Success in its non-branded business for the Holiday 2005 and Spring 2006 seasons. In May 2005, Kids was hard at work on the Fall 2005 season and had started preparing for the Holiday 2005 and Spring 2006 seasons. Kids' designers already had been traveling and shopping internationally to develop ideas for the Spring 2006 season, and they had a good understanding about what Wal-Mart and Target's Spring 2006 needs would be. During their departure from Kids, Dweck and Taxin took this business. I award it to Kids and hold Dweck, Taxin, Success, and Premium liable for the profits that Success and Premium earned from these seasons. [...]

C. Dweck's Personal Expenses

Between 2002 and 2005, Dweck caused Kids to reimburse her $466,948 in personal and business expenses. Dweck conceded that $171,966 were personal expenses that she wrongfully charged to Kids. She claimed she could not determine whether $170,400 were business or personal, but nevertheless asserted that she should not be ordered to repay that amount to Kids. She testified that $124,582 corresponded to legitimate Kids' business expenses.

> Under Delaware law, fiduciaries have a duty to account to their beneficiaries for their disposition of all assets that they manage in a fiduciary capacity. That duty carries with it the burden of proving that the disposition was proper. . . . [I]ncluded within the duty to account is a duty to maintain records that will discharge the fiduciaries' burden, and . . . if that duty is not observed, every presumption will be made against the fiduciaries.

Technicorp Int'l II, Inc. v. Johnston, 2000 WL 713750, at *2 (Del. Ch. May 31, 2000). "If corporate fiduciaries divert corporate assets to themselves for non-corporate purposes, they are liable for the amounts wrongfully diverted." *Id.* at *45.

As a Kids fiduciary, Dweck bore the burden at trial of proving that the challenged expenses were legitimate. Dweck failed to meet her burden. Instead, Dweck testified that she "didn't think Mr. Nasser would mind." Tr. 519. She later explained: "I felt that [the expense reimbursement] was part of, really, part of my compensation. In retrospect, I'm sorry I did it and I made a mistake." Tr. 521.

Dweck accordingly is liable to Kids for a total of $342,366 in expenses, comprising both the $171,966 of admittedly personal expenses and the $170,400 of indeterminate expenses. [...]

4.3.2 Entire Fairness

When fiduciaries of the corporation lose the business judgment presumption, they will have to justify to the court that their actions were entirely fair to the corporation. A defendant director who bears the burden of proving its actions were entirely fair to the corporation has to bear a heavy burden. Unlike the business judgment presumption, which can a defendant can rely on to have a claim dismissed on the pleadings, when a defendant must bear the burden of proving the entire fairness of transaction, the defendant can only do that after a full trial. Consequently, losing the presumption of business judgment and being forced to prove at trial that the actions of the defendants were entirely fair to the corporation is often outcome determinative. Defendant directors will often seek to settle litigation rather than go to trial under the entire fairness standard.

In older cases, the "entire fairness" standard is also known as the "intrinsic fairness" standard or the "inherent fairness" standard.

4.3.2.1 Weinberger v. UOP, Inc.

In Weinberger, the court deals with a common loyalty problem. What are the fiduciary duties of a controlling stockholder in dealing with minority stockholders. In such situations, the controlling stockholder, because of her ability to control and direct management decisions of the corporation, has fiduciary obligations to deal with minority stockholders fairly. Transactions between the controller and the corporation will not receive the protection of the business judgment presumption.

Rather, the controlling stockholder bears the burden of proving the fairness of its dealings with the corporation. The entire fairness standard requires the court to examine two aspects of the board's dealings with the corporation: whether the board dealt fairly with the corporation and whether the challenged transaction was at a fair price to the corporation.

As you read Weinberger, consider the facts and ask yourself if you were advising the controller how, if they were able to do things all over again, they might change things to make sure the actions of the controller and the board comported with the entire fairness standard as described by the court.

457 A.2d 701 (1983)
WEINBERGER v. UOP, INC.

MOORE, Justice:

Signal is a diversified, technically based company operating through various subsidiaries. Its stock is publicly traded on the New York, Philadelphia and Pacific Stock Exchanges. UOP, formerly known as Universal Oil Products Company, was a diversified industrial company engaged in various lines of business, including petroleum and petro-chemical services and related products, construction, fabricated metal products, transportation equipment products, chemicals and plastics, and other products and services including land development, lumber products and waste disposal. Its stock was publicly held and listed on the New York Stock Exchange.

In 1974 Signal sold one of its wholly-owned subsidiaries for $420,000,000 in cash. […] While looking to invest this cash surplus, Signal became interested in UOP as a possible acquisition. Friendly negotiations ensued, and Signal proposed to acquire a controlling interest in UOP at a price of $19 per share. UOP's representatives sought $25 per share. In the arm's length bargaining that followed, an understanding was reached whereby Signal agreed to purchase from UOP 1,500,000 shares of UOP's authorized but unissued stock at $21 per share. […]

The negotiations between Signal and UOP occurred during April 1975, and the resulting tender offer was greatly oversubscribed. However, Signal limited its total purchase of the tendered shares so that, when coupled with the stock bought from UOP, it had achieved its goal of becoming a 50.5% shareholder of UOP.

Although UOP's board consisted of thirteen directors, Signal nominated and elected only six. Of these, five were either directors or employees of Signal. The sixth, a partner in the banking firm of Lazard Freres & Co., had been one of Signal's representatives in the negotiations and bargaining with UOP concerning the tender offer and purchase price of the UOP shares. […]

However, the president and chief executive officer of UOP retired during 1975, and Signal caused him to be replaced by James V. Crawford, a long-time employee and senior executive vice president of one of Signal's wholly-owned subsidiaries. […]

By the end of 1977 Signal basically was unsuccessful in finding other suitable investment candidates for its excess cash, and by February 1978 considered that it had no other realistic acquisitions available to it on a friendly basis. Once again its attention turned to UOP.

The trial court found that at the instigation of certain Signal management personnel, including William W. Walkup, its board chairman, […], a feasibility study was made concerning the possible acquisition of the balance of UOP's outstanding shares. This study was performed by two Signal officers, Charles S. Arledge and Andrew J. Chitiea. Arledge and Chitiea were both directors of UOP in addition to their membership on the Signal board.

Arledge and Chitiea concluded that it would be a good investment for Signal to acquire the remaining 49.5% of UOP shares at any price up to $24 each. Their report was discussed between Walkup and Shumway who, along with Arledge, Chitiea and Brewster L. Arms, internal counsel for Signal, constituted Signal's senior management. […] It was ultimately agreed that a meeting of Signal's executive committee would be called to propose that Signal acquire the remaining outstanding stock of UOP through a cash-out merger in the range of $20 to $21 per share.

The executive committee meeting was set for February 28, 1978. As a courtesy, UOP's president, Crawford, was invited to attend, although he was not a member of Signal's executive committee. On his arrival, and prior to the meeting, Crawford was asked to meet privately with Walkup and Shumway. He was then told of Signal's plan to acquire full ownership of UOP and was asked for his reaction to the proposed price range of $20 to $21 per share. Crawford said he thought such a price would be "generous", and that it was certainly one which should be submitted to UOP's minority shareholders for their ultimate consideration. […]

Thus, it was the consensus that a price of $20 to $21 per share would be fair to both Signal and the minority shareholders of UOP. Signal's executive committee authorized [706] its management "to negotiate" with UOP "for a cash acquisition of the minority ownership in UOP, Inc., with the intention of presenting a proposal to [Signal's] board of directors ... on March 6, 1978". Immediately after this February 28, 1978 meeting, Signal issued a press release stating:

> The Signal Companies, Inc. and UOP, Inc. are conducting
> negotiations for the acquisition for cash by Signal of the 49.5 per

cent of UOP which it does not presently own, announced Forrest
N. Shumway, president and chief executive officer of Signal, and
James V. Crawford, UOP president.

Price and other terms of the proposed transaction have not yet been
finalized and would be subject to approval of the boards of
directors of Signal and UOP, scheduled to meet early next week, the
stockholders of UOP and certain federal agencies.

The announcement also referred to the fact that the closing price of UOP's common stock on that day was $14.50 per share.

Two days later, on March 2, 1978, Signal issued a second press release stating that its management would recommend a price in the range of $20 to $21 per share for UOP's 49.5% minority interest. [...]

Between Tuesday, February 28, 1978 and Monday, March 6, 1978, a total of four business days, Crawford spoke by telephone with all of UOP's non-Signal, i.e., outside, directors. Also during that period, Crawford retained Lehman Brothers to render a fairness opinion as to the price offered the minority for its stock. He gave two reasons for this choice. First, the time schedule between the announcement and the board meetings was short (by then only three business days) and since Lehman Brothers had been acting as UOP's investment banker for many years, Crawford felt that it would be in the best position to respond on such brief notice. Second, James W. Glanville, a long-time director of UOP and a partner in Lehman Brothers, had acted as a financial advisor to UOP for many years. Crawford believed that Glanville's familiarity with UOP, as a member of its board, would also be of assistance in enabling Lehman Brothers to render a fairness opinion within the existing time constraints. [...]

Glanville assembled a three-man Lehman Brothers team to do the work on the fairness opinion. These persons examined relevant documents and information concerning UOP, including its annual reports and its Securities and Exchange Commission filings from 1973 through 1976, as well as its audited financial statements for 1977, its interim reports to shareholders, and its recent and historical market prices and trading volumes. In addition, on Friday, March 3, 1978, two members of the Lehman Brothers team flew to UOP's headquarters in Des Plaines, Illinois, to perform a "due diligence" visit, during the course of which they interviewed Crawford as well as UOP's general counsel, its chief financial officer, and other key executives and personnel.

As a result, the Lehman Brothers team concluded that "the price of either $20 or $21 would be a fair price for the remaining shares of UOP". They telephoned this impression to Glanville, who was spending the weekend in Vermont.

On Monday morning, March 6, 1978, Glanville and the senior member of the Lehman Brothers team flew to Des Plaines to attend the scheduled UOP directors meeting. Glanville looked over the assembled information during the flight. The two had with them the draft of a "fairness opinion letter" in which the price had been left blank. Either during or immediately prior to the directors' meeting, the two-page "fairness opinion letter" was typed in final form and the price of $21 per share was inserted. [...]

A primary issue mandating reversal is the preparation by two UOP directors, Arledge and Chitiea, of their feasibility study for the exclusive use and benefit of Signal. This document was of obvious significance to both Signal and UOP. Using UOP data, it described the advantages to Signal of ousting the minority at a price range of $21-$24 per share.

It is clear from the record that neither Arledge nor Chitiea shared this report with their fellow directors of UOP. We are satisfied that no one else did either. This conduct hardly meets the fiduciary standards applicable to such a transaction. [...] Mr. Shumway, Signal's president, testified that he made sure the Signal outside directors had this report prior to the March 6, 1978 Signal board meeting, but he did not testify that the Arledge-Chitiea report was also sent to UOP's outside directors. [...]

The concept of fairness has two basic aspects: fair dealing and fair price. The former embraces questions of when the transaction was timed, how it was initiated, structured, negotiated, disclosed to the directors, and how the approvals of the directors and the stockholders were obtained. The latter aspect of fairness relates to the economic and financial considerations of the proposed merger, including all relevant factors: assets, market value, earnings, future prospects, and any other elements that affect the intrinsic or inherent value of a company's stock. [...]However, the test for fairness is not a bifurcated one as between fair dealing and price. All aspects of the issue must be examined as a whole since the question is one of entire fairness. However, in a non-fraudulent transaction we recognize that price may be the preponderant consideration outweighing other features of the merger. Here, we address the two basic aspects of fairness separately because we find reversible error as to both. […]

Part of fair dealing is the obvious duty of candor […] one possessing superior knowledge may not mislead any stockholder by use of corporate information to which the latter is not privy. […]. With the well-established Delaware law on the subject, and the Court of Chancery's findings of fact here, it is inevitable that the obvious conflicts posed by Arledge and Chitiea's preparation of their "feasibility study", derived from UOP information, for the sole use and benefit of Signal, cannot pass muster.

The Arledge-Chitiea report is but one aspect of the element of fair dealing. How did this merger evolve? It is clear that it was entirely initiated by Signal. The serious time constraints under which the principals acted were all set by Signal. It had not found a suitable outlet for its excess cash and considered UOP a desirable investment, particularly since it was now in a position to acquire the whole company for itself. For whatever reasons, and they were only Signal's, the entire transaction was presented to and approved by UOP's board within four business days. Standing alone, this is not necessarily indicative of any lack of fairness by a majority shareholder. It was what occurred, or more properly, what did not occur, during this brief period that makes the time constraints imposed by Signal relevant to the issue of fairness.

The structure of the transaction, again, was Signal's doing. So far as negotiations were concerned, it is clear that they were modest at best. Crawford, Signal's man at UOP, never really talked price with Signal, except to accede to its management's statements on the subject, and to convey to Signal the UOP outside directors' view that as between the $20-$21 range under consideration, it would have to be $21. The latter is not a surprising outcome, but hardly arm's length negotiations. […]

As we have noted, the matter of disclosure to the UOP directors was wholly flawed by the conflicts of interest raised by the Arledge-Chitiea report. All of those conflicts were resolved by Signal in its own favor without divulging any aspect of them to UOP.

This cannot but undermine a conclusion that this merger meets any reasonable test of fairness. The outside UOP directors lacked one material piece of information generated by two of their colleagues, but shared only with Signal. True, the UOP board had the

Lehman Brothers' fairness opinion, but that firm has been blamed by the plaintiff for the hurried task it performed, when more properly the responsibility for this lies with Signal. There was no disclosure of the circumstances surrounding the rather cursory preparation of the Lehman Brothers' fairness opinion. Instead, the impression was given UOP's minority that a careful study had been made, when in fact speed was the hallmark. [...] Yet, none of this was disclosed to UOP's minority.

Finally, the minority stockholders were denied the critical information that Signal considered a price of $24 to be a good investment. Since this would have meant over $17,000,000 more to the minority, we cannot conclude that the shareholder vote was an informed one. Under the circumstances, an approval by a majority of the minority was meaningless. [...]

Given these particulars and the Delaware law on the subject, the record does not establish that this transaction satisfies any reasonable concept of fair dealing, [...]

Turning to the matter of price, plaintiff also challenges its fairness. [...]

In this breach of fiduciary duty case, the Chancellor perceived that the approach to valuation was the same as that in an appraisal proceeding. Consistent with precedent, he rejected plaintiff's method of proof and accepted defendants' evidence of value as being in accord with practice under prior case law. This means that the so-called "Delaware block" or weighted average method was employed wherein the elements of value, i.e., assets, market price, earnings, etc., were assigned a particular weight and the resulting amounts added to determine the value per share. This procedure has been in use for decades. [...]. However, to the extent it excludes other generally accepted techniques used in the financial community and the courts, it is now clearly outmoded. It is time we recognize this in appraisal and other stock valuation proceedings and bring our law current on the subject.

While the Chancellor rejected plaintiff's discounted cash flow method of valuing UOP's stock, as not corresponding with "either logic or the existing law" [...] it is significant that this was essentially the focus, i.e., earnings potential of UOP, of Messrs. Arledge and Chitiea in their evaluation of the merger. Accordingly, the standard "Delaware block" or weighted average method of valuation, formerly [713] employed in appraisal and other stock valuation cases, shall no longer exclusively control such proceedings. We believe that a more liberal approach must include proof of value by any techniques or methods which are generally considered acceptable in the financial community and otherwise admissible in court, subject only to our interpretation of 8 *Del.C.* § 262(h),[…] This will obviate the very structured and mechanistic procedure that has heretofore governed such matters. […]

Fair price obviously requires consideration of all relevant factors involving the value of a company. […]

While a plaintiff's monetary remedy ordinarily should be confined to the more liberalized appraisal proceeding herein established, we do not intend any limitation on the historic powers of the Chancellor to grant such other relief as the facts of a particular case may dictate. The appraisal remedy we approve may not be adequate in certain cases, particularly where fraud, misrepresentation, self-dealing, deliberate waste of corporate assets, or gross and palpable overreaching are involved. […] Under such circumstances, the Chancellor's powers are complete to fashion any form of equitable and monetary relief as may be appropriate, including rescissory damages. Since it is apparent that this long completed transaction is too involved to undo, and in view of the Chancellor's discretion, the award, if any, should be in the form of monetary damages based upon entire fairness standards, i.e., fair dealing and fair price.

4.3.2.2 Sinclair Oil Corp. v. Levien

Stockholders do not normally have fiduciary duties with respect to other stockholders. This principle makes sense for a number of reasons. Stockholders with small stakes have no ability to influence the board of directors and therefore should be free from restrictions in their dealings with other stockholders. However, this principle is subject to an exception. When stockholders can, through their ownership position influence and control the direction of the corporation, then those stockholders have fiduciary obligations with respect to minority stockholders. As a result, in such circumstances, controlling stockholders will bear the burden of proving entire fairness when they engage in self-dealing with the corporation.

280 A.2d 717 (1971)
SINCLAIR OIL CORPORATION v. LEVIEN

WOLCOTT, Chief Justice.

This is an appeal by the defendant, Sinclair Oil Corporation (hereafter Sinclair), from an order of the Court of Chancery, 261 A.2d 911 in a derivative action requiring Sinclair to account for damages sustained by its subsidiary, Sinclair Venezuelan Oil Company (hereafter Sinven), organized by Sinclair for the purpose of operating in Venezuela, as a result of dividends paid by Sinven, the denial to Sinven of industrial development, and a breach of contract between Sinclair's wholly-owned subsidiary, Sinclair International Oil Company, and Sinven.

Sinclair, operating primarily as a holding company, is in the business of exploring for oil and of producing and marketing crude oil and oil products. At all times relevant to this litigation, it owned about 97% of Sinven's stock. The plaintiff owns about 3000 of 120,000 publicly held shares of Sinven. Sinven, incorporated in 1922, has been engaged in petroleum operations primarily in Venezuela and since 1959 has operated exclusively in Venezuela.

Sinclair nominates all members of Sinven's board of directors. The Chancellor found as a fact that the directors were not independent of Sinclair. Almost without exception, they were officers, directors, or employees of corporations in the Sinclair complex. By reason of Sinclair's domination, it is clear that Sinclair owed Sinven a fiduciary duty. Getty Oil Company v. Skelly Oil Co., 267 A.2d 883 (Del.Supr. 1970); Cottrell v. Pawcatuck Co., 35 Del. Ch. 309, 116 A.2d 787 (1955). Sinclair concedes this.

The Chancellor held that because of Sinclair's fiduciary duty and its control over Sinven, its relationship with Sinven must meet the test of intrinsic fairness. The [720] standard of intrinsic fairness involves both a high degree of fairness and a shift in the burden of proof. Under this standard the burden is on Sinclair to prove, subject to careful judicial scrutiny, that its transactions with Sinven were objectively fair. Guth v. Loft, Inc., 23 Del.Ch. 255, 5 A.2d 503 (1939); Sterling v. Mayflower Hotel Corp., 33 Del.Ch. 293, 93 A.2d 107, 38 A. L.R.2d 425 (Del.Supr.1952); Getty Oil Co. v. Skelly Oil Co., supra.

347

Sinclair argues that the transactions between it and Sinven should be tested, not by the test of intrinsic fairness with the accompanying shift of the burden of proof, but by the business judgment rule under which a court will not interfere with the judgment of a board of directors unless there is a showing of gross and palpable overreaching. Meyerson v. El Paso Natural Gas Co., 246 A.2d 789 (Del.Ch. 1967). A board of directors enjoys a presumption of sound business judgment, and its decisions will not be disturbed if they can be attributed to any rational business purpose. A court under such circumstances will not substitute its own notions of what is or is not sound business judgment.

We think, however, that Sinclair's argument in this respect is misconceived. When the situation involves a parent and a subsidiary, with the parent controlling the transaction and fixing the terms, the test of intrinsic fairness, with its resulting shifting of the burden of proof, is applied. Sterling v. Mayflower Hotel Corp., supra; David J. Greene & Co. v. Dunhill International, Inc., 249 A.2d 427 (Del.Ch.1968); Bastian v. Bourns, Inc., 256 A.2d 680 (Del.Ch.1969) aff'd. Per Curiam (unreported) (Del.Supr.1970). The basic situation for the application of the rule is the one in which the parent has received a benefit to the exclusion and at the expense of the subsidiary.

Recently, this court dealt with the question of fairness in parent-subsidiary dealings in Getty Oil Co. v. Skelly Oil Co., supra. In that case, both parent and subsidiary were in the business of refining and marketing crude oil and crude oil products. The Oil Import Board ruled that the subsidiary, because it was controlled by the parent, was no longer entitled to a separate allocation of imported crude oil. The subsidiary then contended that it had a right to share the quota of crude oil allotted to the parent. We ruled that the business judgment standard should be applied to determine this contention. Although the subsidiary suffered a loss through the administration of the oil import quotas, the parent gained nothing. The parent's quota was derived solely from its own past use. The past use of the subsidiary did not cause an increase in the parent's quota. Nor did the parent usurp a quota of the subsidiary. Since the parent received nothing from the subsidiary to the exclusion of the minority stockholders of the subsidiary, there was no self-dealing. Therefore, the business judgment standard was properly applied.

A parent does indeed owe a fiduciary duty to its subsidiary when there are parent-subsidiary dealings. However, this alone will not evoke the intrinsic fairness standard.

This standard will be applied only when the fiduciary duty is accompanied by self-dealing — the situation when a parent is on both sides of a transaction with its subsidiary. Self-dealing occurs when the parent, by virtue of its domination of the subsidiary, causes the subsidiary to act in such a way that the parent receives something from the subsidiary to the exclusion of, and detriment to, the minority stockholders of the subsidiary.

We turn now to the facts. The plaintiff argues that, from 1960 through 1966, Sinclair caused Sinven to pay out such excessive dividends that the industrial development of Sinven was effectively prevented, and it became in reality a corporation in dissolution.

From 1960 through 1966, Sinven paid out $108,000,000 in dividends ($38,000,000 [721] in excess of Sinven's earnings during the same period). The Chancellor held that Sinclair caused these dividends to be paid during a period when it had a need for large amounts of cash. Although the dividends paid exceeded earnings, the plaintiff concedes that the payments were made in compliance with 8 Del.C. § 170, authorizing payment of dividends out of surplus or net profits. However, the plaintiff attacks these dividends on the ground that they resulted from an improper motive — Sinclair's need for cash. The Chancellor, applying the intrinsic fairness standard, held that Sinclair did not sustain its burden of proving that these dividends were intrinsically fair to the minority stockholders of Sinven.

Since it is admitted that the dividends were paid in strict compliance with 8 Del.C. § 170, the alleged excessiveness of the payments alone would not state a cause of action. Nevertheless, compliance with the applicable statute may not, under all circumstances, justify all dividend payments. If a plaintiff can meet his burden of proving that a dividend cannot be grounded on any reasonable business objective, then the courts can and will interfere with the board's decision to pay the dividend.

Sinclair contends that it is improper to apply the intrinsic fairness standard to dividend payments even when the board which voted for the dividends is completely dominated. In support of this contention, Sinclair relies heavily on American District Telegraph Co. [ADT] v. Grinnell Corp., (N.Y.Sup.Ct.1969) aff'd. 33 A.D.2d 769, 306 N.Y.S.2d 209 (1969). Plaintiffs were minority stockholders of ADT, a subsidiary of Grinnell. The plaintiffs alleged that Grinnell, realizing that it would soon have to sell its ADT stock because of a pending anti-trust action, caused ADT to pay excessive dividends. Because the dividend payments conformed with applicable statutory law, and the plaintiffs could not prove an abuse of discretion, the court ruled that the complaint did not state a cause of action. Other decisions seem to support Sinclair's contention. In Metropolitan Casualty Ins. Co. v. First State Bank of Temple, 54 S.W.2d 358 (Tex.Civ.App.1932), rev'd. on other grounds, 79 S.W.2d 835 (Sup.Ct. 1935), the court held that a majority of interested directors does not void a declaration of dividends because all directors, by necessity, are interested in and benefited by a dividend declaration. See, also, Schwartz v. Kahn, 183 Misc. 252, 50 N.Y.S. 2d 931 (1944); Weinberger v. Quinn, 264 A.D. 405, 35 N.Y.S.2d 567 (1942).

We do not accept the argument that the intrinsic fairness test can never be applied to a dividend declaration by a dominated board, although a dividend declaration by a dominated board will not inevitably demand the application of the intrinsic fairness standard. Moskowitz v. Bantrell, 41 Del.Ch. 177, 190 A.2d 749 (Del.Supr. 1963). If such a dividend is in essence self-dealing by the parent, then the intrinsic fairness standard is the proper standard. For example, suppose a parent dominates a subsidiary and its board of directors. The subsidiary has outstanding two classes of stock, X and Y. Class X is owned by the parent and Class Y is owned by minority stockholders of the subsidiary. If the subsidiary, at the direction of the parent, declares a dividend on its Class X stock only, this might well be self-dealing by the parent. It would be receiving something from the subsidiary to the exclusion of and detrimental to its minority stockholders. This self-dealing, coupled with the parent's fiduciary duty, would make intrinsic fairness the proper standard by which to evaluate the dividend payments.

Consequently it must be determined whether the dividend payments by Sinven were, in essence, self-dealing by Sinclair. The dividends resulted in great sums of money being transferred from Sinven to Sinclair. However, a proportionate share of this money was received by the minority shareholders of Sinven. Sinclair received nothing from Sinven to the exclusion of its [722] minority stockholders. As such, these dividends were not self-dealing. We hold therefore that the Chancellor erred in applying the intrinsic fairness test as to these dividend payments. The business judgment standard should have been applied.

We conclude that the facts demonstrate that the dividend payments complied with the business judgment standard and with 8 Del.C. § 170. The motives for causing the declaration of dividends are immaterial unless the plaintiff can show that the dividend payments resulted from improper motives and amounted to waste. The plaintiff contends only that the dividend payments drained Sinven of cash to such an extent that it was prevented from expanding.

The plaintiff proved no business opportunities which came to Sinven independently and which Sinclair either took to itself or denied to Sinven. As a matter of fact, with two minor exceptions which resulted in losses, all of Sinven's operations have been conducted in Venezuela, and Sinclair had a policy of exploiting its oil properties located in different countries by subsidiaries located in the particular countries.

From 1960 to 1966 Sinclair purchased or developed oil fields in Alaska, Canada, Paraguay, and other places around the world. The plaintiff contends that these were all opportunities which could have been taken by Sinven. The Chancellor concluded that Sinclair had not proved that its denial of expansion opportunities to Sinven was intrinsically fair. He based this conclusion on the following findings of fact. Sinclair made no real effort to expand Sinven. The excessive dividends paid by Sinven resulted in so great a cash drain as to effectively deny to Sinven any ability to expand. During this same period Sinclair actively pursued a company-wide policy of developing through its subsidiaries new sources of revenue, but Sinven was not permitted to participate and was confined in its activities to Venezuela.

However, the plaintiff could point to no opportunities which came to Sinven. Therefore, Sinclair usurped no business opportunity belonging to Sinven. Since Sinclair received nothing from Sinven to the exclusion of and detriment to Sinven's minority stockholders, there was no self-dealing. Therefore, business judgment is the proper standard by which to evaluate Sinclair's expansion policies.

Since there is no proof of self-dealing on the part of Sinclair, it follows that the expansion policy of Sinclair and the methods used to achieve the desired result must, as far as Sinclair's treatment of Sinven is concerned, be tested by the standards of the business judgment rule. Accordingly, Sinclair's decision, absent fraud or gross overreaching, to achieve expansion through the medium of its subsidiaries, other than Sinven, must be upheld.

Even if Sinclair was wrong in developing these opportunities as it did, the question arises, with which subsidiaries should these opportunities have been shared? No evidence indicates a unique need or ability of Sinven to develop these opportunities. The decision of which subsidiaries would be used to implement Sinclair's expansion policy was one of business judgment with which a court will not interfere absent a showing of gross and palpable overreaching. Meyerson v. El Paso Natural Gas Co., 246 A.2d 789 (Del.Ch.1967). No such showing has been made here.

Next, Sinclair argues that the Chancellor committed error when he held it liable to Sinven for breach of contract.

In 1961 Sinclair created Sinclair International Oil Company (hereafter International), a wholly owned subsidiary used for the purpose of coordinating all of Sinclair's foreign operations. All crude purchases by Sinclair were made thereafter through International.

On September 28, 1961, Sinclair caused Sinven to contract with International whereby Sinven agreed to sell all of its [723] crude oil and refined products to International at specified prices. The contract provided for minimum and maximum quantities and prices. The plaintiff contends that Sinclair caused this contract to be breached in two respects. Although the contract called for payment on receipt, International's payments lagged as much as 30 days after receipt. Also, the contract required International to purchase at least a fixed minimum amount of crude and refined products from Sinven. International did not comply with this requirement.

Clearly, Sinclair's act of contracting with its dominated subsidiary was self-dealing. Under the contract Sinclair received the products produced by Sinven, and of course the minority shareholders of Sinven were not able to share in the receipt of these products. If the contract was breached, then Sinclair received these products to the detriment of Sinven's minority shareholders. We agree with the Chancellor's finding that the contract was breached by Sinclair, both as to the time of payments and the amounts purchased.

Although a parent need not bind itself by a contract with its dominated subsidiary, Sinclair chose to operate in this manner. As Sinclair has received the benefits of this contract, so must it comply with the contractual duties.

Under the intrinsic fairness standard, Sinclair must prove that its causing Sinven not to enforce the contract was intrinsically fair to the minority shareholders of Sinven. Sinclair has failed to meet this burden. Late payments were clearly breaches for which Sinven should have sought and received adequate damages. As to the quantities purchased, Sinclair argues that it purchased all the products produced by Sinven. This, however, does not satisfy the standard of intrinsic fairness. Sinclair has failed to prove that Sinven could not possibly have produced or someway have obtained the contract minimums. As such, Sinclair must account on this claim.

Finally, Sinclair argues that the Chancellor committed error in refusing to allow it a credit or setoff of all benefits provided by it to Sinven with respect to all the alleged damages. The Chancellor held that setoff should be allowed on specific transactions, e. g., benefits to Sinven under the contract with International, but denied an over all setoff against all damages claimed. We agree with the Chancellor, although the point may well be moot in view of our holding that Sinclair is not required to account for the alleged excessiveness of the dividend payments.

We will therefore reverse that part of the Chancellor's order that requires Sinclair to account to Sinven for damages sustained as a result of dividends paid between 1960 and 1966, and by reason of the denial to Sinven of expansion during that period. We will affirm the remaining portion of that order and remand the cause for further proceedings.

** ** ***

4.3.# Who is a Controlling Stockholder?

In *Sinclair v. Levien* where Sinclair Oil Corp owned 97% of the shares in its subsidiary, Sinclair Venezuelan Oil Company, there really was no question that Sinclair was a controlling stockholder with fiduciary obligations to the minority stockholders. However, it is not always so obvious that a stockholder is a controlling stockholder with fiduciary obligations.

In *Kahn v. Lynch Communications Systems, Inc.*, the Supreme Court observed that Delaware courts will deem a stockholder a "controlling stockholder" when the stockholder: (1) owns more than 50% of the voting power of a corporation *or* (2) owns less than 50% of the voting power of the corporation but "exercises control over the business affairs of the corporation."

353

Blocks of 50% more of the voting power obviously create the ability to control the corporation. The 50%+ blockholder has the power to unilaterally replace the board of directors and can thus guide decision-making in the corporation.

That a 50% blockholder is a controller is hardly news. The more interesting question is whether a minority blockholder where the stockholder holds a block of less than 50% can also be deemed a controller. The answer to that question is obviously "yes". For example, a 48% blockholder holds less than majority voting control, but in a world where meeting participation and voting is not universal, 48% will usually be enough to determine the result of contested director elections.

For the court to reach a determination that a minority blockholder is a controller, the minority blockholder must exercise *actual* control over the business affairs of the corporation. In *Tesla Stockholder Litigation*, plaintiffs argued that Elon Musk, a 22.1% stockholder in Tesla had actual control of the corporation notwithstanding his minority position. The court required plaintiffs to demonstrate that Musk "exercised actual domination and control over . . . [the] directors." In this regard, his power must be "so potent that independent directors . . . [could not] freely exercise their judgment."

The court laid out the challenge for plaintiffs in demonstrating control thusly: "The requisite degree of control can be shown to exist generally or 'with regard to the particular transaction that is being challenged.'" Stated differently, when pleading that a minority blockholder is a controlling stockholder, the plaintiff may plead either (or both) of the following: (1) that the minority blockholder actually dominated and controlled the corporation, its board or the deciding committee with respect to the challenged transaction or (2) that the minority blockholder actually dominated and controlled the majority of the board generally. "[W]hether a large blockholder is so powerful as to have obtained the status of a 'controlling stockholder' is intensely factual [and] it is a difficult [question] to resolve on the pleadings. In the case of Tesla, the court reached a determination that with his 22.1% block and control of the board that plaintiffs had demonstrated Musk was the controlling stockholder of Tesla.

4.3.3 Sec. 144 Safe Harbor and Interested Director Transactions

During the 19th century, transactions between the corporation and its directors were commonplace. Such transactions often worked to the advantage of the interested director at the expense of the stockholder. The pernicious effect of such transactions caused legislatures to strictly regulate relationships between corporations and their directors. Through the early 20th century, transactions between a corporation and a director were considered **void**. Over the years, policy with respect to interested director transactions has loosened, but such transactions are still, rightly, looked at with suspicion.

Such transactions are no longer void per se. Section 144 provides for a statutory safe harbor for interested director transactions. Interested director transactions that comply with the requirements of Section 144 will not be considered **void** or **voidable**.

Compliance with the requirements of Section 144 provides a board with a safe harbor only against attacks for **voidability**. Interested director transactions are still subject to attack for potential violations of the duty of loyalty. So, while the challenged transaction might not be void, it could still be unfair and boards may be required to defend the transaction for violations of the duty of loyalty.

The procedures for insulating interested director transactions from attack for purposes of Section 144 provide a partial roadmap for the related **doctrine of stockholder ratification**. Interested director transactions that comply with the requirements of stockholder ratification doctrine will not be subject to attack for potential violations of the duty of loyalty and will receive the benefit of the business judgment presumption.

4.3.3.1 DGCL Sec. 144

The following provision of the statute provides a safe harbor for interested director transactions. If the requirements of the safe harbor are complied with then an interested director transaction will not be void or voidable because of the participation of the director. It may still, however, be subject to attack as a violation of the duty of loyalty and the interested director may be required to prove the entire fairness of the transaction.

§ 144. Interested directors; quorum.

(a) No contract or transaction between a corporation and 1 or more of its directors or officers, or between a corporation and any other corporation, partnership, association, or other organization in which 1 or more of its directors or officers, are directors or officers, or have a financial interest, shall be void or voidable solely for this reason, or solely because the director or officer is present at or participates in the meeting of the board or committee which authorizes the contract or transaction, or solely because any such director's or officer's votes are counted for such purpose, if:

(1) The material facts as to the director's or officer's relationship or interest and as to the contract or transaction are disclosed or are known to the board of directors or the committee, and the board or committee in good faith authorizes the contract or transaction by the affirmative votes of a majority of the disinterested directors, even though the disinterested directors be less than a quorum; or

(2) The material facts as to the director's or officer's relationship or interest and as to the contract or transaction are disclosed or are known to the stockholders entitled to vote thereon, and the contract or transaction is specifically approved in good faith by vote of the stockholders; or

(3) The contract or transaction is fair as to the corporation as of the time it is authorized, approved or ratified, by the board of directors, a committee or the stockholders.

(b) Common or interested directors may be counted in determining the presence of a quorum at a meeting of the board of directors or of a committee which authorizes the contract or transaction.

4.3.3.2 Benihana of Tokyo, Inc. v. Benihana, Inc.

Section 144(a)(1) provides that when a board member's interest is disclosed to or is known by disinterested directors and a majority of the disinterested directors approve the challenged transaction, the board's decision to enter into the transaction will receive the benefit of the §144 safe harbor protection from challenges for voidness and voidability.

Benihana raises a couple of important issues. First, does the disclosure of the director's interest need to be accomplished formally? Or, is it sufficient that the director's interest be common knowledge to the disinterested directors? Second, to the extent a majority of disinterested directors approve the transaction does such an approval provide the interested director and the transaction any additional protection beyond merely protection against the transaction being deemed void or voidable? If a transaction is approved by a majority of disinterested directors who are fully informed about the transaction should that transaction get the protection of the business judgment presumption?

906 A.2d 114 (2006)
BENIHANA OF TOKYO, INC. v. BENIHANA, INC.

BERGER, Justice:

Rocky Aoki founded Benihana of Tokyo, Inc. (BOT), and its subsidiary, Benihana, which own and operate Benihana restaurants in the United States and other countries. Aoki owned 100% of BOT until 1998, when he pled guilty to insider trading charges. In order to avoid licensing problems created by his status as a convicted felon, Aoki transferred his stock to the Benihana Protective Trust. The trustees of the Trust were Aoki's three children (Kana Aoki Nootenboom, Kyle Aoki and Kevin Aoki) and Darwin Dornbush (who was then the family's attorney, a Benihana director, and, effectively, the company's general counsel).

Benihana, a Delaware corporation, has two classes of common stock. There are approximately 6 million shares of Class A common stock outstanding. Each share has 1/10 vote and the holders of Class A common are entitled to elect 25% of the directors. There are approximately 3 million shares of Common stock outstanding. Each share of Common has one vote and the holders of Common stock are entitled to elect the remaining 75% of Benihana's directors. Before the transaction at issue, BOT owned 50.9% of the Common stock and 2% of the Class A stock. The nine member board of directors is classified and the directors serve three-year terms.[1]

In 2003, shortly after Aoki married Keiko Aoki, conflicts arose between Aoki and his children. In August, the children were upset to learn that Aoki had changed his will to give Keiko control over BOT. Joel Schwartz, Benihana's president and chief executive officer, also was concerned about this change in control. He discussed the situation with Dornbush, and they briefly considered various options, including the issuance of sufficient Class A stock to trigger a provision in the certificate of incorporation that would allow the Common and Class A to vote together for 75% of the directors.[2]

The Aoki family's turmoil came at a time when Benihana also was facing challenges. Many of its restaurants were old and outmoded. Benihana hired WD Partners to evaluate its facilities and to plan and design appropriate renovations. The resulting Construction and Renovation Plan anticipated that the project would take at least five years and cost $56 million or more. Wachovia offered to provide Benihana a $60 million line of credit for the Construction and Renovation Plan, but the restrictions Wachovia imposed made it unlikely that Benihana would be able to borrow the full amount.[3] Because the Wachovia line of credit did not assure that Benihana would have the capital it needed, the company retained Morgan Joseph & Co. to develop other financing options.

On January 9, 2004, after evaluating Benihana's financial situation and needs, Fred Joseph, of Morgan Joseph, met with Schwartz, Dornbush and John E. Abdo, the board's executive committee. Joseph expressed concern that Benihana would not have sufficient available capital to complete the Construction and Renovation Plan and pursue appropriate acquisitions. Benihana was conservatively leveraged, and Joseph discussed various financing alternatives, including bank debt, high yield debt, convertible debt or preferred stock, equity and sale/leaseback options.

The full board met with Joseph on January 29, 2004. He reviewed all the financing alternatives that he had discussed with the executive committee, and recommended that Benihana issue convertible preferred stock.[4] Joseph explained that the preferred stock would provide the funds needed for the Construction and Renovation Plan and also put the company in a better negotiating position if it sought additional financing from Wachovia. […]

The board met again on February 17, 2004, to review the terms of the Transaction. The directors discussed Benihana's preferences and Joseph predicted what a buyer likely would expect or require. […]

Shortly after the February meeting, Abdo contacted Joseph and told him that BFC Financial Corporation was interested in buying the new convertible stock.[5] In April 2005, Joseph sent BFC a private placement memorandum. Abdo negotiated with Joseph for several weeks.[6] They agreed to the Transaction on the following basic terms: (i) $20 million issuance in two tranches of $10 million each, with the second tranche to be issued one to three years after the first; (ii) BFC obtained one seat on the board, and one additional seat if Benihana failed to pay dividends for two consecutive quarters; (iii) BFC obtained preemptive rights on any new voting securities; (iv) 5% dividend; (v) 15% conversion premium; (vi) BFC had the right to force Benihana to redeem the preferred stock in full after ten years; and (vii) the stock would have immediate "as if converted" voting rights. Joseph testified that he was satisfied with the negotiations, as he had obtained what he wanted with respect to the most important points.

On April 22, 2004, Abdo sent a memorandum to Dornbush, Schwartz and Joseph, listing the agreed terms of the Transaction. He did not send the memorandum to any other members of the Benihana board. Schwartz did tell Becker, Sturges, Sano, and possibly Pine that BFC was the potential buyer. At its next meeting, held on May 6, 2004, the entire board was officially informed of BFC's involvement in the Transaction. Abdo made a presentation on behalf of BFC and then left the meeting. Joseph distributed an updated board book, which explained that Abdo had approached Morgan Joseph on behalf of BFC, and included the negotiated terms. The trial court found that the board was not informed that Abdo had negotiated the deal on behalf of BFC. But the board did know that Abdo was a principal of BFC. After discussion, the board reviewed and approved the Transaction, subject to the receipt of a fairness opinion.

On May 18, 2004, after he learned that Morgan Joseph was providing a fairness opinion, Schwartz publicly announced the stock issuance. Two days later, Aoki's counsel sent a letter asking the board to abandon the Transaction and pursue other, more favorable, financing alternatives. The letter expressed concern about the directors' conflicts, the dilutive effect of the stock issuance, and its "questionable legality." […] The board then approved the Transaction. […]

On June 8, 2004, Benihana and BFC executed the Stock Purchase Agreement. On June 11, 2004, the board met and approved resolutions ratifying the execution of the Stock Purchase Agreement and authorizing the stock issuance. […]. On July 2, 2004, BOT filed this action against all of Benihana's directors, except Kevin Aoki, alleging breaches of fiduciary duties; and against BFC, alleging that it aided and abetted the fiduciary violations. Three months later, as the parties were filing their pre-trial briefs, the board again reviewed the Transaction. After considering the allegations in the amended complaint, the board voted once more to approve it. [...]

A. Section 144(a)(1) Approval

Section 144 of the Delaware General Corporation Law provides a safe harbor for interested transactions, like this one, if "[t]he material facts as to the director's. . . relationship or interest and as to the contract or transaction are disclosed or are known to the board of directors ... and the board . . . in good faith authorizes the contract or transaction by the affirmative votes of a majority of the disinterested directors. . . ."[11] After approval by disinterested directors, courts review the interested transaction under the business judgment rule,[12] which "is a presumption that in making a business decision, the directors of a corporation acted on an informed basis, in good faith and in the honest belief that the action taken was in the best interest of the company."[13]

BOT argues that § 144(a)(1) is inapplicable because, when they approved the Transaction, the disinterested directors did not know that Abdo had negotiated the terms for BFC.[14] Abdo's role as negotiator is material, according to BOT, because Abdo had been given the confidential term sheet prepared by Joseph and knew which of those terms Benihana was prepared to give up during negotiations. We agree that the board needed to know about Abdo's involvement in order to make an informed decision. The record clearly [121] establishes, however, that the board possessed that material information when it approved the Transaction on May 6, 2004 and May 20, 2004.

Shortly before the May 6 meeting, Schwartz told Becker, Sturges and Sano that BFC was the proposed buyer. Then, at the meeting, Abdo made the presentation on behalf of BFC. Joseph's board book also explained that Abdo had made the initial contact that precipitated the negotiations. The board members knew that Abdo is a director, vice-chairman, and one of two people who control BFC. Thus, although no one ever said, "Abdo negotiated this deal for BFC," the directors understood that he was BFC's representative in the Transaction. As Pine testified, "whoever actually did the negotiating, [Abdo] as a principal would have to agree to it. So whether he sat in the room and negotiated it or he sat somewhere else and was brought the results of someone else's negotiation, he was the ultimate decision-maker."[15] Accordingly, we conclude that the disinterested directors possessed all the material information on Abdo's interest in the Transaction, and their approval at the May 6 and May 20 board meetings satisfies § 144(a)(1).

B. Abdo's alleged fiduciary violation

BOT next argues that the Court of Chancery should have reviewed the Transaction under an entire fairness standard because Abdo breached his duty of loyalty when he used Benihana's confidential information to negotiate on behalf of BFC. This argument starts with a flawed premise. The record does not support BOT's contention that Abdo used any confidential information against Benihana. Even without Joseph's comments at the February 17 board meeting, Abdo knew the terms a buyer could expect to obtain in a deal like this. Moreover, as the trial court found, "the negotiations involved give and take on a number of points" and Benihana "ended up where [it] wanted to be" for the most important terms.[17] Abdo did not set the terms of the deal; he did not deceive the board; and he did not dominate or control the other directors' approval of the Transaction. In short, the record does not support the claim that Abdo breached his duty of loyalty.[18]

C. Dilution of BOT's voting power

Finally, BOT argues that the board's primary purpose in approving the Transaction was to dilute BOT's voting control. BOT points out that Schwartz was concerned about BOT's control in 2003 and even discussed with Dornbush the possibility of issuing a huge number of Class A shares. Then, despite the availability of other financing options, the board decided on a stock issuance, and agreed to give BFC "as if converted" voting rights. According to BOT, the trial court overlooked this powerful evidence of the board's improper purpose.

It is settled law that, "corporate action . . . may not be taken for the sole or [122] primary purpose of entrenchment."[19] Here, however, the trial court found that "the primary purpose of the . . . Transaction was to provide what the directors subjectively believed to be the best financing vehicle available for securing the necessary funds to pursue the agreed upon Construction and Renovation Plan for the Benihana restaurants."[20] That factual determination has ample record support, especially in light of the trial court's credibility determinations. Accordingly, we defer to the Court of Chancery's conclusion that the board's approval of the Transaction was a valid exercise of its business judgment, for a proper corporate purpose.

Conclusion

Based on the foregoing, the judgment of the Court of Chancery is affirmed.

4.3.3.3 Fliegler v. Lawrence

Section 144 provides alternate methods to insulate interested director transactions from attack for voidness. In addition to seeking the approval of a majority of the disinterested directors, a board can seek the approval of the stockholders. Notice that the statute requires only that the challenged transaction is approved by a majority of the stockholders in order to gain the protection of the statutory safe harbor and not necessarily a majority of disinterested stockholders.

Remember the protections of § 144 extend only to the question of void or voidability of an interested director transaction and not further. One can see how there would be many situations where one might not want stockholder approval of an interested director transaction to do much more than simply rescue a transaction from voidness. Where a controlling stockholder approves a transaction with itself (as a director) we may be okay with that transaction not being void, but we might still want the interested director/stockholder to be required to prove the transaction is nevertheless entirely fair to the corporation.

The court in the following case, *Fliegler,* recognizes this problem and makes it clear that for directors who are seeking the additional protection of the business judgment presumption, they would have to do more than just comply with § 144(a)(2). For those directors, they will have to take the additonal step of complying with the requirements of common law stockholder ratification doctrine and seek informed approval of a majority of disinterested stockholders.

361 A.2d 218 (1976)
<u>FLIEGLER v. LAWRENCE</u>

McNEILLY, Justice:

In this shareholder derivative action brought on behalf of Agau Mines, Inc., a Delaware corporation, (Agau) against its officers and directors and United States Antimony Corporation, a Montana corporation (USAC), we are asked to decide whether the individual defendants, in their capacity as directors and officers of both corporations, wrongfully usurped a corporate opportunity belonging to Agau, and whether all defendants wrongfully profited by causing Agau to exercise an option to purchase that opportunity. […]

In November, 1969, defendant, John C. Lawrence (then president of Agau, a publicly held corporation engaged in a dual-phased gold and silver exploratory venture) in his individual capacity, acquired certain antimony properties under a lease-option for $60,000[…] Lawrence offered to [220] transfer the properties, which were then "a raw prospect", to Agau, but after consulting with other members of Agau's board of directors, he and they agreed that the corporation's legal and financial position would not permit acquisition and development of the properties at that time. Thus, it was decided to transfer the properties to USAC, (a closely held corporation formed just for this purpose and a majority of whose stock was owned by the individual defendants) where capital necessary for development of the properties could be raised without risk to Agau through the sale of USAC stock; it was also decided to grant Agau a long-term option to acquire USAC if the properties proved to be of commercial value.

In January, 1970, the option agreement was executed by Agau and USAC. Upon its exercise and approval by Agau shareholders, Agau was to deliver 800,000 shares of its restricted investment stock for all authorized and issued shares of USAC.[…]

In July, 1970, the Agau board resolved to exercise the option, an action which was approved by majority vote of the shareholders in October, 1970. Subsequently, plaintiff instituted this suit on behalf of Agau to recover the 800,000 shares and for an accounting.

Plaintiff contends that because the individual defendants personally profited through the use of Agau's resources, *viz.,* personnel (primarily Lawrence) to develop the USAC properties and stock purchase warrants to secure a $300,000. indebtedness (incurred by

USAC because it could not raise sufficient capital through sale of stock), they must be compelled to account to Agau for that profit. This argument pre-supposes that defendants did in fact so misuse corporate assets; however, the record reveals substantial evidence to support the Vice-Chancellor's conclusion that there was no misuse of either Agau personnel or warrants. Issuance of the warrants in fact enhanced the value of Agau's option at a time when there was reason to believe that USAC's antimony properties had a "considerable potential", and plaintiff did not prove that alleged use of Agau's personnel and equipment was detrimental to the corporation. […]

Nevertheless, our inquiry cannot stop here, for it is clear that the individual defendants stood on both sides of the transaction in implementing and fixing the terms of the option agreement. […]

A.

Preliminarily, defendants argue that they have been relieved of the burden of proving fairness by reason of shareholder ratification of the Board's decision to exercise the option. They rely on 8 Del.C. § 144(a)(2) and *Gottlieb v. Heyden Chemical Corp.,* Del.Supr., 33 Del.Ch. 177, 91 A. 2d 57 (1952).

In *Gottlieb,* this Court stated that shareholder ratification of an "interested transaction", although less than unanimous, shifts the burden of proof to an objecting shareholder to demonstrate that the terms are so unequal as to amount to a gift or waste of corporate assets. Also see *Saxe v. Brady,* 40 Del.Ch. 474, 184 A.2d 602 (1962). The Court explained:

> "[T]he entire atmosphere is freshened and a new set of rules
> invoked where formal approval has been given by a majority of
> independent, fully informed [share]holders." 91 A.2d at 59.

The purported ratification by the Agau shareholders would not affect the burden of proof in this case because the majority of shares voted in favor of exercising the option were cast by defendants in their capacity as Agau shareholders. Only about one-third of the "disinterested" shareholders voted, and we cannot assume that such non-voting shareholders either approved or disapproved. Under these circumstances, we cannot say that "the entire atmosphere has been freshened" and that departure from the objective fairness test is permissible. […] In short, defendants have not established factually a basis for applying *Gottlieb.*

Nor do we believe the Legislature intended a contrary policy and rule to prevail by enacting 8 Del.C. § 144, which provides, in part:

> (a) No contract or transaction between a corporation and 1 or more of its directors or officers, or between a corporation and any other corporation, partnership, association, or other organization in which 1 or more of its directors [222] or officers, are directors or officers, or have a financial interest, shall be void or voidable solely for this reason, or solely because the director or officer is present at or participates in the meeting of the board or committee which authorizes the contract or transaction, or solely because his or their votes are counted for such purpose, if: […]

> (2) The material facts as his relationship or interest and as to the contract or transaction are disclosed or are known to the shareholders entitled to vote thereon, and the contract or transaction is specifically approved in good faith by vote of the shareholders […]

Defendants argue that the transaction here in question is protected by § 144(a)(2)[3] which, they contend, does not require that ratifying shareholders be "disinterested" or "independent"; nor, they argue, is there warrant for reading such a requirement into the statute. […] We do not read the statute as providing the broad immunity for which defendants contend. It merely removes an "interested director" cloud when its terms are met and provides against invalidation of an agreement "solely" because such a director or officer is involved. Nothing in the statute sanctions unfairness to Agau or removes the transaction from judicial scrutiny. […]

4.3.4 Stockholder Ratification Doctrine

For anyone with more than a passing familiarity with the law of agency, stockholder ratification doctrine will sound very familiar. As you remember in the Restatement (3rd) of Agency, §8.06 conduct by an agent that would otherwise constitute a breach of a fiduciary duty does not constitute a breach of duty if the principal consents to the conduct, provided that the agent acts in good faith, discloses all material facts that the agent knows, has reason to know, or should know would reasonably affect the principal's judgment, and the agent otherwise deals fairly with the principal. Full and adequate disclosure of an agent's actions followed by knowing and uncoerced assent by the principal in effect cleanses the otherwise disloyal acts of an agent.

In the context of the corporate law, common law courts have adopted a very similar approach to the unauthorized acts of boards, or agents of the corporation. For example, self-dealing by a board will, upon a stockholder challenge, be subject to the stringent entire fairness standard with the board bearing the burden of proving that it dealt fairly with the corporation. However, where the material facts about those acts are fully disclosed to the stockholders and stockholders have an uncoerced opportunity to vote 'yay or nay' on those actions, board actions so approved by the stockholders will be granted the deference of business judgment rather than be subject to entire fairness review.

Although in a successful ratification case, the board is not required prove entire fairness, in order to establish that the ratification is effective, the board is required to bear the burden of proving that it disclosed to stockholders all the material facts related to the challenged transaction available to it at the time.

Once a board has successfully established that stockholder ratification the effect of such ratification is to shift the substantive test on judicial review of the act from one of fairness to one of "corporate waste".

4.3.4.1 Corwin v. KKR Financial Co.

In *Corwin*, the court takes up the question of what is the appropriate standard of review for a challenged merger transaction during a post-closing damages trial, where the directors are disinterested and the transaction has been approved by an informed vote of the stockholders. In such situations, where the stockholders are fully-informed and their vote has not been coerced, courts will be loathe to substitute their own business judgment for that of the stockholders. This result – essentially ratification by the stockholders – is consistent with the court's previous rulings with which you are already familiar.

125 A.3d 304 (2015)
CORWIN v. <u>KKR FINANCIAL HOLDINGS</u>

STRINE, Chief Justice:

In a well-reasoned opinion, the Court of Chancery held that the business judgment rule is invoked as the appropriate standard of review for a post-closing damages action when a merger that is not subject to the entire fairness standard of review has been approved by a fully informed, uncoerced majority of the disinterested stockholders.[1] For that and other reasons, the Court of Chancery dismissed the plaintiffs' complaint.[2] In this decision, we find that the Chancellor was correct in finding that the voluntary judgment of the disinterested stockholders to approve the merger invoked the business judgment rule standard of review and that the plaintiffs' complaint should be dismissed. For sound policy reasons, Delaware corporate law has long been reluctant to second-guess the judgment of a disinterested stockholder majority that determines that a transaction with a party other than a controlling stockholder is in their best interests.

I. The Court Of Chancery Properly Held That The Complaint Did Not Plead Facts Supporting An Inference That KKR Was A Controlling Stockholder of Financial Holdings

The plaintiffs filed a challenge in the Court of Chancery to a stock-for-stock merger between KKR & Co. L.P. ("KKR") and KKR Financial Holdings LLC ("Financial Holdings") in which KKR acquired each share of Financial Holdings's stock for 0.51 of a share of KKR stock, a 35% premium to the unaffected market price. Below, the plaintiffs' primary argument was that the transaction was presumptively subject to the entire fairness standard of review because Financial Holdings's primary business was financing KKR's leveraged buyout activities, and instead of having employees manage the company's day-to-day operations, Financial Holdings was managed by KKR Financial Advisors, an affiliate of KKR, under a contractual management agreement that could only be terminated by Financial Holdings if it paid a termination fee. As a result, the plaintiffs alleged that KKR was a controlling stockholder of Financial Holdings, which was an LLC, not a corporation.[3]

The defendants filed a motion to dismiss, taking issue with that argument. In a thoughtful and thorough decision, the Chancellor found that the defendants were correct that the plaintiffs' complaint did not plead facts supporting an inference that KKR was Financial Holdings's controlling stockholder.[4] Among other things, the Chancellor noted that KKR owned less than 1% of Financial Holdings's stock, had no right to appoint any directors, and had no contractual right to veto any board action.[5] Although the Chancellor acknowledged the unusual existential circumstances the plaintiffs cited, he noted that those were known at all relevant times by investors, and that Financial Holdings had real assets its independent board controlled and had the option of pursuing any [307] path its directors chose.[6]

In addressing whether KKR was a controlling stockholder, the Chancellor was focused on the reality that in cases where a party that did not have majority control of the entity's voting stock was found to be a controlling stockholder, the Court of Chancery, consistent with the instructions of this Court, looked for a combination of potent voting power[7] and management control such that the stockholder could be deemed to have effective control of the board without actually owning a majority of stock.[8] Not finding that combination here, the Chancellor noted:

> Plaintiffs' real grievance, as I see it, is that [Financial Holdings] was
> structured from its inception in a way that limited its value-
> maximizing options. According to plaintiffs, [Financial Holdings]
> serves as little more than a public vehicle for financing KKR-
> sponsored transactions and the terms of the Management
> Agreement make [Financial Holdings] unattractive as an acquisition
> target to anyone other than KKR because of [Financial Holdings]'s
> operational dependence on KKR and because of the significant cost
> that would be incurred to terminate the Management Agreement. I
> assume all that is true. But, every contractual obligation of a
> corporation constrains the corporation's freedom to operate to
> some degree and, in this particular case, the stockholders cannot
> claim to be surprised. Every stockholder of [Financial Holdings]
> knew about the limitations the Management Agreement imposed on
> [Financial Holdings]'s business when he, she or it acquired shares in

[Financial Holdings]. They also knew that the business and affairs of [Financial Holdings] would be managed by a board of directors that would be subject to annual stockholder elections. At bottom, plaintiffs ask the Court to impose fiduciary obligations on a relatively nominal stockholder, not because of any coercive power that stockholder could wield over the board's ability to independently decide whether or not to approve the merger, but because of pre-existing contractual obligations with that stockholder that constrain the business or strategic options available to the corporation. Plaintiffs have cited no legal authority for that novel proposition, and I decline to create such a rule.[9]

After carefully analyzing the pled facts and the relevant precedent, the Chancellor held:

[308] [T]here are no well-pled facts from which it is reasonable to infer that KKR could prevent the [Financial Holdings] board from freely exercising its independent judgment in considering the proposed merger or, put differently, that KKR had the power to exact retribution by removing the [Financial Holdings] directors from their offices if they did not bend to KKR's will in their consideration of the proposed merger.[10]

Although the plaintiffs reiterate their position on appeal, the Chancellor correctly applied the law and we see no reason to repeat his lucid analysis of this question.

II. The Court of Chancery Correctly Held That The Fully Informed, Uncoerced Vote Of The Disinterested Stockholders Invoked The Business Judgment Rule Standard Of Review

On appeal, the plaintiffs further contend that, even if the Chancellor was correct in determining that KKR was not a controlling stockholder, he was wrong to dismiss the complaint because they contend that if the entire fairness standard did not apply, *Revlon*[11] did, and the plaintiffs argue that they pled a *Revlon* claim against the defendant directors. But, as the defendants point out, the plaintiffs did not fairly argue below that

Revlon applied and even if they did, they ignore the reality that Financial Holdings had in place an exculpatory charter provision, and that the transaction was approved by an independent board majority and by a fully informed, uncoerced stockholder vote.[12] Therefore, the defendants argue, the plaintiffs failed to state a non-exculpated claim for breach of fiduciary duty.

But we need not delve into whether the Court of Chancery's determination that *Revlon* did not apply to the merger is correct for a single reason: it does not matter. Because the Chancellor was correct in determining that the entire fairness standard did not apply to the merger, the Chancellor's analysis of the effect of the uncoerced, informed stockholder vote is outcome-determinative, even if *Revlon* applied to the merger.

As to this point, the Court of Chancery noted, and the defendants point out on appeal, that the plaintiffs did not contest the defendants' argument below that if the merger was not subject to the entire fairness standard, the business judgment standard of review was invoked because the merger was approved by a disinterested stockholder majority.[13] The Chancellor [309] agreed with that argument below, and adhered to precedent supporting the proposition that when a transaction not subject to the entire fairness standard is approved by a fully informed, uncoerced vote of the disinterested stockholders, the business judgment rule applies.[14] Although the Chancellor took note of the possible conflict between his ruling and this Court's decision in *Gantler v. Stephens,*[15] he reached the conclusion that *Gantler* did not alter the effect of legally required stockholder votes on the appropriate standard of review.[16] Instead, the Chancellor read *Gantler* as a decision solely intended to clarify the meaning of the precise term "ratification."[17] He had two primary reasons for so finding. First, he noted that any statement about the effect a statutorily required vote had on the appropriate standard of review would have been dictum because in *Gantler* the Court held that the disclosures regarding the vote in question — a vote on an amendment to the company's charter — were materially misleading.[18] Second, the Chancellor doubted that the Supreme Court would have "overrule[d] extensive Delaware precedent, including Justice Jacobs's own earlier decision in *Wheelabrator,* which involved a statutorily required stockholder vote to consummate a merger" without "expressly stat[ing] such an intention."[19]

On appeal, the plaintiffs make *Gantler* a central part of their argument, even though they did not fairly present this point below. They now argue that *Gantler* bound the Court of Chancery to give the informed stockholder vote no effect in determining the standard of review. They contend that the Chancellor's reading of *Gantler* as a decision focused on the precise term "ratification" and not a decision intended to overturn a deep strain of precedent it never bothered to cite, was incorrect.[20] The plaintiffs also argue that they should be relieved of their failure to argue this point fairly below in the interests of justice.[21]

Although we disagree with the plaintiffs that this sort of case provides a sound basis for relieving a sophisticated party of its failure to present its position properly to the trial court, even if we agreed it would not aid the plaintiffs. No doubt *Gantler* can be read in more than one way, but we agree with the Chancellor's interpretation of that decision and do not accept the plaintiffs' contrary one. Had *Gantler* been intended to unsettle a long-standing body of case law, the decision would likely have said so.[22] Moreover, as the Chancellor noted, the issue presented in this case was not even squarely before the Court in *Gantler* because it found the relevant proxy statement to be materially misleading.[23] To erase any doubt on the part of practitioners, we embrace the Chancellor's well-reasoned decision and the precedent it cites to support an interpretation of *Gantler* as a narrow decision focused on defining a specific legal term, "ratification," and not on the question of what standard of review applies if a transaction not subject to the entire fairness standard is approved by an informed, voluntary vote of disinterested stockholders. This view is consistent with well-reasoned Delaware precedent.[24]

Furthermore, although the plaintiffs argue that adhering to the proposition that a fully informed, uncoerced stockholder vote invokes the business judgment rule would impair the operation of *Unocal*[25] and *Revlon,* or expose stockholders to unfair action by directors without protection, the plaintiffs ignore several factors. First, *Unocal* and *Revlon* are primarily designed to give stockholders and the Court of Chancery the tool of injunctive relief to address important M & A decisions in real time, before closing. They were not tools designed with post-closing money damages claims in mind, the standards they articulate do not match the gross negligence standard for director due care liability under *Van Gorkom*,[26] and with the prevalence of exculpatory charter provisions, due care liability is rarely even available.

Second and most important, the doctrine applies only to fully informed, uncoerced stockholder votes, and if troubling facts regarding director behavior were not disclosed that would have been material to a voting stockholder, then the business judgment rule is not invoked.[27] Here, however, all of the objective facts regarding the board's interests, KKR's interests, and the negotiation process, were fully disclosed.

Finally, when a transaction is not subject to the entire fairness standard, the [313] long-standing policy of our law has been to avoid the uncertainties and costs of judicial second-guessing when the disinterested stockholders have had the free and informed chance to decide on the economic merits of a transaction for themselves. There are sound reasons for this policy. When the real parties in interest — the disinterested equity owners — can easily protect themselves at the ballot box by simply voting no, the utility of a litigation-intrusive standard of review promises more costs to stockholders in the form of litigation rents and inhibitions on risk-taking than it promises in terms of benefits to them.[28] The reason for that is tied to the core rationale of the business judgment rule, which is that judges are poorly positioned to evaluate the wisdom of business decisions and there is little utility to having them second-guess the determination [314] of impartial decision-makers with more information (in the case of directors) or an actual economic stake in the outcome (in the case of informed, disinterested stockholders). In circumstances, therefore, where the stockholders have had the voluntary choice to accept or reject a transaction, the business judgment rule standard of review is the presumptively correct one and best facilitates wealth creation through the corporate form.

For these reasons, therefore, we affirm the Court of Chancery's judgment on the basis of its well-reasoned decision.

Footnotes

[19] *In re KKR Fin. Holdings*, 101 A.3d at 1002.

Aside from the substantial authority cited by the Chancellor, there is additional precedent under Delaware law for the proposition that the approval of the disinterested stockholders in a fully informed, uncoerced vote that was required to consummate a transaction has the effect of invoking the business judgment rule. In citing to these authorities, we note that many of them used the term "ratification" in a looser sense than the clarified and narrow description that was given to that term in the scholarly *Gantler* opinion. Although the nomenclature was less precise, the critical reasoning of these opinions was centered on giving standard of review-invoking effect to a fully informed vote of the disinterested stockholders.

In many of the cases, that effect was given to a statutorily required vote or one required by the certificate of incorporation. *See Stroud v. Grace,* 606 A.2d 75, 83 (Del. 1992) ("Inherent in [enhanced scrutiny] is a presumption that a board acted in the absence of an informed shareholder vote ratifying the challenged action."); *Solomon,* 747 A.2d at 1127, 1133, *aff'd,* 746 A.2d 277 (dismissing a challenge to a spin-off of a subsidiary because a fully informed, uncoerced vote of the stockholders that was required under the corporation's charter invoked the business judgment rule); *In re Lukens Inc. S'holders Litig.,* 757 A.2d 720, 736-38 (Del. Ch. 1999), *aff'd sub nom. Walker v. Lukens, Inc.,* 757 A.2d 1278 (Del. 2000) (holding that the fully informed stockholder approval of a merger invoked the business judgment rule); *In re Gen. Motors Class H S'holders Litig.,* 734 A.2d 611, 616 (Del. Ch. 1999) ("Because the shareholders were afforded the opportunity to decide for themselves [whether to approve charter amendments in connection with a series of transactions] on accurate disclosures and in a non-coercive atmosphere, the business judgment rule applies...."); *Weiss v. Rockwell Int'l. Corp.,* 1989 WL 80345, at *3, *7 (Del. Ch. July 19, 1989), *aff'd,* 574 A.2d 264 (Del. 1990) (dismissing a challenge to a charter amendment because it was approved by a fully informed vote of the disinterested stockholders); *Schiff v. RKO Pictures Corp.,* 104 A.2d 267, 271-72 (Del. Ch. 1954) (finding that the principles established in *Gottlieb v. Heyden Chemical Corp.,* 91 A.2d 57, 58 (Del. 1952), which held that voluntary stockholder approval of a stock option plan invoked the business judgment standard of review, were "equally applicable" to statutorily required stockholder approval of an asset sale to the company's chairman and 30% stockholder, requiring the plaintiffs to show "that the disparity between the money received and the value of the assets sold is so great that the court will infer that those passing judgment are guilty of improper motives or are recklessly indifferent to or intentionally disregarding the interest of the whole body of stockholders"); *Cole v. Nat'l*

Cash Credit Ass'n, 156 A. 183, 188 (Del. Ch. 1931) ("The same presumption of fairness that supports the discretionary judgment of the managing directors must also be accorded to the majority of stockholders whenever they are called upon to speak for the corporation in matters assigned to them for decision, as is the case at one stage of the proceedings leading up to a sale of assets or a merger. No rational ground of distinction can be drawn in this respect between the directors on the one hand and the majority of stockholders on the other."); *MacFarlane v. N. Am. Cement Corp.,* 157 A. 396, 398 (Del. Ch. 1928) ("When, therefore, the law provided that a merger might be effected if approved by the votes of stockholders of each corporation representing two-thirds of its total capital stock, it was no doubt believed that the interests of all the stockholders in the merging companies would be sufficiently safeguarded. Such being the case, it is manifest that the court should not, by its injunctive process, prevent a merger so approved unless it is clear that it would be so injurious and unfair to some minority complaining stockholders as to be shocking, and the court is convinced that it is so grossly unfair to such stockholders as to be fraudulent."); *see also In re Morton's,* 74 A.3d at 663 n.34 ("[W]hen disinterested approval of a sale to an arm's-length buyer is given by a majority of stockholders who have had the chance to consider whether or not to approve the transaction for themselves, there is a long line and sensible tradition of giving deference to the stockholders' voluntary decision, invoking the business judgment rule standard of review...."); *In re S. Peru Copper Corp. S'holder Derivative Litig.,* 52 A.3d 761, 793 n.113 (Del. Ch. 2011) ("[I]t has long been my understanding of Delaware law, that the approval of an uncoerced, disinterested electorate of a merger (including a sale) would have the effect of invoking the business judgment rule standard of review."); *Sample v. Morgan,* 914 A.2d 647, 663 (Del. Ch. 2007) (footnote omitted) ("When uncoerced, fully informed, and disinterested stockholders approve a specific corporate action, the doctrine of ratification, in most situations, precludes claims for breach of duty attacking that action."); *In re PNB Holding Co.,* 2006 WL 2403999, at *14 ("[O]utside the [controlling stockholder] context, proof that an informed, non-coerced majority of the disinterested stockholders approved an interested transaction has the effect of invoking business judgment rule protection for the transaction and, as a practical matter, insulating the transaction from revocation and its proponents from liability."); *Apple Comput., Inc. v. Exponential Tech., Inc.,* 1999 WL 39547, at *7 (Del. Ch. Jan. 21, 1999) (noting that if an informed vote of the stockholders approved an asset sale potentially subject to § 271, that would moot any statutory claim and invoke the business judgment rule); William T. Allen et al., *Function Over Form: A Reassessment of Standards of Review in Delaware Corporation Law*, 56 BUS. LAW. 1287, 1317-18 (2001) [hereinafter *Function Over Form*] ("Under present Delaware law, a fully informed majority vote *of the disinterested stockholders* that approves a transaction (other than a merger with a controlling stockholder) has the effect of insulating the directors from all claims except waste.").

In other cases, the vote may not have been statutorily required, but there was no suggestion that that factor was necessary for the vote to be given effect in determining the judicial standard of review. *See Marciano v. Nakash*, 535 A.2d 400, 405 n.3 (Del. 1987) ("[A]pproval by fully-informed disinterested stockholders ... permits invocation of the business judgment rule...."); *Michelson v. Duncan*, 407 A.2d 211, 224 (Del. 1979) ("`Where there has been independent stockholder ratification of interested director action, the objecting stockholder has the burden of showing that no person of ordinary sound business judgment would say that the consideration received for the options was a fair exchange for the options granted.'" (internal citation omitted)).

[24] *See supra* notes 14 & 19. In addition to the cases previously cited for the proposition that an uncoerced, fully informed vote of the disinterested stockholders invokes the business judgment rule standard of review, the tradition of giving burden-shifting effect to a majority-of-the-minority vote in a controlling stockholder going-private merger also supports our view that a statutorily required vote has historically been taken into account in determining the standard of review. In fact, in the case of *Greene v. Dunhill International, Inc.,* the Court of Chancery refused to invoke the business judgment rule because the merger in question involved a controlling stockholder as the buyer, the court cited to a case invoking the business judgment based on a stockholder vote, and indicating that it stood for the proposition that "[i]n the absence of divided interests, the judgment of the majority stockholders ... is presumed made in good faith and inspired by a bona fides of purpose." 249 A.2d 427, 430 (Del. Ch. 1968) (citing *Cole,* 156 A. at 188). The entire strand of our entire controlling stockholder law, running from *Dunhill,* to *Weinberger v. UOP, Inc.,* 457 A.2d 701 (Del. 1983), to *Kahn v. Lynch,* to *Kahn v. M & F Worldwide Corp.,* 88 A.3d 635 (Del. 2014), has focused on what effect of fully informed, uncoerced approval of the disinterested stockholders should have, and has never

focused on whether the vote was statutorily required. Furthermore, although there has been the requirement that the disinterested vote be determinative in giving standard of review influencing effect to a stockholder vote in a controlling stockholder merger, e.g., by having the merger subject to a majority of the minority condition, this Court has never held that the stockholders had to be asked separately to "ratify" the board's actions for that effect to be given. Rather, it has been the ability of an uncoerced group of informed stockholders to freely accept for themselves whether a transaction was good for them that gave rise to the effect on the standard of review applied in any post-closing challenge.

[27] *See Williams v. Geier*, 671 A.2d 1368, 1380-83 (Del. 1996) (noting that "[a]n otherwise valid stockholder vote may be nullified by a showing that the structure or circumstances of the vote were impermissibly coercive"); *In re Rural Metro Corp.*, 88 A.3d 54, 84 n.10 (Del. Ch. 2014) ("Because the Proxy Statement contained materially misleading disclosures and omissions, this case does not provide any opportunity to consider whether a fully informed stockholder vote would lower the standard of review from enhanced scrutiny to the business judgment rule."); *Huizenga*, 751 A.2d at 898-99 ("If the corporate board failed to provide the voters with material information undermining the integrity or financial fairness of the transaction subject to the vote, no ratification effect will be accorded to the vote and the plaintiffs may press all of their claims.... In this regard, it is noteworthy that Delaware law does not make it easy for a board of directors to obtain `ratification effect' from a stockholder vote. The burden to prove that the vote was fair, uncoerced, and fully informed falls squarely on the board.").

[28] *See Williams*, 671 A.2d at 1381 (where a stockholder vote is statutorily required such as for a merger or a charter amendment, "the stockholders control their own destiny through informed voting," and calling this "the highest and best form of corporate democracy"); *In re Morton's*, 74 A.3d at 663 n.34 ("Traditionally, our equitable law of corporations has applied the business judgment standard of review to sales to arms'-length buyers when an informed, uncoerced vote of the disinterested electorate has approved the transaction. This effect on the standard of review is, of course, only available to disinterested stockholder approval for good reason — only disinterested stockholder approval is a strong assurance of fairness." (internal citations omitted)); *In re*

Netsmart Techs. Inc. S'holders Litig., 924 A.2d 171, 207 (Del. Ch. 2007) ("Delaware corporate law strives to give effect to business decisions approved by properly motivated directors and by informed, disinterested stockholders. By this means, our law seeks to balance the interest in promoting fair treatment of stockholders and the utility of avoiding judicial inquiries into the wisdom of business decisions. Thus, doctrines ... operate to keep the judiciary from second-guessing transactions when disinterested stockholders have had a fair opportunity to protect themselves by voting no."); *In re Lear Corp. S'holder Litig.,* 926 A.2d 94, 114-15 (Del. Ch. 2007) ("Delaware corporation law gives great weight to informed decisions made by an uncoerced electorate. When disinterested stockholders make a mature decision about their economic self-interest, judicial second-guessing is almost completely circumscribed by the doctrine of ratification."); *In re PNB Holding Co.,* 2006 WL 2403999, at *15 ("[W]hen most of the affected minority affirmatively approves the transaction, their self-interested decision to approve is sufficient proof of fairness to obviate a judicial examination of that question."); *Huizenga,* 751 A.2d at 901 ("If fully informed, uncoerced, independent stockholders have approved the transaction, they have ... made the decision that the transaction is a fair exchange. As such, it is difficult to see the utility of allowing litigation to proceed in which the plaintiffs are permitted discovery and a possible trial.... In this day and age in which investors also have access to an abundance of information about corporate transactions from sources other than boards of directors, it seems presumptuous and paternalistic to assume that the court knows better in a particular instance than a fully informed corporate electorate with real money riding on the corporation's performance." (internal citations omitted)); *Effect of Stockholder Approval, supra* note 20, at 1457 n.50 ("There is a gut-level sense of fairness to [the result that the business judgment rule is invoked where there is an uncoerced and fully informed vote of the disinterested stockholders to approve the action of a compromised board]. If the fully informed stockholders conclude collectively that they want an outcome, why should self-appointed stockholder plaintiffs be able to seek to hold directors liable for a decision that a majority of the stockholders endorsed? Absent disclosure violations or coercion, there is something contradictory about stockholders collectively saying, `Yes, I want this merger' and then for the stockholder plaintiffs to seek damages from the directors for having approved the deal and recommended it to the stockholders in the first place."); *cf. Function Over Form, supra* note 19, at 1307 ("If ... the vote is uncoerced and is fully informed, there is no reason why the shareholder vote should not be given that effect, particularly given the [Delaware Supreme Court's] rightful emphasis on the importance of the shareholder franchise and its exercise.").

4.3.4.2 Contours of Section 144 and Stockholder Ratification

The common law doctrine of stockholder ratification is a close cousin of Section 144. It is important to remember that the two, though conceptually similar in some respects, are different in effect.

First, consider why 144(a)(1)'s approval by disinterested directors only provides for protection against an attack for voidness and is not a complete defense against a duty of loyalty attack. In the event, a single director (or something less than a majority of directors) is interested, then it is possible for a board to cleanse an interested transaction for purposes of Section 144. At the same time, the fact that a majority of the directors are disinterested (and presumably independent) means that in a derivative suit alleging a violation of the duty of loyalty by the interested director, the plaintiff would likely be unable to plead sufficient facts under *Aronson* to survive a Rule 23.1 motion to dismiss. On the other hand, where a majority of the board is interested, it would be possible for interested directors to comply with the requirements of Section 144 and have the interested director transaction approved by the disinterested minority. Such an approval, though it would protect a transaction from a voidability challenge, would not be sufficient to prevent a plaintiff from successfully pleading demand futility under *Aronson* in challenge alleging that the interested director transaction constituted a violation of the directors' duty of loyalty to the corporation.

Second, consider how the common law doctrine of stockholder ratification interacts with the requirements of Section 144(a)(2). Section 144(a)(2) provides a statutory safe harbor from voidness challenges for interested director transactions when the transaction in question was approved by stockholders of the corporation. The relevant question for our purposes is what is the effect of an informed stockholder vote on the standard of review.

We already know that a 144(a)(2) vote will provide protection against a voidness challenge, but will it - or should it - make an interested director transaction immune from any fiduciary duty challenge by stockholders? The language of the statute presents an obstacle to relying on stockholder votes for more than protection against voidness challenges. In the obvious example, as in *Fliegler*, the majority stockholder is also the interested party. A statutory provision that permitted an ostensibly bad actor to cleanse their own bad acts seems patently unreasonable. Consequently, Section 144(a)(2), like Section 144(a)(1) cannot be relied on to do more than the statute permits.

In *Lewis v Vogelstein*, 699 A.2d 327 (Del. Ch. 1997), then Chancellor Allen outlined the contours of stockholder ratification in the context of director compensation, a transaction where directors are obviously interested parties, as follows:

> What is the effect under Delaware corporation law of shareholder ratification of an interested transaction? ... In order to state my own understanding I first note that by shareholder ratification I do not refer to every instance in which shareholders vote affirmatively with respect to a question placed before them. I exclude from the question those instances in which shareholder votes are a necessary step in authorizing a transaction. Thus the law of ratification as here discussed has no direct bearing on shareholder action to amend a certificate of incorporation or bylaws. *Cf. Williams v. Geier*, Del.Supr., 671 A.2d 1368 (1996); nor does that law bear on shareholder votes necessary to authorize a merger, a sale of substantially all the corporation's assets, or to dissolve the enterprise. For analytical purposes one can set such cases aside. *1. Ratification generally:* I start with principles broader than those of corporation law. Ratification is a concept deriving from the law of agency which contemplates the *ex post* conferring upon or confirming of the legal authority of an agent in circumstances in which the agent had no authority or arguably had no authority. RESTATEMENT (SECOND) OF AGENCY § 82 (1958). To be effective, of course, the agent must fully disclose all relevant circumstances with respect to the transaction to the principal prior to the ratification. *See, e.g., Breen Air Freight Ltd. v. Air Cargo, Inc., et al.,* 470 F.2d 767, 773 (2d Cir.1972); RESTATEMENT (SECOND) OF AGENCY § 91 (1958). Beyond

that, since the relationship between a principal and agent is fiduciary in character, the agent in seeking ratification must act not only with candor, but with loyalty. Thus an attempt to coerce the principal's consent improperly will invalidate the effectiveness of the ratification. RESTATEMENT (SECOND) OF AGENCY § 100 (1958).Assuming that a ratification by an agent is validly obtained, what is its effect? One way of conceptualizing that effect is that it provides, after the fact, the grant of authority that may have been wanting at the time of the agent's act. Another might be to view the ratification as consent or as an estoppel by the principal to deny a lack of authority. *See* RESTATEMENT (SECOND) OF AGENCY § 103 (1958). In either event the effect of informed ratification is to validate or affirm the act of the agent as the act of the principal. *Id.* § 82.Application of these general ratification principles to shareholder ratification is complicated by three other factors. First, most generally, in the case of shareholder ratification there is of course no single individual acting as principal, but rather a class or group of divergent individuals — the class of shareholders. This aggregate quality of the principal means that decisions to affirm or ratify an act will be subject to collective action disabilities; that some portion of the body doing the ratifying may in fact have conflicting interests in the transaction; and some dissenting members of the class may be able to assert more or less convincingly that the "will" of the principal is wrong, or even corrupt and ought not to be binding on the class. In the case of individual ratification these issues won't arise, assuming that the principal does not suffer from multiple personality disorder. Thus the collective nature of shareholder ratification makes it more likely that following a claimed shareholder ratification, nevertheless, there is a litigated claim on behalf of the principal that the agent lacked authority or breached its duty. The second, mildly complicating factor present in shareholder ratification is the fact that in corporation law the "ratification" that shareholders provide will often not be directed to lack of legal authority of an agent but will relate to the consistency of some authorized director action with the equitable duty of loyalty. Thus shareholder ratification sometimes acts not to confer legal authority — but as in this case — to affirm that action taken is consistent with shareholder interests. Third, when what is "ratified" is a director conflict transaction, the statutory law — in Delaware Section 144 of the Delaware General Corporation Law — may bear on the effect.*2. Shareholder ratification:* These differences between shareholder ratification of director action and classic ratification by a single principal, do lead to a difference in the effect of a valid ratification in the shareholder context. The principal novelty added to ratification law generally by the shareholder context, is the idea — no doubt analogously present in other contexts in which common interests are held — that, in addition to a claim that ratification was defective because of incomplete information or coercion, shareholder ratification is subject to a claim by a member of the class that the ratification is ineffectual (1) because a majority of those affirming the transaction had a conflicting interest with respect to it or (2) because the transaction that is ratified constituted a corporate waste. As to the second of these, it has long been held that shareholders may not ratify a waste except by a unanimous vote. *Saxe v. Brady,*Del.Ch., 184 A.2d 602, 605 (1962). The idea behind this rule is apparently that a transaction that satisfies the high standard of waste constitutes a *gift* of corporate property and no one should be forced against their will to make a gift of their property. *In all events, informed, uncoerced, disinterested shareholder ratification of a transaction in which corporate directors have a material conflict of interest has the effect of protecting the transaction from judicial review except on the basis of waste.* (emphasis added)

In *Gantler v. Stephens* (965 A.2d 695)(2009), the Delaware Supreme provided some clarity on the question of shareholder ratification:

Under current Delaware case law, the scope and effect of the common law doctrine of shareholder ratification is unclear, making it difficult to apply that doctrine in a coherent manner. As the Court of Chancery has noted in *In re Wheelabrator Technologies, Inc., Shareholders Litigation:*

[The doctrine of ratification] might be thought to lack coherence because the decisions addressing the effect of shareholder "ratification" have fragmented that subject into three distinct compartments,... In its "classic" ... form, shareholder ratification describes the situation where shareholders approve board action that, legally speaking, could be accomplished without any shareholder approval.... "[C]lassic" ratification involves the voluntary addition of an independent layer of shareholder approval in circumstances where shareholder approval is not legally required. But "shareholder ratification" has also been used to describe the effect of an informed shareholder vote that was statutorily required for the transaction to have legal existence.... That [the Delaware courts] have used the same term is such highly diverse sets of factual circumstances, without regard to their possible functional differences, suggests that "shareholder ratification" has now acquired an expanded meaning intended to describe any approval of challenged board action by a fully informed vote of shareholders, irrespective of whether that shareholder vote is legally required for the transaction to attain legal existence.

To restore coherence and clarity to this area of our law, we hold that the scope of the shareholder ratification doctrine must be limited to its so-called "classic" form; that is, to circumstances where a fully informed shareholder vote approves director action that does *not* legally require shareholder approval in order to become legally effective. Moreover, the only director action or conduct that can be ratified is that which the shareholders are specifically asked to approve. With one exception, the "cleansing" effect of such a ratifying shareholder vote is to subject the challenged director action to business judgment review, as opposed to "extinguishing" the claim altogether (*i.e.*, obviating all judicial review of the challenged action).

Following *Gantler* and *Vogelstein*, it is clear that an *informed, uncoerced, vote of disinterested stockholders ratifying a transaction in which corporate directors have a material conflict of interest has the effect of providing the interested director transaction to protection of the business judgment presumption.* While such a transaction is still subject to possible attack, the directors' interest may not be the basis of a subsequent challenge.

The court in *Corwin* reaffirmed this basic teaching in the context of a post-merger trial for damages. Some commentators and defendants have attempted to extend *Corwin* further. However, the courts have pushed back. In *Massey Energy Company Derivative and Class Action Litigation* (2017), Chancellor Bouchard provided the following comment on the limits of the reach of *Corwin* and stockholder ratification:

> The policy underlying *Corwin,* to my mind, was never intended to serve as a massive eraser, exonerating corporate fiduciaries for any and all of their actions or inactions *preceding* (ed. emphasis added) their decision to undertake a transaction for which stockholder approval is obtained. Here, in voting on the Merger, the Massey stockholders were asked simply whether or not they wished to accept a specified amount of Alpha shares and cash in exchange for their Massey shares or, alternatively, to stay the course as stockholders of Massey as a standalone enterprise, which would have allowed plaintiffs to press derivative claims. Massey's stockholders were *not* asked in any direct or straightforward way to approve releasing defendants from any liability they may have to the Company for the years of alleged mismanagement that preceded the sale process. Indeed, the proxy statement for the Merger implied just the opposite in stating that control over the derivative claims likely would pass to Alpha as a result of the Merger. To top it off, if defendants' view of *Corwin* were correct, it would have the disconcerting and perverse effect of negating the value of the derivative claims that Alpha paid to acquire along with Massey's other assets.In short, in order to invoke the cleansing effect of a stockholder vote under *Corwin,* there logically must be a far more proximate relationship than exists here between the transaction or issue for which stockholder approval is sought and the nature of the claims to be "cleansed" as a result of a fully-informed vote.

Stockholder ratification will be limited strictly to the claims presented to stockholders. Absent a truly fully-informed vote, stockholders will not be deemed to have ratified director action and directors will not be absolved from wrongdoing.

4.3.4.3 In re Investors Bancorp, Inc. Stockholder Litigation

Because directors have a statutory right to set their own compensation (See DGCL §122(15) and §141(h)), director compensation plans are neither void nor voidable. However, the ability of boards to set their own compensation is not without limits. Director compensation is a quintessential "interested director" transaction. In these cases, directors are deciding the amounts and nature of their own compensation and naturally have at least implicit biases in favor of larger amounts. It is no surprise then that director decisions to set their own compensation are subject to entire fairness review upon a stockholder challenge.

In the case that follows, the Delaware Supreme Court addresses whether stockholder ratification in the form of fully-informed, disinterested stockholder approval of a compensation plan for non-employee directors affords the plan the protection of the business judgment presumption rather than the more exacting entire fairness standard. *Investors Bancorp* also provides a useful overview of the doctrinal development of stockholder ratification for non-employee director compensation.

Note that the discussion in *Investors Bancorp* relates to *director* compensation, not compensation of corporate *executives*. Decisions by the board of directors to compensate corporate executives, like the CEO and other C-level executives who are not simultaneously directors of the corporation, are typically treated like arms-length transactions and granted the protection of the business judgment presumption. Absent a successful attack under the waste standard, claims that the board violated their duty of loyalty to the corporation by approving *executive* compensation plans will typically fail.

177 A.3d 1208 (2017)
In Re Investors Bancorp, Inc. Stockholder Litigation

SEITZ, Justice.

In this appeal we consider the limits of the stockholder ratification defense when directors make equity awards to themselves under the general parameters of an equity incentive plan. In the absence of stockholder approval, if a stockholder properly challenges equity incentive plan awards the directors grant to themselves, the directors must prove that the awards are entirely fair to the corporation. But, when the stockholders have approved an equity incentive plan, the affirmative defense of stockholder ratification comes into play. Stated generally, stockholder ratification means a majority of fully informed, uncoerced, and disinterested stockholders approved board action, which, if challenged, typically leads to a deferential business judgment standard of review.

For equity incentive plans in which the award terms are fixed and the directors have no discretion how they allocate the awards, the stockholders know exactly what they are being asked to approve. But, other plans—like the equity incentive plan in this appeal— create a pool of equity awards that the directors can later award to themselves in amounts and on terms they decide. The Court of Chancery has recognized a ratification defense for such discretionary plans as long as the plan has "meaningful limits" on the awards directors can make to themselves.[1] If the discretionary plan does not contain meaningful limits, the awards, if challenged, are subject to an entire fairness standard of review.

Stockholder ratification serves an important purpose—directors can take self-interested action secure in the knowledge that the stockholders have expressed their approval. But, when directors make discretionary awards to themselves, that discretion must be exercised consistent with their fiduciary duties. Human nature being what it is,[2] self-interested discretionary acts by directors should in an appropriate case be subject to review by the Court of Chancery.

We balance the competing concerns—utility of the ratification defense and the need for judicial scrutiny of certain self-interested discretionary acts by directors—by focusing on the specificity of the acts submitted to the stockholders for approval. When the directors submit their specific compensation decisions for approval by fully informed, uncoerced, and disinterested stockholders, ratification is properly asserted as a defense in support of a motion to dismiss. The same applies for self-executing plans, meaning plans that make awards over time based on fixed criteria, with the specific amounts and terms approved by the stockholders. But, when stockholders have approved an equity incentive plan that gives the directors discretion to grant themselves awards within general parameters, and a stockholder properly alleges that the directors inequitably exercised that discretion, then the ratification defense is unavailable to dismiss the suit, and the directors will be required to prove the fairness of the awards to the corporation.

Here, the Equity Incentive Plan ("EIP") approved by the stockholders left it to the discretion of the directors to allocate up to 30% of all option or restricted stock shares available as awards to themselves. The plaintiffs have alleged facts leading to a pleading stage reasonable inference that the directors breached their fiduciary duties by awarding excessive equity awards to themselves under the EIP. Thus, a stockholder ratification defense is not available to dismiss the case, and the directors must demonstrate the fairness of the awards to the Company. We therefore reverse the Court of Chancery's decision dismissing the complaint and remand for further proceedings consistent with this opinion.

I.

According to the allegations of the complaint, which we must accept as true at this stage of the proceedings,[3] the plaintiffs are stockholders of Investors Bancorp, Inc. ("Investors Bancorp" or the "Company") and were stockholders at the time of the awards challenged in this case. The defendants fall into two groups—ten non-employee director defendants[4] and two executive director defendants.[5]Investors Bancorp, the nominal defendant, is a Delaware corporation with its principal place of business in Short Hills, New Jersey. Investors Bancorp is a holding company for Investors Bank, a New Jersey chartered savings bank with corporate headquarters in Short Hills, New Jersey. The Company operates 143 banking branches in New Jersey and New York. In 2014, after a mutual-to-stock conversion,[6] Investors Bancorp conducted a second-step offering to the public, which is when the plaintiffs acquired their shares. In this second-step offering, the Company sold 219,580,695 shares and raised about $2.15 billion.

The board sets director compensation based on recommendations of the Compensation and Benefits Committee ("Committee"), composed of seven of the ten non-employee directors. In 2014, the non-employee directors were compensated by (i) a monthly cash retainer; (ii) cash awards for attending board and board committee meetings; and (iii) perquisites and personal benefits. The chairman of each committee received an additional annual retainer. As the Court of Chancery noted, the annual compensation for all non-employee directors ranged from $97,200 to $207,005, with $133,340 as the average amount of compensation per director.

In 2014, Cummings, the Company's President and CEO, received (i) a $1,000,000 base salary; (ii) an Annual Cash Incentive Award of up to 150% of his base salary contingent on certain performance goals; and (iii) perquisites and benefits valued at $278,400, which totaled $2,778,700. Cama, the Company's COO and Senior Executive Vice President, received annual compensation consisting of (i) a $675,000 base salary; (ii) an Annual Cash Incentive Award of up to 120% of his base salary; and (iii) perquisites and benefits valued at $180,794, which totaled $1,665,794.[7]

At the end of 2014, following completion of the conversion plan, the Committee met to review 2014 director compensation and set compensation for 2015. Gregory Keshishian, a compensation consultant from GK Partners, Inc., presented to the board a study of director compensation for eighteen publicly held peer companies. According to the study, these companies paid their non-employee directors an average of $157,350 in total compensation. The Company's $133,340 average non-employee director compensation in 2014 fell close to the study average. Following the presentation, the Committee recommended to the board that the non-employee director compensation package remain the same for 2015. The only change was to increase the fees paid for attending committee meetings from $1,500 to $2,500.

The Committee also reviewed the compensation package for executive officers. After GK Partners reviewed peer-average figures with the committee, the committee unanimously recommended no changes to Cummings' or Cama's annual salary, but recommended an increase in the 2015 Annual Cash Incentive Award from 150% to 200%, and 120% to 160% of their base salaries, respectively.[8] The Committee did not discuss any additional equity awards at the December or February meetings.

1214*1214 Just a few months after setting the 2015 board compensation, in March, 2015, the board proposed the 2015 EIP. The EIP was intended to "provide additional incentives for [the Company's] officers, employees and directors to promote [the Company's] growth and performance and to further align their interests with those of [the Company's] stockholders . . . and give [the Company] the flexibility [needed] to continue to attract, motivate and retain highly qualified officers, employees and directors."[9]

The Company reserved 30,881,296 common shares for restricted stock awards, restricted stock units, incentive stock options, and non-qualified stock options for the Company's 1,800 officers, employees, non-employee directors, and service providers. The EIP has limits within each category. Of the total shares, a maximum of 17,646,455 can be issued for stock options or restricted stock awards and 13,234,841 for restricted stock units or performance shares. Those limits are further broken down for employee and non-employee directors:

- A maximum of 4,411,613 shares, in the aggregate (25% of the shares available for stock option awards), may be issued or delivered to any one employee pursuant to the exercise of stock options;

- A maximum of 3,308,710 shares, in the aggregate (25% of the shares available for restricted stock awards and restricted stock units), may be issued or delivered to any one employee as a restricted stock or restricted stock unit grant; and

- The maximum number of shares that may be issued or delivered to all non-employee directors, in the aggregate, pursuant to the exercise of stock options or grants of restricted stock or restricted stock units shall be 30% of all option or restricted stock shares available for awards, "all of which may be granted in any calendar year."[10]

According to the proxy sent to stockholders, "[t]he number, types and terms of awards to be made pursuant to the [EIP] are subject to the discretion of the Committee and have not been determined at this time, and will not be determined until subsequent to stockholder approval."[11] At the Company's June 9, 2015 annual meeting, 96.25% of the voting shares approved the EIP (79.1% of the total shares out-standing).[12]

Three days after stockholders approved the EIP, the Committee held the first of four meetings and eventually approved awards of restricted stock and stock options to all board members. According to the complaint, these awards were not part of the final 2015 compensation package nor discussed in any prior meetings.[13] The first meeting took place on June 12, 2015. The Committee met with Cummings, Cama, Keshishian (the compensation consultant), and representatives from Luse Gorman 1215*1215 (outside counsel) "to begin the process of determining the allocation of shares."[14]

At the second meeting on June 16, 2015, the Committee met with Keshishian, the Luse Gorman representatives, and the full board except Siekerka and Ward, to "gather input" from outside experts and Committee members.[15] They considered a list of the stock options and awards granted by the 164 companies that underwent mutual-to-stock conversions in the last twenty years.[16] Luse Gorman presented an analysis of these companies, selected "based on the size of the company and the size of the equity sold in the second step offering, and the size of the equity plan."[17] The complaint alleges that the first two are arbitrary and the third is "a textbook example of results driven by self-selection bias."[18] The plaintiffs also claim that Luse Gorman did not compare five other companies on the list that met the criteria and had more recently undergone conversions—each of which granted significantly lower awards.[19]

At the third meeting on June 19, 2015, the Committee met with Cummings, Cama, Keshishian, and the representatives from Luse Gorman "to have a thorough discussion of all the major decisions" regarding the allocation of shares.[20] They analyzed the circumstances surrounding the peer companies' awards and discussed the EIP, noting the stockholders' authorization of director awards of up to 30% of the EIP's restricted stock options.[21] Cama proposed and the attendees approved the specific awards—including those to Cama and Cummings.[22]According to the plaintiffs, however, the 2016 Proxy disclosed that Cummings and Cama did not attend meetings when their "compensation is being determined."[23]The Committee held a fourth and final meeting on June 23, 2015 when the entire board, after hearing from Keshishian and the Luse Gorman representatives, "approve[d] all the components of the incentive stock and option grants for Directors and Management."[24]

The board awarded themselves 7.8 million shares.[25] Non-employee directors each received 250,000 stock options—valued at $780,000—and 100,000 restricted shares—valued at $1,254,000; Cashill and Dittenhafer received 150,000 restricted shares—valued at $1,881,000—due to their years of service. The non-employee director awards totaled $21,594,000 and averaged $2,159,400. Peer companies' non-employee awards averaged $175,817. Cummings received 1,333,333 stock options and 1,000,000 restricted shares, valued at $16,699,999 and alleged to be 1,759% higher than the peer companies' average compensation for executive directors. Cama received 1,066,666 stock options and 600,000 restricted shares, valued at $13,359,998 and alleged 1216*1216 to be 2,571% higher than the peer companies' average. […]

After the Company disclosed the awards, stockholders filed three separate complaints in the Court of Chancery alleging breaches of fiduciary duty by the directors for awarding themselves excessive compensation. Following the filing of a consolidated complaint, the defendants moved to dismiss under Court of Chancery Rule 12(b)(6) for failure to state a claim and under Court of Chancery Rule 23.1 for failure to make a demand before filing suit.

The Court of Chancery granted both motions and dismissed the plaintiffs' complaint.[27] Relying on the court's earlier decisions in In re 3COM Corp.[28] and Calma on Behalf of Citrix Systems, Inc. v. Templeton,[29] the court dismissed the complaint against the non-employee directors because the EIP contained "meaningful, specific limits on awards to all director beneficiaries" like the 3COMplan, as opposed to the broad-based plan in Citrix that contained a generic limit covering director and non-director beneficiaries.[30] The court also dismissed the claims directed to the executive directors because the plaintiffs failed to make a pre-suit demand on the board.

We review the Court of Chancery decision dismissing the complaint de novo.[31]

II.

Unless restricted by the certificate of incorporation or bylaws, Section 141(h) of Delaware General Corporation Law ("DGCL") authorizes the board "to fix the compensation of directors."[32] Although authorized to do so by statute, when the board fixes its compensation, it is self-interested in the decision because the directors are deciding how much they should reward themselves for board service.[33] If no other factors are involved, the board's decision will "lie outside the business judgment rule's presumptive protection, so that, where properly challenged, the receipt of self-determined benefits is subject to an affirmative showing that the compensation arrangements are fair to the corporation."[34] In other words, the entire fairness standard of review will apply.[35]

Other factors do sometimes come into play. When a fully informed, uncoerced, and disinterested majority of stockholders approve the board's authorized corporate action, the stockholders are said to have ratified the corporate act. Stockholder ratification of corporate acts applies in different corporate law settings.[36] Here, we address the affirmative defense of stockholder ratification of director self-compensation decisions.

A.

Early Supreme Court cases recognized a ratification defense by directors when reviewing their self-compensation decisions. In the 1952 decision Kerbs v. California Eastern Airways, Inc., a stockholder filed suit against the directors attacking a stock option and profit sharing plan on a number of grounds.[37] As to the stock option plan, 250,000 shares of the corporation's unissued stock were granted in specific amounts to named executives of the corporation at a $1 per share exercise price.[38] The profit sharing plan was based on a mathematical formula tied to the financial performance of the corporation.[39] Both plans were approved at a board meeting where five of the eight directors were beneficiaries of both plans.[40] The stockholders approved the plans.

Addressing the effect of stockholder approval of the stock option plan, our Court held that "ratification cures any voidable defect in the action of the [b]oard. Stockholder ratification of voidable acts of directors 1218*1218 is effective for all purposes unless the action of the directors constituted a gift of corporate assets to themselves or was ultra vires, illegal, or fraudulent."[41] As to the profit sharing plan, the Court viewed things differently because "the effectiveness of such ratification depends upon the type of notice sent to the stockholder and the explanation to them of the plan itself,"[42] and the record on appeal was insufficient to determine the adequacy of the disclosures.[43]

The stock option plan approved by the stockholders in Kerbs was self-executing, meaning once approved by the stockholders, implementing the awards required no discretion by the directors.[44] The Court addressed a similar dispute in a case decided the following day. In Gottlieb v. Heyden Chemical Corp.,[45] the restricted stock option plan granted specific company officers—six of whom were board members—present and future options to purchase fixed amounts of common stock at prices to be set by the board, subject to a price collar. The plan was contingent upon ratification by a majority of the stockholders.[46] In advance of the stockholder meeting, the board disclosed the names of the officers receiving the awards, the number of shares allocated to each, the price per share, and the schedule for future issuances.[47] The stockholders approved the plan.[48]

After initially denying the stockholder's challenge to the plan, on reargument, the Court noted the effect of stockholder ratification. For the current awards specifically approved by the stockholders:

> Where there is stockholder ratification,. . . the burden of proof is shifted to the objector. In such a case the objecting stockholder must convince the court that no person of ordinary sound business judgment would be expected to entertain the view that the consideration furnished by the individual directors is a fair exchange for the options conferred.[49]

But, for the options subject to future awards, the court explained that they were not ratified because the 25,500 shares had not been placed into any contracts prior to approval.[50] The stockholders only approved the allocation of shares "of a certain general pattern," but "nobody [knew] what all of the terms of these future contracts [would] be."[51] The Court concluded that ratification "cannot be taken to have approved specific bargains not yet proposed."[52] 1219*1219 Thus,
after Kerbs and Gottlieb, directors could successfully assert the ratification defense when the stockholders were fully informed and approved stock option plans containing specific director awards. But the award of "specific bargains not yet proposed" could not be ratified by general stockholder approval of the compensation plan.[53]

Our Court has not considered ratification of director self-compensation decisions since Kerbs and Gottlieb. The Court of Chancery has, however, continued to develop this area of the law.

B.

Following the Supreme Court's lead recognizing the ratification defense only when specific acts are presented to the stockholders for approval, the Court of Chancery in Steiner v. Meyerson[54] and Lewis v. Vogelstein[55] recognized the directors' ratification defense when awards made to directors under equity compensation plans were specific as to amounts and value. In Steiner, the stock option plan granted each non-employee director "an option to purchase 25,000 shares upon election to the Telxon board, and an additional 10,000 shares on the anniversary of his election while he remains on the board."[56] In Lewis, the plan provided for two categories of director compensation: (i) one-time grants of 15,000 options per director; and (ii) annual grants of up to 10,000 options per director depending on length of board service.[57] The plans were self-executing, meaning that no further director action was required to implement the awards as they were earned. In both cases, the Court of Chancery held that the stockholders validly ratified the awards, and the standard of review following ratification was waste.[58]

Two Court of Chancery decisions following Steiner and Lewis addressed a twist in previous cases that bears directly on this appeal—the plans approved by the stockholders set upper limits on the amounts to be awarded, but allowed the directors to decide the specific awards or change the conditions of the awards after stockholder approval.[59] In In re 3COM Corp. Shareholders Litigation, the option grants were 1220*1220 based on "specific ceilings on the awarding of options each year" which "differ based on specific categories of service, such as service on a committee, position as a lead director, and chairing the [b]oard."[60] The plaintiff alleged in conclusory fashion that grants made by the board were "lavish and excessive compensation tantamount to a waste of corporate assets."[61] Because the board exercised its discretion within the specific limits approved by the stockholders, the Court of Chancery determined that the stockholder approval of the plan parameters extended to the specific awards made after plan approval.[62] Thus, the directors' post-approval compensation decisions were subject to the business judgment rule standard of review, requiring the directors to show waste.[63]

In Criden v. Steinberg, the Court of Chancery addressed a broad-based stock option plan that allowed the directors to re-price the options after stockholder approval of the plan.[64] The re-pricing decisions, although not submitted to the stockholders for approval, were subject to a business judgment standard of review.[65] According to the court, the stockholders approved a plan setting the re-pricing parameters, and the directors re-priced the options within those parameters.[66]Thus, the directors' decisions were reviewed under a business judgment rule standard of review.

After 3COM and Criden, the Court of Chancery decided Sample v. Morgan.[67] In Sample, the Court addressed two non-employee directors on the compensation committee who awarded 200,000 shares to the company's three employee directors under a management stock incentive plan.[68] A disinterested majority of Randall Bearings' stockholders had previously approved the plan, which authorized up to 200,000 shares, with no parameters on how the shares should be awarded. The court rejected a ratification defense and stated:

> [T]he Delaware doctrine of ratification does not embrace a "blank check" theory. When uncoerced, fully informed, and disinterested stockholders approve a specific corporate action, the doctrine of ratification, in most situations, precludes claims for breach of fiduciary duty attacking that action. But the mere approval by stockholders of a request by directors for the authority to take action within broad parameters does not insulate all future action by the directors within those parameters from attack. Although the fact of stockholder approval might have some bearing on consideration of a fiduciary duty claim in that context, it does not, by itself, preclude such a claim. An essential aspect of our form of corporate law is the balance between law (in the form of statute and contract, including the contracts governing the internal affairs of corporations, such as charters and bylaws) and equity (in the form of concepts of fiduciary duty). Stockholders can entrust directors with broad legal authority precisely because they know that authority 1221*1221 must be exercised consistently with equitable principles of fiduciary duty. Therefore, the entrustment to the [compensation committee] of the authority to issue up to 200,000 shares to key employees under discretionary terms and conditions cannot reasonably be interpreted as a license for the [c]ommittee and other directors making proposals to it to do whatever they

wished, unconstrained by equity. Rather, it is best understood as a
decision by the stockholders to give the directors broad legal
authority and to rely upon the policing of equity to ensure that
authority would be utilized properly. For this reason alone, the
directors' ratification argument fails.[69]

The court in Sample did not address either 3COM or Criden. But, in Seinfeld v.
Slager,[70] the court addressed 3COM and a concern that recognizing ratification for
plans approved by stockholders with only general parameters for making compensation
awards provided insufficient protection from possible self-dealing. The plan
in Seinfeld was a broad-based plan applying to directors, officers, and
employees.[71] Unlike the plan in 3COM, where each category of beneficiaries had an
upper limit on what they could receive, the Seinfeld plan contained a single generic limit
on awards, with no restrictions on how the awards could be distributed to the different
classes of beneficiaries.[72] Rather than essentially approve a blank check, or in the Vice
Chancellor's words—give the directors carte blanche—to make awards as the directors
saw fit, the court required "some meaningful limit imposed by the stockholders on the
[b]oard for the plan to be consecrated by 3COM and receive the blessing of the business
judgment rule."[73]Thus, after Seinfeld, directors could retain the discretion to make
awards after stockholder plan approval, but the plan had to contain meaningful limits on
the awards the directors could make to themselves before ratification could be
successfully asserted.

Finally, in Cambridge Retirement System v. Bosnjak, although the plan did not set forth
the specific compensation awarded to the directors, the specific awards were submitted
to the stockholders for approval.[74] Thus, the court found that the directors could assert
a ratification defense.[75] And, in Calma on Behalf of Citrix Systems, Inc. v.
Templeton, Chancellor Bouchard, after a thorough review of the case law, determined
that directors could not assert a ratification defense when the incentive plan had generic
limits on compensation for all the plan beneficiaries.[76]The court denied a ratification
defense, holding "when the [b]oard sought stockholder approval of the broad
parameters of the plan and the generic limits specified therein, Citrix stockholders were
not asked to approve any action specific to 1222*1222 director compensation."[77]

III.

A.

As ratification has evolved for stockholder-approved equity incentive plans, the courts have recognized the defense in three situations—when stockholders approved the specific director awards; when the plan was self-executing, meaning the directors had no discretion when making the awards; or when directors exercised discretion and determined the amounts and terms of the awards after stockholder approval. The first two scenarios present no real problems. When stockholders know precisely what they are approving, ratification will generally apply. The rub comes, however, in the third scenario, when directors retain discretion to make awards under the general parameters of equity incentive plans. The defendants rely on 3COM and Criden, where the Court of Chancery recognized a stockholder ratification defense even though the directors' self-compensation awards were not submitted for stockholder approval.[78] As noted earlier, in 3COM, the Court of Chancery recognized ratification for director-specific compensation plans, where the plans contained specific limits for awards depending on factors set forth in the plan.[79] In Criden, the court upheld a ratification defense when the plan authorized the directors to re-price the options after stockholder approval.[80]

The court's decisions in 3COM and Criden opened the door to the difficulties raised in this appeal. After those decisions, the Court of Chancery had to square 3COM and Criden—and their expanded use of ratification for discretionary plans— with existing precedent, which only recognized ratification when stockholders approved the specific awards. The Court of Chancery tried to harmonize the decisions by requiring "meaningful limits" on the amounts directors could award to themselves.

We think, however, when it comes to the discretion directors exercise following stockholder approval of an equity incentive plan, ratification cannot be used to foreclose the Court of Chancery from reviewing those further discretionary actions when a breach of fiduciary duty claim has been properly alleged. As the Court of Chancery emphasized in Sample, using an expression coined many years ago, director action is "twice-tested," first for legal authorization, and second by equity.[81] When stockholders approve the general parameters of an equity compensation plan and 1223*1223 allow directors to exercise their "broad legal authority" under the plan, they do so "precisely because they know that authority must be exercised consistently with equitable principles of fiduciary

396

duty."[82] The stockholders have granted the directors the legal authority to make awards. But, the directors' exercise of that authority must be done consistent with their fiduciary duties. Given that the actual awards are self-interested decisions not approved by the stockholders, if the directors acted inequitably when making the awards, their "inequitable action does not become permissible simply because it is legally possible"[83] under the general authority granted by the stockholders.

The Sample case underlines the need for continued equitable review of self-interested discretionary director self-compensation decisions. As noted before, the plaintiffs in Sample alleged that the board adopted "a self-dealing plan to entrench the Company under the then-current management and massively dilute the equity interests of the public holders to benefit management personally."[84] If ratification could be invoked at the outset, those breach of fiduciary duty allegations would be insulated from judicial review. Other cases reinforce the same point—when a stockholder properly alleges that the directors breached their fiduciary duties when exercising their discretion after stockholders approve the general parameters of an equity incentive plan, the directors should have to demonstrate that their self-interested actions were entirely fair to the company.[85]

B.

The Investors Bancorp EIP is a discretionary plan as described above. It covers about 1,800 officers, employees, non-employee directors, and service providers. Specific to the directors, the plan reserves 30,881,296 shares of common stock for restricted stock awards, restricted stock units, incentive stock options, and non-qualified stock options for the Company's officers, employees, non-employee directors, and service providers.[86] Of those reserved shares and other equity, the non-employee directors were entitled to up to 30% of all option and restricted stock shares, all of which could be granted in 1224*1224 any calendar year.[87] But, "[t]he number, types, and terms of the awards to be made pursuant to the [EIP] are subject to the discretion of the Committee and have not been determined at this time, and will not be determined until subsequent to stockholder approval."[88]

When submitted to the stockholders for approval, the stockholders were told that "[b]y approving the Plan, stockholders will give [the Company] the flexibility [it] need[s] to continue to attract, motivate and retain highly qualified officers, employees and directors by offering a competitive compensation program that is linked to the performance of [the Company's] common stock."[89] The complaint alleges that this representation was reasonably interpreted as forward-looking. In other words, by approving the EIP, stockholders understood that the directors would reward Company employees for future performance, not past services.

After stockholders approved the EIP, the board eventually approved just under half of the stock options available to the directors and nearly thirty percent of the shares available to the directors as restricted stock awards, based predominately on a five-year going forward vesting period. The plaintiffs argue that the directors breached their fiduciary duties by granting themselves these awards because they were unfair and excessive.[90] According to the plaintiffs, the stockholders were told the EIP would reward future performance, but the Board instead used the EIP awards to reward past efforts for the mutual-to-stock conversion—which the directors had already accounted for in determining their 2015 compensation packages.[91] Also, according to the plaintiffs, the rewards were inordinately higher than peer companies'. As alleged in the complaint, the Board paid each non-employee director more than $2,100,000 in 2015,[92] which "eclips[ed] director pay at every Wall Street firm."[93] This significantly exceeded the Company's non-employee director compensation in 2014, which ranged from $97,200 to $207,005.[94] It also far surpassed the $198,000 median pay at similarly sized companies and the $260,000 median pay at much larger companies.[95] And the awards were over twenty-three times more than the $87,556 median award granted to other companies' non-employee directors after mutual-to-stock conversions.[96]

In addition, according to the complaint, Cama and Cummings' compensation far exceeded their prior compensation and that of peer companies. Cummings' $20,006,957 total compensation in 2015 was 1225*1225 seven times more than his 2014 compensation package of $2,778,000.[97] And Cama's $15,318,257 compensation was nine times more than his 2014 compensation package of $1,665,794.[98] Cummings' $16,699,999 award was 3,683% higher than the median award other companies granted their CEOs after mutual-to-stock conversions. And Cama's $13,359,998 award was

5,384% higher than the median other companies granted their second-highest paid executives after the conversions.[99]

The plaintiffs have alleged facts leading to a pleading stage reasonable inference that the directors breached their fiduciary duties in making unfair and excessive discretionary awards to themselves after stockholder approval of the EIP. Because the stockholders did not ratify the specific awards the directors made under the EIP, the directors must demonstrate the fairness of the awards to the Company.

IV.

The parties raise a last issue—whether the plaintiffs are excused from making a demand on the board under Court of Chancery Rule 23.1 for the awards made to executive directors Cama and Cummings. The directors do not contest that they are interested for the awards they made to themselves. But, according to the directors, the awards made to the two executive directors were not part of a "single transaction" because these awards were made as part of a series of compensation meetings following the EIP's adoption. Further, they argue, the plaintiffs failed to demonstrate a "quid pro quo" between the non-employee directors and Cama and Cummings. Thus, the non-employee directors claim they would be capable of exercising independent judgment to consider a demand challenging the board's awards to the executive directors.

Demand is futile when, under the particular facts alleged, a reasonable doubt is created that (1) a majority of the board is disinterested and independent, or (2) the challenged transaction was otherwise the product of a valid exercise of business judgment.[100] Although showing a quid pro quo might be one way of proving interestedness or lack of independence, it is not a requirement. Rather, the focus is on the acts being challenged and the relationship between those acts and the directors who approved them. Here, immediately after the Investors Bancorp stockholders approved the EIP, the directors 1226*1226 held a series of nearly contemporaneous meetings that resulted in awards to both the non-employee directors and the executive directors. It is implausible to us that the non-employee directors could independently consider a demand when to do so would require those directors to call into question the grants they made to themselves. In other words, "[i]t strains reason to argue that a defendant-director could act independently to evaluate the merits of bringing a legal action against any of the other defendants if the director participated in the identical challenged misconduct."[101] Thus, demand is excused for the claims made against non-employee and executive directors.

V.

The Investors Bancorp stockholders approved the general parameters of the EIP. The plaintiffs have properly alleged, however, that the directors, when exercising their discretion under the EIP, acted inequitably in granting themselves unfair and excessive awards. Because the stockholders did not ratify the specific awards under the EIP, the affirmative defense of ratification cannot not be used to dismiss the complaint. The plaintiffs have also demonstrated that demand would be futile as to all directors. Thus, the Court of Chancery's decision is reversed, and the case is remanded for further proceedings consistent with this opinion. [...]

4.3.5 Corporate Opportunity Doctrine

Remember that directors have an obligation to act in the best interests of the corporation. However, that charge can sometimes be difficult for even well-meaning directors to operationalize. For example, directors are often experienced business-people with their own relationships and their own business ventures. A common challenge facing directors comes in the form of business opportunities that come to them while they are directors. Which of the opportunities that come to directors properly belong to the corporation and which of them properly belongs to the director can be a vexing question.

If the director gets the answer to that question wrong, she may well find herself on the wrong end of a lawsuit alleging violations of the duty of loyalty for wrongfully benefitting from an opportunity that properly belonged to the corporation. On the other hand, the director may also mistakenly forego personal business opportunities for fear that her duty to the corporation prohibited her from pursuing them.

The corporate opportunity doctrine provides directors an affirmative defense to claims against them for taking a corporate opportunity. If a director can establish that the opportunity offered her was not properly an opportunity for the corporation, then the court will deem the director to have dealt fairly with the corporation.

4.3.5.1 Broz v. Cellular Information Systems, Inc.

673 A.2d 148 (1996)
BROZ v.CELLULAR INFORMATION SYSTEMS, INC.

VEASEY, Chief Justice:

The Court of Chancery decided that the defendant, a corporate director, breached his fiduciary duty by not formally presenting to the corporation an opportunity which had come to the director individually and independent of the director's relationship with the corporation. […]

We conclude that, although a corporate director may be shielded from liability by offering to the corporation an opportunity which has come to the director independently and individually, the failure of the director to present the opportunity does not necessarily result in the improper usurpation of a corporate opportunity. […]

Broz has been the President and sole stockholder of RFBC since 1992. RFBC owns and operates an FCC license area, known as the Michigan-4 Rural Service Area Cellular License ("Michigan-4"). The license entitles RFBC to provide cellular telephone service to a portion of rural Michigan. Although Broz' efforts have been devoted primarily to the business operations of RFBC, he also served as an outside director of CIS at the time of the events at issue in this case. CIS was at all times fully aware of Broz' relationship with RFBC and the obligations incumbent upon him by virtue of that relationship.

In April of 1994, Mackinac Cellular Corp. ("Mackinac") sought to divest itself of Michigan-2, the license area immediately adjacent to Michigan-4. To this end, Mackinac contacted Daniels & Associates ("Daniels") and arranged for the brokerage firm to seek potential purchasers for Michigan-2. In compiling a list of prospects, Daniels included

RFBC as a likely candidate. In May of 1994,[…]Daniels, contacted Broz and broached the subject of RFBC's possible acquisition of Michigan-2. […]

Michigan-2 was not, however, offered to CIS. Apparently, Daniels did not consider CIS to be a viable purchaser for Michigan-2 in light of CIS' recent financial difficulties. [152] The record shows that, at the time Michigan-2 was offered to Broz, CIS had recently emerged from lengthy and contentious Chapter 11 proceedings. Pursuant to the Chapter 11 Plan of Reorganization, CIS entered into a loan agreement that substantially impaired the company's ability to undertake new acquisitions or to incur new debt. […]

During the period from early 1992 until the time of CIS' emergence from bankruptcy in 1994, CIS divested itself of some fifteen separate cellular license systems.[2] CIS contracted to sell four additional license areas on May 27, 1994,[3] leaving CIS with only five remaining license areas, all of which were outside of the Midwest.

On June 13, 1994, following a meeting of the CIS board, Broz spoke with CIS' Chief Executive Officer, Richard Treibick ("Treibick"), concerning his interest in acquiring Michigan-2. Treibick communicated to Broz that CIS was not interested in Michigan-2.[4] Treibick further stated that he had been made aware of the Michigan-2 opportunity prior to the conversation with Broz, and that any offer to acquire Michigan-2 was rejected[…] Broz contacted another CIS director, Peter Schiff ("Schiff"), to discuss the possible acquisition of Michigan-2 by RFBC. Schiff, like Treibick, indicated that CIS had neither the wherewithal nor the inclination to purchase Michigan-2. In late September of 1994, Broz also contacted Stanley Bloch ("Bloch"), a director and counsel for CIS, to request that Bloch represent RFBC in its dealings with Mackinac. Bloch agreed to represent RFBC, and, like Schiff and Treibick, expressed his belief that CIS was not at all interested in the transaction. Ultimately, all the CIS directors testified at trial that, had Broz inquired at that time, they each would have expressed the opinion that CIS was not interested in Michigan-2[…]

On August 2, 1994, PriCellular commenced a tender offer for all outstanding shares of CIS at $2.00 per share. […]

On August 6, September 6 and September 21, 1994, Broz submitted written offers to Mackinac for the purchase of Michigan-2. During this time period, PriCellular also began negotiations with Mackinac to arrange an option for the purchase of Michigan-2.

PriCellular's interest in Michigan-2 was fully disclosed to CIS' chief executive, Treibick, who did not express any interest in Michigan-2, and was actually incredulous that PriCellular would want to acquire the license. Nevertheless, CIS was fully aware that PriCellular and Broz were bidding for Michigan-2 and did not interpose CIS in this bidding war.

On November 14, 1994, Broz agreed to pay Mackinac $7.2 million for the Michigan-2 license. […]

Nine days later, on November 23, 1994, PriCellular completed its financing and closed its tender offer for CIS. Prior to that point, PriCellular owned no equity interest in CIS. Subsequent to the consummation of the PriCellular tender offer for CIS, members of the CIS board of directors, including Broz, were discharged and replaced with a slate of PriCellular nominees. On March 2, 1995, this action was commenced by CIS in the Court of Chancery.

At trial in the Court of Chancery, […] CIS asserted that Broz breached his fiduciary duty to CIS and its stockholders. CIS admits that, at the time the opportunity was offered to Broz, the board of CIS would not have been interested in Michigan-2, but CIS asserts that Broz usurped the opportunity nevertheless. CIS claims that Broz was required to look not just to CIS, but to the articulated business plans of PriCellular, to determine whether PriCellular would be interested in acquiring Michigan-2. Since Broz failed to do this and acquired Michigan-2 without first considering the interests of PriCellular in its capacity as a potential acquiror of CIS, CIS contends that Broz must be held to account for breach of fiduciary duty.

IV. APPLICATION OF THE CORPORATE OPPORTUNITY DOCTRINE

The doctrine of corporate opportunity represents but one species of the broad fiduciary duties assumed by a corporate director or officer. A corporate fiduciary agrees to place the interests of the corporation before his or her own in appropriate circumstances.[…] The classic statement of the doctrine is derived from the venerable case of *Guth v. Loft, Inc.* In *Guth,* this Court held that:

> if there is presented to a corporate officer or director a business
> opportunity which the corporation is financially able to undertake,
> is, from its nature, in the line of the corporation's business and is of
> practical advantage to it, is one in which the corporation has an
> interest or a reasonable expectancy, and, by embracing the
> opportunity, the self-interest of the officer or director will be
> brought into conflict with that of the corporation, the law will not
> permit him to seize the opportunity for himself.

Guth, 5 A.2d at 510-11.

The corporate opportunity doctrine, as delineated by *Guth* and its progeny, holds [155] that a corporate officer or director may not take a business opportunity for his own if: (1) the corporation is financially able to exploit the opportunity; (2) the opportunity is within the corporation's line of business; (3) the corporation has an interest or expectancy in the opportunity; and (4) by taking the opportunity for his own, the corporate fiduciary will thereby be placed in a position inimicable to his duties to the corporation. The Court in *Guth* also derived a corollary which states that a director or officer *may* take a corporate opportunity if: (1) the opportunity is presented to the director or officer in his individual and not his corporate capacity; (2) the opportunity is not essential to the corporation; (3) the corporation holds no interest or expectancy in the opportunity; and (4) the director or officer has not wrongfully employed the resources of the corporation in pursuing or exploiting the opportunity. *Guth,* 5 A.2d at 509.

Thus, the contours of this doctrine are well established. It is important to note, however, that the tests enunciated in *Guth* and subsequent cases provide guidelines to be considered by a reviewing court in balancing the equities of an individual case. No one factor is dispositive and all factors must be taken into account insofar as they are applicable. Cases involving a claim of usurpation of a corporate opportunity range over a multitude of factual settings. Hard and fast rules are not easily crafted to deal with such an array of complex situations. As this Court noted in *Johnston v. Greene,* Del. Supr., 121 A.2d 919 (1956), the determination of "[w]hether or not a director has appropriated for himself something that in fairness should belong to the corporation is `a factual question to be decided by reasonable inference from objective facts.'" *Id.* at 923 (quoting *Guth,* 5

A.2d at 513). In the instant case, we find that the facts do not support the conclusion that Broz misappropriated a corporate opportunity.

We note at the outset that Broz became aware of the Michigan-2 opportunity in his individual and not his corporate capacity. As the Court of Chancery found, "Broz did not misuse proprietary information that came to him in a corporate capacity nor did he otherwise use any power he might have over the governance of the corporation to advance his own interests." 663 A.2d at 1185. This fact is not the subject of serious dispute. In fact, it is clear from the record that Mackinac did not consider CIS a viable candidate for the acquisition of Michigan-2. Accordingly, Mackinac did not offer the property to CIS. In this factual posture, many of the fundamental concerns undergirding the law of corporate opportunity are not present (*e.g.,* misappropriation of the corporation's proprietary information). [...]

We turn now to an analysis of the factors relied on by the trial court. First, we find that CIS was not financially capable of exploiting the Michigan-2 opportunity.[...] The record shows that CIS was in a precarious financial position at the time Mackinac presented the Michigan-2 opportunity to Broz. Having recently emerged from lengthy and contentious bankruptcy proceedings, CIS was not in a position to commit capital to the acquisition of new assets. Further, the loan agreement entered into by CIS and its creditors severely limited the discretion of CIS as to the acquisition of new assets and substantially restricted the ability of CIS to incur new debt.

While it may be said with some certainty that the Michigan-2 opportunity was within CIS' line of business, it is not equally clear that CIS had a cognizable interest or expectancy in the license.[7] Under the third factor laid down by this Court in *Guth,* for an opportunity to be deemed to belong to the fiduciary's corporation, the corporation must have an interest or expectancy in that opportunity. [...] Despite the fact that the nature of the Michigan-2 opportunity was historically close to the core operations of CIS, changes were in process. At the time the opportunity was presented, CIS was actively engaged in the process of divesting its cellular license holdings. CIS' articulated business plan did not involve any new acquisitions. [...] Thus, CIS had no [157] interest or expectancy in the Michigan-2 opportunity.[...]).

Finally, the corporate opportunity doctrine is implicated only in cases where the fiduciary's seizure of an opportunity results in a conflict between the fiduciary's duties to the corporation and the self-interest of the director as actualized by the exploitation of the opportunity. In the instant case, Broz' interest in acquiring and profiting from Michigan-2 created no duties that were inimicable to his obligations to CIS. [...] CIS was fully aware of Broz' potentially conflicting duties. Broz, however, comported himself in a manner that was wholly in accord with his obligations to CIS. Broz took care not to usurp any opportunity which CIS was willing and able to pursue. Broz sought only to compete with an outside entity, PriCellular, for acquisition of an opportunity which both sought to possess. Broz was not obligated to refrain from competition with PriCellular. Therefore, the totality of the circumstances indicates that Broz did not usurp an opportunity that properly belonged to CIS. [...]

In concluding that Broz had usurped a corporate opportunity, the Court of Chancery placed great emphasis on the fact that Broz had not formally presented the matter to the CIS board. [...]

The teaching of *Guth* and its progeny is that the director or officer must analyze the situation *ex ante* to determine whether the opportunity is one rightfully belonging to the corporation. If the director or officer believes, based on one of the factors articulated above, that the corporation is not entitled to the opportunity, then he may take it for himself. Of course, presenting the opportunity to the board creates a kind of "safe harbor" for the director, which removes the specter of a *post hoc* judicial determination that the director or officer has improperly usurped a corporate opportunity. Thus, presentation avoids the possibility that an error in the fiduciary's assessment of the situation will create future liability for breach of fiduciary duty. It is not the law of Delaware that presentation to the board is a necessary prerequisite to a finding that a corporate opportunity has not been usurped. [...]

The corporate opportunity doctrine represents a judicially crafted effort to harmonize the competing demands placed on corporate fiduciaries in a modern business environment. The doctrine seeks to reduce the possibility of conflict between a director's duties to the corporation and interests unrelated to that role. In the instant case, Broz adhered to his obligations to CIS. [...]

Therefore, we hold that Broz did not breach his fiduciary duties to CIS.

4.3.5.2 In re eBay Inc. S'Holders Litigation

2004 WL 253521

In re EBAY INC. SHAREHOLDERS LITIGATION

No. C.A. 19988-NC.

Court of Chancery of Delaware.

Submitted Sept. 16, 2003.

CHANDLER, J.

Shareholders of eBay, Inc. filed these consolidated derivative actions against certain eBay directors and officers for usurping corporate opportunities. [1] Plaintiffs allege that eBay's investment banking advisor, Goldman Sachs Group, engaged in "spinning," a practice that involves allocating shares of lucrative initial public offerings of stock to favored clients. In effect, the plaintiff shareholders allege that Goldman Sachs bribed certain eBay insiders, using the currency of highly profitable investment opportunities-opportunities that should have been offered to, or provided for the benefit of, eBay rather than the favored insiders. Plaintiffs accuse Goldman Sachs of aiding and abetting the corporate insiders breach of their fiduciary duty of loyalty to eBay.

The individual eBay defendants, as well as Goldman Sachs, have moved to dismiss these consolidated actions for failure to state a claim and for failure to make a pre-suit demand on eBay's board of directors as required under Chancery Court Rule 23.1. For reasons I briefly discuss below, I deny all of the defendants' motions to dismiss.

I. BACKGROUND FACTS

The facts, as alleged in the complaint, are straightforward. In 1995, defendants Pierre M. Omidyar and Jeffrey Skoll founded nominal defendant eBay, a Delaware corporation, as a sole proprietorship. eBay is a pioneer in online trading platforms, providing a virtual auction community for buyers and sellers to list items for sale and to bid on items of interest. In 1998, eBay retained Goldman Sachs and other investment banks to underwrite an initial public offering of common stock. Goldman Sachs was the lead underwriter. The stock was priced at $18 per share. Goldman Sachs purchased about 1.2 million shares. Shares of eBay stock became immensely valuable during 1998 and 1999, rising to $175 per share in early April 1999. Around that time, eBay made a secondary offering, issuing 6.5 million shares of common stock at $170 per share for a total of $1.1 billion. Goldman Sachs again served as lead underwriter. Goldman Sachs was asked in 2001 to serve as eBay's financial advisor in connection with an acquisition by eBay of PayPal, Inc. For these services, eBay has paid Goldman Sachs over $8 million.

During this same time period, Goldman Sachs "rewarded" the individual defendants by allocating to them thousands of IPO shares, managed by Goldman Sachs, at the initial offering price. Because the IPO market during this particular period of time was extremely active, prices of initial stock offerings often doubled or tripled in a single day. Investors who were well connected, either to Goldman Sachs or to similarly situated investment banks serving as IPO underwriters, were able to flip these investments into instant profit by selling the equities in a few days or even in a few hours after they were initially purchased.

The essential allegation of the complaint is that Goldman Sachs provided these IPO share allocations to the individual defendants to show appreciation for eBay's business and to enhance Goldman Sachs' chances of obtaining future eBay business. In addition to co-founding eBay, defendant Omidyar has been eBay's CEO, CFO and President. He is eBay's largest stockholder, owning more than 23% of the company's equity. Goldman Sachs allocated Omidyar shares in at least forty IPOs at the initial offering price. Omidyar resold these securities in the public market for millions of dollars in profit. Defendant Whitman owns 3.3% of eBay stock and has been President, CEO and a director since early 1998. Whitman also has been a director of Goldman Sachs since 2001. Goldman Sachs allocated Whitman shares in over a 100 IPOs at the initial offering price. Whitman sold these equities in the open market and reaped millions of dollars in profit. Defendant Skoll, in addition to co-founding eBay, has served in various positions at the company, including Vice-President of Strategic Planning and Analysis and President. He served as an eBay director from December 1996 to March 1998. Skoll is eBay's second largest stockholder, owning about 13% of the company. Goldman Sachs has allocated Skoll shares in at least 75 IPOs at the initial offering price, which Skoll promptly resold on the open market, allowing him to realize millions of dollars in profit. Finally, defendant Robert C. Kagle has served as an eBay director since June 1997.

Goldman Sachs allocated Kagle shares in at least 25 IPOs at the initial offering price. Kagle promptly resold these equities, and recorded millions of dollars in profit.

II. ANALYSIS

[...]

B. Corporate Opportunity

4 Plaintiffs have stated a claim that defendants usurped a corporate opportunity of eBay. Defendants insist that Goldman Sachs' IPO allocations to eBay's insider directors were "collateral investments opportunities" that arose by virtue of the inside directors status as wealthy individuals. They argue that this is not a corporate opportunity within the corporation's line of business or an opportunity in which the corporation had an interest or expectancy. [3] These arguments are unavailing.

First, no one disputes that eBay financially was able to exploit the opportunities in question. Second, eBay was in the business of investing in securities. The complaint alleges that eBay "consistently invested a portion of its cash on hand in marketable securities." According to eBay's 1999 10-K, for example, eBay had more than $550 million invested in equity and debt securities. eBay invested more than $181 million in "short-term investments" and $373 million in "long-term investments." Thus, investing was "a line of business" of eBay. Third, the facts alleged in the complaint suggest that investing was integral to eBay's cash management strategies and a significant part of its business. Finally, it is no answer to say, as do defendants, that IPOs are risky investments. It is undisputed that eBay was never given an opportunity to turn down the IPO allocations as too risky. [4]

Defendants also argue that to view the IPO allocations in question as corporate opportunities will mean that every advantageous investment opportunity that comes to an officer or director will be considered a corporate opportunity. On the contrary, the allegations in the complaint in this case indicate that unique, below-market price investment opportunities were offered by Goldman Sachs to the insider defendants as financial inducements to maintain and secure corporate business. This was not an instance where a broker offered advice to a director about an investment in a marketable security. The conduct challenged here involved a large investment bank that regularly did business with a company steering highly lucrative IPO allocations to select insider directors and officers at that company, allegedly both to reward them for past business and to induce them to direct future business to that investment bank. This is a far cry from the defendants' characterization of the conduct in question as merely "a broker's investment recommendations" to a wealthy client.

Nor can one seriously argue that this conduct did not place the insider defendants in a position of conflict with their duties to the corporation. One can realistically characterize these IPO allocations as a form of commercial discount or rebate for past or future investment banking services. Viewed pragmatically, it is easy to understand how steering such commercial rebates to certain insider directors places those directors in an obvious conflict between their self-interest and the corporation's interest. It is noteworthy, too, that the Securities and Exchange Commission has taken the position that "spinning" practices violate the obligations of broker-dealers under the "Free-riding and Withholding Interpretation" rules. [5] As the SEC has explained, "the purpose of the interpretation is to protect the integrity of the public offering system by ensuring that members make a bona fide public distribution of 'hot issue' securities and do not withhold such securities for their own benefit or use the securities to reward other persons who are in a position to direct future business to the member." [6]

*5 Finally, even if one assumes that IPO allocations like those in question here do not constitute a corporate opportunity, a cognizable claim is nevertheless stated on the common law ground that an agent is under a duty to account for profits obtained personally in connection with transactions related to his or her company. The complaint gives rise to a reasonable inference that the insider directors accepted a commission or gratuity that rightfully belonged to eBay but that was improperly diverted to them. Even if this conduct does not run afoul of the corporate opportunity doctrine, it may still constitute a breach of the fiduciary duty of loyalty. [7] Thus, even if one does not consider Goldman Sachs' IPO allocations to these corporate insiders-allocations that generated millions of dollars in profit-to be a corporate opportunity, the defendant directors were nevertheless not free to accept this consideration from a company, Goldman Sachs, that was doing significant business with eBay and that arguably intended the consideration as an inducement to maintaining the business relationship in the future. [8] […]

III. CONCLUSION

For all of the above reasons, I deny the defendants' motions to dismiss the complaint in this consolidated action.

4.3.6 Duty of Good Faith

The ubiquity of exculpation provisions in charters as well as precedent like *Malpiede v. Townson* have made it extremely difficult – if not impossible – for shareholder plaintiffs to succeed on claims that simply allege violations of the duty of care. In response to foreclosing that avenue, shareholder plaintiffs have brought other theories to court in attempts to generate monetary liability for otherwise disinterested directors when their decision-making process has fallen short of the mark.

Duty of good faith claims are just one such theory. In the good faith claims, plaintiffs argue that otherwise disinterested directors inaction or decision-making was so poor that it exceeds gross negligence – the standard of a duty of care claim – and rises to the level of a violation of the duty of good faith.

The object of these theories is to work around the limitations of exculpation provisions. To the extent they are successful, such theories might be able to generate monetary liability for disinterested directors.

Courts have heard these theories and have responded by narrowing the possible set of circumstances of a successful good faith claim.

4.3.6.1 Oversight Claims

It is not uncommon that when a corporation makes a decision that results in a loss for the corporation that stockholders will be unhappy. In some cases, stockholders may well sue the board for the lack of propriety of the decision leading to the loss. However, absent some indicia of a violation of the duty of loyalty, such claims are a very thin reed upon which to rest one's litigation hopes. Oftentimes, plaintiffs will advance a theory that directors violated their duty of good faith due to inadequate oversight of the corporation leading to a nonexculpable loss. In one such case, *Caremark*, the court noted the good faith theory advanced by the plaintiffs "is possibly the most difficult theory in corporation law upon which a plaintiff might hope to win a judgment."

Following the financial crisis of 2008, plaintiffs brought a series of claims against the major banks alleging directors failed in their oversight obligations of the banks leading to catastrophic losses. *Citigroup* demonstrates just how difficult it is for plaintiffs to win on this legal theory.

4.3.6.1.1 Stone v. Ritter

A common good faith claim is that directors violated their duty of good faith the corporation by failing to provide adequate oversight, resulting in avoidable losses to the corporation. These "oversight claims" are also known as *Caremark* claims after a case where the issue of oversight liability was dealt with in dicta. In *Stone*, the Delaware Supreme Court adopts the reasoning of *Caremark* and applies the standard to facts before it.

911 A.2d 362 (2006)
William STONE v. C. Dowd RITTER

HOLLAND, Justice:

This is an appeal from a final judgment of the Court of Chancery dismissing a derivative complaint against fifteen present and former directors of AmSouth Bancorporation ("AmSouth"), a Delaware corporation. The plaintiffs-appellants, William and Sandra Stone, are AmSouth shareholders and filed their derivative complaint without making a pre-suit demand on AmSouth's board of directors (the "Board"). The Court of Chancery held that the plaintiffs had failed to adequately plead that such a demand would have been futile. The Court, therefore, dismissed the derivative complaint under Court of Chancery Rule 23.1.

The Court of Chancery characterized the allegations in the derivative complaint as a "classic *Caremark* claim," a claim that derives its name from *In re Caremark Int'l Deriv. Litig.*[1] In *Caremark*, the Court of Chancery recognized that: "[g]enerally where a claim of directorial liability for corporate loss is predicated upon ignorance of liability creating activities within the corporation . . . only a sustained or systematic failure of the board to

412

exercise oversight—such as an utter failure to attempt to assure a reasonable information and reporting system exists—will establish the lack of good faith that is a necessary condition to liability."

In this appeal, the plaintiffs acknowledge that the directors neither "knew [n]or should have known that violations of law were occurring," *i.e.,* that there were no "red flags" before the directors. Nevertheless, the plaintiffs argue that the Court of Chancery erred by dismissing the derivative complaint which alleged that "the defendants had utterly failed to implement any sort of statutorily required monitoring, reporting or information controls that would have enabled them to learn of problems requiring their attention." The defendants argue that the plaintiffs' assertions are contradicted by the derivative complaint itself and by the documents incorporated therein by reference.

[365] Consistent with our opinion in *In re Walt Disney Co. Deriv Litig,* we hold that *Caremark* articulates the necessary conditions for assessing director oversight liability.[3] We also conclude that the *Caremark* standard was properly applied to evaluate the derivative complaint in this case. Accordingly, the judgment of the Court of Chancery must be affirmed.

Facts

This derivative action is brought on AmSouth's behalf by William and Sandra Stone, who allege that they owned AmSouth common stock "at all relevant times." The nominal defendant, AmSouth, is a Delaware corporation with its principal executive offices in Birmingham, Alabama. During the relevant period, AmSouth's wholly-owned subsidiary, AmSouth Bank, operated about 600 commercial banking branches in six states throughout the southeastern United States and employed more than 11,600 people.

In 2004, AmSouth and AmSouth Bank paid $40 million in fines and $10 million in civil penalties to resolve government and regulatory investigations pertaining principally to the failure by bank employees to file "Suspicious Activity Reports" ("SARs"), as required by the federal Bank Secrecy Act ("BSA")[4] and various anti-money-laundering ("AML") regulations[…]No fines or penalties were imposed on AmSouth's directors, and no other regulatory action was taken against them.

The government investigations arose originally from an unlawful "Ponzi" scheme operated by Louis D. Hamric, II and Victor G. Nance. In August 2000, Hamric, then a licensed attorney, and Nance, then a registered investment advisor with Mutual of New York, contacted an AmSouth branch bank in Tennessee to arrange for custodial trust accounts to be created for "investors" in a "business venture." That venture (Hamric and Nance represented) involved the construction of medical clinics overseas. In reality, Nance had convinced more than forty of his clients to invest in promissory notes bearing high rates of return, by misrepresenting the nature and the risk of that investment. […]

The Hamric-Nance scheme was discovered in March 2002, when the investors did not receive their monthly interest payments. […]

The authorities examined AmSouth's compliance with its reporting and other obligations under the BSA. On November 17, 2003, the USAO advised AmSouth that it was the subject of a criminal investigation. On October 12, 2004, AmSouth and the USAO entered into a Deferred Prosecution Agreement ("DPA") in which AmSouth agreed: first, to the filing by USAO of a one-count Information in the United States District Court for the Southern District of Mississippi, charging AmSouth with failing to file SARs; and second, to pay a $40 million fine. In conjunction with the DPA, the USAO issued a "Statement of Facts," which noted that although in 2000 "at least one" AmSouth employee suspected that Hamric was involved in a possibly illegal scheme, AmSouth failed to file SARs in a timely manner. In neither the Statement of Facts nor anywhere else did the USAO ascribe any blame to the Board or to any individual director.

On October 12, 2004, the Federal Reserve and the Alabama Banking Department concurrently issued a Cease and Desist Order against AmSouth, requiring it, for the first time, to improve its BSA/AML program. That Cease and Desist Order required AmSouth to (among other things) engage an independent consultant "to conduct a comprehensive review of the Bank's AML Compliance program and make recommendations, as appropriate, for new policies and procedures to be implemented by the Bank." KPMG Forensic Services ("KPMG") performed the role of independent consultant and issued its report on December 10, 2004 (the "KPMG Report").

Also on October 12, 2004, FinCEN and the Federal Reserve jointly assessed a $10 million civil penalty against AmSouth for operating an inadequate anti-money-laundering program and for failing to file SARs. In connection with that assessment, FinCEN issued a written Assessment of Civil Money Penalty (the "Assessment"), which included detailed "determinations" regarding AmSouth's BSA compliance procedures. FinCEN found that "AmSouth violated the suspicious activity reporting requirements of the Bank Secrecy Act," and that "[s]ince April 24, 2002, AmSouth has been in violation of the anti-money-laundering program requirements of the Bank Secrecy Act." Among FinCEN's specific determinations were its conclusions that "AmSouth's [AML compliance] program lacked adequate board and management oversight," and that "reporting to management for the purposes of monitoring and oversight of compliance activities was materially deficient." AmSouth neither admitted nor denied FinCEN's determinations in this or any other forum.

Demand Futility and Director Independence

It is a fundamental principle of the Delaware General Corporation Law that "[t]he business and affairs of every corporation organized under this chapter shall be managed by or under the direction of a board of directors. . . ."[6] Thus, "by its very nature [a] derivative action impinges on the managerial freedom of directors."[7] Therefore, the right of a stockholder to prosecute a derivative suit is limited to situations where either the stockholder has demanded the directors pursue a corporate claim and the directors have wrongfully refused to do so, or where demand is excused because the directors are incapable of making an impartial decision regarding whether to institute such litigation.[8] Court of Chancery Rule 23.1, accordingly, requires that the complaint in a derivative action "allege with particularity the efforts, if any, made by the plaintiff to obtain the action the plaintiff desires from the directors [or] the reasons for the plaintiff's failure to obtain the action or for not making the effort."[9]

In this appeal, the plaintiffs concede that "[t]he standards for determining demand futility in the absence of a business decision" are set forth in *Rales v. Blasband.*[10] To excuse demand under *Rales,* "a court must determine whether or not the particularized factual allegations of a derivative stockholder complaint create a reasonable doubt that, as of the time the complaint is filed, the board of directors could have properly exercised its independent and disinterested business judgment in responding to a demand."[11] The plaintiffs attempt to satisfy the *Rales* test in this proceeding by asserting that the incumbent defendant directors "face a substantial likelihood of liability" that renders them "personally interested in the outcome of the decision on whether to pursue the claims asserted in the complaint," and are therefore not disinterested or independent.[12]

Critical to this demand excused argument is the fact that the directors' potential personal liability depends upon whether or not their conduct can be exculpated by the section 102(b)(7) provision contained in the AmSouth certificate of incorporation.[13] Such a provision can exculpate directors from monetary liability for a breach of the duty of care, but not for conduct that is not in good faith or a breach of the duty of loyalty.[14] The standard for assessing a director's potential personal liability for failing to act in good faith in discharging his or her oversight responsibilities has evolved beginning with our decision in *Graham v. Allis-Chalmers Manufacturing Company*,[15] through the Court of Chancery's *Caremark* decision to our most recent decision in *Disney*.[16] A brief discussion of that evolution will help illuminate the standard that we adopt in this case.

Graham and Caremark

Graham was a derivative action brought against the directors of Allis-Chalmers for failure to prevent violations of federal anti-trust laws by Allis-Chalmers employees. There was no claim that the Allis-Chalmers directors knew of the employees' conduct that resulted in the corporation's liability. Rather, the plaintiffs claimed that the Allis-Chalmers directors *should have known* of the illegal conduct by the corporation's employees. In *Graham*, this Court held that "*absent cause for suspicion* there is no duty upon the directors to install and operate a corporate system of espionage to ferret out wrongdoing which they have no reason to suspect exists."[17]

In *Caremark*, the Court of Chancery reassessed the applicability of our holding in *Graham* when called upon to approve a settlement of a derivative lawsuit brought against the directors of Caremark International, Inc. The plaintiffs claimed that the Caremark directors should have known that certain officers and employees of Caremark were involved in violations of the federal Anti-Referral Payments Law. That law prohibits health care providers from paying any form of remuneration to induce the referral of Medicare or Medicaid patients. The plaintiffs claimed that the *Caremark* directors breached their fiduciary duty for having "allowed a situation to develop and continue which exposed the corporation to enormous legal liability and that in so doing they violated a duty to be active monitors of corporate performance."[18]

In evaluating whether to approve the proposed settlement agreement in *Caremark,* the Court of Chancery narrowly construed our holding in *Graham* "as standing for the proposition that, absent grounds to suspect deception, neither corporate boards nor senior officers can be charged with wrongdoing simply for assuming the integrity of employees and the honesty of their dealings on the company's behalf."[19] The *Caremark* Court opined it would be a "mistake" to interpret this Court's decision in *Graham* to mean that:

> corporate boards may satisfy their obligation to be reasonably informed concerning the corporation, without assuring themselves that information and reporting systems exist in the organization that are reasonably designed to provide to senior management and to the board itself timely, accurate information sufficient to allow management and the board, each within its scope, to reach informed judgments concerning both the corporation's compliance with law and its business performance.[20]

To the contrary, the *Caremark* Court stated, "it is important that the board exercise a good faith judgment that the corporation's information and reporting system is in concept and design adequate to assure the board that appropriate information will come to its attention in a timely manner as a matter of ordinary operations, so that it may satisfy its responsibility."[21] The *Caremark* Court recognized, however, that "the duty to act in good faith to be informed cannot be thought to require directors to possess detailed information about all aspects of the operation of the enterprise."[22] The Court of Chancery then formulated the following standard for assessing the liability of directors where the directors are unaware of employee [369] misconduct that results in the corporation being held liable:

> Generally where a claim of directorial liability for corporate loss is predicated upon ignorance of liability creating activities within the corporation, as in *Graham* or in this case, . . . only a sustained or systematic failure of the board to exercise oversight—such as an

utter failure to attempt to assure a reasonable information and reporting system exists—will establish the lack of good faith that is a necessary condition to liability.[23]

Caremark Standard Approved

As evidenced by the language quoted above, the *Caremark* standard for so-called "oversight" liability draws heavily upon the concept of director failure to act in good faith. That is consistent with the definition(s) of bad faith recently approved by this Court in its recent *Disney*[24] decision, where we held that a failure to act in good faith requires conduct that is qualitatively different from, and more culpable than, the conduct giving rise to a violation of the fiduciary duty of care (i.e., gross negligence).[25] In *Disney*, we identified the following examples of conduct that would establish a failure to act in good faith:

> A failure to act in good faith may be shown, for instance, where the fiduciary intentionally acts with a purpose other than that of advancing the best interests of the corporation, where the fiduciary acts with the intent to violate applicable positive law, or where the fiduciary intentionally fails to act in the face of a known duty to act, demonstrating a conscious disregard for his duties. There may be other examples of bad faith yet to be proven or alleged, but these three are the most salient.[26]

The third of these examples describes, and is fully consistent with, the lack of good faith conduct that the *Caremark* court held was a "necessary condition" for director oversight liability, i.e., "a sustained or systematic failure of the board to exercise oversight—such as an utter failure to attempt to assure a reasonable information and reporting system exists. . . ."[27] Indeed, our opinion in *Disney* cited *Caremark* with approval for that proposition.[28] Accordingly, the Court of Chancery applied the correct standard in assessing whether demand was excused in this case where failure to exercise oversight was the basis or theory of the plaintiffs' claim for relief.

It is important, in this context, to clarify a doctrinal issue that is critical to understanding fiduciary liability under *Caremark* as we construe that case. The phraseology used in *Caremark* and that we employ here—describing the lack of good faith as a "necessary

418

condition to liability"—is deliberate. The purpose of that formulation is to communicate that a failure to act in good faith is not conduct that results, *ipso facto,* in the direct imposition of fiduciary liability.[29] The failure to act in [370] good faith may result in liability because the requirement to act in good faith "is a subsidiary element[,]" i.e., a condition, "of the fundamental duty of loyalty."[30] It follows that because a showing of bad faith conduct, in the sense described in *Disney* and *Caremark,* is essential to establish director oversight liability, the fiduciary duty violated by that conduct is the duty of loyalty.

This view of a failure to act in good faith results in two additional doctrinal consequences. First, although good faith may be described colloquially as part of a "triad" of fiduciary duties that includes the duties of care and loyalty,[31] the obligation to act in good faith does not establish an independent fiduciary duty that stands on the same footing as the duties of care and loyalty. Only the latter two duties, where violated, may directly result in liability, whereas a failure to act in good faith may do so, but indirectly. The second doctrinal consequence is that the fiduciary duty of loyalty is not limited to cases involving a financial or other cognizable fiduciary conflict of interest. It also encompasses cases where the fiduciary fails to act in good faith. As the Court of Chancery aptly put it in *Guttman,* "[a] director cannot act loyally towards the corporation unless she acts in the good faith belief that her actions are in the corporation's best interest."[32]

We hold that *Caremark* articulates the necessary conditions predicate for director oversight liability: (a) the directors utterly failed to implement any reporting or information system or controls; *or* (b) having implemented such a system or controls, consciously failed to monitor or oversee its operations thus disabling themselves from being informed of risks or problems requiring their attention. In either case, imposition of liability requires a showing that the directors knew that they were not discharging their fiduciary obligations.[33] Where directors fail to act in the face of a known duty to act, thereby demonstrating a conscious disregard for their responsibilities,[34] they breach their duty of loyalty by failing to discharge that fiduciary obligation in good faith.[35]

Chancery Court Decision

The plaintiffs contend that demand is excused under Rule 23.1 because AmSouth's directors breached their oversight duty and, as a result, face a "substantial likelihood of liability" as a result of their "utter failure" to act in good faith to put into place policies and procedures to ensure compliance with BSA and AML obligations. The Court of Chancery found that the plaintiffs did not plead the existence of "red flags"—"facts showing that the board ever was aware that AmSouth's internal controls were inadequate, that these inadequacies would result in illegal activity, and that the board chose to do nothing about problems it allegedly knew existed." In dismissing the derivative complaint in this action, the Court of Chancery concluded:

> This case is not about a board's failure to carefully consider a material corporate decision that was presented to the [371] board. This is a case where information was not reaching the board because of ineffective internal controls. . . . With the benefit of hindsight, it is beyond question that AmSouth's internal controls with respect to the Bank Secrecy Act and anti-money laundering regulations compliance were inadequate. Neither party disputes that the lack of internal controls resulted in a huge fine—$50 million, alleged to be the largest ever of its kind. The fact of those losses, however, is not alone enough for a court to conclude that a majority of the corporation's board of directors is disqualified from considering demand that AmSouth bring suit against those responsible.[36]

This Court reviews *de novo* a Court of Chancery's decision to dismiss a derivative suit under Rule 23.1.[37]

Reasonable Reporting System Existed

The KPMG Report evaluated the various components of AmSouth's longstanding BSA/AML compliance program. The KPMG Report reflects that AmSouth's Board dedicated considerable resources to the BSA/AML compliance program and put into place numerous procedures and systems to attempt to ensure compliance. According to KPMG, the program's various components exhibited between a low and high degree of compliance with applicable laws and regulations. […]

Complaint Properly Dismissed

In this case, the adequacy of the plaintiffs' assertion that demand is excused depends on whether the complaint alleges facts sufficient to show that the defendant *directors* are potentially personally liable for the failure of non-director bank *employees* to file SARs. Delaware courts have recognized that "[m]ost of the decisions that a corporation, acting through its human agents, makes are, of course, not the subject of director attention."[39] Consequently, a claim that directors are subject to personal liability for employee failures is "possibly the most difficult theory in corporation law upon which a plaintiff might hope to win a judgment."[40]

For the plaintiffs' derivative complaint to withstand a motion to dismiss, "only a sustained or systematic failure of the board to exercise oversight—such as an utter failure to attempt to assure a reasonable information and reporting system exists—will establish the lack of good faith that is a necessary condition to liability."[41] As the *Caremark* decision noted:

> Such a test of liability—lack of good faith as evidenced by sustained or systematic failure of a director to exercise reasonable oversight— is quite high. But, a demanding test of liability in the oversight context is probably beneficial to corporate shareholders as a class, as it is in the board decision context, since it makes board service by qualified persons more likely, while continuing to act as a stimulus to *good faith performance of duty* by such directors.[42]

The KPMG Report—which the plaintiffs explicitly incorporated by reference into their derivative complaint—refutes the assertion that the directors "never took the necessary steps . . . to ensure that a reasonable BSA compliance and reporting system existed." KPMG's findings reflect [373] that the Board received and approved relevant policies and procedures, delegated to certain employees and departments the responsibility for filing SARs and monitoring compliance, and exercised oversight by relying on periodic reports from them. Although there ultimately may have been failures by employees to report deficiencies to the Board, there is no basis for an oversight claim seeking to hold the directors personally liable for such failures by the employees.

With the benefit of hindsight, the plaintiffs' complaint seeks to equate a bad outcome with bad faith. The lacuna in the plaintiffs' argument is a failure to recognize that the directors' good faith exercise of oversight responsibility may not invariably prevent employees from violating criminal laws, or from causing the corporation to incur significant financial liability, or both, as occurred in *Graham, Caremark* and this very case. In the absence of red flags, good faith in the context of oversight must be measured by the directors' actions "to assure a reasonable information and reporting system exists" and not by second-guessing after the occurrence of employee conduct that results in an unintended adverse outcome.[43] Accordingly, we hold that the Court of Chancery properly applied *Caremark* and dismissed the plaintiffs' derivative complaint for failure to excuse demand by alleging particularized facts that created reason to doubt whether the directors had acted in good faith in exercising their oversight responsibilities.

4.3.6.1.2 In re Citigroup Inc. Shareholder Derivative Litigation

In the wake of the Financial Crisis of 2008, stockholders were rightly upset. Boards of corporate America took what in hindsight appear to have been excess risk and helped push the entire economy to the brink of collapse. The case that follows, *Citigroup*, is typical of the derivative claims brought following the financial crisis. In essence, the plaintiffs argument is that the defendant board mismanaged the company and missed obvious signs ('red flags') that things were heading in the wrong direction.

Stockholders seek to hold directors accountable for the resulting failure in corporate performance. These claims are a version of *Caremark* oversight claims. Though rather than charging directors with missing misconduct of corporate officers, plaintiffs are charging directors with taking on excessive business risk. Remember, such claims must take the form of derivative claims. Consequently, plaintiffs must plead demand futility. This opinion is an opinion on a Rule 23.1 motion to dismiss.

964 A.2d 106 (2009)
In re CITIGROUP INC. SHAREHOLDER DERIVATIVE LITIGATION.

CHANDLER, Chancellor.

This is a shareholder derivative action brought on behalf of Citigroup Inc. ("Citigroup" or the "Company"), seeking to recover for the Company its losses arising from exposure to the subprime lending market. Plaintiffs, shareholders of Citigroup, brought this action against current and former directors and officers of Citigroup, alleging, in essence, that the defendants breached their fiduciary duties by failing to properly monitor and manage the risks the Company faced from problems in the subprime lending market and for failing to properly disclose Citigroup's exposure to subprime assets. Plaintiffs allege that there were extensive "red flags" that should have given defendants notice of the problems that were brewing in the real estate and credit markets and that defendants ignored these warnings in the pursuit of short term profits and at the expense of the Company's long term viability. […]

Citigroup is a global financial services company whose businesses provide a broad range of financial services to consumers and businesses. Citigroup was incorporated in Delaware in 1988 and maintains its principal executive offices in New York, New York.

Defendants in this action are current and former directors and officers of Citigroup. The complaint names thirteen members of the Citigroup board of directors on November 9, 2007, when the first of plaintiffs' now-consolidated derivative actions was filed.[1] Plaintiffs allege that a majority of the director defendants were members of the Audit and Risk Management Committee ("ARM Committee") in 2007 and were considered audit committee financial experts as defined by the Securities and Exchange Commission. […]

B. Citigroup's Exposure to the Subprime Crisis

Plaintiffs allege that since as early as 2006, defendants have caused and allowed Citigroup to engage in subprime lending[2] that ultimately left the Company exposed to massive losses by late 2007.[3] Beginning in late 2005, house prices, which many believe were artificially inflated by speculation and easily available credit, began to [113] plateau, and then deflate. Adjustable rate mortgages issued earlier in the decade began to reset, leaving many homeowners with significantly increased monthly payments. Defaults and foreclosures increased, and assets backed by income from residential mortgages began to decrease in value. By February 2007, subprime mortgage lenders began filing for bankruptcy and subprime mortgages packaged into securities began experiencing increasing levels of delinquency. In mid-2007, rating agencies downgraded bonds backed by subprime mortgages.

Much of Citigroup's exposure to the subprime lending market arose from its involvement with collateralized debt obligations ("CDOs")—repackaged pools of lower rated securities that Citigroup created by acquiring asset-backed securities, including residential mortgage backed securities ("RMBSs"),[4] and then selling rights to the cash flows from the securities in classes, or tranches, with different levels of risk and return. Included with at least some of the CDOs created by Citigroup was a "liquidity put"—an option that allowed the purchasers of the CDOs to sell them back to Citigroup at original value.

According to plaintiffs, Citigroup's alleged $55 billion subprime exposure was in two areas of the Company's Securities & Banking Unit. The first portion totaled $11.7 billion and included securities tied to subprime loans that were being held until they could be added to debt pools for investors. The second portion included $43 billion of super-senior securities, which are portions of CDOs backed in part by RMBS collateral.[5]

By late 2007, it was apparent that Citigroup faced significant losses on its subprime-related assets, including the following as alleged by plaintiffs:

> • *October 1, 2007:* Citigroup announced it would write-down approximately $1.4 billion on funded and unfunded highly leveraged finance commitments.

> • *October 15, 2007:* Citigroup issued a press release reporting a net income of $2.38 billion, a 57% decline from the Company's prior year results.

> • *November 4, 2007:* Citigroup announced significant declines on the fair value of the approximately $55 billion in the Company's U.S. subprime-related direct exposures, and estimated that further write downs would be between $8 and $11 billion.

> • *November 6, 2007:* Citigroup disclosed that it provided $7.6 billion of emergency financing to the seven SIVs the Company operated after they were unable to repay maturing debt. The SIVs drew on the $10 billion of so-called committed liquidity provided by Citigroup. On December 13, 2007 Citigroup bailed out seven of its

affiliated SIVs by bringing $49 billion in assets onto its balance sheet and taking full responsibility for the SIVs' $49 billion worth of assets.

• *January 15, 2008:* Citigroup announced it would take an additional $18.1 billion write-down for the fourth quarter 2007 and a quarterly loss of $9.83 billion. Citigroup also announced that the Company lowered its dividend to $0.32 per share, a 40% decline from the Company's previous dividend disbursement.

• By March 2008, Citigroup shares traded below book value and the Company announced that it would lay off an additional 2,000 employees, bringing Citigroup's total layoff since the beginning of the subprime market crisis to more than 6,000.

• July 18, 2008: Citigroup announced it lost $2.5 billion in the second quarter, largely caused by $7.2 billion of write-downs of Citigroup's investments in mortgages and other loans and by weakness in the consumer market.

Plaintiffs also allege that Citigroup was exposed to the subprime mortgage market through its use of SIVs. Banks can create SIVs by borrowing cash (by selling commercial paper) and using the proceeds to purchase loans; in other words, the SIVs sell short term debt and buy longer-term, higher yielding assets. According to plaintiffs, Citigroup's SIVs invested in riskier assets, such as home equity loans, rather than the low-risk assets traditionally used by SIVs.

The problems in the subprime market left Citigroup's SIVs unable to pay their investors. The SIVs held subprime mortgages that had decreased in value, and the normally liquid commercial paper market became illiquid. Because the SIVs could no longer meet their cash needs by attracting new investors, they had to sell assets at allegedly "fire sale" prices. In November 2007, Citigroup disclosed that it provided $7.6 billion of emergency financing to the seven SIVs the Company operated after they were unable to repay maturing debt. Ultimately, Citigroup was forced to bail out seven of its affiliated

SIVs by bringing $49 billion in assets onto its balance sheet, notwithstanding that Citigroup previously represented that it would manage the SIVs on an arms-length basis.

Plaintiffs' Claims

Plaintiffs allege that defendants are liable to the Company for breach of fiduciary duty for (1) failing to adequately oversee and manage Citigroup's exposure to the problems in the subprime mortgage market, even in the face of alleged "red flags" and (2) failing to ensure that the Company's financial reporting and other disclosures were thorough and accurate.[6] As will be more fully explained below, the "red flags" alleged in the eighty-six page Complaint are generally statements from public documents that reflect worsening [115] conditions in the financial markets, including the subprime and credit markets, and the effects those worsening conditions had on market participants, including Citigroup's peers. By way of example only, plaintiffs' "red flags" include the following:

> • *May 27, 2005:* Economist Paul Krugman of the *New York Times* said he saw "signs that America's housing market, like the stock market at the end of the last decade, is approaching the final, feverish stages of a speculative bubble."

> • *May 2006:* Ameriquest Mortgage, one of the United States' leading wholesale subprime lenders, announced the closing of each of its 229 retail offices and reduction of 3,800 employees.

> • *February 12, 2007:* ResMae Mortgage, a subprime lender, filed for bankruptcy. According to *Bloomberg,* in its Chapter 11 filing, ResMae stated that "[t]he subprime mortgage market has recently been crippled and a number of companies stopped originating loans and United States housing sales have slowed and defaults by borrowers have risen."

> • *April 18, 2007:* Freddie Mac announced plans to refinance up to $20 billion of loans held by subprime borrowers who would be unable to afford their adjustable-rate mortgages at the reset rate.

• *July 10, 2007:* Standard and Poor's and Moody's downgraded bonds backed by subprime mortgages.

• *August 1, 2007:* Two hedge funds managed by Bear Stearns that invested heavily in subprime mortgages declared bankruptcy.

• *August 9, 2007:* American International Group, one of the largest United States mortgage lenders, warned that mortgage defaults were spreading beyond the subprime sector, with delinquencies becoming more common among borrowers in the category just above subprime.

• *October 18, 2007:* Standard & Poor's cut the credit ratings on $23.35 billion of securities backed by pools of home loans that were offered to borrowers during the first half of the year. The downgrades even hit securities rated AAA, which was the highest of the ten investment-grade ratings and the rating of government debt.[7]

Plaintiffs also allege that the director defendants and certain other defendants are liable to the Company for waste for: (1) allowing the Company to purchase $2.7 billion in subprime loans from Accredited Home Lenders in March 2007 and from Ameriquest Home Mortgage in September 2007; (2) authorizing and not suspending the Company's share repurchase program in the first quarter of 2007, which allegedly resulted in the Company buying its own shares at "artificially inflated prices;" (3) approving a multi-million dollar payment and benefit package for defendant Prince upon his retirement as Citigroup's CEO in November 2007; and (4) allowing the Company to invest in SIVs that were unable to pay off maturing debt.

THE MOTION TO DISMISS UNDER RULE 23.1

A. The Legal Standard for Demand Excused

The decision whether to initiate or pursue a lawsuit on behalf of the corporation is generally within the power and responsibility of the board of directors.[25] This follows from the "cardinal precept of the General Corporation Law of the State of Delaware ... that directors, rather than shareholders, manage the business and affairs of the corporation."[26] Accordingly, in order to cause the corporation to pursue litigation, a shareholder must either (1) make a pre-suit demand by presenting the allegations to the corporation's directors, requesting that they bring suit, and showing that they wrongfully refused to do so, or (2) plead facts showing that demand upon the board would have been futile.[27] Where, as here, a plaintiff does not make a pre-suit demand on the board of directors, the complaint must plead with particularity facts showing that a demand on the board would have been futile.[28] The purpose of the demand requirement is not to insulate defendants from liability; rather, the demand requirement and the strict requirements of factual particularity under Rule 23.1 "exist[] to preserve the primacy of board decisionmaking regarding legal claims belonging to the corporation."[29]

Under the familiar *Aronson* test, to show demand futility, plaintiffs must provide particularized factual allegations that raise a reasonable doubt that "(1) the directors are disinterested and independent [or] (2) the challenged transaction was otherwise the product of a valid exercise of business judgment."[30] Where, however, plaintiffs complain of board inaction and do not challenge a specific decision of the board, there is no "challenged transaction," and the ordinary *Aronson* analysis does not apply.[31] Instead, to show demand futility where the subject of the derivative suit is not a business decision of the board, a plaintiff must allege particularized facts that "create a reasonable doubt that, as of the time the complaint is filed, the board of directors could have properly exercised its independent and disinterested business judgment in responding to a demand."[32]

In evaluating whether demand is excused, the Court must accept as true the well pleaded factual allegations in the Complaint. […]To establish that demand is excused under Rule 23.1, the pleadings must comply with "stringent requirements of factual particularity" and set forth "particularized factual statements that are essential to the [121] claim."[33] "A prolix complaint larded with conclusory language ... does not comply with these fundamental pleading mandates."[34] […]

Demand is not excused solely because the directors would be deciding to sue themselves.[35] Rather, demand will be excused based on a possibility of personal director liability only in the rare case when a plaintiff is able to show director conduct that is "so egregious on its face that board approval cannot meet the test of business judgment, and a substantial likelihood of director liability therefore exists."[36]

B. Demand Futility Regarding Plaintiffs' Fiduciary Duty Claims

Plaintiffs' argument is based on a theory of director liability famously articulated by former-Chancellor Allen in *In re Caremark*.[…]

In *Stone v. Ritter,* the Delaware Supreme Court approved the *Caremark* standard for director oversight liability and made clear that liability was based on the concept of good faith, which the *Stone* Court held was embedded in the fiduciary duty of loyalty and did not constitute a freestanding fiduciary duty that [123] could independently give rise to liability.[…]

Thus, to establish oversight liability a plaintiff must show that the directors *knew* they were not discharging their fiduciary obligations or that the directors demonstrated a *conscious* disregard for their responsibilities such as by failing to act in the face of a known duty to act.[46] The test is rooted in concepts of bad faith; indeed, a showing of bad faith is a *necessary condition* to director oversight liability.[47]

1. Plaintiffs' Caremark Allegations

Plaintiffs' theory of how the director defendants will face personal liability is a bit of a twist on the traditional *Caremark* claim. In a typical *Caremark* case, plaintiffs argue that the defendants are liable for damages that arise from a failure to properly monitor or oversee employee misconduct or violations of law. […]

In contrast, plaintiffs' *Caremark* claims are based on defendants' alleged failure to properly monitor Citigroup's *business risk,* specifically its exposure to the subprime mortgage market. In their answering brief, plaintiffs allege that the director defendants are personally liable under *Caremark* for failing to "make a good faith [124] attempt to follow the procedures put in place or fail[ing] to assure that adequate and proper corporate information and reporting systems existed that would enable them to be fully informed regarding Citigroup's risk to the subprime mortgage market."[49] Plaintiffs point to so-called "red flags" that should have put defendants on notice of the problems in the subprime mortgage market and further allege that the board should have been especially conscious of these red flags because a majority of the directors (1) served on the Citigroup board during its previous Enron related conduct and (2) were members of the ARM Committee and considered financial experts.

Although these claims are framed by plaintiffs as *Caremark* claims, plaintiffs' theory essentially amounts to a claim that the director defendants should be personally liable to the Company because they failed to fully recognize the risk posed by subprime securities. When one looks past the lofty allegations of duties of oversight and red flags used to dress up these claims, what is left appears to be plaintiff shareholders attempting to hold the director defendants personally liable for making (or allowing to be made) business decisions that, in hindsight, turned out poorly for the Company. Delaware Courts have faced these types of claims many times and have developed doctrines to deal with them—the fiduciary duty of care and the business judgment rule. These doctrines properly focus on the decision-making process rather than on a substantive evaluation of the merits of the decision. This follows from the inadequacy of the Court, due in part to a concept known as hindsight bias,[50] to properly evaluate whether corporate decision-makers made a "right" or "wrong" decision.

The business judgment rule "is a presumption that in making a business decision the directors of a corporation acted on an informed basis, in good faith and in the honest belief that the action taken was in the best interests of the company."[51] The burden is on plaintiffs, the party challenging the directors' decision, to rebut this presumption.[52] Thus, absent an allegation of interestedness or disloyalty to the corporation, the business judgment rule prevents a judge or jury from second guessing director decisions if they were the product of a rational process and the directors availed themselves of all material and reasonably available information. The standard of director liability under the business judgment rule "is predicated upon concepts of gross negligence."[53]

Additionally, Citigroup has adopted a provision in its certificate of incorporation pursuant to 8 *Del. C.* § 102(b)(7) that exculpates directors from personal liability for violations of fiduciary duty, except for, among other things, breaches of the duty of loyalty or actions or omissions not in good faith or that involve intentional misconduct or a knowing violation of law. Because the director defendants are "exculpated from liability for certain conduct, `then a serious threat of liability may only be found to exist if the plaintiff pleads a [125] *non-exculpated* claim against the directors based on particularized facts.'"[54] Here, plaintiffs have not alleged that the directors were interested in the transaction and instead root their theory of director personal liability in bad faith.

The Delaware Supreme Court has stated that bad faith conduct may be found where a director "intentionally acts with a purpose other than that of advancing the best interests of the corporation, ... acts with the intent to violate applicable positive law, or ... intentionally fails to act in the face of a known duty to act, demonstrating a conscious disregard for his duties."|[...] A plaintiff can thus plead bad faith by alleging with particularity that a director *knowingly* violated a fiduciary duty or failed to act in violation of a *known* duty to act, demonstrating a *conscious* disregard for her duties.

Turning now specifically to plaintiffs' *Caremark* claims, one can see a similarity between the standard for assessing oversight liability and the standard for assessing a disinterested director's decision under the duty of care when the company has adopted an exculpatory provision pursuant to § 102(b)(7). In either case, a plaintiff can show that the director defendants will be liable if their acts or omissions constitute bad faith. A plaintiff can show bad faith conduct by, for example, properly alleging particularized facts that show that a director *consciously* disregarded an obligation to be reasonably informed about the business and its risks or *consciously* disregarded the duty to monitor and oversee the business.

[...]The presumption of the business judgment rule, the protection of an exculpatory § 102(b)(7) provision, and the difficulty of proving a *Caremark* claim together function to place an extremely high burden on a plaintiff to state a claim for personal director liability for a failure to see the extent of a company's business risk.

[...]To the extent the Court allows shareholder plaintiffs to succeed on a theory that a director is liable for a failure to monitor business risk, the Court risks undermining the well settled policy of Delaware law by inviting Courts to perform a hindsight evaluation of the reasonableness or prudence of directors' business decisions. Risk has been defined as the chance that a return on an investment will be different that expected. The essence of the business judgment of managers and directors is deciding how the company will evaluate the trade-off between risk and return. Businesses—and particularly financial institutions—make returns by taking on risk; a company or investor that is willing to take on more risk can earn a higher return. Thus, in almost any business transaction, the parties go into the deal with the knowledge that, even if they have evaluated the situation correctly, the return could be different than they expected.

It is almost impossible for a court, in hindsight, to determine whether the directors of a company properly evaluated risk and thus made the "right" business decision.[58] In any investment there is a chance that returns will turn out lower than expected, and generally a smaller chance that they will be far lower than expected. When investments turn out poorly, it is possible that the decision-maker evaluated the deal correctly but got "unlucky" in that a huge loss—the probability of which was very small—actually happened. It is also possible that the decision-maker improperly evaluated the risk posed by an investment and that the company suffered large losses as a result.

Business decision-makers must operate in the real world, with imperfect information, limited resources, and an uncertain future. To impose liability on directors for making a "wrong" business decision would cripple their ability to earn returns for investors by taking business risks. Indeed, this kind of judicial second guessing is what the business judgment rule was designed to prevent, and even if a complaint is framed under a *Caremark* theory, this Court will not abandon such bedrock principles of Delaware fiduciary duty law. [...]

The allegations in the Complaint amount essentially to a claim that Citigroup suffered large losses and that there were certain warning signs that could or should have put defendants on notice of the business [127] risks related to Citigroup's investments in subprime assets. Plaintiffs then conclude that because defendants failed to prevent the Company's losses associated with certain business risks, they must have consciously ignored these warning signs or knowingly failed to monitor the Company's risk in accordance with their fiduciary duties.[59] Such conclusory allegations, however, are not sufficient to state a claim for failure of oversight that would give rise to a substantial likelihood of personal liability, which would require particularized factual allegations demonstrating bad faith by the director defendants.

Plaintiffs do not contest that Citigroup had procedures and controls in place that were designed to monitor risk. Plaintiffs admit that Citigroup established the ARM Committee and in 2004 amended the ARM Committee charter to include the fact that one of the purposes of the ARM Committee was to assist the board in fulfilling its oversight responsibility relating to policy standards and guidelines for risk assessment and risk management.[...]

Plaintiffs nevertheless argue that the director defendants breached their duty of oversight either because the oversight mechanisms were not adequate or because the director defendants did not make a good faith effort to comply with the established oversight procedures. [...]

Plaintiffs argue that demand is excused because a majority of the director defendants face a substantial likelihood of personal liability because they were charged with management of Citigroup's risk as members of the ARM Committee and as audit committee financial experts and [128] failed to properly oversee and monitor such risk.[[...]

The warning signs alleged by plaintiffs are not evidence that the directors consciously disregarded their duties or otherwise acted in bad faith; at most they evidence that the directors made bad business decisions. The "red flags" in the Complaint amount to little more than portions of public documents that reflected the worsening conditions in the subprime mortgage market and in the economy generally. Plaintiffs fail to plead "particularized facts suggesting that the Board was presented with `red flags' alerting it to potential misconduct" at the Company.[...] Nothing about plaintiffs' "red flags" supports plaintiffs' conclusory allegation that "defendants have not made a good faith attempt to assure that adequate and proper corporate information and reporting systems existed that would enable them to be fully informed regarding Citigroup's risk to the subprime mortgage market."[...]

The Complaint and plaintiffs' answering brief repeatedly make the conclusory allegation that the defendants have breached their duty of oversight, but nowhere do plaintiffs adequately explain what the director defendants actually did or failed to do that would constitute such a violation. Even while admitting that Citigroup had a risk monitoring system in place, plaintiffs seem to conclude that, because the director defendants (and the ARM Committee members in particular) were charged with monitoring Citigroup's risk, then they must be found liable because Citigroup experienced losses as a result of exposure [130] to the subprime mortgage market. The only factual support plaintiffs provide for this conclusion are "red flags" that actually amount to nothing more than signs of continuing deterioration in the subprime mortgage market. These types of conclusory allegations are exactly the kinds of allegations that do not state a claim for relief under *Caremark*.

To recognize such claims under a theory of director oversight liability would undermine the long established protections of the business judgment rule. It is well established that the mere fact that a company takes on business risk and suffers losses—even catastrophic losses—does not evidence misconduct, and without more, is not a basis for personal director liability.[…] That there were signs in the market that reflected worsening conditions and suggested that conditions may deteriorate even further is not an invitation for this Court to disregard the presumptions of the business judgment rule and conclude that the directors are liable because they did not properly evaluate business risk. What plaintiffs are asking the Court to conclude from the presence of these "red flags" is that the directors failed to see the extent of Citigroup's business risk and therefore made a "wrong" business decision by allowing Citigroup to be exposed to the subprime mortgage market. […]

4.3.7 Violations of the law and the duty of loyalty

Sometimes in the popular press or in the media (movies, television, etc.) you will see discussions about how directors of the corporation might have a fiduciary obligation to pursue corporate profits even if to do so requires the corporation to adopt a policy of violating the law. Nothing can be further from the truth. Delaware courts, as well as other state courts, have repeatedly and unequivocally ruled that directors who adopt corporate policies to violate the law are not acting in the best interests of the corporation and are, therefore, disloyal directors.

Given that certificates of incorporation limit the purpose of the corporation for "any lawful purpose for which a corporation may be organized." If a corporate board pursues, as a matter of corporate policy, activities which are illegal or contrary to a positive law, then such acts are also *ultra vires*, or outside the scope of permitted activities for corporate activity.

In addition, directors are not exculpated from financial liability under §102(b)(7) for "acts or omissions not in good faith or which involve intentional misconduct or a knowing violation of the law." Consequently, a director who intentionally causes the firm to violate the law has violated their duty of good faith (i.e. loyalty) to the corporation and may be subject to financial liability.

Below are a series of representative cases on this same point.

TW Services v SWT Acquisition Corp

Chancellor Allen described the duty of loyalty as requiring directors to endeavor to "manage the corporation within the law, with due care and in a way intended to maximize the long run interests of shareholders."

TW Servs., Inc. v. SWT Acquisition Corp., C.A. Nos. 10427, 10298, 1989 WL 20290, at *7 (Del. Ch. Mar. 2, 1989)

Metro Commc'n Corp. BVI v. Advanced Mobilecomm Techs. Inc.

Holding that if directors engaged in unlawful bribery for the purpose of helping the corporation obtain governmental permits, they have violated their "duty of loyalty" and further stating that "[u]nder Delaware law, a fiduciary may not choose to manage an entity in an illegal fashion, even if the fiduciary believes that the illegal activity will result in profits for the entity."

Metro Commc'n Corp. BVI v. Advanced Mobilecomm Techs. Inc., 854 A.2d 121, 131, 163–64 (Del. Ch. 2004)

Guttman v. Huang

"[O]ne cannot act loyally as a corporate director by causing the corporation to violate the positive laws it is obliged to obey."

Guttman v. Huang, 823 A.2d 492, 506 (Del. Ch. 2003)

Miller v. Am. Tel. & Tel. Co.

"[D]irectors must be restrained from engaging in activities which are against public policy."

Miller v. Am. Tel. & Tel. Co., 507 F.2d 759, 762 (3d Cir. 1974)

Roth v. Robertson

"Where the directors and officers of a corporation engage in ultra vires transactions [illegal acts], and they cause loss to the corporation, they must be held jointly and severally liable for such damages."

Roth v. Robertson, 118 N.Y.S. 351, 353 (N.Y. Gen. Term 1909)

Desimone

"Directors have no authority knowingly to cause the corporation to become a rogue, exposing the corporation to penalties from criminal and civil regulators."

Desimone, 924 A.2d at 934.

In addition to a fiduciary duty claim against the directors for knowingly causing the corporation to violate a positive law, upon an application by the state Department of Justice, Delaware courts can, and do, revoke the corporate charters of firms that have been involved in corporate criminal activity. For example, Backpage.com, LLC ran a notorious website that faciliated sex trafficking. In its November 2018 application for revocation, the Delaware Attorney Gerneral restated the Delaware corporate law's view on law breaking activities of corporations:

> Delaware law has never permitted or condoned the use of business entities formed under its laws for unlawful or nefarious purposes, and thus Defendants' guilty pleas are proof that Defendants, and their principals, have abused and misused not only Defendants' powers and privileges, but their very existences, in perhaps the most reprehensible manner possible. Having abandoned the responsibilities that come with status as Delaware limited liability companies, Defendants must be forever denied the rights and privileges that also come with that status, and their certificates of formation must therefore be canceled.

> **Denn v. Backpage.com** (Nov. 2018)

4.3.8 Duty of Candor

A final fiduciary duty is the duty of candor or the duty of disclosure. Like good faith, the duty of candor is not an independent fiduciary duty, but rather - depending on the circumstances - a subsidiary element of the duty of loyalty or care. The duty of candor implicates a series of legal obligations under both state corporate law and Federal securities laws. The *Wayport* case that follows summarizes how the duty of candor is implicated depending on the circumstance.

4.3.8.1 In Re Wayport Inc. Litigation

In the following case Vice Chancellor Laster takes the opportunity in a disclosure case to outline the four varieties of disclosure obligations that directors have. Each one of them implicates either care or loyalty and implicates a different aspect of the law.

IN RE WAYPORT, INC. LITIGATION.
Consol. C.A. No. 4167-VCL.
Court of Chancery of Delaware.

LASTER, Vice Chancellor.

The plaintiffs sued for damages arising out of their sales of stock in Wayport, Inc. ("Wayport" or the "Company"). Vice Chancellor Lamb granted the defendants' motion to dismiss in part, and his rulings represent law of the case. *See Latesco, L.P. v. Wayport, Inc.,* 2009 WL 2246793 (Del. Ch. July 24, 2009) (the "Dismissal Opinion"). The litigation proceeded to trial against the remaining defendants on claims for breach of fiduciary duty, aiding and abetting a breach of fiduciary duty, common law fraud, and equitable fraud. Judgment is entered in favor of plaintiff Brett Stewart and against defendant Trellis Partners Opportunity Fund, L.P. ("Trellis Opportunity Fund") in the amount of $470,000, subject to an adjustment to be calculated by the parties in accordance with this opinion, plus pre- and post-judgment interest at the legal rate, compounded quarterly. Judgment otherwise is entered against the plaintiffs and in favor of the defendants. […]

A. The Claim For Breach Of Fiduciary Duty

The plaintiffs contended at trial that Trellis, NEA, Williams, and Wayport breached their fiduciary duties of loyalty. The plaintiffs did not carry their burden of proof, and judgment is entered in favor of the defendants on the fiduciary duty claim.

1. The Nature Of The Fiduciary Duty Claim

The plaintiffs contended that the defendants owed them fiduciary duties that included a duty to disclose material information when they purchased the plaintiffs' shares. Directors of a Delaware corporation owe two fiduciary duties: care and loyalty. *Stone ex rel. AmSouth Bancorporation v. Ritter,* 911 A.2d 362, 370 (Del. 2006). The "duty of disclosure is not an independent duty, but derives from the duties of care and loyalty." *Pfeffer v. Redstone,* 965 A.2d 676, 684 (Del. 2009) (internal quotation marks omitted). The duty of disclosure arises because of "the application in a specific context of the board's fiduciary duties . . . ." *Malpiede v. Townson,* 780 A.2d 1075, 1086 (Del. 2001). Its scope and requirements depend on context; the duty "does not exist in a vacuum." *Stroud v. Grace,* 606 A.2d 75, 85 (Del. 1992). When confronting a disclosure claim, a court therefore must engage in a contextual specific analysis to determine the source of the duty, its requirements, and any remedies for breach. *See* Lawrence A. Hamermesh, *Calling Off the Lynch Mob: The Corporate Director's Fiduciary Disclosure Duty,* 49 Vand. L. Rev. 1087, 1099 (1996). Governing principles have been developed for recurring scenarios, four of which are prominent.

The first recurring scenario is classic common law ratification, in which directors seek approval for a transaction that does not otherwise require a stockholder vote under the DGCL. *See Gantler v. Stephens,* 965 A.2d 695, 713 (Del. 2009) (describing ratification in its classic form); *id.* at 713 n.54 (distinguishing "the common law doctrine of shareholder ratification" from "the effect of an approving vote of disinterested shareholders" under 8 *Del. C.* § 144). If a director or officer has a personal interest in a transaction that conflicts with the interests of the corporation or its stockholders generally, and if the board of directors asks stockholders to ratify the transaction, then the directors have a duty "to disclose all facts that are material to the stockholders' consideration of the transaction and that are or can reasonably be obtained through their position as directors." Hamermesh, *supra,* at 1103. The failure to disclose material information in this context will eliminate any effect that a favorable stockholder vote otherwise might have for the validity of the transaction or for the applicable standard of review. *Id.*; *see Gantler,* 965 A.2d at 713 ("With one exception, the `cleansing' effect of such a ratifying shareholder vote is to subject the challenged director action to business judgment review, as opposed to `extinguishing' the claim altogether (*i.e.,* obviating all judicial review of the challenged action)."); *id.* at 713 n.54 ("The only species of claim that shareholder ratification can validly extinguish is a claim that the directors lacked the authority to take action that was later ratified. Nothing herein should be read as altering the well-established principle that void acts such as fraud, gift, waste and ultra vires acts cannot be ratified by a less than unanimous shareholder vote.").

A second and quite different scenario involves a request for stockholder action. When directors submit to the stockholders a transaction that requires stockholder approval (such as a merger, sale of assets, or charter amendment) or which requires a stockholder investment decision (such as tendering shares or making an appraisal election), but which is not otherwise an interested transaction, the directors have a duty to "exercise reasonable care to disclose all facts that are material to the stockholders' consideration of the transaction or matter and that are or can reasonably be obtained through their position as directors." Hamermesh, *supra,* at 1103; *see Stroud,* 606 A.2d at 84 ("[D]irectors of Delaware corporations [have] a fiduciary duty to disclose fully and fairly all material information within the board's control when it seeks shareholder action."). A failure to disclose material information in this context may warrant an injunction against, or rescission of, the transaction, but will not provide a basis for damages from defendant directors absent proof of (i) a culpable state of mind or non-exculpated gross negligence, (ii) reliance by the stockholders on the information that was not disclosed, and (iii) damages proximately caused by that failure. *See Loudon v. Archer-Daniels-Midland Co.,* 700 A.2d 135, 146-47 (Del. 1997).

A third scenario involves a corporate fiduciary who speaks outside of the context of soliciting or recommending stockholder action, such as through "public statements made to the market," "statements informing shareholders about the affairs of the corporation," or public filings required by the federal securities laws. *Malone v. Brincat,* 722 A.2d 5, 11 (Del. 1998). In that context, directors owe a duty to stockholders not to speak falsely:

> Whenever directors communicate publicly or directly with
> shareholders about the corporation's affairs, with or without a
> request for shareholder action, directors have a fiduciary duty to
> shareholders to exercise due care, good faith and loyalty. It follows *a*
> *fortiori* that when directors communicate publicly or directly with
> shareholders about corporate matters the *sine qua non* of directors'
> fiduciary duty to shareholders is honesty.

Id. at 10. "[D]irectors who knowingly disseminate false information that results in corporate injury or damage to an individual stockholder violate their fiduciary duty, and may be held accountable in a manner appropriate to the circumstances." *Id.* at 9; *see id.* at 14 ("When the directors are not seeking shareholder action, but are deliberately misinforming shareholders about the business of the corporation, either directly or by a public statement, there is a violation of fiduciary duty."). Breach "may result in a derivative claim on behalf of the corporation," "a cause of action for damages," or "equitable relief . . . ." *Id.*

The fourth scenario arises when a corporate fiduciary buys shares directly from or sells shares directly to an existing outside stockholder. Hamermesh, *supra,* at 1103. Under the "special facts doctrine" adopted by the Delaware Supreme Court in *Lank v. Steiner,* 224 A.2d 242 (Del. 1966), a director has a fiduciary duty to disclose information in the context of a private stock sale "only when a director is possessed of special knowledge of future plans or secret resources and deliberately misleads a stockholder who is ignorant of them." *Id.* at 244. If this standard is met, a duty to speak exists, and the director's failure to disclose material information is evaluated within the framework of common law fraud. If the standard is not met, then the director does not have a duty to speak and is liable only to the same degree as a non-fiduciary would be. It bears emphasizing that the duties that exist in this context do not apply to purchases or sales in impersonal secondary markets. *See* Hamermesh, *supra,* at 1153 & n.296. Transactions in the public markets are distinctly different. *See, e.g., In re Am. Int'l Gp., Inc.,* 965 A.2d 763, 800 (Del. Ch. 2009), *aff'd,* 11 A.3d 228 (Del. 2011) (TABLE); *In re Oracle Corp.,* 867 A.2d 904, 932-33, 953 (Del. Ch. 2004), *aff'd,* 872 A.2d 960 (Del. 2005); *Guttman v. Huang,* 823 A.2d 492, 505 (Del. Ch. 2003).

The current case originally raised the second, third, and fourth scenarios, but only the fourth remains. Count I of the complaint was titled "Breach of Fiduciary Duty of Disclosure." Dkt. 25 at 20. At the motion to dismiss stage, it was understood to invoke the second scenario, *viz.*, the duty of disclosure in the context of a request for stockholder action. Vice Chancellor Lamb dismissed Count I on the grounds that "a call for an individual stockholder to sell his shares does not, without more, qualify as a call for stockholder action." Dismissal Op. at *6 n.18.

Count II of the complaint was titled "Breach of Fiduciary Duty of Loyalty." Dkt. 25 at 21. At the motion to dismiss stage, it was understood to invoke both the third scenario (the duty under *Malone* not to engage in deliberate falsehoods) and the fourth scenario (the duty to speak that a fiduciary may have in the context of a direct purchase of shares from a stockholder). As to the former, Vice Chancellor Lamb recognized that the "corporation and its officers and directors are, of course, subject to the underlying duty of loyalty not to make false statements or otherwise materially misrepresent the facts in such a way as to defraud the stockholder in any such negotiation [over the purchase of shares]." Dismissal Op. at *6 n.19 (citing *Malone,* 722 A.2d at 10). He held, however, that the complaint pled "no facts whatsoever to suggest that the company, or its directors or officers, made any knowingly false statements . . . ." *Id.* He therefore dismissed Count II as to the Company and the director defendants, effectively disposing of the *Malone* claim. As to the latter, Vice Chancellor Lamb denied the motion to dismiss, holding that Count II implicated the "normal standard of fraud, *as applied to transactions between corporate insiders* . . . ." Dismissal Op. at *5 (emphasis added). In a footnote, Vice Chancellor Lamb contrasted this variety of fraud with "the affirmative-misrepresentation or intentional concealment species of fraud (that is, the forms of fraud that do not require a duty to speak)" that applies to non-fiduciaries. *Id.* at *5 n.17. This remaining aspect of Count II was litigated and tried. […]

5 Corporate Waste

Although we all think we know what a waste is, the concept of corporate waste has a very specific meaning. As a legal standard, corporate waste claims are – along with good faith claims – among some of the hardest claims for plaintiffs to succeed on. Chancellor Allen observed that a successful waste claim is much like the Loch Ness monster:

"[T]he waste theory represents a theoretical exception to the statement very rarely encountered in the world of real transactions. There surely are cases of fraud; of unfair self-dealing and, much more rarely negligence. But rarest of all — and indeed like Nessie [of Loch Ness fame], possibly non-existent — would be the case of disinterested business people making non-fraudulent deals (non-negligently) that meet the legal standard of waste!" (Steiner v. Meyerson, Del. Ch., C.A. No. 13139, Allen, C. (July 18, 1995), Mem. Op. at 2, 1995 WL 441999.)

The judicial standard for determination of corporate waste is well developed. A waste entails an exchange of corporate assets for consideration so disproportionately small as to lie beyond the range at which any reasonable person might be willing to trade. Most often the claim is associated with a transfer of corporate assets that serves no corporate purpose; or for which no consideration at all is received. Such a transfer is in effect a gift. If, however, there is *any substantial* consideration received by the corporation, and if there is a *good faith judgment* that in the circumstances the transaction is worthwhile, there should be no finding of waste, even if the fact finder would conclude *ex post* that the transaction was unreasonably risky. Courts are ill-fitted to attempt to weigh the "adequacy" of consideration under the waste standard or, *ex post,* to judge appropriate degrees of business risk (Lewis v. Vogelstein, 699 A. 2d 327, 336 (1997).

Nevertheless, corporate waste claims are not uncommon. In recent years, plaintiffs have brought many corporate waste claims against boards for their executive compensation practices. Few – if any – of these claims are ever successful.

5.1 In Re The Goldman Sachs Group, Inc. Shareholder Litigation

In recent years executive compensation has soared to almost unimaginable levels. It is not uncommon to see headlines about an executive being paid multiple million dollars a year to run a failing business. You have probably seen headlines like those and thought to yourself: "What a waste." You wouldn't be alone.

Following the financial crisis of 2008 a number of very high profile cases were brought on behalf of stockholders against boards alleging among other things that the compensation schemes deployed by boards amounted to a "corporate waste" and that they even created incentives that encouraged excessive risk-taking, bringing the entire economy to the brink of collapse. Goldman Sachs, the case that follows, is an example of such a case. The court is asked to rule on whether the executive compensation plan approved by the board amounted to a "corporate waste". As you will see this standard is very difficult to meet.

IN RE THE GOLDMAN SACHS GROUP, INC. SHAREHOLDER LITIGATION
Civil Action No. 5215-VCG
Court of Chancery of Delaware

GLASSCOCK, Vice Chancellor.

The Plaintiffs allege that the Director Defendants breached their fiduciary duties by approving the compensation structure discussed above. Additionally, the Plaintiffs claim that the payments under this compensation structure constituted corporate waste. […]

C. Compensation

Goldman employed a "pay for performance" philosophy linking the total compensation of its employees to the company's performance.[11] Goldman has used a Compensation Committee since at least 2006 to oversee the development and implementation of its compensation scheme.[12] The Compensation Committee was responsible for reviewing and approving the Goldman executives' annual compensation.[13] To fulfill their charge, the Compensation Committee consulted with senior management about management's projections of net revenues and the proper ratio of compensation and benefits expenses to net revenues (the "compensation ratio").[14] Additionally, the Compensation Committee compared Goldman's compensation ratio to that of Goldman's competitors such as Bear Stearns, Lehman Brothers, Merrill Lynch, and Morgan Stanley. The

Compensation Committee would then approve a ratio and structure that Goldman would use to govern Goldman's compensation to its employees.[15]

The Plaintiffs allege that from 2007 through 2009, the Director Defendants approved a management-proposed compensation structure that caused management's interests to diverge from those of the stockholders.[16] According to the Plaintiffs, in each year since 2006 the Compensation Committee approved the management-determined compensation ratio, which governed "the total amount of funds available to compensate all employees including senior executives," without any analysis.[17] Although the total compensation paid by Goldman varied significantly each year, total compensation as a percentage of net revenue remained relatively constant.[18] Because management was awarded a relatively constant percentage of total revenue, management could maximize their compensation by increasing Goldman's total net revenue and total stockholder equity.[19] The Plaintiffs contend that this compensation structure led management to pursue a highly risky business strategy that emphasized short term profits in order to increase their yearly bonuses.[20] [...]

E. The Plaintiffs' Claims

The Plaintiffs allege that the Director Defendants breached their fiduciary duties by [...] (2) committing waste by "approving a compensation ratio to Goldman employees in an amount so disproportionately large to the contribution of management, as opposed to capital as to be unconscionable."[50] [...]

3. Waste

The Plaintiffs also contend that Goldman's compensation levels were unconscionable and constituted waste. To sustain their claim that demand would be futile, the Plaintiffs must raise a reasonable doubt that Goldman's compensation levels were the product of a valid business judgment. Specifically, to excuse demand on a waste claim, the Plaintiffs must plead particularized allegations that "overcome the general presumption of good faith by showing that the board's decision was so egregious or irrational that it could not have been based on a valid assessment of the corporation's best interests."[152]

"[W]aste entails an exchange of corporate assets for consideration so disproportionately small as to lie beyond the range at which any reasonable person might be willing to trade."[153] Accordingly, if "there is any *substantial* consideration received by the corporation, and if there is a *good faith judgment* that in the circumstances the transaction is worthwhile, there should be no finding of waste."[154] The reason being, "[c]ourts are ill-fitted to attempt to weigh the `adequacy' of consideration under the waste standard or, *ex post,* to judge appropriate degrees of business risk."[155] Because of this, "[i]t is the essence of business judgment for a board to determine if a particular individual warrant[s] large amounts of money."[156]

The Plaintiffs' waste allegations revolve around three premises: that Goldman's pay per employee is significantly higher than its peers, that Goldman's compensation ratios should be compared to hedge funds and other shareholder funds to reflect Goldman's increasing reliance on proprietary trading as opposed to traditional investment banking services, and that Goldman's earnings and related compensation are only the result of risk taking.

The Plaintiffs consciously do not identify a particular individual or person who received excessive compensation, but instead focus on the average compensation received by each of Goldman's 31,000 employees.[157] The Plaintiffs allege that "Goldman consistently allocated and distributed anywhere from two to six times the amounts that its peers distributed to each employee,"[158] and the Plaintiffs provide comparisons of Goldman's average pay per employee to firms such as Morgan Stanley, Bear Stearns, Merrill Lynch, Citigroup, and Bank of America.[159] The Plaintiffs note that these firms are investment banks, but do not provide any indication of why these firms are comparable to Goldman or their respective primary areas of business. The Plaintiffs do not compare trading segment to trading segment or any other similar metric. A broad assertion that Goldman's board devoted more resources to compensation than did other firms, standing alone, is not a particularized factual allegation creating a reasonable doubt that Goldman's compensation levels were the product of a valid business judgment.

The Plaintiffs urge that, in light of Goldman's increasing reliance on proprietary trading, Goldman's employees' compensation should be compared against a hedge fund or other shareholder fund.[160] The Plaintiffs allege that Goldman's compensation scheme is equal to 2% of net assets and 45% of the net income produced, but a typical hedge fund is only awarded 2% of net assets and 20% of the net income produced.[161] The Plaintiffs paradoxically assert that "no hedge fund manager may command compensation for managing assets at the annual rate of 2% of net assets and 45% of net revenues," but then immediately acknowledge that in fact there are hedge funds that have such compensation schemes.[162] It is apparent to me from the allegations of the complaint that while the majority of hedge funds may use a "2 and 20" compensation scheme, this is not the exclusive method used too set such compensation. Even if I were to conclude that a hedge fund or shareholder fund would be an appropriate yardstick with which to measure Goldman's compensation package and "even though the amounts paid to defendants exceeded the industry average," I fail to see a "shocking disparity" between the percentages that would render them "legally excessive."[163]

In the end, while the Goldman employees may not have been doing, in the words of the complaint and Defendant Blankfein, "God's Work,"[164] the complaint fails to present facts that demonstrate that the work done by Goldman's 31,000 employees was of such limited value to the corporation that no reasonable person in the directors' position would have approved their levels of compensation.[165] Absent such facts, these decisions are the province of the board of directors rather than the courts.[166] Without examining the payment to a specific individual, or group of individuals, and what was specifically done in exchange for that payment, I am unable to determine whether a transaction is "so one sided that no business person of ordinary, sound judgment could conclude that the corporation has received adequate consideration."[167]

The closest the Plaintiffs come to pleading waste with any factual particularity is in regards to the payment to the Trading and Principal Investment segment in 2008. The Plaintiffs allege that in 2008 "the Trading and Principal Investments segment produced $9.06 billion in net revenue, but, as a result of discretionary bonuses paid to employees, lost more than $2.7 billion for the [stockholders]."[168] The Plaintiffs' allegations, however, are insufficient to raise a reasonable doubt that Goldman's compensation levels in this segment were the product of a valid business judgment. As a strictly pedagogic exercise, imagine a situation where one half of the traders lost money, and the other half made the same amount of money, so that the firm broke even. Even if no bonus was awarded to the half that lost money, a rational manager would still want to award a bonus to the half that did make money in order to keep that talent from leaving. Since net trading gains were $0, these bonuses would cause a net loss, but there would

446

not be a waste of corporate assets because there was adequate consideration for the bonuses. Without specific allegations of unconscionable transactions and details regarding who was paid and for what reasons they were paid, the Plaintiffs fail to adequately plead demand futility on the basis of waste.

Finally, the Plaintiffs herald the fact that during the sub-prime crisis the Director Defendants continued to allocate similar percentages of net revenue as compensation while the firm was engaged in risky transactions; however, "there should be no finding of waste, even if the fact finder would conclude *ex post* that the transaction was unreasonably risky. Any other rule would deter corporate boards from the optimal rational acceptance of risk."[169] Because this complaint lacks a particular pleading that an individual or group of individuals was engaged in transactions so unconscionable that no rational director could have compensated them, the Plaintiffs have failed to raise a reasonable doubt that the compensation decisions were not the product of a valid business judgment. […]

5.2 Seinfeld v. Slager

Stockholder challenges to excessive executive compensation packages are relatively common. For the most part, such challenges are extremely difficult for plaintiffs to win. In most instances, the executives' pay is approved by a disinterested board of directors. As you already know, a disinterested board making an informed decision will receive the protection of the business judgment presumption when the decision to pay an executive a large amount of money is challenged by stockholders. Because it is extremely difficult to plead demand futility in such cases, they are often characterized as "waste" claims in order to access *Aronson*'s second prong.

Some believe that boards have an obligation to minimize tax liability or to avoid paying taxes. Such a view has never been supported by any corporate law doctrine. Nevertheless, that fact does not stop some litigants from bringing challenges against board decisions with respect to tax strategy. Such challenges, assuming a disinterested and reasonably informed board are doomed for failure. Consequently, plaintiffs who bring such claims are left to characterize such claims as "waste" claims.

One area where plaintiffs are more successful is in claims against directors, rather than executives, for director compensation. Although directors are expressly authorized by statute to set their own pay (DGCL 141(h)), the levels of such pay can give courts pause. Plaintiffs are obviously more successful in such cases because by their nature, directors are interested parties in their own pay. Consequently, plaintiffs are much more likely to succeed in overcoming *Aronson*'s demand futility pleading burden.

In Seinfeld, the court deals with all three of these issues.

SEINFELD v. SLAGER
Court of Chancery of Delaware.
Submitted: April 25, 2012

GLASSCOCK, Vice Chancellor.

I. BACKGROUND

A. Parties

The Plaintiff, Frank David Seinfeld, is a stockholder of Republic Services, Inc. ("Republic" or the "Company"), who has held Republic stock during all relevant times.

Defendant Republic is a Delaware corporation that engages in waste hauling and waste disposal.[1]

Defendants James E. O'Connor, Donald W. Slager, John W. Croghan, James W. Crownover, William J. Flynn, David I. Foley, Michael Larson, Nolan Lehmann, W. Lee Nutter, Ramon A. Rodriguez, Allan Sorensen, John M. Trani, and Michael W. Wickham are members of Republic's board of directors (collectively, the "Defendant Directors"). [...]

II. STANDARDS OF REVIEW

The Defendants have moved to dismiss all claims under Court of Chancery Rule 12(b)(6) for failure to state a claim. Except for the excessive compensation claim, the Defendants have also moved to dismiss pursuant to Rule 23.1, on the basis that the

Plaintiff has failed to make demand or plead particularized facts that demonstrate demand futility.

The Plaintiff alleges that demand is excused for all his claims because the challenged transactions were not the product of a valid exercise of business judgment. The Plaintiff also alleges that demand is futile because the Defendants were interested or lacked independence in the stock option claim and the excessive compensation claim. [...]

C. Demand Futility

The Plaintiff challenges affirmative decisions by Republic's board and has failed to make pre-suit demand; therefore, to show demand futility, under the well-known *Aronson* test, the Plaintiff must allege particularized facts that raise a reason to doubt that "(1) the directors are disinterested and independent [or] (2) the challenged transaction was otherwise the product of a valid exercise of business judgment."[12] Under the first prong of *Aronson,* a director is interested if he sits on both sides of a transaction or derives a benefit from a transaction that is not shared by the corporation or all stockholders generally.[13] A director is not interested merely because he is named as a defendant in a suit, and generally, an inference of financial interest is not imputed to a director solely because he receives customary compensation for his board service.[14] When addressing *Aronson*'s second prong, there is a presumption that the business judgment rule applies, and the plaintiff must rebut this presumption by pleading "particularized facts to create a reasonable doubt that either (1) the action was taken honestly and in good faith or (2) the board was adequately informed in making the decision."[15]

D. Waste

Demand may be excused under the second prong of *Aronson* if a plaintiff properly pleads a waste claim.[16] In a derivative suit, this Court analyzes each of the challenged transactions individually to determine demand futility.[17] The Plaintiff here alleges that he has adequately pled waste for each of his claims and that demand should be excused.

"[T]he doctrine of waste is a residual protection for stockholders that polices the outer boundaries of the broad field of discretion afforded directors by the business judgment rule."[18] As such, a plaintiff faces an uphill battle in bringing a waste claim, and a plaintiff "must allege particularized facts that lead to a reasonable inference that the director defendants authorized `an exchange that is so one sided that no business person of ordinary, sound judgment could conclude that the corporation has received adequate consideration.'"[19] "Where, however, the corporation has received `any substantial consideration' and where the board has made `a good faith judgment that in the circumstances the transaction was worthwhile,' a finding of waste is inappropriate, even if hindsight proves that the transaction may have been ill-advised."[20] This Court has described the waste standard as "an extreme test, very rarely satisfied by a shareholder plaintiff, because if under the circumstances any reasonable person might conclude that the deal made sense, then the judicial inquiry ends."[21] The rationale behind these stringent requirements is that "[c]ourts are ill-fitted to attempt to weigh the adequacy of consideration under the waste standard or, *ex post,* to judge the appropriate degrees of business risk."[22]

E. Taxes

The Plaintiff argues that demand should be excused under *Aronson*'s second prong on the ground that he has properly pleaded that the Defendants failed to minimize taxes. The Plaintiff appears to contend that there is an independent duty to minimize taxes, or alternatively that the failure to minimize taxes is *per se* a waste of corporate assets. The Plaintiff, however, does not point to any Delaware jurisprudence for this position; instead, the Plaintiff presents a smattering of inapposite cases from various other jurisdictions which I find logically unpersuasive.[23]

This Court has concluded that "there is no general fiduciary duty to minimize taxes."[24] There are a variety of reasons why a company may choose or not choose to take advantage of certain tax savings,[25] and generally a company's tax policy "typif[ies] an area of corporate decision-making best left to management's business judgment, so long as it is exercised in an appropriate fashion."[26] I am not foreclosing the theoretical possibility that under certain circumstances overpayment of taxes might be the result of a breach of a fiduciary duty.[27] I am simply noting that a decision to pursue or forgo tax savings is generally a business decision for the board of directors. Accordingly, despite the Plaintiff's contentions, Delaware law is clear that there is no separate duty to minimize taxes, and a failure to do so is not automatically a waste of corporate assets.

Using the above standards, I now address the Plaintiff's claims and the facts relevant thereto.

III. FACTS AND ANALYSIS

A. Past Consideration

Defendant O'Connor worked for Republic, serving as its CEO and a member of its board, for 10 years.[28] During this time, O'Connor was compensated for his services.[29] O'Connor signed an employment agreement (the "Employment Agreement") with the company, effective May 14, 2009, that provided him with retirement benefits such as a $10 million payment, health benefits, and stock options.[30] On June 24, 2010, the Company accepted O'Connor's retirement as CEO, to be effective on January 1, 2011;[31] however, the next day, on June 25, 2010, O'Connor signed a "Retirement Agreement" with the Company that provided him with a variety of retirement benefits in return for stated consideration, which included a release of claims and an assurance that his retirement occurred on "mutually acceptable terms."[32] One of the benefits conferred on O'Connor was a $1.8 million cash payment, given, according to the explicit terms of the Retirement Agreement, "to reward [O'Connor] for [his] long service to the Company."[33]

The Plaintiff contends that this $1.8 million payment was a gift constituting a waste of corporate assets. The Plaintiff alleges that the $1.8 million payment was not included in the May 14, 2009, employment agreement—and thus was not contractually required—and further argues that there is nothing in the expressed purpose of the payment—reward for service—indicating that the amount was reasonable in light of the services rendered[…]The Plaintiff, therefore, asserts that this $1.8 million payment was retroactive compensation, constituting a gift or waste.[35] The Defendants point to the Retirement Agreement and argue that O'Connor provided consideration for the $1.8 million payment, and also point out that the Plaintiff has failed to allege that the $1.8 million payment was unreasonable in light of O'Connor's past service to the company.[36] […]

1. Payment for Services Already Rendered

Earlier decisions of Delaware courts held that payment for services previously rendered and compensated generally would constitute a waste of corporate assets.[39] This Court has recognized, however, that there may be many sufficient reasons for a board to award a severance or retirement bonus.[40] Accordingly, the Court has declined to substitute its judgment for that of the board, even absent a contractual basis for the bonus, where the retroactive payment was not unreasonable under the circumstances.[41] [...]

In *Zucker v. Andreessen*, this Court recently addressed whether a generous severance package given to a departing executive in exchange for general releases constituted waste.[51] The plaintiff alleged that the company had no contractual obligation to provide the departing executive with a severance and the company could have avoided paying the executive severance because the company had grounds to terminate him for cause.[52] The *Zucker* court found that the general releases provided at least some consideration, that a portion of the severance pay awarded could represent reasonable compensation for past performance, and that an amicable severance of ties may have had some value.[53] The plaintiff, therefore, had not adequately pleaded that the severance package constituted waste, and the *Zucker* court dismissed the waste claim there under Rule 23.1.

[...]

2. Past Consideration and Waste

Employment compensation decisions are core functions of a board of directors, and are protected, appropriately, by the business judgment rule.[55] A plaintiff, as here, alleging waste arising from the decision of an independent board concerning employee compensation has set himself a Herculean, and perhaps Sisyphean, task. "Where . . . the corporation has received `any substantial consideration' and where the board has made `a good faith judgment that in the circumstances the transaction was worthwhile,' a finding of waste is inappropriate, even if hindsight proves that the transaction may have been ill-advised."[56]

A board of directors may have a variety of reasons for awarding an executive bonuses for services already rendered. For instance, awarding retroactive compensation to an employee who stays with the company may encourage him to continue his employment.[57] In the case of a retiring employee, the award may serve as a signal to current and future employees that they, too, might receive extra compensation at the end of their tenure if they successfully serve their term. Other factors may also properly influence the board, including ensuring a smooth and harmonious transfer of power, securing a good relationship with the retiring employee, preventing future embarrassing disclosure and lawsuits, and so on. Therefore, an informed and disinterested decision whether or not to award an employee a reasonable bonus for services that have already been rendered, for which the employee has already been compensated, properly falls within a board's business judgment.

Looked at in this light, the question then becomes whether the Employment Agreement was a transaction so lacking in value to the Company that no reasonable director could have been in favor of it; in other words, was the transaction so one-sided that it amounted to waste. The fact that an employee has already been compensated for his work goes directly to whether compensation is reasonable and whether there is a rational basis for "directors to conclude that the amount and form of compensation is appropriate and likely to be beneficial for the company."[58] This fact alone, however, is not determinative. It is simply another, albeit important, factor to be considered.

[…] The Retirement Agreement, considered as a whole, is clear from its explicit terms that it provided the cash bonus as part of a package intended to secure a general release, to provide continuity in the Board, and to ensure that O'Connor's separation from the Company was amicable.[60] It is clear, therefore, that there was some consideration for the benefits provided to O'Connor.[61]

Moreover, the Plaintiff fails to plead—let alone specifically allege—that the amount of the retirement bonus was unreasonable.[62] The Plaintiff only points to the Board's own description, in the Retirement Agreement itself, that the $1.8 million cash bonus was "to reward [O'Connor] for [his] long service to the Company."[63] The Plaintiff conflates "reward" with unreasonable gift. Most bonuses carry with them an aspect of reward for service, as the word bonus itself necessarily conveys. While the Plaintiff has adequately pleaded that the cash retirement bonus was not contractually required and was meant to, among other factors spelled out in the Retirement Agreement, reward O'Connor's service, he has failed to allege with particularity that the bonus was not made in good faith.

The Plaintiff's complaint is void of allegations which, if true, would lead to the conclusion that the retirement bonus, though retroactive and not required by prior contract, constituted waste. O'Connor had been CEO for ten years. He was Chairman of the Board of Directors. The Company had an interest in seeing that his separation was amicable, that he completed his term on the board, and that any potential sources of post-termination litigation were foreclosed, as well as in incentivizing O'Connor's successor and other employees. As part of his retirement package, the Board provided a cash bonus of $1.8 million. Is that bonus, in light of all the circumstances that were known to the board, "too much?" That is a core question for the Board of Directors. Because the Plaintiff has failed to plead with particularity facts that indicate that the amount of this bonus was unreasonable or that otherwise establish waste, the claim must be dismissed.

B. Incentive Award

In addition to challenging the $1.8 million payment to O'Connor, the Plaintiff attacks a $1.25 million incentive award also paid to O'Connor upon his retirement.[64] The Plaintiff contends that by paying O'Connor this award, Republic's compensation plan will be rendered non-tax-deductible.[65] The Plaintiff does not assert that the Defendant Directors were interested in the transaction; instead, the Plaintiff argues that demand is excused because the loss of this tax deduction constitutes a waste of company assets.[66]

1. The Taxman Cometh?

[…] § 162(m) provides that annual compensation in excess of $1 million is not tax-deductible unless the compensation is granted pursuant to a performance-based, stockholder-approved plan that contains pre-established, objective criteria. […]

The Company has such a stockholder-approved compensation plan, the Executive Incentive Plan (the "EIP").[68] Under the EIP, the Company pays performance bonuses to participating employees for meeting or exceeding certain performance goals, as measured by the Company's financial results.[…]

O'Connor participated in the EIP in 2009 and 2010[75] and had an employment contract, effective February 21, 2007, which provided that the Company would pay him upon his retirement the "full target amount" of his performance bonuses, i.e., the amount he would have received if he had worked for the entire bonus period and achieved his performance goal, with no pro-rata reduction.[76] This contract provided, therefore, that O'Connor would receive "the full target amount" of his performance bonuses regardless of whether O'Connor actually met the performance goal or worked for the entire applicable period..[…]

The Plaintiff's waste claim is that, hypothetically, O'Connor's compensation scheme will lead to an unnecessary payment to the federal government in the future, in the form of a greater tax bill.[89] The Plaintiff's waste claim, concerning the Board's decision to award O'Connor the full target amount, is unusual because the alleged tax ramifications have not actually occurred and there is nothing in the record suggesting when, if ever, they will occur.

This argument is facially unsound. I find that the decision of an independent board to rely, in setting compensation, on a revenue ruling of the IRS, is within the business judgment of the board, and that the Plaintiff's waste claim arising from this decision must be dismissed. […]

C. Stock Plan Awards

The Company also compensates employees through its 2007 Stock Incentive Plan (the "Stock Plan"), which allows the Company to grant stock awards to its employees, officers, and directors.[95] The Stock Plan's stated purpose is to "enable the Company to attract, retain, reward and motivate" employees, officers, and directors, and to "incentivize them to expend maximum effort for the growth and success of the Company."[96] The Stock Plan is administered by a committee of non-employee members of the Board, or if no committee exists, by the Board itself (the "Committee");[97] however, "with respect to the grant of Awards to non-employee directors, the Committee shall be the Board."[98] […]

The Defendant Directors are participants in the Stock Plan, and pursuant to it have awarded themselves time-vesting restricted stock units.[107] In 2009, the Board gave each Defendant Director, except O'Connor, restricted stock units worth $743,700. […] The Plaintiff alleges that the Defendant Directors' annual compensation far exceeds the compensation of directors by one of the Company's peers.[111]

Because the Defendant Directors awarded themselves these units, the Plaintiff asserts that they are interested in the transaction.[112] The Plaintiff contends that this compensation constitutes waste because the awards are unreasonable and are not tax-deductible.[…]

In *In re 3COM Corp. Shareholders Litigation,* the plaintiff contended that members of 3COM's board violated their fiduciary duties and wasted corporate assets when they granted themselves stock options under 3COM's stockholder approved Director Stock Option Plan.[115] The *3COM* plaintiff asserted that because the directors granted themselves the options under this plan, this transaction was a self-interested one and the plaintiff's claim should be reviewed under the entire fairness standard.[116] Then-Vice Chancellor Steele found that corporate directors who "administer a stockholder approved director stock option plan are entitled to the protection of the business judgment rule, and in absence of waste, a total failure of consideration, they do not breach their duty of loyalty by acting consistently with the terms of the stockholder-approved plan."[117] The Vice Chancellor explained:

> I do not see this as a case of directors independently or unilaterally granting themselves stock options, but instead a case where stock options accrued to these directors under the terms of an established option plan with *sufficiently defined terms.* One cannot plausibly contend that the directors structured and implemented a self-interested transaction inconsistent with the interests of the corporation and its shareholders when the shareholders knowingly set the parameters of the Plan, approved it in advance, and the directors implemented the Plan according to its terms. Precedent in this Court clearly establishes that "self-interested" director transactions made under a stock option plan approved by the corporation's shareholders are entitled to the benefit of the business judgment rule.[118]

Here, even though the stockholders approved the plan, the Defendant Directors are interested in self-dealing transactions under the Stock Plan. The Stock Plan lacks sufficient definition to afford the Defendant Directors protection under the business judgment rule. The sufficiency of definition that anoints a stockholder-approved option or bonus plan with business judgment rule protection exists on a continuum. Though the stockholders approved this plan, there must be some *meaningful* limit imposed by the stockholders on the Board for the plan to be consecrated by *3COM* and receive the blessing of the business judgment rule, else the "sufficiently defined terms" language of

3COM is rendered toothless. A stockholder-approved *carte blanche* to the directors is insufficient. The more definite a plan, the more likely that a board's compensation decision will be labeled disinterested and qualify for protection under the business judgment rule. If a board is free to use its absolute discretion under even a stockholder-approved plan, with little guidance as to the *total* pay that can be awarded, a board will ultimately have to show that the transaction is entirely fair.

In reading the Complaint and the Stock Plan, I find no effective limits on the total amount of pay that can be awarded through time-vesting restricted stock units. The plan before me confers on the Defendant Directors the theoretical ability to award themselves as much as tens of millions of dollars per year, with few limitations; therefore, I find that the Defendant Directors are interested in the decision to award themselves a substantial bonus. While the Defendant Directors may be able to show that the amounts they awarded themselves are entirely fair, their motion to dismiss must be denied with respect to this claim.

2. Time-Vesting Stock Options Granted to Employees

The Plaintiff's next claim addresses the Board's decision to award to employees certain forms of compensation instead of others. The Plaintiff alleges that while the Stock Plan allows the Board to grant both time-vesting and performance-vesting units, the Board breached its duties by only granting non-tax-deductible time-vesting [...]

The Plaintiff alleges that the Defendant Directors' choice to award only time-vesting stock units contravened the Stock Plan because granting time-vesting units did not sufficiently align the Covered Employees' interests with the stockholders' and did not incentivize the Covered Employees to expend "maximum efforts."[122] The Plaintiff argues that the Defendant Directors breached their duty of loyalty by not following the terms of the Stock Plan. The Plaintiff also contends that the Defendant Directors' decision wasted corporate assets because the time-vesting units were not tax deductible.[123] The Plaintiff, in support of his position, asserts that three of Republic's "peer group companies" award mainly performance-based stock compensation.[124]

The Plaintiff is challenging quintessential Board decisions: how much to pay employees and how to allocate company assets efficiently.[125] The Plaintiff's contention is that Republic could have received a lower tax bill, while achieving better results, if the Board had chosen performance-vesting units instead of time-vesting units. As discussed above, "there is no general fiduciary duty to minimize taxes,"[126] and the fact that higher taxes were paid, without more, is insufficient to sustain a waste claim. [...]

 In other words, the Plaintiff mainly disagrees with a business decision by the Board; this disagreement does not state a cognizable claim. [...]

6 Insider Trading

Anyone familiar with the law of agency will very quickly understand why insider trading is so troublesome. When an insider uses the information of the corporation for their own benefit, the agent violates their duty of loyalty to the corporation. Over the years, the jurisprudence of insider trading has evolved to meet the changing landscape of the marketplace. In the following cases we start with classical insider trading theory and then progress to more modern evolutions including liability for insider trading under Federal misappropriation theory.

6.1 State-based liability

State-based insider trading liability takes the form a derivative action by stockholders against insiders. In such an action, the basic claim is that directors (or "insiders") used confidential information of the corporation for their own benefit and not for the benefit of the corporation. As a derivative action based, state-based insider trading liability is prosecuted by stockholders and not by state regulators or the SEC. *Oracle* as well as the *Guttman v. Huang* cases from earlier in the semester are examples of stockholders bringing derivative suits against board members who have allegedly engaged in insider trading in the stock of the corporation.

Consistent with other derivative actions, in state-based insider trading cases, the remedy, if any, is paid to the corporation in the form of disgorgement of profits. Because the state-based action is derivative, neither stockholders nor any governmental entity is entitled to receive any of the profits disgorged as a remedy. Those illicit profits are paid back to the corporation and are not paid as fines to the SEC or any other regulator. In addition, state-based insider trading liability is civil and not criminal.

6.1.1 Kahn v. KKR & Co.

23 A.3d 831 (2011)
KAHN v. KOLBERG KRAVIS ROBERTS & CO.

STEELE, Chief Justice:

The Appellants in this derivative action, Linda Kahn and Alan Spiegal, who are shareholders of Primedia, Inc., appeal the Court of Chancery's decision granting the Primedia Special Litigation Committee's Motion to Dismiss claims arising out of a series of alleged violations of fiduciary duty by defendants, Kohlberg, Kravis, Roberts & Co., Primedia, Inc., and other Primedia officers and directors. Because we do not agree with the Court of Chancery's interpretation of a *Brophy* claim as explained in *Pfeiffer*, we must reverse the Court of Chancery's judgment of dismissal and remand the case for further proceedings consistent with this Opinion.

I. FACTS AND PROCEDURAL HISTORY

The nominal defendant in this action is Primedia, Inc., (the Company) a Delaware corporation whose main executive offices are located in New York City. Primedia's business involves ownership of media properties and brands that "connect buyers and sellers through print publications, websites, events, newsletters, and video programs." [...]

Defendant below/appellee Kohlberg Kravis Roberts & Co. L.P. is an investment partnership that specializes in management buyouts of business entities. KKR indirectly controlled a majority of the common stock of Primedia. [...]

B. The Facts

On December 19, 2001, Primedia's board of directors approved a plan for Primedia to acquire up to $100 million dollars of its preferred shares, at 50% to 60% of redemption value, in exchange for common stock. As of December 19, 2001, KKR controlled approximately 60% of Primedia's outstanding stock and had three of its designees on Primedia's board. At the May 16, 2002 board meeting, Primedia's directors authorized an additional $100 million in buybacks of its preferred shares. On May 21, 2002, Primedia's KKR directors authored an advisory memo to KKR's Investment Committee and Portfolio Committee containing an update on Primedia's second quarter performance and advocating the purchase of Primedia's preferred shares. The May 21st memo contained nonpublic information about Primedia.

At some point in 2002, KKR sought from the Primedia board of directors permission for KKR to purchase Primedia's preferred shares, as long as Primedia was not purchasing those shares in the market. On July 2, 2002, Primedia director (and General

460

Counsel) Beverley Chell circulated the unanimous written consent to the disinterested directors. After receiving advice from outside counsel, Chell circulated the written consent to Primedia's entire board on July 8, 2002. The written consent stated, in part, that KKR's purchase of up to $50 million in Primedia preferred stock was acceptable and not a usurpation of corporate opportunity. The board purportedly executed the written consent on July 8, 2002, without any serious deliberations. The record is unclear when the written consent actually became effective, because the original version's signature page bore no date and at least one signature was not received until July 12, 2002. On July 3, 2002, KKR formed ABRA III LLC as an investment vehicle to purchase Primedia's preferred shares, and ABRA began purchasing preferred shares on July 8, 2002. Between July 8 and November 5, 2002, KKR (through ABRA) purchased over $75 million of Primedia's preferred stock, an amount that exceeded the $50 million limit allowed by the written consent.

On September 26, 2002, Primedia's board of directors met and approved the sale of one of its biggest assets, the American Baby Group, for approximately $115 million in cash. Primedia did not publicly disclose the American Baby Group sale until November 4, 2002. Between September 26 and November 4, 2002, KKR spent $39 million[11] to acquire Primedia's preferred stock. On November 5, 2002, Primedia's board of directors decided to explore repurchasing Primedia preferred shares. ABRA made its last purchase of Primedia's preferred shares on November 5, 2002. […]

II. ANALYSIS

[…]

B. Brophy Does Not Require an Element of Harm to the Corporation Before Disgorgement is an Available Remedy and to the Extent Pfeiffer Conflicts With This Holding, It is Wrong.

We review a trial judge's legal conclusions *de novo*.[10] The Vice Chancellor's analysis focused on the SLC's investigation of three issues: (1) the *Brophy* claim based on the May 21st Insider Information Memo; (2) the *Brophy* claim based on the agreement to sell American Baby Group; and (3) the Breach of Contract Claim based on the backdated written consent and the $50 million restriction.[11] The Vice Chancellor applied the two-part *Zapata* standard to the SLC's motion to dismiss.[12] The first prong of the *Zapata* standard analyzes the independence and good faith of the committee members, the quality of its investigation and the reasonableness of its conclusions.[13] Under *Zapata's* first prong, the Vice Chancellor found the SLC based its decision on an independently thorough investigation of the claims merits and a cost benefit analysis of pursuing the claims.[14] The Vice Chancellor found that the SLC met its burden under the first prong of *Zapata,* but rather than granting the motion to dismiss immediately, the Vice Chancellor addressed *Zapata's* discretionary second prong.[15]

Under *Zapata's* second prong, which is purely discretionary, the court looks at a claim that may be sustainable but that the SLC decided should not be pursued for other reasons.[16] The Court of [837] Chancery's function under *Zapata's* second prong is to "strik[e] a balance between `legitimate corporate claims' as expressed in the derivative shareholder suit and the corporation's best interest as ascertained by the Special Litigation Committee."[17] Here, the Vice Chancellor started from "the proposition that there is a *Brophy* claim [ ] that would blow by a motion to dismiss on failure to state a claim."[18] Then the Vice Chancellor held that under the law, as explained in *Pfeiffer v. Toll,* disgorgement is not an available remedy for most of the *Brophy* claims.[19] But, *Pfeiffer's* holding—which requires a plaintiff to show that the corporation suffered actual harm before bringing a *Brophy* claim—is not a correct statement of our law. To the extent *Pfeiffer v. Toll* conflicts with our current interpretation of *Brophy v. Cities Service Co., Pfeiffer* cannot be Delaware law.

In the venerable case of *Brophy v. Cities Service Co.,* one of the defendants was an employee who had acquired inside information that the corporate plaintiff was about to enter the market and purchase its own shares. Using this confidential information, the employee, who was not an officer, bought a large block of shares and, after the corporation's purchases had caused the price to rise, resold them at a profit.[20] Because the employee defendant occupied a position of trust and confidence within the plaintiff corporation, the court found his relationship analogous to that of a fiduciary.[21] The employee defendant argued that the plaintiff had failed to state a claim because "it [did] not appear that the corporation suffered any loss through his purchase of its stock."[22] The Court of Chancery expressly rejected that argument, stating that:

> In equity, when the breach of confidential relation by an employee
> is relied on and an accounting for any resulting profit is sought, loss

> to the corporation need not be charged in the complaint. . . . Public
> policy will not permit an employee occupying a position of trust and
> confidence toward his employer to abuse that relation to his own
> profit, regardless of whether his employer suffers a loss.[23]

Thus, actual harm to the corporation is not required for a plaintiff to state a claim under *Brophy.* In *Brophy,* the court relied on the principles of restitution and equity, citing the Restatement of the Law of Restitution § 200, comment a, for the proposition that a fiduciary cannot use confidential corporate information for his own benefit.[24] As the court recognized in *Brophy,* [838] it is inequitable to permit the fiduciary to profit from using confidential corporate information. Even if the corporation did not suffer actual harm, equity requires disgorgement of that profit.[25]

This Court has cited *Brophy* approvingly when discussing how the duty of loyalty governs the misuse of confidential corporate information by fiduciaries.[26] In *In re Oracle Corp. Deriv. Litig.,*[27] we affirmed the Court of Chancery's articulation of the elements essential for a plaintiff to prevail on a *Brophy* claim. The plaintiff must show that: "1) the corporate fiduciary possessed material, nonpublic company information; and 2) the corporate fiduciary used that information improperly by making trades because she was motivated, in whole or in part, by the substance of that information."[28]

In *Pfeiffer v. Toll,* the plaintiff stockholder brought a derivative action against the defendants, who were eight members of the Toll Brothers' board of directors, to recover damages suffered by the company from their alleged insider trading.[29] Pfeiffer claimed that the defendants sold significant amounts of Toll Brothers stock from December 2004 through September 2005 while in possession of material, non-public information about Toll Brothers' future prospects.[30] Specifically, Toll Brothers was projecting 20% growth in net income for 2006 and 2007, and its stock price more than doubled from December 2004 to July 2005. During this same period, the director defendants allegedly sold 14 million shares of stock for over $615 million. Based on those sales, which were inconsistent with past trading patterns and were suspicious in their timing and amount, Pfeiffer asserted a derivative claim for breach of fiduciary duty under *Brophy.*

The defendants moved to dismiss the complaint, arguing, among other things, that *Brophy* is an outdated precedent in light of the federal securities laws, which govern insider trading claims. While on [839] one hand upholding *Brophy* as good law,[31] the Court of Chancery concluded that "[t]he purpose of a *Brophy* claim is to remedy harm to the corporation."[32] By focusing on that harm, it "disposes of the defendants' contentions that Brophy is a misguided vehicle for recovering the same trading losses that are addressed by the federal securities laws . . . [and] the contention that *Brophy* grants a remedy without underlying harm."[33] Next, the Vice Chancellor concluded that the harm to the corporation "is generally not measured by insider trading gains or reciprocal losses."[34] Citing to this Court's precedent on two occasions, the Vice Chancellor found that Delaware law "does not provide a class-wide remedy for market based-harm"[35] and "interpreting *Brophy* as a basis for recovering those measures of damages would conflict with [those holdings]."[36] Moreover, the court found that "disgorgement of insider trading profits. . . is also not the appropriate measure of damages because insiders who trade on an impersonal market typically are not engaging in the type of self-dealing transaction to which a disgorgement remedy historically applies."[37] The court also held that market trading "typically does not involve the usurpation of a corporate opportunity, where disgorgement has been the preferred remedy."[38]

To that end, the Vice Chancellor concluded that in the context of a *Brophy* claim, disgorgement is "theoretically available" in two circumstances: (1) "when a fiduciary engages directly in actual fraud and benefits from trading on the basis of the fraudulent information;" and (2) "if the insider used confidential corporate information to compete directly with the corporation."[39] *Brophy,* in the Vice Chancellor's view, was an example of the second circumstance where disgorgement is an [840] appropriate remedy.[40] But, in most circumstances a corporation would only be able to recover for "actual harm causally related (in both the actual and proximate sense) to the breach of the duty of loyalty"—for example "costs and expenses for regulatory proceedings and internal investigations, fees paid to counsel and other professionals, fines paid to regulators, and judgments in litigation."[41]

We decline to adopt *Pfeiffer's* thoughtful, but unduly narrow, interpretation of *Brophy* and its progeny. We also disagree with the *Pfeiffer* court's conclusion that the purpose of *Brophy* is to "remedy harm to the corporation." In fact, *Brophy* explicitly held that the corporation did not need to suffer an actual loss for there to be a viable claim.[42]

464

Importantly, *Brophy* focused on preventing a fiduciary wrongdoer from being unjustly enriched.[43] Moreover, we have found no cases requiring that the corporation suffer actual harm for a plaintiff to bring a *Brophy* claim.[44] To read *Brophy* as applying only where the corporation has suffered actual harm improperly limits its holding.

We decline to adopt *Pfeiffer's* interpretation that would limit the disgorgement remedy to a usurpation of corporate opportunity or cases where the insider used confidential corporate information to compete directly with the corporation. *Brophy* was not premised on either of those rationales. Rather, *Brophy* focused on the public policy of preventing unjust enrichment based on the misuse of confidential corporate information.[45] Just as the *Brophy* court relied on the seminal decision in *Guth v. Loft*,[46] we also rely on the *Guth* court's rationale in this case, and refuse to restrict disgorgement in *Brophy* cases as *Pfeiffer* suggests.

> The rule, inveterate and uncompromising in its rigidity, does not
> rest upon the narrow ground of injury or damage to the corporation
> resulting from a betrayal of confidence, but upon a broader
> foundation of a wise public policy that, for the purpose of removing
> all temptation, extinguishes all possibility of profit flowing from a
> breach of the confidence imposed by the fiduciary relation.[47]

Given *Guth's* eloquent articulation of Delaware's public policy and the fact that "Delaware law dictates that the scope of recovery for a breach of the duty of loyalty is not to be determined narrowly,"[48] we find no reasonable public policy ground to restrict the scope of disgorgement remedy in *Brophy* cases—irrespective of arguably parallel remedies grounded in federal securities law. […]

6.2 Federal-based liability

In additional to state-based liability, traders trading on the basis of inside information may also be liable under the federal securities laws. Federal insider trading liability carries with it potentially both civil and criminal liability. Like state-based liability, federal liability for insider trading is derived from the common law. There is no federal statute that explicitly prohibits insider trading. Rather, courts have interpreted Section 10b of the Securities Act of 1934, the Act's anti-fraud provision, as prohibiting insider trading.

With respect to liability under the Federal law, please note that the Securities Exchange Commission and the Department of Justice have concurrent jurisdiction over the enforcement of the securities laws. When the Department of Justice brings a case, it will be a criminal case. When the SEC brings a case, the liability will be solely civil. The main differences between civil and criminal cases can be found in the remedies available (fines v. jail) as well as the burdens of proof that the government must bear.

6.2.1 Rule 10b-5

§ 240.10b-5 Employment of manipulative and deceptive devices.

It shall be unlawful for any person, directly or indirectly, by the use of any means or instrumentality of interstate commerce, or of the mails or of any facility of any national securities exchange,

> (a) To employ any device, scheme, or artifice to defraud, (b) To make any untrue statement of a material fact or to omit to state a material fact necessary in order to make the statements made, in the light of the circumstances under which they were made, not misleading, or (c) To engage in any act, practice, or course of business which operates or would operate as a fraud or deceit upon any person,

in connection with the purchase or sale of any security.

6.2.2 SEC v. Texas Gulf Sulphur Co.

The following case, *Texas Gulf Sulphur*, is an early federal insider trading case. In TGS, the court starts from the position that insiders, as fiduciaries, have an obligation not to use the corporation's information for their personal benefit. As fiduciaries, insiders have an obligation to "disclose" the confidential inside information, or "abstain from trading" while in possession of the corporation's material, confidential inside information. Questions arise as to what information is material and when is information no longer confidential such that an insider may freely trade on it.

401 F.2d 833 (1968)
SEC v. TEXAS GULF SULPHUR

[…]

THE FACTUAL SETTING

This action derives from the exploratory activities of TGS begun in 1957 on the Canadian Shield in eastern Canada. In March of 1959, aerial geophysical surveys were conducted over more than 15,000 square miles of this area by a group led by defendant Mollison, a mining engineer and a Vice President of TGS. The group included defendant Holyk, TGS's chief geologist, defendant Clayton, an electrical engineer and geophysicist, and defendant Darke, a geologist. These operations resulted in the detection of numerous anomalies, i. e., extraordinary variations in the conductivity of rocks, one of which was on the Kidd 55 segment of land located near Timmins, Ontario.

On October 29 and 30, 1963, Clayton conducted a ground geophysical survey on the northeast portion of the Kidd 55 segment which confirmed the presence of an anomaly and indicated the necessity of diamond core drilling for further evaluation. Drilling of the initial hole, K-55-1, at the strongest part of the anomaly was commenced on November 8 and terminated on November 12 at a depth of 655 feet. Visual estimates by Holyk of the core of K-55-1 indicated an average copper content of 1.15% and an average zinc content of 8.64% over a length of 599 feet. This visual estimate convinced TGS that it was desirable to acquire the remainder of the Kidd 55 segment, and in order to facilitate this acquisition TGS President Stephens instructed the exploration group to keep the results of K-55-1 confidential and undisclosed even as to other officers, directors, and employees of TGS. The hole was concealed and a barren core was intentionally drilled off the anomaly. Meanwhile, the core of K-55-1 had been shipped to Utah for chemical assay which, when received in early December, revealed an average mineral content of 1.18% copper, 8.26% zinc, and 3.94% ounces of silver per ton over a length of 602 feet. These results were so remarkable that neither Clayton, an experienced geophysicist, nor four other TGS expert witnesses, had ever seen or heard of a comparable initial exploratory drill hole in a base metal deposit. So, the trial court concluded, "There is no doubt that the drill core of K-55-1 was unusually [844] good and that it excited the interest and speculation of those who knew about it." Id. at 282. By March 27, 1964, TGS decided that the land acquisition program had advanced to such a point that the company might well resume drilling, and drilling was resumed on March 31.

During this period, from November 12, 1963 when K-55-1 was completed, to March 31, 1964 when drilling was resumed, certain of the individual defendants listed in fn. 2, supra, and persons listed in fn. 4, supra, said to have received "tips" from them, purchased TGS stock or calls thereon. Prior to these transactions these persons had owned 1135 shares of TGS stock and possessed no calls; thereafter they owned a total of 8235 shares and possessed 12,300 calls. […]

Meanwhile, rumors that a major ore strike was in the making had been circulating throughout Canada. On the morning of Saturday, April 11, Stephens at his home in Greenwich, Conn. read in the New York Herald Tribune and in the New York Times unauthorized reports of the TGS drilling which seemed to infer a rich strike from the fact that the drill cores had been flown to the United States for chemical assay. Stephens immediately contacted Fogarty at his [845] home in Rye, N. Y., who in turn telephoned and later that day visited Mollison at Mollison's home in Greenwich to obtain a current report and evaluation of the drilling progress.[7] The following morning, Sunday, Fogarty again telephoned Mollison, inquiring whether Mollison had any further information and told him to return to Timmins with Holyk, the TGS Chief Geologist, as soon as possible "to move things along." With the aid of one Carroll, a public relations consultant, Fogarty drafted a press release designed to quell the rumors, which release, after having been channeled through Stephens and Huntington, a TGS attorney, was issued at 3:00 P. M. on Sunday, April 12, and which appeared in the morning newspapers of general circulation on Monday, April 13. It read in pertinent part as follows:

> NEW YORK, April 12 — The following statement was made today by Dr. Charles F. Fogarty, executive vice president of Texas Gulf Sulphur Company, in regard to the company's drilling operations near Timmins, Ontario, Canada. Dr. Fogarty said:
>
> "During the past few days, the exploration activities of Texas Gulf Sulphur in the area of Timmins, Ontario, have been widely reported in the press, coupled with rumors of a substantial copper discovery there. These reports exaggerate the scale of operations, and mention

plans and statistics of size and grade of ore that are without factual basis and have evidently originated by speculation of people not connected with TGS.

"The facts are as follows. TGS has been exploring in the Timmins area for six years as part of its overall search in Canada and elsewhere for various minerals — lead, copper, zinc, etc. During the course of this work, in Timmins as well as in Eastern Canada, TGS has conducted exploration entirely on its own, without the participation by others. Numerous prospects have been investigated by geophysical means and a large number of selected ones have been core-drilled. These cores are sent to the United States for assay and detailed examination as a matter of routine and on advice of expert Canadian legal counsel. No inferences as to grade can be drawn from this procedure.

"Most of the areas drilled in Eastern Canada have revealed either barren pyrite or graphite without value; a few have resulted in discoveries of small or marginal sulphide ore bodies.

"Recent drilling on one property near Timmins has led to preliminary indications that more drilling would be required for proper evaluation of this prospect. The drilling done to date has not been conclusive, but the statements made by many outside quarters are unreliable and include information and figures that are not available to TGS.

"The work done to date has not been sufficient to reach definite conclusions and any statement as to size and grade of ore would be premature and possibly misleading. When we have progressed to the point where reasonable and logical conclusions can be made, TGS will issue a definite statement to its stockholders and to the public in order to clarify the Timmins project."

* * * * * *

The release purported to give the Timmins drilling results as of the release date, April 12. From Mollison Fogarty had been told of the developments through 7:00 P. M. on April 10, and of [846] the remarkable discoveries made up to that time, detailed supra, which discoveries, according to the calculations of the experts who testified for the SEC at the hearing, demonstrated that TGS had already discovered 6.2 to 8.3 million tons of proven ore having gross assay values from $26 to $29 per ton. TGS experts, on the other hand, denied at the hearing that proven or probable ore could have been calculated on April 11 or 12 because there was then no assurance of continuity in the mineralized zone.

The evidence as to the effect of this release on the investing public was equivocal and less than abundant. On April 13 the New York Herald Tribune in an article head-noted "Copper Rumor Deflated" quoted from the TGS release of April 12 and backtracked from its original April 11 report of a major strike but nevertheless inferred from the TGS release that "recent mineral exploratory activity near Timmins, Ontario, has provided preliminary favorable results, sufficient at least to require a step-up in drilling operations." Some witnesses who testified at the hearing stated that they found the release encouraging. On the other hand, a Canadian mining security specialist, Roche, stated that "earlier in the week [before April 16] we had a Dow Jones saying that they [TGS] didn't have anything basically" and a TGS stock specialist for the Midwest Stock Exchange became concerned about his long position in the stock after reading the release. The trial court stated only that "While, in retrospect, the press release may appear gloomy or incomplete, this does not make it misleading or deceptive on the basis of the facts then known." Id. at 296.

Meanwhile, drilling operations continued. [...]

While drilling activity ensued to completion, TGC officials were taking steps toward ultimate disclosure of the discovery. On April 13, a previously-invited reporter for The Northern Miner, a Canadian mining industry journal, visited the drillsite, interviewed Mollison, Holyk and Darke, and prepared an article which confirmed a 10 million ton ore strike. This report, after having been submitted to Mollison and returned to the reporter unamended on April 15, was published in the April 16 issue. A statement relative to the extent of the discovery, in substantial part drafted by Mollison, was given to the Ontario Minister of Mines for release to the Canadian media. Mollison and Holyk

470

expected it to be released over the airways at 11 P. M. on April 15th, but, for undisclosed reasons, it was not released until 9:40 A. M. on the 16th. An official detailed statement, announcing a strike of at least 25 million tons of ore, based on the drilling data set forth above, was read to representatives of American financial media from 10:00 A. M. to 10:10 or 10:15 A. M. on April 16, and appeared over Merrill Lynch's private wire at 10:29 A. M. and, somewhat later than [847] expected, over the Dow Jones ticker tape at 10:54 A. M.

Between the time the first press release was issued on April 12 and the dissemination of the TGS official announcement on the morning of April 16, the only defendants before us on appeal who engaged in market activity were Clayton and Crawford and TGS director Coates. Clayton ordered 200 shares of TGS stock through his Canadian broker on April 15 and the order was executed that day over the Midwest Stock Exchange. Crawford ordered 300 shares at midnight on the 15th and another 300 shares at 8:30 A. M. the next day, and these orders were executed over the Midwest Exchange in Chicago at its opening on April 16. Coates left the TGS press conference and called his broker son-in-law Haemisegger shortly before 10:20 A. M. on the 16th and ordered 2,000 shares of TGS for family trust accounts of which Coates was a trustee but not a beneficiary; Haemisegger executed this order over the New York and Midwest Exchanges, and he and his customers purchased 1500 additional shares.

During the period of drilling in Timmins, the market price of TGS stock fluctuated but steadily gained overall. On Friday, November 8, when the drilling began, the stock closed at 17 3/8 on Friday, November 15, after K-55-1 had been completed, it closed at 18. After a slight decline to 16 3/8 by Friday, November 22, the price rose to 20 7/8 by December 13, when the chemical assay results of K-55-1 were received, and closed at a high of 24 1/8 on February 21, the day after the stock options had been issued. It had reached a price of 26 by March 31, after the land acquisition program had been completed and drilling had been resumed, and continued to ascend to 30 1/8 by the close of trading on April 10, at which time the drilling progress up to then was evaluated for the April 12th press release. On April 13, the day on which the April 12 release was disseminated, TGS opened at 30 1/8, rose immediately to a high of 32 and gradually tapered off to close at 30 7/8. It closed at 30¼ the next day, and at 29 3/8 on April 15.

On April 16, the day of the official announcement of the Timmins discovery, the price climbed to a high of 37 and closed at 36 3/8. By May 15, TGS stock was selling at 58¼.

I. THE INDIVIDUAL DEFENDANTS

A. *Introductory*

Rule 10b-5, 17 CFR 240.10b-5, on which this action is predicated, provides:

> It shall be unlawful for any person, directly or indirectly, by the use of any means or instrumentality of interstate commerce, or of the mails, or of any facility of any national securities exchange,
>
> (1) to employ any device, scheme, or artifice to defraud,
>
> (2) to make any untrue statement of a material fact or to omit to state a material fact necessary in order to make the statements made, in the light of the circumstances under which they were made, not misleading, or
>
> (3) to engage in any act, practice, or course of business which operates or would operate as a fraud or deceit upon any person,
>
> in connection with the purchase or sale of any security.

Rule 10b-5 was promulgated pursuant to the grant of authority given the SEC by Congress in Section 10(b) of the Securities Exchange Act of 1934 (15 U.S.C. § 78j(b).[...] The Act and the Rule apply to the transactions here, all of which were consummated on exchanges. [...] Whether predicated on traditional fiduciary concepts, [...] or on the "special facts" doctrine, [...] the Rule is based in policy on the justifiable expectation of the securities marketplace that all investors trading on impersonal exchanges have relatively equal access to material information, [...]The essence of the Rule is that anyone who, trading for his own account in the securities of a corporation has "access, directly or indirectly, to information intended to be available only for a corporate purpose and not for the personal benefit of anyone" may not take "advantage of such information knowing it is unavailable to those with whom he is dealing," i. e., the investing public. Matter of Cady, Roberts & Co., 40 SEC 907, 912 (1961). Insiders, as directors or management officers are, of course, by this Rule,

472

precluded from so unfairly dealing, but the Rule is also applicable to one possessing the information who may not be strictly termed an "insider" within the meaning of Sec. 16(b) of the Act. Cady, Roberts, supra. Thus, anyone in possession of material inside information must either disclose it to the investing public, or, if he is disabled from disclosing it in order to protect a corporate confidence, or he chooses not to do so, must abstain from trading in or recommending the securities concerned while such inside information remains undisclosed. So, it is here no justification for insider activity that disclosure was forbidden by the legitimate corporate objective of acquiring options to purchase the land surrounding the exploration site; if the information was, as the SEC contends, material,[9] its possessors should have kept out of the market until disclosure was accomplished.[…]

B. Material Inside Information

An insider is not, of course, always foreclosed from investing in his own company merely because he may be more familiar with company operations than are outside investors. An insider's duty to disclose information or his duty to abstain from dealing in his company's securities arises only in "those situations which are essentially extraordinary in nature and which are reasonably certain to have a substantial effect on the market price of the security if [the extraordinary situation is] disclosed." […]

Nor is an insider obligated to confer upon outside investors the benefit of his superior financial or other expert analysis by disclosing his educated guesses or predictions. […] The only regulatory objective is that access to material information be enjoyed equally, but this objective requires nothing more than the disclosure of basic facts so that outsiders may draw upon their own evaluative expertise in reaching their own investment decisions with knowledge equal to that of the insiders.

This is not to suggest, however, as did the trial court, that "the test of materiality must necessarily be a conservative one, particularly since many actions under Section 10(b) are brought on the basis of hindsight," […]in the sense that the materiality of facts is to be assessed solely by measuring the effect the knowledge of the facts would have upon prudent or conservative investors. […], "The basic test of materiality * * * is whether a *reasonable* man would attach importance * * * in determining his choice of action in the transaction in question.[…] Such a fact is a material fact and must be effectively disclosed to the investing public prior to the commencement of insider trading in the

473

corporation's securities. The speculators and chartists of Wall and Bay Streets are also "reasonable" investors entitled to the same legal protection afforded conservative traders.[10] Thus, material facts include not only information disclosing the earnings and distributions of a company but also those facts which affect the probable future of the company and those which may affect the desire of investors to buy, sell, or hold the company's securities. [...]

Our survey of the facts found below conclusively establishes that knowledge of the results of the discovery hole, K-55-1, would have been important to a reasonable investor and might have affected the price of the stock.[12] On April 16, The Northern Miner, a trade publication in wide circulation among mining stock specialists, called K-55-1, the discovery hole, "one of the most impressive drill holes completed in modern times."[13] Roche, a Canadian broker whose firm specialized in mining securities, characterized the importance to investors of the results of K-55-1. He stated that the completion of "the first drill hole" with "a 600 foot drill core is very very significant * * * anything over 200 feet is considered very significant and 600 feet is just beyond your wildest imagination." He added, however, that it "is a natural thing to buy more stock once they give you the first drill hole." Additional testimony revealed that the prices of stocks of other companies, albeit less diversified, smaller firms, had increased substantially solely on the basis of the discovery of good anomalies or even because of the proximity of their lands to the situs of a potentially major strike.

Finally, a major factor in determining whether the K-55-1 discovery was a material fact is the importance attached to the drilling results by those who knew about it. In view of other unrelated recent developments favorably affecting TGS, participation by an informed person in a regular stock-purchase program, or even sporadic trading by an informed person, might lend only nominal support to the inference of the materiality of the K-55-1 discovery; nevertheless, the timing by those who knew of it of their stock purchases and their purchases of *short-term* calls — purchases in some cases by individuals who had never before purchased calls or even TGS stock — virtually compels the inference that the insiders were influenced by the drilling results. [...]. No reason appears why outside investors, perhaps better acquainted with speculative modes of investment and with, in many cases, perhaps more capital at their disposal for intelligent speculation, would have been less influenced, and would not have been similarly motivated to invest if they had known what the insider investors knew about the K-55-1 discovery. [...]

The core of Rule 10b-5 is the implementation of the Congressional purpose that all investors should have equal access to the rewards of participation [852] in securities transactions. It was the intent of Congress that all members of the investing public should be subject to identical market risks, — which market risks include, of course the risk that one's evaluative capacity or one's capital available to put at risk may exceed another's capacity or capital. The insiders here were not trading on an equal footing with the outside investors. They alone were in a position to evaluate the probability and magnitude of what seemed from the outset to be a major ore strike; they alone could invest safely, secure in the expectation that the price of TGS stock would rise substantially in the event such a major strike should materialize, but would decline little, if at all, in the event of failure, for the public, ignorant at the outset of the favorable probabilities would likewise be unaware of the unproductive exploration, and the additional exploration costs would not significantly affect TGS market prices. Such inequities based upon unequal access to knowledge should not be shrugged off as inevitable in our way of life, or, in view of the congressional concern in the area, remain uncorrected.

We hold, therefore, that all transactions in TGS stock or calls by individuals apprised of the drilling results[14] of K-55-1 were made in violation of Rule 10b-5.[...] The geologist Darke possessed undisclosed material information and traded in TGS securities. Therefore we reverse the dismissal of the action as to him and his personal transactions. [...]

With reference to Huntington, the trial court found that he "had no detailed knowledge as to the work" on the Kidd-55 segment, 258 F.Supp. 281. Nevertheless, the evidence shows that he knew about and participated in TGS's land acquisition program which followed the receipt of the K-55-1 drilling results, and that on February 26, 1964 he purchased 50 shares of TGS stock. Later, on March 16, he helped prepare a letter for Dr. Holyk's signature in which TGS made a substantial offer for lands near K-55-1, and on the same day he, who had never before purchased calls on any stock, purchased a call on 100 shares of TGS stock. We are satisfied that these purchases in February and March, coupled with his readily inferable and probably reliable, understanding of the highly favorable nature of preliminary operations on the Kidd segment, demonstrate that Huntington possessed material inside information such as to make his purchase violative of the Rule and the Act. [...]

Appellant Crawford, who ordered[17] the purchase of TGS stock shortly before the TGS April 16 official announcement, and defendant Coates, who placed orders with and communicated the news to his broker immediately after the official announcement was read at the TGS-called press conference, concede that they were in possession of material information. They contend, however, that their purchases were not proscribed purchases for the news had already been effectively disclosed. We disagree.

The trial court's finding that "he sought to, and did, `beat the news,'" 258 F.Supp. at 287, is well documented by the record. The rumors of a major ore strike which had been circulated in Canada and, to a lesser extent, in New York, had been disclaimed by the TGS press release of April 12, which significantly promised the public an official detailed announcement when possibilities had ripened into actualities. The abbreviated announcement to the Canadian press at 9:40 A.M. on the 16th by the Ontario Minister of Mines and the report carried by The Northern Miner, parts of which had sporadically reached New York on the morning of the 16th through reports from Canadian affiliates to a few New York investment firms, are assuredly not the equivalent of the official 10-15 minute announcement which was not released to the American financial press until after 10:00 A.M. Crawford's orders had been [854] placed before that. Before insiders may act upon material information, such information must have been effectively disclosed in a manner sufficient to insure its availability to the investing public. Particularly here, where a formal announcement to the entire financial news media had been promised in a prior official release known to the media, all insider activity must await dissemination of the promised official announcement.

Coates was absolved by the court below because his telephone order was placed shortly before 10:20 A.M. on April 16, which was after the announcement had been made even though the news could not be considered already a matter of public information. 258 F. Supp. at 288. This result seems to have been predicated upon a misinterpretation of dicta in *Cady,Roberts,* where the SEC instructed insiders to "keep out of the market until the established procedures for public release of the information are *carried out* instead of hastening to execute transactions in advance of, and in frustration of, the objectives of the release," 40 SEC at 915 (emphasis supplied). The reading of a news release, which prompted Coates into action, is merely the first step in the process of dissemination required for compliance with the regulatory objective of providing all investors with an equal opportunity to make informed investment judgments. Assuming that the contents of the official release could instantaneously be acted upon,[18] at the minimum Coates should have waited until the news could reasonably have been expected to appear over the media of widest circulation, the Dow Jones broad tape, rather than hastening to insure an advantage to himself and his broker son-in-law.[19] […]

6.2.3 Tipper/Tippee Liability

What about liability for insider trading in situations where the trading does not involve an insider? The knottiest of these problems involve situations where insiders have tipped outsiders who then trade.

Tipping is a direct challenge to the classical insider trading doctrine and requires some development of the law. Because the recipient of inside information does not have a fiduciary duty to the shareholders or the corporation, classical insider trading theory does not extend to recipients of inside information. Courts have responded to these situations by finding ways to extend liability to recipients of inside information, "tippees". Because courts built tippee liability for insider trading on the scaffolding of fiduciary duty, the reach of liability can at times be limited.

6.2.3.1 Dirks v. SEC

463 U.S. 646 (1983)
DIRKS v. SECURITIES AND EXCHANGE COMMISSION
Supreme Court of United States.

JUSTICE POWELL delivered the opinion of the Court.

Petitioner Raymond Dirks received material nonpublic information from "insiders" of a corporation with which he had no connection. He disclosed this information to investors who relied on it in trading in the shares of the corporation. The question is whether Dirks violated the antifraud provisions of the federal securities laws by this disclosure. […]

In 1973, Dirks was an officer of a New York broker-dealer firm who specialized in providing investment analysis of insurance company securities to institutional investors.[1] On [649] March 6, Dirks received information from Ronald Secrist, a former officer of Equity Funding of America. Secrist alleged that the assets of Equity Funding, a diversified corporation primarily engaged in selling life insurance and mutual funds, were vastly overstated as the result of fraudulent corporate practices. Secrist also stated that various regulatory agencies had failed to act on similar charges made by Equity Funding employees. He urged Dirks to verify the fraud and disclose it publicly.

Dirks decided to investigate the allegations. He visited Equity Funding's headquarters in Los Angeles and interviewed several officers and employees of the corporation. The senior management denied any wrongdoing, but certain corporation employees corroborated the charges of fraud. Neither Dirks nor his firm owned or traded any Equity Funding stock, but throughout his investigation he openly discussed the information he had obtained with a number of clients and investors. Some of these persons sold their holdings of Equity Funding securities, including five investment advisers who liquidated holdings of more than $16 million.[2]

While Dirks was in Los Angeles, he was in touch regularly with William Blundell, the Wall Street Journal's Los Angeles bureau chief. Dirks urged Blundell to write a story on the fraud allegations. Blundell did not believe, however, that such a massive fraud could go undetected and declined to [650] write the story. He feared that publishing such damaging hearsay might be libelous.

During the 2-week period in which Dirks pursued his investigation and spread word of Secrist's charges, the price of Equity Funding stock fell from $26 per share to less than $15 per share. This led the New York Stock Exchange to halt trading on March 27. Shortly thereafter California insurance authorities impounded Equity Funding's records and uncovered evidence of the fraud. Only then did the Securities and Exchange Commission (SEC) file a complaint against Equity Funding[3] and only then, on April 2, did the Wall Street Journal publish a front-page story based largely on information assembled by Dirks. Equity Funding immediately went into receivership.[4]

The SEC began an investigation into Dirks' role in the exposure of the fraud. After a hearing by an Administrative Law Judge, the SEC found that Dirks had aided and abetted violations of[...] SEC Rule 10b-5, 17 CFR § 240.10b-5 (1983),[7] by repeating the allegations of fraud to members of the investment community who later sold their Equity Funding stock. The SEC concluded: "Where `tippees' — regardless of their motivation or occupation — come into possession of material `corporate information that they know is confidential and know or should know came from a corporate insider,' they must either publicly disclose that information or refrain from trading." [...] Recognizing, however, that Dirks "played an important role in bringing [Equity Funding's] massive fraud [652] to light,"[...]

II

In the seminal case of *In re Cady, Roberts & Co.,* 40 S. E. C. 907 (1961), the SEC recognized that the common law in some jurisdictions imposes on "corporate `insiders,' particularly officers, directors, or controlling stockholders" an "affirmative duty of disclosure . . . when dealing in securities." *Id.,* at 911, and n. 13.[10]The SEC found that not only did breach of this common-law duty also establish the elements of a Rule 10b-5 violation,[11] but that individuals other than corporate insiders could be obligated either to disclose material nonpublic information[12] before trading or to abstain from trading altogether.*Id.,* at 912. In *Chiarella,* we accepted the two elements set out in *Cady, Roberts* for establishing a Rule 10b-5 violation: "(i) the existence of a relationship affording access to inside information intended to be available only for a corporate purpose, and (ii) the unfairness of allowing a corporate insider to take advantage of that information [654] by trading without disclosure." 445 U. S., at 227. In examining whether Chiarella had an obligation to disclose or abstain, the Court found that there is no general duty to disclose before trading on material nonpublic information,[13] and held that "a duty to disclose under § 10(b) does not arise from the mere possession of nonpublic market information."*Id.,* at 235. Such a duty arises rather from the existence of a fiduciary relationship.[...]

In an inside-trading case this fraud derives from the "inherent unfairness involved where one takes advantage" of "information intended to be available only for a corporate purpose and not for the personal benefit of anyone." [...]. Thus, an insider will be

479

liable under Rule 10b-5 for inside trading only where he fails to disclose material nonpublic information before trading on it and thus makes "secret profits." […]

III

We were explicit in *Chiarella* in saying that there can be no duty to disclose where the person who has traded on inside information "was not [the corporation's] agent, . . . was not a fiduciary, [or] was not a person in whom the sellers [of the securities] had placed their trust and confidence." […] Not to require such a fiduciary relationship, we recognized, would "depar[t] radically from the established doctrine that duty arises from a specific relationship between [655] two parties" and would amount to "recognizing a general duty between all participants in market transactions to forgo actions based on material, nonpublic information." […]. This requirement of a specific relationship between the shareholders and the individual trading on inside information has created analytical difficulties for the SEC and courts in policing tippees who trade on inside information. Unlike insiders who have independent fiduciary duties to both the corporation and its shareholders, the typical tippee has no such relationships.[14] In view of this absence, it has been unclear how a tippee acquires the *Cady, Roberts* duty to refrain from trading on inside information. […]

In effect, the SEC's theory of tippee liability in both cases appears rooted in the idea that the antifraud provisions require equal information among all traders. This conflicts with the principle set forth in *Chiarella* that only some persons, under some circumstances, will be barred from trading while in possession of material nonpublic information.[16] Judge Wright correctly read our opinion in *Chiarella* as repudiating any notion that all traders must enjoy equal information before trading: "[T]he `information' theory is rejected. Because the disclose-or-refrain duty is extraordinary, it attaches only when a party has legal obligations other than a mere duty to comply with the general antifraud proscriptions in the federal securities laws."[…] We reaffirm today that "[a] duty [to disclose] [658] arises from the relationship between parties . . . and not merely from one's ability to acquire information because of his position in the market." […]

B

The conclusion that recipients of inside information do not invariably acquire a duty to disclose or abstain does not mean that such tippees always are free to trade on the information. The need for a ban on some tippee trading is clear. Not only are insiders forbidden by their fiduciary relationship from personally using undisclosed corporate information to their advantage, but they also may not give such information to an outsider for the same improper purpose of exploiting the information for their personal gain.[...]. As we noted in *Chiarella*, "[t]he tippee's obligation has been viewed as arising from his role as a participant after the fact in the insider's breach of a fiduciary duty." [...

Thus, some tippees must assume an insider's duty to the shareholders not because they receive inside information, but rather because it has been made available to them *improperly*.[19] And for Rule 10b-5 purposes, the insider's disclosure is improper only where it would violate his *Cady, Roberts* duty. Thus, a tippee assumes a fiduciary duty to the shareholders of a corporation not to trade on material nonpublic information only when the insider has breached his fiduciary duty to the shareholders by disclosing the information to the tippee and the tippee knows or should know that there has been a breach.[...]

C

In determining whether a tippee is under an obligation to disclose or abstain, it thus is necessary to determine whether the insider's "tip" constituted a breach of the insider's fiduciary duty. All disclosures of confidential corporate information [662] are not inconsistent with the duty insiders owe to shareholders. In contrast to the extraordinary facts of this case, the more typical situation in which there will be a question whether disclosure violates the insider's *Cady, Roberts* duty is when insiders disclose information to analysts. [...] In some situations, the insider will act consistently with his fiduciary duty to shareholders, and yet release of the information may affect the market. For example, it may not be clear — either to the corporate insider or to the recipient analyst — whether the information will be viewed as material nonpublic information. Corporate officials may mistakenly think the information already has been disclosed or that it is not material enough to affect the market. Whether disclosure is a breach of duty therefore depends in large part on the purpose of the disclosure. This standard was identified by the SEC itself in *Cady, Roberts:* a purpose of the securities laws was to eliminate "use of inside information for personal advantage." [...]Thus, the test is whether the insider personally will benefit, directly or indirectly, from his disclosure. Absent some personal gain, there has been no breach of duty to stockholders. And absent a breach by the insider, there is no derivative breach.[...]

But to determine whether the disclosure itself "deceive[s], manipulate[s], or defraud[s]" shareholders, [...] the initial inquiry is whether there has been a breach of duty by the insider. This requires courts to focus on objective criteria, *i. e.,* whether the insider receives a direct or indirect personal benefit from the disclosure, such as a pecuniary gain or a reputational benefit that will translate into future earnings. [...] Brudney, Insiders, Outsiders, and Informational Advantages Under the Federal Securities [664] Laws, 93 Harv. L. Rev. 322, 348 (1979) ("The theory . . . is that the insider, by giving the information out selectively, is in effect selling the information to its recipient for cash, reciprocal information, or other things of value for himself. . ."). There are objective facts and circumstances that often justify such an inference. For example, there may be a relationship between the insider and the recipient that suggests a *quid pro quo* from the latter, or an intention to benefit the particular recipient. The elements of fiduciary duty and exploitation of nonpublic information also exist when an insider makes a gift of confidential information to a trading relative or friend. The tip and trade resemble trading by the insider himself followed by a gift of the profits to the recipient.

Determining whether an insider personally benefits from a particular disclosure, a question of fact, will not always be easy for courts. But it is essential, we think, to have a guiding principle for those whose daily activities must be limited and instructed by the SEC's inside-trading rules, and we believe that there must be a breach of the insider's fiduciary duty before the tippee inherits the duty to disclose or abstain. In contrast, the rule adopted by the SEC in this case would have no limiting principle.[24]

IV

Under the inside-trading and tipping rules set forth above, we find that there was no actionable violation by Dirks.[25] It is undisputed that Dirks himself was a stranger to Equity Funding, with no pre-existing fiduciary duty to its shareholders.[26] He took no action, directly or indirectly, that induced the shareholders or officers of Equity Funding to repose trust or confidence in him. There was no expectation by Dirks' sources that he would keep their information in confidence. Nor did Dirks misappropriate or illegally obtain the information about Equity Funding. Unless the insiders breached their *Cady, Roberts* duty to shareholders in disclosing the nonpublic information to Dirks, he breached no duty when he passed it on to investors as well as to the Wall Street Journal.

It is clear that neither Secrist nor the other Equity Funding employees violated their *Cady, Roberts* duty to the corporation's shareholders by providing information to Dirks.[27] The tippers received no monetary or personal benefit for revealing Equity Funding's secrets, nor was their purpose to make a gift of valuable information to Dirks. As the facts of this case clearly indicate, the tippers were motivated by a desire to expose the fraud.[…] In the absence of a breach of duty to shareholders by the insiders, there was no derivative breach by Dirks. See n. 20, *supra.* Dirks therefore could not have been "a participant after the fact in [an] insider's breach of a fiduciary duty." *Chiarella,* 445 U. S., at 230, n. 12.

V

We conclude that Dirks, in the circumstances of this case, had no duty to abstain from use of the inside information that he obtained. The judgment of the Court of Appeals therefore is

Reversed.

6.2.3.2 SEC v. Switzer

Not all tippees will be subject to liability for trading on a corporation's material, confidential inside information. In the case that follows, the court tests the limits of liability for tippees.

590 F.Supp. 756 (1984)
SEC v. SWITZER

United States District Court, W.D. Oklahoma.

SAFFELS, District Judge, Sitting by Designation.

This action brought by the Securities and Exchange Commission [hereinafter SEC] was tried to the court on March 19-22, 1984. It involved allegations of violations of Section

10(b) of the Securities Exchange Act of 1934 and violations of Commission Rule 10b-5. [...]

6. Barry L. Switzer resides at 2811 Castlewood Drive, Norman, Oklahoma (73070). At all times mentioned in the complaint, Switzer was the head football coach at the University of Oklahoma in Norman, Oklahoma. [...]

13. Texas International Company [hereinafter TIC] is a Delaware corporation with principal offices located in Oklahoma City, Oklahoma. At all times mentioned in the complaint, TIC was engaged in, among other things, exploration for and development of oil and natural gas properties. At all times mentioned in the complaint, TIC's common stock was registered with the SEC pursuant to Section 12(b) of the Securities Exchange Act [15 U.S.C. 78*l*(b)] and was traded on the New York Stock Exchange, as well as other exchanges. On or about June 18, 1982, a wholly-owned subsidiary of TIC merged with Phoenix Resources Company [hereinafter Phoenix] and Phoenix became a wholly-owned subsidiary of TIC. At all times mentioned in the complaint prior to the merger, TIC owned in excess of fifty percent (50%) of the common stock of Phoenix, and, by reason of such ownership position, controlled Phoenix through election of three of the five members of the Phoenix Board of Directors.

14. Prior to the merger, Phoenix, the successor to King Resources Company, was a Maine corporation with principal offices located in Oklahoma City, Oklahoma. At all times mentioned in the complaint prior to the merger, Phoenix engaged in, among other things, exploration for and development of oil and natural gas properties. At all times mentioned in the complaint prior to the merger, Phoenix's common stock was registered with the SEC pursuant to Section 12(b) of the Securities Exchange Act [15 U.S.C. 78*l* (b)] and was traded in the Over-the-Counter securities market on the National Association of Securities Dealers Automated Quotation System. [...]

32. Barry Switzer is a well-recognized "celebrity" in Oklahoma and elsewhere. He has an interest in the oil and gas industry, as he is personally involved in various ventures within the industry.

33. Over the past several years, defendants Switzer, Kennedy, Deem, Smith, Hodges, Amyx and Hoover have acted together in varying combinations of persons (or in

various groups of persons) in making investments. They have formed partnerships such as S & H Investments, Waverly Ltd., and Hodges, Amyx, Cross and Hodges, to assist them in their investment ventures. Often times, they trade on rumors or gossip they hear within the investing community. Profits and losses occurring as a result of stock investments made through these partnerships are shared by the members of the partnerships.

34. TIC had been considering various options for either consolidating or separating TIC and Phoenix for some time prior to its approaching Morgan Stanley on June 4 or 5, 1981. Rumors concerning these various options were circulating within the investing oil and gas community prior to June 4 or 5, 1981.

35. On June 6, 1981, four days prior to the public announcement concerning Phoenix, a state invitational secondary school track meet was held at John Jacobs Field on the University of Oklahoma campus. The track meet was a day long event. Several hundred spectators attended, including Barry Switzer, who arrived at the meet between 10:00 and 10:30 a.m. to watch his son compete, and George and Linda Platt, who arrived between 9:00 and 10:00 a.m. to watch their son compete. Soon after Switzer's arrival at the track meet, he and G. Platt recognized and greeted each other. Neither Switzer nor G. Platt knew that the other would be attending the meet.

36. G. Platt was a supporter of Oklahoma University football and had met Switzer at a few social engagements prior to June of 1981. TIC was a sponsor of Switzer's football show, "Play Back." G. Platt had had season tickets to the OU football games for approximately five years. G. Platt had obtained autographs from Switzer for G. Platt's minor children, and had had his secretary telephone Switzer to request that his season tickets be upgraded. Upgrading of tickets was extended as a courtesy by Switzer to many season ticket holders. On at least two occasions Switzer had phoned G. Platt requesting continued sponsorship by TIC of Switzer's football television program. These calls were made at the urging of Tom Goodgame, General Manager of the television station which then produced "Play Back." As of June 5, 1981, Switzer knew that G. Platt was Chairman of the Board of TIC and further knew that TIC was a substantial shareholder of Phoenix because Switzer was a stockholder in TIC and thereby knew Phoenix was a subsidiary.

37. Neither G. Platt nor his wife Linda are particularly impressed by Switzer. They view him as "just a nice fellow."

38. Upon first greeting each other at the track meet, G. Platt and Switzer exchanged pleasantries. Switzer then departed and continued on through the bleachers.

39. Throughout the course of the day, G. Platt and Linda Platt generally remained in one place in the bleachers. Switzer, however, throughout the day moved around a great deal, at times speaking with his son or other participants and their families, signing autographs and watching the different events on the field. While moving about, Switzer joined the Platts to visit with them about three to five times. During these visits Switzer and the Platts talked about their sons' participation in the meet, the oil and gas business, the economy, football and their respective personal investments.

40. G. Platt and Switzer did not have any conversations regarding Phoenix or Morgan Stanley, nor did they have any conversations regarding any mergers, acquisitions, take-overs or possible liquidations of Phoenix in which Morgan Stanley would play a part. G. Platt did not make [762] any stock recommendations to Switzer, nor did he intentionally communicate material, non-public corporate information to Switzer about Phoenix during their conversations at the track meet. The information that Switzer heard at the track meet about Phoenix was overheard and was not the result of an intentional disclosure by G. Platt.

41. Sometime in the afternoon, after his last conversation with G. Platt, Switzer laid down on a row of bleachers behind the Platts to sunbathe while waiting for his son's next event. While Switzer was sunbathing, he overheard G. Platt talking to his wife about his trip to New York the prior day. In that conversation, G. Platt mentioned Morgan Stanley and his desire to dispose of or liquidate Phoenix. G. Platt further talked about several companies bidding on Phoenix. Switzer also overheard that an announcement of a "possible" liquidation of Phoenix might occur the following Thursday. Switzer remained on the bleachers behind the Platts for approximately twenty minutes then got up and continued to move about.

42. At this time Switzer had no knowledge as to whether the information he had overheard was confidential.

43. G. Platt was not conscious of Switzer's presence on the bleachers behind him that day, nor that Switzer had overheard any conversation.

44. G. Platt had returned home late the previous day from his meetings in New York, and his wife was to leave town for an entire week on the following day. Having minor children, it is the Platts' common practice to try to arrange for G. Platt to be at home when his wife is out of town. The day of the track meet provided the Platts with an opportunity to discuss their respective plans for the up-coming week. During this discussion, G. Platt's prior business activities in New York and its resultant obligations and appointments were mentioned. In addition, when G. Platt appears distracted, it is not uncommon for his wife to inquire of him what is on his mind. On these occasions, he will talk to her about his problems, even though she does not have an understanding of nor interest in business matters. On the day of the track meet, Phoenix was weighing upon the mind of G. Platt, as it had been for the past several years, prompting G. Platt to talk to his wife about it.

45. On June 6, 1981, after the track meet, Switzer returned home and looked up the price of Phoenix in the paper. He then had dinner with Sedwyn Kennedy, a close friend of both his and defendant Lee Allan Smith. In the past, they had all made investments through their partnership, SKS. Switzer told Kennedy he had overheard a conversation about the possible liquidation of Phoenix and that it would probably occur or be announced the next Thursday. Switzer told him the source was a gentlemen who was an executive with TIC. Switzer did not tell Kennedy the man was G. Platt. Switzer and Kennedy are close friends and have known each other since 1966.

46. By the end of the evening, Switzer and Kennedy had each expressed an intention to purchase Phoenix stock. [...]

48. On or about Monday, June 8, 1981, Kennedy purchased five thousand (5,000) shares of Phoenix stock at Forty-Two and 75/100 Dollars ($42.75) per share through the S&H Investments account; and on or about Tuesday, June 9, 1981, after further discussions with Deem, Kennedy purchased an additional one thousand (1,000) shares of Phoenix at Forty-Nine Dollars ($49) per share. (See stipulated fact No. 15, *supra*.) [...]

61. G. Platt did not share in the profits made through the transactions in Phoenix stock by Switzer, Kennedy, Deem, Smith, Hodges, Amyx and Hoover, nor did he receive any other financial benefit as a result of those transactions.

62. G. Platt did not receive any direct or indirect pecuniary gain nor any reputational benefit likely to translate into future earnings due to Switzer's inadvertent receipt of the information regarding Phoenix.

63. G. Platt did not make any gift to Switzer at this time, nor has he ever made a gift to Switzer.

64. Neither Switzer, Kennedy, Smith, Deem, Hodges, Amyx nor Hoover has ever been employed by or been an officer or director of Phoenix or TIC, nor have any of these defendants ever had any business relationship with Phoenix or with G. Platt personally. None of these defendants is a relative or personal friend of G. Platt.

65. None of the defendants had a relationship of trust and confidence with Phoenix, its shareholders or G. Platt. […]

3. It is undisputed that G. Platt was an insider in regard to both TIC and Phoenix as of June 6, 1981.

4. Switzer, Kennedy, Deem, Smith, Hodges, Amyx and Hoover were not insiders of Phoenix. None of them had any fiduciary duty to the stockholders of TIC or Phoenix by virtue of their positions. None of them were employed by Phoenix, nor did they have any position of trust or confidence with Phoenix. These defendants were strangers to Phoenix and had no preexisting fiduciary duties to the shareholders of Phoenix. In its recent opinion of *Dirks v. Securities Exchange Commission,* 463 U.S. 646, 103 S.Ct. 3255, 77 L.Ed.2d 911 (1983), the United States Supreme Court addressed tippee liability. The court pointed out that, unlike insiders who have independent fiduciary duties to both the corporation and its shareholders, the typical tippee has no such fiduciary relationship. In view of the absence of this fiduciary relationship, the court notes it has been unclear how a tippee acquires the *Cady, Roberts* duty to disclose or refrain from trading on inside information first stated in *In re Cady, Roberts & Co.,* 40 S.E.C. 907 (1961). Although the SEC, in *Dirks,* urged the court to accept what has become known as the "information" theory, which in essence states that anyone knowingly receiving non-public, material

information acquires an insider fiduciary duty to disclose or abstain from trading, the court rejected this theory as they had in *Chiarella v. United States,* 445 U.S. 222, 100 S.Ct. 1108, 63 L.Ed.2d 348 (1980). The court in *Dirks* stated: "We reaffirm today that `[a] duty [to disclose] arises from the relationship between parties ... and not merely from one's ability to acquire information because of his position in the market.'" *Dirks,* 103 S.Ct. at 3263, quoting from *Chiarella v. United States,* 445 U.S. at 232-33, n. 14, 100 S.Ct. at 1116 n. 14. The court further stated in *Dirks:* "As we emphasized in *Chiarella,* mere possession of non-public information does not give rise to a duty to disclose or abstain; only a specific relationship does that. And we do not believe that the mere receipt of information from an insider creates such a special relationship between the tippee and the corporation's shareholders." 103 S.Ct. at 3262, n. 15.

6. Essentially, in *Dirks* the court found that the *Cady, Roberts* duty of a tippee "to disclose or abstain" is *derivative* from that of the insider's duty. The court stated:

> ... [S]ome tippees must assume an insider's duty to the shareholders not because they receive inside information, but rather because it has been made available to them *improperly.* And for Rule 10b-5 purposes, the insider's disclosure is improper only where it would violate his *Cady, Roberts* duty. Thus, a tippee assumes a fiduciary duty to the shareholders of a corporation not to trade on material nonpublic information only when the insider has breached his fiduciary duty to the shareholders by disclosing the information to the tippee and the tippee knows or should know that there has been a breach. As Commissioner Smith perceptively observed in *Investors Management Co.:* `[T]ippee responsibility must be related back to insider responsibility by a necessary finding that the tippee knew the information was given to him in breach of a duty by a person having a special relationship to the issuer not to disclose the information .... `44 S.E.C., at 651 (concurring in the result). Tipping thus properly is viewed only as a means of indirectly violating [766] the *Cady, Roberts* disclose-or-abstain rule.

[...]

7. Thus, only when a disclosure is made for an "improper purpose" will such a "tip" constitute a breach of an insider's duty, and only when there has been a breach of an insider's duty which the "tipee" knew or should have known constituted such a breach will there be "tippee" liability sufficient to constitute a violation of § 10(b) and Commission Rule 10b-5.

8. In *Dirks,* the court held that a disclosure is made for an "improper purpose" when an insider personally will benefit, directly or indirectly, from his disclosure. That court stated: "Absent some personal gain, there has been no breach of duty to stockholders. And absent a breach by the insider [to his stockholders], there is no derivative breach [by the tippee].*Dirks,* 103 S.Ct. at 3265.

9. G. Platt did not breach a fiduciary duty to stockholders of Phoenix for purposes of Rule 10b-5 liability nor § 10(b) liability, when he disclosed to his wife at the track meet of June 6, 1981, that there was going to be a possible liquidation of Phoenix.

10. This information was given to Mrs. Platt by G. Platt for the purpose of informing her of his up-coming business schedule so that arrangements for child care could be made.

11. The information was inadvertently overheard by Switzer at the track meet.

12. Rule 10b-5 does not bar trading on the basis of information inadvertently revealed by an insider. […]

14. G. Platt did not personally benefit, directly or indirectly, monetarily or otherwise from the inadvertent disclosure.

15. As noted above, *Dirks* set forth a two-prong test for purposes of determining whether a tippee has acquired a fiduciary duty. First, it must be shown that an insider breached a fiduciary duty to the shareholders by disclosing inside information; and, second, it must be shown that the tippee knew or should have known that there had been a breach by the insider.*Dirks,* 103 S.Ct. at 3264.

16. G. Platt did not breach a duty to the shareholders of Phoenix, and thus plaintiff failed to meet its burden of proof as to the first prong established in *Dirks.* Since G. Platt did not breach a fiduciary duty to Phoenix shareholders, Switzer did not acquire nor assume a fiduciary duty to Phoenix's shareholders, and because Switzer did not

acquire a fiduciary duty to Phoenix shareholders, any information he passed on to defendants Smith, Hodges, Amyx, Hoover, Kennedy and Deem was not in violation of Rule 10b-5. […]

On the basis of the above findings of fact and conclusions of law, the court orders judgment in favor of defendants.

6.2.3.3 A note on US v Newman

The classic tipper-tippee scenario in insider trading prosecutions involves a corporate insider who, in exchange for a personal benefit, discloses material nonpublic information to an outsider, who then later trades in reliance on this inside information. For many years, courts leaned on increasingly vague assertions of "personal benefit" received by tippers to assign liability to remote tippees. In some cases, courts have been willing to "daisy chain" to recipients of inside information who are extremely remote from the original source.

In *United States v. Newman* the Second Circuit reduced the liability of remote tippees by holding that a tippee cannot be convicted unless the tippee "knows of the personal benefit received by the insider in exchange for the disclosure." In addition, *Newman* held the "personal benefit" received by the tipper "must be of some consequence" and must be a true *quid pro quo*, rejecting the notion that mere friendship and association could meet this requirement.

From the *Newman* opinion:

> [T]he Government presented evidence that a group of financial analysts exchanged information they obtained from company insiders, both directly and more often indirectly. Specifically, the Government alleged that these analysts received information from insiders at Dell and NVIDIA disclosing those companies' earnings numbers before they were publicly released in Dell's May 2008 and August 2008 earnings announcements and NVIDIA's May 2008 earnings announcement. These analysts then passed the inside information to their portfolio managers, including Newman and Chiasson, who, in turn, executed trades in Dell and NVIDIA stock,

491

earning approximately $4 million and $68 million, respectively, in profits for their respective funds. Newman and Chiasson were several steps removed from the corporate insiders and there was no evidence that either was aware of the source of the inside information. With respect to the Dell tipping chain, the evidence established that Rob Ray of Dell's investor relations department tipped information regarding Dell's consolidated earnings numbers to Sandy Goyal, an analyst at Neuberger Berman. Goyal in turn gave the information to Diamondback analyst Jesse Tortora. Tortora in turn relayed the information to his manager Newman as well as to other analysts including Level Global analyst Spyridon "Sam" Adondakis. Adondakis then passed along the Dell information to Chiasson, making Newman and Chiasson three and four levels removed from the inside tipper, respectively. ...Newman and Chiasson moved for a judgment of acquittal pursuant to Federal Rule of Criminal Procedure 29. They argued that there was no evidence that the corporate insiders provided inside information in exchange for a personal benefit which is required to establish tipper liability under *Dirks v. S.E.C.,*463 U.S. 646, 103 S.Ct. 3255, 77 L.Ed.2d 911 (1983). Because a tippee's liability derives from the liability of the tipper, Newman and Chiasson argued that they could not be found guilty of insider trading. Newman and Chiasson also argued that, even if the corporate insiders had received a personal benefit in exchange for the inside information, there was no evidence that they knew about any such benefit. Absent such knowledge, appellants argued, they were not aware of, or participants in, the tippers' fraudulent breaches of fiduciary duties to Dell or NVIDIA, and could not be convicted of insider trading under *Dirks.* ...In light of *Dirks,* we find no support for the Government's contention that knowledge of a breach of the duty of confidentiality without knowledge of the personal benefit is sufficient to impose criminal liability. Although the Government might like the law to be different, nothing in the law requires a symmetry of information in the nation's securities markets. The Supreme Court explicitly repudiated this premise not only in *Dirks,* but in a predecessor case, *Chiarella v. United States.* In *Chiarella,* the Supreme Court rejected this Circuit's conclusion that "the federal securities laws have created a system providing equal access to information necessary for reasoned and intelligent investment decisions.... because [material non-public] information gives certain buyers or sellers an unfair advantage over less informed buyers and sellers." 445 U.S. at 232, 100 S.Ct. 1108. The Supreme Court emphasized that "[t]his reasoning suffers from [a] defect.... [because] not every instance of financial unfairness constitutes fraudulent activity under § 10(b)." *Id. See also United States v. Chestman,* 947 F.2d 551, 578 (2d Cir. 1991) (Winter, J., concurring) ("[The policy rationale [for prohibiting insider trading] stops well short of prohibiting all trading on material nonpublic information. Efficient capital markets depend on the protection of property rights in information. However, they also require that persons who acquire and act on information about companies be able to profit from the information they generate....")]. Thus, in both *Chiarella* and *Dirks,* the Supreme Court affirmatively established that insider trading liability is based on breaches of fiduciary duty, not on informational asymmetries. This is a critical limitation on insider trading liability that protects a corporation's interests in confidentiality while promoting efficiency in the nation's securities markets. As noted above, *Dirks* clearly defines a breach of fiduciary duty as a breach of the duty of confidentiality in exchange for a personal benefit. ... Accordingly, we conclude that a tippee's knowledge of the insider's breach necessarily requires knowledge that the insider disclosed confidential information in exchange for personal benefit. In reaching this conclusion, we join every other district court to our knowledge—apart from Judge Sullivan—that has confronted this question. ...Our conclusion also comports with well-settled principles of substantive criminal law. As the Supreme Court explained in *Staples v. United States*, under the common law, *mens rea*, which requires that the defendant know the facts that make his conduct illegal, is a necessary element in every crime. Such a requirement is particularly appropriate in insider trading cases where we have acknowledged "it is easy to imagine a ... trader who receives a tip and is unaware that his conduct was illegal and therefore wrongful." *United States v. Kaiser*. This is also a statutory requirement, because only "willful" violations are subject to criminal provision. *See United States v. Temple* ("`Willful' repeatedly has been defined in the criminal context as intentional, purposeful, and voluntary, as distinguished from accidental or negligent").In sum, we hold that to sustain an insider trading conviction against a tippee, the Government must prove each of the following elements beyond a reasonable doubt: that (1) the corporate insider was entrusted with a fiduciary duty; (2) the corporate insider breached his fiduciary duty by (a) disclosing confidential information to a tippee (b) in exchange for a personal benefit; (3) the tippee knew of the tipper's breach, that is, he knew the information was confidential and divulged for personal benefit; and (4) the tippee still used that information to trade in a security or tip another individual for personal benefit.

6.2.3.4 US v. Chestman

There are many situations in which it might be unreasonable for the court to seek evidence of a breach of fiduciary duty. For example, where a spouse learns inside information and trades on it. The courts and SEC have adapted in response to those situations.

In addition to the holding in this case, the court in US v. Chestman provides a nice summary of the two theories of Federal insider trading liability: classical and misappropriation. In addition, the court also lays out its understanding of the role of fiduciary duties in establishing liability. In his dissent, Judge Winter summarizes a policy argument against insider trading based in property rights over corporate information and hints at an efficiency argument for permitting some insider trading.

494

947 F.2d 551 (1991)
U.S. v. CHESTMAN

MESKILL, Circuit Judge, joined by CARDAMONE, PRATT, MINER and
ALTIMARI, Circuit Judges:

The issues spring from the alleged insider trading of defendant Robert Chestman. A jury
found Chestman guilty of thirty-one counts of insider trading and perjury: […] (2) ten
counts of securities fraud in violation of section 10(b), 18 U.S.C. § 2, and 17 C.F.R. §
240.10b-5 (1988) (Rule 10b-5), […]

On *in banc* reconsideration, we conclude that the Rule 14e-3(a) convictions should be
affirmed and that the Rule 10b-5 […]

BACKGROUND

Robert Chestman is a stockbroker. Keith Loeb first sought Chestman's services in 1982,
when Loeb decided to consolidate his and his wife's holdings in Waldbaum, Inc.
(Waldbaum), a publicly traded company that owned a large supermarket chain. During
their initial meeting, Loeb told Chestman that his wife was a grand-daughter of Julia
Waldbaum, a member of the board of directors of Waldbaum and the wife of its
founder. Julia Waldbaum also was the mother of Ira Waldbaum, the president and
controlling shareholder of Waldbaum. From 1982 to 1986, Chestman executed several
transactions involving Waldbaum restricted and common stock for Keith Loeb. To
facilitate some of these trades, Loeb sent Chestman a copy of his wife's birth certificate,
which indicated that his wife's mother was Shirley Waldbaum Witkin.

On November 21, 1986, Ira Waldbaum agreed to sell Waldbaum to the Great Atlantic
and Pacific Tea Company (A & P). The resulting stock purchase agreement required Ira
to tender a controlling block of Waldbaum shares to A & P at a price of $50 per share.
Ira told three of his children, all employees of Waldbaum, about the pending sale two
days later, admonishing them to keep the news quiet until a public announcement. […]

In spite of Ira's counsel, Shirley told her daughter, Susan Loeb, on November 24 that Ira
was selling the company. Shirley warned Susan not to tell anyone except her husband,
Keith Loeb, because disclosure could ruin the sale. The next day, Susan told her

husband about the pending tender offer and cautioned him not to tell anyone because "it could possibly ruin the sale."

The following day, November 26, Keith Loeb telephoned Robert Chestman at 8:59 a.m. Unable to reach Chestman, Loeb left a message asking Chestman to call him "ASAP." According to Loeb, he later spoke with Chestman between 9:00 a.m. and 10:30 a.m. that morning and told Chestman that he had "some definite, some accurate information" that Waldbaum was about to be sold at a "substantially higher" price than its market value. Loeb asked Chestman several times what he thought Loeb should do. Chestman responded that he could not advise Loeb what to do "in a situation like this" and that Loeb would have to make up his own mind.

That morning Chestman executed several purchases of Waldbaum stock. At 9:49 a.m., he bought 3,000 shares for his own account at $24.65 per share. Between 11:31 a.m. and 12:35 p.m., he purchased an additional 8,000 shares for his clients' discretionary accounts at prices ranging from $25.75 to $26.00 per share. One of the discretionary accounts was the Loeb account, for which Chestman bought 1,000 shares.

Before the market closed at 4:00 p.m., Loeb claims that he telephoned Chestman a second time. During their conversation Loeb again pressed Chestman for advice. Chestman repeated that he could not advise Loeb "in a situation like this," but then said that, based on his research, Waldbaum was a "buy." Loeb subsequently ordered 1,000 shares of Waldbaum stock.

Chestman presented a different version of the day's events. Before the SEC and at trial, he claimed that he had purchased Waldbaum stock based on his own research. He stated that his purchases were consistent with previous purchases of Waldbaum stock and other retail food stocks and were supported by reports in trade publications as well as the unusually high trading volume of the stock on November 25. He denied having spoken to Loeb about Waldbaum stock on the day of the trades.

At the close of trading on November 26, the tender offer was publicly announced. Waldbaum stock rose to $49 per share the next business day. In December 1986 Loeb learned that the National Association [556] of Securities Dealers had started an investigation concerning transactions in Waldbaum stock. Loeb contacted Chestman who, according to Loeb, "reassured" him that Chestman had bought the stock for

Loeb's account based on his research. Loeb called Chestman again in April 1987 after learning of an SEC investigation into the trading of Waldbaum stock. Chestman again stated that he bought the stock based on research. Similar conversations ensued. After one of these conversations, Chestman asked Loeb what his "position" was, Loeb replied, "I guess it's the same thing." Loeb subsequently agreed, however, to cooperate with the government. The terms of his cooperation agreement required that he disgorge the $25,000 profit from his purchase and sale of Waldbaum stock and pay a $25,000 fine.

A grand jury returned an indictment on July 20, 1988, charging Chestman with the following counts of insider trading and perjury:[…] ten counts of securities fraud in violation of Rule 10b-5, […]. After a jury trial, Chestman was found guilty on all counts.

Chestman appealed. […]

B. Rule 10b-5

Chestman's Rule 10b-5 convictions were based on the misappropriation theory, which provides that "one who misappropriates nonpublic information in breach of a fiduciary duty and trades on that information to his own advantage violates Section 10(b) and Rule 10b-5." *SEC v. Materia,* 745 F.2d 197, 203 (2d Cir.1984), *cert. denied,* 471 U.S. 1053, 105 S.Ct. 2112, 85 L.Ed.2d 477 (1985). With respect to the shares Chestman purchased on behalf of Keith Loeb, Chestman was convicted of aiding and abetting Loeb's misappropriation of nonpublic information in breach of a duty Loeb owed to the Waldbaum family and to his wife Susan. As to the shares Chestman purchased for himself and his other clients, Chestman was convicted as a "tippee" of that same misappropriated information. Thus, while Chestman is the defendant in this case, the alleged misappropriator was Keith Loeb. The government agrees that Chestman's convictions cannot be sustained unless there was sufficient evidence to show that (1) Keith Loeb breached a duty owed to the Waldbaum family or Susan Loeb based on a fiduciary or similar relationship of trust and confidence, and (2) Chestman knew that Loeb had done so. We have heretofore never applied the misappropriation theory — and its predicate requirement of a fiduciary breach — in the context of family relationships. As a prologue to that analysis, we canvass past Rule 10b-5 jurisprudence.

Section 10(b) prohibits the use "in connection with the purchase or sale of any security ... [of] any manipulative or deceptive device or contrivance in contravention of such rules and regulations as the Commission may prescribe." 15 U.S.C. § 78j(b). Pursuant to that mandate, the SEC promulgated Rule 10b-5, which, in pertinent part, makes it unlawful "[t]o employ any device, scheme, or artifice to defraud" or "[t]o engage in any act ... which operates ... as a fraud or deceit upon any person, in connection with the purchase or sale of any security." 17 C.F.R. § 240.10b-5 (1988). While more than one interpretation has been given to this expansive language, fraud has remained the centerpiece of a Rule 10b-5 criminal violation. At this juncture, two general theories of Rule 10b-5 fraud have emerged to fill the interstitial gaps of the rule.

1. Traditional Theory of Rule 10b-5 Liability

The traditional theory of insider trader liability derives principally from the Supreme Court's holdings in *Chiarella*, 445 [565] U.S. 222, 100 S.Ct. 1108, and *Dirks v. SEC*, 463 U.S. 646, 103 S.Ct. 3255, 77 L.Ed.2d 911 (1983). A securities trader commits Rule 10b-5 fraud, the *Chiarella* Court held, only if he "fails to disclose material information prior to the consummation of a transaction ... when he is under a duty to do so." *Chiarella*, 445 U.S. at 228, 100 S.Ct. at 1114. The *Chiarella* Court then delineated when a person possessing material nonpublic information owes such a duty — what it called "[t]he obligation to disclose or abstain" from trading. *Id.* at 227, 100 S.Ct. at 1114. It held that this duty "does not arise from the mere possession of nonpublic market information." *Id.* at 235, 100 S.Ct. at 1118. That is, the duty inquiry does not turn on whether the parties to the transaction have "equal information." *Dirks*, 463 U.S. at 657, 103 S.Ct. at 3263 (construing *Chiarella*). Rather, a duty to disclose or abstain arises only from "`a fiduciary or other similar relation of trust and confidence between [the parties to the transaction].'" *Chiarella*, 445 U.S. at 228, 100 S.Ct. at 1114 (quoting Restatement (Second) of Torts § 551(2)(a) (1976)).

In *Dirks*, an action concerning the liability of a tippee of material nonpublic information, the Court built on its holding in *Chiarella*. *Dirks* again rejected a parity of information theory of Rule 10b-5 liability, reiterating the "requirement of a specific relationship between the shareholders and the individual trading on inside information." *Dirks*, 463 U.S. at 655, 103 S.Ct. at 3261. It then examined when a tippee inherits a fiduciary duty to the corporation's shareholders to disclose or refrain from trading. Noting the "derivative" nature of tippee liability, *id.* at 659, 103 S.Ct. at 3264, the Court held that tippee liability attaches only when an "insider has breached his fiduciary duty to the shareholders by disclosing the information to the tippee and the tippee knows or should know that there has been a breach."*Id.* at 660, 103 S.Ct. at 3264.

Dirks established, in *dictum,* an additional means by which erstwhile outsiders become fiduciaries of a corporation's shareholders. Justice Powell explained:

> Under certain circumstances, such as where corporate information is revealed legitimately to an underwriter, accountant, lawyer, or consultant working for the corporation, these outsiders may become fiduciaries of the shareholders. The basis for recognizing this fiduciary duty is not simply that such persons acquired nonpublic corporate information, but rather that they have entered into a special confidential relationship in the conduct of the business of the enterprise and are given access to information solely for corporate purposes.... For such a duty to be imposed, however, the corporation must expect the outsider to keep the disclosed nonpublic information confidential, and the relationship at least must imply such a duty.

Id. at 655 n. 14, 103 S.Ct. at 3262 n. 14 (citations omitted). This theory clothes an outsider with temporary insider status when the outsider obtains access to confidential information solely for corporate purposes in the context of "a special confidential relationship." The temporary insider thereby acquires a correlative fiduciary duty to the corporation's shareholders.

Binding these strands of Rule 10b-5 liability are two principles — one, the predicate act of fraud must be traceable to a breach of duty to the purchasers or sellers of securities,[2] two, a fiduciary duty does [566] not run to the purchasers or sellers solely as a result of one's possession of material nonpublic information.

2. Misappropriation Theory

The second general theory of Rule 10b-5 liability, the misappropriation theory, has not yet been the subject of a Supreme Court holding,[3] but has been adopted in the Second, Third, Seventh and Ninth Circuits. *See, e.g., SEC v. Cherif,* 933 F.2d 403 (7th Cir.1991);

SEC v. Clark, 915 F.2d 439 (9th Cir.1990); *Rothberg v. Rosenbloom,* 771 F.2d 818 (3d Cir.1985), *rev'd on other grounds after remand,* 808 F.2d 252 (3d Cir.1986), *cert. denied,* 481 U.S. 1017, 107 S.Ct. 1895, 95 L.Ed.2d 501 (1987); *United States v. Newman,* 664 F.2d 12 (2d Cir. 1981), *aff'd after remand,* 722 F.2d 729 (2d Cir.1983), *cert. denied,* 464 U.S. 863, 104 S.Ct. 193, 78 L.Ed.2d 170 (1983). Under this theory, a person violates Rule 10b-5 when he misappropriates material nonpublic information in breach of a fiduciary duty or similar relationship of trust and confidence and uses that information in a securities transaction. *See, e.g., Carpenter,* 791 F.2d at 1028-29; *Materia,* 745 F.2d at 201; *Newman,* 664 F.2d at 17-18. In contrast to *Chiarella* and *Dirks,* the misappropriation theory does not require that the buyer or seller of securities be defrauded. *Newman,* 664 F.2d at 17. Focusing on the language "fraud or deceit upon *any* person" (emphasis added), we have held that the predicate act of fraud may be perpetrated on the source of the nonpublic information, even though the source may be unaffiliated with the buyer or seller of securities.*See Carpenter,* 791 F.2d at 1032. To date we have applied the theory only in the context of employment relationships. *See Carpenter,* 791 F.2d at 1032 (financial columnist breached duty to his newspaper); *Materia,* 745 F.2d at 202 (copyholder breached duty to his printing company); *Newman,* 664 F.2d at 17 (investment banker breached duty to his firm). District courts in this Circuit have applied the theory in other settings as well as in the employment context. *See, e.g., United States v. Willis,* 737 F.Supp. 269 (S.D.N.Y.1990) (denying motion to dismiss indictment of psychiatrist who traded on the basis of information obtained from patient, in breach of duty arising from relationship of trust and confidence); *United States v. Reed,* 601 F.Supp. 685 (S.D.N.Y.), *rev'd on other grounds,* 773 F.2d 477 (2d Cir.1985) (allegation that son breached fiduciary duty to father, a corporate director, withstood motion to dismiss indictment); *SEC v. Musella,* 578 F.Supp. 425 (S.D.N.Y.1984) (office services manager of law firm breached duty to law firm and its clients by trading on the basis of material nonpublic information acquired in the course of his employment).

One point at which the misappropriation theory and the traditional theory of insider trading merge warrants brief consideration. Our first applications of the misappropriation theory, in *Newman* and *Materia,* concerned conduct that occurred before the Supreme Court's holding in *Dirks. Dirks* noted that an outsider could obtain temporary insider status by gaining access to confidential information through certain relationships with a corporation — as, for example, an underwriter, lawyer or consultant. 463 U.S. at 655 n. 14, 103 S.Ct. at 3262 n. 14. A temporary insider theory of prosecution might well have covered the activities of the investment banker in *Newman* and the printer in *Materia*. In *Newman* and *Materia*, the defendants appeared to have "entered into a special confidential relationship in the conduct of the business of the enterprise and [were] given access to information solely for corporate purposes." *Dirks*, 463 U.S. at 655 n. 14, 103 S.Ct. at 3262 n. 14. In view of the [567] overlap between *Newman* and *Materia* on the one hand and the *Dirks* concept of temporary insiders on the other, we arguably did not break ranks with the traditional theory of insider trading until our holding in *Carpenter*. In *Carpenter* none of the prongs of liability under the traditional theory applied. That is, the defendants did not owe the people with whom they traded a duty to disclose or abstain from trading — absent resurrection of the twice-rejected parity of information theory. *Carpenter*, then, represents the first fact pattern we have considered that is clearly beyond the pale of the traditional theory of insider trading.

After *Carpenter*, the fiduciary relationship question takes on special importance. This is because a fraud-on-the-source theory of liability extends the focus of Rule 10b-5 beyond the confined sphere of fiduciary/shareholder relations to fiduciary breaches of any sort, a particularly broad expansion of 10b-5 liability if the add-on, a "similar relationship of trust and confidence," is construed liberally. One concern triggered by this broadened inquiry is that fiduciary duties are circumscribed with some clarity in the context of shareholder relations but lack definition in other contexts. *See generally Reed*, 601 F.Supp. 685 (and authorities cited therein). Tethered to the field of shareholder relations, fiduciary obligations arise within a narrow, principled sphere. The existence of fiduciary duties in other common law settings, however, is anything but clear. Our Rule 10b-5 precedents under the misappropriation theory, moreover, provide little guidance with respect to the question of fiduciary breach, because they involved egregious fiduciary breaches arising solely in the context of employer/employee associations. *See Carpenter*, 791 F.2d at 1028 ("It is clear that defendant Winans ... breached a duty of confidentiality to his employer"); *Newman*, 664 F.2d at 17 ("we need spend little time on the issue of fraud and deceit"); *Materia*, 745 F.2d at 201 (same). For these reasons we tread cautiously in extending the misappropriation theory to new relationships, lest our efforts to construe Rule 10b-5 lose method and predictability, taking over "the whole corporate universe." *United States v. Chiarella,* 588 F.2d 1358, 1377 (2d Cir.1978) (Meskill, *J.,* dissenting) (quoting *Santa Fe Industries, Inc. v. Green,* 430 U.S. 462, 480, 97 S.Ct. 1292, 1304, 51 L.Ed.2d 480 (1977)), *rev'd,* 445 U.S. 222, 100 S.Ct. 1108, 63 L.Ed.2d 348 (1980). [...]

4. Application of the Law of Fiduciary Duties

The alleged misappropriator in this case was Keith Loeb. According to the government's theory of prosecution, Loeb breached a fiduciary duty to his wife Susan and the Waldbaum family when he disclosed to Robert Chestman information concerning a pending tender offer for Waldbaum stock. Chestman was convicted as an aider and abettor of the misappropriation and as a tippee of the misappropriated information. Convictions under both theories, the government concedes, required the government to establish two critical elements — Loeb breached a fiduciary duty to Susan Loeb or to the Waldbaum family and Chestman knew that Loeb had done so.

Chestman challenges the sufficiency of the evidence to establish each of these elements of the convictions. Although such a challenge carries a "heavy burden," *United States v. Chang An-Lo,* 851 F.2d 547, 553 (2d Cir.), *cert. denied,* 488 U.S. 966, 109 S.Ct. 493, 102 L.Ed.2d 530 (1988), that burden was carried here.

We have little trouble finding the evidence insufficient to establish a fiduciary relationship or its functional equivalent between Keith Loeb and the Waldbaum family. The government presented only two pieces of evidence on this point. The first was that Keith was an extended member of the Waldbaum family, specifically the family patriarch's (Ira Waldbaum's) "nephew-in-law." The second piece of evidence concerned Ira's discussions of the business with family members. "My children," Ira Waldbaum testified, "have always been involved with me and my family and they know we never speak about business outside of the family." His earlier testimony indicates that the "family" to which he referred were his "three children who were involved in the business."

Lending this evidence the reasonable inferences to which it is entitled, *United States v. Zabare,* 871 F.2d 282, 286 (2d Cir.), *cert. denied,* 493 U.S. 856, 110 S.Ct. 161, 107 L.Ed.2d 119 (1989), it falls short of establishing the relationship necessary for fiduciary obligations. Kinship alone does not create the necessary relationship. The government proffered nothing more to establish a fiduciary-like association. It did not show that Keith Loeb had been brought into the family's inner circle, whose members, it appears, discussed confidential business information either because they were kin or because they worked together with Ira Waldbaum. Keith was not an employee of Waldbaum and there was no showing that he participated in confidential communications regarding the business. The critical information was gratuitously communicated to him. The disclosure did not serve the interests of Ira Waldbaum, his children or the Waldbaum company. Nor was there any evidence that the alleged relationship was characterized by influence or reliance of any sort. Measured against the principles of fiduciary relations, the evidence does not support a finding that Keith Loeb and the [571] Waldbaum family shared either a fiduciary relation or its functional equivalent.

The government's theory that Keith breached a fiduciary duty of confidentiality to Susan suffers from similar defects. The evidence showed: Keith and Susan were married; Susan admonished Keith not to disclose that Waldbaum was the target of a tender offer; and the two had shared and maintained confidences in the past.

Keith's status as Susan's husband could not itself establish fiduciary status. Nor, absent a pre-existing fiduciary relation or an express agreement of confidentiality, could the coda — "Don't tell." That leaves the unremarkable testimony that Keith and Susan had shared and maintained generic confidences before. The jury was not told the nature of these past disclosures and therefore it could not reasonably find a relationship that inspired fiduciary, rather than normal marital, obligations.

In the absence of evidence of an explicit acceptance by Keith of a duty of confidentiality, the context of the disclosure takes on special import. While acceptance may be implied, it must be implied from a pre-existing fiduciary-like relationship between the parties. Here the government presented the jury with insufficient evidence from which to draw a rational inference of implied acceptance. Susan's disclosure of the information to Keith served no purpose, business or otherwise. The disclosure also was unprompted. Keith did not induce her to convey the information through misrepresentation or subterfuge. Superiority and reliance, moreover, did not mark this relationship either before or after the disclosure of the confidential information. Nor did Susan's dependence on Keith to act in her interests for some purpose inspire the disclosure. The government failed even to establish a pattern of sharing business confidences between the couple. The government, therefore, failed to offer sufficient evidence to establish the functional equivalent of a fiduciary relation.

In sum, because Keith owed neither Susan nor the Waldbaum family a fiduciary duty or its functional equivalent, he did not defraud them by disclosing news of the pending tender offer to Chestman. Absent a predicate act of fraud by Keith Loeb, the alleged misappropriator, Chestman could not be derivatively liable as Loeb's tippee or as an aider and abettor. Therefore, Chestman's Rule 10b-5 convictions must be reversed. [...]

WINTER, Circuit Judge (joined by OAKES, Chief Judge, NEWMAN, KEARSE, and McLAUGHLIN, Circuit Judges), concurring in part and dissenting in part:

[...]

b) Property Rights in Inside Information

One commentator has attempted to explain the Supreme Court decisions in terms of the business-property rationale for banning insider trading mentioned in *Cady, Roberts & Co. See* Easterbrook, *supra,* at 309-39. That rationale may be summarized as follows. Information is perhaps the most precious commodity in commercial markets. It is expensive to produce, and, because it involves facts and ideas that can be easily photocopied or carried in one's head, there is a ubiquitous risk that those [577] who pay to produce information will see others reap the profit from it. Where the profit from an activity is likely to be diverted, investment in that activity will decline. If the law fails to protect property rights in commercial information, therefore, less will be invested in generating such information. *Id.* at 313.

For example, mining companies whose investments in geological surveys have revealed valuable deposits do not want word of the strike to get out until they have secured rights to the land.[3] If word does get out, the price of the land not only will go up, but other mining companies may also secure the rights. In either case, the mining company that invested in geological surveys (including the inevitably sizeable number of unsuccessful drillings) will see profits from that investment enjoyed by others. If mining companies are unable to keep the results of such surveys confidential, less will be invested in them.

Similarly, firms that invest money in generating information about other companies with a view to some form of combination will maintain secrecy about their efforts, and if secrecy cannot be maintained, less will be invested in acquiring such information. Hostile acquirers will want to keep such information secret lest the target mount defensive actions or speculators purchase the target's stock. Even when friendly negotiations with the other company are undertaken, the acquirer will often require the target corporation to maintain secrecy about negotiations, lest the very fact of negotiation tip off others on the important fact that the two firms think a combination might be valuable. *See, e.g., Staffin v. Greenberg,* 672 F.2d 1196, 1207 n. 12 (3d Cir.1982) ("If, as is often the case, a merger will benefit both the acquired company and its shareholders, an insider may be obliged to maintain strict confidentiality to avoid ruining the corporate opportunity through premature disclosure. Indeed, the record is clear in this case that [the buyer] very nearly withdrew from merger discussions upon hearing of [the seller's] ... press release."); *Flamm v. Eberstadt,* 814 F.2d 1169, 1174-79 (7th Cir.) ("[P]otential acquires ... may fear that premature disclosure may spark competition that will deprive them of part of the value of their effort, so that bids in a world of early disclosure will be lower than bids in a world of deferred disclosure."), *cert. denied,* 484 U.S. 853, 108 S.Ct. 157, 98 L.Ed.2d 112 (1987). In the instant matter, A & P made secrecy a condition of its acquisition of Waldbaum's.

Insider trading may reduce the return on information in two ways. First, it creates incentives for insiders to generate or disclose information that may disregard the welfare of the corporation. Easterbrook, *supra,* at 332-33. That risk is not implicated by the facts in the present case, and no further discussion is presently required.

Second, insider trading creates a risk that information will be prematurely disclosed by such trading, and the corporation will lose part or all of its property in that information. *Id.* at 331. Although trades by an insider may rarely affect market price, others who know of the insider's trading may notice that a trader is unusually successful, or simply perceive unusual activity in a stock and guess the information and/or make piggyback trades.[4]*Id.* at 336. A broker who executes a trade for a geologist or for a financial printer may well draw relevant conclusions. Or, as in the instant matter, the trader, Loeb, may tell his or her broker about the inside information, who may then trade on his or her account, on clients' accounts, or may tell [578] friends and relatives. One inside trader has publicly attributed his exposure in part to the fact that the bank through which he made trades piggybacked on the trades, as did the broker who made the trades for the bank. *See* Levine, *The Inside Story of An Inside Trader,* Fortune, May 21, 1990, at 80. Once activity in a stock reaches an unusual stage, others may guess the reason for the trading — the corporate secret. Insider trading thus increases the risk that confidential information acquired at a cost may be disclosed. If so, the owner of the information may lose its investment.

This analysis provides a policy rationale for prohibiting insider trading when the property rights of a corporation in information are violated by traders. However, the rationale stops well short of prohibiting all trading on material nonpublic information. Efficient capital markets depend on the protection of property rights in information. However, they also require that persons who acquire and act on information about companies be able to profit from the information they generate so long as the method by which the information is acquired does not amount to a form of theft. A rule commanding equal access would result in a securities market governed by relative degrees of ignorance because the profit motive for independently generating information about companies would be substantially diminished. Easterbrook, *supra,* at 313-14. Under such circumstances, the pricing of securities would be less accurate than in circumstances in which the production of information is encouraged by legal protection.

One may speculate that it was for these reasons that the Supreme Court declined in *Chiarella* to adopt a broad ban on trading on material nonpublic information[5] and then imposed in *Dirks* a breach of fiduciary duty requirement — not running to those with whom the trader buys or sells. Under the *Dirks* rule, insider trading is illegal only where the trader has received the information as a result of the trader's or tipper's breach of a duty to keep information confidential.

The misappropriation theory adopted by several circuits fits within this rationale. Misappropriation also involves the misuse of confidential information in a way that risks making information public in a fashion similar to trading by corporate insiders. In *U.S. v. Carpenter,* 791 F.2d 1024 (2d Cir.1986), *aff'd,* 484 U.S. 19, 108 S.Ct. 316, 98 L.Ed.2d 275 (1987), for example, where the information belonged to the *Wall Street Journal* rather than to the corporations whose shares were traded, the misuse of information created an

506

incentive on the part of the traders to create false information that might affect the efficiency of the market's pricing of the corporations' stock. Moreover, the potential for piggybacking would add to that inefficiency.

It must be noted, however, that, although the rationale set out above provides a policy for prohibiting a specific kind of insider trading, any obvious relationship to Section 10(b) is presently missing because theft rather than fraud or deceit, seems the gravamen of the prohibition. Indeed, *Carpenter* analogized the conduct there to embezzlement. 791 F.2d at 1033 n. 11. Nevertheless, the law is far enough down this road — indeed, the Insider Trading Sanctions Act seems premised on Section 10(b)'s applicability — that a court of appeals has no option but to continue the route. [...]

6.2.3.5 Rule 10b5-2 Duties of trust or confidence

Preliminary Note to § 240.10b5-2:

This section provides a non-exclusive definition of circumstances in which a person has a duty of trust or confidence for purposes of the "misappropriation" theory of insider trading under Section 10(b) of the Act and Rule 10b-5. The law of insider trading is otherwise defined by judicial opinions construing Rule 10b-5, and Rule 10b5-2 does not modify the scope of insider trading law in any other respect.

 (a) *Scope of Rule*. This section shall apply to any violation of Section 10(b) of the Act (15 U.S.C. 78j(b)) and § 240.10b-5 thereunder that is based on the purchase or sale of securities on the basis of, or the communication of, material nonpublic information misappropriated in breach of a duty of trust or confidence.

(b) *Enumerated "duties of trust or confidence."* For purposes of this section, a "duty of trust or confidence" exists in the following circumstances, among others:

> (1) Whenever a person agrees to maintain information in confidence;

> (2) Whenever the person communicating the material nonpublic information and the person to whom it is communicated have a history, pattern, or practice of sharing confidences, such that the recipient of the information knows or reasonably should know that the person communicating the material nonpublic information expects that the recipient will maintain its confidentiality; or

(3) Whenever a person receives or obtains material nonpublic information from his or her spouse, parent, child, or sibling; *provided,* however, that the person receiving or obtaining the information may demonstrate that no duty of trust or confidence existed with respect to the information, by establishing that he or she neither knew nor reasonably should have known that the person who was the source of the information expected that the person would keep the information confidential, because of the parties' history, pattern, or practice of sharing and maintaining confidences, and because there was no agreement or understanding to maintain the confidentiality of the information.

6.2.4 Misappropriation Theory

Classical insider trading theory generates liability for insiders, temporary insiders, and tippees in the event any of them trade in the stock of the corporation to which they own a fiduciary duty while in possession of material inside information.

However, this classical theory has an obvious limitation. Under the classical theory of insider trading, there is no liability if the insider uses the material inside information of the corporation to trade in the stock of ANOTHER corporation and not the corporation to which the insider has a fiduciary duty.

The following cases lay out the courts' response to the limitations of the classical insider trading theory while holding on to its fiduciary duty core.

6.2.4.1 Carpenter v. United States

484 U.S. 19 (1987)
CARPENTER ET AL. v. UNITED STATES

JUSTICE WHITE delivered the opinion of the Court.

Petitioners Kenneth Felis and R. Foster Winans were convicted of violating § 10(b) of the Securities Exchange Act of [21] 1934, 48 Stat. 891, 15 U. S. C. § 78j(b),[2] and Rule 10b-5, 17 CFR § 240. 10b-5 (1987).[3][…]

In 1981, Winans became a reporter for the Wall Street Journal (the Journal) and in the summer of 1982 became one of the two writers of a daily column, "Heard on the Street." That column discussed selected stocks or groups of stocks, giving positive and negative information about those stocks and taking "a point of view with respect to investment in the stocks that it reviews." 612 F. Supp., at 830. Winans regularly interviewed corporate executives to put together interesting perspectives on the stocks that would be highlighted in upcoming columns, but, at least for the columns at issue here, none contained corporate inside information or any "hold for release" information. […]

The official policy and practice at the Journal was that prior to publication, the contents of the column were the Journal's confidential information. Despite the rule, with which Winans was familiar, he entered into a scheme in October 1983 with Peter Brant and petitioner Felis, both connected with the Kidder Peabody brokerage firm in New York City, to give them advance information as to the timing and contents of the "Heard" column. This permitted Brant and Felis and another conspirator, David Clark, a client of Brant, to buy or sell based on the probable impact of the column on the market. Profits were to be shared. The conspirators agreed that the scheme would not affect the journalistic purity of the "Heard" column, and the District Court did not find that the contents of any of the articles were altered to further the profit potential of petitioners' stock-trading scheme. […]. Over a 4-month period, the brokers made prepublication trades on the basis of information given them by Winans about the contents of some 27 "Heard" columns. The net profits from these trades were about $690,000.

In November 1983, correlations between the "Heard" articles and trading in the Clark and Felis accounts were noted at Kidder Peabody and inquiries began. Brant and Felis denied knowing anyone at the Journal and took steps to conceal the trades. Later, the Securities and Exchange Commission began an investigation. Questions were met by denials both by the brokers at Kidder Peabody and by Winans at the Journal. As the investigation progressed, the conspirators quarreled, and on March 29, 1984, Winans and Carpenter went to the SEC and revealed the entire scheme. […]

The District Court found, and the Court of Appeals agreed, that Winans had knowingly breached a duty of confidentiality [24] by misappropriating prepublication information regarding the timing and contents of the "Heard" column, information that had been gained in the course of his employment under the understanding that it would not be revealed in advance of publication and that if it were, he would report it to his employer. It was this appropriation of confidential information that underlay both the securities laws and mail and wire fraud counts. With respect to the § 10(b) charges, the courts below held that the deliberate breach of Winans' duty of confidentiality and concealment of the scheme was a fraud and deceit on the Journal. Although the victim of the fraud, the Journal, was not a buyer or seller of the stocks traded in or otherwise a market participant, the fraud was nevertheless considered to be "in connection with" a purchase or sale of securities within the meaning of the statute and the rule. The courts reasoned that the scheme's sole purpose was to buy and sell securities at a profit based on advance information of the column's contents.[…]

Petitioners argue that the Journal's interest in prepublication confidentiality for the "Heard" columns is no more than an intangible consideration outside the reach of § 1341; nor does that law, it is urged, protect against mere injury to reputation. […] The Journal, as Winans' employer, was defrauded of much more than its contractual right to his honest and faithful service, an interest too ethereal in itself to fall within the protection of the mail fraud statute, which "had its origin in the desire to protect individual property rights." […] Here, the object of the scheme was to take the Journal's confidential business information — the publication schedule and contents of the "Heard" column — and its intangible nature does not make it any less "property" protected by the mail and wire fraud statutes. […]

Both courts below expressly referred to the Journal's interest in the confidentiality of the contents and timing of the "Heard" column as a property right, 791 F. 2d, at 1034-1035; 612 F. Supp., at 846, and we agree with that conclusion. […] Confidential business information has long been recognized as property. […]"Confidential information acquired or compiled by a corporation in the course and conduct of its business is a species of property to which the corporation has the exclusive right and benefit, and which a court of equity will protect through the injunctive process or other appropriate remedy." 3 W. Fletcher, Cyclopedia of Law of Private Corporations § 857.1, p. 260 (rev. ed. 1986) (footnote omitted). The Journal had a property right in keeping confidential and making exclusive use, prior to publication, of the schedule and contents of the "Heard" column. […]

Petitioners' arguments that they did not interfere with the Journal's use of the information or did not publicize it and deprive the Journal of the first public use of it, see Reply Brief for Petitioners 6, miss the point. The confidential information was generated from the business, and the business had a right to decide how to use it prior to disclosing it to the public. […]

We cannot accept petitioners' further argument that Winans' conduct in revealing prepublication information was no more than a violation of workplace rules and did not amount to fraudulent activity that is proscribed by the mail fraud statute. […]

The District Court found that Winans' undertaking at the Journal was not to reveal prepublication information about his column, a promise that became a sham when in violation of his duty he passed along to his co-conspirators confidential information belonging to the Journal, pursuant to an ongoing scheme to share profits from trading in anticipation of the "Heard" column's impact on the stock market. […] As the New York courts have recognized: "It is well established, as a general proposition, that a person who acquires special knowledge or information by virtue of a confidential or fiduciary relationship with another is not free [28] to exploit that knowledge or information for his own personal benefit but must account to his principal for any profits derived therefrom." […]

We have little trouble in holding that the conspiracy here to trade on the Journal's confidential information is not outside the reach of the mail and wire fraud statutes, provided the other elements of the offenses are satisfied. The Journal's business information that it intended to be kept confidential was its property; the declaration to that effect in the employee manual merely removed any doubts on that score and made the finding of specific intent to defraud that much easier. Winans continued in the employ of the Journal, appropriating its confidential business information for his own use, all the while pretending to perform his duty of safeguarding it. In fact, he told his editors twice about leaks of confidential information not related to the stock-trading scheme, 612 F. Supp., at 831, demonstrating both his knowledge that the Journal viewed information concerning the "Heard" column as confidential and his deceit as he played the role of a loyal employee. Furthermore, the District Court's conclusion that each of the petitioners acted with the required specific intent to defraud is strongly supported by the evidence. […]

The judgment below is *Affirmed.*

6.2.4.2 U.S. v. O'Hagan

521 U.S. 642 (1997)
UNITED STATES v. O'HAGAN

Justice Ginsburg, delivered the opinion of the Court.

Respondent James Herman O'Hagan was a partner in the law firm of Dorsey & Whitney in Minneapolis, Minnesota. In July 1988, Grand Metropolitan PLC (Grand Met), a company based in London, England, retained Dorsey & Whitney as local counsel to represent Grand Met regarding a potential tender offer for the common stock of the Pillsbury Company, headquartered in Minneapolis. Both Grand Met and Dorsey & Whitney took precautions to protect the confidentiality of Grand Met's tender offer plans. O'Hagan did no work on the Grand Met representation. [...]

On August 18, 1988, while Dorsey & Whitney was still representing Grand Met, O'Hagan began purchasing call options for Pillsbury stock. Each option gave him the right to purchase 100 shares of Pillsbury stock by a specified date in September 1988. Later in August and in September, O'Hagan made additional purchases of Pillsbury call options. By the end of September, he owned 2,500 unexpired Pillsbury options, apparently more than any other individual investor. [...]When Grand Met announced its tender offer in October, the price of Pillsbury stock rose to nearly $60 per share. O'Hagan then sold his Pillsbury call options and common stock, making a profit of more than $4.3 million.

The Securities and Exchange Commission (SEC or Commission) initiated an investigation into O'Hagan's transactions, culminating in a 57-count indictment. The indictment alleged that O'Hagan defrauded his law firm and its client, Grand Met, by using for his own trading purposes material, nonpublic information regarding Grand Met's planned tender offer. *Id.,* at 8.[2] According to the indictment, O'Hagan used the profits he gained through this trading to conceal his previous embezzlement and conversion of unrelated client trust funds. *Id.,*[...]

In pertinent part, § 10(b) of the Exchange Act provides:

> "It shall be unlawful for any person, directly or indirectly, by the use of any means or instrumentality of interstate commerce or of the mails, or of any facility of any national securities exchange—

. . . . .

> "(b) To use or employ, in connection with the purchase or sale of any security registered on a national securities exchange or any security not so registered, any manipulative or deceptive device or contrivance in contravention of such rules and regulations as the [Securities and Exchange] Commission may prescribe as necessary or appropriate in the public interest or for the protection of investors." 15 U. S. C. § 78j(b). [651] The statute thus proscribes (1) using any deceptive device (2) in connection with the purchase or sale of securities, in contravention of rules prescribed by the Commission. The provision, as written, does not confine its coverage to deception of a purchaser or seller of securities, see *United States* v. *Newman,* 664 F. 2d 12, 17 (CA2 1981); rather, the statute reaches any deceptive device used "in connection with the purchase or sale of any security."

Pursuant to its § 10(b) rulemaking authority, the Commission has adopted Rule 10b—5, which, as relevant here, provides:

> "It shall be unlawful for any person, directly or indirectly, by the use of any means or instrumentality of interstate commerce, or of the mails or of any facility of any national securities exchange,

513

"(a) To employ any device, scheme, or artifice to defraud, [or]

. . . . .

"(c) To engage in any act, practice, or course of business which
operates or would operate as a fraud or deceit upon any person, "in
connection with the purchase or sale of any security." 17 CFR §
240.10b—5 (1996).

Liability under Rule 10b—5, our precedent indicates, does not extend beyond conduct
encompassed by § 10(b)'s prohibition. […]

Under the "traditional" or "classical theory" of insider trading liability, § 10(b) and Rule
10b—5 are violated when a corporate insider trades in the securities of his corporation
[652] on the basis of material, nonpublic information. Trading on such information
qualifies as a "deceptive device" under § 10(b), we have affirmed, because "a relationship
of trust and confidence [exists] between the shareholders of a corporation and those
insiders who have obtained confidential information by reason of their position with
that corporation." *Chiarella* v. *United States,* 445 U. S. 222, 228 (1980). That relationship,
we recognized, "gives rise to a duty to disclose [or to abstain from trading] because of
the `necessity of preventing a corporate insider from . . . tak[ing] unfair advantage of . . .
uninformed . . . stockholders.' " *Id.,* at 228-229 (citation omitted). The classical theory
applies not only to officers, directors, and other permanent insiders of a corporation, but
also to attorneys, accountants, consultants, and others who temporarily become
fiduciaries of a corporation. See *Dirks* v. *SEC,* 463 U. S. 646, 655, n. 14 (1983).

The "misappropriation theory" holds that a person commits fraud "in connection with"
a securities transaction, and thereby violates § 10(b) and Rule 10b—5, when he
misappropriates confidential information for securities trading purposes, in breach of a
duty owed to the source of the information. […]Under this theory, a fiduciary's
undisclosed, self-serving use of a principal's information to purchase or sell securities, in
breach of a duty of loyalty and confidentiality, defrauds the principal of the exclusive use
of that information. In lieu of premising liability on a fiduciary relationship between
company insider and purchaser or seller of the company's stock, the misappropriation
theory premises liability on a fiduciary-turned-trader's deception of those who entrusted
him with access to confidential information.

514

The two theories are complementary, each addressing efforts to capitalize on nonpublic information through the purchase or sale of securities. The classical theory targets a corporate insider's breach of duty to shareholders with whom the insider transacts; the misappropriation theory outlaws [653] trading on the basis of nonpublic information by a corporate "outsider" in breach of a duty owed not to a trading party, but to the source of the information. The misappropriation theory is thus designed to "protec[t] the integrity of the securities markets against abuses by `outsiders' to a corporation who have access to confidential information that will affect th[e] corporation's security price when revealed, but who owe no fiduciary or other duty to that corporation's shareholders." [...]

Deception through nondisclosure is central to the theory of liability for which the Government seeks recognition. As counsel for the Government stated in explanation of the theory at oral argument: "To satisfy the common law rule that a trustee may not use the property that [has] been entrusted [to] him, there would have to be consent. To satisfy the requirement of the Securities Act that there be no deception, there would only have to be disclosure."[...]

Full disclosure forecloses liability under the misappropriation theory: Because the deception essential to the misappropriation theory involves feigning fidelity to the source of information, if the fiduciary discloses to the source that he plans to trade on the nonpublic information, there is no "deceptive device" and thus no § 10(b) violation—although the fiduciary-turned trader may remain liable under state law for breach of a duty of loyalty.[8]

We turn next to the § 10(b) requirement that the misappropriator's deceptive use of information be "in connection with [656] the purchase or sale of [a] security." This element is satisfied because the fiduciary's fraud is consummated, not when the fiduciary gains the confidential information, but when, without disclosure to his principal, he uses the information to purchase or sell securities. [...]

The misappropriation theory comports with § 10(b)'s language, which requires deception "in connection with the purchase or sale of any security," not deception of an identifiable purchaser or seller. The theory is also well tuned to an animating purpose of the Exchange Act: to insure honest securities markets and thereby promote investor confidence. See 45 Fed. Reg. 60412 (1980) (trading on misappropriated information "undermines the integrity of, and investor confidence in, the securities markets"). Although informational disparity is inevitable in the securities markets, investors likely would hesitate to venture their capital in a market where trading based on misappropriated nonpublic information is unchecked by law. An investor's informational disadvantage vis-à-vis a misappropriator with material, nonpublic information [659] stems from contrivance, not luck; it is a disadvantage that cannot be overcome with research or skill. […]

In sum, considering the inhibiting impact on market participation of trading on misappropriated information, and the congressional purposes underlying § 10(b), it makes scant sense to hold a lawyer like O'Hagan a § 10(b) violator if he works for a law firm representing the target of a tender offer, but not if he works for a law firm representing the bidder. The text of the statute requires no such result.[10] The misappropriation at issue here was properly made the subject of a § 10(b) charge because it meets the statutory requirement that there be "deceptive" conduct "in connection with" securities transactions. […]

The judgment of the Court of Appeals for the Eighth Circuit is reversed, and the case is remanded for further proceedings consistent with this opinion.

It is so ordered.

6.2.4.3 SEC v. Dorozhko

Like tipper/tippee liability, there are limits to use of misappropriation theory. In Dorozhko, the Second Circuit extends misappropriation theory in a novel way. Dorozhko involves a Ukrainian hacker who steals inside information and then trades on it. The lack of a fiduciary relationship to the source of the information should mean there is no liability under misappropriation theory. However, here the court agrees with the SEC's theory and extends liability but in a novel way, suggesting that fiduciary relationships are not actually required in order to establish liability under 10b-5.

574 F.3d 42 (2009)
SEC v. DOROZHKO

JOSÉ A. CABRANES, Circuit Judge:

We are asked to consider whether, in a civil enforcement lawsuit brought by the United States Securities and Exchange Commission ("SEC") under Section 10(b) [44] of the Securities Exchange Act of 1934 ("Section 10(b)"), computer hacking may be "deceptive" where the hacker did not breach a fiduciary duty in fraudulently obtaining material, nonpublic information used in connection with the purchase or sale of securities. For the reasons stated herein, we answer the question in the affirmative. […]

In early October 2007, defendant Oleksandr Dorozhko, a Ukranian national and resident, opened an online trading account with Interactive Brokers LLC ("Interactive Brokers") and deposited $42,500 into that account. At about the same time, IMS Health, Inc. ("IMS") announced that it would release its third-quarter earnings during an analyst conference call scheduled for October 17, 2007 at 5 p.m.—that is, after the close of the securities markets in New York City. IMS had hired Thomson Financial, Inc. ("Thomson") to provide investor relations and web-hosting services, which included managing the online release of IMS's earnings reports.

Beginning at 8:06 a.m. on October 17, and continuing several times during the morning and early afternoon, an anonymous computer hacker attempted to gain access to the IMS earnings report by hacking into a secure server at Thomson prior to the report's official release. At 2:15 p.m.—minutes after Thomson actually received the IMS data—that hacker successfully located and downloaded the IMS data from Thomson's secure server.

Beginning at 2:52 p.m., defendant—who had not previously used his Interactive Brokers account to trade—purchased $41,670.90 worth of IMS "put" options that would expire on October 25 and 30, 2007.[1] These purchases represented approximately 90% of all purchases of "put" options for IMS stock for the six weeks prior to October 17. In purchasing these options, which the SEC describes as "extremely risky," defendant was betting that IMS's stock price would decline precipitously (within a two-day expiration period) and significantly (by greater than 20%). […]

At 4:33 p.m.—slightly ahead of the analyst call—IMS announced that its earnings per share were 28% below "Street" expectations, *i.e.,* the expectations of many Wall Street analysts. When the market opened the next morning, October 18, at 9:30 a.m., IMS's stock price sank approximately 28% almost immediately—from $29.56 to $21.20 per

517

share. Within six minutes of the market opening, defendant had sold all of his IMS options, realizing a net profit of $286,456.59 overnight.

Interactive Brokers noticed the irregular trading activity and referred the matter to the SEC, which now alleges that defendant was the hacker. [...] On October 29, 2007, the SEC sought and received from the United States District Court for the Southern District of New York (Naomi Reice Buchwald, *Judge*) a temporary restraining order freezing the proceeds of the "put" option transactions in defendant's brokerage [45] account. [...]

On January 8, 2008, in a thoughtful and careful opinion, the District Court denied the SEC's request for a preliminary injunction because the SEC had not shown a likelihood of success. Specifically, the District Court ruled that computer hacking was not "deceptive" within the meaning of Section 10(b) as defined by the Supreme Court. According to the District Court, "a breach of a fiduciary duty of disclosure is a required element of any `deceptive' device under § 10b." [...]The District Court reasoned that since defendant was a corporate outsider with no special relationship to IMS or Thomson, he owed no fiduciary duty to either. Although computer hacking might be fraudulent and might violate a number of federal and state criminal statutes, the District Court concluded that this behavior did not violate Section 10(b) without an accompanying breach of a fiduciary duty.

On appeal, the SEC maintains its theory that the fraud in this case consists of defendant's alleged computer hacking, which involves various misrepresentations. The SEC does not argue that defendant breached any fiduciary duties as part of his scheme. In this critical regard, we recognize that the SEC's claim against defendant—a corporate outsider who owed no fiduciary duties to the source of the information—is not based on either of the two generally accepted theories of insider trading. *See United States v. Cusimano,* 123 F.3d 83, 87 (2d Cir.1997) (distinguishing "the traditional theory of insider trading, under which a corporate insider trades in the securities of his own corporation on the basis of material, non-public information," from "the misappropriation theory, [under which] § 10(b) and Rule 10b-5 are violated whenever a person trades while in knowing possession of material, non-public information that has been gained in violation of a fiduciary duty to its source"). The SEC's claim is nonetheless based on a claim of fraud, and we turn our attention to whether this fraud is "deceptive" within the meaning of Section 10(b). [...]

"Section 10(b) prohibits the use or employ, in connection with the purchase or sale of any security . . ., [of] any manipulative or deceptive device or contrivance in contravention of such rules and regulations as the [SEC] may prescribe." 15 U.S.C. § 78j(b)[2] The instant case requires us to [46] decide whether the "device" in this case—computer hacking—could be "deceptive."[3]

In construing the text of any federal statute, we first consider the precedents that bind us as an intermediate appellate court—namely, the holdings of the Supreme Court and those of prior panels of this Court, which provide definitive interpretations of otherwise ambiguous language. Insofar as those precedents fail to resolve an apparent ambiguity, we examine the text of the statute itself, interpreting provisions in light of their ordinary meaning and their contextual setting. […]

The District Court determined that the Supreme Court has interpreted the "deceptive" element of Section 10(b) to require a breach of a fiduciary duty. […] ("[T]he Supreme Court has in a number of opinions carefully established that the essential component of a § 10(b) violation is a breach of a fiduciary duty to disclose or abstain that coincides with a securities transaction."). The District Court reached this conclusion by relying principally on three Supreme Court opinions: *Chiarella v. United States,* 445 U.S. 222, 100 S.Ct. 1108, 63 L.Ed.2d 348 (1980), *United States v. O'Hagan,* 521 U.S. 642, 117 S.Ct. 2199, 138 L.Ed.2d 724 (1997), and *SEC v. Zandford,* 535 U.S. 813, 122 S.Ct. 1899, 153 L.Ed.2d 1 (2002). We consider each of these cases in turn.

In *Chiarella,* the defendant was employed by a financial printer and used information passing through his office to trade securities offered by acquiring and target companies. In a criminal prosecution, [47] the government alleged that the defendant committed fraud by not disclosing to the market that he was trading on the basis of material, nonpublic information. The Supreme Court held that defendant's "silence," or nondisclosure, was not fraud because he was under no obligation to disclose his knowledge of inside information. "When an allegation of fraud is based upon nondisclosure, there can be no fraud absent a duty to speak. We hold that a duty to disclose under § 10(b) does not arise from the mere possession of nonpublic market information." 445 U.S. at 235, 100 S.Ct. 1108; *see also United States v. Chestman,* 947 F.2d 551, 575 (2d Cir. 1991) (Winter, J., concurring in part and dissenting in part) (stating that, after *Chiarella,* "silence cannot constitute a fraud absent a duty to speak owed to those who are injured"). Justice Blackmun, joined by Justice Marshall, dissented. In their view, stealing information from an employer was fraudulent within the meaning of Section 10(b) because the statute was designed as a "catchall" provision to protect investors from unknown risks. *Id.* at 246, 100 S.Ct. 1108 (Blackmun, *J.,* dissenting). According to Justice Blackmun, the majority had "confine[d]" the meaning of fraud "by imposition of a requirement of a `special relationship' akin to fiduciary duty before the statute gives rise to a duty to disclose or to abstain from trading upon material, nonpublic information." *Id.*[4]

In *O'Hagan,* the defendant was an attorney who traded in securities based on material, nonpublic information regarding his firm's clients. As in *Chiarella,* the government alleged that the defendant had committed fraud through "silence" because the defendant had a duty to disclose to the source of the information (his client) that he would trade on the information. The Supreme Court agreed, noting that "[d]eception through nondisclosure is central to the theory of liability for which the Government seeks recognition." 521 U.S. at 654, 117 S.Ct. 2199. "[I]f the fiduciary discloses to the source that he plans to trade on the nonpublic information, there is no `deceptive device' and thus no § 10(b) violation—although the fiduciary-turned-trader may remain liable under state law for breach of a duty of loyalty." *Id.* at 655, 117 S.Ct. 2199.

In *Zandford,* the defendant was a securities broker who traded under a client's account and transferred the proceeds to his own account. The Fourth Circuit held that the defendant's fraud was not "in connection with" the purchase or sale of a security because it was mere theft that happened to involve securities, rather than true securities fraud. The Supreme Court reversed in a unanimous opinion, observing that Section 10(b) "should be construed not technically and restrictively, but flexibly to effectuate its remedial purposes." 535 U.S. at 819, 122 S.Ct. 1899. Although the Court warned that not "every common-law fraud that happens to involve securities [is] a violation of § 10(b)," *id.* at 820, 122 S.Ct. 1899, the defendant's scheme was a single plan to deceive, rather than a series of independent frauds, and was therefore "in connection with" the purchase or sale of a security, *id.* at 825, 122 S.Ct. 1899. In a final footnote, the Court offered the following observation: "[I]f the [48] broker told his client he was stealing the client's assets, that breach of fiduciary duty might be in connection with a sale of securities, but it would not involve a deceptive device or fraud." 535 U.S. at 825 n. 4,

122 S.Ct. 1899. In the instant case, the District Court interpreted the *Zandford* footnote as an "explicit[ ] acknowledg[ment] that Zandford would not be liable under § 10(b) if he *had* disclosed to Wood that he was planning to steal his money." *Dorozhko*, 606 F.Supp.2d at 338.

The District Court concluded that in *Chiarella, O'Hagan,* and *Zandford,* the Supreme Court developed a requirement that any "deceptive device" requires a breach of a fiduciary duty. In applying that interpretation to the instant case, the District Court ruled that "[a]lthough [defendant] may have broken the law, he is not liable in a civil action under § 10(b) because he owed no fiduciary or similar duty either to the source of his information or to those he transacted with in the market." [...] At least one of our sister circuits has made the same observation relying on the same precedent. [...]

In our view, none of the Supreme Court opinions relied upon by the District Court— much less the sum of all three opinions — establishes a fiduciary-duty requirement as an element of every violation of Section 10(b). In *Chiarella, O'Hagan,* and *Zandford,* the theory of fraud was silence or nondisclosure, not an affirmative misrepresentation. The Supreme Court held that remaining silent was actionable only where there was a duty to speak, arising from a fiduciary relationship. In *Chiarella,* the Supreme Court held that there was no deception in an employee's silence because he did not have duty to speak. [...] In *O'Hagan,* an attorney who traded on client secrets had a fiduciary duty to inform his firm that he was trading on the basis of the confidential information. [...]Even in *Zandford,* which dealt principally with the statutory requirement that a deceptive device be used "in connection with" the purchase or sale of a security, the defendant's fraud consisted of not telling his brokerage client—to whom he owed a fiduciary duty—that he was stealing assets from the account. [...]

Chiarella, O'Hagan, and *Zandford* all stand for the proposition that nondisclosure in breach of a fiduciary duty "satisfies § 10(b)'s requirement . . . [of] a `deceptive device or contrivance,'" [...]. However, what is sufficient is not always what is necessary, and none of the Supreme Court opinions considered by the District Court *require* a fiduciary relationship as an element of an actionable securities claim under Section 10(b). [...] Even if a person does not have a fiduciary duty to "disclose or abstain from trading," there is nonetheless an affirmative obligation in commercial dealings not to mislead. [...]

In this case, the SEC has not alleged that defendant fraudulently remained silent in the face of a "duty to disclose or abstain" from trading. Rather, the SEC argues that defendant affirmatively misrepresented himself in order to gain access to material, nonpublic information, which he then used to trade. We are aware of no precedent of the Supreme Court or our Court that forecloses or prohibits the SEC's straightforward theory of fraud.[6] Absent a controlling precedent that "deceptive" has a more limited meaning than its ordinary meaning, we see no reason to complicate the enforcement of Section 10(b) by divining new requirements. In reaching this conclusion, we are mindful of the Supreme Court's oft-repeated instruction that Section 10(b) "should be construed not technically and restrictively, but flexibly to effectuate its remedial purposes." […]

In its ordinary meaning, "deceptive" covers a wide spectrum of conduct involving cheating or trading in falsehoods. *See* Webster's International Dictionary […] In light of this ordinary meaning, it is not at all surprising that Rule 10b-5 equates "deceit" with "fraud." […]

The District Court—summarizing the SEC's allegations—described the computer hacking in this case as "employ[ing] electronic means to trick, circumvent, or bypass computer security in order to gain unauthorized access to computer systems, networks, and information . . . and to steal such data." […] On appeal, the SEC adds a further gloss, arguing that, in general, "[computer [51] h]ackers either (1) `engage in false identification and masquerade as another user[']. . . or (2) `exploit a weakness in [an electronic] code within a program to cause the program to malfunction in a way that grants the user greater privileges.'" […]In our view, misrepresenting one's identity in order to gain access to information that is otherwise off limits, and then stealing that information is plainly "deceptive" within the ordinary meaning of the word. It is unclear, however, that exploiting a weakness in an electronic code to gain unauthorized access is "deceptive," rather than being mere theft. Accordingly, depending on how the hacker gained access, it seems to us entirely possible that computer hacking could be, by definition, a "deceptive device or contrivance" that is prohibited by Section 10(b) and Rule 10b-5.

[…]Having established that the SEC need not demonstrate a breach of fiduciary duty, we now remand to the District Court to consider, in the first instance, whether the computer hacking in this case involved a fraudulent misrepresentation that was "deceptive" within the ordinary meaning of Section 10(b). [...]

7 Takeovers

The merger transaction is probably one of the most significant events possible in the life of a corporation. Because mergers are so important to the corporation, they are regulated quite closely. Although the corporate law typically grants great deference to the decisions of boards of directors, when boards take actions in the context of pursuing a sale or defending against an unwanted offer, courts are more apt to enquire into process relied on by the board. In the following sections we explore both the mechanics of the merger transaction as well as the fiduciary duties of directors in the merger scenario.

7.1 Statutory Mergers

The statutory merger is the building block of all M&A activity. The provisions that follow provide an outline for the mechanics of the statutory merger transaction. Although the statutory mergers described in Section 251 involve two Delaware corporations, statutory mergers under other provisions of the code permit mergers between corporations and other business forms, including business forms from other states. The mechanics of those transactions are not substantially dissimilar from the process outlined in Section 251 below.

7.1.1 DGCL Sec 251

§ 251. Merger or consolidation of domestic corporations.

(a) Any 2 or more corporations existing under the laws of this State may merge into a single corporation, which may be any 1 of the constituent corporations or may consolidate into a new corporation formed by the consolidation, pursuant to an agreement of merger or consolidation, as the case may be, complying and approved in accordance with this section.

(b) The board of directors of each corporation which desires to merge or consolidate shall adopt a resolution approving an agreement of merger or consolidation and declaring its advisability. The agreement shall state:

>   (1) The terms and conditions of the merger or consolidation;

(2) The mode of carrying the same into effect;

(3) In the case of a merger, such amendments or changes in the certificate of incorporation of the surviving corporation as are desired to be effected by the merger (which amendments or changes may amend and restate the certificate of incorporation of the surviving corporation in its entirety), or, if no such amendments or changes are desired, a statement that the certificate of incorporation of the surviving corporation shall be its certificate of incorporation;

(4) In the case of a consolidation, that the certificate of incorporation of the resulting corporation shall be as is set forth in an attachment to the agreement;

(5) The manner, if any, of converting the shares of each of the constituent corporations into shares or other securities of the corporation surviving or resulting from the merger or consolidation, or of cancelling some or all of such shares, and, if any shares of any of the constituent corporations are not to remain outstanding, to be converted solely into shares or other securities of the surviving or resulting corporation or to be cancelled, the cash, property, rights or securities of any other corporation or entity which the holders of such shares are to receive in exchange for, or upon conversion of such shares and the surrender of any certificates evidencing them, which cash, property, rights or securities of any other corporation or entity may be in addition to or in lieu of shares or other securities of the surviving or resulting corporation; and

(6) Such other details or provisions as are deemed desirable, including, without limiting the generality of the foregoing, a provision for the payment of cash in lieu of the issuance or recognition of fractional shares, interests or rights, or for any other arrangement with respect thereto, consistent with § 155 of this title. […]

(c) The agreement required by subsection (b) of this section shall be submitted to the stockholders of each constituent corporation at an annual or special meeting for the purpose of acting on the agreement. Due notice of the time, place and purpose of the meeting shall be mailed to each holder of stock, whether voting or nonvoting, of the corporation at the stockholder's address as it appears on the records of the corporation, at least 20 days prior to the date of the meeting. The notice shall contain a copy of the agreement or a brief summary thereof. At the meeting, the agreement shall be considered and a vote taken for its adoption or rejection. If a majority of the outstanding stock of the corporation entitled to vote thereon shall be voted for the adoption of the agreement, that fact shall be certified on the agreement by the secretary or assistant secretary of the corporation, provided that such certification on the agreement shall not be required if a certificate of merger or consolidation is filed in lieu of filing the agreement. If the agreement shall be so adopted and certified by each constituent corporation, it shall then be filed and shall become effective, in accordance with § 103 of this title. In lieu of filing the agreement of merger or consolidation required by this section, the surviving or resulting corporation may file a certificate of merger or consolidation, executed in accordance with § 103 of this title, which states:

> (1) The name and state of incorporation of each of the constituent corporations;

> (2) That an agreement of merger or consolidation has been approved, adopted, executed and acknowledged by each of the constituent corporations in accordance with this section;

> (3) The name of the surviving or resulting corporation;

> (4) In the case of a merger, such amendments or changes in the certificate of incorporation of the surviving corporation as are desired to be effected by the merger (which amendments or changes may amend and restate the certificate of incorporation of the surviving corporation in its entirety), or, if no such amendments or changes are desired, a statement that the certificate of incorporation of the surviving corporation shall be its certificate of incorporation;

> (5) In the case of a consolidation, that the certificate of incorporation of the resulting corporation shall be as set forth in an attachment to the certificate;

> (6) That the executed agreement of consolidation or merger is on file at an office of the surviving corporation, stating the address thereof; and

(7) That a copy of the agreement of consolidation or merger will be furnished by the surviving corporation, on request and without cost, to any stockholder of any constituent corporation.

(d) Any agreement of merger or consolidation may contain a provision that at any time prior to the time that the agreement (or a certificate in lieu thereof) filed with the Secretary of State becomes effective in accordance with § 103 of this title, the agreement may be terminated by the board of directors of any constituent corporation notwithstanding approval of the agreement by the stockholders of all or any of the constituent corporations; in the event the agreement of merger or consolidation is terminated after the filing of the agreement (or a certificate in lieu thereof) with the Secretary of State but before the agreement (or a certificate in lieu thereof) has become effective, a certificate of termination or merger or consolidation shall be filed in accordance with § 103 of this title. [...]

(e) In the case of a merger, the certificate of incorporation of the surviving corporation shall automatically be amended to the extent, if any, that changes in the certificate of incorporation are set forth in the agreement of merger.

(f) Notwithstanding the requirements of subsection (c) of this section, unless required by its certificate of incorporation, no vote of stockholders of a constituent corporation surviving a merger shall be necessary to authorize a merger if (1) the agreement of merger does not amend in any respect the certificate of incorporation of such constituent corporation, (2) each share of stock of such constituent corporation outstanding immediately prior to the effective date of the merger is to be an identical outstanding or treasury share of the surviving corporation after the effective date of the merger, and (3) either no shares of common stock of the surviving corporation and no shares, securities or obligations convertible into such stock are to be issued or delivered under the plan of merger, or the authorized unissued shares or the treasury shares of common stock of the surviving corporation to be issued or delivered under the plan of merger plus those initially issuable upon conversion of any other shares, securities or obligations to be issued or delivered under such plan do not exceed 20% of the shares of common stock of such constituent corporation outstanding immediately prior to the effective date of the merger. No vote of stockholders of a constituent corporation shall be necessary to authorize a merger or consolidation if no shares of the stock of such corporation shall have been issued prior to the adoption by the board of directors of the resolution approving the agreement of merger or consolidation. If an agreement of merger is adopted by the constituent corporation surviving the merger, by action of its board of directors and without any vote of its stockholders pursuant to this subsection, the secretary or assistant secretary of that corporation shall certify on the agreement that the agreement has been adopted pursuant to this subsection and, (1) if it has been adopted pursuant to the first sentence of this subsection, that the conditions specified in that sentence have been satisfied, or (2) if it has been adopted pursuant to the second sentence of this subsection, that no shares of stock of such corporation were issued prior to the adoption by the board of directors of the resolution approving the agreement of merger or consolidation, provided that such certification on the agreement shall not be required if a certificate of merger or consolidation is filed in lieu of filing the agreement. The agreement so adopted and certified shall then be filed and shall become effective, in accordance with § 103 of this title. Such filing shall constitute a representation by the person who executes the agreement that the facts stated in the certificate remain true immediately prior to such filing. […]

7.2 Board Obligations in the Takeover Context

Decisions whether or not to sell the corporation are like other business decisions taken by the board. Absent special circumstances such decisions are going to be subject to the business judgment presumption.

The cases that follow some of these special circumstances are present. The courts have developed the intermediate standard – a preliminary inquiry – to assist the courts in determining whether in a given fact scenario the court should deploy the business judgment presumption or whether the actions of the a board should be subject to the more intensive entire fairness scrutiny.

These fact scenarios include situations when the board adopts defenses to fend off an unwanted buyer, or when the board of its own accord decides to engage in a sale of control of the corporation, or when the board takes an action that might interfere with stockholders' voting rights. Each of these situations will engender additional judicial scrutiny before they are allowed to stand.

7.2.1 Unocal Corp. v. Mesa Petroleum Co.

Board decisions typically receive the deferential presumption of business judgment. However, in some sets of facts it may be difficult to ascertain immediately whether actions taken by the board are in fact acts taken by a fully informed, disinterested board acting in the best interests of the corporation or if they are acting to entrench themselves and not in the best interests of the corporation.

For example, when a board unilaterally adopts defensive measures in response to a perceived threat to its corporate policy or effectiveness, that decision might be motivated by a desire to protect the corporation from some outside threat (best case scenario) or it could also be motivated by a desire to entrench disloyal managers (worst case scenario).

In such situations, those board decisions will be subject to a preliminary review (the intermediate standard) before the court determines whether to subject those decisions to deferential business judgment or the more exacting entire fairness standard. The nature of this review is an inquiry into the motivations behind board actions and then a determination about the reasonableness of the means adopted by the board. In testing the motive and means of the board, the burden is on the board to show that it was properly motivated and that the means it adopted were reasonable.

To the extent the board is able to establish it was properly motivated and acted reasonably, the board's actions will receive the presumption of business judgment. On the other hand, if the board was not properly motivated or if the defensive measures adopted by the board are not reasonable, the board's decision will be subject to entire fairness review. Because entire fairness review places such a heavy burden on defendants, resolution of the preliminary inquiry laid out in *Unocal* will often times be outcome determinative.

493 A.2d 946 (1985)
UNOCAL CORPORATION v. MESA PETROLEUM CO.

MOORE, Justice.

We confront an issue of first impression in Delaware — the validity of a corporation's self-tender for its own shares which excludes from participation a stockholder making a hostile tender offer for the company's stock. [...]

On April 8, 1985, Mesa, the owner of approximately 13% of Unocal's stock, commenced a two-tier "front loaded" cash tender offer for 64 million shares, or approximately 37%, of Unocal's outstanding stock at a price of $54 per share. The "back-end" was designed to eliminate the remaining publicly held shares by an exchange of securities purportedly worth $54 per share. However, pursuant to an order entered by the United States District Court for the Central District of California on April 26, 1985, Mesa issued a supplemental proxy statement to Unocal's stockholders disclosing that the securities offered in the second-step merger would be highly subordinated, and that Unocal's capitalization would differ significantly from its present [950] structure. Unocal has rather aptly termed such securities "junk bonds".[3]

Unocal's board consists of eight independent outside directors and six insiders. It met on April 13, 1985, to consider the Mesa tender offer. Thirteen directors were present, and the meeting lasted nine and one-half hours. The directors were given no agenda or written materials prior to the session. However, detailed presentations were made by legal counsel regarding the board's obligations under both Delaware corporate law and the federal securities laws. The board then received a presentation from Peter Sachs on behalf of Goldman Sachs & Co. (Goldman Sachs) and Dillon, Read & Co. (Dillon Read) discussing the bases for their opinions that the Mesa proposal was wholly inadequate. Mr. Sachs opined that the minimum cash value that could be expected from a sale or orderly liquidation for 100% of Unocal's stock was in excess of $60 per share. [...]

Mr. Sachs also presented various defensive strategies available to the board if it concluded that Mesa's two-step tender offer was inadequate and should be opposed. One of the devices outlined was a self-tender by Unocal for its own stock with a reasonable price range of $70 to $75 per share. The cost of such a proposal would cause the company to incur $6.1-6.5 billion of additional debt, and a presentation was made informing the board of Unocal's ability to handle it. The directors were told that the primary effect of this obligation would be to reduce exploratory drilling, but that the company would nonetheless remain a viable entity.

The eight outside directors, comprising a clear majority of the thirteen members present, then met separately with Unocal's financial advisors and attorneys. Thereafter, they unanimously agreed to advise the board that it should reject Mesa's tender offer as inadequate, and that Unocal should pursue a self-tender to provide the stockholders with a fairly priced alternative to the Mesa proposal. The board then reconvened and unanimously adopted a resolution rejecting as grossly inadequate Mesa's tender offer. Despite the nine and one-half hour length of the meeting, no formal decision was made on the proposed defensive self-tender.

On April 15, the board met again with four of the directors present by telephone [951] and one member still absent.[4] This session lasted two hours. Unocal's Vice President of Finance and its Assistant General Counsel made a detailed presentation of the proposed terms of the exchange offer. A price range between $70 and $80 per share was considered, and ultimately the directors agreed upon $72. The board was also advised about the debt securities that would be issued, and the necessity of placing restrictive covenants upon certain corporate activities until the obligations were paid. The board's decisions were made in reliance on the advice of its investment bankers, including the terms and conditions upon which the securities were to be issued. Based upon this advice, and the board's own deliberations, the directors unanimously approved the exchange offer. Their resolution provided that if Mesa acquired 64 million shares of Unocal stock through its own offer (the Mesa Purchase Condition), Unocal would buy the remaining 49% outstanding for an exchange of debt securities having an aggregate par value of $72 per share. [...]

Unocal's exchange offer was commenced on April 17, 1985, and Mesa promptly challenged it by filing this suit in the Court of Chancery. On April 22, the Unocal board met again and was advised by Goldman Sachs and Dillon Read to waive the Mesa Purchase Condition as to 50 million shares. This recommendation was in response to a perceived concern of the shareholders that, if shares were tendered to Unocal, no shares would be purchased by either offeror. The directors were also advised that they should tender their own Unocal stock into the exchange offer as a mark of their confidence in it.

Another focus of the board was the Mesa exclusion. Legal counsel advised that under Delaware law Mesa could only be excluded for what the directors reasonably believed to be a valid corporate purpose. The directors' discussion centered on the objective of adequately compensating shareholders at the "back-end" of Mesa's proposal, which the latter would finance with "junk bonds". To include Mesa would defeat that goal, because under the proration aspect of the exchange offer (49%) every Mesa share accepted by Unocal would displace one held by another stockholder. Further, if Mesa were permitted to tender to Unocal, the latter would in effect be financing Mesa's own inadequate proposal. […]

On April 29, 1985, the Vice Chancellor temporarily restrained Unocal from proceeding with the exchange offer unless it included Mesa. […]

Unocal immediately sought certification of an interlocutory appeal to this Court pursuant to Supreme Court Rule 42(b). […]

On May 13, 1985 the Court of Chancery certified this interlocutory appeal to us as a question of first impression, and we accepted it on May 14. The entire matter was scheduled on an expedited basis.[5]

II.

The issues we address involve these fundamental questions: Did the Unocal board have the power and duty to oppose a takeover threat it reasonably perceived to be harmful to the corporate enterprise, and if so, is its action here entitled to the protection of the business judgment rule?

Mesa contends that the discriminatory exchange offer violates the fiduciary duties Unocal owes it. Mesa argues that because of the Mesa exclusion the business judgment rule is inapplicable, because the directors by tendering their own shares will derive a financial benefit that is not available to *all* Unocal stockholders. Thus, it is Mesa's ultimate contention that Unocal cannot establish that the exchange offer is fair to *all* shareholders, and argues that the Court of Chancery was correct in concluding that Unocal was unable to meet this burden.

Unocal answers that it does not owe a duty of "fairness" to Mesa, given the facts here. Specifically, Unocal contends that its board of directors reasonably and in good faith concluded that Mesa's $54 two-tier tender offer was coercive and inadequate, and that Mesa sought selective treatment for itself. Furthermore, Unocal argues that the board's approval of the exchange offer was made in good faith, on an informed basis, and in the exercise of due care. Under these circumstances, Unocal contends that its directors properly employed this device to protect the company and its stockholders from Mesa's harmful tactics.

III.

We begin with the basic issue of the power of a board of directors of a Delaware corporation to adopt a defensive measure of this type. Absent such authority, all other questions are moot. Neither issues of fairness nor business judgment are pertinent without the basic underpinning of a board's legal power to act.

The board has a large reservoir of authority upon which to draw. Its duties and responsibilities proceed from the inherent powers conferred by 8 *Del.C.* § 141(a), respecting management of the corporation's "business and affairs".[6] Additionally, the powers here being exercised derive from 8 *Del.C.* § 160(a), conferring broad authority upon a corporation to deal in its own stock.[7] From this it is now well established that in the acquisition of its shares a [954] Delaware corporation may deal selectively with its stockholders, provided the directors have not acted out of a sole or primary purpose to entrench themselves in office. [...]

Finally, the board's power to act derives from its fundamental duty and obligation to protect the corporate enterprise, which includes stockholders, from harm reasonably perceived, irrespective of its source. [...] Thus, we are satisfied that in the broad context of corporate governance, including issues of fundamental corporate change, a board of directors is not a passive instrumentality.[8]

Given the foregoing principles, we turn to the standards by which director action is to be measured. In *Pogostin v. Rice,*[...]we held that the business judgment rule, including the standards by which director conduct is judged, is applicable in the context of a takeover. [...]The business judgment rule is a "presumption that in making a business decision the directors of a corporation acted on an informed basis, in good faith and in the honest belief that the action taken was in the best interests of the company." *Aronson v. Lewis,*[...]A hallmark of the business judgment rule is that a court will not substitute its judgment for that of the board if the latter's decision can be "attributed to any rational business purpose." *Sinclair Oil Corp. v. Levien,*[...]

When a board addresses a pending takeover bid it has an obligation to determine whether the offer is in the best interests of the corporation and its shareholders. In that respect a board's duty is no different from any other responsibility it shoulders, and its decisions should be no less entitled to the respect they otherwise would be accorded in the realm of business judgment.[9]*See also Johnson v. Trueblood,* 629 F.2d 287, 292-293 (3d Cir.1980). There are, however, certain caveats to a proper exercise of this function. Because of the omnipresent specter that a board may be acting primarily in its own interests, rather than those of the corporation and its shareholders, there is an enhanced duty which calls for judicial examination at the threshold before the protections of the business judgment rule may be conferred. [...]

In the face of this inherent conflict directors must show that they had reasonable grounds for believing that a danger to corporate policy and effectiveness existed because of another person's stock ownership. [...]However, they satisfy that burden "by showing good faith and reasonable investigation...." [...] Furthermore, such proof is materially enhanced, as here, by the approval of a board comprised of a majority of outside independent directors who have acted in accordance with the foregoing standards. [...]

IV.

A.

In the board's exercise of corporate power to forestall a takeover bid our analysis begins with the basic principle that corporate directors have a fiduciary duty to act in the best interests of the corporation's stockholders. [...]As we have noted, their duty of care extends to protecting the corporation and its owners from perceived harm whether a threat originates from third parties or other shareholders.[10] But such powers are not absolute. A corporation does not have unbridled discretion to defeat any perceived threat by any Draconian means available.

The restriction placed upon a selective stock repurchase is that the directors may not have acted solely or primarily out of a desire to perpetuate themselves in office. [...]The standard of proof [...]is designed to ensure that a defensive measure to thwart or impede a takeover is indeed motivated by a good faith concern for the welfare of the corporation and its stockholders, which in all circumstances must be free of any fraud or other misconduct. […]However, this does not end the inquiry.

B.

A further aspect is the element of balance. If a defensive measure is to come within the ambit of the business judgment rule, it must be reasonable in relation to the threat posed. This entails an analysis by the directors of the nature of the takeover bid and its effect on the corporate enterprise. *Examples of such concerns may include: inadequacy of the price offered, nature and timing of the offer, questions of illegality, the impact on "constituencies" other than shareholders (i.e., creditors, customers, employees, and perhaps even the community generally), the risk of nonconsummation, and the quality of securities being offered in the exchange. See* Lipton and Brownstein, *Takeover Responses and Directors' Responsibilities: An Update,* p. 7, ABA National Institute on the Dynamics of Corporate Control (December 8, 1983). While not a controlling factor, it also seems to us that a board may reasonably consider the basic stockholder interests at stake, including those of short term speculators, whose actions may have fueled the coercive aspect of the offer at the expense of the long term investor.[11] Here, the threat posed was viewed by the Unocal board as a grossly inadequate two-tier coercive tender offer coupled with the threat of greenmail.

Specifically, the Unocal directors had concluded that the value of Unocal was substantially above the $54 per share offered in cash at the front end. Furthermore, they determined that the subordinated securities to be exchanged in Mesa's announced squeeze out of the remaining shareholders in the "back-end" merger were "junk bonds" worth far less than $54. It is now well recognized that such offers are a classic coercive measure designed to stampede shareholders into tendering at the first tier, even if the price is inadequate, out of fear of what they will receive at the back end of the transaction.[12] Wholly beyond the coercive aspect of an inadequate two-tier tender offer, the threat was posed by a corporate raider with a national reputation as a "greenmailer".[13]

In adopting the selective exchange offer, the board stated that its objective was either to defeat the inadequate Mesa offer or, should the offer still succeed, provide the 49% of its stockholders, who would otherwise be forced to accept "junk bonds", with $72 worth of senior debt. We find that both purposes are valid.

However, such efforts would have been thwarted by Mesa's participation in the exchange offer. First, if Mesa could tender its shares, Unocal would effectively be subsidizing the former's continuing effort to buy Unocal stock at $54 per share. Second, Mesa could not, by definition, fit within the class of shareholders being protected from its own coercive and inadequate tender offer.

Thus, we are satisfied that the selective exchange offer is reasonably related to the threats posed. [...]

Mesa contends that it is unlawful, and the trial court agreed, for a corporation to discriminate in this fashion against one shareholder. It argues correctly that no case has ever sanctioned a device that precludes a raider from sharing in a benefit available to all other stockholders. However, as we have noted earlier, the principle of selective stock repurchases by a Delaware corporation is neither unknown nor unauthorized. *Cheff v. Mathes,* 199 A.2d at 554; *Bennett v. Propp,* 187 A.2d at 408; *Martin v. American Potash & Chemical Corporation,* 92 A.2d at 302; *Kaplan v. Goldsamt,* 380 A.2d at 568-569; *Kors v. Carey,* 158 A.2d at 140-141; 8 *Del. C.* § 160. The only difference is that heretofore the approved transaction was the payment of "greenmail" to a raider or dissident posing a threat to the corporate enterprise. All other stockholders were denied such favored treatment, and given Mesa's past history of greenmail, its claims here are rather ironic.

However, our corporate law is not static. It must grow and develop in response to, indeed in anticipation of, evolving concepts and needs. Merely because the General Corporation Law is silent as to a specific matter does not mean that it is prohibited. [...]

More recently, as the sophistication of both raiders and targets has developed, a host of other defensive measures to counter such ever mounting threats has evolved and received judicial sanction. These include defensive charter amendments and other devices bearing some rather exotic, but apt, names: Crown Jewel, White Knight, Pac Man, and Golden Parachute. Each has highly selective features, the object of which is to deter or defeat the raider.

Thus, while the exchange offer is a form of selective treatment, given the nature of the threat posed here the response is neither unlawful nor unreasonable. If the board of directors is disinterested, has acted in good faith and with due care, its decision in the absence of an abuse of discretion will be upheld as a proper exercise of business judgment. [...]

In conclusion, there was directorial power to oppose the Mesa tender offer, and to undertake a selective stock exchange made in good faith and upon a reasonable investigation pursuant to a clear duty to protect the corporate enterprise. Further, the selective stock repurchase plan chosen by Unocal is reasonable in relation to the threat that the board rationally and reasonably believed was posed by Mesa's inadequate and coercive two-tier tender offer. Under those circumstances the board's action is entitled to be measured by the standards of the business judgment rule. Thus, unless it is shown by a preponderance of the evidence that the directors' decisions were primarily based on perpetuating themselves in office, or some other breach of fiduciary duty such as fraud, overreaching, lack of good faith, or being uninformed, a Court will not substitute its judgment for that of the board. [...]

7.2.2 Revlon, Inc. v. MacAndrews & Forbes Holdings

When a board, under *Unocal*, is asked to justify its decision to adopt defensive measures by identifying some threat to the corporation or corporate policy, the board generally has broad discretion in identifying the threat. The court in *Unocal* noted that boards may be permitted to consider "the impact on "constituencies" other than shareholders (i.e., creditors, customers, employees, and perhaps even the community generally)". That is to say, the board is permitted to take a long-term view and consider the potential impact of a threat on the many constituencies that the corporation requires over the long term.

Revlon provides us with an alternative application of *Unocal*'s intermediate standard. In situations like *Revlon* where the board has decided of its own accord to look to the short term by engaging in a sale of control of the corporation, then the board may no longer consider long-term constituencies. When the board has focused on the short term, then the only cognizable threat to corporate policy are those that affect value in the short term. If a board in a *Revlon*-like situation adopts defenses, it will have to justify them as reasonable in relation to the threat posed to the corporation in the short run.

In the *Revlon* opinion that follows notice how the court applies *Unocal*'s intermediate standard before and after a break up of the corporation becomes imminent.

506 A.2d 173 (1986)
REVLON, INC. v. MacANDREWS & FORBES HOLDINGS, INC.

MOORE, Justice:

The prelude to this controversy began in June 1985, when Ronald O. Perelman, chairman of the board and chief executive officer of Pantry Pride, met with his counterpart at Revlon, Michel C. Bergerac, to discuss a friendly acquisition of Revlon by Pantry Pride. Perelman suggested a price in the range of $40-50 per share, but the meeting ended with Bergerac dismissing those figures as considerably below Revlon's intrinsic value. All subsequent Pantry Pride overtures were rebuffed, perhaps in part based on Mr. Bergerac's strong personal antipathy to Mr. Perelman.

Thus, on August 14, Pantry Pride's board authorized Perelman to acquire Revlon, either through negotiation in the $42-$43 per share range, or by making a hostile tender offer at $45. Perelman then met with Bergerac and outlined Pantry Pride's alternate approaches. Bergerac remained adamantly opposed to such schemes and conditioned any further discussions of the matter on Pantry Pride executing a standstill agreement prohibiting it from acquiring Revlon without the latter's prior approval.

On August 19, the Revlon board met specially to consider the impending threat of a hostile bid by Pantry Pride.[3] At the meeting, Lazard Freres, Revlon's investment [177] banker, advised the directors that $45 per share was a grossly inadequate price for the company. Felix Rohatyn and William Loomis of Lazard Freres explained to the board that Pantry Pride's financial strategy for acquiring Revlon would be through "junk bond" financing followed by a break-up of Revlon and the disposition of its assets. With proper timing, according to the experts, such transactions could produce a return to Pantry Pride of $60 to $70 per share, while a sale of the company as a whole would be in the "mid 50" dollar range. Martin Lipton, special counsel for Revlon, recommended two defensive measures: first, that the company repurchase up to 5 million of its nearly 30 million outstanding shares; and second, that it adopt a Note Purchase Rights Plan. Under this plan, each Revlon shareholder would receive as a dividend one Note Purchase Right (the Rights) for each share of common stock, with the Rights entitling the holder to exchange one common share for a $65 principal Revlon note at 12%

538

interest with a one-year maturity. The Rights would become effective whenever anyone acquired beneficial ownership of 20% or more of Revlon's shares, unless the purchaser acquired all the company's stock for cash at $65 or more per share. In addition, the Rights would not be available to the acquiror, and prior to the 20% triggering event the Revlon board could redeem the rights for 10 cents each. Both proposals were unanimously adopted.

Pantry Pride made its first hostile move on August 23 with a cash tender offer for any and all shares of Revlon at $47.50 per common share and $26.67 per preferred share, subject to (1) Pantry Pride's obtaining financing for the purchase, and (2) the Rights being redeemed, rescinded or voided.

The Revlon board met again on August 26. The directors advised the stockholders to reject the offer. Further defensive measures also were planned. On August 29, Revlon commenced its own offer for up to 10 million shares, exchanging for each share of common stock tendered one Senior Subordinated Note (the Notes) of $47.50 principal at 11.75% interest, due 1995, and one-tenth of a share of $9.00 Cumulative Convertible Exchangeable Preferred Stock valued at $100 per share. Lazard Freres opined that the notes would trade at their face value on a fully distributed basis.[4] Revlon stockholders tendered 87 percent of the outstanding shares (approximately 33 million), and the company accepted the full 10 million shares on a pro rata basis. The new Notes contained covenants which limited Revlon's ability to incur additional debt, sell assets, or pay dividends unless otherwise approved by the "independent" (nonmanagement) members of the board.

At this point, both the Rights and the Note covenants stymied Pantry Pride's attempted takeover. The next move came on September 16, when Pantry Pride announced a new tender offer at $42 per share, conditioned upon receiving at least 90% of the outstanding stock. […] While this offer was lower on its face than the earlier $47.50 proposal, Revlon's investment banker, Lazard Freres, described the two bids as essentially equal in view of the completed exchange offer.

The Revlon board held a regularly scheduled meeting on September 24. The directors rejected the latest Pantry Pride offer and authorized management to negotiate with other parties interested in acquiring Revlon. Pantry Pride remained determined in its efforts and continued to make cash bids for the company, offering $50 per share on September 27, and raising its bid to $53 on October 1, and then to $56.25 on October […]

 In the meantime, Revlon's negotiations with Forstmann […]had produced results. […]the directors unanimously agreed to a leveraged buyout by Forstmann. The terms of this accord were as follows: each stockholder would get $56 cash per share; management would purchase stock in the new company by the exercise of their Revlon "golden parachutes";[5] Forstmann would assume Revlon's $475 million debt incurred by the issuance of the Notes; and Revlon would redeem the Rights and waive the Notes covenants for Forstmann or in connection with any other offer superior to Forstmann's. The board did not actually remove the covenants at the October 3 meeting, because Forstmann then lacked a firm commitment on its financing, but accepted the Forstmann capital structure, and indicated that the outside directors would waive the covenants in due course. Part of Forstmann's plan was to sell Revlon's Norcliff Thayer and Reheis divisions to American Home Products for $335 million. Before the merger, Revlon was to sell its cosmetics and fragrance division to Adler & Shaykin for $905 million. These transactions would facilitate the purchase by Forstmann or any other acquiror of Revlon.

When the merger, and thus the waiver of the Notes covenants, was announced, the market value of these securities began to fall. […]One director later reported (at the October 12 meeting) a "deluge" of telephone calls from irate noteholders, and on October 10 the Wall Street Journal reported threats of litigation by these creditors.

Pantry Pride countered with a new proposal on October 7, raising its $53 offer to $56.25, subject to nullification of the Rights, a waiver of the Notes covenants, and the election of three Pantry Pride directors to the Revlon board. […]Pantry Pride announced that it would engage in fractional bidding and top any Forstmann offer by a slightly higher one. It is also significant that Forstmann, to Pantry Pride's exclusion, had been made privy to certain Revlon financial data. Thus, the parties were not negotiating on equal terms.

Privately armed with Revlon data, Forstmann met on October 11 with Revlon's special counsel and investment banker. On October 12, Forstmann made a new $57.25 per share offer, based on several conditions.[6] The principal demand was a lock-up option to purchase Revlon's Vision Care and National Health Laboratories divisions for $525 million, some $100-$175 million below the value ascribed to them by Lazard Freres, if another acquiror got 40% of Revlon's shares. Revlon also was required to accept a no-shop provision. The Rights and Notes covenants had to be removed as in the October 3 agreement. There would be a $25 million cancellation fee to be placed in escrow, and released to Forstmann if the new agreement terminated or if another acquiror got more than 19.9% of Revlon's stock. Finally, there would be no participation by Revlon management in the merger. In return, Forstmann agreed to support the par value [179] of the Notes, which had faltered in the market, by an exchange of new notes. Forstmann also demanded immediate acceptance of its offer, or it would be withdrawn. The board unanimously approved Forstmann's proposal because: (1) it was for a higher price than the Pantry Pride bid, (2) it protected the noteholders, and (3) Forstmann's financing was firmly in place.[7] The board further agreed to redeem the rights and waive the covenants on the preferred stock in response to any offer above $57 cash per share. The covenants were waived, contingent upon receipt of an investment banking opinion that the Notes would trade near par value once the offer was consummated.

Pantry Pride, which had initially sought injunctive relief from the Rights plan on August 22, filed an amended complaint on October 14 challenging the lock-up, the cancellation fee, and the exercise of the Rights and the Notes covenants. Pantry Pride also sought a temporary restraining order to prevent Revlon from placing any assets in escrow or transferring them to Forstmann. Moreover, on October 22, Pantry Pride again raised its bid, with a cash offer of $58 per share conditioned upon nullification of the Rights, waiver of the covenants, and an injunction of the Forstmann lock-up. [...]

The ultimate responsibility for managing the business and affairs of a corporation falls on its board of directors. 8 Del.C. § 141(a).[8] In discharging this function the directors owe fiduciary duties of care and loyalty to the corporation and its shareholders. [...] These principles apply with equal force when a board approves a corporate merger pursuant to 8 Del.C. § 251(b);[9]Smith v. Van Gorkom, Del.Supr., 488 A.2d 858, 873 (1985); and of course they are the bedrock of our law regarding corporate takeover issues. [...]While the business judgment rule may be applicable to the actions of corporate directors responding to takeover threats, the principles upon which it is founded — care, loyalty and independence — must first be satisfied.[10]Aronson v. Lewis, 473 A.2d at 812.

If the business judgment rule applies, there is a "presumption that in making a business decision the directors of a corporation acted on an informed basis, in good faith and in the honest belief that the action taken was in the best interests of the company." […]However, when a board implements anti-takeover measures there arises "the omnipresent specter that a board may be acting primarily in its own interests, rather than those of the corporation and its shareholders ..." […]This potential for conflict places upon the directors the burden of proving that they had reasonable grounds for believing there was a danger to corporate policy and effectiveness, a burden satisfied by a showing of good faith and reasonable investigation. *Id.* at 955. In addition, the directors must analyze the nature of the takeover and its effect on the corporation in order to ensure balance — that the responsive action taken is reasonable in relation to the threat posed. […]

The first relevant defensive measure adopted by the Revlon board was the Rights Plan, which would be considered a "poison pill" in the current language of corporate takeovers — a plan by which shareholders receive the right to be bought out by the corporation at a substantial premium on the occurrence of a stated triggering event. *S*[…] the board clearly had the power to adopt the measure. […]Thus, the focus becomes one of reasonableness and purpose.

The Revlon board approved the Rights Plan in the face of an impending hostile takeover bid by Pantry Pride at $45 per share, a price which Revlon reasonably concluded was grossly inadequate. […] In adopting the Plan, the board protected the shareholders from a hostile takeover at a price below the company's intrinsic value, while retaining sufficient flexibility to address any proposal deemed to be in the stockholders' best interests.

To that extent the board acted in good faith and upon reasonable investigation. Under the circumstances it cannot be said that the Rights Plan as employed was unreasonable, considering the threat posed. Indeed, the Plan was a factor in causing Pantry Pride to raise its bids from a low of $42 to an eventual high of $58. At the time of its adoption the Rights Plan afforded a measure of protection consistent with the directors' fiduciary duty in facing a takeover threat perceived as detrimental to corporate interests. […]Far from being a "show-stopper," as the plaintiffs had contended in *Moran,* the measure spurred the bidding to new heights, a proper result of its implementation. *S*[…]

Although we consider adoption of the Plan to have been valid under the circumstances, its continued usefulness was rendered moot by the directors' actions on October 3 and October 12. At the October 3 meeting the board redeemed the Rights conditioned upon consummation of a merger with Forstmann, but further acknowledged that they would also be redeemed to facilitate any more favorable offer. On October 12, the board unanimously passed a resolution redeeming the Rights in connection with any cash proposal of $57.25 or more per share. Because all the pertinent offers eventually equalled or surpassed that amount, the Rights clearly were no longer any impediment in the contest for Revlon. This mooted any question of their propriety under [...]*Unocal.*

The second defensive measure adopted by Revlon to thwart a Pantry Pride takeover was the company's own exchange offer for 10 million of its shares. [...]

The Revlon directors concluded that Pantry Pride's $47.50 offer was grossly inadequate. In that regard the board acted in good faith, and on an informed basis, with reasonable grounds to believe that there existed a harmful threat to the corporate enterprise. The adoption of a defensive measure, reasonable in relation to the threat posed, was proper and fully accorded with the powers, duties, and responsibilities conferred upon directors under our law. [...]

However, when Pantry Pride increased its offer to $50 per share, and then to $53, it became apparent to all that the break-up of the company was inevitable. The Revlon board's authorization permitting management to negotiate a merger or buyout with a third party was a recognition that the company was for sale. The duty of the board had thus changed from the preservation of Revlon as a corporate entity to the maximization of the company's value at a sale for the stockholders' benefit. This significantly altered the board's responsibilities under the *Unocal* standards. It no longer faced threats to corporate policy and effectiveness, or to the stockholders' interests, from a grossly inadequate bid. The whole question of defensive measures became moot. The directors' role changed from defenders of the corporate bastion to auctioneers charged with getting the best price for the stockholders at a sale of the company. [...]

This brings us to the lock-up with Forstmann and its emphasis on shoring up the sagging market value of the Notes in the face of threatened litigation by their holders. Such a focus was inconsistent with the changed concept of the directors' responsibilities at this stage of the developments. [...]

The original threat posed by Pantry Pride — the break-up of the company — had become a reality which even the directors embraced. Selective dealing to fend off a hostile but determined bidder was no longer a proper objective. Instead, obtaining the highest price for the benefit of the stockholders should have been the central theme guiding director action. Thus, the Revlon board could not make the requisite showing of good faith by preferring the noteholders and ignoring its duty of loyalty to the shareholders. The rights of the former already were fixed by contract. […]The noteholders required no further protection, and when the Revlon board entered into an auction-ending lock-up agreement with Forstmann on the basis of impermissible considerations at the expense of the shareholders, the directors breached their primary duty of loyalty.

The Revlon board argued that it acted in good faith in protecting the noteholders because *Unocal* permits consideration of other corporate constituencies. […]However, such concern for non-stockholder interests is inappropriate when an auction among active bidders is in progress, and the object no longer is to protect or maintain the corporate enterprise but to sell it to the highest bidder. […]

In conclusion, the Revlon board was confronted with a situation not uncommon in the current wave of corporate takeovers. A hostile and determined bidder sought the company at a price the board was convinced was inadequate. The initial defensive tactics worked to the benefit of the shareholders, and thus the board was able to sustain its *Unocal* burdens in justifying those measures. However, in granting an asset option lock-up to Forstmann, we must conclude that under all the circumstances the directors allowed considerations other than the maximization of shareholder profit to affect their judgment, and followed a course that ended the auction for Revlon, absent court intervention, to the ultimate detriment of its shareholders. No such defensive measure can be sustained when it represents a breach of the directors' fundamental duty of care. *See Smith v. Van Gorkom,* Del.Supr., 488 A.2d 858, 874 (1985). In that context the board's action is not entitled to the deference accorded it by the business judgment rule.

7.2.3 Paramount Communications, Inc. v. Time Inc.

In *Time*, the court is asked to clarify exactly when a board's actions will be reviewed under the standard announced in *Unocal* and *Revlon*.

571 A.2d 1140 (1989)
PARAMOUNT COMMUNICATIONS, INC. v. TIME INC.

HORSEY, Justice:

Paramount Communications, Inc. ("Paramount")[…] filed suits in the Delaware Court of Chancery seeking a preliminary injunction to halt Time's tender offer for 51% of Warner Communication, Inc.'s ("Warner") outstanding shares at $70 cash per share.[…]

Shareholder Plaintiffs also assert a claim based on *Revlon v. MacAndrews & Forbes Holdings, Inc.,* Del.Supr., 506 A.2d 173 (1986). They argue that the original Time-Warner merger agreement of March 4, 1989 resulted in a change of control which effectively put Time up for sale, thereby triggering *Revlon* duties. Those plaintiffs argue that Time's board breached its *Revlon* duties by failing, in the face of the change of control, to maximize shareholder value in the immediate term.

Applying our standard of review, we affirm the Chancellor's ultimate finding and conclusion under *Unocal.* We find that Paramount's tender offer was reasonably perceived by Time's board to pose a threat to Time and that the Time board's "response" to that threat was, under the circumstances, reasonable and proportionate. Applying *Unocal,* we reject the argument that the only corporate threat posed by an all-shares, all-cash tender offer is the possibility of inadequate value.

We also find that Time's board did not by entering into its initial merger agreement with Warner come under a *Revlon* duty either to auction the company or to maximize short-term shareholder value, notwithstanding the unequal share exchange. Therefore, the Time board's original plan of merger with Warner was subject only to a business judgment rule analysis. *See Smith v. Van Gorkom,* Del.Supr., 488 A.2d 858, 873-74 (1985).[2]

I

Time is a Delaware corporation with its principal offices in New York City. Time's traditional business is publication of magazines and books; however, Time also provides pay television programming through its Home Box Office, Inc. and Cinemax subsidiaries. In addition, Time owns and operates cable television franchises through its subsidiary, American Television and Communication Corporation. During the relevant time period, Time's board consisted of sixteen directors. Twelve of the directors were "outside," nonemployee directors. Four of the directors were also officers of the company.[...]

As early as 1983 and 1984, Time's executive board began considering expanding Time's operations into the entertainment industry. [...] This expansion, as the Chancellor noted, was predicated upon two considerations: first, Time's desire to have greater control, in terms of quality and price, over the film products delivered by way of its cable network and franchises; and second, Time's concern over the increasing globalization of the world economy. Some of Time's outside directors, especially Luce and Temple, had opposed this move as a threat to the editorial integrity and journalistic focus of Time.[4] Despite this concern, the board recognized that a [1144] vertically integrated video enterprise to complement Time's existing HBO and cable networks would better enable it to compete on a global basis. [...]

The board's consensus was that a merger of Time and Warner was feasible, but only if Time controlled the board of the resulting corporation and thereby preserved a management committed to Time's journalistic integrity. To accomplish this goal, the board stressed the importance of carefully defining in advance the corporate governance provisions that would control the resulting entity. Some board members expressed concern over whether such a business combination would place Time *"in play."* The board discussed the wisdom of adopting further defensive measures to lessen such a possibility.[5] [...]

From the outset, Time's board favored an all-cash or cash and securities acquisition of Warner as the basis for consolidation. [...]Warner insisted on a stock swap in order to preserve its shareholders' equity in the resulting corporation. Time's officers, on the other hand, made it abundantly clear that Time would be the acquiring corporation and that Time would control the resulting board. Time refused to permit itself to be cast as the "acquired" company.

Negotiations ended when the parties reached an impasse. Time's board refused to compromise on its position on corporate governance. Time, and particularly its outside directors, viewed the corporate governance provisions as critical for preserving the "Time Culture" through a pro-Time management at the top. […]

Warner and Time resumed negotiations in January 1989. The catalyst for the resumption of talks was a private dinner between Steve Ross and Time outside director, Michael Dingman. Dingman was able to convince Ross that the transitional nature of the proposed co-CEO arrangement did not reflect a lack of confidence in Ross. […]Negotiations resumed and many of the details of the original stock-for-stock exchange agreement remained [1146] intact. […]

 The parties ultimately agreed upon an exchange rate favoring Warner of .465. On that basis, Warner stockholders would have owned approximately 62%[7] of the common stock of Time-Warner.

On March 3, 1989, Time's board, with all but one director in attendance, met and unanimously approved the stock-for-stock merger with Warner. Warner's board likewise approved the merger. The agreement called for Warner to be merged into a wholly-owned Time subsidiary with Warner becoming the surviving corporation. The common stock of Warner would then be converted into common stock of Time at the agreed upon ratio. Thereafter, the name of Time would be changed to Time-Warner, Inc.

The rules of the New York Stock Exchange required that Time's issuance of shares to effectuate the merger be approved by a vote of Time's stockholders. The Delaware General Corporation Law required approval of the merger by a majority of the Warner stockholders. Delaware law did not require any vote by Time stockholders. […]

At its March 3, 1989 meeting, Time's board adopted several defensive tactics. Time entered an automatic share exchange agreement with Warner. Time would receive 17,292,747 shares of Warner's outstanding common stock (9.4%) and Warner would receive 7,080,016 shares of Time's outstanding common stock (11.1%). Either party could trigger the exchange. Time sought out and paid for "confidence" letters from various banks with which it did business. In these letters, the banks promised not to finance any third-party attempt to acquire Time. Time argues these agreements served only to preserve the confidential relationship between itself and the banks. The Chancellor found these agreements to be inconsequential and futile attempts to "dry up" money for a hostile takeover. Time also agreed to a "no-shop" clause, preventing Time from considering any other consolidation proposal, thus relinquishing [1147] its power to consider other proposals, regardless of their merits. Time did so at Warner's insistence. Warner did not want to be left "on the auction block" for an unfriendly suitor, if Time were to withdraw from the deal. […]

Time representatives lauded the lack of debt to the United States Senate and to the President of the United States. Public reaction to the announcement of the merger was positive. Time-Warner would be a media colossus with international scope. The board scheduled the stockholder vote for June 23; and a May 1 record date was set. On May 24, 1989, Time sent out extensive proxy statements to the stockholders regarding the approval vote on the merger. In the meantime, with the merger proceeding without impediment, the special committee had concluded, shortly after its creation, that it was not necessary either to retain independent consultants, legal or financial, or even to meet. Time's board was unanimously in favor of the proposed merger with Warner; and, by the end of May, the Time-Warner merger appeared to be an accomplished fact.

On June 7, 1989, these wishful assumptions were shattered by Paramount's surprising announcement of its all-cash offer to purchase all outstanding shares of Time for $175 per share. The following day, June 8, the trading price of Time's stock rose from $126 to $170 per share. Paramount's offer was said to be "fully negotiable."[8]

Time found Paramount's "fully negotiable" offer to be in fact subject to at least three conditions. First, Time had to terminate its merger agreement and stock exchange agreement with Warner, and remove certain other of its defensive devices, including the redemption of Time's shareholder rights. Second, Paramount had to obtain the required cable franchise transfers from Time in a fashion acceptable to Paramount in its sole discretion. Finally, the offer depended upon a judicial determination that section 203 of the General Corporate Law of Delaware (The Delaware Anti-Takeover Statute) was inapplicable to any Time-Paramount merger. […]

On June 8, 1989, Time formally responded to Paramount's offer. Time's chairman and CEO, J. Richard Munro, sent an aggressively worded letter to Paramount's CEO, Martin Davis. Munro's letter attacked Davis' personal integrity and called Paramount's offer "smoke and mirrors." […]

548

Over the following eight days, Time's board met three times to discuss Paramount's $175 offer. The board viewed Paramount's offer as inadequate and concluded that its proposed merger with Warner was the better course of action. [...]

In June, Time's board of directors met several times. [...]

At these June meetings, certain Time directors expressed their concern that Time stockholders would not comprehend the long-term benefits of the Warner merger. Large quantities of Time shares were held by institutional investors. The board feared that even though there appeared to be wide support for the Warner transaction, Paramount's cash premium would be a tempting prospect to these investors. [...]

 Time's board decided to recast its consolidation with Warner into an outright cash and securities acquisition of Warner by Time; and Time so informed Warner. Time accordingly restructured its proposal to acquire Warner as follows: Time would make an immediate all-cash offer for 51% of Warner's outstanding stock at $70 per share. The remaining 49% would be purchased at some later date for a mixture of cash and securities worth $70 per share. To provide the funds required for its outright acquisition of Warner, Time would assume 7-10 billion dollars worth of debt, thus eliminating one of the principal transaction-related benefits of the original merger agreement. Nine billion dollars of the total purchase price would be allocated to the purchase of Warner's goodwill. [...]

On June 23, 1989, Paramount raised its all-cash offer to buy Time's outstanding stock to $200 per share. Paramount still professed that all aspects of the offer were negotiable. Time's board met on June 26, 1989 and formally rejected Paramount's $200 per share second offer. The board reiterated its belief that, despite the $25 increase, the offer was still inadequate. The Time board maintained that the Warner transaction offered a greater long-term value for the stockholders and, unlike Paramount's offer, did not pose a threat to Time's survival and its "culture." Paramount then filed this action in the Court of Chancery.

II

The Shareholder Plaintiffs first assert a *Revlon* claim. They contend that the March 4 Time-Warner agreement effectively put Time up for sale, triggering *Revlon* duties, requiring Time's board to enhance short-term shareholder value and to treat all other

549

interested acquirors on an equal basis. The Shareholder Plaintiffs base this argument on two facts: (i) the ultimate Time-Warner exchange ratio of .465 favoring Warner, resulting in Warner shareholders' receipt of 62% of the combined company; and (ii) the subjective intent of Time's directors as evidenced in their statements that the market might perceive the Time-Warner merger as putting Time up "for sale" and their adoption of various defensive measures. […]

The Court of Chancery posed the pivotal question presented by this case to be: Under what circumstances must a board of directors abandon an in-place plan of corporate development in order to provide its shareholders with the option to elect and realize an immediate control premium? As applied to this case, the question becomes: Did Time's board, having developed a strategic plan of global expansion to be launched through a business combination with Warner, come under a fiduciary duty to jettison its plan and put the corporation's future in the hands of its shareholders?

While we affirm the result reached by the Chancellor, we think it unwise to place undue emphasis upon long-term versus short-term corporate strategy. Two key predicates underpin our analysis. First, Delaware law imposes on a board of directors the duty to manage the business and affairs of the corporation. 8 *Del.C.* § 141(a). This broad mandate includes a conferred authority to set a corporate course of action, including time frame, designed to enhance corporate profitability. Thus, the question of "long-term" versus "short-term" values is largely irrelevant because directors, generally, are obliged to chart a course for a corporation which is in its best interests without regard to a fixed investment horizon. Second, absent a limited set of circumstances as defined under *Revlon,* a board of directors, while always required to act in an informed manner, is not under any *per se* duty to maximize shareholder value in the short term, even in the context of a takeover.[12] In our view, the pivotal question presented by this case is: "Did Time, by entering into the proposed merger with Warner, put itself up for sale?" A resolution of that issue through application of *Revlon* has a significant bearing upon the resolution of the derivative *Unocal* issue.

A.

We first take up plaintiffs' principal *Revlon* argument, summarized above. In rejecting this argument, the Chancellor found the original Time-Warner merger agreement not to constitute a "change of control" and concluded that the transaction did not trigger *Revlon* duties. The Chancellor's conclusion is premised on a finding that "[b]efore the merger agreement was signed, control of the corporation existed in a fluid aggregation of unaffiliated shareholders representing a voting majority — in other words, in the market." The Chancellor's findings of fact are supported by the record and his conclusion is correct as a matter of law. However, we premise our rejection of plaintiffs' *Revlon* claim on different grounds, namely, the absence of any substantial evidence to conclude that Time's board, in negotiating with Warner, made the dissolution or break-up of the corporate entity inevitable, as was the case in *Revlon.*

Under Delaware law there are, generally speaking and without excluding other possibilities, two circumstances which may implicate *Revlon* duties. The first, and clearer one, is when a corporation initiates an active bidding process seeking to sell itself or to effect a business reorganization involving a clear break-up of the company. *See, e.g., Mills Acquisition Co. v. Macmillan, Inc,* Del.Supr., 559 A.2d 1261 (1988). However, *Revlon* duties may also be triggered where, in response to a bidder's offer, a target abandons its long-term strategy and seeks an alternative transaction involving the breakup of the company[…] If, however, the board's reaction to a hostile tender offer is found to constitute only a defensive response and not an abandonment of the corporation's continued existence, *Revlon* duties are not triggered, though *Unocal* [1151] duties attach[…]

Plaintiffs rely on the subjective intent of Time's board of directors and principally upon certain board members' expressions of concern that the Warner transaction *might* be viewed as effectively putting Time up for sale. […]

We agree with the Chancellor that such evidence is entirely insufficient to invoke *Revlon* duties; and we decline to extend *Revlon*'s application to corporate transactions simply because they might be construed as putting a corporation either "in play" or "up for sale." *See Citron v. Fairchild Camera,* Del.Supr., 569 A.2d 53, (1989); *Macmillan,* 559 A.2d at 1285 n. 35. The adoption of structural safety devices alone does not trigger *Revlon.*[15] Rather, as the Chancellor stated, such devices are properly subject to a *Unocal* analysis.

Finally, we do not find in Time's recasting of its merger agreement with Warner from a share exchange to a share purchase a basis to conclude that Time had either abandoned its strategic plan or made a sale of Time inevitable.[16] The Chancellor found that although the merged Time-Warner company would be large (with a value approaching approximately $30 billion), recent takeover cases have proven that acquisition of the combined company might nonetheless be possible. [...] The legal consequence is that *Unocal* alone applies to determine whether the business judgment rule attaches to the revised agreement. [...]

In *Unocal*, we held that before the business judgment rule is applied to a board's adoption of a defensive measure, the burden will lie with the board to prove (a) reasonable grounds for believing that a danger to corporate policy and effectiveness existed; and (b) that the defensive measure adopted was reasonable in relation to the threat posed. *Unocal*, 493 A.2d 946. Directors satisfy the first part of the *Unocal* test by demonstrating good faith and reasonable investigation. We have repeatedly stated that the refusal to entertain an offer may comport with a valid exercise of a board's business judgment. [...]

Paramount would have us hold that only if the value of Paramount's offer were determined to be clearly inferior to the value created by management's plan to merge with Warner could the offer be viewed — objectively — as a threat.

Implicit in the plaintiffs' argument is the view that a hostile tender offer can pose only two types of threats: the threat of coercion that results from a two-tier offer promising unequal treatment for nontendering shareholders; and the threat of inadequate value from an all-shares, all-cash offer at a price below what a target board [1153] in good faith deems to be the present value of its shares. *See, e.g., Interco,*[...] Since Paramount's offer was all-cash, the only conceivable "threat," plaintiffs argue, was inadequate value.[17] We disapprove of such a narrow and rigid construction of *Unocal*, for the reasons which follow.

Plaintiffs' position represents a fundamental misconception of our standard of review under *Unocal* principally because it would involve the court in substituting its judgment as to what is a "better" deal for that of a corporation's board of directors. To the extent that the Court of Chancery has recently done so in certain of its opinions, we hereby reject such approach as not in keeping with a proper *Unocal* analysis. *See, e.g., Interco,* 551 A.2d 787, and its progeny; *but see TW Services, Inc. v. SWT Acquisition Corp.,* Del.Ch., C.A. No. 1047, Allen, C. 1989 WL 20290 (March 2, 1989).

The usefulness of *Unocal* as an analytical tool is precisely its flexibility in the face of a variety of fact scenarios. *Unocal* is not intended as an abstract standard; neither is it a structured and mechanistic procedure of appraisal. Thus, we have said that directors may consider, when evaluating the threat posed by a takeover bid, the "inadequacy of the price offered, nature and timing of the offer, questions of illegality, the impact on `constituencies' other than shareholders ... the risk of nonconsummation, and the quality of securities being offered in the exchange." [...] The open-ended analysis mandated by *Unocal* is not intended to lead to a simple mathematical exercise:[...] To engage in such an exercise is a distortion of the *Unocal* process and, in particular, the application of the second part of *Unocal*'s test, discussed below.

In this case, the Time board reasonably determined that inadequate value was not the only legally cognizable threat that Paramount's all-cash, all-shares offer could present. Time's board concluded that Paramount's eleventh hour offer posed other threats. One concern was that Time shareholders might elect to tender into Paramount's cash offer in ignorance or a mistaken belief of the strategic benefit which a business combination with Warner might produce. [...]

We turn to the second part of the *Unocal* analysis. [...]

Paramount argues that, assuming its tender offer posed a threat, Time's response was unreasonable in precluding Time's shareholders from accepting the tender offer or receiving a control premium in the immediately foreseeable future. Once again, the contention stems, we believe, from a fundamental misunderstanding of where the power of corporate governance lies. Delaware law confers the management of the corporate enterprise to the stockholders' duly elected board representatives. 8 *Del.C.* § 141(a). The fiduciary duty to manage a corporate enterprise includes the selection of a time frame for achievement of corporate goals. That duty may not be delegated to the stockholders. [...] Directors are not obliged to abandon a deliberately conceived corporate plan for a short-term shareholder profit unless there is clearly no basis to sustain the corporate strategy. [...]

We have found that even in light of a valid threat, management actions that are coercive in nature or force upon shareholders a management-sponsored alternative to a hostile offer may be struck down as unreasonable and non-proportionate responses.[...]

Here, on the record facts, the Chancellor found that Time's responsive action to Paramount's tender offer was not aimed at [1155] "cramming down" on its shareholders a management-sponsored alternative, but rather had as its goal the carrying forward of a pre-existing transaction in an altered form.[19] Thus, the response was reasonably related to the threat. The Chancellor noted that the revised agreement and its accompanying safety devices did not preclude Paramount from making an offer for the combined Time-Warner company or from changing the conditions of its offer so as not to make the offer dependent upon the nullification of the Time-Warner agreement. Thus, the response was proportionate. […]

7.2.4 Paramount Communications Inc. v. QVC Networks Inc.

The court in QVC returns to the question of application of the intermediate standard under Revlon. Ultimately, QVC will become a very important case in the development and application of the Revlon standard. In QVC, the court makes it clear that Revlon is not about a new standard of review but rather, akin to Unocal, it is an inquiry into the motive and means of the board.

If the board's motive is impaired by conflicts of interest, or if the board's means in defending its decision merge with a preferred party are draconian, the court will apply the entire fairness standard to a review of that decision. If not, then the a board's decision to engage in a sale of control transaction will get the presumption of business judgment, even if that decision is not perfect or, in hindsight, appears unwise.

637 A.2d 34 (1994)
PARAMOUNT COMMUNICATIONS INC. v. QVC NETWORK INC.

VEASEY, Chief Justice.

In this appeal we review an order of the Court of Chancery dated November 24, 1993 (the "November 24 Order"), preliminarily enjoining certain defensive measures designed to facilitate a so-called strategic alliance between Viacom Inc. ("Viacom") and Paramount Communications Inc. ("Paramount") approved by the board of directors of Paramount (the "Paramount Board" or the "Paramount directors") and to thwart an unsolicited, more valuable, tender offer by QVC Network Inc. ("QVC"). In affirming, we hold that the sale of control in this case, which is at the heart of the proposed strategic alliance, implicates enhanced judicial scrutiny of the conduct of the Paramount

Board under *Unocal Corp. v. Mesa Petroleum Co.,* Del. Supr., 493 A.2d 946 (1985), and *Revlon, Inc. v. MacAndrews & Forbes Holdings, Inc.,* Del.Supr., 506 A.2d 173 (1986). We further hold that the conduct of the Paramount Board was not reasonable as to process or result. […]

I. FACTS

Paramount is a Delaware corporation with its principal offices in New York City. Approximately 118 million shares of Paramount's common stock are outstanding and traded on the New York Stock Exchange. The majority of Paramount's stock is publicly held by numerous unaffiliated investors. Paramount owns and operates a diverse group of entertainment businesses, including motion picture and television studios, book publishers, professional sports teams, and amusement parks. […]

Viacom is a Delaware corporation with its headquarters in Massachusetts. Viacom is controlled by Sumner M. Redstone ("Red-stone"), its Chairman and Chief Executive Officer, who owns indirectly approximately 85.2 percent of Viacom's voting Class A stock and approximately 69.2 percent of Viacom's nonvoting Class B stock through National Amusements, Inc. ("NAI"), an entity 91.7 percent owned by Redstone. […]

QVC is a Delaware corporation with its headquarters in West Chester, Pennsylvania. QVC has several large stockholders, including Liberty Media Corporation, Comcast Corporation, Advance Publications, Inc., and Cox Enterprises Inc. Barry Diller ("Diller"), the Chairman and Chief Executive Officer of QVC, is also a substantial stockholder. […]

Beginning in the late 1980s, Paramount investigated the possibility of acquiring or merging with other companies in the entertainment, media, or communications industry. Paramount considered such transactions to be desirable, and perhaps necessary, in order to keep pace with competitors in the rapidly evolving field of entertainment and communications. Consistent with its goal of strategic expansion, Paramount made a tender offer for Time Inc. in 1989, but was ultimately unsuccessful. *See Paramount Communications, Inc. v. Time Inc.,* Del. Supr., 571 A.2d 1140 (1990) ("*Time-Warner*").

Although Paramount had considered a possible combination of Paramount and Viacom as early as 1990, recent efforts to explore such a transaction began at a dinner meeting between Redstone and Davis on April 20, 1993. […]

It was tentatively agreed that Davis would be the chief executive officer and Redstone would be the controlling stockholder of the combined company, but the parties could not reach agreement on the merger price and the terms of a stock option to be granted to Viacom. With respect to price, Viacom offered a package of cash and stock (primarily Viacom Class B nonvoting stock) with a market value of approximately $61 per share, but Paramount wanted at least $70 per share.

Shortly after negotiations broke down in July 1993, two notable events occurred. First, Davis apparently learned of QVC's potential interest in Paramount, and told Diller over lunch on July 21, 1993, that Paramount was not for sale. Second, the market value of Viacom's Class B nonvoting stock increased from $46.875 on July 6 to $57.25 on August 20. QVC claims (and Viacom disputes) that this price increase was caused by open market purchases of such stock by Redstone or entities controlled by him.

[39] On August 20, 1993, discussions between Paramount and Viacom resumed when Greenhill arranged another meeting between Davis and Redstone. After a short hiatus, the parties negotiated in earnest in early September, and performed due diligence with the assistance of their financial advisors, Lazard Freres & Co. ("Lazard") for Paramount and Smith Barney for Viacom. On September 9, 1993, the Paramount Board was informed about the status of the negotiations and was provided information by Lazard, including an analysis of the proposed transaction.

On September 12, 1993, the Paramount Board met again and unanimously approved the Original Merger Agreement whereby Paramount would merge with and into Viacom. The terms of the merger provided that each share of Paramount common stock would be converted into 0.10 shares of Viacom Class A voting stock, 0.90 shares of Viacom Class B nonvoting stock, and $9.10 in cash. In addition, the Paramount Board agreed to amend its "poison pill" Rights Agreement to exempt the proposed merger with Viacom. The Original Merger Agreement also contained several provisions designed to make it more difficult for a potential competing bid to succeed. We focus, as did the Court of Chancery, on three of these defensive provisions: a "no-shop" provision (the "No-Shop Provision"), the Termination Fee, and the Stock Option Agreement.

First, under the No-Shop Provision, the Paramount Board agreed that Paramount would not solicit, encourage, discuss, negotiate, or endorse any competing transaction unless: (a) a third party "makes an unsolicited written, bona fide proposal, which is not subject to any material contingencies relating to financing"; and (b) the Paramount Board determines that discussions or negotiations with the third party are necessary for the Paramount Board to comply with its fiduciary duties.

Second, under the Termination Fee provision, Viacom would receive a $100 million termination fee if: (a) Paramount terminated the Original Merger Agreement because of a competing transaction; (b) Paramount's stockholders did not approve the merger; or (c) the Paramount Board recommended a competing transaction.

The third and most significant deterrent device was the Stock Option Agreement, which granted to Viacom an option to purchase approximately 19.9 percent (23,699,000 shares) of Paramount's outstanding common stock at $69.14 per share if any of the triggering events for the Termination Fee occurred. In addition to the customary terms that are normally associated with a stock option, the Stock Option Agreement contained two provisions that were both unusual and highly beneficial to Viacom: (a) Viacom was permitted to pay for the shares with a senior subordinated note of questionable marketability instead of cash, thereby avoiding the need to raise the $1.6 billion purchase price (the "Note Feature"); and (b) Viacom could elect to require Paramount to pay Viacom in cash a sum equal to the difference between the purchase price and the market price of Paramount's stock (the "Put Feature"). Because the Stock Option Agreement was not "capped" to limit its maximum dollar value, it had the potential to reach (and in this case did reach) unreasonable levels.

After the execution of the Original Merger Agreement and the Stock Option Agreement on September 12, 1993, Paramount and Viacom announced their proposed merger. In a number of public statements, the parties indicated that the pending transaction was a virtual certainty. Redstone described it as a "marriage" that would "never be torn asunder" and stated that only a "nuclear attack" could break the deal. Redstone also called Diller and John Malone of Tele-Communications Inc., a major stockholder of QVC, to dissuade them from making a competing bid.

Despite these attempts to discourage a competing bid, Diller sent a letter to Davis on September 20, 1993, proposing a merger in which QVC would acquire Paramount for approximately $80 per share, consisting of 0.893 shares of QVC common stock and $30 in cash. […]

On October 21, 1993, QVC filed this action and publicly announced an $80 cash tender offer for 51 percent of Paramount's outstanding shares (the "QVC tender offer"). Each remaining share of Paramount common stock would be converted into 1.42857 shares of QVC common stock in a second-step merger. The tender offer was conditioned on, among other things, the invalidation of the Stock Option Agreement, which was worth over $200 million by that point.[5] QVC contends that it had to commence a tender offer because of the slow pace of the merger discussions and the need to begin seeking clearance under federal antitrust laws.

Confronted by QVC's hostile bid, which on its face offered over $10 per share more than the consideration provided by the Original Merger Agreement, Viacom realized that it would need to raise its bid in order to remain competitive. Within hours after QVC's tender offer was announced, Viacom entered into discussions with Paramount concerning a revised transaction. These discussions led to serious negotiations concerning a comprehensive amendment to the original Paramount-Viacom transaction. In effect, the opportunity for a "new deal" with Viacom was at hand for the Paramount Board. With the QVC hostile bid offering greater value to the Paramount stockholders, the Paramount Board had considerable leverage with Viacom.

At a special meeting on October 24, 1993, the Paramount Board approved the Amended Merger Agreement and an amendment to the Stock Option Agreement. The Amended Merger Agreement was, however, essentially the same as the Original Merger Agreement, except that it included a few new provisions. One provision related to an $80 per share cash tender offer by Viacom for 51 percent of Paramount's stock, and another changed the merger consideration so that each share of Paramount would be converted into 0.20408 shares of Viacom Class A voting stock, 1.08317 shares of Viacom Class B nonvoting stock, and 0.20408 shares of a new series of Viacom convertible preferred stock. The Amended Merger Agreement also added a provision giving Paramount the right not to amend its Rights Agreement to exempt Viacom if the Paramount Board determined that such an amendment would be inconsistent with its fiduciary duties because another offer constituted a "better alternative."[6] Finally, the Paramount Board was given the power to terminate the Amended Merger Agreement if it withdrew its recommendation of the Viacom transaction or recommended a competing transaction.

Although the Amended Merger Agreement offered more consideration to the Paramount stockholders and somewhat more flexibility to the Paramount Board than did the Original Merger Agreement, the defensive measures designed to make a competing bid more difficult were not removed or modified. [41] In particular, there is no evidence in the record that Paramount sought to use its newly-acquired leverage to eliminate or modify the No-Shop Provision, the Termination Fee, or the Stock Option Agreement when the subject of amending the Original Merger Agreement was on the table. [...]

On November 6, 1993, Viacom unilaterally raised its tender offer price to $85 per share in cash and offered a comparable increase in the value of the securities being proposed in the second-step merger. [...]

QVC responded to Viacom's higher bid on November 12 by increasing its tender offer to $90 per share and by increasing the securities for its second-step merger by a similar amount. [...]

At its meeting on November 15, 1993, the Paramount Board determined that the new QVC offer was not in the best interests of the stockholders. The purported basis for this conclusion was that QVC's bid was excessively conditional. The Paramount Board did not communicate with QVC regarding the status of the conditions because it believed that the No-Shop Provision prevented such communication in the absence of firm financing. Several Paramount directors also testified that they believed the Viacom transaction would be more advantageous to Paramount's future business prospects than a QVC transaction.[7] Although a number of materials were distributed to the Paramount Board describing the Viacom and QVC transactions, the only quantitative analysis of the consideration to be received by the stockholders under each proposal was based on then-current market prices of the securities involved, not on the anticipated value of such securities at the time when the stockholders would receive them.[8]

The preliminary injunction hearing in this case took place on November 16, 1993. On November 19, Diller wrote to the Paramount Board to inform it that QVC had obtained financing commitments for its tender offer and that there was no antitrust obstacle to the offer. [...]

II. APPLICABLE PRINCIPLES OF ESTABLISHED DELAWARE LAW

The General Corporation Law of the State of Delaware (the "General Corporation Law") and the decisions of this Court have repeatedly recognized the fundamental principle that the management of the business and affairs of a Delaware corporation is entrusted to its directors, who are the duly elected and authorized representatives of the [42] stockholders. 8 *Del.C.* § 141(a); *Aronson v. Lewis,* Del.Supr., 473 A.2d 805, 811-12 (1984); *Pogostin v. Rice,* Del.Supr., 480 A.2d 619, 624 (1984). Under normal circumstances, neither the courts nor the stockholders should interfere with the managerial decisions of the directors. The business judgment rule embodies the deference to which such decisions are entitled. […]

Nevertheless, there are rare situations which mandate that a court take a more direct and active role in overseeing the decisions made and actions taken by directors. In these situations, a court subjects the directors' conduct to enhanced scrutiny to ensure that it is reasonable.[9] The decisions of this Court have clearly established the circumstances where such enhanced scrutiny will be applied. *E.g., Unocal,* 493 A.2d 946; *Moran v. Household Int'l, Inc.,* Del.Supr., 500 A.2d 1346 (1985); *Revlon,* 506 A.2d 173; *Mills Acquisition Co. v. Macmillan, Inc.,* Del.Supr., 559 A.2d 1261 (1989); *Gilbert v. El Paso Co.,* Del.Supr., 575 A.2d 1131 (1990). The case at bar implicates two such circumstances: (1) the approval of a transaction resulting in a sale of control, and (2) the adoption of defensive measures in response to a threat to corporate control.

A. The Significance of a Sale or Change of Control

When a majority of a corporation's voting shares are acquired by a single person or entity, or by a cohesive group acting together, there is a significant diminution in the voting power of those who thereby become minority stockholders. Under the statutory framework of the General Corporation Law, many of the most fundamental corporate changes can be implemented only if they are approved by a majority vote of the stockholders. […]

In the absence of devices protecting the minority stockholders,[12] stockholder votes are likely to become mere formalities where there is a majority stockholder. […] Absent effective protective provisions, minority stockholders must rely for protection solely on the fiduciary duties owed to them by the directors and the majority stockholder, since the minority stockholders have lost the power to influence corporate direction through the ballot. The acquisition of majority status and the consequent privilege of exerting the powers of majority ownership come at a price. That price is usually a control premium which recognizes not only the value of a control block of shares, but also compensates the minority stockholders for their resulting loss of voting power.

In the case before us, the public stockholders (in the aggregate) currently own a majority of Paramount's voting stock. Control of the corporation is not vested in a single person, entity, or group, but vested in the fluid aggregation of unaffiliated stockholders. In the event the Paramount-Viacom transaction is consummated, the public stockholders will receive cash and a minority equity voting position in the surviving corporation. Following such consummation, there will be a controlling stockholder who will have the voting power to: (a) elect directors; (b) cause a break-up of the corporation; (c) merge it with another company; (d) cash-out the public stockholders; (e) amend the certificate of incorporation; (f) sell all or substantially all of the corporate assets; or (g) otherwise alter materially the nature of the corporation and the public stockholders' interests. Irrespective of the present Paramount Board's vision of a long-term strategic alliance with Viacom, the proposed sale of control would provide the new controlling stockholder with the power to alter that vision.

Because of the intended sale of control, the Paramount-Viacom transaction has economic consequences of considerable significance to the Paramount stockholders. Once control has shifted, the current Paramount stockholders will have no leverage in the future to demand another control premium. As a result, the Paramount stockholders are entitled to receive, and should receive, a control premium and/or protective devices of significant value. There being no such protective provisions in the Viacom-Paramount transaction, the Paramount directors had an obligation to take the maximum advantage of the current opportunity to realize for the stockholders the best value reasonably available.

B. The Obligations of Directors in a Sale or Change of Control Transaction

The consequences of a sale of control impose special obligations on the directors of a corporation.[13] In particular, they have the obligation of acting reasonably to seek the transaction offering the best value reasonably available to the stockholders. The courts will apply enhanced scrutiny to ensure that the directors have acted reasonably. [...]

In the sale of control context, the directors must focus on one primary objective — to secure the transaction offering the best value reasonably available for the stockholders — and they must exercise their fiduciary duties to further that end. […]

Barkan teaches some of the methods by which a board can fulfill its obligation to seek the best value reasonably available to the stockholders. […] These methods are designed to determine the existence and viability of possible alternatives. They include conducting an auction, canvassing the market, etc. Delaware law recognizes that there is "no single blueprint" that directors must follow. […]

In determining which alternative provides the best value for the stockholders, a board of directors is not limited to considering only the amount of cash involved, and is not required to ignore totally its view of the future value of a strategic alliance. […]Instead, the directors should analyze the entire situation and evaluate in a disciplined manner the consideration being offered. Where stock or other non-cash consideration is involved, the board should try to quantify its value, if feasible, to achieve an objective comparison of the alternatives.[14] In addition, the board may assess a variety of practical considerations relating to each alternative, including:

> [an offer's] fairness and feasibility; the proposed or actual financing for the offer, and the consequences of that financing; questions of illegality; ... the risk of nonconsum[m]ation;... the bidder's identity, prior background and other business venture experiences; and the bidder's business plans for the corporation and their effects on stockholder interests.

[…] While the assessment of these factors may be complex, [45] the board's goal is straightforward: Having informed themselves of all material information reasonably available, the directors must decide which alternative is most likely to offer the best value reasonably available to the stockholders.

C. Enhanced Judicial Scrutiny of a Sale or Change of Control Transaction

Board action in the circumstances presented here is subject to enhanced scrutiny. Such scrutiny is mandated by: (a) the threatened diminution of the current stockholders' voting power; (b) the fact that an asset belonging to public stockholders (a control premium) is being sold and may never be available again; and (c) the traditional concern of Delaware courts for actions which impair or impede stockholder voting rights (see *supra* note 11). In *Macmillan,* this Court held:

> When *Revlon* duties devolve upon directors, this Court will continue
> to exact an enhanced judicial scrutiny at the threshold, as in *Unocal,*
> before the normal presumptions of the business judgment rule will
> apply.[15]

559 A.2d at 1288. The *Macmillan* decision articulates a specific two-part test for analyzing board action where competing bidders are not treated equally:[16]

> In the face of disparate treatment, the trial court must first examine
> whether the directors properly perceived that shareholder interests
> were enhanced. In any event the board's action must be reasonable
> in relation to the advantage sought to be achieved, or conversely, to
> the threat which a particular bid allegedly poses to stockholder
> interests. […]

The key features of an enhanced scrutiny test are: (a) a judicial determination regarding the adequacy of the decisionmaking process employed by the directors, including the information on which the directors based their decision; and (b) a judicial examination of the reasonableness of the directors' action in light of the circumstances then existing. The directors have the burden of proving that they were adequately informed and acted reasonably.

Although an enhanced scrutiny test involves a review of the reasonableness of the substantive merits of a board's actions,[17] a court should not ignore the complexity of the directors' task in a sale of control. There are many business and financial considerations implicated in investigating and selecting the best value reasonably available. The board of directors is the corporate decisionmaking body best equipped to make these judgments. Accordingly, a court applying enhanced judicial scrutiny should be deciding whether the directors made a reasonable decision, not a perfect decision. If a board selected one of several reasonable alternatives, a court should not second-guess that choice even though it might have decided otherwise or subsequent events may have cast doubt on the board's determination. Thus, courts will not substitute their business judgment for that of the directors, but will determine if the directors' decision was, on balance, within a range of reasonableness. [...].

D. Revlon and Time-Warner Distinguished

The Paramount defendants and Viacom assert that the fiduciary obligations and the enhanced judicial scrutiny discussed above are not implicated in this case in the absence of a "break-up" of the corporation, and that the order granting the preliminary injunction should be reversed. This argument is based on their erroneous interpretation of our decisions in *Revlon* and *Time-Warner*.

In *Revlon*, we reviewed the actions of the board of directors of Revlon, Inc. ("Revlon"), which had rebuffed the overtures of Pantry Pride, Inc. and had instead entered into an agreement with Forstmann Little & Co. ("Forstmann") providing for the acquisition of 100 percent of Revlon's outstanding stock by Forstmann and the subsequent break-up of Revlon. Based on the facts and circumstances present in *Revlon*, we held that "[t]he directors' role changed from defenders of the corporate bastion to auctioneers charged with getting the best price for the stockholders at a sale of the company." 506 A.2d at 182. We further held that "when a board ends an intense bidding contest on an insubstantial basis, ... [that] action cannot withstand the enhanced scrutiny which *Unocal* requires of director conduct." *Id.* at 184.

It is true that one of the circumstances bearing on these holdings was the fact that "the break-up of the company . . . had become a reality which even the directors embraced." *Id.* at 182. It does not follow, however, that a "break-up" must be present and "inevitable" before directors are subject to enhanced judicial scrutiny and are required to pursue a transaction that is calculated to produce the best value reasonably available to the stockholders. In fact, we stated in *Revlon* that "when bidders make relatively similar offers, or dissolution of the company becomes inevitable, the directors cannot fulfill their enhanced *Unocal* duties by playing favorites with the contending factions." *Id.* at 184 (emphasis added). *Revlon* thus does not hold that an inevitable dissolution or "break-up" is necessary.

The decisions of this Court following *Revlon* reinforced the applicability of enhanced scrutiny and the directors' obligation to seek the best value reasonably available for the stockholders where there is a pending sale of control, regardless of whether or not there is to be a break-up of the corporation. In *Macmillan,* this Court held:

> We stated in *Revlon,* and again here, that in a sale of corporate control the responsibility of the directors is to get the highest value reasonably attainable for the shareholders.

559 A.2d at 1288 (emphasis added). In *Barkan,* we observed further:

> We believe that the general principles announced in *Revlon,* in *Unocal Corp. v. Mesa Petroleum Co.,* Del.Supr., 493 A.2d 946 (1985), and in *Moran v. Household International, Inc.,* Del.Supr., 500 A.2d 1346 (1985) govern this case and every case in which a fundamental change of corporate control occurs or is contemplated.

567 A.2d at 1286 (emphasis added).

Although *Macmillan* and *Barkan* are clear in holding that a change of control imposes on directors the obligation to obtain the best value reasonably available to the stockholders, the Paramount defendants have interpreted our decision in *Time-Warner* as requiring a corporate break-up in order for that obligation to apply. The facts in *Time-Warner,* however, were quite different from the facts of this case, and refute Paramount's position here. In *Time-Warner,* the Chancellor held that there was no change of control in the original stock-for-stock merger between Time and Warner because Time would be owned by a fluid aggregation of unaffiliated stockholders both before and after the merger:

> If the appropriate inquiry is whether a change in control is contemplated, the answer must be sought in the specific circumstances surrounding the transaction. Surely under some circumstances a stock for stock merger could reflect a transfer of corporate control. That would, for example, plainly be the case here if Warner were a private company. But where, as [47] here, the shares of both constituent corporations are widely held, corporate control can be expected to remain unaffected by a stock for stock merger. This in my judgment was the situation with respect to the

original merger agreement. When the specifics of that situation are reviewed, it is seen that, aside from legal technicalities and aside from arrangements thought to enhance the prospect for the ultimate succession of [Nicholas J. Nicholas, Jr., president of Time], neither corporation could be said to be acquiring the other. Control of both remained in a large, fluid, changeable and changing market.

The existence of a control block of stock in the hands of a single shareholder or a group with loyalty to each other does have real consequences to the financial value of "minority" stock. The law offers some protection to such shares through the imposition of a fiduciary duty upon controlling shareholders. But here, effectuation of the merger would not have subjected Time shareholders to the risks and consequences of holders of minority shares. This is a reflection of the fact that no control passed to anyone in the transaction contemplated. The shareholders of Time would have "suffered" dilution, of course, but they would suffer the same type of dilution upon the public distribution of new stock.

Paramount Communications Inc. v. Time Inc., Del.Ch., No. 10866, 1989 WL 79880, Allen, C. (July 17, 1989), reprinted at 15 Del.J.Corp.L. 700, 739 (emphasis added). Moreover, the transaction actually consummated in *Time-Warner* was not a merger, as originally planned, but a sale of Warner's stock to Time.

In our affirmance of the Court of Chancery's well-reasoned decision, this Court held that "The Chancellor's findings of fact are supported by the record and his conclusion is correct as a matter of law." 571 A.2d at 1150 (emphasis added). Nevertheless, the Paramount defendants here have argued that a break-up is a requirement and have focused on the following language in our *Time-Warner* decision:

> However, we premise our rejection of plaintiffs' *Revlon* claim on different grounds, namely, the absence of any substantial evidence to conclude that Time's board, in negotiating with Warner, made the dissolution or break-up of the corporate entity inevitable, as was the case in *Revlon*.

Under Delaware law there are, generally speaking and without excluding other possibilities, two circumstances which may implicate *Revlon* duties. The first, and clearer one, is when a corporation initiates an active bidding process seeking to sell itself or to effect a business reorganization involving a clear break-up of the company. However, *Revlon* duties may also be triggered where, in response to a bidder's offer, a target abandons its long-term strategy and seeks an alternative transaction involving the breakup of the company.

Id. at 1150 (emphasis added) (citation and footnote omitted).

The Paramount defendants have misread the holding of *Time-Warner*. Contrary to their argument, our decision in *Time-Warner* expressly states that the two general scenarios discussed in the above-quoted paragraph are not the only instances where "*Revlon* duties" may be implicated. The Paramount defendants' argument totally ignores the phrase "without excluding other possibilities." Moreover, the instant case is clearly within the first general scenario set forth in *Time-Warner*. The Paramount Board, albeit unintentionally, had "initiate[d] an active bidding process seeking to sell itself" by agreeing to sell control of the corporation to Viacom in circumstances where another potential acquiror (QVC) was equally interested in being a bidder.

The Paramount defendants' position that both a change of control and a break-up are required must be rejected. Such a holding would unduly restrict the application of *Revlon*, is inconsistent with this Court's decisions in *Barkan* and *Macmillan*, and has no basis in policy. There are few events that have a more significant impact on the stockholders than a sale of control or a corporate breakup. Each event represents a fundamental [48] (and perhaps irrevocable) change in the nature of the corporate enterprise from a practical standpoint. It is the significance of each of these events that justifies: (a) focusing on the directors' obligation to seek the best value reasonably available to the stockholders; and (b) requiring a close scrutiny of board action which could be contrary to the stockholders' interests.

Accordingly, when a corporation undertakes a transaction which will cause: (a) a change in corporate control; or (b) a breakup of the corporate entity, the directors' obligation is to seek the best value reasonably available to the stockholders. This obligation arises because the effect of the Viacom-Paramount transaction, if consummated, is to shift control of Paramount from the public stockholders to a controlling stockholder, Viacom. Neither *Time-Warner* nor any other decision of this Court holds that a "break-up" of the company is essential to give rise to this obligation where there is a sale of control.

III. BREACH OF FIDUCIARY DUTIES BY PARAMOUNT BOARD

We now turn to duties of the Paramount Board under the facts of this case and our conclusions as to the breaches of those duties, which warrant injunctive relief.

A. The Specific Obligations of the Paramount Board

Under the facts of this case, the Paramount directors had the obligation: (a) to be diligent and vigilant in examining critically the Paramount-Viacom transaction and the QVC tender offers; (b) to act in good faith; (c) to obtain, and act with due care on, all material information reasonably available, including information necessary to compare the two offers to determine which of these transactions, or an alternative course of action, would provide the best value reasonably available to the stockholders; and (d) to negotiate actively and in good faith with both Viacom and QVC to that end.

Having decided to sell control of the corporation, the Paramount directors were required to evaluate critically whether or not all material aspects of the Paramount-Viacom transaction (separately and in the aggregate) were reasonable and in the best interests of the Paramount stockholders in light of current circumstances, including: the change of control premium, the Stock Option Agreement, the Termination Fee, the coercive nature of both the Viacom and QVC tender offers,[18] the No-Shop Provision, and the proposed disparate use of the Rights Agreement as to the Viacom and QVC tender offers, respectively.

These obligations necessarily implicated various issues, including the questions of whether or not those provisions and other aspects of the Paramount-Viacom transaction (separately and in the aggregate): (a) adversely affected the value provided to the Paramount stockholders; (b) inhibited or encouraged alternative bids; (c) were enforceable contractual obligations in light of the directors' fiduciary duties; and (d) in the end would advance or retard the Paramount directors' obligation to secure for the Paramount stockholders the best value reasonably available under the circumstances.

The Paramount defendants contend that they were precluded by certain contractual provisions, including the No-Shop Provision, from negotiating with QVC or seeking alternatives. Such provisions, whether or not they are presumptively valid in the abstract, may not validly define or limit the directors' fiduciary duties under Delaware law or prevent the Paramount directors from carrying out their fiduciary duties under Delaware law. To the extent such provisions are inconsistent with those duties, they are invalid and unenforceable. *See Revlon*, 506 A.2d at 184-85.

Since the Paramount directors had already decided to sell control, they had an obligation [49] to continue their search for the best value reasonably available to the stockholders. This continuing obligation included the responsibility, at the October 24 board meeting and thereafter, to evaluate critically both the QVC tender offers and the Paramount-Viacom transaction to determine if: (a) the QVC tender offer was, or would continue to be, conditional; (b) the QVC tender offer could be improved; (c) the Viacom tender offer or other aspects of the Paramount-Viacom transaction could be improved; (d) each of the respective offers would be reasonably likely to come to closure, and under what circumstances; (e) other material information was reasonably available for consideration by the Paramount directors; (f) there were viable and realistic alternative courses of action; and (g) the timing constraints could be managed so the directors could consider these matters carefully and deliberately.

B. The Breaches of Fiduciary Duty by the Paramount Board

The Paramount directors made the decision on September 12, 1993, that, in their judgment, a strategic merger with Viacom on the economic terms of the Original Merger Agreement was in the best interests of Paramount and its stockholders. Those terms provided a modest change of control premium to the stockholders. The directors also decided at that time that it was appropriate to agree to certain defensive measures (the Stock Option Agreement, the Termination Fee, and the No-Shop Provision) insisted upon by Viacom as part of that economic transaction. Those defensive measures, coupled with the sale of control and subsequent disparate treatment of competing bidders, implicated the judicial scrutiny of *Unocal, Revlon, Macmillan,* and their progeny.

We conclude that the Paramount directors' process was not reasonable, and the result achieved for the stockholders was not reasonable under the circumstances.

When entering into the Original Merger Agreement, and thereafter, the Paramount Board clearly gave insufficient attention to the potential consequences of the defensive measures demanded by Viacom. The Stock Option Agreement had a number of unusual and potentially "draconian"[19] provisions, including the Note Feature and the Put Feature. Furthermore, the Termination Fee, whether or not unreasonable by itself, clearly made Paramount less attractive to other bidders, when coupled with the Stock Option Agreement. Finally, the No-Shop Provision inhibited the Paramount Board's ability to negotiate with other potential bidders, particularly QVC which had already expressed an interest in Paramount.[20]

Throughout the applicable time period, and especially from the first QVC merger proposal on September 20 through the Paramount Board meeting on November 15, QVC's interest in Paramount provided the opportunity for the Paramount Board to seek significantly higher value for the Paramount stockholders than that being offered by Viacom. QVC persistently demonstrated its intention to meet and exceed the Viacom offers, and [50] frequently expressed its willingness to negotiate possible further increases.

The Paramount directors had the opportunity in the October 23-24 time frame, when the Original Merger Agreement was renegotiated, to take appropriate action to modify the improper defensive measures as well as to improve the economic terms of the Paramount-Viacom transaction. Under the circumstances existing at that time, it should have been clear to the Paramount Board that the Stock Option Agreement, coupled with the Termination Fee and the No-Shop Clause, were impeding the realization of the best value reasonably available to the Paramount stockholders. Nevertheless, the Paramount Board made no effort to eliminate or modify these counterproductive devices, and instead continued to cling to its vision of a strategic alliance with Viacom. Moreover, based on advice from the Paramount management, the Paramount directors considered the QVC offer to be "conditional" and asserted that they were precluded by the No-Shop Provision from seeking more information from, or negotiating with, QVC.

By November 12, 1993, the value of the revised QVC offer on its face exceeded that of the Viacom offer by over $1 billion at then current values. This significant disparity of value cannot be justified on the basis of the directors' vision of future strategy, primarily because the change of control would supplant the authority of the current Paramount Board to continue to hold and implement their strategic vision in any meaningful way. Moreover, their uninformed process had deprived their strategic vision of much of its credibility. *See Van Gorkom,* 488 A.2d at 872; *Cede v. Technicolor,* 634 A.2d at 367; *Hanson Trust PLC v. ML SCM Acquisition Inc.,* 2d Cir., 781 F.2d 264, 274 (1986).

When the Paramount directors met on November 15 to consider QVC's increased tender offer, they remained prisoners of their own misconceptions and missed opportunities to eliminate the restrictions they had imposed on themselves. Yet, it was not "too late" to reconsider negotiating with QVC. The circumstances existing on November 15 made it clear that the defensive measures, taken as a whole, were problematic: (a) the No-Shop Provision could not define or limit their fiduciary duties; (b) the Stock Option Agreement had become "draconian"; and (c) the Termination Fee, in context with all the circumstances, was similarly deterring the realization of possibly higher bids. Nevertheless, the Paramount directors remained paralyzed by their uninformed belief that the QVC offer was "illusory." This final opportunity to negotiate on the stockholders' behalf and to fulfill their obligation to seek the best value reasonably available was thereby squandered.[21]

IV. VIACOM'S CLAIM OF VESTED CONTRACT RIGHTS

Viacom argues that it had certain "vested" contract rights with respect to the No-Shop Provision and the Stock Option Agreement.[22] In effect, Viacom's argument is that the Paramount directors could enter into an agreement in violation of their fiduciary duties and then render Paramount, and ultimately its stockholders, liable for failing to carry out an agreement in violation of those duties. Viacom's protestations about vested rights are without merit. This Court has found that those defensive measures were improperly designed to deter potential bidders, and that such measures do not meet the reasonableness test to which they must be subjected. They are consequently invalid and unenforceable under the facts of this case.

The No-Shop Provision could not validly define or limit the fiduciary duties of the Paramount directors. To the extent that a contract, or a provision thereof, purports to require a board to act or not act in such a fashion as to limit the exercise of fiduciary duties, it is invalid and unenforceable. *Cf. Wilmington Trust v. Coulter,* 200 A.2d at 452-54.

Despite the arguments of Paramount and Viacom to the contrary, the Paramount directors could not contract away their fiduciary obligations. Since the No-Shop Provision was invalid, Viacom never had any vested contract rights in the provision.

As discussed previously, the Stock Option Agreement contained several "draconian" aspects, including the Note Feature and the Put Feature. While we have held that lock-up options are not *per se* illegal, *see Revlon*, 506 A.2d at 183, no options with similar features have ever been upheld by this Court. Under the circumstances of this case, the Stock Option Agreement clearly is invalid. Accordingly, Viacom never had any vested contract rights in that Agreement.

Viacom, a sophisticated party with experienced legal and financial advisors, knew of (and in fact demanded) the unreasonable features of the Stock Option Agreement. It cannot be now heard to argue that it obtained vested contract rights by negotiating and obtaining contractual provisions from a board acting in violation of its fiduciary duties. As the Nebraska Supreme Court said in rejecting a similar argument in *ConAgra, Inc. v. Cargill, Inc.,* 222 Neb. 136, 382 N.W.2d 576, 587-88 (1986), "To so hold, it would seem, would be to get the shareholders coming and going." Likewise, we reject Viacom's arguments and hold that its fate must rise or fall, and in this instance fall, with the determination that the actions of the Paramount Board were invalid.

V. CONCLUSION

The realization of the best value reasonably available to the stockholders became the Paramount directors' primary obligation under these facts in light of the change of control. That obligation was not satisfied, and the Paramount Board's process was deficient. The directors' initial hope and expectation for a strategic alliance with Viacom was allowed to dominate their decisionmaking process to the point where the arsenal of defensive measures established at the outset was perpetuated (not modified or eliminated) when the situation was dramatically altered. QVC's unsolicited bid presented the opportunity for significantly greater value for the stockholders and enhanced negotiating leverage for the directors. Rather than seizing those opportunities, the Paramount directors chose to wall themselves off from material information which was reasonably available and to hide behind the defensive measures as a rationalization for refusing to negotiate with QVC or seeking other alternatives. Their view of the strategic alliance likewise became an empty rationalization as the opportunities for higher value for the stockholders continued to develop.

It is the nature of the judicial process that we decide only the case before us — a case which, on its facts, is clearly controlled by established Delaware law. Here, the proposed change of control and the implications thereof were crystal clear. In other cases they may be less clear. The holding of this case on its facts, coupled with the holdings of the principal cases discussed herein where the issue of sale of control is implicated, should provide a workable precedent against which to measure future cases.

8 Appendix: Corporate Documents

8.1 Restated Articles of Incorporation of Green Bay Packers, Inc.

Below you will find the text of the restated articles of incorporation for the Green Bay Packers, Inc., the football team of the NFL. These articles were filed with the Wisconsin secretary of states on June 12, 2007.

RESTATED ARTICLES OF INCORPORATION OF

GREEN BAY PACKERS, INC.

Pursuant to Section 180. I 007 of the Wisconsin Business Corporation Law, these Restated Articles of Incorporation shall supersede and take the place of the corporation's heretofore existing Amended and Restated Articles of Incorporation and all amendments thereto.

ARTICLE I

The undersigned have associated and do hereby associate themselves together for . the purpose of forming a corporation under Chapter 180 of the Wisconsin Statutes and acts amendatory thereof and supplemental thereto. That this association shall be a community project intended to promote community welfare and that its purposes shall be exclusively charitable and that ·incidental to *its* purposes, it shall have the right to conduct athletic contests, operate a football team, or such other similar projects for the purpose of carrying out its charitable purposes, which purposes shall be carried on within the State of Wisconsin,· and especially within the County of Brown, in said State.

ARTICLE II

The name of the corporation shall be the GREEN BAY PACKERS, INC., and its Location shall be in the City of Green Bay, Brown County, Wisconsin.

ARTICLE III

A. Authorized Stock. The total number of shares of all classes of capital stock that said corporation shall have the authority to issue is ten million (10,000,000) shares of common stock having no par value ("Common Stock").

B. Preemptive Rights. Notwithstanding Section 180.1705 of the Wisconsin Business Corporation Law (or any successor provision to such section), the holders of Common Stock shall not have a preemptive right to acquire unissued shares of Common Stock.

C. Limitation on Issuances of Stock. After 8:00 a.m. (Central Time) on November 14,1997 (the "Effective Time,), the corporation shall be entitled to issue up to one million (1,000,000) authorized but unissued states of Common Stock upon the authority of the board of directors of the corporation in accordm1ce with applicable law7 but the corporation shall not issue any shares in excess of such amount unless, in addition to the authority of the board of directors of the corporation in accordance with applicable law, the issuance of such excess shares shall have been approved by the affirmative vote of the holders of seventy percent (70%) of the shares of Common Stock outstanding prior to the issuance of such excess shares.

ARTICLE IV

The number of directors constituting the initial board of directors of the corporation is three (3) and thereafter the number of directors shall be such number (not less than three (3)) as is fixed from time to time by the bylaws. Said directors may be classified as authorized from time to time by the bylaws.

ARTICLE V

The bylaws may provide regulations for the person holding the stock, when such stock may be transferred, when the stock may be redeemed and the conditions under which stock may be transferred and new stockholders admitted to the corporation. Notwithstanding the foregoing, after the· Effective Time, Common Stock is redeemable at the option of the corporation at a price of $0.025 per share of Common Stock only in the event the board of directors of the corporation determines the stockholder cannot be located after the corporation has expended reasonable time and effort attempting to locate the stockholder and a period of five years *has* elapsed since the stockholder's last contact with the corporation.

ARTICLE VI

The corporation shall be non-profit sharing and its purpose shall be exclusively for charitable purposes and that its profit shall be donated to the Green Bay Packers Foundation, but that the Green Bay Packers, Inc. can make contributions to any lo al charitable institutions; that no stockholder shall receive any dividend, pecuniary profit or emolument by virtue of his being a stockholder.

That should there be a dissolution of the Green Bay Packers, Inc., the players shall be subject to the National Football League Rules, but that the undivided profits and assets of the. Green Bay Packers, Inc. shall go to the Green Bay Packers Foundation for distribution to community programs, charitable causes, and such other similar cause to which the Foundation deems appropriate.

ARTICLE VII

The board of directors shall have the right to create a capital reserve to provide for the acquisitions and maintenance of its plant, equipment and players and said funds shall be preserved and no distribution made to any done under the charitable clause of the Articles of Incorporation, except when in the judgment of the board of directors it shall be deemed advisable.

ARTICLE VIII

The registered office of the Green Bay Packers, Inc. is 1265 Lombardi Avenue, P.O. Box. l0628, Green Bay, Wisconsin 54307-0628, and its registered agent is Jason G. Wied whose address is 1265 Lombardi Avenue, P.O. Box 10628. Green Bay, Wisconsin 54307-0628.

ARTICLE IX

These articles may be amended in the manner authorized by law.

ARTICLE X

Twenty (20) per cent of the outstanding stock of the corporation shall constitute a quorum at any meeting, special or annual, and such quorum shall be capable of transacting any business.

CERTIFICATION

The undersigned, the duly elected and acting Chairman and Secretary of the Green Bay Packers, Inc., a Wisconsin corporation, in accordance with Section 180.1007 of the Wisconsin Business Corporation Law, DO HEREBY CERTIFY THAT:

1. The name of the corporation is Green Bay Packers, Inc.

2. The foregoing Restated Articles of Incorporation, which do not contain amendments to the corporation's articles of incorporation requiring stockholder approval, were adopted by the corporation's Board of Directors on May 30, 2007. ·

IN WITNESS WHEREOF, the undersigned have executed these Restated Articles of Incorporation on behalf of the corporation this 30th day of May, 2007.

GREEN BAY PACKERS, INC.

/s/ Robert E. Harlan

Robert E. Harlan, Chairman

By /s/ Peter Platten

Peter M. Platten ill, Secretary

8.2 Facebook, Inc. Restated Certificate of Incorporation

Below you will find the text of Facebook's certificate of incorporation as filed with the SEC on May 22, 2012.

Facebook, Inc.

RESTATED CERTIFICATE OF INCORPORATION

Facebook, Inc., a Delaware corporation, hereby certifies as follows.

1. The name of the corporation is Facebook, Inc. The date of filing its original Certificate of Incorporation with the Secretary of State was July 29, 2004, under the name TheFacebook, Inc.

2. The Restated Certificate of Incorporation of the corporation attached hereto as Exhibit A, which is incorporated herein by this reference, and which restates, integrates and further amends the provisions of the Certificate of Incorporation of this corporation as heretofore amended and/or restated, has been duly adopted by the corporation's Board of Directors and by the stockholders in accordance with Sections 242 and 245 of the General Corporation Law of the State of Delaware, with the approval of the corporation's stockholders having been given by written consent without a meeting in accordance with Section 228 of the General Corporation Law of the State of Delaware.

IN WITNESS WHEREOF, this corporation has caused this Restated Certificate of Incorporation to be signed by its duly authorized officer and the foregoing facts stated herein are true and correct.

Dated: May 22, 2012   FACEBOOK, INC.

By: /s/ Mark Zuckerberg
Name: Mark Zuckerberg
Title: Chief Executive Officer

FACEBOOK, INC.

RESTATED CERTIFICATE OF INCORPORATION

ARTICLE I: NAME

The name of the corporation is Facebook, Inc.

ARTICLE II: AGENT FOR SERVICE OF PROCESS

The address of the corporation's registered office in the State of Delaware is 2711 Centerville Road, Suite 400, Wilmington, County of New Castle, 19808. The name of the registered agent of the corporation at that address is Corporation Service Company.

ARTICLE III: PURPOSE

The purpose of the corporation is to engage in any lawful act or activity for which corporations may be organized under the General Corporation Law of the State of Delaware ("*General Corporation Law*").

ARTICLE IV: AUTHORIZED STOCK

1. Total Authorized.

The total number of shares of all classes of capital stock that the corporation has authority to issue is 9,241,000,000 shares, consisting of: 5,000,000,000 shares of Class A Common Stock, $0.000006 par value per share ("*Class A Common Stock*"), 4,141,000,000 shares of Class B Common Stock, $0.000006 par value per share ("*Class B Common Stock*" and together with the Class A Common Stock, the "*Common Stock*") and 100,000,000 shares of Preferred Stock, $0.000006 par value per share. The number of authorized shares of Class A Common Stock or Class B Common Stock may be increased or decreased (but not below the number of shares thereof then outstanding) by the affirmative vote of the holders of capital stock representing a majority of the voting power of all the then-outstanding shares of capital stock of the corporation entitled to vote thereon, irrespective of the provisions of Section 242(b)(2) of the General Corporation Law.

2. Designation of Additional Shares

2.1 The Board of Directors is authorized, subject to any limitations prescribed by the laws of the State of Delaware, by resolution or resolutions, to provide for the issuance of the shares of Preferred Stock in one or more series, and, by filing a certificate of designation pursuant to the applicable law of the State of Delaware ("*Certificate of Designation*"), to establish from time to time the number of shares to be included in each such series, to fix the designation, powers (including voting powers), preferences and relative, participating, optional or other rights, if any, of the shares of each such series and any qualifications, limitations or restrictions thereof, and to increase (but not above the total number of authorized shares of such class) or decrease (but not below the number of shares of such series then outstanding) the number of shares of any such series. The number of authorized shares of Preferred Stock may also be increased or decreased (but not below the number of shares thereof then outstanding) by the affirmative vote of the holders of a majority of the voting power of all the then-outstanding shares of capital stock of the corporation entitled to vote thereon, without a separate vote of the holders of the Preferred Stock or any series thereof, irrespective of the provisions of Section 242(b)(2) of the General Corporation Law, unless a vote of any such holders is required pursuant to the terms of any Certificate of Designation designating a series of Preferred Stock.

2.2 Except as otherwise expressly provided in any Certificate of Designation designating any series of Preferred Stock pursuant to the foregoing provisions of this ARTICLE IV, any new series of Preferred Stock may be designated, fixed and determined as provided herein by the Board of Directors without approval of the holders of Common Stock or the holders of Preferred Stock, or any series thereof, and any such new series may have powers, preferences and rights, including, without limitation, voting powers, dividend rights, liquidation rights, redemption rights and conversion rights, senior to, junior to or pari passu with the rights of the Common Stock, the Preferred Stock, or any future class or series of Preferred Stock or Common Stock.

3. Rights of Class A Common Stock and Class B Common Stock.

3.1 <u>Equal Status</u>. Except as otherwise provided in this Restated Certificate of Incorporation or required by applicable law, shares of Class A Common Stock and Class B Common Stock shall have the same rights and powers, rank equally (including as to dividends and distributions, and upon any liquidation, dissolution or winding up of the corporation), share ratably and be identical in all respects and as to all matters.

3.2 <u>Voting Rights</u>. Except as otherwise expressly provided by this Restated Certificate of Incorporation or as provided by law, the holders of shares of Class A Common Stock and Class B Common Stock shall (a) at all times vote together as a single class on all matters (including the election of directors) submitted to a vote or for the consent (if action by written consent of the stockholders is permitted at such time under this Restated Certificate of Incorporation) of the stockholders of the corporation, (b) be entitled to notice of any stockholders' meeting in accordance with the Bylaws of the corporation and (c) be entitled to vote upon such matters and in such manner as may be provided by applicable law. Except as otherwise expressly provided herein or required by applicable law, each holder of Class A Common Stock shall have the right to one (1) vote per share of Class A Common Stock held of record by such holder and each holder of Class B Common Stock shall have the right to ten (10) votes per share of Class B Common Stock held of record by such holder.

3.3 <u>Dividend and Distribution Rights</u>. Shares of Class A Common Stock and Class B Common Stock shall be treated equally, identically and ratably, on a per share basis, with respect to any dividends or distributions as may be declared and paid from time to time by the Board of Directors out of any assets of the corporation legally available therefor; *provided, however*, that in the event a dividend is paid in the form of shares of Class A Common Stock or Class B Common Stock (or rights to acquire such shares), then holders of Class A Common Stock shall receive shares of Class A Common Stock (or rights to acquire such shares, as the case may be) and holders of Class B Common Stock shall receive shares of Class B Common Stock (or rights to acquire such shares, as the case may be), with holders of shares of Class A Common Stock and Class B Common Stock receiving, on a per share basis, an identical number of shares of Class A Common Stock or Class B Common Stock, as applicable. Notwithstanding the foregoing, the Board of Directors may pay or make a disparate dividend or distribution per share of Class A Common Stock or Class B Common Stock (whether in the amount of such dividend or distribution payable per share, the form in which such dividend or distribution is payable, the timing of the payment, or otherwise) if such disparate dividend or distribution is approved in advance by the affirmative vote (or written consent if action by written consent of stockholders is permitted at such time under this Restated Certificate of Incorporation) of the holders of a majority of the outstanding shares of Class A Common Stock and Class B Common Stock, each voting separately as a class.

3.4 <u>Subdivisions, Combinations or Reclassifications</u>. Shares of Class A Common Stock or Class B Common Stock may not be subdivided, combined or reclassified unless the shares of the other class are concurrently therewith proportionately subdivided, combined or reclassified in a manner that maintains the same proportionate equity ownership between the holders of the outstanding Class A Common Stock and Class B Common Stock on the record date for such subdivision, combination or reclassification; *provided, however*, that shares of one such class may be subdivided, combined or reclassified in a different or disproportionate manner if such subdivision, combination or reclassification is approved in advance by the affirmative vote (or written consent if action by written consent of stockholders is permitted at such time under this Restated Certificate of Incorporation) of the holders of a majority of the outstanding shares of Class A Common Stock and Class B Common Stock, each voting separately as a class.

3.5 <u>Liquidation, Dissolution or Winding Up</u>. Subject to the preferential or other rights of any holders of Preferred Stock then outstanding, upon the dissolution, liquidation or winding up of the corporation, whether voluntary or involuntary, holders of Class A Common Stock and Class B Common Stock will be entitled to receive ratably all assets of the corporation available for distribution to its stockholders unless disparate or different treatment of the shares of each such class with respect to distributions upon any such liquidation, dissolution or winding up is approved in advance by the affirmative vote (or written consent if action by written consent of stockholders is permitted at such time under this Restated Certificate of Incorporation) of the holders of a majority of the outstanding shares of Class A Common Stock and Class B Common Stock, each voting separately as a class.

3.6 <u>Merger or Consolidation</u>. In the case of any distribution or payment in respect of the shares of Class A Common Stock or Class B Common Stock upon the consolidation or merger of the Corporation with or into any other entity, or in the case of any other transaction having an effect on stockholders substantially similar to that resulting from a consolidation or merger, such distribution or payment shall be made ratably on a per share basis among the holders of the Class A Common Stock and Class B Common Stock as a single class; *provided, however,* that shares of one such class may receive different or disproportionate distributions or payments in connection with such merger, consolidation or other transaction if (i) the only difference in the per share distribution to the holders of the Class A Common Stock and Class B Common Stock is that any securities distributed to the holder of a share Class B Common Stock have ten times the voting power of any securities distributed to the holder of a share of Class A Common Stock, or (ii) such merger, consolidation or other transaction is approved by the affirmative vote (or written consent if action by written consent of stockholders is permitted at such time under this Restated Certificate of Incorporation) of the holders of a majority of the outstanding shares of Class A Common Stock and Class B Common Stock, each voting separately as a class.

3.7 Change of Control Class B Vote. Until the first date on which the outstanding shares of Class B Common Stock represent less than thirty-five percent (35%) of the total voting power of the then outstanding shares of the corporation then entitled to vote generally in the election of directors, the corporation shall not consummate a Change in Control Transaction (as defined in Section 4 of this ARTICLE IV) without first obtaining the affirmative vote (or written consent if action by written consent of stockholders is permitted at such time under this Restated Certificate of Incorporation) of the holders of a majority of the then outstanding shares of Class B Common Stock, voting as a separate class, in addition to any other vote required by applicable law, this Restated Certificate of Incorporation or the Bylaws.

3.8 Conversion of Class B Common Stock.

(a) Voluntary Conversion. Each share of Class B Common Stock shall be convertible into one (1) fully paid and nonassessable share of Class A Common Stock at the option of the holder thereof at any time upon written notice to the corporation. Before any holder of Class B Common Stock shall be entitled to voluntarily convert any shares of such Class B Common Stock, such holder shall surrender the certificate or certificates therefor (if any), duly endorsed, at the principal corporate office of the corporation or of any transfer agent for the Class B Common Stock, and shall give written notice to the corporation at its principal corporate office, of the election to convert the same and shall state therein the name or names (i) in which the certificate or certificates representing the shares of Class A Common Stock into which the shares of Class B Common Stock are so converted are to be issued if such shares are certificated or (ii) in which such shares are to be registered in book entry if such shares are uncertificated. The corporation shall, as soon as practicable thereafter, issue and deliver at such office to such holder of Class B Common Stock, or to the nominee or nominees of such holder, a certificate or certificates representing the number of shares of Class A Common Stock to which such holder shall be entitled as aforesaid (if such shares are certificated) or, if such shares are uncertificated, register such shares in book-entry form. Such conversion shall be deemed to have been made immediately prior to the close of business on the date of such surrender of the shares of Class B Common Stock to be converted following or contemporaneously with the written notice of such holder's election to convert required by this Section 3.8(a), and the person or persons entitled to receive the shares of Class A Common Stock issuable upon such conversion shall be treated for all purposes as the record holder or holders of such shares of Class A Common Stock as of such date. Each share of Class B Common Stock that is converted pursuant to this Section 3.8(a) shall be retired by the corporation and shall not be available for reissuance.

(b) Automatic Conversion. (i) Each share of Class B Common Stock shall be automatically, without further action by the holder thereof, converted into one (1) fully paid and nonassessable share of Class A Common Stock, upon the occurrence of a Transfer (as defined in Section 4 of this ARTICLE IV), other than a Permitted Transfer (as defined in Section of this ARTICLE IV), of such share of Class B Common Stock and (ii) all shares of Class B Common Stock shall be automatically, without further action by any holder thereof, converted into an identical number of shares of Class A Common Stock at such date and time, or the occurrence of an event, specified by the affirmative vote (or written consent if action by written consent of stockholders is permitted at such time under this Restated Certificate of Incorporation) of the holders of a majority of the then outstanding shares Class B Common Stock, voting as a separate class (the occurrence of an event described in clause (i) or (ii) of this Section 3.8(b), a "*Conversion Event*"). Each outstanding stock certificate that, immediately prior to a Conversion Event, represented one or more shares of Class B Common Stock subject to such Conversion Event shall, upon such Conversion Event, be deemed to represent an equal number of shares of Class A Common Stock, without the need for surrender or exchange thereof. The corporation shall, upon the request of any holder whose shares of Class B Common Stock have been converted into shares of Class A Common Stock as a result of a Conversion Event and upon surrender by such holder to the corporation of the outstanding certificate(s) formerly representing such holder's shares of Class B Common Stock (if any), issue and deliver to such holder certificate(s) representing the shares of Class A Common Stock into which such holder's shares of Class B Common Stock were converted as a result of such Conversion Event (if such shares are certificated) or, if such shares are uncertificated, register such shares in book-entry form. Each share of Class B Common Stock that is converted pursuant to this Section 3.8(b) of ARTICLE IV shall thereupon be retired by the corporation and shall not be available for reissuance.

(c) The corporation may, from time to time, establish such policies and procedures, not in violation of applicable law or the other provisions of this Restated Certificate, relating to the conversion of the Class B Common Stock into Class A Common Stock, as it may deem necessary or advisable in connection therewith. If the corporation has reason to believe that a Transfer giving rise to a conversion of shares of Class B Common Stock into Class A Common Stock has occurred but has not theretofore been reflected on the books of the corporation, the corporation may request that the holder of such shares furnish affidavits or other evidence to the corporation as the corporation deems necessary to determine whether a conversion of shares of Class B Common Stock to Class A Common Stock has occurred, and if such holder does not within ten (10) days after the date of such request furnish sufficient evidence to the corporation (in the manner provided in the request) to enable the corporation to determine that no such conversion has occurred, any such shares of Class B Common Stock, to the extent not previously converted, shall be automatically converted into shares of Class A Common Stock and the same shall thereupon be registered on the books and records of the corporation. In connection with any action of stockholders taken at a meeting or by written consent (if action by written consent of stockholders is permitted at such time under this Restated Certificate of Incorporation), the stock ledger of the corporation shall be presumptive evidence as to who are the stockholders entitled to vote in person or by proxy at any meeting of stockholders or in connection with any such written consent and the class or classes or series of shares held by each such stockholder and the number of shares of each class or classes or series held by such stockholder.

3.9 <u>Reservation of Stock</u>. The corporation shall at all times reserve and keep available out of its authorized but unissued shares of Class A Common Stock, solely for the purpose of effecting the conversion of the shares of Class B Common Stock, such number of shares of Class A Common Stock as shall from time to time be sufficient to effect the conversion of all outstanding shares of Class B Common Stock into shares of Class A Common Stock.

3.10 <u>Protective Provision</u>. The corporation shall not, whether by merger, consolidation or otherwise, amend, alter, repeal or waive Sections 3 or 4 of this Article IV (or adopt any provision inconsistent therewith), without first obtaining the affirmative vote (or written consent if action by written consent of stockholders is permitted at such time under this Restated Certificate of Incorporation) of the holders of a majority of the then outstanding shares of Class B Common Stock, voting as a separate class, in addition to any other vote required by applicable law, this Restated Certificate of Incorporation or the Bylaws.

4. Definitions. For purposes of this Restated Certificate of Incorporation:

4.1 "<u>Change in Control Transaction</u>" means the occurrence of any of the following events:

(a) the sale, lease, exchange, encumbrance or other disposition (other than licenses that do not constitute an effective disposition of all or substantially all of the assets of the corporation and its subsidiaries taken as a whole, and the grant of security interests in the ordinary course of business) by the corporation of all or substantially all of the corporation's assets; or

(b) the merger or consolidation of the corporation with or into any other entity, other than a merger or consolidation that would result in the Class B Common Stock of the corporation outstanding immediately prior thereto continuing to represent (either by remaining outstanding or by being converted into voting securities of the surviving entity or its sole parent entity) more than fifty percent (50%) of the total voting power represented by the voting securities of the corporation or such surviving entity or its sole parent entity outstanding immediately after such merger or consolidation.

4.2 "Charitable Trust" means a trust that is exempt from taxation under Section 501(c)(3) of the United States Internal Revenue Code of 1986, as amended (or any successor provision thereto) (whether a determination letter with respect to such exemption is issued before, at or after the Covered Security Date), and further includes any successor entity that is exempt from taxation under Section 501(c)(3) (or any successor provision thereto) upon a conversion of, or transfer of all or substantially all of the assets of, a Charitable Trust to such successor entity (whether a determination letter with respect to such successor's exemption is issued before, at or after the conversion date).

4.3 "Covered Security Date" means May 14, 2012

4.4 "Family Member" shall mean with respect to any natural person who is a Qualified Stockholder, the spouse, parents, grandparents, lineal descendents, siblings and lineal descendants of siblings of such Qualified Stockholder. Lineal descendants shall include adopted persons, but only so long as they are adopted during minority.

4.5 "Qualified Stockholder" shall mean (a) the registered holder of a share of Class B Common Stock as of the Covered Security Date; (b) the initial registered holder of any shares of Class B Common Stock that are originally issued by the corporation after the Covered Security Date pursuant to the exercise or conversion of options or warrants or settlement of restricted stock units (RSUs) that, in each case, are outstanding as of the Covered Security Date; (c) each natural person who Transferred shares of or equity awards for Class B Common Stock (including any option or warrant exercisable or convertible into or any RSU that can be settled in shares of Class B Common Stock) to a Permitted Entity that is or becomes a Qualified Stockholder pursuant to subclauses (a) or (b) of this Section 4.5; and (d) a Permitted Transferee.

4.6 "Parent" of an entity shall mean any entity that directly or indirectly owns or controls a majority of the voting power of the voting securities of such entity.

4.7 "Permitted Entity" shall mean with respect to a Qualified Stockholder (a) a Permitted Trust solely for the benefit of (i) such Qualified Stockholder, (ii) one or more Family Members of such Qualified Stockholder, (iii) any other Permitted Entity of such Qualified Stockholder and/or (iv) any entity that is described in Sections 501(c)(3), 170(b)(1)(A), 170(c), 2055(a) or 2522(a) of the United States Internal Revenue Code of

1986, as amended (or any successor provision thereto), (b) any general partnership, limited partnership, limited liability company, corporation or other entity exclusively owned by (i) such Qualified Stockholder, (ii) one or more Family Members of such Qualified Stockholder and/or (iii) any other Permitted Entity of such Qualified Stockholder, (c) any Charitable Trust created by a Qualified Stockholder, which Charitable Trust was (x) validly created and (y) a registered holder of shares of capital stock of the corporation, in each case prior to the Covered Security Date (whether or not it continuously holds such shares of capital stock or any other shares of capital stock of the corporation at all times before or after the Covered Security Date), (d) the personal representative of the estate of a Qualified Stockholder upon the death of such Qualified Stockholder solely to the extent the executor is acting in the capacity as personal representative of such estate, (e) a revocable living trust, which revocable living trust is itself both a Permitted Trust and a Qualified Stockholder, during the lifetime of the natural person grantor of such trust, or (f) a revocable living trust, which revocable living trust is itself both a Permitted Trust and a Qualified Stockholder, following the death of the natural person grantor of such trust, solely to the extent that such shares are held in such trust pending distribution to the beneficiaries designated in such trust. Except as explicitly provided for herein, a Permitted Entity of a Qualified Stockholder shall not cease to be a Permitted Entity of that Qualified Stockholder solely by reason of the death of that Qualified Stockholder.

4.8 "Permitted Transfer" shall mean, and be restricted to, any Transfer of a share of Class B Common Stock:

(a) by a Qualified Stockholder (or the estate of a deceased Qualified Stockholder) to (i) one or more Family Members of such Qualified Stockholder, or (ii) any Permitted Entity of such Qualified Stockholder; or (iii) to such Qualified Stockholder's revocable living trust, which revocable living trust is itself both a Permitted Trust and a Qualified Stockholder;

(b) by a Permitted Entity of a Qualified Stockholder to (i) such Qualified Stockholder or one or more Family Members of such Qualified Stockholder, or (ii) any other Permitted Entity of such Qualified Stockholder; or

(c) by a Qualified Stockholder that is a natural person or revocable living trust to an entity that is exempt from taxation under Section 501(c)(3) of the United States Internal

Revenue Code of 1986, as amended (or any successor provision thereto) (a "501(c)(3) Organization") or an entity that is exempt from taxation under Section 501(c)(3) and described in Section 509(a)(3) of United States Internal Revenue Code of 1986, as amended (or any successor provision thereto) (a "Supporting Organization"), as well as any Transfer by a 501(c)(3) Organization to a Supporting Organization of which such 501(c)(3) Organization (x) is a supported organization (within the meaning of Section 509(f)(3) of the United States Internal Revenue Code of 1986, as amended (or any successor provision thereto)), and (y) has the power to appoint a majority of the board of directors, provided that such 501(c)(3) Organization or such Supporting Organization irrevocably elects, no later than the time such share of Class B Common Stock is Transferred to it, that such share of Class B Common Stock shall automatically be converted into Class A Common Stock upon the death of such Qualified Stockholder or the natural person grantor of such Qualified Stockholder.

4.9 "Permitted Transferee" shall mean a transferee of shares of Class B Common Stock received in a Transfer that constitutes a Permitted Transfer.

4.10 "Permitted Trust" shall mean a bona fide trust where each trustee is (a) a Qualified Stockholder, (b) a Family Member of a Qualified Stockholder, (c) a professional in the business of providing trustee services, including private professional fiduciaries, trust companies and bank trust departments, or (d) solely in the case of any such trust established by a natural person grantor prior to the Covered Security Date, any other bona fide trustee.

4.11 "Transfer" of a share of Class B Common Stock shall mean, directly or indirectly, any sale, assignment, transfer, conveyance, hypothecation or other transfer or disposition of such share or any legal or beneficial interest in such share, whether or not for value and whether voluntary or involuntary or by operation of law (including by merger, consolidation or otherwise), including, without limitation, a transfer of a share of Class B Common Stock to a broker or other nominee (regardless of whether there is a corresponding change in beneficial ownership), or the transfer of, or entering into a binding agreement with respect to, Voting Control (as defined below) over such share by proxy or otherwise. A "Transfer" shall also be deemed to have occurred with respect to a share of Class B Common Stock beneficially held by (i) an entity that is a Permitted Entity, if there occurs any act or circumstance that causes such entity to no longer be a

Permitted Entity or (ii) an entity that is a Qualified Stockholder, if there occurs a Transfer on a cumulative basis, from and after the Covered Security Date, of a majority of the voting power of the voting securities of such entity or any direct or indirect Parent of such entity, other than a Transfer to parties that are, as of the Covered Security Date, holders of voting securities of any such entity or Parent of such entity. Notwithstanding the foregoing, the following shall not be considered a "Transfer" within the meaning of this ARTICLE IV:

(a) the granting of a revocable proxy to officers or directors of the corporation at the request of the Board of Directors in connection with actions to be taken at an annual or special meeting of stockholders or in connection with any action by written consent of the stockholders solicited by the Board of Directors (if action by written consent of stockholders is permitted at such time under this Restated Certificate of Incorporation);

(b) entering into a voting trust, agreement or arrangement (with or without granting a proxy) solely with stockholders who are holders of Class B Common Stock, which voting trust, agreement or arrangement (i) is disclosed either in a Schedule 13D filed with the Securities and Exchange Commission or in writing to the Secretary of the corporation, (ii) either has a term not exceeding one (1) year or is terminable by the holder of the shares subject thereto at any time and (iii) does not involve any payment of cash, securities, property or other consideration to the holder of the shares subject thereto other than the mutual promise to vote shares in a designated manner;

(c) the pledge of shares of Class B Common Stock by a stockholder that creates a mere security interest in such shares pursuant to a bona fide loan or indebtedness transaction for so long as such stockholder continues to exercise Voting Control over such pledged shares; *provided, however,* that a foreclosure on such shares or other similar action by the pledgee shall constitute a "Transfer" unless such foreclosure or similar action qualifies as a "Permitted Transfer" at such time; or

(d) any change in the trustees or the person(s) and/or entity(ies) having or exercising Voting Control over shares of Class B Common Stock (i) of a Charitable Trust that qualifies as a Permitted Entity pursuant to ARTICLE IV, Section 4.7 above, or (ii) of a Permitted Entity *provided* that following such change such Permitted Entity continues to be a Permitted Entity pursuant to ARTICLE IV, Section 4.7 above.

4.12 "Voting Control" shall mean, with respect to a share of Class B Common Stock, the power (whether exclusive or shared) to vote or direct the voting of such share by proxy, voting agreement or otherwise.

4.13 "Voting Threshold Date" shall mean 5:00 p.m. (Eastern Time) on the first day falling on or after the date on which the outstanding shares of Class B Common Stock represent less than a majority of the total voting power of the then outstanding shares of the corporation then entitled to vote generally in the election of directors.

ARTICLE V: AMENDMENT OF BYLAWS

The Board of Directors of the corporation shall have the power to adopt, amend or repeal the Bylaws of the corporation. Any adoption, amendment or repeal of the Bylaws of the corporation by the Board of Directors shall require the approval of a majority of the Whole Board. For purposes of this Restated Certificate of Incorporation, the term "*Whole Board*" shall mean the total number of authorized directors whether or not there exist any vacancies in previously authorized directorships. The stockholders shall also have power to adopt, amend or repeal the Bylaws of the corporation. Prior to the Voting Threshold Date, in addition to any vote of the holders of any class or series of stock of the corporation required by applicable law or by this Restated Certificate of Incorporation (including any Preferred Stock issued pursuant to a Certificate of Designation), such adoption, amendment or repeal of the Bylaws of the corporation by the stockholders shall require the affirmative vote of a majority in voting power of all of the then outstanding shares of capital stock of the corporation entitled to vote generally in the election of directors, voting together as a single class. From and after the Voting Threshold Date, in addition to any vote of the holders of any class or series of stock of the corporation required by applicable law or by this Restated Certificate of Incorporation (including any Preferred Stock issued pursuant to a Certificate of Designation), such adoption, amendment or repeal of the Bylaws of the corporation by the stockholders shall require the affirmative vote of the holders of at least two-thirds of the voting power of all of the then-outstanding shares of the capital stock of the corporation entitled to vote generally in the election of directors, voting together as a single class.

ARTICLE VI: MATTERS RELATING TO THE BOARD OF DIRECTORS

1. Director Powers. The business and affairs of the corporation shall be managed by or under the direction of the Board of Directors. In addition to the powers and authority expressly conferred upon them by statute or by this Restated Certificate of Incorporation or the Bylaws of the corporation, the directors are hereby empowered to exercise all such powers and do all such acts and things as may be exercised or done by the corporation.

2. Number of Directors. Subject to the rights of the holders of any series of Preferred Stock to elect additional directors under specified circumstances, the number of directors shall be fixed from time to time exclusively by resolution adopted by a majority of the Whole Board.

3. Classified Board. Subject to the rights of the holders of any series of Preferred Stock to elect additional directors under specified circumstances, immediately following the Voting Threshold Date, the directors shall be divided, with respect to the time for which they severally hold office, into three classes designated as Class I, Class II and Class III, respectively (the "*Classified Board*"). The Board of Directors may assign members of the Board of Directors in office immediately prior to the Classified Board becoming effective to the several classes of the Classified Board, which assignments shall become effective at the same time the Classified Board becomes effective. Directors shall be assigned to each class in accordance with a resolution or resolutions adopted by a majority of the Board of Directors, with the number of directors in each class to be divided as nearly equal as reasonably possible. The initial term of office of the Class I directors shall expire at the corporation's first annual meeting of stockholders following the date on which the Classified Board becomes effective, the initial term of office of the Class II directors shall expire at the corporation's second annual meeting of stockholders following the date on which the Classified Board becomes effective, and the initial term of office of the Class III directors shall expire at the corporation's third annual meeting of stockholders following the date on which the Classified Board becomes effective. At each annual meeting of stockholders following the date on which the Classified Board becomes effective, directors elected to succeed those directors of the class whose terms then expire shall be elected for a term of office to expire at the third succeeding annual meeting of stockholders after their election.

4. Term and Removal. Each director shall hold office until such director's successor is elected and qualified, or until such director's earlier death, resignation or removal. Any director may resign at any time upon notice to the corporation given in writing or by any electronic transmission permitted in the corporation's Bylaws or in accordance with applicable law. Subject to the rights of the holders of any series of Preferred Stock with respect to directors elected thereby, from and after the effectiveness of the Classified Board, no director may be removed except for cause and only by the affirmative vote of the holders of at least a majority of the voting power of the then-outstanding shares of capital stock of the corporation then entitled to vote at an election of directors voting together as a single class. No decrease in the number of directors constituting the Whole Board shall shorten the term of any incumbent director.

5. Board Vacancies. Subject to the rights of the holders of any series of Preferred Stock to elect directors under specified circumstances, from and after the effectiveness of the Classified Board, any vacancy occurring in the Board of Directors for any cause, and any newly created directorship resulting from any increase in the authorized number of directors, shall (unless (a) the Board of Directors determines by resolution that any such vacancy or newly created directorship shall be filled by the stockholders or (b) otherwise required by applicable law) be filled only by the affirmative vote of a majority of the directors then in office, even if less than a quorum, or by a sole remaining director, and not by the stockholders. Any director elected in accordance with the preceding sentence shall hold office for a term expiring at the annual meeting of stockholders at which the term of office of the class to which the director has been elected expires or until such director's successor shall have been duly elected and qualified.

6. Vote by Ballot. Election of directors need not be by written ballot.

ARTICLE VII: DIRECTOR LIABILITY; INDEMNIFICATION

1. Limitation of Liability. To the fullest extent permitted by law, no director of the corporation shall be personally liable to the corporation or its stockholders for monetary damages for breach of fiduciary duty as a director. Without limiting the effect of the preceding sentence, if the General Corporation Law is hereafter amended to authorize the further elimination or limitation of the liability of a director, then the liability of a director of the corporation shall be eliminated or limited to the fullest extent permitted by the General Corporation Law, as so amended.

2. Indemnification. The corporation shall indemnify to the fullest extent permitted by law any person made or threatened to be made a party to an action or proceeding, whether criminal, civil, administrative or investigative, by reason of the fact that he, his testator or intestate is or was a director or officer of the corporation or any predecessor of the Corporation, or serves or served at any other enterprise as a director or officer at the request of the corporation or any predecessor to the corporation.

3. Change in Rights. Neither any amendment nor repeal of this ARTICLE VII, nor the adoption of any provision of this Restated Certificate of Incorporation inconsistent with this ARTICLE VII, shall eliminate or reduce the effect of this Article VII in respect of any matter occurring, or any action or proceeding accruing or arising or that, but for this Article VII, would accrue or arise, prior to such amendment, repeal or adoption of an inconsistent provision.

ARTICLE VIII: MATTERS RELATING TO STOCKHOLDERS

1. No Action by Written Consent of Stockholders. Subject to the rights of the holders of any series of Preferred Stock with respect to actions by the holders of shares of such series, from and after the Voting Threshold Date, (a) no action shall be taken by the stockholders of the corporation except at a duly called annual or special meeting of stockholders and (b) no action shall be taken by the stockholders of the corporation by written consent.

2. Special Meeting of Stockholders. Subject to the rights of the holders of any series of Preferred Stock with respect to actions by the holders of shares of such series, special meetings of the stockholders of the corporation may be called only by the Board of Directors acting pursuant to a resolution adopted by a majority of the Whole Board, the Chief Executive Officer, President or the Chairperson of the Board, and may not be called by any other person or persons. Business transacted at special meetings of stockholders shall be confined to the purpose or purposes stated in the notice of meeting.

3. Advance Notice of Stockholder Nominations. Advance notice of stockholder nominations for the election of directors of the corporation and of business to be brought by stockholders before any meeting of stockholders of the corporation shall be given in the manner provided in the Bylaws of the corporation.

4. Business Combinations. The corporation elects not to be governed by Section 203 of the General Corporation Law.

ARTICLE IX: CHOICE OF FORUM

Unless the corporation consents in writing to the selection of an alternative forum, the Court of Chancery of the State of Delaware shall, to the fullest extent permitted by law, be the sole and exclusive forum for (1) any derivative action or proceeding brought on behalf of the corporation, (2) any action asserting a claim of breach of a fiduciary duty owed by, or other wrongdoing by, any director, officer, employee or agent of the corporation to the corporation or the corporation's stockholders, (3) any action asserting a claim arising pursuant to any provision of the General Corporation Law or the corporation's Restated Certificate of Incorporation or Bylaws, (4) any action to interpret, apply, enforce or determine the validity of the corporation's Restated Certificate of Incorporation or Bylaws or (5) any action asserting a claim governed by the internal affairs doctrine, in each such case subject to said Court of Chancery having personal jurisdiction over the indispensable parties named as defendants therein. Any person or entity purchasing or otherwise acquiring any interest in shares of capital stock of the corporation shall be deemed to have notice of and consented to the provisions of this ARTICLE IX.

ARTICLE X: AMENDMENT OF RESTATED CERTIFICATE OF INCORPORATION

The corporation reserves the right to amend or repeal any provision contained in this Restated Certificate of Incorporation in the manner prescribed by the laws of the State of Delaware and all rights conferred upon stockholders are granted subject to this reservation; *provided, however*, that, notwithstanding any other provision of this Restated Certificate of Incorporation or any provision of applicable law that might otherwise permit a lesser vote or no vote, but in addition to any vote of the holders of any class or series of the capital stock of this corporation required by applicable law or by this Restated Certificate of Incorporation, from and after the Voting Threshold Date, any amendment to or repeal of this ARTICLE X or ARTICLE V, ARTICLE VI, ARTICLE VII, ARTICLE VIII or ARTICLE IX of this Restated Certificate of Incorporation (or the adoption of any provision inconsistent therewith) shall require the affirmative vote of the holders of at least two-thirds of the voting power of the then outstanding shares of capital stock of the corporation entitled to vote generally in the election of directors, voting together as a single class.

* * * * * * * * * *

8.3 Slack Technologies, Inc. Restated Certificate of Incorporation

SLACK TECHNOLOGIES, INC.
AMENDED AND RESTATED CERTIFICATE OF INCORPORATION

Slack Technologies, Inc. (the "**Corporation**"), a corporation organized and existing under the laws of the State of Delaware, hereby certifies as follows:

A. The Corporation was originally incorporated pursuant to the General Corporation Law of the State of Delaware (the "**DGCL**") on February 25, 2009 under the name Tiny Spec, Inc., which name was subsequently amended to Tiny Speck, Inc. on March 5, 2009, which name was subsequently amended to Slack Technologies, Inc. on July 17, 2014.

B. This Amended and Restated Certificate of Incorporation was duly adopted in accordance with Sections 242 and 245 of the DGCL, and has been duly approved by the written consent of the stockholders of the Corporation in accordance with Section 228 of the DGCL.

C. The Amended and Restated Certificate of Incorporation of the Corporation is hereby amended and restated in its entirety to read as follows:

ARTICLE I

The name of the Corporation is Slack Technologies, Inc.

ARTICLE II

The address of the Corporation's registered office in the State of Delaware is 3500 South DuPont Highway, City of Dover, County of Kent, 19901. The name of its registered agent at such address is Incorporating Services, Ltd.

ARTICLE III

The purpose of the Corporation is to engage in any lawful act or activity for which corporations may be organized under the DGCL.

ARTICLE IV

A.   Classes of Stock. The total number of shares of capital stock that the Corporation shall have authority to issue is 5,800,000,000, consisting of the following: 5,000,000,000 shares of Class A Common Stock, par value $0.0001 per share ("**Class A Common Stock**"), 700,000,000 shares of Class B Common Stock, par value $0.0001 per share ("**Class B Common Stock**"), and 100,000,000 shares of undesignated Preferred Stock, par value $0.0001 per share ("**Preferred Stock**").

B.   Rights of Preferred Stock. The Board of Directors of the Corporation (the "**Board of Directors**") is authorized, subject to any limitations prescribed by law but to the fullest extent permitted by law, to provide by resolution for the designation and issuance of shares of Preferred Stock in one or more series, and to establish from time to time the number of shares to be included in each such series, and to fix the designation, powers (which may include, without limitation, full, limited or no voting powers), preferences, and relative, participating, optional or other rights of the shares of each such series and any qualifications, limitations or restrictions thereof, and to file a certificate pursuant to the applicable law of the State of Delaware (such certificate being hereinafter referred to as a "**Preferred Stock Designation**"), setting forth such resolution or resolutions.

C.   Vote to Increase or Decrease Authorized Shares of Preferred Stock. The number of authorized shares of Preferred Stock may be increased or decreased (but not below the number of shares thereof then outstanding) by the affirmative vote of the holders of a majority of the voting power of all of the outstanding shares of capital stock of the Corporation entitled to vote thereon, without a separate class vote of the holders of Preferred Stock, or any separate series votes of any series thereof, unless a vote of any such holders is required pursuant to the terms of any Preferred Stock Designation.

D.   Rights of Class A Common Stock and Class B Common Stock. The relative powers, rights, qualifications, limitations and restrictions granted to or imposed on the shares of Class A Common Stock and Class B Common Stock are as follows:

1.   Voting Rights.

(a)   General Right to Vote Together; Exception. Except as otherwise expressly provided herein or required by applicable law, the holders of Class A Common Stock and Class B Common Stock shall vote together as one class on all matters submitted to a vote of the stockholders; *provided, however,* subject to the terms of any Preferred Stock Designation, the number of authorized shares of Class A Common Stock or Class B Common Stock may be increased or decreased (but not below the number of shares thereof then outstanding) by the affirmative vote of the holders of a majority of the voting power of the capital stock of the Corporation entitled to vote.

(b)   Votes Per Share. Except as otherwise expressly provided herein or required by applicable law, on any matter that is submitted to a vote of the stockholders, each holder of Class A Common Stock shall be entitled to one (1) vote for each such share, and each holder of Class B Common Stock shall be entitled to ten (10) votes for each such share.

2.   Identical Rights. Except as otherwise expressly provided herein or required by applicable law, shares of Class A Common Stock and Class B Common Stock shall have the same rights and privileges and rank equally, share ratably and be identical in all respects as to all matters, including, without limitation:

(a)   Dividends and Distributions. Shares of Class A Common Stock and Class B Common Stock shall be treated equally, identically and ratably, on a per share basis, with respect to any Distribution paid or distributed by the Corporation, unless different treatment of the shares of each such class is approved by the affirmative vote of the holders of a majority of the outstanding shares of Class A Common Stock and by the affirmative vote of the holders of a majority of the outstanding shares of Class B Common Stock, each voting separately as a class; *provided, however,* that in the event a Distribution is paid in the form of Class A Common Stock or Class B Common Stock (or Rights to acquire such stock), then holders of Class A Common Stock shall receive Class A Common Stock (or Rights to acquire such stock, as the case may be) and holders of Class B Common Stock shall receive Class B Common Stock (or Rights to acquire such stock, as the case may be).

(b) <u>Subdivision or Combination</u>. If the Corporation in any manner subdivides or combines the outstanding shares of Class A Common Stock or Class B Common Stock, the outstanding shares of the other such class will be subdivided or combined in the same proportion and manner, unless different treatment of the shares of each such class is approved by the affirmative vote of the holders of a majority of the outstanding shares of Class A Common Stock and by the affirmative vote of the holders of a majority of the outstanding shares of Class B Common Stock, each voting separately as a class.

(c) <u>Equal Treatment in a Change of Control or any Merger Transaction</u>. In connection with any Change of Control Transaction, shares of Class A Common Stock and Class B Common Stock shall be treated equally, identically and ratably, on a per share basis, with respect to any consideration into which such shares are converted or any consideration paid or otherwise distributed to stockholders of the Corporation, unless different treatment of the shares of each such class is approved by the affirmative vote of the holders of a majority of the outstanding shares of Class A Common Stock and by the affirmative vote of the holders of a majority of the outstanding shares of Class B Common Stock, each voting separately as a class. Any merger or consolidation of the Corporation with or into any other entity, which is not a Change of Control Transaction, shall require approval by the affirmative vote of the holders of a majority of the outstanding shares of Class A Common Stock and by the affirmative vote of the holders of a majority of the outstanding shares of Class B Common Stock, each voting separately as a class, unless (i) the shares of Class A Common Stock and Class B Common Stock remain outstanding and no other consideration is received in respect thereof or (ii) such shares are converted on a pro rata basis into shares of the surviving or parent entity in such transaction having identical rights to the shares of Class A Common Stock and Class B Common Stock, respectively.

3. <u>Conversion of Class B Common Stock</u>.

(a) <u>Voluntary Conversion</u>. Each one (1) share of Class B Common Stock shall be convertible into one (1) share of Class A Common Stock at the option of the holder thereof at any time upon written notice to the transfer agent of the Corporation.

(b) <u>Automatic Conversion</u>. Shares of Class B Common Stock shall automatically, without any further action, convert into an equal number of shares of Class A Common Stock upon the earlier of:

(i) a Transfer of such share; *provided, however,* that no such automatic conversion shall occur in the case of a Transfer by a Class B Stockholder to any of the persons or entities listed in clauses (A) through (G) below (each, a "**Permitted Transferee**") and from any such Permitted Transferee back to such Class B Stockholder and/or any other Permitted Transferee established by or for such Class B Stockholder:

(A) a family member of such Class B Stockholder, which shall include with respect to any natural person who is a Class B Stockholder, the spouse, domestic partner, parents, grandparents, lineal descendants, siblings and lineal descendants of siblings of such Class B Stockholder; and *provided, further,* that lineal descendants shall include adopted persons, but only so long as they are adopted while a minor;

(B)   a trust for the benefit of such Class B Stockholder or persons other than the Class B Stockholder so long as the Class B Stockholder and/or family members of such Class B Stockholder have sole dispositive power and exclusive Voting Control with respect to the shares of Class B Common Stock held by such trust; *provided* such Transfer does not involve any payment of cash, securities, property or other consideration to the Class B Stockholder (other than as a settlor or beneficiary of such trust) and, *provided, further,* that in the event such Class B Stockholder and/or family members of such Class B Stockholder no longer have sole dispositive power and exclusive Voting Control with respect to the shares of Class B Common Stock held by such trust, each share of Class B Common Stock then held by such trust shall automatically convert into one (1) fully paid and nonassessable share of Class A Common Stock;

(C)   the beneficiaries or trustee of a trust; so long as the original grantor of the trust (the "**Grantor**") and/or family members of such Grantor have sole dispositive power and exclusive Voting Control with respect to the shares of Class B Common Stock, *provided* that in the event such Grantor and/or family members of such Grantor no longer have sole dispositive power and exclusive Voting Control with respect to the shares of Class B Common Stock, each share of Class B Common Stock then held shall automatically convert into one (1) fully paid and nonassessable share of Class A Common Stock;

(D)   a trust under the terms of which such Class B Stockholder has retained a "qualified interest" within the meaning of §2702(b)(1) of the Internal Revenue Code (or successor provision) and/or a reversionary interest so long as the Class B Stockholder and/or family members of such Class B Stockholder have sole dispositive power and exclusive Voting Control with respect to the shares of Class B Common Stock held by such trust; *provided, however,* that in the event such Class B Stockholder and/or family members of such Class B Stockholder no longer have sole dispositive power and exclusive Voting Control with respect to the shares of Class B Common Stock held by such trust, each share of Class B Common Stock then held by such trust shall automatically convert into one (1) fully paid and nonassessable share of Class A Common Stock;

(E)   an Individual Retirement Account, as defined in Section 408(a) of the Internal Revenue Code (or successor provision), or a pension, profit sharing, stock bonus or other type of plan or trust of which such Class B Stockholder is a participant or beneficiary and which satisfies the requirements for qualification under Section 401 of the Internal Revenue Code (or successor provision); *provided* that in each case such Class B Stockholder has sole dispositive power and exclusive Voting Control with respect to the shares of Class B Common Stock held in such account, plan or trust, and *provided, further,* that in the event the Class B Stockholder no longer has sole dispositive power and exclusive Voting Control with respect to the shares of Class B Common Stock held by such account, plan or trust, each share of Class B Common Stock then held by such trust shall automatically convert into one (1) fully paid and nonassessable share of Class A Common Stock;

(F)   a corporation, partnership or limited liability company in which such Class B Stockholder and/or family members of such Class B Stockholder directly, or indirectly through one or more Permitted Transferees, own shares, partnership interests or membership interests, as applicable, with sufficient Voting Control in the corporation, partnership or limited liability company, as applicable, or otherwise have legally enforceable rights, such that the Class B Stockholder and/or family members of such Class B Stockholder retain sole dispositive power and exclusive Voting Control with respect to the shares of Class B Common Stock held by such corporation, partnership or limited liability company; *provided, however,* that in the event the Class B Stockholder and/or family members of such Class B Stockholder no longer own sufficient shares, partnership interests or membership interests, as applicable, or no longer has sufficient legally enforceable rights to ensure the Class B Stockholder and/or family members of such Class B Stockholder retain sole dispositive power and exclusive Voting Control with respect to the shares of Class B Common Stock held by such corporation, partnership or limited liability company, as applicable, each share of Class B Common Stock then held by such corporation, partnership or limited liability company, as applicable, shall automatically convert into one (1) fully paid and nonassessable share of Class A Common Stock; or

(G)   an Affiliate of a Class B Stockholder; *provided, however,* that the person or entity holding sole dispositive power and exclusive Voting Control with respect to the shares of Class B Common Stock being Transferred (the "**Controlling Person**") retains, directly or indirectly, sole dispositive power and exclusive Voting Control with respect to the shares following such Transfer; *provided, further,* that in the event the Controlling Person no longer has sole dispositive power and exclusive Voting Control with respect to the shares of Class B Common Stock Transferred to such Affiliate, each such share of Class B Common Stock Transferred to such Affiliate shall automatically convert into one (1) share of Class A Common Stock unless such transaction is otherwise approved by the Corporation.

(ii)   the date specified by a written notice and certification request of the Corporation to the holder of such share of Class B Common Stock requesting a certification, in a form satisfactory to the Corporation, verifying such holder's ownership of Class B Common Stock and confirming that a conversion to Class A Common Stock has not occurred, which date shall not be less than sixty (60) calendar days after the date of such notice and certification request; *provided, however,* that no such automatic conversion pursuant to this subsection (ii) shall occur in the case of a Class B Stockholder or its Permitted Transferees that furnishes a certification satisfactory to the Corporation prior to the specified date.

(c)   <u>Conversion Upon Death or Incapacity of a Class B Stockholder</u>. Each share of Class B Common Stock held of record by a Class B Stockholder who is a natural person, or by such Class B Stockholder's Permitted Transferees, shall automatically, without any further action, convert into one share of Class A Common Stock upon the death or Incapacity of such Class B Stockholder.

(d)   <u>Automatic Conversion of All Outstanding Class B Common Stock</u>. Each one (1) share of Class B Common Stock shall automatically, without any further action, convert into one (1) share of Class A Common Stock upon the date specified by affirmative vote of the holders of at least sixty-six and two-thirds percent (66-2/3%) of the outstanding shares of Class B Common Stock, voting as a single class.

(e)   <u>Final Conversion of Class B Common Stock</u>. On the Final Conversion Date, each one (1) outstanding share of Class B Common Stock shall automatically, without any further action, convert into one (1) share of Class A Common Stock. Following such conversion, the reissuance of all shares of Class B Common Stock shall be prohibited, and such shares shall be retired and cancelled in accordance with

Section 243 of the DGCL and the filing by the Secretary of State of the State of Delaware required thereby, and upon such retirement and cancellation, all references to Class B Common Stock in this Amended and Restated Certificate of Incorporation shall be eliminated.

(f) <u>Procedures</u>. The Corporation may, from time to time, establish such policies and procedures relating to the conversion of Class B Common Stock to Class A Common Stock and the general administration of this dual class stock structure, including the issuance of stock certificates (or the establishment of book-entry positions) with respect thereto, as it may deem necessary or advisable, and may request that holders of shares of Class B Common Stock furnish affidavits or other proof to the Corporation as it deems necessary to verify the ownership of Class B Common Stock and to confirm that a conversion to Class A Common Stock has not occurred. A determination by the Secretary of the Corporation that a Transfer results in a conversion to Class A Common Stock shall be conclusive and binding.

(g) <u>Immediate Effect of Conversion</u>. In the event of a conversion of shares of Class B Common Stock to shares of Class A Common Stock pursuant to this Section D.3, such conversion(s) shall be deemed to have been made at the time that the Corporation's transfer agent receives the written notice required, the time that the Transfer of such shares occurred, the death or Incapacity of the Class B Stockholder or immediately upon the Final Conversion Date, as applicable. Upon any conversion of Class B Common Stock to Class A Common Stock, all rights of the holder of such shares of Class B Common Stock shall cease and the person or persons in whose names or names the certificate or certificates (or book-entry position(s)) representing the shares of Class B Common Stock) are to be issued shall be treated for all purposes as having become the record holder or holders of such number of shares of Class A Common Stock into which such shares of Class B Common Stock were convertible. Shares of Class B Common Stock that are converted into shares of Class A Common Stock as provided in this Section D.3 shall be retired and shall not be reissued.

(h) <u>Reservation of Stock</u>. The Corporation shall at all times reserve and keep available out of its authorized but unissued shares of Class A Common Stock, solely for the purpose of effecting the conversion of the shares of Class B Common Stock, such number of its shares of Class A Common Stock as shall from time to time be sufficient to effect the conversion of all outstanding shares of Class B Common Stock into shares of Class A Common Stock.

E. <u>No Further Issuances</u>. Except for the issuance of Class B Common Stock issuable upon exercise of Rights outstanding at the Effective Time or a dividend payable in accordance with <u>Article IV</u>, Section D.2(a), the Corporation shall not at any time after the Effective Time issue any additional shares of Class B Common Stock, unless such issuance is approved by the affirmative vote of the holders of a majority of the outstanding shares of Class B Common Stock. After the Final Conversion Date, the Corporation shall not issue any additional shares of Class B Common Stock.

ARTICLE V

The following terms, where capitalized in this Amended and Restated Certificate of Incorporation, shall have the meanings ascribed to them in this <u>Article V</u>:

"**Affiliate**" means with respect to any specified person, any other person who or which, directly or indirectly, controls, is controlled by, or is under common control with such specified person, including, without limitation, any general partner, managing member, officer, director or manager of such person and any venture capital, private equity, investment advisor or other investment fund now or hereafter existing that is controlled by one or more general partners or managing members of, or is under common investment management (or shares the same management, advisory company or investment advisor) with, such person.

"**Change of Control Share Issuance**" means the issuance by the Corporation, in a transaction or series of related transactions, of voting securities representing more than two percent (2%) of the total voting power (assuming Class A Common Stock and Class B Common Stock each have one (1) vote per share) of the Corporation before such issuance to any person or persons acting as a group as contemplated in Rule 13d-5(b) under the Exchange Act (or any successor provision) that immediately prior to such transaction or series of related transactions held fifty percent (50%) or less of the total voting power of the Corporation (assuming Class A Common Stock and Class B Common Stock each have one (1) vote per share), such that, immediately following such transaction or series of related transactions, such person or group of persons would hold more than fifty percent (50%) of the total voting power of the Corporation (assuming Class A Common Stock and Class B Common Stock each have one (1) vote per share).

"**Change of Control Transaction**" means (i) the sale, lease, exclusive license, exchange, or other disposition (other than liens and encumbrances created in the ordinary course of business, including liens or encumbrances to secure indebtedness for borrowed money that are approved by the Corporation's Board of Directors, so long as no foreclosure occurs in respect of any such lien or encumbrance) of all or substantially all of the Corporation's property and assets (which shall for such purpose include the property and assets of any direct or indirect subsidiary of the Corporation), *provided that* any sale, lease, exclusive license, exchange or other disposition of property or assets exclusively between or among the Corporation and any direct or indirect subsidiary or subsidiaries of the Corporation shall not be deemed a "**Change of Control Transaction**"; (ii) the merger, consolidation, business combination, or other similar transaction of the Corporation with any other entity, other than a merger, consolidation, business combination, or other similar transaction that would result in the voting securities of the Corporation outstanding immediately prior thereto continuing to represent (either by remaining outstanding or by being converted into voting securities of the surviving entity or its parent) more than fifty percent (50%) of the total voting power represented by the voting securities of the Corporation *and* more than fifty percent (50%) of the total number of outstanding shares of the Corporation's capital stock, in each case as outstanding immediately after such merger, consolidation, business combination, or other similar transaction, and the stockholders of the Corporation immediately prior to the merger, consolidation, business combination, or other similar transaction own voting securities of the Corporation, the surviving entity or its parent immediately following the merger, consolidation, business combination, or other similar transaction in substantially the same proportions (vis-à-vis each other) as such stockholders owned the voting securities of the Corporation immediately prior to the transaction; (iii) a recapitalization, liquidation, dissolution, or other similar transaction involving the Corporation, other than a recapitalization, liquidation, dissolution, or other similar transaction that would result in the voting securities of the Corporation outstanding immediately prior thereto continuing to represent (either by remaining outstanding or being converted into voting securities of the surviving entity or its parent) more than fifty percent (50%) of the total voting power represented by the voting securities of the Corporation *and* more than fifty percent (50%) of the total number of outstanding shares of the Corporation's capital stock, in each case as outstanding immediately after such recapitalization, liquidation, dissolution or other similar transaction, and the stockholders of the Corporation immediately prior to the recapitalization, liquidation, dissolution or other similar transaction own voting securities of the Corporation, the surviving entity or its parent immediately following the recapitalization, liquidation, dissolution or other similar transaction in substantially the same proportions (vis-à-vis each other) as such stockholders owned the voting securities of the Corporation immediately prior to the transaction; and (iv) any Change of Control Share Issuance.

"**Class B Stockholder**" means (i) the registered holder of a share of Class B Common Stock at the Effective Time and (ii) the registered holder of any shares of Class B Common Stock that are originally issued by the Corporation after the Effective Time.

"**Distribution**" means (i) any dividend or distribution of cash, property or shares of the Corporation's capital stock; and (ii) any distribution following or in connection with any liquidation, dissolution or winding up of the Corporation, either voluntary or involuntary.

"**Effective Time**" means the acceptance of this Amended and Restated Certificate of Incorporation for filing by the Secretary of State of the State of Delaware.

"**Exchange Act**" means the United States Securities Exchange Act of 1934, as amended.

"**Final Conversion Date**" means 5:00 p.m. in New York City, New York on the first Trading Day falling on or after the tenth (10th) year anniversary of the Effective Time.

"**Incapacity**" shall mean that such holder is incapable of managing his or her financial affairs under the criteria set forth in the applicable probate code that can be expected to result in death or which has lasted or can be expected to last for a continuous period of not less than six (6) months as determined by a licensed medical practitioner. In the event of a dispute regarding whether a Class B Stockholder has suffered an Incapacity, no Incapacity of such holder will be deemed to have occurred unless and until an affirmative ruling regarding such Incapacity has been made by a court of competent jurisdiction.

"**Independent Directors**" means the members of the Board of Directors designated as independent directors in accordance with the requirements of the Securities Exchange that are generally applicable to companies with common equity securities listed thereon (or if the Corporation's equity securities are not listed for trading on a Securities Exchange, the requirements of a Securities Exchange generally applicable to companies with common equity securities listed thereon).

"**Rights**" means any option, warrant, restricted stock unit, conversion right or contractual right of any kind to acquire shares of the Corporation's authorized but unissued capital stock.

"**Securities Exchange**" means, at any time, the registered national securities exchange on which the Corporation's equity securities are then principally listed or traded, which shall be the New York Stock Exchange or Nasdaq Global Market (or similar national quotation system of the Nasdaq Stock Market) ("**Nasdaq**") or any successor exchange of either the New York Stock Exchange or Nasdaq.

"**Trading Day**" means any day on which the Securities Exchange is open for trading.

"**Transfer**" of a share of Class B Common Stock shall mean any sale, assignment, transfer, conveyance, hypothecation or other transfer or disposition of such share or any legal or beneficial interest in such share, whether or not for value and whether voluntary or involuntary or by operation of law. A "**Transfer**" shall also include, without limitation, (i) a transfer of a share of Class B Common Stock to a broker or other nominee (regardless of whether or not there is a corresponding change in beneficial ownership) or (ii) the transfer of, or entering into a binding agreement with respect to, Voting Control over a share of Class B Common Stock by proxy or otherwise; *provided, however*, that the following shall not be considered a "**Transfer**": (a) the grant of a proxy to officers or directors of the Corporation at the request of the Board of Directors of the Corporation in connection with actions to be taken at an annual or special meeting of stockholders; (b) entering into a voting agreement that provides for the grant of a voting proxy to the Chief Executive Officer of the Corporation; (c) the pledge of shares of Class B Common Stock by a Class B Stockholder that creates a mere security interest in such shares pursuant to a *bona fide* loan or indebtedness transaction so long as the Class B Stockholder continues to exercise Voting Control over such pledged shares; *provided, however*, that a foreclosure on such shares of Class B Common Stock or other similar action by the pledge shall constitute a "**Transfer**"; (d) the fact that, as of the Effective Time or at any time after the Effective Time, the spouse of any Class B Stockholder possesses or obtains an interest in such holder's shares of Class B Common Stock arising solely by reason of the application of the community property laws of any jurisdiction, so long as no other event or circumstance shall exist or have occurred that constitutes a "**Transfer**" of such shares of Class B Common Stock; (e) entering into a trading plan pursuant to Rule 10b5-1 under the Exchange Act with a broker or other nominee; *provided, however*, that a sale of such shares of Class B Common Stock pursuant to such plan shall constitute a "**Transfer**" at the time of such sale; or (f) entering into a support, voting, tender or similar agreement, arrangement or understanding (with or without granting a proxy) in connection with a Change of Control Transaction; *provided, however,* that such Change of Control Transaction was approved by a majority of the Independent Directors then in office.

"**Voting Control**" with respect to a share of Class B Common Stock means the exclusive power (whether directly or indirectly) to vote or direct the voting of such share of Class B Common Stock by proxy, voting agreement, or otherwise.

ARTICLE VI

A. <u>General Powers</u>. The business and affairs of the Corporation shall be managed by or under the direction of the Board of Directors.

B. <u>Number of Directors; Election</u>. Subject to the rights of holders of any series of Preferred Stock with respect to the election of directors, the number of directors that constitutes the entire Board of Directors of the Corporation shall be fixed solely by resolution of the Board of Directors. Subject to the rights of holders of any series of Preferred Stock with respect to the election of directors, each director of the Corporation shall hold office until the expiration of the term for which he or she is elected and until his or her successor has been duly elected and qualified or until his or her earlier resignation, death or removal.

C. <u>Classified Board Structure</u>. From and after the Effective Time, and subject to the rights of holders of any series of Preferred Stock with respect to the election of directors, the directors of the Corporation shall be divided into three (3) classes as nearly equal in size as is practicable, hereby designated Class I, Class II and Class III. The Board of Directors may assign members of the Board of Directors already in office to such classes at the time such classification becomes effective. The term of office of the initial Class I directors shall expire at the first regularly-scheduled annual meeting of stockholders following the Effective Time, the term of office of the initial Class II directors shall expire at the second annual meeting of stockholders following the Effective

Time and the term of office of the initial Class III directors shall expire at the third annual meeting of stockholders following the Effective Time. At each annual meeting of stockholders, commencing with the first regularly-scheduled annual meeting of stockholders following the Effective Time, each of the successors elected to replace the directors of a Class whose term shall have expired at such annual meeting shall be elected to hold office until the third annual meeting next succeeding his or her election and until his or her respective successor shall have been duly elected and qualified.

Notwithstanding the foregoing provisions of this Article VI, each director shall serve until his or her successor is duly elected and qualified or until his or her death, resignation, or removal. Subject to the rights of holders of any series of Preferred Stock with respect to the election of directors, if the number of directors is hereafter changed, any newly created directorships or decrease in directorships shall be so apportioned among the classes as to make all classes as nearly equal in number as is practicable, provided that no decrease in the number of directors constituting the Board of Directors shall shorten the term of any incumbent director.

D. Removal; Vacancies. Subject to the rights of holders of any series of Preferred Stock with respect to the election of directors, for so long as the Board of Directors is divided into classes pursuant to Article VI Section C, any director may be removed from office by the stockholders of the Corporation only for cause. Vacancies occurring on the Board of Directors for any reason and newly created directorships resulting from an increase in the authorized number of directors may be filled only by vote of a majority of the remaining members of the Board of Directors, although less than a quorum, or by a sole remaining director, at any meeting of the Board of Directors. A person so elected by the Board of Directors to fill a vacancy or newly created directorship shall hold office until the next election of the class for which such director shall have been chosen and until his or her successor shall be duly elected and qualified.

ARTICLE VII

A. Written Ballot. Elections of directors need not be by written ballot unless the Bylaws of the Corporation (the "**Bylaws**") shall so provide.

B. Amendment of Bylaws. In furtherance and not in limitation of the powers conferred by statute, the Board of Directors is expressly authorized to adopt, amend or repeal the Bylaws of the Corporation.

C. Special Meetings. Special meetings of the stockholders may be called only by (i) the Board of Directors pursuant to a resolution adopted by a majority of the Board of Directors; (ii) the chairman of the Board of Directors; or (iii) the chief executive officer of the Corporation.

D. No Stockholder Action by Written Consent. Subject to the rights of the holders of any series of Preferred Stock, no action shall be taken by the stockholders of the Corporation except at an annual or special meeting of the stockholders called in accordance with the Bylaws, and no action shall be taken by the stockholders by written consent.

E. No Cumulative Voting. No stockholder will be permitted to cumulate votes at any election of directors.

ARTICLE VIII

To the fullest extent permitted by the DGCL, as it presently exists or may hereafter be amended from time to time, a director of the Corporation shall not be personally liable to the Corporation or its stockholders for monetary damages for breach of any fiduciary duties as a director. If the DGCL is amended to authorize corporate action further eliminating or limiting the personal liability of directors, then the liability of a director of the Corporation shall be eliminated or limited to the fullest extent permitted by the DGCL, as so amended.

Neither any amendment nor repeal of this Article VIII, nor the adoption of any provision of the Corporation's Amended Certificate of Incorporation inconsistent with this Article VIII, shall eliminate or reduce the effect of this Article VIII in respect of any matter occurring, or any cause of action, suit or proceeding accruing or arising or that, but for this Article VIII, would accrue or arise, prior to such amendment, repeal or adoption of an inconsistent provision.

ARTICLE IX

Subject to any provisions in the Bylaws of the Corporation related to indemnification of directors or officers of the Corporation, the Corporation shall indemnify, to the fullest extent permitted by applicable law, any director or officer of the Corporation who was or is a party or is threatened to be made a party to any threatened, pending or completed action, suit or proceeding, whether civil, criminal, administrative or investigative (a "**Proceeding**") by reason of the fact that he or she is or was a director, officer, employee or agent of the Corporation or is or was serving at the request of the Corporation as a director, officer, employee or agent of another corporation, partnership, joint venture, trust or other enterprise, including service with respect to employee benefit plans, against expenses (including attorneys' fees), judgments, fines and amounts paid in settlement actually and reasonably incurred by such person in connection with any such Proceeding.

The Corporation shall have the power to indemnify, to the extent permitted by the DGCL, as it presently exists or may hereafter be amended from time to time, any employee or agent of the Corporation who was or is a party or is threatened to be made a party to any Proceeding by reason of the fact that he or she is or was a director, officer, employee or agent of the Corporation or is or was serving at the request of the Corporation as a director, officer, employee or agent of another corporation, partnership, joint venture, trust or other enterprise, including service with respect to employee benefit plans, against expenses (including attorneys' fees), judgments, fines and amounts paid in settlement actually and reasonably incurred by such person in connection with any such Proceeding.

A right to indemnification or to advancement of expenses arising under a provision of this Amended and Restated Certificate of Incorporation or the Bylaws of the Corporation shall not be eliminated or impaired by an amendment to this Amended and Restated Certificate of Incorporation or the Bylaws of the Corporation after the occurrence of the act or omission that is the subject of the Proceeding for which indemnification or advancement of expenses is sought, unless the provision in effect at the time of such act or omission explicitly authorizes such elimination or impairment after such action or omission has occurred.

ARTICLE X

If any provision of this Amended and Restated Certificate of Incorporation becomes or is declared on any ground by a court of competent jurisdiction to be illegal, unenforceable or void, portions of such provision, or such provision in its entirety, to the extent necessary, shall be severed from this Amended and Restated Certificate of Incorporation, and the court will replace such illegal, void or unenforceable provision of this Amended and Restated Certificate of Incorporation with a valid and enforceable provision that most accurately reflects the Corporation's intent, in order to achieve, to the maximum extent possible, the same economic, business and other purposes of the illegal, void or unenforceable provision. The balance of this Amended and Restated Certificate of Incorporation shall be enforceable in accordance with its terms.

Except as provided in ARTICLE VIII and ARTICLE IX above, the Corporation reserves the right to amend, alter, change or repeal any provision contained in this Amended and Restated Certificate of Incorporation, in the manner now or hereafter prescribed by statute, and all rights conferred upon stockholders herein are granted subject to this reservation; *provided, however,* that, notwithstanding any other provision of this Amended and Restated Certificate of Incorporation or any provision of law that might otherwise permit a lesser vote or no vote, but in addition to any vote of the holders of any class or series of the stock of this Corporation required by law or by this Amended and Restated Certificate of Incorporation, the affirmative vote of the holders of at least sixty-six and two-thirds percent (66-2/3%) of the voting power of the outstanding shares of stock of the Corporation entitled to vote generally in the election of directors, voting together as a single class, shall be required to amend or repeal, or adopt any provision of this Amended and Restated Certificate of Incorporation inconsistent with, ARTICLE VI, ARTICLE VII, ARTICLE VIII, ARTICLE IX or this ARTICLE X.

* * *

IN WITNESS WHEREOF, this Amended and Restated Certificate of Incorporation has been signed on behalf of the Corporation by its duly authorized officer effective this 20th day of June, 2019.

SLACK TECHNOLOGIES, INC.

By: /s/ S. Butterfield
_____
        Stewart Butterfield
        Chief Executive Officer

8.3 Slack Technologies, Inc. Amended & Restated Bylaws

AMENDED AND RESTATED BYLAWS
OF
SLACK TECHNOLOGIES, INC.
(effective upon the effectiveness of the corporation's registration statement on Form S-1)

ARTICLE I
CORPORATE OFFICES

1.1   Registered Office. The registered office of Slack Technologies, Inc. (the "**corporation**") shall be fixed in its certificate of incorporation, as the same may be amended from time to time.

1.2　Other Offices. The corporation's board of directors may at any time establish other offices at any place or places where the corporation is qualified to do business.

<h1 style="text-align:center">ARTICLE II</h1>
<h2 style="text-align:center">MEETINGS OF STOCKHOLDERS</h2>

2.1　Place of Meetings. Meetings of stockholders shall be held at any place, within or outside the State of Delaware, designated by the board of directors. The board of directors may, in its sole discretion, determine that a meeting of stockholders shall not be held at any place, but may instead be held solely by means of remote communication as authorized by Section 211(a)(2) of the General Corporation Law of the State of Delaware (the "**DGCL**"). In the absence of any such designation or determination, stockholders' meetings shall be held at the corporation's principal executive office.

2.2　Annual Meeting. The annual meeting of stockholders shall be held on such date, at such time, and at such place (if any) within or without the State of Delaware as shall be designated from time to time by the board of directors and stated in the corporation's notice of the meeting. At the annual meeting, directors shall be elected and any other proper business, brought in accordance with Section 2.4 of these bylaws, may be transacted. The board of directors may cancel, postpone or reschedule any previously scheduled annual meeting at any time, before or after the notice for such meeting has been sent to the stockholders.

2.3　Special Meeting.

(i)　A special meeting of the stockholders, other than those required by statute, may be called at any time by (A) the board of directors, (B) the chairperson of the board of directors or (C) the chief executive officer, but a special meeting may not be called by any other person or persons. The board of directors may cancel, postpone or reschedule any previously scheduled special meeting at any time, before or after the notice for such meeting has been sent to the stockholders.

(ii)　The notice of a special meeting shall include the purpose for which the meeting is called. Only such business shall be conducted at a special meeting of stockholders as shall have been brought before the meeting by or at the direction of the board of directors, chairperson of the board of directors or chief executive officer. Nothing contained in this Section 2.3(ii) shall be construed as limiting, fixing or affecting the time when a meeting of stockholders called by action of the board of directors may be held.

2.4　Advance Notice Procedures

(i)　Advance Notice of Stockholder Business. At an annual meeting of the stockholders, only such business shall be conducted as shall have been properly brought before the meeting. To be properly brought before an annual meeting, business must be brought: (A) pursuant to the corporation's proxy materials with respect to such meeting, (B) by or at the direction of the board of directors, or (C) by a stockholder of the corporation who (1) is a stockholder of record at the time of the giving of the notice required by this Section 2.4(i) and on the record date for the determination of stockholders entitled to vote at the annual meeting and (2) has timely complied in proper written form with the notice procedures set forth in this Section 2.4(i). In addition, for business to be properly brought before an annual meeting by a stockholder, such business must be a proper matter for stockholder action pursuant to these bylaws and applicable law. For the avoidance of doubt, except for proposals properly made in accordance with Rule 14a-8 under the Securities and Exchange Act of 1934, as amended, or any successor thereto (the "**1934 Act**"), and the regulations thereunder (or any successor rule and in any case as so amended), clause (C) above shall be the exclusive means for a stockholder to bring business before an annual meeting of stockholders.

(a) To comply with clause (C) of Section 2.4(i) above, a stockholder's notice must set forth all information required under this Section 2.4(i) and must be timely received by the secretary of the corporation. To be timely, a stockholder's notice must be received by the secretary at the principal executive offices of the corporation not later than the 90th day nor earlier than the 120th day before the one-year anniversary of the date on which the corporation first mailed its proxy materials or a notice of availability of proxy materials (whichever is earlier) for the preceding year's annual meeting; *provided, however,* that in the event that no annual meeting was held in the previous year or if the date of the annual meeting is advanced by more than 30 days prior to or delayed by more than 60 days after the one-year anniversary of the date of the previous year's annual meeting, then, for notice by the stockholder to be timely, it must be so received by the secretary not earlier than the close of business on the 120th day prior to such annual meeting and not later than the close of business on the later of (i) the 90th day prior to such annual meeting, or (ii) the tenth day following the day on which Public Announcement (as defined below) of the date of such annual meeting is first made. In no event shall any adjournment, rescheduling or postponement of an annual meeting or the announcement thereof commence a new time period for the giving of a stockholder's notice as described in this Section 2.4(i)(a). "**Public Announcement**" shall mean disclosure in a press release reported by the Dow Jones News Service, Associated Press or a comparable national news service, in a document publicly filed by the corporation with the Securities and Exchange Commission pursuant to Section 13, 14 or 15(d) of the 1934 Act.

(b) To be in proper written form, a stockholder's notice to the secretary must set forth as to each matter of business the stockholder intends to bring before the annual meeting: (1) a brief description of the business intended to be brought before the annual meeting, the text of the proposal or business (including the text of any resolutions proposed for consideration
and in the event that such business includes a proposal to amend the bylaws, the language of the proposed amendment) and the reasons for conducting such business at the annual meeting, (2) the name and address, as they appear on the corporation's books, of the stockholder proposing such business and any Stockholder Associated Person (as defined below), (3) the class and number of shares of the corporation that are held of record or are beneficially owned by the stockholder or any Stockholder Associated Person and any

derivative positions held or beneficially held by the stockholder or any Stockholder Associated Person, (4) whether and the extent to which any hedging or other transaction or series of transactions has been entered into by or on behalf of such stockholder or any Stockholder Associated Person with respect to any securities of the corporation, and a description of any other agreement, arrangement or understanding (including any short position or any borrowing or lending of shares), the effect or intent of which is to mitigate loss to, or to manage the risk or benefit from share price changes for, or to increase or decrease the voting power of, such stockholder or any Stockholder Associated Person with respect to any securities of the corporation, (5) any material interest of the stockholder or a Stockholder Associated Person in such business, (6) a statement whether either such stockholder or any Stockholder Associated Person will deliver a proxy statement and/or form of proxy to holders of at least the percentage of the voting power of the corporation's voting shares required under applicable law to carry the proposal and/or otherwise to solicit proxies or votes from stockholders in support of such proposal and (7) any other information relating to such stockholder or Stockholder Associated Person, if any, required to be disclosed in a proxy statement or other filings required to be made in connection with solicitations of proxies for, the proposal pursuant to and in accordance with Section 14(a) of the 1934 Act and the rules and regulations promulgated thereunder (such information provided and statements made as required by clauses (1) through (7), a "**Business Solicitation Statement**"). In addition, to be in proper written form, a stockholder's notice to the secretary must be supplemented not later than ten days following the record date for the determination of stockholders entitled to notice of the meeting to disclose the information contained in clauses (3) and (4) above as of the record date. For purposes of this Section 2.4, a "**Stockholder Associated Person**" of any stockholder shall mean (i) any person controlling, directly or indirectly, or acting in concert with, such stockholder, (ii) any beneficial owner of shares of stock of the corporation owned of record or beneficially by such stockholder and on whose behalf the proposal or nomination, as the case may be, is being made, or (iii) any person controlling, controlled by or under common control with such person referred to in the preceding clauses (i) and (ii).

(c)   Without exception, no business shall be conducted at any annual meeting except in accordance with the provisions set forth in this Section 2.4(i) and, if applicable, Section 2.4(ii). In addition, business proposed to be brought by a stockholder may not be brought before the annual meeting if such stockholder or a Stockholder Associated Person, as applicable, takes action contrary to the representations made in the Business Solicitation Statement applicable to such business or if the Business Solicitation Statement applicable to such business contains an untrue statement of a material fact or omits to state a material fact necessary to make the statements therein not misleading. The chairperson of the annual meeting shall, if the facts warrant, determine and declare at the annual meeting that business was not properly brought before the annual meeting and in accordance with the provisions of this Section 2.4(i), and, if the chairperson should so determine, he or she shall so declare at the annual meeting that any such business not properly brought before the annual meeting shall not be conducted.

(ii)   Advance Notice of Director Nominations at Annual Meetings. Notwithstanding anything in these bylaws to the contrary, only persons who are nominated in accordance with the procedures set forth in this Section 2.4(ii) shall be eligible for election or re-election as directors at an annual meeting of stockholders. Nominations of persons for election to the board of directors of the corporation shall be made at an annual meeting of stockholders only (A) by or at the direction of the board of directors or (B) by a stockholder of the corporation who (1) was a stockholder of record at the time of the giving of the notice required by this Section 2.4(ii) and on the record date for the determination of stockholders entitled to vote at the annual meeting and (2) has complied with the notice procedures set forth in this Section 2.4(ii). In addition to any other applicable requirements, for a nomination to be made by a stockholder, the stockholder must have given timely notice thereof in proper written form to the secretary of the corporation.

(a)   To comply with clause (B) of Section 2.4(ii) above, a nomination to be made by a stockholder must set forth all information required under this Section 2.4(ii) and must be received by the secretary of the corporation at the principal executive offices of the corporation at the time set forth in, and in accordance with, the final three sentences of Section 2.4(i)(a) above; *provided additionally, however,* that in the event that the number of directors to be elected to the board of directors is increased and there is no Public Announcement naming all of the nominees for director or specifying the size of the increased board made by the corporation at least ten days before the last day a stockholder may deliver a notice of nomination pursuant to the foregoing provisions, a stockholder's notice required by this Section 2.4(ii) shall also be considered timely, but only with respect to nominees for any new positions created by such increase, if it shall be received by the secretary of the corporation at the principal executive offices of the corporation not later than the close of business on the tenth day following the day on which such Public Announcement is first made by the corporation.

(b)   To be in proper written form, such stockholder's notice to the secretary must set forth:

(1)   as to each person (a "**nominee**") whom the stockholder proposes to nominate for election or re-election as a director: (A) the name, age, business address and residence address of the nominee, (B) the principal occupation or employment of the nominee, (C) the class and number of shares of the corporation that are held of record or are beneficially owned by the nominee and any derivative positions held or beneficially held by the nominee, (D) whether and the extent to which any hedging or other transaction or series of transactions has been entered into by or on behalf of the nominee with respect to any securities of the corporation, and a description of any other agreement, arrangement or understanding (including any short position or any borrowing or lending of shares), the effect or intent of which is to mitigate loss to, or to manage the risk or benefit of share price changes for, or to increase or decrease the

voting power of the nominee, (E) a description of all arrangements or understandings between or among any of the stockholder, each nominee and/or any other person or persons (naming such person or persons) pursuant to which the nominations are to be made by the stockholder or relating to the nominee's potential service on the board of directors, (F) a written statement executed by the nominee acknowledging that as a director of the corporation, the nominee will owe a fiduciary duty under Delaware law with respect to the corporation and its stockholders, and (G) any other information relating to the nominee that would be required to be disclosed about such nominee if proxies were being solicited for the election of the nominee as a director, or that is otherwise required, in each case pursuant to Regulation 14A under the 1934 Act (including without limitation the nominee's written consent to being named in the proxy statement, if any, as a nominee and to serving as a director if elected); and

(2) as to such stockholder giving notice, (A) the information required to be provided pursuant to clauses (2) through (5) of Section 2.4(i)(b) above, and the supplement referenced in the second sentence of Section 2.4(i)(b) above (except that the references to "business" in such clauses shall instead refer to nominations of directors for purposes of this paragraph), and (B) a statement whether either such stockholder or Stockholder Associated Person will deliver a proxy statement and/or form of proxy to holders at least the percentage of the corporation's voting shares reasonably believed by such stockholder or Stockholder Associated Person to be necessary to elect such nominee(s) (such information provided and statements made as required by clauses (A) and (B) above, a "**Nominee Solicitation Statement**").

(c) At the request of the board of directors, any person nominated by a stockholder for election as a director must furnish to the secretary of the corporation (1) that information required to be set forth in the stockholder's notice of nomination of such person as a director as of a date subsequent to the date on which the notice of such person's nomination was given and (2) such other information as may reasonably be required by the corporation to determine the eligibility of such proposed nominee to serve as an independent director of the corporation or that could be material to a reasonable stockholder's understanding of the independence, or lack thereof, of such nominee; in the absence of the furnishing of such information if requested, such stockholder's nomination shall not be considered in proper form pursuant to this Section 2.4(ii).

(d) Without exception, no person shall be eligible for election or re-election as a director of the corporation at an annual meeting of stockholders unless nominated in accordance with the provisions set forth in this Section 2.4(ii). In addition, a nominee shall not be eligible for election or re-election if a stockholder or Stockholder Associated Person, as applicable, takes action contrary to the representations made in the Nominee Solicitation Statement applicable to such nominee or if the Nominee Solicitation Statement applicable to such nominee contains an untrue statement of a material fact or omits to state a material fact necessary to make the statements therein not misleading. The chairperson of the annual meeting shall, if the facts warrant, determine and declare at the annual meeting that a nomination was not made in accordance with the provisions prescribed by these bylaws, and if the chairperson should so determine, he or she shall so declare at the annual meeting, and the defective nomination shall be disregarded.

(iii) <u>Advance Notice of Director Nominations for Special Meetings</u>.

(a) For a special meeting of stockholders at which directors are to be elected pursuant to Section 2.3, nominations of persons for election to the board of directors shall be made only (1) by or at the direction of the board of directors or (2) by any stockholder of the corporation who (A) is a stockholder of record at the time of the giving of the notice required by this Section 2.4(iii) and on the record date for the determination of stockholders entitled to vote at the special meeting and (B) delivers a timely written notice of the nomination to the secretary of
the corporation that includes the information set forth in Sections 2.4(ii)(b) and (ii)(c) above. To be timely, such notice must be received by the secretary at the principal executive offices of the corporation not earlier than the close of business on the 120th day prior to such meeting and not later than the close of business on the later of the 90th day prior to such special meeting or the tenth day following the day on which Public Announcement is first made of the date of the special meeting and of the nominees proposed by the board of directors to be elected at such meeting. In no event shall any adjournment, rescheduling or postponement of a special meeting or the announcement thereof commence a new time period for the giving of a stockholder's notice. A person shall not be eligible for election or re-election as a director at a special meeting unless the person is nominated (i) by or at the direction of the board of directors or (ii) by a stockholder in accordance with the notice procedures set forth in this Section 2.4(iii). In addition, a nominee shall not be eligible for election or re-election if a stockholder or Stockholder Associated Person, as applicable, takes action contrary to the representations made in the Nominee Solicitation Statement applicable to such nominee or if the Nominee Solicitation Statement applicable to such nominee contains an untrue statement of a material fact or omits to state a material fact necessary to make the statements therein not misleading.

(b) The chairperson of the special meeting shall, if the facts warrant, determine and declare at the meeting that a nomination or business was not made in accordance with the procedures prescribed by these bylaws, and if the chairperson should so determine, he or she shall so declare at the meeting, and the defective nomination or business shall be disregarded.

(iv) <u>Other Requirements and Rights</u>. In addition to the foregoing provisions of this Section 2.4, a stockholder must also comply with all applicable requirements of state law and of the 1934 Act and the rules and regulations thereunder with respect to the matters set forth in this Section 2.4, including, with respect to business such stockholder intends to bring before the annual meeting that involves a proposal that such stockholder requests to be included in the corporation's proxy statement, the requirements of Rule 14a-8 (or any successor provision) under the 1934 Act. Nothing in this Section 2.4 shall be deemed to affect any right of the corporation to omit a proposal from the corporation's proxy statement pursuant to Rule 14a-8 (or any successor provision) under the 1934 Act.

Notwithstanding the foregoing provisions of this Section 2.4, unless otherwise required by law, if the stockholder (or a qualified representative of the stockholder) does not appear at the annual or special meeting of stockholders of the corporation to present a nomination or proposed business, such nomination shall be disregarded and such proposed business shall not be transacted, notwithstanding that proxies in respect of such vote may have been received by the corporation. For purposes of this Section 2.4, to be considered a qualified representative of the stockholder, a person must be a duly authorized officer, manager or partner of such stockholder or must be authorized by a writing executed by such stockholder or an electronic transmission delivered by such stockholder to act for such stockholder as proxy at the meeting of stockholders and such person must produce such writing or electronic transmission, or a reliable reproduction of the writing or electronic transmission, at the meeting of stockholders.

2.5   Notice of Stockholders' Meetings. Whenever stockholders are required or permitted to take any action at a meeting, a written notice of the meeting shall be given which shall state the place, if any, date and hour of the meeting, the means of remote communications, if any, by which stockholders and proxy holders may be deemed to be present in person and vote at such meeting, the record date for determining the stockholders entitled to vote at the meeting, if such date is different from the record date for determining stockholders entitled to notice of the meeting, and, in the case of a special meeting, the purpose or purposes for which the meeting is called. Except as otherwise provided in the DGCL, the certificate of incorporation or these bylaws, the written notice of any meeting of stockholders shall be given not less than 10 nor more than 60 days before the date of the meeting to each stockholder entitled to vote at such meeting as of the record date for determining the stockholders entitled to notice of the meeting.

2.6   Quorum. The holders of a majority of the voting power of the stock issued and outstanding and entitled to vote, present in person or represented by proxy, shall constitute a quorum for the transaction of business at all meetings of the stockholders, unless otherwise required by law, the certificate of incorporation, these bylaws or the rules of any applicable stock exchange. Where a separate vote by a class or series or classes or series is required, a majority of the voting power of the issued and outstanding shares of such class or series or classes or series, present in person or represented by proxy, shall constitute a quorum entitled to take action with respect to that vote on that matter, except as otherwise required by law, the certificate of incorporation, these bylaws or the rules of any applicable stock exchange.

Whether or not a quorum is present at a meeting of stockholders, the chairperson of the meeting shall have power to adjourn the meeting from time to time, without notice other than announcement at the meeting.

2.7   Adjourned Meeting; Notice. When a meeting is adjourned to another time or place, unless these bylaws otherwise require, notice need not be given of the adjourned meeting if the time, place, if any, thereof, and the means of remote communications, if any, by which stockholders and proxy holders may be deemed to be present in person and vote at such adjourned meeting are announced at the meeting at which the adjournment is taken. At the adjourned meeting, the corporation may transact any business which might have been transacted at the original meeting. If the adjournment is for more than 30 days, a notice of the adjourned meeting shall be given to each stockholder of record entitled to vote at the meeting. If after the adjournment a new record date for stockholders entitled to vote is fixed for the adjourned meeting, the board of directors shall fix a new record date for notice of such adjourned meeting in accordance with Section 213(a) of the DGCL and Section 2.11 of these bylaws, and shall give notice of the adjourned meeting to each stockholder of record entitled to vote at such adjourned meeting as of the record date fixed for notice of such adjourned meeting.

2.8 <u>Conduct of Business</u>. The chairperson of any meeting of stockholders shall determine the order of business and the procedure at the meeting, including such regulation of the manner of voting and the conduct of business. The chairperson of any meeting of stockholders shall be designated by the board of directors; in the absence of such designation, the chairperson of the board, if any, the chief executive officer (in the absence of the chairperson) or the lead independent director (in the absence of the chairperson of the board and the chief executive officer), or in their absence any other executive officer of the corporation, shall serve as chairperson of the stockholder meeting.

2.9 <u>Voting</u>. The stockholders entitled to vote at any meeting of stockholders shall be determined in accordance with the provisions of Section 2.11 of these bylaws, subject to Section 217 (relating to voting rights of fiduciaries, pledgors and joint owners of stock) and Section 218 (relating to voting trusts and other voting agreements) of the DGCL.

Except as may be otherwise provided in the certificate of incorporation, each stockholder shall be entitled to one vote for each share of capital stock held by such stockholder.

Except as otherwise required by law, the certificate of incorporation, these bylaws or the rules of any applicable stock exchange, in all matters other than the election of directors, the affirmative vote of a majority of the voting power of the shares, present in person or represented by proxy, at the meeting and entitled to vote on the subject matter shall be the act of the stockholders. Except as otherwise required by law, the certificate of incorporation, these bylaws or the rules of any applicable stock exchange, directors shall be elected by a plurality of the voting power of the shares, present in person or represented by proxy, at the meeting and entitled to vote on the election of directors. Where a separate vote by a class or series or classes or series is required, in all matters other than the election of directors, the affirmative vote of the majority of the voting power of shares of such class or series or classes or series, present in person or represented by proxy, at the meeting shall be the act of such class or series or classes or series, except as otherwise provided by law, the certificate of incorporation, these bylaws or the rules of any applicable stock exchange.

2.10   No Stockholder Action By Written Consent Without A Meeting. Subject to the rights of the holders of the shares of any series of preferred stock or any other class of stock or series thereof that have been expressly granted the right to take action by written consent, any action required or permitted to be taken by the stockholders of the corporation must be effected at a duly called annual or special meeting of stockholders of the corporation and may not be effected by any consent in writing by such stockholders.

2.11   Record Dates. In order that the corporation may determine the stockholders entitled to notice of any meeting of stockholders or any adjournment thereof, the board of directors may fix a record date, which record date shall not precede the date upon which the resolution fixing the record date is adopted by the board of directors and which record date shall not be more than 60 nor less than 10 days before the date of such meeting. If the board of directors so fixes a date, such date shall also be the record date for determining the stockholders entitled to vote at such meeting unless the board of directors determines, at the time it fixes such record date, that a later date on or before the date of the meeting shall be the date for making such determination.

If no record date is fixed by the board of directors, the record date for determining stockholders entitled to notice of and to vote at a meeting of stockholders shall be at the close of business on the day next preceding the day on which notice is given, or, if notice is waived, at the close of business on the day next preceding the day on which the meeting is held.

A determination of stockholders of record entitled to notice of or to vote at a meeting of stockholders shall apply to any adjournment of the meeting; provided, however, that the board of directors may fix a new record date for determination of stockholders entitled to vote at the adjourned meeting, and in such case shall also fix as the record date for stockholders entitled to notice of such adjourned meeting the same or an earlier date as that fixed for determination of stockholders entitled to vote in accordance with the provisions of Section 213 of the DGCL and this Section 2.11 at the adjourned meeting.

In order that the corporation may determine the stockholders entitled to receive payment of any dividend or other distribution or allotment of any rights or the stockholders entitled to exercise any rights in respect of any change, conversion or exchange of stock, or for the purpose of any other lawful action, the board of directors may fix a record date, which record date shall not precede the date upon which the resolution fixing the record date is adopted, and which record date shall be not more than 60 days prior to such action. If no record date is fixed, the record date for determining stockholders for any such purpose shall be at the close of business on the day on which the board of directors adopts the resolution relating thereto.

2.12   Proxies. Each stockholder entitled to vote at a meeting of stockholders may authorize another person or persons to act for such stockholder by proxy authorized by an instrument in writing or by a transmission permitted by law filed in accordance with the procedure established for the meeting, but no such proxy shall be voted or acted upon after three years from its date, unless the proxy provides for a longer period. The revocability of a proxy that states on its face that it is irrevocable shall be governed by the provisions of Section 212 of the DGCL. A written proxy may be in the form of a telegram, cablegram, or other means of electronic transmission which sets forth or is submitted with information from which it can be determined that the telegram, cablegram, or other means of electronic transmission was authorized by the stockholder.

2.13   List of Stockholders Entitled to Vote. The officer who has charge of the stock ledger of the corporation shall prepare and make, at least 10 days before every meeting of stockholders, a complete list of the stockholders entitled to vote at the meeting; *provided, however,* if the record date for determining the stockholders entitled to vote is less than 10 days before the meeting date, the list shall reflect the stockholders entitled to vote as of the tenth day before the meeting date, arranged in alphabetical order, and showing the address of each stockholder and the number of shares registered in the name of each stockholder. The corporation shall not be required to include electronic mail addresses or other electronic contact information on such list. Such list shall be open to the examination of any stockholder for any purpose germane to the meeting for a period of at least 10 days prior to the meeting: (i) on a reasonably accessible electronic network; *provided* that the information required to gain access to such list is provided with the notice of the meeting, or (ii) during ordinary business hours, at the corporation's principal place of business. In the event that the corporation determines to make the list available on an electronic network, the corporation may take reasonable steps to ensure that such information is available only to stockholders of the corporation. If the meeting is to be held at a place, then a list of stockholders entitled to vote at the meeting shall be produced and kept at the time and place of the meeting during the whole time thereof, and may be examined by any stockholder who is present. If the meeting is to be held solely by means of remote communication, then such list shall also be open to the examination of any stockholder during the whole time of the meeting on a reasonably accessible electronic network, and the information required to access such list shall be provided with the notice of the meeting. Such list shall presumptively determine the identity of the stockholders entitled to vote at the meeting and the number of shares held by each of them.

2.14   Inspectors of Election. Before any meeting of stockholders, the board of directors shall appoint an inspector or inspectors of election to act at the meeting or its adjournment. The number of inspectors shall be either one or three. If any person appointed as inspector fails to appear or fails or refuses to act, then the chairperson of the meeting may, and upon the request of any stockholder or a stockholder's proxy shall, appoint a person to fill that vacancy; *provided further* that, in any case, if no inspector or alternate is able to act at a meeting of stockholders, the chairperson of the meeting shall appoint at least one inspector to act at the meeting.

Each inspector, before entering upon the discharge of his or her duties, shall take and sign an oath to execute faithfully the duties of inspector with strict impartiality and according to the best of his or her ability. Such inspectors shall:

(i)   determine the number of shares outstanding and the voting power of each, the number of shares represented at the meeting, the existence of a quorum, and the authenticity, validity, and effect of proxies;

(ii)   receive votes, ballots or consents;

(iii)   hear and determine all challenges and questions in any way arising in connection with the right to vote;

(iv)   count and tabulate all votes or consents;

(v)   determine when the polls shall close;

(vi)   determine the result; and

(vii)   do any other acts that may be proper to conduct the election or vote with fairness to all stockholders.

The inspectors of election shall perform their duties impartially, in good faith, to the best of their ability and as expeditiously as is practical. If there are three inspectors of election, the decision, act or certificate of a majority is effective in all respects as the decision, act or certificate of all. Any report or certificate made by the inspectors of election is prima facie evidence of the facts stated therein.

ARTICLE III
DIRECTORS

3.1   <u>Powers</u>. The business and affairs of the corporation shall be managed by or under the direction of the board of directors, except as may be otherwise provided in the DGCL or the certificate of incorporation.

3.2   <u>Number of Directors</u>. The board of directors shall consist of one or more members, each of whom shall be a natural person. Unless the certificate of incorporation fixes the number of directors, the number of directors shall be determined from time to time by resolution of the board of directors. No reduction of the authorized number of directors shall have the effect of removing any director before that director's term of office expires.

3.3   <u>Election, Qualification and Term of Office Of Directors</u>. Except as provided in Section 3.4 of these bylaws, each director, including a director elected to fill a vacancy, shall hold office until the expiration of the term for which elected and until such director's successor is elected and qualified or until such director's earlier death, resignation or removal. Directors need not be stockholders unless so required by the certificate of incorporation or these bylaws. The certificate of incorporation or these bylaws may prescribe other qualifications for directors.

In accordance with the provisions of the certificate of incorporation, the directors of the corporation shall be divided into three classes.

3.4   <u>Resignation and Vacancies</u>. Any director may resign at any time upon notice given in writing or by electronic transmission to the corporation. A resignation is effective when the resignation is delivered unless the resignation specifies a later effective date or an effective date determined upon the happening of an event or events. A resignation which is conditioned upon the director failing to receive a specified vote for reelection as a director may provide that it is irrevocable. Unless otherwise provided in the certificate of incorporation or these bylaws, when one or more directors resign from the board of directors, effective at a future date, a majority of the directors then in office, including those who have so resigned, shall have power to fill such vacancy or vacancies, the vote thereon to take effect when such resignation or resignations shall become effective.

Unless otherwise provided in the certificate of incorporation or these bylaws, vacancies and newly created directorships resulting from any increase in the authorized number of directors elected by all of the stockholders having the right to vote as a single class shall be filled only by a majority of the directors then in office, although less than a quorum, or by a sole remaining director. If the directors are divided into classes, a person so elected by the directors then in office to fill a vacancy or newly created directorship shall hold office until the next election of the class for which such director shall have been chosen and until his or her successor shall have been duly elected and qualified.

If at any time, by reason of death or resignation or other cause, the corporation should have no directors in office, then any officer or any stockholder or an executor, administrator, trustee or
guardian of a stockholder, or other fiduciary entrusted with like responsibility for the person or estate of a stockholder, may call a special meeting of stockholders in accordance with the provisions of the certificate of incorporation or these bylaws, or may apply to the Delaware Court of Chancery for a decree summarily ordering an election as provided in Section 211 of the DGCL.

If, at the time of filling any vacancy or any newly created directorship, the directors then in office constitute less than a majority of the whole board of directors (as constituted immediately prior to any such increase), the Court of Chancery may, upon application of any stockholder or stockholders holding at least 10% of the voting power of the voting stock at the time outstanding having the right to vote for such directors, summarily order an election to be held to fill any such vacancies or newly created directorships, or to replace the directors chosen by the directors then in office as aforesaid, which election shall be governed by the provisions of Section 211 of the DGCL as far as applicable.

3.5 <u>Place of Meetings; Meetings By Telephone</u>. The board of directors may hold meetings, both regular and special, either within or outside the State of Delaware.

Unless otherwise restricted by the certificate of incorporation or these bylaws, members of the board of directors, or any committee designated by the board of directors, may participate in a meeting of the board of directors, or any committee, by means of conference telephone or other communications equipment by means of which all persons participating in the meeting can hear each other, and such participation in a meeting shall constitute presence in person at the meeting.

3.6 <u>Regular Meetings</u>. Regular meetings of the board of directors may be held without notice at such time and at such place as shall from time to time be determined by the board of directors.

3.7   Special Meetings; Notice. Special meetings of the board of directors for any purpose or purposes may be called at any time by the chairperson of the board of directors, the chief executive officer, the president, the secretary or a majority of the authorized number of directors, at such times and places as he or she or they shall designate.

Notice of the time and place of special meetings shall be:

(i)   delivered personally by hand, by courier or by telephone;

(ii)   sent by United States first-class mail, postage prepaid;

(iii)   sent by facsimile; or

(iv)   sent by electronic mail,

directed to each director at that director's address, telephone number, facsimile number or electronic mail address, as the case may be, as shown on the corporation's records.

If the notice is (i) delivered personally by hand, by courier or by telephone, (ii) sent by facsimile or (iii) sent by electronic mail, it shall be delivered or sent at least 24 hours before the time of the holding of the meeting. If the notice is sent by United States mail, it shall be deposited in the United States mail at least four days before the time of the holding of the meeting. Any oral notice may be communicated to the director. The notice need not specify the place of the meeting (if the meeting is to be held at the corporation's principal executive office) nor the purpose of the meeting.

3.8   Quorum; Voting. At all meetings of the board of directors, a majority of the total authorized number of directors shall constitute a quorum for the transaction of business. If a quorum is not present at any meeting of the board of directors, then the directors present thereat may adjourn the meeting from time to time, without notice other than announcement at the meeting, until a quorum is present. A meeting at which a quorum is initially present may continue to transact business notwithstanding the withdrawal of directors, if any action taken is approved by at least a majority of the required quorum for that meeting.

The vote of a majority of the directors present at any meeting at which a quorum is present shall be the act of the board of directors, except as may be otherwise specifically provided by statute, the certificate of incorporation or these bylaws.

If the certificate of incorporation provides that one or more directors shall have more or less than one vote per director on any matter, every reference in these bylaws to a majority or other proportion of the directors shall refer to a majority or other proportion of the votes of the directors.

3.9   Board Action By Written Consent Without A Meeting. Unless otherwise restricted by the certificate of incorporation or these bylaws, any action required or permitted to be taken at any meeting of the board of directors, or of any committee thereof, may be taken without a meeting if all members of the board of directors or committee, as the case may be, consent thereto in writing or by electronic transmission and the writing or writings or electronic transmission or transmissions are filed with the minutes of proceedings of the board of directors or committee. Such filing shall be in paper form if the minutes are maintained in paper form and shall be in electronic form if the minutes are maintained in electronic form. Any person (whether or not then a director) may provide, whether through instruction to an agent or otherwise, that a consent to action will be effective at a future time (including a time determined upon the happening of an event), no later than 60 days after such instruction is given or such provision is made and such consent shall be deemed to have been given for purposes of this Section 3.9 at such effective time so long as such person is then a director and did not revoke the consent prior to such time. Any such consent shall be revocable prior to its becoming effective.

     3.10   <u>Fees and Compensation of Directors</u>. Unless otherwise restricted by the certificate of incorporation or these bylaws, the board of directors shall have the authority to fix the compensation of directors.

     3.11   <u>Removal of Directors</u>. A director may be removed from office by the stockholders of the corporation only as provided in the certificate of incorporation. No reduction of the authorized number of directors shall have the effect of removing any director prior to the expiration of such director's term of office.

ARTICLE IV
COMMITTEES

     4.1   <u>Committees of Directors</u>. The board of directors may designate one or more committees, each committee to consist of one or more of the directors of the corporation. The board of directors may designate one or more directors as alternate members of any committee, who may replace any absent or disqualified member at any meeting of the committee. In the absence or disqualification of a member of a committee, the member or members thereof present at any meeting and not disqualified from voting, whether or not such member or members constitute a quorum, may unanimously appoint another member of the board of directors to act at the meeting in the place of any such absent or disqualified member. Any such committee, to the extent provided in the resolution of the board of directors or in these bylaws, shall have and may exercise all the powers and authority of the board of directors in the management of the business and affairs of the corporation, and may authorize the seal of the corporation to be affixed to all papers that may require it; but no such committee shall have the power or authority to (i) approve or adopt, or recommend to the stockholders, any action or matter (other than the election or removal of directors) expressly required by the DGCL to be submitted to stockholders for approval, or (ii) adopt, amend or repeal any bylaw of the corporation.

     4.2   <u>Committee Minutes</u>. Each committee shall keep regular minutes of its meetings and report the same to the board of directors when required.

     4.3   <u>Meetings and Action of Committees</u>. Meetings and actions of committees shall be governed by, and held and taken in accordance with, the provisions of:

         (i)   Section 3.5 (place of meetings and meetings by telephone);

         (ii)   Section 3.6 (regular meetings);

         (iii)   Section 3.7 (special meetings and notice);

         (iv)   Section 3.8 (quorum; voting);

         (v)   Section 7.5 (waiver of notice); and

(vi)   Section 3.9 (action without a meeting)

with such changes in the context of those bylaws as are necessary to substitute the committee and its members for the board of directors and its members. However:

(i)   the time of regular meetings of committees may be determined either by resolution of the board of directors or by resolution of the committee;

(ii)   special meetings of committees may also be called by resolution of the board of directors; and

(iii)   notice of special meetings of committees shall also be given to all alternate members, who shall have the right to attend all meetings of the committee.

The board of directors or a committee may adopt rules for the government of any committee not inconsistent with the provisions of these bylaws.

Any provision in the certificate of incorporation providing that one or more directors shall have more or less than one vote per director on any matter shall apply to voting in any committee or subcommittee, unless otherwise provided in the certificate of incorporation or these bylaws.

4.4   Subcommittees. Unless otherwise provided in the certificate of incorporation, these bylaws or the resolutions of the board of directors designating the committee, a committee may create one or more subcommittees, each subcommittee to consist of one or more members of the committee, and delegate to a subcommittee any or all of the powers and authority of the committee.

ARTICLE V
OFFICERS

5.1   Officers. The officers of the corporation shall be a president and a secretary. The corporation may also have, at the discretion of the board of directors, a chairperson of the board of directors, a vice chairperson of the board of directors, a chief executive officer, a chief financial officer or treasurer, one or more vice presidents, one or more assistant vice presidents, one or more assistant treasurers, one or more assistant secretaries, and any such other officers as may be appointed in accordance with the provisions of these bylaws. Any number of offices may be held by the same person.

5.2   Appointment of Officers. The board of directors shall appoint the officers of the corporation, except such officers as may be appointed in accordance with the provisions of Sections 5.3 of these bylaws, subject to the rights, if any, of an officer under any contract of employment.

5.3   Subordinate Officers. The board of directors may appoint, or empower the chief executive officer or, in the absence of a chief executive officer, the president, to appoint, such other officers and agents as the business of the corporation may require. Each of such officers and agents shall hold office for such period, have such authority, and perform such duties as are provided in these bylaws or as the board of directors may from time to time determine.

5.4   Removal and Resignation of Officers. Subject to the rights, if any, of an officer under any contract of employment, any officer may be removed, either with or without cause, by an affirmative vote of the majority of the board of directors at any regular or special meeting of the board of directors or, except in the case of an officer chosen by the board of directors, by any officer upon whom such power of removal may be conferred by the board of directors.

Any officer may resign at any time by giving written notice to the corporation. Any resignation shall take effect at the date of the receipt of that notice or at any later time specified in that notice. Unless otherwise specified in the notice of resignation, the acceptance of the resignation shall not be necessary to make it effective. Any resignation is without prejudice to the rights, if any, of the corporation under any contract to which the officer is a party.

5.5 <u>Vacancies In Offices</u>. Any vacancy occurring in any office of the corporation shall be filled by the board of directors or as provided in Section 5.3.

5.6 <u>Representation of Shares of Other Entities</u>. The chairperson of the board of directors, the president, any vice president, the treasurer, the secretary or assistant secretary of this corporation, or any other person authorized by the board of directors or the president or a vice president, is authorized to vote, represent, and exercise on behalf of this corporation all rights incident to any and all shares or other equity interests of any other corporation or corporations or entity or entities standing in the name of this corporation, including the right to act by written consent. The authority granted herein may be exercised either by such person directly or by any other person authorized to do so by proxy or power of attorney duly executed by such person having the authority.

5.7 <u>Authority and Duties of Officers</u>. All officers of the corporation shall respectively have such authority and perform such duties in the management of the business of the corporation as may be designated from time to time by the board of directors or the stockholders and, to the extent not so provided, as generally pertain to their respective offices, subject to the control of the board of directors.

ARTICLE VI
STOCK

6.1 <u>Stock Certificates; Partly Paid Shares</u>. The shares of the corporation shall be represented by certificates; *provided* that the board of directors may provide by resolution or resolutions that some or all of any or all classes or series of its stock shall be uncertificated shares. Any such resolution shall not apply to shares represented by a certificate until such certificate is surrendered to the corporation. Every holder of stock represented by certificates shall be entitled to have a certificate signed by, or in the name of the corporation by any two authorized officers of the corporation, which shall include, without limitation, the chairperson of the board of directors, the vice-chairperson of the board of directors, the president, any vice-president, the treasurer, any assistant treasurer, the secretary and any assistant secretary of the corporation, representing the number of shares registered in certificate form. Any or all of the signatures on the certificate may be a facsimile. In case any officer, transfer agent or registrar who has signed or whose facsimile signature has been placed upon a certificate has ceased to be such officer, transfer agent or registrar before such certificate is issued, it may be issued by the corporation with the same effect as if such person were such officer, transfer agent or registrar at the date of issue. The corporation shall not have power to issue a certificate in bearer form.

The corporation may issue the whole or any part of its shares as partly paid and subject to call for the remainder of the consideration to be paid therefor. Upon the face or back of each stock certificate issued to represent any such partly-paid shares, or upon the books and records of the corporation in the case of uncertificated partly-paid shares, the total amount of the consideration to be paid therefor and the amount paid thereon shall be stated. Upon the declaration of any dividend on fully-paid shares, the corporation shall declare a dividend upon partly-paid shares of the same class, but only upon the basis of the percentage of the consideration actually paid thereon.

6.2   Special Designation On Certificates. If the corporation is authorized to issue more than one class of stock or more than one series of any class, then the powers, the designations, the preferences, and the relative, participating, optional or other special rights of each class of stock or series thereof and the qualifications, limitations or restrictions of such preferences and/or rights shall be set forth in full or summarized on the face or back of the certificate that the corporation shall issue to represent such class or series of stock; *provided, however*, that, except as otherwise provided in Section 202 of the DGCL, in lieu of the foregoing requirements there may be set forth on the face or back of the certificate that the corporation shall issue to represent such class or series of stock, a statement that the corporation will furnish without charge to each stockholder who so requests the powers, designations, preferences and relative, participating, optional or other special rights of each class of stock or series thereof and the qualifications, limitations or restrictions of such preferences and/or rights. Within a reasonable time after the issuance or transfer of uncertificated stock, the corporation shall send to the registered owner thereof a written notice containing the information required to be set forth or stated on certificates pursuant to this Section 6.2 or Sections 151, 156, 202(a) or 218(a) of the DGCL or with respect to this Section 6.2 a statement that the corporation will furnish without charge to each stockholder who so requests the powers, designations, preferences and relative, participating, optional or other special rights of each class of stock or series thereof and the qualifications, limitations or restrictions of such preferences and/or rights. Except as otherwise expressly provided by law, the rights and obligations of the holders of uncertificated stock and the rights and obligations of the holders of certificates representing stock of the same class and series shall be identical.

6.3   Lost Certificates. Except as provided in this Section 6.3, no new certificates for shares shall be issued to replace a previously issued certificate unless the latter is surrendered to the corporation and cancelled at the same time. The corporation may issue a new certificate of stock or uncertificated shares in the place of any certificate theretofore issued by it, alleged to have been lost, stolen or destroyed, and the corporation may require the owner of the lost, stolen or destroyed certificate, or such owner's legal representative, to give the corporation a bond sufficient to indemnify it against any claim that may be made against it on account of the alleged loss, theft or destruction of any such certificate or the issuance of such new certificate or uncertificated shares.

6.4   Dividends. The board of directors, subject to any restrictions contained in the certificate of incorporation or applicable law, may declare and pay dividends upon the shares of the corporation's capital stock.

The board of directors may set apart out of any of the funds of the corporation available for dividends a reserve or reserves for any proper purpose and may abolish any such reserve. Such purposes shall include but not be limited to equalizing dividends, repairing or maintaining any property of the corporation, and meeting contingencies.

6.5   Transfer of Stock. Transfers of record of shares of stock of the corporation shall be made only upon its books by the holders thereof, in person or by an attorney duly authorized, and, subject to Section 6.3 of these bylaws, if such stock is certificated, upon the surrender of a certificate or certificates for a like number of shares, properly endorsed or accompanied by proper evidence of succession, assignation or authority to transfer.

6.6   Stock Transfer Agreements. The corporation shall have power to enter into and perform any agreement with any number of stockholders of any one or more classes of stock of the corporation to restrict the transfer of shares of stock of the corporation of any one or more classes owned by such stockholders in any manner not prohibited by the DGCL.

6.7   Registered Stockholders. The corporation:

(i)   shall be entitled to recognize the exclusive right of a person registered on its books as the owner of shares to receive dividends and to vote as such owner;

(ii)   shall be entitled to hold liable for calls and assessments the person registered on its books as the owner of shares; and

(iii)   shall not be bound to recognize any equitable or other claim to or interest in such share or shares on the part of another person, whether or not it shall have express or other notice thereof, except, in each case, as otherwise provided by the laws of Delaware.

ARTICLE VII
MANNER OF GIVING NOTICE AND WAIVER

7.1   Notice of Stockholders' Meetings. Notice of any meeting of stockholders, if mailed, is given when deposited in the United States mail, postage prepaid, directed to the stockholder at such stockholder's address as it appears on the corporation's records. An affidavit of the secretary or an assistant secretary of the corporation or of the transfer agent or other agent of the corporation that the notice has been given shall, in the absence of fraud, be *prima facie* evidence of the facts stated therein.

7.2   Notice By Electronic Transmission. Without limiting the manner by which notice otherwise may be given effectively to stockholders pursuant to the DGCL, the certificate of incorporation or these bylaws, any notice to stockholders given by the corporation under any provision of the DGCL, the certificate of incorporation or these bylaws shall be effective if given by a form of electronic transmission consented to by the stockholder to whom the notice is given. Any such consent shall be revocable by the stockholder by written notice to the corporation. Any such consent shall be deemed revoked if:

(i) the corporation is unable to deliver by electronic transmission two consecutive notices given by the corporation in accordance with such consent; and

(ii) such inability becomes known to the secretary or an assistant secretary of the corporation or to the transfer agent, or other person responsible for the giving of notice.

However, the inadvertent failure to treat such inability as a revocation shall not invalidate any meeting or other action.

Any notice given pursuant to the preceding paragraph shall be deemed given:

(i) if by facsimile telecommunication, when directed to a number at which the stockholder has consented to receive notice;

(ii) if by electronic mail, when directed to an electronic mail address at which the stockholder has consented to receive notice;

(iii) if by a posting on an electronic network together with separate notice to the stockholder of such specific posting, upon the later of (A) such posting and (B) the giving of such separate notice; and

(iv) if by any other form of electronic transmission, when directed to the stockholder.

An affidavit of the secretary or an assistant secretary or of the transfer agent or other agent of the corporation that the notice has been given by a form of electronic transmission shall, in the absence of fraud, be *prima facie* evidence of the facts stated therein.

An "**electronic transmission**" means any form of communication, not directly involving the physical transmission of paper, that creates a record that may be retained, retrieved, and reviewed by a recipient thereof, and that may be directly reproduced in paper form by such a recipient through an automated process.

Notice by a form of electronic transmission shall not apply with respect to Sections 164, 296, 311, 312 or 324 of the DGCL.

7.3   Notice To Stockholders Sharing An Address. Except as otherwise prohibited under the DGCL, without limiting the manner by which notice otherwise may be given effectively to stockholders, any notice to stockholders given by the corporation under the provisions of the DGCL, the certificate of incorporation or these bylaws shall be effective if given by a single written notice to stockholders who share an address if consented to by the stockholders at that address to whom such notice is given. Any such consent shall be revocable by the stockholder by written notice to the corporation. Any stockholder who fails to object in writing to the corporation, within 60 days of having been given written notice by the corporation of its intention to send the single notice, shall be deemed to have consented to receiving such single written notice.

7.4   Notice To Person With Whom Communication Is Unlawful. Whenever notice is required to be given, under the DGCL, the certificate of incorporation or these bylaws, to any person with whom communication is unlawful, the giving of such notice to such person shall not be required and there shall be no duty to apply to any governmental authority or agency for a license or permit to give such notice to such person. Any action or meeting which shall be taken or held without notice to any such person with whom communication is unlawful shall have the same force and effect as if such notice had been duly given. In the event that the action taken by the corporation is such as to require the filing of a certificate under the DGCL, the certificate shall state, if such is the fact and if notice is required, that notice was given to all persons entitled to receive notice except such persons with whom communication is unlawful.

7.5 <u>Waiver of Notice</u>. Whenever notice is required to be given under any provision of the DGCL, the certificate of incorporation or these bylaws, a written waiver, signed by the person entitled to notice, or a waiver by electronic transmission by the person entitled to notice, whether before or after the time of the event for which notice is to be given, shall be deemed equivalent to notice. Attendance of a person at a meeting shall constitute a waiver of notice of such meeting, except when the person attends a meeting for the express purpose of objecting at the beginning of the meeting, to the transaction of any business because the meeting is not lawfully called or convened. Neither the business to be transacted at, nor the purpose of, any regular or special meeting of the stockholders need be specified in any written waiver of notice or any waiver by electronic transmission unless so required by the certificate of incorporation or these bylaws.

ARTICLE VIII
FORUM FOR CERTAIN ACTIONS

Unless the corporation consents in writing to the selection of an alternative forum, the sole and exclusive forum for (i) any derivative action or proceeding brought on behalf of the corporation, (ii) any action asserting a claim of breach of a fiduciary duty owed by any director, officer or other employee or stockholder of the corporation to the corporation or the corporation's stockholders, (iii) any action asserting a claim arising pursuant to any provision of the DGCL, the certificate of incorporation or these bylaws or as to which the DGCL confers jurisdiction on the Court of Chancery of the State of Delaware or (iv) any action asserting a claim governed by the internal affairs doctrine shall be a state or federal court located within the state of Delaware, in all cases subject to the court's having personal jurisdiction over the indispensable parties named as defendants. Any person or entity purchasing or otherwise acquiring any interest in shares of capital stock of the corporation shall be deemed to have notice of and consented to the provisions of this bylaw. Notwithstanding the foregoing, any action asserting claims under the Securities Act of 1933, as amended may be brought in state or federal court, subject to applicable law.

ARTICLE IX
INDEMNIFICATION

9.1 <u>Indemnification of Directors and Officers In Third Party Proceedings</u>. Subject to the other provisions of this Article IX, the corporation shall indemnify, to the fullest extent permitted by the DGCL, as now or hereinafter in effect, any person who was or is a party or is threatened to be made a party to any threatened, pending or completed action, suit or proceeding, whether civil, criminal, administrative or investigative (a "**Proceeding**") (other than an action by or in the right of the corporation) by reason of the fact that such person is or was a director or officer of the corporation, or is or was a director or officer of the corporation serving at the request of the corporation as a director, officer, employee or agent of another corporation, partnership, joint venture, trust or other enterprise, against expenses (including attorneys' fees), judgments, fines and amounts paid in settlement actually and reasonably incurred by such person in connection with such Proceeding if such person acted in good faith and in a manner such person reasonably believed to be in or not opposed to the best interests of the corporation, and, with respect to any criminal action or proceeding, had no reasonable cause to believe such person's conduct was unlawful. The termination of any Proceeding by judgment, order, settlement, conviction, or upon a plea of *nolo contendere* or its equivalent, shall not, of itself, create a presumption that the person did not act in good faith and in a manner which such person reasonably believed to be in or not opposed to the best interests of the corporation, and, with respect to any criminal action or proceeding, had reasonable cause to believe that such person's conduct was unlawful.

9.2   Indemnification of Directors and Officers in Actions by or in the Right of the Corporation. Subject to the other provisions of this Article IX, the corporation shall indemnify, to the fullest extent permitted by the DGCL, as now or hereinafter in effect, any person who was or is a party or is threatened to be made a party to any threatened, pending or completed action or suit by or in the right of the corporation to procure a judgment in its favor by reason of the fact that such person is or was a director or officer of the corporation, or is or was a director or officer of the corporation serving at the request of the corporation as a director, officer, employee or agent of another corporation, partnership, joint venture, trust or other enterprise against expenses (including attorneys' fees) actually and reasonably incurred by such person in connection with the defense or settlement of such action or suit if such person acted in good faith and in a manner such person reasonably believed to be in or not opposed to the best interests of the corporation; except that no indemnification shall be made in respect of any claim, issue or matter as to which such person shall have been adjudged to be liable to the corporation unless and only to the extent that the Court of Chancery or the court in which such action or suit was brought shall determine upon application that, despite the adjudication of liability but in view of all the circumstances of the case, such person is fairly and reasonably entitled to indemnity for such expenses which the Court of Chancery or such other court shall deem proper.

9.3   Successful Defense. To the extent that a present or former director or officer of the corporation has been successful on the merits or otherwise in defense of any action, suit or proceeding described in Section 9.1 or Section 9.2, or in defense of any claim, issue or matter therein, such person shall be indemnified against expenses (including attorneys' fees) actually and reasonably incurred by such person in connection therewith.

9.4   Indemnification of Others. Subject to the other provisions of this Article IX, the corporation shall have power to indemnify its employees and agents to the extent not prohibited by the DGCL or other applicable law. The board of directors shall have the power to delegate to such person or persons as the board shall in its discretion determine the determination of whether employees or agents shall be indemnified.

9.5   Advance Payment of Expenses. Expenses (including attorneys' fees) actually and reasonably incurred by a current officer or director of the corporation in defending any Proceeding shall be paid by the corporation in advance of the final disposition of such Proceeding upon receipt of a written request therefor (together with documentation reasonably evidencing such expenses) and an undertaking by or on behalf of the person to repay such amounts if it shall ultimately be determined that the person is not entitled to be indemnified under this Article IX or the DGCL.

Such expenses (including attorneys' fees) incurred by former directors and officers or other employees and agents of the corporation or by persons serving at the request of the corporation as directors, officers, employees or agents of another corporation, partnership, joint venture, trust or other enterprise may be so paid upon such terms and conditions, if any, as the corporation deems appropriate. The right to advancement of expenses shall not apply to any claim for which indemnity is excluded pursuant to these bylaws, but shall apply to any Proceeding referenced in Section 9.6(ii) or 9.6(iii) prior to a determination that the person is not entitled to be indemnified by the corporation. The right to advancement of expenses shall not apply to any claim for which indemnity is excluded pursuant to these bylaws, but shall apply to any Proceeding referenced in Section 9.6(ii) or 9.6(iii) prior to a determination that the person is not entitled to be indemnified by the corporation.

9.6   Limitation On Indemnification. Subject to the requirements in Section 9.3 and the DGCL, the corporation shall not be obligated to indemnify any person pursuant to this Article IX in connection with any Proceeding (or any part of any Proceeding):

(i)   for which payment has actually been made to or on behalf of such person under any statute, insurance policy, indemnity provision, vote or otherwise, except with respect to any excess beyond the amount paid;

(ii)   for an accounting or disgorgement of profits pursuant to Section 16(b) of the 1934 Act, or similar provisions of federal, state or local statutory law or common law, if such person is held liable therefor (including pursuant to any settlement arrangements);

(iii)   for any reimbursement of the corporation by such person of any bonus or other incentive-based or equity-based compensation or of any profits realized by such person from the sale of securities of the corporation, as required in each case under the 1934 Act (including any such reimbursements that arise from an accounting restatement of the corporation pursuant to Section 304 of the Sarbanes-Oxley Act of 2002 (the "**Sarbanes-Oxley Act**"), or the payment to the corporation of profits arising from the purchase and sale by such person of securities in violation of Section 306 of the

Sarbanes-Oxley Act), if such person is held liable therefor (including pursuant to any settlement arrangements);

(iv)   initiated by such person, including any Proceeding (or any part of any Proceeding) initiated by such person against the corporation or its directors, officers, employees, agents or other indemnitees, unless (a) the board of directors authorized the Proceeding (or the relevant part of the Proceeding) prior to its initiation, (b) the corporation provides the indemnification, in its sole discretion, pursuant to the powers vested in the corporation under applicable law, (c) otherwise required to be made under Section 9.7 or (d) otherwise required by applicable law; or

(v)   if prohibited by applicable law; *provided, however,* that if any provision or provisions of this Article IX shall be held to be invalid, illegal or unenforceable for any reason whatsoever: (1) the validity, legality and enforceability of the remaining provisions of this Article IX (including, without limitation, each portion of any paragraph or clause containing any such provision held to be invalid, illegal or unenforceable, that is not itself held to be invalid, illegal or unenforceable) shall not in any way be affected or impaired thereby; and (2) to the fullest extent possible, the provisions of this Article IX (including, without limitation, each such portion of any paragraph or clause containing any such provision held to be invalid, illegal or unenforceable) shall be construed so as to give effect to the intent manifested by the provision held invalid, illegal or unenforceable.

9.7   Determination; Claim. If a claim for indemnification or advancement of expenses under this Article IX is not paid in full within 60 days after receipt by the corporation of the written request therefor, the claimant shall be entitled to an adjudication by a court of competent jurisdiction of his or her entitlement to such indemnification or advancement of expenses. The corporation shall indemnify such person against any and all expenses that are incurred by such person in connection with any action for indemnification or advancement of expenses from the corporation under this Article IX, to the extent such person is successful in such action, and to the extent not prohibited by law. In any such suit, the corporation shall, to the fullest extent not prohibited by law, have the burden of proving that the claimant is not entitled to the requested indemnification or advancement of expenses.

9.8   Non-Exclusivity of Rights. The indemnification and advancement of expenses provided by, or granted pursuant to, this Article IX shall not be deemed exclusive of any other rights to which those seeking indemnification or advancement of expenses may be entitled under the certificate of incorporation or any statute, bylaw, agreement, vote of stockholders or disinterested directors or otherwise, both as to action in such person's official capacity and as to action in another capacity while holding such office. The corporation is specifically authorized to enter into individual contracts with any or all of its directors, officers, employees or agents respecting indemnification and advancement of expenses, to the fullest extent not prohibited by the DGCL or other applicable law.

9.9   Insurance. The corporation may purchase and maintain insurance on behalf of any person who is or was a director, officer, employee or agent of the corporation, or is or was serving at the request of the corporation as a director, officer, employee or agent of another corporation, partnership, joint venture, trust or other enterprise against any liability asserted against such person and incurred by such person in any such capacity, or arising out of such person's status as such, whether or not the corporation would have the power to indemnify such person against such liability under the provisions of the DGCL.

9.10   Survival. The rights to indemnification and advancement of expenses conferred by this Article IX shall continue as to a person who has ceased to be a director, officer, employee or agent and shall inure to the benefit of the heirs, executors and administrators of such a person.

9.11   Effect of Repeal or Modification. A right to indemnification or to advancement of expenses arising under a provision of the certificate of incorporation or a bylaw shall not be eliminated or impaired by an amendment to the certificate of incorporation or these bylaws after the occurrence of the act or omission that is the subject of the civil, criminal, administrative or investigative action, suit or proceeding for which indemnification or advancement of expenses is sought, unless the provision in effect at the time of such act or omission explicitly authorizes such elimination or impairment after such action or omission has occurred.

9.12   Certain Definitions. For purposes of this Article IX, references to the "**corporation**" shall include, in addition to the resulting corporation, any constituent corporation (including any constituent of a constituent) absorbed in a consolidation or merger which, if its separate existence had continued, would have had power and authority to indemnify its directors, officers, employees or agents, so that any person who is or was a director, officer, employee or agent of such constituent corporation, or is or was serving at the request of such constituent corporation as a director, officer, employee or agent of another corporation, partnership, joint venture, trust or other enterprise, shall stand in the same position under the provisions of this Article IX with respect to the resulting or surviving corporation as such person would have with respect to such constituent corporation if its separate existence had continued. For purposes of this Article IX, references to "**other enterprises**" shall include employee benefit plans; references to "**fines**" shall include any excise taxes assessed on a person with respect to an employee benefit plan; and references to "**serving at the request of the corporation**" shall include any service as a director, officer, employee or agent of the corporation which imposes duties on, or involves services by, such director, officer, employee or agent with respect to an employee benefit plan, its participants or beneficiaries; and a person who acted in good faith and in a manner such person reasonably believed to be in the interest of the participants and beneficiaries of an employee benefit plan shall be deemed to have acted in a manner "**not opposed to the best interests of the corporation**" as referred to in this Article IX.

ARTICLE X
GENERAL MATTERS

10.1   Execution of Corporate Contracts and Instruments. Except as otherwise provided by law, the certificate of incorporation or these bylaws, the board of directors may authorize any officer or officers, or agent or agents, to enter into any contract or execute any document or instrument in the name of and on behalf of the corporation; such authority may be general or confined to specific instances. Unless so authorized or ratified by the board of directors or within the agency power of an officer, no officer, agent or employee shall have any power or authority to bind the corporation by any contract or engagement or to pledge its credit or to render it liable for any purpose or for any amount.

10.2   Fiscal Year. The fiscal year of the corporation shall be fixed by resolution of the board of directors and may be changed by the board of directors.

10.3   Seal. The corporation may adopt a corporate seal, which may be altered by the board of directors. The corporation may use the corporate seal by causing it or a facsimile thereof to be impressed or affixed or in any other manner reproduced.

10.4   Construction; Definitions. Unless the context requires otherwise, the general provisions, rules of construction, and definitions in the DGCL shall govern the construction of these bylaws. Without limiting the generality of this provision, the singular number includes the plural, the plural number includes the singular, and the term "**person**" includes both a corporation and a natural person.

ARTICLE XI
AMENDMENTS

These bylaws may be adopted, amended or repealed by the stockholders entitled to vote; *provided, however,* that the affirmative vote of the holders of at least sixty-six and two-thirds percent (66-2/3%) of the total voting power of outstanding voting securities, voting together as a single class, shall be required for the stockholders of the corporation to alter, amend or repeal, or adopt any provision of these bylaws. The board of directors shall also have the power to adopt, amend or repeal bylaws.

A bylaw amendment adopted by stockholders which specifies the votes that shall be necessary for the election of directors shall not be further amended or repealed by the board of directors.

46191319R00352

Made in the USA
San Bernardino, CA
04 August 2019